Dr. Dobb's Toolbook of C

The Editors of Dr. Dobb's Journal

A Brady Book
Published by Prentice Hall Press
New York, New York 10023

Dr. Dobb's Toolbook of C

Copyright © 1986 by Brady Communications Company, Inc.
All rights reserved
including the right of reproduction
in whole or in part in any form.

A Brady Book
Published by Prentice Hall Press
A Division of Simon & Schuster, Inc.
Gulf + Western Building
One Gulf + Western Plaza
New York, New York 10023

PRENTICE HALL PRESS is a trademark of Simon & Schuster, Inc.

Manufactured in the United States of America

1 2 3 4 5 6 7 8 9 10

Library of Congress Cataloging-in-Publication Data
Main entry under title:
  Dr. Dobb's toolbook of C.

  1. C (Computer program language)—Addresses, essays, lectures. I. Dr. Dobb's journal.
II. Title: Doctor Dobb's toolbook of C.
QA76.73.C15D7 1986   005.13'3   85-24276
ISBN 0-89303-615-3 (case)
ISBN 0-89303-599-8 (paper)

Special volume discounts are available by contacting the Special Sales Department, Englewood Cliffs, NJ 07632.

Contents

1 The C Programming Language   **1**
    Linguistic History of C   1
    Type Structure of C   5
    Statements and Control Flow   10
    Operators and Expressions   12
    Structure of Programs   16
    C Preprocessor   18
    Environmental Considerations   19
    Experience with C   21
    Conclusions and Future Directions   25
    References   26

2 Putting C on a Microcomputer: The Original Small-C   **27**

3 C Notebook: Selections from Dr. Dobb's First C Column   **33**
    Part 1 Layout of C Code   34
        A Possible Solution   37
    Part 2 Linker Formats and Runtime Libraries   48
        Link Formats   48
    Part 3 Memory Models   52
        Background   52
        Environment Block Address   57
        Allocation of Memory   57
    Part 4 C Input-Output Functions and Language Philosophy   59
        Low Level Input-Output in C   59
    Part 5 Scientific Uses   65

GPR: General Purpose Routines   66
How to Use the Integrator   72
Part 6 X: Extended C Grammar   74
Language Extensibility   74
Part 7 Wish Lists   88
Programming Philosophy   88
Conclusion   92

4 How Compilers Work   139
Anatomy of a Compiler   139
Notes   147

5 The Small-C Compiler   153
Differences   154
New Features Explained   155
Availability   161

6 A New Library for Small-C   231
Library Organization   232
System Functions   233
Conclusion   253
Availability   254

7 Small-Mac: An Assembler for Small-C   309
Concepts and Facilities   310
Using Small-Mac Programs   324
  MAC: The Small-Mac Assembler   324
  Description   324
  LNK: Small-Mac Linkage Editor   327
  Description   328
  LGO: Small-Mac Load-and-Go Loader   332
  LIB: Small-Mac Library Manager   333
  CMIT: Small-Mac Configuration Utility (Compile Machine Instruction Tables   337
  DREL: Dump Relocatable Object Files   340
  Availability   341

8 P: A Small-C Preprocessor   427
Features   428
Implementation   431
Installation   433

9 Getargs: A Command-Line Argument Processor   465
Getargs()   466
Command-Line Switch Formats   466

CONTENTS   v

        Using Getargs()   467
        Conclusion   469

10   Cross-Reference Generator in C: A Program Conversion Aid   479

11   CC: A Driver for Small-C   493
        Features   493
        Implementation   495
        Installation   497

12   CP/M BDOS and BIOS Calls for C   511
        Installation   512

13   Small-Tools: Programs for Text Processing   519
        The Small-Tools Package   519
        Small-Tools Concepts and Facilities   522
        Program Descriptions   528
        Installation   567
        Availability   568

14   Grep.c: A Generalized, Regular Expression Parser in C   655
        Regular Expressions   656
        Technical Description   658
        Conclusion   668

15   Optimizing Strings in C   699
        Some Further Thoughts   703

Limits of Liability and Disclaimer of Warranty

The author(s) and publisher of this book have used their best efforts in preparing this book and the programs contained in it. These efforts include the development, research, and testing of the theories and programs to determine their effectiveness. The author(s) and publisher make no warranty of any kind, expressed or implied, with regard to these programs or the documentation contained in this book. The author(s) and publisher shall not be liable in any event for incidental or consequential damages in connection with, or arising out of, the furnishing, performance, or use of these programs.

MS/DOS is a trademark of Microsoft Corp.
CP/M is a trademark of Digital Research, Inc.
Unix is a trademark of AT&T Bell Laboratories

PREFACE

The C programming language is becoming more popular for several reasons. The language is both powerful and concise: it's high-level enough to write significant programs, but it still gives you access to the machine at a very low level. Perhaps, most importantly, C is portable (or at least as portable as a programming language can be). Consequently a large body of C language software tools has been developed, though it's hard sometimes to separate the useful programs from the chaff.

Though C is a good language, it's unfortunately difficult to learn. It can be obscure to the point of unintelligibility and textbooks on the language never seem to address real-world programming problems.

This book addresses both of these problems. Reading through functioning C programs is one of the best ways to learn the language and this is a book of functioning programs. It's useful to see how others have solved problems similar to the one you're working on right now. The book goes beyond intellectual exercises though; the programs here are useful in their own right. An entire C compiler, with all its support routines, is given here, as are versions of various utility programs such as Grep and a C program cross reference generator. Though many of these have appeared in Dr. Dobb's over the years, there are quite a few unpublished programs here too. Jim Hendrix has augmented his version of the Small-C compiler with an assembler, linker, librarian and an improved I/O library. He's also contributed a set of text management tools, à la Kernighan and Plauger. In addition to the programs, Anthony Skjellum has distilled all his "C Programmer's Notebook" columns into a single essay. Skjellum's column was an interesting forum on C related topics and the version included here provides much food for thought. Most of the programs that were once in the magazine have been updated and improved from their original versions. Bugs have been fixed and some additional functions have been added.

To my knowledge this book is the most comprehensive set of C software tools available. The C programming community owes its thanks to the authors whose labor is reproduced in this volume. The programs presented here represent several man-years of labor, and they are being given to us for free. As a group, they represent an invaluable resource, and it is through this sort of selfless giving that the programming art can advance.

1
THE C PROGRAMMING LANGUAGE

by D.M. Ritchie, S.C. Johnson, M.E. Lesk, and B.W. Kernighan

This chapter appeared in DDJ #45 (May 1980); the authors, who work at Bell Laboratories in Murray Hill, New Jersey, originally wrote the article in 1978.
    Copyright © 1978, American Telephone and Telegraph Company; reprinted by permission.

    C is a general purpose programming language featuring economy of expression, modern control flow and data structure capabilities, and a rich set of operators and data types.
    C is not a "very high-level" language nor a big one and is not specialized to any particular area of application. Its generality and an absence of restrictions make it more convenient and effective for many more tasks than supposedly more powerful languages. C has been used for a wide variety of programs, including the Unix operating system, the C compiler itself, and essentially all Unix application software. The language is sufficiently expressive and efficient to have completely displaced assembly language programming on Unix.
    C was originally written for the PDP-11 under Unix, but the language is not tied to any particular hardware or operating system. C compilers run on a wide variety of machines, including the Honeywell 6000, the IBM System/370, and the Interdata 8/32.

Linguistic History of C

The C language in use today (Kernighan and Ritchie, 1978) is the product of several years of evolution. Many of its most important ideas stem from the considerably older, but still quite vital, language BCPL (Richards, 1969) developed by Martin Richards. The influence of BCPL on C proceeded indirectly through the language B (Johnson and Kernighan, 1973), which was written by Ken Thompson in 1970 for the first Unix system on the PDP-11.

Although neither B nor C could really be considered dialects of BCPL, they all have several characteristic features in common:

1. All are able to express the fundamental flow-control constructions required for well-structured programs: statement grouping, decision-making (if), looping (while) with the termination test either at the top or the bottom of the loop, and branching out to a sequence of possible cases (switch). It is interesting that BCPL provided these constructions in 1967, well before the current vogue for structured programming.

2. All three languages include the concept of *pointer* and provide the ability to do address arithmetic.

3. In all three languages, the arguments to functions are passed by copying the value of the argument, and it is impossible for the function to change the actual argument. To achieve "call by reference," a pointer may be passed explicitly, and the function may change the object to which the pointer points. Any function is allowed to be recursive, and its local variables are typically "automatic" or specific to each invocation.

4. All three languages are rather low-level, in that, they deal with the same sorts of objects that most computers do. BCPL and B restrict their attention almost completely to machine words, whereas C widens its horizons somewhat to characters and (possibly multiword) integers, and floating-point numbers. None deals directly with composite objects such as character strings, sets, lists, or arrays considered as a whole. The languages themselves do not define any storage allocation facility beside static definition and the stack discipline provided by the local variables of functions; likewise, I/O is not part of any of these languages. All these higher mechanisms must be provided by explicitly called routines from libraries.

B and BCPL differ mainly in their syntax, and many differences stem from the very small size of the first B compiler (fewer than 4K 18-bit words on the PDP-7). Several constructions in BCPL encourage a compiler to maintain a representation of the entire program in memory. In BCPL, for example,

```
valof $(
    ...
    resultis expression
    ...
$)
```

is syntactically an expression. It provides a way of packaging a block of many statements into a sort of unnamed internal procedure yielding a single result (delivered by the resultis statement). The valof construction can occur in the middle of any expression, and can be arbitrarily large. The B language avoided the difficulties caused by this and some other constructions by rigorously simplifying (and in some cases adjusting to personal taste) the syntax of BCPL.

Despite many syntactic changes, B remained close to BCPL semantically. The most characteristic feature of both languages is their nearly identical treatment of addresses (pointers). They support a model of the storage of the machine consisting of a sequence of equal-sized cells, into which values can be placed; in typical implementations, these cells are machine words. Each identifier in a program corresponds to a cell, and a cell may contain a variety of values. Most often the value is an integer, or perhaps a representation of a character. All the cells, however, are numbered; the address of a cell is just the integer giving its ordinal position. BCPL has a unary operator *lv* (in some versions, and also in B and C, shortened to &) that, when applied to a name, yields the address of the cell corresponding to the name. The inverse operator *rv* (later *) yields the value in the cell pointed to. Thus the statement

```
px = &x;
```

of B assigns to px the number that can be interpreted as the address of x; the statements

```
y = *px + 2;
*px = 5;
```

first use the value in the cell pointed to by px (which is the same cell as x) and then assign 5 to this cell.

Arrays in BCPL and B are intimately tied up with pointers. An array declaration, which might in BCPL be written

```
let Array = vec 10
```

and in B

```
auto Array[10];
```

creates a single cell named *Array* and initializes it with the address of the first in a sequence of 10 unnamed cells containing the array itself. Since the quantity stored in *Array* is just the address of the cell of the first element of the array, the expression

```
Array + i
```

is the address of the *ith* element, counting from zero. Likewise, applying the indirection operator,

```
*(Array + i)
```

refers to the value of the *ith* member of the array. This operation is so frequent that special syntax was invented to express it:

```
Array[i]
```

Thus, despite its asymmetric appearance, subscripting is a commutative operation; the above example could equally well be written

```
i[Array]
```

In BCPL and B there is only one type of object, the machine word, so when the same language operator is applied to two operands, the calculation actually carried out must always be the same. Thus, for example, if the programmer wants to do floating-point arithmetic, the "+" operator notation cannot be used, since it implies an integer addition. Instead (in a version of BCPL for the GE 635), a "." was placed in front of each operator that had floating-point operands. As may be appreciated, this was a frequent source of errors.

The machine model implied by the definitions of BCPL and B is simple and self-consistent. It is, however, inadequate for many purposes, and on many machines it causes inefficiencies when implemented. The problems became evident to us after B began to be used heavily on the first PDP-11 version of Unix. The first problem followed from the fact that the PDP-11, like several machines (including, for example, the IBM System/370) is byte-addressed; a machine address refers to any of several bytes (characters) in a word, not the word alone. Most obviously, the word orientation of B cuts us off from any convenient ability to access bytes. Equally important was the fact that, before any address could be used, it had to be shifted left by one place. The reason for this is simple: there are two bytes per PDP-11 word. On the one hand, the language guaranteed that if 1 was added to an address quantity, it would point to the next word; on the other hand, the machine architecture required that word addresses be even and equal to the byte number of the first byte in the word. Since there was no way to distinguish cells containing ordinary integers from those containing pointers, the only solution visible was to represent pointers as word numbers and then, at the point of use, convert to the byte representation by multiplication by 2.

Yet another problem was introduced by the desire to provide for floating-point arithmetic. The PDP-11 supports two floating-point formats, one of which requires two words, the other four. In neither case was it satisfactory to use the trick used on the GE 635 (operator like ".+") because there was no way to represent the requirement for a single data item occupying four or eight bytes. This problem did not arise on the 635 because integers and single-precision floating-point both require only one word.

Thus, the problems evidenced by B led us to design a new language that (after a brief period under the name NB) was dubbed C. The major advance provided by C is its typing structure, which completely solved the difficulties mentioned above. Each declaration in a C program specifies (sometimes implicitly) a *type*, which determines how much storage the object requires and how it is to be interpreted. The original fundamental types provided were single character (byte), integer, single-precision floating-point, and double-precision floating-point. (Others discussed below were added later.) Thus in the program

```
double a, b;
...
a = b + 3;
```

the compiler can determine from the declarations of *a* and *b* the fact that they require four words of storage each, that the "+" means a double-precision floating add, and that "3" must be converted to floating.

Of course, the idea of typing variables is in no way original with C; in fact, it was the general rule among the most widely used and influential languages, including Algol, Fortran, and PL/1. Nevertheless, the introduction of types marked an important change in our own thinking. The typeless nature of BCPL and B had seemed to promise a great simplification in the implementation, understanding, and use of these languages. By the time C was created (circa 1972), advocates of languages such as Algol 68 and Pascal strongly recommended an enforced type structure on psychological grounds; but even disregarding their arguments, the typeless nature of BCPL and B seemed inappropriate, for purely technological reasons, to the available hardware.

Type Structure of C

The introduction of types in C, although a major departure from the tradition of BCPL and B, was done in such a way that many of the characteristic usages of the earlier languages survived. To some extent, this continuity was an attempt to preserve as much as possible of the considerable corpus of existing software written in B, but even more important, especially in retrospect, was the desire to minimize the intellectual distance between past and future ways of expression.

Pointers, Arrays, and Address Arithmetic

One clear example of the similarity of C to the earlier languages is its treatment of pointers and arrays. In C an array of 10 integers might be declared

```
int Array[10];
```

which is identical to the corresponding declaration in B. (Arrays begin at zero; the elements of *Array* are *Array[0]*,...,*Array[9]*.) As discussed above, the B implementation caused a cell named *Array* to be allocated and initialized with a pointer to ten otherwise unnamed cells to hold the array. In C, the effect is a bit different; ten integers are allocated, and the first is associated with the name *Array*. But C also includes a general rule that, whenever the name of an array appears in an expression, it is converted to a pointer to the first member of the array. Strictly speaking, we should say, for this example, it is converted to an *integer pointer* since all C pointers are associated with a particular type to which they point. In most usages, the actual effects of the slightly different meanings of *Array* are indistinguishable. Thus in the C expression

```
Array + i
```

the identifier *Array* is converted to a pointer to the first element of the array; *i* is scaled (if required) before it is added to the pointer. For a byte-addressed machine, the scale factor is the number of bytes in an integer; for a word-addressed machine the scale factor is unity. In any event, the result is a pointer to the *ith* member of the array. Likewise identical in effect to the interpretation of B,

```
*(Array + i)
```

is the *ith* member itself, and

```
Array[i]
```

is another notation for the same thing. In all these cases, of course, should *Array* be an array of, or pointer to, some objects other than integers, the scale factor is adjusted appropriately. The pointer arithmetic, as written, is independent of the type of object to which the pointer points and indeed of the internal representation of the pointer.

Derived Types

As mentioned above, the basic types in C were originally *int*, which represents an integer in the basic size provided by the machine architecture; *char*, which represents a single byte; *float*, a single-precision floating-point number; and *double*, double-precision floating-point. Over the years, *long*, *short*, and *unsigned* integers have been added. In current C implementations, long is at least 32 bits; short is usually 16 bits; and int remains the natural size for the machine at hand. Unsigned integers exist mainly to squeeze an extra bit out of the machine, since the sign bit need not be represented.

In addition to these basic types, C provides a conceptually infinite hierarchy of derived types, which are formed by composition of the basic types with *pointers, arrays, structures, unions,* and *functions*. Examples of pointer and array declarations have already been exhibited; another is

```
double *vecp, vector[100];
```

which declares a pointer *vecp* to double-precision floating numbers, and an array *vector* of the same kind of objects. The size of an array, when specified, must always be a constant.

A structure is an aggregate of one or more objects, usually of various types, which can be treated as a unit. C structures are essentially the same as records in languages such as Pascal, and semantically, though not syntactically, like PL/1 and Cobol structures. Thus:

```
struct tag {
        int             i;
        float           f;
        char            c[3];
};
```

defines a template, called *tag*, for a structure containing three *members:* an integer *i*, a floating-point number *f*, and a three-character array *c*. The declaration

```
struct tag x, y[10], *p;
```

declares a structure x of this type, an array y of 10 such structures, and a pointer *p* to this kind of structure. The hierarchical nature of derived types is clearly evident here: y is an array of structures whose members include an array of characters. References to individual members of structures use the "." operator.

```
x.i
x.f
y[i].c[0]
(*p).c[1]
```

Parentheses in the last line are necessary because the . binds more tightly than the *. It turns out that pointers to structures are so common that special syntax is called for to express structure access through a pointer.

```
p->c[1]
p->i
```

This soon becomes more natural than the equivalent

```
(*p).c[1]
(*p).i
```

A union can hold, at different times, objects of different types, with the compiler keeping track of size and alignment requirements. Unions provide a way to manipulate different kinds of data in a single part of storage, without embedding machine-dependent information (such as the relative sizes of int and float) in a program. For example, the union u, declared

```
union {
        int     i;
        float   f;
}u;
```

can hold either an int (written u.i) or a float (written u.f). Regardless of the machine it is compiled on, it will be large enough to hold either one of these quantities. A union is syntactically identical to a structure; it may be considered as a structure in which all the members begin at the same offset. Unions in C are more analogous to PL/1's CALL than to the unions of Algol 68 or the variant records of Pascal, because it is the responsibility of the programmer to avoid referring to a union that does not currently contain an object of the implied type.

A function is a subprogram that returns an object of a given type:

```
unsigned unsf();
```

declares a function that returns unsigned. The type of a function ignores the number and types of its arguments, although in general the call and the definition must agree.

Type Definition

The syntax of declarations borrows from that of expressions. The key idea is that a declaration, say

```
int     ... ;
```

contains a part "..." that, if it appeared in an expression, would be of type int. The constructions seen so far, for example,

```
int     *lptr;
int     lfunc();
int     iarr[10];
```

exhibit this approach, but more complicated declarations are common. For example:

```
int     *funcptr();
int     (*ptrfunc)();
```

declare respectively a function that returns a pointer to an integer, and a pointer to a function that returns an integer. The extra parentheses in the second are needed to make the * apply directly to ptrfunc, since the implicit function-call operator () binds more tightly than *. Functions are not variables, so arrays or structures of functions are not permitted. However, a pointer to a function, such as ptrfunc, may be stored, copied, passed as an argument, returned by a function, and so on, just as any other pointer.

Arrays of pointers are frequently used instead of multidimensional arrays. The usage of *a* and *b* when declared

```
int     a[10][10];
int     *b[10];
```

may be similar, in that $a[5][5]$ and $b[5][5]$ are both legal references to a single int, but *a* is a true array: all 100 storage cells have been allocated, and the conventional rectangular subscript calculation is done. For *b*, however, the declaration has only allocated 10 pointers; each must be set to point to an array of integers. Assuming each does point to a 10-element array, then there will be 100 storage cells set aside, plus the 10 cells for the pointers. Thus, the array of pointers uses slightly more space and may require an extra initialization step, but it has two advantages: it trades an indirection for a subscript multiplication, and it permits the rows of the array to be of different lengths. (That is, each element of *b* need not point to a 10-element vector; one may point to 2 elements, another to 20.) Particularly with strings whose lengths are not known in advance, an array of pointers is often used instead of a multidimensional array. Every C main program gets access to its invoking command line in this form, for example.

The idea of specifying types by appropriating some of the syntax of expressions seems to be original with C, and for the simpler cases, it works well. Occasionally some rather ornate types are needed, and the declaration may be a bit hard to interpret. For example, a pointer to an array of pointers to functions, each returning an int, would be written

```
int (*(*funnyarray)[])();
```

that is certainly opaque, although understandable enough if read from the inside out. In an expression, *funnyarray* might appear as

```
i = (*(*funnyarray)[j])(k);
```

The corresponding Algol 68 declaration is

```
ref [] ref proc int
```
funnyarray

when read from left to right in correspondence with the informal description of the type if ref is taken to be the equivalent of C's "pointer to." The Algol may be clearer, but both are hard to grasp.

Statements and Control Flow

Control flow in C differs from other languages primarily in details of syntax. As in PL/1, semicolons are used to terminate statements, not to separate them. Most statements are just expressions followed by a semicolon; since assignments are expressions, there is no need for a special assignment statement.

Statements are grouped with braces { and }, rather than with words such as begin-end or do-od, because the more concise form seems much easier to read and is certainly easier to type. A sequence of statements enclosed in { } is syntactically a single statement.

The if-else statement has the form

```
if (expression)
        statement
else
        statement
```

The *expression* is evaluated; if it is "true" (that is, if *expression* has a nonzero value), the first *statement* is done. If it is "false" (*expression* is zero), and if there is an else part, the second *statement* is executed instead. The else part is optional; if it is omitted in a sequence of nested if's, the resulting ambiguity is resolved in the usual way by associating the else with the nearest previous else-less if.

The switch statement provides a multiway branch depending on the value of an integer expression:

```
switch (expression){
    case const:
            code
    case const:
            code
    ...
    default:
            code
}
```

The expression is evaluated and compared against the various cases, which are labeled with distinct integer constant values. If any case matches, execution begins at that point. If no case matches but there is a default statement, execution begins there; otherwise, no part of the switch is executed.

The cases are just labels, and so control may flow from one case to the next. Although this permits multiple labels on cases, it also means that in general most cases must be terminated with an explicit exit from the switch (the break statement below).

The switch construction is part of C's legacy from BCPL; it is so useful and so easy to provide that the lack of a corresponding facility of acceptable generality in languages ranging from Fortran through Algol 68, and even to Pascal (which does not provide for a default), must be considered a real failure of imagination in language designers.

C provides three kinds of loops. The while is simply

```
while (expression)
    statement
```

The *expression* is evaluated; if it is true (nonzero), the *statement* is executed, and then the process repeats. When *expression* becomes false (zero), execution terminates.

The do statement is a test-at-the-bottom loop:

```
do
    statement
while (expression);
```

statement is performed once, then *expression* is evaluated. If it is true, the loop is repeated; otherwise it is terminated.

The for loop is reminiscent of similarly named loops in other languages, but rather more general. The for statement

```
for (expr1;expr2;expr3)
    statement
```

is equivalent to

```
expr1;
while (expr2){
        statement
        expr3;
}
```

Grammatically, the three components of a for loop are expressions. Any of the three parts can be omitted, although the semicolons must remain. If *expr1* or *expr3* is left out, it is simply dropped from the expansion. If the test, *expr2*, is not present, it is taken as permanently true, so

```
for (;;){
        ...
}
```

is an "infinite" loop, to be broken by other means, for example by break, below.

The "for" statement keeps the loop control components together and visible at the top of the loop, as in the idiomatic

```
for (i = 0; i < N; i = i + 1)
```

which processes the first N elements of an array, the analogue of the Fortran or PL/1 DO loop. The for is more general, however. The test is reevaluated on each pass through the loop, and there is no restriction on changing the variables involved in any of the expressions in the for statement. The controlling variable i retains its value regardless of how the loop terminates. And since the components of a for are arbitrary expressions, for loops are not restricted to arithmetic progressions. For example, the classic walk along a linked list is

```
for (p = top; p! = NULL; p = p -> next)
    . . .
```

There are two statements for controlling loops. The break statement, as mentioned, causes an immediate exit from the immediately enclosing while, for, do, and switch. The continue statement causes the next iteration of the immediately enclosing loop to begin. The statements break and continue are asymmetric, since continue does not apply to switch.

Finally, C provides the oft-maligned goto statement. Empirically, goto's are not used much, at least not on our system. The operating system itself, for example, contains 98 goto statements in some 8300 lines; the PDP-11 C compiler, in 9660 lines, has 147. Essentially, all of these implement some form of branch to the top or bottom of a loop, or to error recovery code.

Operators and Expressions

C has been characterized as having a relatively rich set of operators. Some of these are quite conventional. For example, the basic binary arithmetic operators are +, −, *, and /. To these, C adds the modulus operator %: m%n is the remainder when m is divided by n.

Besides the basic logical or bitwise operators & (bitwise AND) and | (bitwise OR), there are also the binary operators ^ (bitwise exclusive OR), >> (right shift), and << (left shift), and the unary operator ~ (ones complement). These operators apply to all integers; C provides no special bit-string type.

The relational operators are the usual >, >=, <, <=, == (equality test), and != (inequality test). They have the value 1 if the stated relation is true, 0 if not.

The unary pointer operators * (for indirection) and & (for taking the address) were described earlier. When y is such as to make the expressions &*y or

`*&y` legal, either is just equal to y. Note that & and `*` are used as both binary and unary operators (with different meanings).

The simplest assignment is written =, and is used conventionally: the value of the expression on the right is stored in the object whose address is on the left. In addition, most binary operators can be combined with assignment by writing

```
a op= b
```

which has the effect of

```
a = a op b
```

except that *a* is only evaluated once. For example,

```
x += 3
```

is the same as

```
x = x + 3
```

if x is just a variable, but

```
p[i + j + 1] += 3
```

adds 3 to the element selected from the array p, calculating the subscript only once, and, more importantly, requiring it to be written out only once. Compound assignment operators also seem to correspond well to the way we think; "add 3 to x" is said, if not written, much more commonly than "assign x + 3 to x."

Assignment expressions have a value, just like other expressions, and may be used in larger expressions. For example, the multiple assignment

```
i = j = k = 0;
```

is a by-product of this fact, not a special case. Another very common instance is the nesting of an assignment in the condition part of an if statement or a loop, as in

```
while ((c = getchar())!= EOF)...
```

which fetches a character with the function getchar, assigns it to *c*, then tests whether the result is an end-of-file marker. (Parentheses are needed because the precedence of the assignment = is lower than that of the relational !=.)

C provides two novel operators for incrementing and decrementing variables. The increment operator + + adds 1 to its operand; the decrement operator − − subtracts 1. Thus the statement

```
++i;
```

increments i. The unusual aspect is that + + and − − may be used either as prefix operators (before the variable, as in + +i), or postfix (after the variable as in i+ +). In both cases, the effect is to increment i. But the expression + +i increments i *before* using its value, while i+ + increments i *after* its value has been used. If i is 5, then

```
x = i++;
```

sets x to 5, but

```
x = ++i;
```

sets x to 6. In both cases, i becomes 6.
For example:

```
stack[i++] = ... ;
```

pushes a value on a stack stored in array *stack* indexed by *i*, whereas

```
... = stack [--i];
```

retrieves the value and pops the stack. Of course, when the quantity incremented or decremented is a pointer, appropriate scaling is done, just as if the 1 were added explicitly:

```
*stackp ++= ... ;
... = *--stackp;
```

are analogous to the previous example, this time using a stack pointer instead of an index.

Tests may be combined with the logical connectives && (AND), | | (OR), and ! (truth value negation). The && and | | guarantee left-to-right evaluation, with termination as soon as the truth value is known. For example, in the test

```
if (i <= N && array[i] > 0 ...
```

if i is greater than N, then array[i] (presumably at that point an out-of-bounds reference) will not be accessed. This predictable behavior is especially convenient, and much preferable to the explicitly random order of evaluation promised by most other languages. Most C programs rely heavily on the properties of && and | |.

Finally, the *conditional expression*, written with the ternary operator ?:, provides an analogue of if-else in expressions. In the expression

```
e1 ? e2 : e3
```

the expression *e1* is evaluated first. If it is nonzero (true), then the expression *e2* is evaluated, and that is the value of the conditional expression. Otherwise, *e3* is evaluated, and that is the value. Only one of *e2* and *e3* is evaluated. Thus to set z to the maximum of *a* and *b*,

```
z = (a > b) ? a : b; /* z = max(a, b) */
```

We have already discussed how integers are scaled appropriately in pointer arithmetic. C does several other automatic conversions between data types, more freely than Pascal, for example, but without the wild abandon of PL/1. In all contexts, char variables and constants are promoted to int. This is particularly handy in a code such as

```
n = c - '0';
```

which assigns to n the integer value of the character stored in *c*, by subtracting the value of the character '0'. Generally, the basic types fall into only two classes, integral and floating-point; char variables, and the various lengths of int's, are taken to be representations of the same kind of thing. They occupy different amounts of storage, but are essentially compatible. Boolean values as such do not exist; relational or truth-value expressions have value 1 if true, 0 if false.

Variables of type int are converted to floating-point when combined with floats or doubles and in fact all floating arithmetic is carried out in double precision, so floats are widened to double in expressions.

Conversions that involve "narrowing" an expression (for example, when a longer value is assigned to a shorter) are also well behaved. Floating-point values are converted to integer by truncation; integers convert to shorter integers or characters by dropping high-order bits.

When a conversion is desired, but is not implicit in the context, it is possible to force a conversion by an explicit operator called a *cast*. The expression

```
(type) expression
```

is a new expression whose type is that specified in *type*. For example, the sin routine expects an argument of type double; in the statement

```
x = sin((double)n);
```

the value of n is converted to double before being passed to *sin*.

Structure of Programs

Complete programs consist of one or more files containing function and data declarations. Thus, syntactically, a program is made up of a sequence of declarations; executable code appears inside functions. Conventionally, the runtime system arranges to call a function named main to start execution.

The language distinguishes the notions of *declaration* and *definition*. A declaration merely announces the properties of a variable (such as its type); a definition declares a variable and also allocates storage for it or, in the case of a function, supplies the code.

Functions

The notion of *function* in C includes the subroutines and functions of Fortran and the procedures of most other languages. A function call is written

```
name(arglist)
```

where the parentheses are required even if the argument list is empty. All functions may be used recursively.

Arguments are passed by value, so the called function cannot in any way affect the actual argument with which it was called. This permits the called program to use its formal arguments as conveniently initialized local variables. Call by value also eliminates the class of errors, familiar to Fortran programmers, in which a constant is passed to a subroutine that tries to alter the corresponding argument. An array name as an actual argument, however, is converted to a pointer to the first array element (as it always is), so the effect is as if arrays were called by reference; given the pointer, the called function can work its will on the individual elements of the array. When a function must return a value through its argument list, an explicit pointer may be passed, and the function references the ultimate target through this pointer. For example, the function *swap(px, py)* interchanges two integers pointed to by its arguments:

```
swap(px,py)              /* flip int's
                            pointed to by px and py */.
int *px, *py;
int temp;
{
   temp = *px;
   *px = *py;
   *py = temp;
}
```

This also demonstrates the form of a function definition: the name is followed by an argument list; the arguments are declared, and the body of the function is a block, or compound statement, enclosed in braces. Declarations of local variables may follow the opening brace.

A function returns a value by

```
return expression;
```

The *expression* is automatically coerced to the type that the function returns. By default, functions are assumed to return *int*; if this is not the case, the function must be declared both in the calling routine and when it is defined. For example, a function definition is

```
double sqrt(x)      / *returns square root of x */
double x;
{
        ...
}
```

In the caller, the declaration is

```
double y, sqrt();

y = sqrt(y);
```

A function argument may be any of the basic types or a pointer, but not an array, structure, union, or function. The same is true of the value returned by a function. (The most recent versions of the language, still not standard everywhere, permit structures and unions as arguments and values of functions, and allow them to be assigned.)

Data

Data declared at the top level (that is, outside the body of any function definition) is static in lifetime, and exists throughout the execution of the program. Variables declared within a function body are by default *automatic*: they come into existence when the function is entered and vanish when it is exited. Automatic variables may be declared to be *register* variables; when possible they will be placed in machine registers, which may result in smaller, faster code. The *register* declaration is only considered a hint to the compiler; no hardware register names are mentioned, and the hint may be ignored if the compiler wishes.

Static variables exist throughout the execution of a program, and retain their values across function calls. Static variables may be local to a function or (if defined at the top level) common to several functions.

External variables have the same lifetime as static, but they are also accessible to programs from other source files. That is, all references to an identically named external variable are references to the same thing.

The "storage class" of a variable can be explicitly announced in its declaration:

```
static int x;
extern double y[10];
```

More often the defaults for the context are sufficient. Inside a function, the default is auto (for automatic). Outside a function, at the top level, the default is extern. Since automatic and register variables are specific to a particular call of a particular function, they cannot be declared at the top level. Neither top-level variables nor functions explicitly declared static are visible to functions outside the file in which they appear.

Scope

Declarations may appear either at the top level or at the head of a block (compound statement). Declarations in an inner block temporarily override those of identically named variables outside. The scope of a declaration persists until the end of its block, or until the end of the file, if it was at the top level.

Since function definitions may be given only at the top level (that is, they may not be nested), there are no internal procedures. They have been forbidden not for any philosophical reason, but only to simplify the implementation. It has turned out that the ability to make certain functions and data invisible to programs in other files (by explicitly declaring them static) is sufficient to provide one of their most important uses, namely hiding their names from other functions. (However, it is not possible for one function to access the internal variables of another, as internal procedures could do.) Similarly, the ability to conceal functions and data in one file from access by another satisfies some of the most crucial requirements of modular programming (as in languages such as Alphard, CLU, and Euclid), even though it does not satisfy them all.

C Preprocessor

It is well recognized that the "magic numbers" in a program are a sign of bad programming. Most languages, therefore, provide a way to define the symbolic names for constants, so that the value of a magic number need be specified in only one place, and the rest of the code can refer to the value by some mnemonic name. In C such a mechanism is available, but it is not part of the syntax of the language; instead, symbolic naming is provided by a macro preprocessor automatically invoked as part of every C compilation. For example, given the definitions

```
#define     PI    3.14159
#define     E     2.71284
```

the preprocessor replaces all occurrences of a defined name by the corresponding defining string. (Uppercase names are normally chosen to emphasize that these are not variables.) Thus, when the programmer recognizes that he or she has written an incorrect value for E, only the definition line has to be changed to

```
#define     E     2.71828
```

instead of each instance of the constant in the program.

Providing this service by a macro preprocessor instead of by syntax has some significant advantages. The replacement test is not restricted to being numbers; any string of characters is permitted. Furthermore, the token being replaced need not be a variable, although it must have the form of a name. For example, we can define

```
#define     forever     for(;;)
```

and then write an infinite loop as

```
forever {
    ...
}
```

The macro preprocessor also permits macros to have arguments; this capability is heavily used by some I/O packages.

A second service of the C macro preprocessor is *library file include*; a source line of the form

```
#include    "name"
```

causes the contents of the filename to be interpolated into the source at that point (includes may be nested). This feature is much used, especially in larger programs, for making sure that all the source files of the program are supplied with identical #defines, global data declarations, and the like.

Environmental Considerations

By intent, the C language confines itself to facilities that can be mapped relatively efficiently and directly into machine instructions. For example, writing matrix operations that look exactly like scalar operations is possible in some programming languages and occasionally misleads programmers into believing that matrix operations are as cheap as scalar operations. More important, restricting the domain of the C compiler to those areas where it knows how to do a relatively efficient job provides the freedom to design subroutine libraries for the remaining tasks without constraining them to fit into some language specification. When the compiler cannot implement some facility without heavy costs in nonportability, complexity, or efficiency, there are many benefits to leaving out such a facility: it simplifies the language and the compiler, frequently without inconveniencing users (who often reject a high-cost built-in operation and do it themselves anyway).

At present, C is restricted to simple operations on simple data types. As a result, although the C area of operation is comparatively clean and pleasant, users must know something about the polluting effects of the environment to get most jobs done. A program can always access the raw system calls on each system, if very close interaction with the operating system is needed, but standard library routines have been implemented in each C environment that try to encourage portability while retaining speed and flexibility. The basic areas covered by the standard library at present are storage allocation, string handling, and I/O. Additional libraries and utilities are available for such areas as graphics, coroutine sequencing, execution time monitoring, and parsing.

The only automatic storage management service provided by C itself is the stack discipline for automatic variables. Two subroutines exist for more flexible storage handling. The function calloc(n,s) returns a pointer to a properly aligned storage block that will hold n items each of which is s bytes long. Normally s is obtained from the sizeof pseudo-function, a compile-time function that yields the size in bytes of a variable or data type. To return a block obtained from calloc to the free storage pool, cfree(p) may be called, where p is a value returned by a previous call to calloc.

Another set of routines deals with string handling. There is no "string" data type, but an array of characters, with a convention that the end of a string is indicated by a null byte, can be used for the same purpose. The most commonly used string routines perform the functions of copying one string to another, comparing two strings, and computing a string length. More sophisticated string operations can often be performed using the I/O routines, which are described next.

Most of the routines in the standard library deal with input and output. Most C programmers use stream I/O, although there is no reason why record I/O could not be used with the language. There are three default streams: the standard input, the standard output, and the error output. The most elementary routines for dealing with these streams are getchar(), which reads a character from the standard input, and putchar(c), which writes the character c on the standard output. In the environments in which C programs run, it is generally possible to redirect these streams to files or other programs; the program itself does not change and is unaware of the redirection.

The most common output data function is

```
printf(format, data1, data2,...)
```

which performs data conversion for formatted output. The string format is copied to the standard output, except that when a conversion specification introduced by a % character is found in format it is replaced by the value of the next data argument, converted according to the specification. For example,

```
printf("n = %d, x = %f", n, x);
```

prints n as a decimal integer and x as a floating-point number, as in

```
n = 17, x = 12.34
```

A similar function scanf performs formatted input conversion.

All the routines mentioned have versions that operate on streams other than the standard input or output, and printf and scanf variants may also process a string, to allow for in-memory format conversion. Other routines in the I/O library transmit whole lines between memory and files, and check for error or end-of-file status.

Many other routines and utilities are used with C, somewhat more on Unix than on other systems. As an example, it is possible to compile and load a C program so that when the program is run, data is collected on the number of times each function is called and how long it executes. This profile pinpoints the parts of the program that dominate the run time.

Experience with C

Compilers exist for the most widely used machines at Bell Laboratories (the IBM S/370, Honeywell 6000, PDP-11) and perhaps ten others. Several hundred programmers within Bell Laboratories and many outside use C as their primary programming language.

Favorable Experiences

C has completely displaced assembly language in Unix programs. All application code, the C compiler itself, and the operating system (except for about 1000 lines of initial bootstrap, and so on) are written in C. Although compilers or interpreters are available under Unix for Fortran, Pascal, Algol 68, Snobol, APL, and other languages, most programmers make little use of them. Since C is a relatively low-level language, it is adequately efficient to prevent people from resorting to *assembler*, and yet sufficiently terse and expressive that its users prefer it to PL/1 or other very large languages.

A language that does not have everything is actually easier to program in than some that do. The limitations of C often imply shorter manuals and easier training and adaptation. Language design, especially when done by a committee, often tends toward including all doubtful features, since there is no quick answer to the advocate who insists that the new feature will be useful to some and can be ignored by others. This results in long manuals and hierarchies of "experts" who know progressively larger subsets of the language. In practice, if a feature is not used often enough to be familiar and does not complete some structure of syntax or semantics, it should probably be left out. Otherwise, the manual and compiler get bulky, the users get surprises, and it becomes harder and harder to maintain and use the language. It is also desirable to avoid language features that cannot be compiled efficiently; programmers like to feel that the cost of a statement is comparable to the difficulty in writing it. C has thus avoided implementing operations in the language that would have to be performed by subroutine call. As compiler technology improves, some extensions (such as structure assignment) are being made in C, but always with some principles in mind.

One direction for possible expansion of the language has been explicitly avoided. Although C is much used for writing operating systems and associated software, there are no facilities for multiprogramming, parallel operations, synchronization, or process control. We believe that making these operations primitives of the language is inappropriate, mostly because language design is hard enough in itself without incorporating into it the design of operating systems. Language facilities of this sort tend to make strong assumptions about the underlying operating system that may match very poorly what it actually does.

Unfavorable Experiences

The design and implementation of C can (or could) be criticized on several points. Here we discuss some of the more vulnerable aspects of the language.

Language Level. Some users complain that C is an insufficiently high-level language; for example, they want string data types and operations, or variable-size multidimensional arrays, or generic functions. Sometimes a suggested extension merely involves lifting some restriction. For example, allowing variable-size arrays would actually simplify the language specification, since it would only involve allowing general expressions in place of constants in certain contexts.

Many other extensions are plausible; since the low level of C was praised in the previous section as an advantage of the language, most will not be further discussed. One is worthy of mention, however. The C language provides no facility for I/O, leaving this job to library routines. The following fragment illustrates one difficulty with this approach:

```
printf("%d\n",x);
```

The problem arises on machines on which int is not the same as long: x may not be long; if it were, the program must be written

```
printf("%ld\n",x);
```

so as to tell printf the length of x. Thus, changing the type of x involves changing not only its declaration, but also other parts of the program. If I/O were built into the language, the association between the type of an expression and the format in which it is printed could be reconciled by the compiler.

Type Safety. C has traditionally been permissive in checking whether an expression is used in a context appropriate to its type. A complete list of examples would be long, but two of the most important should illustrate sufficiently. The types of formal arguments of functions are in general not known, and in any case are not checked by the compiler against the actual arguments at each call. Thus in the statement

```
s = sin(1)
```

the fact that the *sin* routine takes a floating-point argument is not noticed until the erroneous result is detected by the programmer.

In the structure reference

```
p->memb
```

p is simply assumed to point to a structure of which *memb* is a member; *p* might even be an integer and not a pointer at all.

Much of the explanation, if not justification, for such laxity is the typeless nature of C's predecessor languages. Fortunately, a justification need no longer be attempted, since a program is now available that detects all common type mismatches. This utility, called lint because it picks bits of fluff from programs, examines a set of files and complains about a great many dubious constructions, ranging from unused or uninitialized variables through the type errors mentioned. Programs that pass unscathed through lint seemingly enjoy freedom from type errors to the same degree as do Algol 68 programs, with a few exceptions: unions are not checked dynamically, and explicit escapes are available that in effect turn off checking.

Some languages, such as Pascal and Euclid, allow the writer to specify that the value of a given variable may assume only a given subrange of the integers. This facility is often connected with the usage of arrays, in that any array index must be a variable or expression whose type specifies a subset of the set given by the bounds of the array. This approach is not without theoretical difficulties, as suggested by Habermann (1973). In itself it does not solve the problems of variables assuming unexpected values or of accessing outside array bounds; such things must (in general) be detected dynamically. Still, the extra information provided by specifying the permissible range for each variable provides valuable information for the compiler and any verifier program. C has no corresponding facility.

One of the characteristic features of C is its rather complete integration of the notion of pointer and of address arithmetic. Some writers, notably Hoare (1975), have argued against the very notion of pointer. We feel, however, that the facilities offered by pointers are too valuable to give up lightly.

Syntax Peculiarities. Some people are annoyed by the terseness of expression that is one of the characteristics of the language. We view C's short operators and general lack of noise as a benefit. For example, the use of braces {} for grouping instead of begin and end seems appropriate in view of the frequency of the operation. The use of braces even fits well into ordinary mathematical notation.

Terseness can lead to code that is hard to read, however. For example,

```
*++*argv
```

where *argv* has been declared char **argv (pointer to an array of character pointers) means: select the character pointer pointed at by argv (*argv) increment it by one (++*argv), then retrieve the character that *that* pointer points at (*++*argv). This is concise and efficient but reminiscent of APL.

An example of a minor problem is the comment convention, which is PL/1's /*...*/. Comments do not nest, so an effort to "comment out" a section of code will fail if that section contains a comment. And several of us can testify that it is surprisingly hard to recognize when an "end comment" delimiter has been botched, so that the comment silently continues until the next comment is reached, deleting a line or two of code. It would be more convenient if a single unique character were reserved to introduce a comment, and if comments were always terminated at an end of line.

Semantic Peculiarities. There are some occasionally surprising operator precedences. For example,

```
a >> 4 + 5
```

shifts right by 9. Perhaps worse,

```
(x & MASK) == 0
```

must be parenthesized to associate the proper way. Users learn quickly to parenthesize such doubtful cases; and when feasible, lint warns of suspicious expressions (including both of these).

We have already mentioned the fact that the case actions in a switch flow through, unless explicitly broken. In practice, users write so many switch statements that they become familiar with this behavior, and some even prefer it.

Some problems arise from machine differences that are reflected, perhaps unnecessarily, onto the semantics of C. For example, the PDP-11 does sign extension on byte retrieves, so that a character (viewed arithmetically) can have a value ranging from -128 to $+127$, rather than 0 to $+255$. Although the reference manual makes it quite clear that the precise range of a char variable is machine dependent, programmers occasionally succumb to the temptation of using the full range that their local machine can represent, forgetting that their programs may not work on another machine. The fundamental problem, of course, is that C permits small numbers, as well as genuine characters, to be stored in char variables. This might not be necessary if, for example, the notion of subranges (explained above) were introduced into the language.

Miscellaneous. C was developed and is generally used in a highly responsive interactive environment, and accordingly the compiler provides few of the services usually associated with batch compilers. For example, it prepares no listing of the source program, no cross-reference table, and no indication of the nature of the generated code. Such facilities are available, but they are separate programs, not parts of the compiler. Programmers used to batch environments may find it hard to live without giant listings; we would find it hard to use them.

Conclusions and Future Directions

C has continued to develop in recent years, mostly by upwardly compatible extensions, occasionally by restrictions against manifestly nonportable or illegal programs that happened to be compiled into something useful. The most recent major changes were motivated by the extension of C to other machines, and the resulting emphasis on portability. The advent of union, and of casts reflects a desire to be more precise about types, when using other machines becomes a prospect. These changes have had relatively little effect on programmers who remained entirely on the Unix system. Of more importance was a new library, that changed the use of a "portable" library from an option into an effective standard, while increasing the efficiency of the library so that users would not object.

It is more difficult, of course, to speculate about the future. C is now encountering more and more foreign environments, and this is producing many demands for C to adapt itself to the hardware, and particularly to the operating systems, of other machines. Bit fields, for example, are a response to a request to describe externally imposed data layouts. Similarly, the procedures for external storage allocation and referencing have been made tighter to conform to requirements on other systems. Portability of the basic language seems well handled, but interactions with operating systems grow ever more complex. These lead to requests for more sophisticated data descriptions and initializations, and even for assembler windows. Further changes of this sort are likely.

What is not likely is a fundamental change in the level of the language. Realistically, the very acceptance of C has compelled changes to be made only most cautiously and compatibly. Should the pressure for improvements become too strong for the language to accommodate, C would probably have to be left as is, and a totally new language developed. We leave it to the reader to speculate on whether it should be called D or P.

References

Habermann, A. N., 1973. "Critical Comments on the Programming Language Pascal." *Acta Informatica*, 3, pp. 47–58.

Hoare, C. A. R., 1975. "Data Reliability." *ACM SIGPLAN Notices*, 10 (June), pp. 528–533.

Johnson, S. C., and Kernighan, B. W., 1973. "The Programming Language B." Computer Science Tech Report No. 8, Bell Laboratories (January).

Kernighan, B. W., and Ritchie, D. M., 1978. *The C Programming Language*. Englewood Cliffs, N.J.: Prentice-Hall.

Richards, M., 1969. "BCPL: A Tool for Compiler Writing and Systems Programming." *Proceedings AFIPS SJCC*, 34, pp. 557–566.

2
PUTTING C ON A MICROCOMPUTER: THE ORIGINAL SMALL-C

by Ron Cain

The article from which this excerpt is taken originally appeared in DDJ #45 (July 1980).

I had to have a compiler for my home computer.
There was no doubt about it: after programming nearly every day in BLISS and then reading about C, Pascal, LISP, and all the other various languages becoming available, it made no sense at all to continue programming in assembly language.
However, the question arose: Which language?
Surprisingly, the decision was not difficult. Since I do mostly system programming (editors, music-board drivers, modem talkers, faster versions of Life, and so on) rather than application programming (accounting programs, solar eclipse predictors, and so on), the choice boiled down to two: C or BLISS. Besides having the most esoteric names of the group, both possess the strengths of system programming languages—that is to say, they both have a slightly better notion of computer architectures than strictly application-oriented languages in terms of accessing bytes and words, and neither wastes time doing "garbage collection" or keeping track of legal array subscripting. Both are intended to produce fairly fast (usually inline) code to get the job done with the least amount of overhead.
After looking around the marketplace, I decided C was the appropriate choice if I expected to produce code usable by others. However, another thing also became obvious: the C compilers available either cost a lot of money, ran only on CP/M, or both. Having neither a lot of money nor CP/M (the second by choice), I had to think of an alternate approach.

The first step came by way of the Tiny-C Interpreter offered by Tiny-C Associates. For a mere $40, I was able to buy the source code of a working C interpreter. I intended to use it to run the C programs I would write until something bigger and better came along. I sent off the money, got the huge white notebook in the mail, and after a couple weeks of typing, had it up and running. Let me be another of many praising the product. The documentation, clarity of print, and ease of implementation were all exceedingly good.

It gave me a few weeks to evaluate the C language as well as the interpreter. It became obvious after a short time that the language was very easy to use and to follow. It also became obvious that the interpreter, though an excellent implementation, was too slow for my needs. Modem to disk programs like to think in terms of microseconds, not milliseconds, and the former was not to be had with an interpreter. Clearly, a third approach was needed.

The solution was obvious: I had to write the compiler myself. (I said obvious, not easy.)

So, after gathering a thick stack of paper and getting ready to produce the (I hoped) last vast 8080 programming effort, I wrote a few lines, and . . . reconsidered.

What better use of a systems programming language could there be than to write a compiler? And what better language could be used than the one the compiler would ultimately support? Ideas began to gel, and pieces began to fit together. I already had the interpreter. Even though it was slow, it might be just the ticket to bootstrap my way onto the machine. And so it began.

Considering I had never even seen a compiler before, and had not done any lengthy programs in C, everything came together in a remarkably short period of time. Chalk that up to the ease of use of the language. The ability to have variables local to individual routines made the recursive-descent expression parser fit together literally in hours. A few weeks of a couple of hours per night saw the compiler begin to take shape. A few obstacles appeared along the way; probably the worst was when I discovered I didn't have enough memory for the entire compiler to reside in the memory along with the interpreter. One demonic session with the editor, deleting all comments (gulp) and shortening all names, brought it to size and solved that problem. The compiler's still recovering from that early trauma. Eventually, there came an evening when all such little problems were solved, and the compiler, running under the interpreter, accepted a small C program and produced an 8080 program.

At that point, I refined the compiler, removed subtle errors, and discovered I still didn't have enough memory for the compiler, the interpreter, and the symbol table that a program as large as the compiler itself required. So I asked around, eventually got access to a Unix system, and spent a couple more weeks refining the compiler without regard to memory or interpreters. This exercise helped remove some of the less obvious syntax errors not caught by the interpreter and necessitated modifying the compiler to accept the true C syntax rather than the slightly modified syntax used by the interpreter. After this upgrade, the compiler was beginning to look like a true C compiler, and there came a time it ran under Unix and accepted as input itself.

So, finally, I was able to take the equivalent 8080 code for the compiler back to my machine at home to complete it. The generated code was assembled, run, and once again the compiler was submitted to itself. The results of this inbreeding highlighted errors in the generated 8080 code that had thus far been hidden. I set those aright, compiled the compiler once again, then used the output to compile the compiler again, and then one more time (sounds like an infinite loop?) compiled the compiler. When the code generated by this great-grandson was byte-for-byte identical to the code generated by Unix way back when, and all subsequent offspring produced such twins, I decided the language could be considered working.

Once it was working, I decided it would save people in a similar situation a lot of parallel effort if I made it available.

For those of you who are interested in getting a compiler for a structured language on your home machines, I'd feel flattered if you'd consider the one published here. And if you are the sort who is looking for a systems programming language, you are undoubtedly the sort who would modify this to fit your own needs. Therefore, a few vital statistics are in order.

In a nutshell, the compiler:

- Is written in C
- Accepts as input a text file written in C
- Produces as output a text file of 8080 mnemonics

The syntax it accepts is a subset of the standard C language. Within this subset, it does not depart from the standard syntax, which means the listing shown here can compile and run under Unix. Although the subset is limited to make the compiler simpler and therefore does not accept just any pre-existing C program, the programs you can write with it are authentic and will be compatible with more complete compilers.

The features of standard C this compiler does *not* support are:

- Floating-point data types
- Structures (or unions)
- Multiple dimension arrays

The aim was not to support the full C language, but rather to support enough of a subset to be able to create C programs that would be compatible with standard C. Then, as the compiler expanded, more and more features could be added to bring it closer in compatibility with other systems.

Currently, the allowable data types are *char* (8-bit data element) and *int* (16-bit data element). Obviously, this means the compiler is an integer-only subset of the language—that means it will not handle floating-point numbers. Actually, all internal arithmetic operations assume 16-bit integers, meaning 8-bit character elements are sign-extended prior to use.

Allowable modifiers of the two basic types are;

1. type *name—declares name to be a pointer to an element of the specified type.

2. type name[]—syntactically identical to the above pointer declaration.

3. type name[constant]—declares an array of "constant" size where each array element is of the specified type.

If you've worked with C before, you know just about everything is done with pointers. It lets you exploit the architecture of the CPU by giving access to all addressable memory. Unlike standard C, you can't use more than one modifier per declaration, meaning, it will not accept something like int (*name)[]. This does not present a terrible restriction, but it must be mentioned. Since no run-time checking is made on the legality of pointer usage, it is a trivial matter to access any byte in memory, and a not-at-all-trivial problem finding which routine is clobbering some random location. You can see why pointers have been lumped with goto's as the bane of the code maintainers and modifiers.

Already, a couple of distributors or private parties have the C programming language working on other machines or are planning it....

This brings up interesting points. If you haven't already made the intuitive leap to the power behind writing the compiler in the same language it supports, it lies in the ability to compile itself. This means users with extra memory can add additional features to the basic compiler, compile it with the old compiler, and a new and more powerful version will exist.

If you have a working compiler on one CPU and want to bootstrap your way to another kind of processor, you need only change the code-generating portions of the compiler (all grouped into the final sections of the listing) to make code for the new machine, compile that compiler, and once again, you have a new language. Sort of like cloning.

Personally, I've developed the language about as far as I needed it for the things I originally intended. However, I am still interested in hearing what modifications are found useful, what machines it eventually wanders onto, and any other interesting paths this language takes.

If you get the language running on your home system, make mods to it, make it run on another CPU, or are in a position to make copies of your work for others with similar CPUs, I would appreciate hearing about it in *Dr. Dobb's.*

I think it's an excellent opportunity to learn how a compiler works and at the same time establish the necessary groundwork for a C community.

[Note: The listing for the Small-C compiler rev. 1.1 (ten pages of small print) is still available as a reprint from DDJ. Version 1.1, adapted to CP/M and with certain improvements, is also available from The Code Works in Goleta, California.]

Putting C on a Microcomputer: The Original Small-C

The following letter from Ron Cain appeared in DDJ #76 (February 1983).

The December [1982] issue of *Dr. Dobb's Journal* [#74] containing the first installment of version 2 of Small-C was definitely a welcome sight. With all the bug corrections and improvements for version 1.0 that have been dribbling in these last couple years, it was becoming clear that someone would just have to sit down and pull together all the pieces.

Marlin Ouverson [then DDJ editor] approached me with the idea of an official rewrite of the little compiler. Though I was eager to give it a try, there was simply no way to find all the spare time required to do it right. At the same time, it was clear (at least to me) that there were some pretty respectable Small-C experts emerging from the readership of *Dr. Dobb's* who were quite possibly more familiar with the original compiler than I (odd thought, that).

So Marlin and I pondered the problem and soon realized there was one name that had appeared more than once in regard to Small-C: J. E. Hendrix. But could we ask him to do it? Marlin contacted him and, well, you can see the results.

I want to make it quite clear that my only role in this was sending to Jim a rather open-ended wish list. From my suggestions (most of which he had already anticipated or even implemented), and from those of Neal Block and Dr. James Van Zandt, Jim somehow found the time necessary to fix the old bugs, check our improvement wish lists, and toss in some compile-time options of his own. I consider the finished product excellent.

Some readers may wish for features not yet implemented (naturally, any programmer wants all the language features possible). Jim is as aware of those as anyone. However, my own feeling is that he chose exactly the right place to stop development, chase out the bugs, and get the language into print. It is the same decision I made many months (and features) ago.

I have no doubt that this new version represents far more work than the original (which was less than a month of spare time in the doing). And because of that, it is a much more generous gift.

3
C NOTEBOOK: SELECTIONS FROM DR. DOBB'S FIRST C COLUMN

by Anthony Skjellum

This chapter is based on a set of columns that appeared in DDJ #84 to #100 (September 1983 to February 1984). The original ten columns, entitled "C/Unix Programmer's Notebook," covered both the C language and the Unix operating system. This chapter contains programs and discussions from nine of the columns related specifically to C.

The C language was already popular when the first C/Unix column appeared. Today, it is even more widely used. Yet despite the proliferation of C books in bookstores, most of these books are for beginners. That means new users have virtually no source for additional information, once they have exhausted the value of beginning books. The material in this chapter is tutorial and therefore should prove interesting to both advanced novices and more seasoned users. I have reorganized the columns by topic to improve readability, added several footnotes and comments, and made some corrections and additions.

What follows is not just a set of useful programs and documentation. Mostly, it is a discussion about the C language, including programming style, language extensions, and runtime libraries. Importantly, a significant percentage of the commentary came from readers who responded to my comments and proposals with their own often different ideas and conceptions. In retrospect, I am convinced that this interaction is what makes the following pages both informative and interesting.

Part 1

LAYOUT OF C CODE

The C language is one of the few standards that applies to a wide variety of computers. *The C Programming Language*, by Brian W. Kernighan and Dennis B. Ritchie (Prentice-Hall, 1978), defines a standard language and runtime library, and also discusses implementation differences in several minicomputer implementations. The book does not define a standard for the layout and presentation of C code, considering this as a matter of personal taste. After reading a lot of C programs from many sources, I have decided that programmers pay too little attention to this aspect of C programming. In this section, I will explain the problem, suggest a standard for C code layout, and propose a possible solution.

Whenever I receive a new piece of C code, I always check to see how the programmer has presented the code. A clear presentation with many comments and an uncluttered look is important for maintaining such code and for aiding other programmers who must understand it. More often than not, the code looks something like the following:

```
main(){printf("Hello world\n");
}
```

In this case the programmer hasn't formatted the program properly. This makes it difficult to follow the inherent block structure of the language. The cluttered look that results from improper indentation is often also accompanied by a paucity of comments. The resulting code is usually hard to understand, improve, or debug.

The style presented in Kernighan and Ritchie (K&R) is consistent, but not optimal, since it does not present blocks and block nesting in the clearest way possible. For example, an *if...else* loop appears as follows:

```
if ((fp = fopen(argv[1],"r")) == NULL) { /* not found */
        fprintf(stderr,"%s not found\n",argv[1]);
        exit(1);
} else {                   /* the file is present */
        fprintf(stderr,"%s is on-line\n",argv[1]);
        fclose(fp);
}
```

Using the same fragment, I prefer the following format:

```
if((fp = fopen(argv[1],"r")) == NULL)   /* not found */
{
        fprintf(stderr,"%s not found\n",argv[1]);
        exit(1);   /* exit with error status 1 */
}
else    /* the file is present */
{
        fprintf(stderr,"%s is on-line\n",argv[1]);
        fclose(fp); /* close the file */
}
```

In the second form, eight-space (standard) tabs are used for indentation (as opposed to the six-space indentation used by the book). Braces are almost always on their own lines and the lowest level braces appear at the left margin. Braces indicate the nesting level of the expression that invoked them, and their contents are themselves indented an additional level. Only one statement is placed on a line, and comments are added liberally to make the code more understandable. Finally, the space used by K&R between keywords and their parenthetical expressions is omitted. (Note: In the amended standard discussed below, this space is optional but recommended. Originally, I didn't think a space in this context added readability, so I recommended that it be omitted (see Table 3-1)).

This example illustrates the layout standard I am proposing, summarized in Table 3-1. The purpose of proposing this standard is to induce C programmers to think more carefully about the layout and presentation of their C code. Clearly, there is more to programming than the layout of the code. The data structures and program structures used are crucial in producing a good piece of software. However, without good layout, the best program may be difficult to understand, maintain, or improve.

Table 3-1.
Proposed Standard for C Code Layout, Preliminary Version

1. Standard tabs are used for program indentation.
    a. Four space tabs may be used, if desired, after column 56. This is permitted to prevent line wrap on 80-column displays.
2. A brace is generally on a line by itself.
    a. The lowest level braces appear on the left margin.
    b. Comments may appear on lines containing a brace, but only after the brace.
    c. Braces are indented to the same depth as the statement that invoked the block they frame.
    d. In variable initializations, the opening brace may be placed on the same line as the equal sign, but the closing brace must have the same indentation as the opening one.
    e. In general, no statements may appear on the same line as a brace.
3. A block begins with a left brace and ends with a right brace. Its contents are indented an extra level to indicate the nesting depth.

Table 3-1 (continued).

    a. Whenever a block is longer than 24 lines (a standard CRT page), a comment should follow the closing brace to indicate the block that the brace closes.
        i. This applies to whole functions as well as regular blocks.
        ii. This rule should also be applied with shorter blocks when block nesting makes the code complex and these comments improve the readability.
    b. The opening and closing braces of a block are always indented identically.
    c. The case/default labels of a switch statement are always indented a level, like statements in a block. The statements that follow these labels are always indented an extra level to improve readability.
    d. Regular labels (destinations for *goto*'s) are always placed at the left margin, regardless of nesting depth.
    e. When a null block is used (for example, {}), it may appear on the same line as statements (for example, *do* {} *while(expr);*).
    f. If a single statement is used instead of a block, it is indented a single level, just as if it were surrounded by braces.
        i. Null statements (that is, just a ";") are indented in the same way as regular statements.

4. White space is added in expressions and assignments to improve readability.
    a. Relational operators are delimited by single spaces.
    b. Equal signs are delimited by single spaces.
    c. Unary operators are not separated by space from their operands.
    d. Parentheses are added to improve readability in complex expressions, even if they are not required to produce correct evaluation.
        i. A *return* statement always has a set of parentheses surrounding its expression.
    e. No white space character is placed between function names and their parenthesized argument list.
    f. No white space character is placed between a keyword (for example, *if*) and its parenthesized argument.

5. Comments are added liberally to make the program read easily.
    a. If a comment requires more than one line, the start/end comment tokens are placed on lines containing no comment text. In this case, the start/end tokens are indented identically.
    b. If a comment fits on a single line, the start/end tokens must also be placed on that line.

6. Variables are always declared, even if your version of C has a default type. Always explain the purpose of your variables.
    a. Declare the variables in logical groups, and include a comment on the same line as the declaration to describe the function(s) of the variable(s).
    b. Avoid numerous declarations on a single line.
    c. Explain complex pointer declarations.
    d. Variable names are always lowercase only.
    e. External variable declarations may be indented a single level for greater readability.

7. Constants created with #*define* are always uppercase. Macros created with #*define* may be uppercase or lowercase.
    a. As with variables, constants should have explanatory comments to explain their purpose.
    b. Macros should be explained via comments to avoid misunderstandings about their uses. This is especially important since macros tend to be cryptic.

Table 3-1 (continued).

    c. Restrict #*define* statements to the beginning of code files (that is, before the first function). This avoids the potential for redefinition and other confusion.

8. Other items

    a. The *else..if(expr)* construct is placed on a single line as if it were a single keyword.
    b. Function names are always lowercase.

9. Portability considerations

    a. When using a nonstandard C feature, always prepare a portable alternative that may be selected via conditional compilation.
    b. Indicate any subtle uses of sign extension and type conversions made by your program or your specific compiler.
    c. Indicate any deviations in the way your compiler handles pointer arithmetic.
    d. Include the ampersand operator (&) when you pass pointers to structures, even if your compiler doesn't require it. Someone else's compiler may support passing structures.
    e. Indicate any deviations of your runtime library from the standard.
    f. Indicate any deviation in the (argc,argv) command line conventions made by your compiler.

A Possible Solution

Even if a layout standard had been described in *The C Programming Language*, some programmers would deviate from it. To provide programmers with the code layouts they prefer, C beautifiers are created. Such programs take C code as input, and by adding/removing white space characters, reformat the C code to some individual layout specification. This allows each programmer to distribute code in a standard layout, while using his or her preferred layout standard for local copies of the code.

    Beautifiers already exist. For example, Berkeley Unix has a beautifier called CB. This program is fairly simpleminded, but it can convert totally unformatted C code (one using the minimum amount of white space) into the K&R-type layout. More ambitious beautifiers can be created, and this is left for readers to work on.

Modifying the Proposed Layout Standard: Questions of White Space

Several readers took exception to one point concerning the proposed layout standard. This was point *4f*, which states, "No white space character is placed between a keyword (for example, if) and its parenthesized argument." David D. Clark of State College, Pennsylvania, wrote, "In general, I like your coding standard suggestions. My only strong objection is your idea of omitting spaces between reserved words [and their arguments]. It makes them look like function invocations."

Tim Smith of Evanston, Illinois, noted, "I think a single space between a function name and the initial opening parenthesis, or after ifs and elses, looks better.

Guy Scharf of Mountain View, California, wrote, "*4f.* I have a strong preference to *always* put a space between a reserved word (*if, while*) and its parenthesized argument. This adds legibility for me."

Finally, Charlie Brady of New South Wales, Australia, wrote, "The only real beef I have with you is the formatting of keywords and their parenthetical expressions. I can see no reason to depart from Kernighan and Ritchie on this point, and a number of reasons for maintaining their convention. First, a flow control construct is semantically distinct from a function call, and a formatting difference is a reasonable way of distinguishing them. Second, the formatting difference simplifies the use of a text editor for such tasks as constructing structure charts. Third, your recommendation departs from at least three extant recommended standards, namely Kernighan and Ritchie, Thomas Plum, (*Programming Standards and Guidelines*, Plum Hall, 1981) and Tim Lang ("Formatting," *AUGEN*, 4(1), January, 1982). (The C standard proposed by Lang is compatible with the one described in Table 3-1.)

After considering the above remarks, I have concluded that the space does serve a useful purpose. Therefore, I suggest point 4f be changed to read: "A single white character is (optionally) placed between a keyword (for example, *if*) and its parenthesized argument." (Making the white space character optional is another point for debate.) I think it should be optional, but recommended. I don't think that adding a space for function call invocations would be beneficial, as suggested by Mr. Smith.

Another question concerning white space insertion comes in connection with argument lists. The original standard does not indicate if spaces should be included. I think that a comma should be directly adjacent to the argument that it follows, and that a single white space should follow each comma to add legibility. I am also convinced that parentheses should be adjacent to the argument(s) they enclose. Thus (in agreement with Tim Lang's article, mentioned above) I would write

```
x = atan(sin(y));
```

and not

```
x = atan( sin( y ) );
```

Yet another point is that binary operators should be delimited by white space. Thus, the following statement lacks sufficient white space

```
v = sin(ln(1.0+x));
```

whereas this expression is properly formed

v = sin(ln(1.0 + x));

Finally, Section 4 needs to be updated to include a style specification for pointer references. I think that that operators "." and "->" should not be delimited by spaces from the objects they act on. This point and the three above are formalized in Table 3-2 as additions to Section 4.

Table 3-2.
Additions to Section 4 of Proposed Standard for C Code Layout

4. b. Binary operators (for example, +, -, /, but not "->" and ".") and assignment operators (for example, =, *=, &=) are delimited by white space.
   g. Parentheses should be adjacent to the argument(s) they enclose.
   h. A comma is bound to the argument that precedes and should be followed by a single space.
   i. Operators such as "->" and "." (used in pointer references) directly bind to their arguments with no intervening spaces.

The Lang article points out a circumstance under which point 4g need not be followed. This occurs when complicated conditional expressions of the form "*keyword* (expr)" are split over several lines. For example, you need not use a crowded expression, as follows:

```
if((a == 1) && (b == 2) && (c == 3) && ((d == 4) || (d == 5)))
{
        /* operations performed if conditional true */
        ...
}
```

Instead, you can select a much more readable form:

```
if      /* we make multiline expression look like a block */
(
        (a == 1) &&
        (b == 2) &&
        (c == 3) &&
        ((d == 4) || (d == 5))
)
(
        /* operations performed if conditional true */
        ...
}
```

In this example, the parentheses are placed on lines by themselves, since they bracket a multiline expression, much like braces enclose the statements of a block.

Another point of minor objection was the tabulation method specified by the standard (point *1a*). Steve Newberry of Los Altos, California, stated, "Upon one point I do feel compelled to argue with you, and that is the tab convention: The *depth* of the tab stop on a given page is of far less significance to the readability of that page than is the *consistency* of the depth. I *really* don't want to use different size tabs on the same page."

Tim Smith wrote, "I personally follow most all of his suggestions on how to actually format the code on the line and page, with only two exceptions. I *always* use 4-space tab stops."

I agree that having a single tab size is the preferable way to write C code. Standard tabs give more openness to the code and make various parts of a program easier to pick out. My rationale for large horizontal tabbing is the same as for vertical tabbing. I want the program's significant portions to stand out. However, I propose adding point *1b* to the standard: "Four-space tabs may be used in lieu of standard tabs in cases where a subprogram includes highly nested segments." I would also include point *1c*: "Only one of the two tabbing conventions should be employed in any given program module."

Some currently available screen editors provide a feature called horizontal scrolling. With horizontal scrolling, you can view a window of your file in both the vertical and horizontal directions. Thus, files with lines longer than the display device may be handled intelligently. Under such circumstances, there is no real disadvantage to using standard tabs to any desired nesting depth, which is permitted by point *1a* of the proposed standard.

Other Corrections

Charlie Brady noted that point *3e* is unnecessary. Point *3e* was: "When a null block is used (for example, {}), it may appear on the same line as other statements (for example, *do* {} *while(expr)*;)." Mr. Brady wrote, "Another minor point of disagreement concerns the use of the null block ({}). This is never necessary, and I believe that the null statement (;) is clearer. It should be emphasized that the null statement *deserves* a line of its own. Your example:

```
do {} while(expr);
```

is more simply written

```
while (expr)
    ;
```

In accordance with Mr. Brady's remark, I propose replacing point *3e* with the following: "The null block ({}) can always be avoided. Instead of a null block, use the null statement." I also would add point *3f-ii*: "The null statement is always on a line by itself."

Documentation Standards

In addition to a code layout standard, James Halstead of Joliet, Illinois, has proposed a basic documentation standard. He wrote, "I strongly suggest that the original standards one through nine be renumbered two through ten so that the first and foremost standard may be inserted."

The documentation standard suggested by Mr. Halstead is presented in Table 3-3. In including this as part of the proposed standard. I chose to place it in section 0 to avoid renumbering. (Asterisks indicate slight additions I made.)

Table 3-3.
Documentation Standard for C (per Halstead)

0. Identification Description (I.D.) information must appear at the the beginning of each C language source file.
    a. The recommended format is:
        i. Begin comment (/*).
        ii. Space.
        iii. Title (identification name normally = filename).
   *   iv. Subtitle (that is, what program system does this file belong to).
        v. Space.
        vi. Classification (see below).
        vii. Year.
        viii. Owner.
        ix. Status (see below).
   *   x. Current version number and brief history.
        xi. Date.
        xii. Functional/structural description in brief.
  *   xiii. Portability synopsis.
  *   xiv. Space.
        xv. End Comment (*/).
  *   xvi. Space.
    b. The program classification (a-vi) is one (or more) of the following:
        i. Public-domain.
        ii. Copyright.
   *   iii. Copyright: released for noncommercial purposes.
        iv. Unclassified.
        v. Secret.
   *   vi. Freeware [voluntary contribution software]
        vii. No classification.
    c. The program status (a-ix) is one of the following:
        i. Outline.
        ii. Draft.
        iii. Test (alpha, beta, and so on).
        iv. Release.

In addition to Section 0, I think a basic documentation standard for functions would also be useful. Such a standard is presented in Table 3-4. I have placed this under section 10, since function documentation is a distinct task from module documentation, as described in section 0 (Table 3-3).

Table 3-4.
Documentation Standard for Functions

10. Each function should contain the following minimum documentation:
    a. A general explanation of the function performed.
    b. Its name, and a description of its arguments including their types and legal values.
    c. A description of the functional return value, if any.
    d. A list of nonstandard functions used by the function.
    e. A list of external variables used and/or modified by the function.
    f. A description of the error handling characteristics of the function.
    g. A valid calling sequence example, if practical.

Other Proposals

Several other readers made suggestions for the standard. Tim Smith proposed several that merit discussion. They are presented in Table 3-5 with the point numbers they receive as part of the standard:

Table 3-5.
Smith's Revisions to Code Standard

(5c). Don't nest comments, even if your preprocessor/compiler allows it.

(6f). If there are many declarations, whether on one line or many, alphabetize them.

(9g). Restrict variable and function names to 7 well-chosen characters, even if your compiler allows more.

Steve Newberry wrote the following about standards: "I applaud your interest in establishing a standard format convention for C programs. However, I feel that your effort would have more impact if tied to support of Tom Plum's book *C Programming Standards and Guidelines, Version U (Unix and offspring)*, third edition, January 1982. Presented in this manner, your proposed formatting standard would be seen as a consistent extension of a more general set of standards already in wide circulation."

Other Points of View

Although most readers were favorable to the idea of a C format standard, Douglas M. Potter of Seattle, Washington, wrote, "I afraid I don't see much advantage of your proposed standard over theirs [Kernighan and Ritchie]. In both cases, the size of the ident is too large, I always run out of room on the right side with a tab sized ident. I also find that nobody uses enough white space."

John F. Draffen of Texas City, Texas, wrote me a detailed letter on why he didn't like the idea: "I am writing to express my objections.... In the first place, I do not think a standard of this type is either necessary or desirable. The layout has nothing to do with portability, which to my mind is the only excuse for a standard. It seems to me that it is hard enough to get people to agree on necessary standards. In the second place, I do not agree with many of your suggestions on style. One of the nice things about C that it shares with Fortran is its relative conciseness. I do not like to see code strung out unnecessarily. C does not interject unnecessary constructions, and I think that introducing unnecessary white space, excessive indentation and meaningless comments is a kind of gingerbread that we can do without." Mr. Draffen's style philosophy is listed in Table 3-6.

Table 3-6.
Draffen's C Style Philosophy

1. Punctuation should be used sparingly. The insertion of unnecessary white space should be avoided.
2. Block structure should be indicated by indentation. Excessive indentation should be avoided.
3. Comments and program code should be separated. Comments on the same line as code should be displaced far enough to the right that they do not obscure the code.
4. Comments should be meaningful. Comments that do no more than repeat what has already been said by the code should be avoided.

I differ with Mr. Draffen on several counts. First and foremost, portability is not the sole subject of importance in programming. The ability to maintain, understand, correct, and enhance code is of great importance. To understand someone else's code (or your own code at a later date) requires some formatting. Comments that seem less than essential to the programmer must sometimes be included for the sake of others. This is immensely important. It is often difficult for programmers to know how to comment their code, since they usually cannot know the level of sophistication of later readers. Thus, it is often better to include a few extra comments than to comment code sparsely.

I suggested previously that users should maintain their code in the form that they prefer. However, code distributed to others could (and should) meet some minimum standard of neatness (formatting) and presentation. Some of this can be provided by a beautifier, but most must be done by the programmer.

As a final note on C layout, I'm including an insightful paragraph from Tim Smith. It suggests why so much C code is so poorly formatted and commented: "I don't think that you will ever get Unix wizards to follow these recommendations. I should have noted that I use Skjellum-like conventions when I'm writing micro-based applications. When I'm maintaining Unix sources, I stick with the standard Unix conventions, which are pretty much K&R standard. Unix whizzes think that aligning curly braces is irrelevant, since vi, the editor that 90% of them use, will always let you find the top or bottom match for any brace automatically. Also, and probably more important, Unix system users always debug by staring at their CRTs, never from printouts (that's for Cobol programmers), and the goal is to reduce the number of lines of a function, so that as much of it as possible will fit on a screen. Seeing a *whole line* taken up by just an opening brace must drive them crazy, and some of them will even close blocks on the end of a line of code (yecch!)"

A C Style Reference

I have included some general references about C style above. Since I wrote of that discussion, I've run into another paper on the subject. Although the formatting is different from what I prefer, I think this paper is well worth attention: *A C Style Sheet* by Martin Minow of Digital Equipment Corporation. (The article lists an address, so perhaps this is the best way to acquire a copy: Martin Minow, DEC, 146 Main Street, MLO 3-3/U8, Maynard, MA 01754.) It includes a list of references from which the work is "abstracted."

The most important point of the foregoing discussion is that programmers need to pay attention to more than just their algorithms. The questions of code layout and documentation require consideration. Using a self-consistent set of guidelines in preparing code and documentation can only help to improve the quality of the finished product.

For reader reference, the complete amended standard is included in Table 3-7.

Table 3-7.
Amended Proposal for C Code Layout

0. Identification Description (I.D.) information must appear at the beginning of each C language source file.
    a. The recommended format is:
        i. Begin comment (/*).
        ii. Space.
        iii. Title (identification name normally = filename).
        iv. Subtitle (that is, what program system does this file belong to).
        v. Space.
        vi. Classification (see below).
        vii. Year.
        viii. Owner.
        ix. Status (see below).
        x. Current Version number and brief history.
        xi. Date.
        xii. Functional/Structural Description in brief.
        xiii. Portability synopsis.

Table 3-7 (continued).

      xiv. Space.
      xv. End Comment (*/).
      xvi. Space.
  b. The program classification (a-vi) is one (or more) of the following:
      i. Public-domain.
      ii. Copyright.
      iii. Copyright: released for noncommercial purposes.
      iv. Unclassified.
      v. Secret.
      vi. Freeware [voluntary contribution software]
      vii. No classification.
  c. The program status (a-ix) is one of the following:
      i. Outline.
      ii. Draft.
      iii. Test (alpha, beta, and so on).
      iv. Release.

1. Standard tabs are used for program indentation.
   a. Four space tabs may be used, if desired, after column 56. This is permitted to prevent line wrap on 80-column displays.
   b. Four-space tabs may be used in lieu of standard tabs in cases where a subprogram includes highly nested segments.
   c. Only one of the two tabbing conventions should be employee in any given program module.

2. A brace is generally on a line by itself.
   a. The lowest level braces appear on the left margin.
   b. Comments may appear on lines containing a brace, but only after the brace.
   c. Braces are indented to the same depth as the statement that invoked the block they frame.
   d. In variable initializations, the opening brace may be placed on the same line as the equal sign, but the closing brace must have the same indentation as the opening one.
   e. In general, no statements may appear on the same line as a brace.

3. A block begins with a left brace and ends with a right brace. Its contents are indented an extra level to indicate the nesting depth.
   a. Whenever a block is longer than 24 lines (a standard CRT page), a comment should follow the closing brace to indicate the block the brace closes.
      i. This applies to whole functions as well as regular blocks.
      ii. This rule should also be applied with shorter blocks when block nesting makes the code complex and these comments improve the readability.
   b. The opening and closing braces of a block are always indented identically.
   c. The case/default labels of a switch statement are always indented a level, like statements in a block. The statements that follow these labels are always indented an extra level to improve readability.
   d. Regular labels (destinations for *goto's*) are always placed at the left margin, regardless of nesting depth.
   e. The null block {} can always be avoided. Instead of a null block, use the null statement.
   f. If a single statement is used instead of a block, it is indented a single level, just as if it were surrounded by braces.

Table 3-7 (continued).

     i. Null statements (that is, just a ";") are indented in the same way as regular statements.
    ii. The null statement is always on a line by itself.

4. White space is added in expressions and assignments to improve readability.
    a. Relational operators are delimited by single spaces.
    b. Binary operators (for example, +, -, /, but not "->" and ".") and assignment operators (for example, =, *=, &=) are delimited by white space.
    c. Unary operators are not separated by space from their operands.
    d. Parentheses are added to improve readability in complex expressions, even if they are not required to produce correct evaluation.
        i. A *return* statement always has a set of parentheses surrounding its expression.
    e. No white space character is placed between function names and their parenthesized argument list.
    f. A single white character is (optionally) placed between a keyword (for example, *if*) and its parenthesized argument.
    g. Parentheses should be adjacent to the argument(s) they enclose.
    h. A comma is bound to the argument that precedes and should be followed by a single space.
    i. Operators such as "->" and "." (used in pointer references) directly bind to their arguments with no intervening spaces.

5. Comments are added liberally to make the program read easily.
    a. If a comment requires more than one line, the start/end comment tokens are placed on lines containing no comment text. In this case, the start/end tokens are indented identically.
    b. If a comment fits on a single line, the start/end tokens must also be placed on that line.
    c. Do not nest comments, even if your preprocessor/compiler allows it.

6. Variables are always declared, even if your version of C has a default type. Always explain the purpose of your variables.
    a. Declare the variables in logical groups, and include a comment on the same line as the declaration to describe the function(s) of the variable(s).
    b. Avoid numerous declarations on a single line.
    c. Explain complex pointer declarations.
    d. Variable names are always lowercase only.
    e. External variable declarations may be indented a single level for greater readability.
    f. If there are many declarations, whether on one line or many, alphabetize them.

7. Constants created with #*define* are always uppercase. Macros created with #*define* may be uppercase or lowercase.
    a. As with variables, constants should have explanatory comments to explain their purpose.
    b. Macros should be explained via comments to avoid misunderstandings about their uses. This is especially important since macros tend to be cryptic.
    c. Restrict #*define* statements to the beginning of code files (that is, before the first function). This avoids the potential for redefinition and other confusion.

Table 3-7 (continued).

8. Other items.
    a. The *else..if(expr)* construct is placed on a single line as if it were a single keyword.
    b. Function names are always lowercase.
9. Portability considerations.
    a. When using a nonstandard C feature, always prepare a portable alternative that may be selected via conditional compilation.
    b. Indicate any subtle uses of sign extension and type conversions made by your program or your specific compiler.
    c. Indicate any deviations in the way your compiler handles pointer arithmetic.
    d. Include the ampersand operator (&) when you pass pointers to structures, even if your compiler doesn't require it. Someone else's compiler may support passing structures.
    e. Indicate any deviations of your runtime library from the standard.
    f. Indicate any deviation in the (argc,argv) command line conventions made by your compiler.
    g. Restrict variable and function names to 7 well-chosen characters, even if your compiler allows more.
10. Each function should contain the following minimum documentation:
    a. A general explanation of the function performed.
    b. Its name and a description of its arguments including their types and legal values.
    c. A description of the functional return value, if any.
    d. A list of nonstandard functions used by the function.
    e. A list of external variables used and/or modified by the function.
    f. A description of the error handling characteristics of the function.
    g. A valid calling sequence example, if practical.

Part 2

LINKER FORMATS AND RUNTIME LIBRARIES

The C Programming Language defines a standard runtime library for C. Some of the features provided are feasible only under Unix. Thus, for CP/M, CP/M-86, and MS-DOS implementations, only part of the runtime library can be supported. Yet some C compilers do not provide a compatible subset library. The result is code that cannot be easily transported from compiler to compiler, or machine to machine. Thus, such compilers negate one of the primary purposes of the C programming language: portability.

The BDS C Compiler is one such software product. It is an excellent subset compiler, but its runtime library is incompatible with the standard. After using BDS C for more than three years, I have accumulated a significant collection of useful subroutines and programs. Unfortunately, some of this software depends heavily on the BDS C runtime library. This code requires significant work before it can be used with another compiler. So be aware of this pitfall and be prepared to live with the consequences if you choose a compiler with a nonstandard runtime library.

BDS C is not the only compiler whose runtime library is nonstandard. The Whitesmith C compilers use their own too. However, since Whitesmith compilers are available for many different environments, portability between Whitesmith compilers is immediate. Nevertheless, I prefer code written for use with the standard library and compilers that support that library in full or subset form.

Link Formats

Besides incompatible runtime libraries, there is the question of subroutine linkage and linkage editor formats. Once again, BDS C is nonstandard. That is, it uses its own linker instead of conforming to the Microsoft .REL format. (Some 8080/Z80 compilers do support the standard, such as the Q/C compiler from The Code Works). Compatibility with the .REL format is a considerable blessing, if you plan to link other software to your C programs.

The lack of linkage compatibility is not limited to the CP/M-80 world. A wide variety of C compilers sold for MS-DOS and CP/M-86 fail to use the appropriate standard. Most notably, older releases of Computer Innovations's C86 compiler used its own internal format. Furthermore, the DESMET C compiler has its own library format and linkage procedure. This made it virtually impossible to use C86 to produce subroutines for other compiled languages under MS-DOS or CP/M-86. (Note: Fortunately, newer versions of most MS-DOS and CP/M-86 C compilers can produce Microsoft-format object code.)

The reasons for the incompatibility are probably manifold. The usual response from the companies producing the incompatible products is that they prefer their own format to Microsoft's. Why is this? I suppose this results from programmers who don't care about standards or just didn't consider that the users would find a compatible linkage format useful. In any case, be aware of the linkage format used by the C compilers you select.

Reader Responses on Link Formats

Readers had a lot to say about incompatibility between link formats. Guy Scharf of Mountain View, California, wrote, "I find the incompatibility of linkage editor formats to be a real problem. For example, I want to use Digital Research's Access Manager and Display Manager 86 with C. I would prefer CI-86 (because I am used to it) but have to switch to DRI's C because of the link format. Another compiler to learn and idiosyncrasies to surmount." He concluded, "I'm not sure what to do about this problem (except complain)."

David D. Clark of State College, Pennsylvania, wrote, "The big problem isn't really the format of linkable files. Even compilers that use Microsoft's M80 and L80 will not allow linkage to code produced by different compilers. The function calling protocols vary tremendously from compiler to compiler. BDS C and Q/C have fairly straightforward function calling protocols. Eco-C, on the other hand, has a tortuous function-calling sequence. And even though Q/C and Eco-C use the Microsoft assembler and linker, the code files produced by them are not compatible."

The problem that Mr. Clark mentions is also present in the 8086 (MS-DOS, CP/M-86) world. Code from different compilers cannot be mixed because:

- Each requires its own main function
- A wide variety of link formats exist
- Calling conventions differ between compilers.

The first two points are essentially insurmountable problems from the user's point of view. However, the third point can be overcome by adding dummy routines to convert calling conventions.

Mr. Clark makes some additional points concerning the deficiencies of the 8080 Microsoft .REL (relocatable) format (these are of interest since many 8080 C compilers rely on this format):

1. M80 and DRI's RMAC assemblers only support six unique characters (all uppercase). This is awkward for many purposes.
2. Although the .REL format can apparently handle seven unique characters, neither M80 nor RMAC support this.
3. Apparently the .REL format, M80, and L80 were designed to work with the Fortran-80 compiler, which permits only six character symbols. This is an old standard, and does not reflect the needs of today's compilers. The absence of case sensitivity in symbols is especially limiting.

It is obvious that an enhanced standard is necessary for the CP/M-80 world. Even under MS-DOS, where Microsoft has enhanced the linkage editor format, problems still exist.

Microsoft's MS-DOS linkage format supports long symbols (31 unique characters) and has case sensitivity. Thus, it overcomes the objections that Mr. Clark posed for the 8080 .REL system. However, one problem still exists: the dichotomy between object modules and libraries. Because of this dichotomy, the MS-DOS linker always includes the full contents of a .OBJ module during linking. However, libraries are searched. To make a library efficient, each function must be compiled into its own .OBJ file. Each .OBJ file becomes a single sub-block in the library; all the functions of that sub-block file are included at program linkage. If libraries and object modules were equivalent, this problem would be overcome since the functions of an object module would be separable during linking.

Runtime Libraries

Nonstandard runtime libraries are a plague to programmers. They inhibit portability and introduce bugs when software is transported between different compilers. Charles Brady of New South Wales, Australia, wrote, "An enormous contribution to standardization of C programs would be the publication of a standard I/O library for BDS C with, if necessary, a modified runtime package. The fast and efficient compiler, particularly with the symbolic debugger tool, provides an inviting environment for software development. It is a great pity that this means abundant nonstandard C. As there is no inherent reason why this should be the case . . . someone should be able to . . . produce a Unix-compatible I/O library."

This point is especially well-taken in view of the large amount of BDS C software available through the C User's Group of McPhearson, Kansas.

In the case of the runtime library itself, there is a clear standard. This standard is spelled out in *The C Programming Language*. Compilers need only support a proper subset appropriate to the environment in which they work.

BDS C Runtime Solution

Alex Cameron of Malvern (Victoria), Australia, had the following comments: "I couldn't help responding to your notes on the nonstandard nature of some of

BDS C's runtime routines. There is probably little doubt that most of us gladly suffer its irregularities because of its speed, low price, and because it is arguably one of the finest C compilers around—all this notwithstanding, I still find the nonstandard buffered file functions such as *fopen* the most frustrating, simply because of the need to continually declare buffers."

Listing 3-1 (stdlib3.c) is Mr. Cameron's proposed solution to this problem under BDS C.

More on Libraries and Portability

Mike Meyer of Norman, Oklahoma, wrote the following concerning libraries and portability: "To add some constructive comment, I'd like to point out that relying on library utilities for things does *not* guarantee portability. For instance, many C implementations won't have the Unix math(3) library or the qsort(3) routines. Of note is that the current AT&T Unix distribution doesn't include the dbm(3) routines from Unix version 7. I used those routines to fix the 'everything is line-oriented ASCII' problem with Unix, and [people at] some of the AT&T sites that don't have that library complained when they received copies of my software."

This is an interesting point that I had not considered. It adds more complexity to the idea of C/Unix software portability. What libraries can and cannot be assumed when writing a program? Is it okay to think of libraries such as CURSES as standard?

Part 3

MEMORY MODELS

This section concerns the memory model concepts of the 8086 and how this affects C compilers implemented for this microprocessor family. I discuss the advantages and drawbacks of several memory models used by existing C compilers, and present code to help overcome some limitations of small memory model compilers.

For readers who are not interested in the details of 8086 C compilers, large memory models, or long pointers, there is still some interesting material in this column. Specifically, several routines included here illustrate real-life code to interface C and assembly language. Most compiler manuals are terse on this subject, so some actual code may help drive home the concepts involved.

Background

Before plunging into a discussion of memory models, a brief introduction to the 8086 architecture is necessary. This material will help to illustrate why there are different addressing schemes used by different compilers.

The 8086/88 microprocessors support 20-bit addressing. This allows the microprocessor to address in excess of one million bytes. However, all the registers are 16 bits wide. This implies that some segmentation scheme must be used to address more than 64K bytes of memory. The technique used involves four 16-bit segment registers: CS, DS, ES, SS. These registers are the code-segment, data-segment, extra-segment, and stack-segment registers, respectively. Depending on the instruction used, different segment registers come into play in determining the complete 20-bit address. In forming a complete address, the segment address is always shifted left, four bits. Note that a segment register by itself addresses memory on 16-byte boundaries. Sixteen-byte regions addressable by segment registers are known as paragraphs. Although paragraphs and paragraph alignment are not normally of interest to C programmers, they are sometimes important when you are developing assembly language interface code for C.

To discuss long pointers, a special notation is used. Since the address is split, it is written in the form:

```
segment:byte_pointer
```

where *segment* is the segment, and *byte pointer* is the 16-bit low-order part of the address. A typical example of such an address would be "es:bx," which means "segment specified by es register and offset from this segment specified by the bx register." This notation is used throughout the listings included with this column.

Machine instructions often differentiate between intersegment and intrasegment operations. For example, there are "far" and "near" CALL instructions.

8080 Memory Model

The 8080 memory model is just what the name implies. All segment registers are set equally, so that only a total of 64K is available for a program. This model is seen mostly under CP/M-86, but is occasionally used by MS-DOS programs. None of the C compilers that I have seen restrict programs to this model.

Small Memory Model

Many programs can work comfortably with only 64K of data space and 64K of program space. Such a model results when the CS and DS registers are set to different blocks of memory (up to 64k each). Normally, ES and SS are set equal to DS, so that all data and stack memory resides in the same block of memory. This model is fine as long as programs and data requirements are small enough to fit within the 64K limits. Many C compilers only support this model.

Large Memory Model

In a large memory model, all addresses refer to the full 20-bit range. All subroutine calls are "far" calls, and all data is referred to with long pointers. Long pointers include a segment and byte address pointer (thus occupying 32 bits). Only a few C compilers support this model. The reason that most compilers don't support this model is the greater complexity of code generation. I will mention more on this later.

Small Code / Large Data Model

A useful hybrid of the small and large memory models is the only one where 64K of program space is provided, but long pointers are used for data. This model offers speed advantages for programs that require more data storage, but are small to moderate in code size.

Large Code / Small Data Model

One other possibility would be a large-code/small-data model, which would be used for programs with small data requirements but large code requirements.

Large Stack Feature

One type of model, not yet considered, is one that supports a large stack. A large stack would support more than 64K of items. Implementing this feature would slow program execution significantly, since stack references would be complicated.

Which model is better?

As long as a C program can fit within the small memory model, there is a distinct speed advantage in using this model. The large memory model produces longer (and somewhat slower) programs because of the greater generality of each instruction produced (ability to refer to 1024K instead of 64K of memory requires longer pointers and more checks). Since the 8086 doesn't provide many instructions to manipulate the long pointers, many additional instructions must be generated for pointer-related operations (which also include all memory references.) Specific examples of the lack of 8086 instructions involve incrementing and decrementing long pointers. Note that a long pointer is not just a 32-bit word. The upper 16 bits is a segment address, which must be treated accordingly when crossing 64K boundaries. Examples of implementing these features in software are included in Listing 3-6 (llint.asm; examples: linc and ldec functions).

Thus, all models have drawbacks. Speed is gained at the expense of (essentially) unlimited program/data space. Use the large memory model for big programs that use big chunks of data. Otherwise, stick with the small model.

Drawbacks of the Small Memory Model

Assuming that you use the small memory model (by choice or because of your compiler), everything will run smoothly until you have to deal with memory outside the C data address space. For example, it might be nice to use large buffers for copying files or keeping help information. Another possibility would involve accessing special locations in the memory map.

You can implement the ability to use long pointers in a small memory model with relative ease. A set of such routines is presented in Listings 3-2 to 3-6.

The Long Pointer Package

The Long Pointer Package supplements a C environment by allowing references to memory locations anywhere in the 20-bit address map. This is done by defining a new data type LPTR (via a typedef):

```
typedef union __lptr
{
        long   _llong;      /* long format */
        char   _lstr[4];    /* character format */
        LWORD  _lword;      /* long-word format */
} LPTR;
```

where LWORD is defined as the following structure:

```
typedef struct __lword
{
        unsigned _addr;     /* address */
        unsigned _segm;     /* segment */
} LWORD;
```

This format for LPTR makes the addresses defined directly compatible with normal long pointers used at the assembly level. These long pointers are stored in the 8080 style: least significant byte of address first, most significant byte of segment last.

The lowest level routines that support long memory references are, of necessity, coded in assembly language. The routines that implement many of the lowest level functions in a noncompiler-specific way are included in Listing 3-5 (llsup.asm). Routines that implement functions for Aztec C86 (a typical 8086 C compiler) version 1.05i are included in Listing 3-6 (llint.asm). You may have to modify these routines for other C compilers, if register usage or stack arrangements differ.

To use the routines with C programs, you must include the header file lsup.h at the beginning of modules that use or refer to LPTR data types. The "lsup.h" file refers to "_lsup.h" also. These two headers are presented in Listings 3-3 and 3-4, respectively.

Supported Functions

The package supports several functions involving long pointers. There are routines to add offsets to long pointers, copy memory between long pointers, and return data addressed by long pointers. A complete list of these functions is included in Table 3-8, which also mentions the file in which the function is located.

Table 3-8.
Functions Involving Long Pointers

```
file: lsup.c   (some C support routines)
    lassign(dest,source)      assign long pointers
    llstrcpy(dest,source)     long string copy
    lprint(lptr)              debugging routine for printing LPTRs

file: llint.asm (Aztec C dependent support routines)

    flptr(lptr,sptr)          form a long pointer from a normal
                              short C (ds relative) pointer
    lchr(lptr)                return character addressed by long
                              pointer
    lint(lptr)                returns int/unsigned addressed by
                              long ptr.
    l_stchr(lptr,chr)         stores char at location lptr
    l_stint(lptr,intgr)       stores int  at location lptr
    lload(dest,lptr,len)      general purpose copy to short
                              pointer area (ds relative) from
                              long pointer area
    lstor(lptr,src,len)       reverse if lload()
    linc(lptr)                increment long pointer
    ldec(lptr)                decrement long pointer
    ladd(lptr,offset)         add unsigned offset to lptr
    lsub(lptr,offset)         subtract unsigned offset from lptr
    lsum(lptr,offset)         add signed offset to lptr
    lcopy(dest,src,len)       general purpose long to long copy
                              (can copy up to 1024K of memory)

file: llsup.asm (compiler independent functions)

    linc                      increment a long pointer
    ldec                      decrement a long pointer
    ladd                      add an unsigned offset to a long
                              pointer
    lsub                      sub an unsigned offset from a long
                              pointer
    lsum                      add a signed offset to a long pointer
    lcopy                     general copy routine
```

An Example:

One useful application of long pointers under MS-DOS 2.0 involves accessing a program's environment block. The environment block is a Unix-like set of environment variables and values. This is normally used to affect some particular aspects of program execution. Specifics about the environment address are in-

Environment Block Address

C compilers under MS-DOS normally produce .EXE files. For .EXE files, a program segment prefix is created by DOS 2.0 and later. The segment address of this prefix is es:0 when the user program begins. At offset 002ch from this address is stored the segment address of the environment table. Only a segment is stored: the offset from the segment is again zero. Thus, the contents of es:2ch is the address of the environment block.

Normally, C compilers have a maintenance routine that is given control at the start of program execution. For Aztec C86, this routine is called $begin and is located in the calldos.asm module included with the compiler. The user must define an external variable in calldos.asm for the benefit of env.c, in order for the segment address to be accessible as a long pointer. The procedure for this operation is detailed in the comments included in Listing 3-7 (env.c).

Allocation of Memory

If a C program intends to use DOS memory allocation in conjunction with the long pointers, it must also be sure to shrink its memory allocation using the MS-DOS SETBLOCK function. This is normally done in the initial maintenance routine of the C runtime system. For Aztec C this must be done in $begin.

The example program env.c (Listing 3-7) reads the environment block and displays the contents of the whole block on the console. In effect, it provides the same listing feature as the MS-DOS SET command.

Long Pointer Corrections

Bruce Komusin wrote from Monaco to point out some errors in the assembly-language routines: "I just read your article ... about long pointers for C. I never [have] used C, but I know 8086 assembler. From your listing of llsup.asm, it is apparent that you overlooked the fact that the 8086 affects the flags when doing INC or DEC [instructions] for 16-bit [quantities]. This is a common error because it is different on the 8080. So, for example, you can save bytes and time in the routine *linc* by removing the "OR BX,BX."

Although this is just an inefficient coding, Mr. Komusin pointed out a real bug: "However, I really wrote this letter to warn you about *ldec*. Of course, it will not work as is because of the 'DEC BX' changing the zero flag set up by the 'OR BX,BX.' I suggest a change ... that fixes everything:"

```
ldec        proc    near
            or      bx,bx
            jnz     ldec_1
            mov     ax,es
            sub     ax,1000h
            mov     es,ax
ldec_1:     dec     bx
            ret
ldec        endp
```

Beyond the basic fixes, Mr. Komusin suggested some increases in efficiency: "However, here are some points about execution speed and byte efficiency. It is much faster to 'fall through' a conditional jump than to actually jump. So, if possible, it is always a good idea to arrange the code so that the normal case falls through and only the exceptional case jumps. As a side benefit, the exceptional case can then be shared."

Listing 3-8 contains a full set of improved routines.

With the package of C and assembly language functions that support long pointers under a small memory model environment, users can enjoy the best of both worlds: access to arbitrary amounts/locations of memory, while retaining the efficiency of short pointers for regular code and pointer operations. For compilers that only support the small model, this package allows access to features previously off-limits to 8086 C programmers.

Part 4

C INPUT-OUTPUT FUNCTIONS AND LANGUAGE PHILOSOPHY

The C language and its runtime library are distinct concepts. The following discussion brings to light important topics concerning the state of C and its runtime library. It also helps to distinguish C from other popular languages.

Low Level Input-Output in C

Patrick Cawood of Los Angeles, California, wrote, "I read with great interest your... article [DDJ #86, December 1983] on tendencies in Unix to produce poor operator interaction programs. I seem to have met some of the same in C.... To provide a secure operator interface, [you do] not echo a keyboard character to the screen until it has been examined and approved by the program. But the *getch()* function automatically echoes—even line feeds, up arrows, [and so on]!! Function *putch()* provides an automatic line feed after printing on the screen!!... I simply cannot believe that anyone would wittingly design these functions as they are, or fail to provide any alternative hardware interfaces—especially considering some of the tasks I've heard were written in C. But perhaps these people writing serious software were all forced to write their own hardware interfaces."

The problem Mr. Cawood referred to exists in several non-Unix C compilers. To begin with, let's review the problem in the Unix environment. Under Unix, putc() and getc() acquire and return a single character, respectively. However, to offload the host system, many terminal interface boards programmatically handle user input-output in lines. Thus, before any input is received by the host, you must enter a whole line. Naturally, the characters are echoed by the terminal interface hardware/firmware, and only limited line editing is permitted. On output, a whole line is buffered before transmission to the terminal. This process can be overcome by use of the "raw" terminal mode (raw implies no host character processing). In this mode, the program is completely responsible for input-output. This mode is much more expensive in terms of input-output cost, since the host must handle an interrupt for each input character and perform an output request for each printed character. However, this is the only way for a program to get full control of what is entered, and what appears on the display device.

With the introduction of C to microcomputers, compiler implementers often based the behavior of the runtime libraries on their Unix experiences rather than on *The C Programming Language*. Thus, whole lines are prebuffered by typical C runtime libraries before a single character is received by getc(). Conversely, a whole line of output is internally buffered before it is printed on the display. Thus, the runtime libraries of microcomputer C compilers often emulate the terminal hardware found on real Unix systems. However, this is not what putc() and getc() are supposed to do. In the truest sense, raw mode is the fundamental terminal mode. These functions should really work on a character-by-character basis. C libraries should permit selection between the "raw" and "cooked" modes (and echo, no-echo) and thus permit input-output flexibility without resorting to assembly language routines.

One C compiler that correctly handles the low-level input-output is the Q/C compiler from The Code Works. For example, single characters are only required when a getchar() call is made. However, it doesn't seem possible to turn off the echo. Nevertheless, this can be effected under Q/C, since The Code Works is kind enough to provide runtime and compiler source code.

Comments about C Input-Output

Mike Meyer wrote, "What you haven't seemed to realize is that almost every flaw in Unix also appears in C. C is terse, doesn't protect the user, and is poorly documented. The only documentation for C is K&R, which may be well written, but is vague and inconsistent on all the points you turn to when you start implementing the language on new machines. To make matters worse, nobody (and I do mean *nobody*) sells a compiler that conforms to K&R, not even AT&T. I don't think anybody ever has, in any case. AT&T distributes a version of *pcc* [portable C compiler] that met K&R internally, but I think that by the time it was released externally, C had grown past K&R."

Gerald I. Evenden of North Falmouth, Massachusetts, responded about C input-output as follows, with quite a different point of view: "I was very disturbed with a basic concept about the C programming language that you kept implying in your column . . . First of all, I suggest that you carefully read the beginning paragraph of chapter 7 of Kernighan and Ritchie's *The C Programming Language*. It begins with, 'Input and output are not part of the C language. . .' What remains is a description of I/O procedures contained in a standard UNIX library that will take care of most filter types of functional operations. I have generally found them to be quite adequate for most programming efforts involving stream data and simple question-answer type of console I/O."

I am aware of the distinction between the C language definition and the standard input-output library. In teaching students how to program in C, this is one of the first points I emphasize: C is a language that gives no special favoritism to a specific set of input-output routines. One standard set does exist, and this is the Unix standard. I consider this an essential feature of C, but I believe a discussion of a real C compiler environment cannot always be separated from a discussion of the support library that comes with it. I also maintain that the Unix input-output library is more than adequate for dealing with stream operations. Mr. Evenden summarizes the distinction between C and C input-output as follows: "The beauty of C is that it doesn't have [a] plethora of specialized built-in functions, but rather provides programmers with a rich facility to build tools required for their own, and occasionally specialized, needs. Obviously, we shouldn't have to redesign all the wheels needed, so most suppliers of C compilers include a library of functions patterned after the Unix libraries. But remember, there is absolutely no requirement to use them if they don't fit your needs, and they should only be viewed as a preliminary toolkit."

One point that merits further exploration is that of portability. It is well and good to preach the separation of C and C input-output, but only software that uses standard Unix input-output calls (and routines built on them) have a prayer of being moved readily between different machines or even between different compilers on the same machines.

In this regard, Mr. Evenden wrote, "I suspect that your problem with getc [and similar expressions] is related to screen editing and control, which is a category of program that doesn't fall into the filter class of function emphasized by Unix (and its libraries), and I certainly agree that these functions don't work in this case . . . the astute programmer writes rawin() and rawout() to satisfy those needs. There's nothing to prevent it and everything to encourage it. . . The worst possible outcome of the problems posed in your article is to even remotely suggest rewriting the current stream I/O functions. Their current form is a de facto standard and a consistency of implementation is expected by most C programmers."

I really don't expect anyone to throw away the existing stream functions. Not only would this be unreasonable, it would also be undesirable. However, clean raw input-output should be supported; it needn't be reinvented each time a Unix programmer discovers that stream input-output is inconvenient for interactive purposes. In discussing a similar worry expressed by Mr. Meyer, I summarized my argument by stating that interactive programs comprise a large fraction of those run by Unix users, and that when programmers write an interactive program, they do not usually want the user to be treated like an input file.

Despite the extremely outspoken way Mr. Evenden lectured me in his letter, we agree in many respects. However, some things he brought up demand careful examination. He stated, "The principal point of this complaint is that you should be a little more careful of what you are talking about. Writing about problems with C I/O is impossible, since C I/O doesn't exist. However, your less experienced readers will take your complaint to heart and decide that C is a useless language because Mr. Skjellum and others don't like the optional I/O library supplied with their compiler. If you were more positive in your approach, you would be telling readers how to write their own procedures to do specialized console I/O on Unix, CP/M, and so on. I've done it on both CP/M and Unix and found it to be a piece of cake in both cases, and I never gave the getc group a second thought when it was obvious it was not meant for the job at hand."

I have based my comments on several years of experience with C under Unix, CP/M, VMS, and so on. It is necessary to come to grips with reality. C input-output, although optional, is normally what users must utilize to deal with a problem at hand; consequently, inexperienced users must lean more heavily on the standard library than experienced users. It is meaningful to discuss C input-output. It does exist, and Mr. Evenden discussed several points about it before stating that the topic is beyond the realm of discussion. Inexperienced users learn by reading dialogue between others who have seen problems in their own work. Censoring this information to "protect" such users from disenchantment with C is an unacceptable alternative.

We have not reached the computer millennium. C and Unix as existing tools have flaws and drawbacks. Only through discussion can we seek solutions and create improved future systems. The idea of restricting discussions based on semantic points seems to be contrary to that goal. Some other writers have taken the approach that C and Unix are "wonderful" tools and heap praise on them in review after review. Certain factions feel highly insulted if this approach is not followed. In an evolving field, it makes sense to criticize as part of the learning process. That is why I include Mr. Evenden's final remarks, because I think that he has drawn a counterproductive conclusion from an understandable point of view: "C is not a perfect language, but it certainly beats what's in second place. Consequently, my enthusiasm about C makes me very chauvinistic about misplaced and invalid criticisms. I have a couple minor complaints about some aspects of C, but I bite my tongue when I think about the dark ages. After several happy years with Algol in the 1960s, I was sentenced to over ten years of Fortran purgatory before being born again with C. I guard this language jealously, and you had better be careful of what you write or I'll curse you to a task of debugging 10,000 lines of Basic code."

Based on the above discussion, Mr. Evenden sent in further comments, which appear next.

An August Response

Mr. Evenden was extremely displeased with my comments about C, because he felt that they could convey the wrong impressions to the uninitiated. Furthermore, he felt it unfair for me to discuss C I/O libraries without strongly disclaiming that C and its libraries are completely separate concepts (which they indeed are). He now wrote, "In regard to your response to my letter... I must expand upon some of my earlier points and make some additional comments. In addition, please excuse the excesses of a middle-age curmudgeon. Scars acquired in numerous battles of the computer wars tend to create a knee-jerk reaction when I sense potentially deviant and dangerous thought processes. I wanted to emphasize that the compiler and the support library are distinct entities, and we must be careful to maintain the distinction. When I talk of C, I am referring to the compiler . . . when I talk about the C library, I am referring to what is currently a vague and poorly defined item."

The original concept of a C library is defined in *The C Programming Language*. There are other libraries available on Unix systems, but these vary from installation to installation, and from version to version. I agree with Mr. Evenden that the words *C Library* are currently vague. Indeed, we should standardize functions that are not inherently Unix-only features. For example, we should include the following:

- "block" input-output (read, write and relatives)
- stream input-output functions (fopen, fwrite, fputc)
- memory allocation functions (calloc, malloc ...)
- setjmp/longjmp procedures
- alarm (but not signal, since Unix-dependent)
- exit
- scanf, printf, and relatives

Furthermore, we should include the Unix math library, since these are fundamental routines (for example, sin(), exp()). Readers may wish to formulate an exact list for exclusion and inclusion.

Mr. Evenden continued, "This sensitivity to the compiler-library problem is caused by having to deal with compilers where too many features that should have been relegated to the support library were included as part of the compiler [that is, language definition]. For example, Fortran gives us READ, WRITE, and a few other input-output support operations that must be treated by the compiler as special operations, since the syntax does not match normal external module calls (of course, external modules are involved, but they are transparent to the programmer). When specialized input-output is required that can't be handled by these statements, all sorts of contortions are done by the programmer to get around these restrictions . . . typically these gyrations are specific to the host system. In addition, many manufacturers compound a bad situation by supplying a compiler with supplementary functions to provide access to unique features of their system. Good-bye, transportability!"

Mr. Evenden is 100 percent correct. Fortran's implicit connection of input-output functions to the language is a terrible failing. Pascal also suffers from this malady, even though it is a newer, structured language. Evenden continued with the following remarks: "In the case of C, compiler users do not have to go out of their way to handle special input-output syntax, and programmers utilizing the typical C library can go to basically three levels of input-output to handle the problem:

- Basic block 'read'-'write'
- Buffered (stream) input-output with the getc(), putc() functions
- Fortran-like scanf() and printf() operations.

This is an excellent example of building-block code: the read-write level is the lowest level and is the only place where we have to deal with the host machine's operating system; each successive level uses the previous level's entries. Application programmers can thus choose the starting level best suited to the job and add the remaining tiers of code to perform the task."

Given this buildup of the C library, Mr. Evenden returned to the reasons for his original objections: "One of the principal fears I have is that if we get to talking of the C compiler and a standard library in one breath, we will find some well-meaning ignoramus developing a C compiler with built-in input-output functions (or, for that matter, other 'special' features). In this situation, our input-output is engraved in stone and we will be forced back into the same situation involved in Fortran coding. With C, we can individually or collectively trash the input-output part of the library in favor of some new software and still preserve the compiler itself. In addition, the old software is still good as long as we maintain a working copy of the old library. We often cannot do this if the compiler has been rewritten. I would much rather try to transport a program where a few specialized routines had to be rewritten than have to deal with compiler variations."

To summarize, the principal points Mr. Evenden made (and with which I agree) are:

1. Computer languages like C are superior because they segregate their library from the language definition.
2. Because of this, the language offers greater maintainability, even through revisions of the libraries, because we can retain old libraries more readily than whole compiler environments.
3. Specialized applications can completely ignore the standard software library without any loss of power.
4. When informing or teaching people about C, we must emphasize this unique feature to ensure that it is retained in future incarnations of the language. I hope that future languages will also be constructed in this way.

Mr. Evenden, to summarize his point of view, stated, "The problem of C libraries and what is a 'standard' C function is not yet resolved and needs further discussion. Tight binding of C and Unix is unfortunate, and we need to disassociate the two if we are to encourage non-Unix use of C and transportable C software. An important part of this unbinding is specifying a viable C library that can be installed without ambiguity and omission on a wide range of operating systems."

This is similar to what I mentioned above. I encourage readers to work along these lines.

Part 5

SCIENTIFIC USES

The purpose of this section is to illustrate scientific uses of the C programming language by examples and to present routines useful in conjunction with scientific programming—some general and others that implement specific numerical algorithms. This material is intended for specific audiences. The first audience is the group of die-hard programmers who refuse to change languages and continue to produce useful programs in outdated languages. Not only is this of greater expense to themselves, but it also cheats others by locking them into Fortran or other old-fashioned languages. For them, I want to illustrate the elegance and versatility of C.

The second audience (which may also include the first as a subset) are those users interested in scientific applications but who may not have used C for this purpose. This section is intended to illustrate that C is completely acceptable for such purposes, and the code shows how general concepts can be presented. (I make no attempt to survey scientific applications where C could be used, but merely to include some nontrivial examples). Finally, for those readers who don't fit into the above categories, the general purpose routines will still prove interesting.

I present three programming systems. The first is a set of general purpose subroutines designed to simplify the process of user-program interaction and to provide a straightforward means for handling erroneous input. The input mechanisms are not particularly sophisticated, but emphasize structure in the user's program. The routines make range checking so automatic that the programmer has no excuse for omitting such checks, regardless of how "quickly" a program is to be completed. Providing these routines to novice programmers in the classroom has eliminated a lot of frustration over using the scanf() function.

The second and third programming systems illustrate Runge-Kutta integration. The Runge-Kutta formalism is a standard numerical technique for handling the numerical integration of one or more ordinary first-order differential equations. Interested readers may wish to consult the book *Numerical Analysis*, by Richard L. Burden and others (Prindle, Weber, Schmidt Publishers, second edition, 1981). This is the source for the algorithms presented in the code and is also a fine reference for introductory numerical methods. The choice of Runge-Kutta routines as examples was based on their widespread use in scientific work. (Note: Interested readers may wish to consult the article "C Instead of Fortran?," *Computer Language*, 2(2), February 1985.) In this article, I describe more of the advantages of C for scientific and engineering applications.

Acknowledgments

The general purpose library has received extensive use by Caltech students during the past eighteen months. Thanks are due to Scott Lewicki and Russell Natter, who each discovered minor details that caused major errors.

The Runge-Kutta code was developed by Michael J. Roberts and myself. Mr. Roberts developed the major portion of the RKSYS (multiple equations) routines as a project for Caltech's Physics 20 course: Introduction to Computational Physics. We spent approximately sixty hours altogether in developing, testing, and debugging this code. Mr. Roberts also wrote the original version of the documentation for RKSYS, included in modified form as Table 3-12.

GPR: General Purpose Routines

The general purpose library consists of five subroutines. Four of these subroutines deal with input. The fifth, a simple facility for printing files to the console, is called display() and will be considered separately from the input functions.

The other routines are iinp(), finp(), sinp() and cinq(). The first three provide integer, floating-point, and string input, respectively. The fourth is a yes-no question processor. The exact calling sequences for each of the routines is provided in Table 3-9.

Table 3-9.
Calling Sequences for General Purpose Routines

1. int iinp(prompt,cflag,low,high);

    char *prompt: optional prompt string to be printed before input
    char cflag: checking flag: if nonzero, range checking is performed
    int low
    int high: low, high are (inclusive) range checking values

    iinp() repeats input until a valid number is entered; the valid number is the function's return value.

2. double finp(prompt,cflag,low,high);

    char *prompt: optional prompt string to be printed before input
    char cflag: checking flag: if nonzero, range checking is performed
    double low
    double high: low, high are (inclusive) range checking values

    finp() repeats input until a valid number is entered; the valid number is the function's return value

Table 3-9 (continued).

3. len = sinp(prompt,string,length);

   int len: length of entered string
   char *prompt: optional prompt string to be printed before input
   int length: maximum length of input string

   sinp() ignores leading spaces.

4. retn = cinq(prompt);

   int retn: 1 --> 'Y' was typed, 0 --> 'N' was typed
   char *prompt: optional prompt string to be printed before input

5. retn = display(fname);
   int retn: 0 --> success, -1 --> failure
   char *fname: null-terminated name of file

   display() prints the specified file on the standard output device.

Traditionally, user input is effected by a sequence of instructions, such as the following sequence for entering an integer:

```
#define MIN 10
#define MAX 100
...

int input;
...

while (1)      /* input loop */
{
        printf("Enter input variable --> ");

        if (scanf("%u",&input) != 1)    /* get variable */
        {
                drain();        /* drain spurious characters */
                continue;       /* skip range checks */
        }

        /* do range checking */

        if ((input >= MIN) && (input <= MAX))
                break;          /* we are done */

        printf("\nNumber out of range\n");

} /* keep looping until scanf() can read a variable */
```

Entering this sequence repeatedly can be tedious from a programmatical point of view, so error checking is often omitted. This practice leads to programs that do not handle users' mistakes intelligently. The GPR routines allow the above sequence to be replaced by a single line of code:

    input = iinp("Enter input variable -->",1,MIN,MAX);

Since using the GPR input functions is easier than using scanf(), this variety of function should be well received, and it can be used in lieu of scanf() for most purposes. A further advantage of these functions is that they unclutter the program. More sophisticated checking will still need to be included explicitly; the input functions do only range checking.

The display() function was included to encourage users to provide online help/documentation along with their programs. This function allows users to print out additional text whenever appropriate. With this function, a trivial online help facility can be created; a help feature is almost always appropriate, but is usually omitted.

The GPR routines are in Listing 3-9. The current list is not exhaustive, but intended only to suggest a trend for additional routines.

RK4: Runge-Kutta Algorithm

The general purpose library simplifies the task of correct input. Now let's consider a scientific application of C: single equation Runge-Kutta integration. Before introducing the code, some background is required.

Start with a differential equation in the canonical form

$$y' = f(y,t)$$

where y' is the first derivative of y with respect to t and f(y,t) is a piecewise continuous function of its arguments. In addition to the differential equation, you are given an initial condition:

$$y(t=0) = y0$$

where y0 is some real constant (for example, 35.1). These two equations uniquely specify the solution y(t), which is as yet unknown. The need for numerical techniques arise when the differential equation cannot be solved analytically.

There are many possible numerical approaches to the solution of this equation, but considering them is beyond the scope of the current discussion. For now, it is sufficient to state that a technique exists called RK4 (Runge-Kutta fourth order) that can solve the equation numerically with known error characteristics. Solution of a typical equation is presented in Listing 3-10 for the equation

$y'(t) = 1 + t - y$

with the initial condition

$y(t=0) = 5.0$

Since this equation can also be solved analytically, a comparison is made with the exact solution to demonstrate error characteristics of the method. The analytical solution turns out to be

$y(t) = t + 5.0*\exp(-t)$

This latter result can be deduced by inspection.

The Runge-Kutta algorithm and code is presented in Listing 3-11. Readers interested in more information should consult the book by Burden and others, cited above. Calling sequences are described in Table 3-10.

Table 3-10.
RK4: Runge-Kutta Integrator

Description:

File: RK4.C, Subroutine Library. Listing 3-11
    The C language call is as follows:
        rk4(function,a,b,n,alpha,t,w);
where:

function	returns the right-hand side f(y,t) of the system.
a	is the start of the interval of integration
b	is the end of the interval of integration
n	is the number of integration steps
alpha	is the initial value y(0) = alpha
t	is the array where the times will be stored
w	is where the approximations to y will be stored

The formal C definitions for the function and its parameters are:

1. rk4(): n step integrator

   ```
   rk4(function,a,b,n,alpha,t,w)
   double (*function)();   /* function giving f(t,y) */
   double a;               /* beginning of interval */
   double b;               /* end of interval */
   int n;                  /* number of steps in interval */
   double alpha;           /* initial condition for y */
   double t[];             /* array for returning T[i] values */
   double w[];             /* array for returning W[i] values */
   ```

2. rk4_1(): 1 step integrator

   ```
   rk4_1(function,h,time,yapprox)
   double (*function)();       /* Pointer to function to integrate */
   ```

```
    double h;              /* Step size */
    double time;           /* Current time step */
    double *yapprox;       /* Current approximation of function */
```

RKSYS: *Systems of Differential Equations*

Imagine now that you have a set (system) of N first-order ordinary differential equations:

$$y_i{'}(t) = f_i(t, y_1, y_2, ..., y_n) \qquad (i = 1, 2, ... N)$$

This problem is useful for solving other systems, too, since sets of linear differential equations involving higher-order derivatives can be transformed to larger systems of the above variety (see Burden). Thus, a program that can solve the above system has reasonably wide applicability.

Unfortunately, the problem is more complicated for N equations than for one equation, as is evident from Table 3-11, in which the more general Runge-Kutta software is described. (Listing 3-12 contains the actual code.) Listings 3-13 and 3-14 are example programs that use rk4n() to solve small systems of equations. Listing 3-13 implements the same problem as Listing 3-10, but using rk4n() instead of rk4() to perform the integration.

Table 3-11.
RK System Solver (RKSYS)

```
Files:      RKS.C          Subroutine library: Listing 3-12
            RKST1.C        Test program #1:    Listing 3-13
            RKST2.         Test program #2:    Listing 3-14

            The format of the C language call is as follows:

                rk4n(function,wsource,wstore,m,a,b,n,alpha,t,kuttas);

where:

            function       is a pointer to the function that will return the
                           first derivatives of each function in your system.
                           It will be called as:

                                function(j,i,tval,rk_comp)

                           where:
                                    j       is the current time step
                                    i       is the current function
                                            number (0, 1, ..., m-1).
                                    tval    is the current time value
                                    rk_comp is a pointer to a function that your
                                            derivative function must call as:
```

Table 3-11 (continued).

> > rk_comp(r,j,i)
> > where:
> > > n is the function number in the system (0,...m-1) of the function you wish to evaluate.
> > > j is the time step.
> > > i is the current function number.

wsource	is a pointer to your function that will return a W value (which will have been stored by the user's WSTORE routine -- you need only worry about storing and returning these values, not the values themselves). It will be called as:
	     wsource(j,i)
	
	 where:
	     j is the current time step.
	     i is the current function number.

wstore	is a pointer to the user's function that will store values of W (see wsource above). It is called as:
	
	     wstore(j,i,value)
	
	 where:
	     j is the current time step.
	     i is the current function number.
	     value is the value to be stored for that location.
	
	 Note: wsource(j,i) should be equal to "value" after wstore(j,i,value).

m	is the number of equations in your system.
a	is the starting time value for the interval.
b	is the ending time value for the interval.
n	is the number of points into which the interval is to be broken.
alpha	is a one-dimensional array of the initial values. The value alpha[0] is the first function at time = a, alpha[1] is the second, and so on.
t	is a one-dimensional array where rk4n() will store the time values as it calculates them. It must be at least as large as n.
kuttas	is a two-dimensional array, the size of whose second

Table 3-11 (continued).

element is 4 (that is, kuttas[][4]). It will be the storage area for "k" values as they are calculated.

The formal C definitions for the function and its parameters are:

```
double rk4n(function,wsource,wstore,m,a,b,n,alpha,t,kuttas)
double (*function)();
double (*wsource)();
double (*wstore)();
int m;
double a;
double b;
int n;
double alpha[];
double t[];
double kuttas[][4];
```

Comments on array sizes, (*wsource)(), (*wstore)():

The (*wstore)() function should trap out-of-bound storage requests that result as a natural part of the rk4n() algorithm. A more elegant solution is to make the array size used by (*wstore)() one greater than the number of steps.

How to Use the Integrator

The rk4n() subroutine will solve a system of first-order differential equations as specified by the calling program, using the Runge-Kutta order four integrator described in Burden and others, pages 239–240; see also page 205.

The calling program must provide information for the rk4n() subroutine for it to solve the system of differential equations. This information must consist of:

- The first derivatives of each of the functions in the system
- Subroutines to store and retrieve values as the functions are integrated
- Initial conditions for each of the functions
- The range over which the function will be integrated
- Storage areas for the time and intermediate "K" value arrays.

The information must be provided in a specific order and format, which is described in Table 3-11.

By studying the Runge-Kutta routines, you will notice the central importance of pointers to functions in the organization of the code. Using this concept effectively allows the software to be completely divorced of the specifics of your program.

In this section, three sets of example routines were presented. This code was included to demonstrate how scientific applications and related software is actually implemented in C. Studying the examples should help you gain insight into the use of C for similar undertakings.

Availability

All the code presented with Part 5 is copyright 1983, 1984 (c) by the California Institute of Technology (Caltech), Pasadena, CA 91125. All rights reserved. This code may be freely distributed, used for all noncommercial purposes, but may not be sold for profit.

Part 6

X: EXTENDED C GRAMMAR

The first five sections have been devoted to C as it exists in the real world. In this section, I discuss some proposals for increasing the power and flexibility of C. Many languages go through regular upgrades and improvements (for example, Fortran IV, Fortran 66, and Fortran 77). C has undergone fewer changes than other popular languages. The lack of upgrades is probably due mainly to C's lack of intrinsic functions, but clearly points to the basic elegance and power of C.

I am aware of only a few upgrades beyond the language definition specified in *The C Programming Language* (K&R). These are enumerated types and structure assignment. Both features were introduced with Unix version 7 and are detailed in Unix 7 documentation. Structure assignment is useful in what follows, but type enumeration will not be mentioned. Therefore, although our definition is based on the Unix 7 version of C, this is not likely to confuse those who have access only to *The C Programming Language*.

Purists may argue that I have no business recommending changes or upgrades to C. Others may argue that many of the suggestions can be implemented via compiler preprocessors or by function calls and need not be part of the language. (This second point is discussed below.) In order to head off the criticism that I am "tampering" with the C language, I offer my recommendations as a new language grammar based on C but called X. I chose the letter X to denote language extensibility, which is the main point of the following proposals.

Language Extensibility

Most languages allow user-defined functions and subroutines, and many newer languages allow user-defined data types. Extensible languages such as Forth and APL allow functions, operators, and data types to be added to the programming environment in a way that makes them equivalent in stature to predefined operations. C retains tremendous flexibility by excluding intrinsic functions, but it does not allow user-defined types to be treated as easily as ints, longs, or floats. Specifically, you cannot extend the definitions of operators such as addition or multiplication to new data types created with typedef. This means that function calls must be used; although this is a completely viable approach, it lacks elegance. This concept is illustrated in the following example.

I need to define a data type called COMPLEX, which will function like Fortran's complex data type. This data type is used for handling complex numbers of the form A + iB, where i is the imaginary unit and A and B are real numbers. This might be done with the following definition:

```
typedef struct   /* complex number type definition */
{
        double _creal;      /* real part */
        double _cimag;      /* imaginary part */
} COMPLEX;
```

I will work with several variables of type COMPLEX (for example, alpha and beta), which are defined as follows:

```
COMPLEX alpha, beta;   /* alpha and beta are complex #'s */
```

Up to this point, I have treated the complex data type equivalently to built-in types. You can also work with pointers to or arrays of COMPLEX, so there is no deficiency along these lines. However, to assign, add, multiply, or subtract these COMPLEX variables, subroutines would have to be invented. Subroutines for two representative operations are illustrated in Figure 3-1.

Figure 3-1. Subroutines for two representative operations.

```
Assignment:  alpha = A + iB; /* pseudo code */

Function:
        calling sequence    (K&R C):    cassign(&alpha,A,B);
        calling sequence    (Unix 7 C): alpha = cassign(A,B);

        function definition (K&R C):

                cassign(comp,a,b)
                COMPLEX *comp;
                double a,b;
                {
                        comp->_creal = a;
                        comp->_cimag = b;
                }

        function definition (Unix 7 C):

                COMPLEX cassign(a,b)
                double a,b;
                {
                        COMPLEX temp;   /* temporary variable */
```

Figure 3-1 (continued).

```
            temp._creal = a;
            temp._cimag = b;
            return(temp);   /* return structure */
    }
```

Addition: gamma = alpha + beta; /* pseudo code */

Function:
    calling sequence   (K&R C):   cadd(&gamma,&alpha,&beta);
    calling sequence   (Unix 7 C): gamma = cadd(alpha,beta);

function definition (K&R C):

```
    cadd(gamma,alpha,beta)
    COMPLEX *gamma; /* destination */
    COMPLEX *alpha; /* addend */
    COMPLEX *beta;  /* augend */
    {
            gamma->_creal = alpha->_creal + beta->_creal;
            gamma->_cimag = alpha->_cimag + beta->_cimag;
    }
```

function definition (Unix 7 C):

```
    COMPLEX cadd(alpha,beta)
    COMPLEX alpha,beta; /* addend, augend */
    {
            COMPLEX temp; /* temporary */

            temp._creal = alpha._creal + beta._creal;
            temp._cimag = alpha._cimag + beta._cimag;
            return(temp);
    }
```

The pseudo-code presented with the subroutines in Figure 3-1 is the most convenient way to specify the operations desired. If the data types had been intrinsic, you could have used similar real C statements in lieu of subroutines. To use +, *, or other operators with the COMPLEX data type, you must introduce a mechanism for defining these operations.

Operators

How could you specify new operations? For example, how would you define addition for the complex data type? The following type of definition could be used to extend addition to the COMPLEX type:

```
COMPLEX oper `+`(alpha,beta)      /* X grammar */
COMPLEX alpha,beta;
{
        COMPLEX __temp; /* temporary */
        __temp._creal = alpha._creal + beta._creal;
        __temp._cimag = alpha._cimag + beta._cimag;

        return(__temp); /* return result */
}
```

The keyword *oper* is new: oper indicates that the following definition is for an operator. The *return* keyword used in function calls also appears with a similar meaning. Since COMPLEX precedes oper, this defines an operation over the COMPLEX data type. Since there are two arguments (alpha, beta), the operator is binary. Finally, note that the + is enclosed in graven accents. Quoting by graven accents is chosen as a way to distinguish operator names. Quotation will not always be needed.

To use this new operator (and assuming that = had also been defined), the following statement could be used:

```
gamma = alpha + beta;    /* add complex numbers */
```

Note that I have omitted the graven accents. Since the + can be distinguished from keywords or identifiers in this context, quoting is not required. The operator definition specified above gives the X compiler a means to evaluate the addition request specified in the example statement. The parser would break this statement down until it could pass an argument garnered from the left and right of the addition operator, much as it does with intrinsic operators and data types. Whether this results in a subroutine call or inline code would depend on the compiler's implementation.

More on Operators

Operators turn out to be a powerful and useful concept. We needn't limit ourselves to defining standard operations for new types. There is nothing to stop the definition of arbitrary operators. A crude facility already exists for this in C via the parameterized #define statement. However, the above facility is more general and more consistent with the syntax of C than the preprocessor #define approach. To encompass the generation of inline code as provided by #define, include the *inline* adjective, which could be used as follows:

```
COMPLEX inline oper `-`(alpha,beta) /* subtraction
inline */
...
```

This keyword would instruct the compiler to generate inline code (as opposed to a subroutine call) whenever possible. Its use is analogous to the use of the *register* adjective: the compiler complies when feasible and silently ignores the request when it cannot comply.

In some cases, C definitions can be shortened when no ambiguity exists (for example, "unsigned" instead of "unsigned int"). Therefore, "inline" would replace "inline oper" in practice. Furthermore, operators would by default work on and return integers, as functions do by default.

Other Uses for Operators

In my view, operators would be used not only to define existing operations over new data types, but also for specifying other operations over new as well as existing data types. These new operators would normally have alphanumeric names and would thus require quoting in graven accents when they appear in expressions. For example, we define the operation of NAND (negated and) for integers as follows (no graven accents are required in the definition but are required in the below invocation):

```
int oper nand(a,b)
int a,b;
{
        return(~(a & b));
}
```

To use this in an actual expression, you would have to quote the nand:

```
c = a `nand` b;
```

Operator Hierarchy

C already has a built-in hierarchy for known operations. The most reasonable approach is to give user-defined operators the lowest priority. This might require more parentheses, but seems logical.

Pointers to Operators

C provides the facility to use pointers to functions. It could potentially prove useful to have pointers to operators as well. A function's address is specified by its name without trailing parentheses. Unfortunately, operator names are used in this way to indicate the operation they represent. To remove the ambiguity in requesting the pointer, the operator name could be parenthesized (for example, (+) or (`nand`)).

Using pointers to operators implies that defined operations must have subroutines associated with them. Thus, truly inline operators could have no pointers associated with them.

Dichotomy of Operators and Functions

Functions and operators are almost the same thing. However, the compiler must know if an operator is binary or unary. Therefore, its definition must be available before use. On the other hand, arguments to C functions are not checked for number or type. Therefore, I choose to keep operators and functions separate, although there is nothing to prevent operators using function calls.

To avoid lexical conflicts, operator and function names would have to be different. This is also desirable from a programming viewpoint, to avoid confusion and errors.

Other Proposals

With the addition of operators, the X grammar provides a much more consistent programming environment than standard C. However, there are some other points that deserve consideration. The first of these is providing a means to handle subroutines with a variable number of arguments. This is considered first.

Since C makes no assumptions about its function library, users are free to write their own, should the standard functions prove inadequate. However, users cannot properly handle functions with variable number of arguments, as must be done by printf(), scanf(), and their relatives. You can solve this problem by introducing a typing adjective called vec, which is short for vector. This adjective is used to indicate that the number of arguments to the function is variable. For example, the fictitious function my_printf(), which allows variable arguments (and returns an integer), would be defined as follows:

```
vec int my_printf(argcnt,argvec)
int argcnt;
char *argvec[];
{
        /* code goes here */
}
```

A function declared with vec always has two arguments: argcnt, argvec. These variables are analogous to main()'s (argc,argv) pair. Before use, a definition of the form:

```
vec my_printf();
```

would be included in each file where my_printf() is referenced. This definition causes command-line arguments to be processed normally: the right-most argument is pushed (placed on the stack) first, and the left-most last, when code is generated. However, the two additional arguments argcnt and argvec are also stacked. The argvec variable points to the stack location where the first real argument is located. Since normal stacks are push-down, this should provide the arguments in the correct order. The argument argcnt contains the number of arguments plus one to account for argvec. This makes it completely analogous to argc. The argument argvec always contains an address, but this is not very useful, if no arguments were specified in the function call.

To illustrate the stacking mechanism, imagine that you invoke my_printf() as follows:

```
my_printf(arg1,arg2,arg3,arg4,arg5);
```

For this specific call, the stacking arrangment (excluding any special register saves) would look as specified in Figure 3-2. Note that argcnt is six (five arguments) for this case, as described above.

It might be worthwhile to have variable argument calls, even if the function was not declared as using this calling convention. To allow this, you introduce the ellipsis (...) concept into the argument string. If my_printf() were not declared as vec, you could force variable argument format as follows:

```
my_printf(arg1,arg2,arg3,arg4,arg5...);
```

Always including the ellipsis for this variety of call seems to improve readability, but is not required to remain compatible with current C usage.

Fixed Arguments

The argvec variable always points to the first variable specified on the command line. However, the function definition could still explicitly declare a finite number of arguments that it may wish to examine more directly. For example, if the first argument of my_printf() were a control string, you could declare my_printf() as follows:

```
vec int my_printf(argcnt,argvec,control_string);
int argcnt;
char **argvec;
char *control_string;
```

Notice that contents of control_string would be meaningless if argcnt were less than two.

Figure 3-2. Memory layout for a variable argument function call.

```
                  --------------------
                  -    Low memory    -
                  --------------------
                  -       ...        -
                  --------------------
                  -   argcnt = 6     -
                  --------------------
                  -  argvec = ADDR   -
                  --------------------
          ADDR:   -      arg1        -
                  --------------------
                  -      arg2        -
                  --------------------
                  -      arg3        -
                  --------------------
                  -      arg4        -
                  --------------------
                  -      arg5        -
                  --------------------
                  -       ...        -
                  --------------------
                  -   High memory    -
                  --------------------
```

One final note about variable argument control is that it enhances a function's ability to detect incorrect input. With reference to printf(), Kernighan and Ritchie state, "A warning: printf uses its first argument to decide how many arguments follow and what their types are. It will get confused, if there are not enough arguments or if they are the wrong type." If implemented with the vec arrangement, printf() could at least know if it has been given the right number of arguments. It still would not know if they were of the correct types.

Variable Length Automatic Arrays

Another element of the X grammar is the ability to declare automatic arrays that possess variable length. Since stack displacements are computed at each entry to a block, this only forces a computed size allocation. At worst, a memory allocation mechanism must be tied into the compiler. This latter restriction can be serious if C is used in a very low level environment, such as in operating system development. So you can readily see the use of this feature, X requires the use of the *var* adjective in conjunction with such definitions. For most purposes, it offers a welcome enhancement. Where it is inappropriate, you should disable this feature via a compiler switch.

As a general example, you can declare a variable length array in the following routine:

```
/* declare an array of integers one larger than
argument */
array_test(length)
int length;
{
        var int test[length+1]; /* declare array */
        ...
}
```

A New Looping Structure

Many loops are unconditional with breaks generated only from within. Therefore, it is often useful to have an unconditional looping command. This avoids a lot of "while(1)" sequences. This could be implemented as follows:

```
                    loop
                    {
                            ... code ...
                    }
replaces
                    while(1)
                    {
                            ... code ...
                    }
```

Preprocessors and Related Comments

Preprocessors could be used to implement several of the X features mentioned above. The statements and expressions would be expanded by the preprocessor into standard function calls. The preprocessor would also provide subroutines from definitions, as needed. New data types could certainly be handled in this way. However, changes to the C parser must be made in order to handle the vec and var features. Trivial additions such as loop can be handled with the existing C preprocessor.

Some programmers may argue that no additions are needed, since most of the features outlined above can be achieved through function calls. In my view, the X grammar makes C more (and not less) consistent because it allows both intrinsic and user-defined types to be handled similarly. It also allows greater portability by defining a means through which variable argument functions can be handled uniformly. In summation, it turns C into an extensible language while adding only a few new keywords.

In this section, I have suggested an enhanced C grammar, denoted X to indicate extensibility. It is the (Unix 7) C language with enhancements designed to allow the incorporation of user-specified operators into programs. This should provide more flexible and consistent reference to user-defined data types. Also mentioned were variable length automatic arrays (var) and a mechanism for allowing variable argument functions (vec). Finally, the use of preprocessors for implementing these ideas was mentioned.

Now let's turn to reader response to these proposals.

Comments on the X Grammar

I received several comments about the X grammar. John M. Gamble of Batavia, Ohio, wrote, "Your column on extensions to the C language was very interesting. I have a few comments: (1) To keep analogy between functions and opers, I think it should be legal to declare static opers."

This sounds fine, but what is a static oper? Since I'm not sure what Mr. Gamble means, I can't really comment. He continued, "(2) I have trouble thinking of any justification for adding one more reserved word (loop) just to do what 'for(;;)' does just as well. If it really offends your eye, couldn't you just use #define to substitute for it?"

I agree. I only mentioned *loop* because I wanted an efficient way to specify an unconditional loop. This is fine, since for(;;) shouldn't produce unnecessary instructions in object code. Mr. Gamble continued his list of comments as follows: "(3) I think your method of declaring argument lists in vec functions is too limited to be practical. A function list is not analogous to argv, which deals only with character strings. A function, after all, deals with all sorts of variables. To get around this problem, I have thought of two possible solutions: (a)Require that the first argument be a string equivalent to printf's control string. Quite frankly, I dislike this solution. Deciphering the control string would be a pain, and the code needed to deal with this pain would probably ruin C's reputation for compact code. (b)Declare the types of the argument list members in the function itself. This would be efficient and easy to modify later on. For example, say that you wish to have some integer variables, and you wish to exchange their values so that they are in [numerical] order. Rather than going through the trouble of inserting the values in an array, calling a sorting routine, and recovering the values from the array, a vec function called sort_them() might be easier to use. The declaration might be as follows:

```
vec int sort_them(argcnt, argvec)
int argcnt;
int *argvec[]; /* Integer arguments */
{
```

```
    /*
     * exchange the values of the argvec array
     * here
     *
     */
}
```

If you wanted to make the function more flexible by allowing the ordering to be user-specified, you could have the first argument be a function. Then the declaration would resemble this:

```
vec int sort_them(argcnt, argvec)
int argcnt;
int *(argvec[0])();
int *argvec[];              /* The rest are integers */
{
    /* etc. */
}
```

Of course, you are not limited to integer pointers. A vec function could just as easily have arguments of all sorts. Such an example is:

```
vec char *dunno(argcnt, argvec)
int     argcnt;
char    *argvec[0];
long    *argvec[1];
double  *argvec[2];
COMPLEX *argvec[3];
int     *argvec[];    /* rest are integers */
{
    /*
     * Here we have a function whose first four arguments
     * are respectively: char, long, double, and COMPLEX
     * pointers. Anything after that is an integer
     *
     */
}
```

Since the argvec array consists of pointers only, the addresses of the argument list are passed in, not the values. Therefore, register variables may not be used in the list. Also, since passing addresses is the default, we can drop the & before each variable [in the calling sequence]."

I think Mr. Gamble's ideas are valid and are consistent with my original intentions for an extended grammar. Does anyone else have further comments about vec functions?

Gerald Evenden of North Falmouth, Massachusetts, responded as follows: "Your thoughts about adding definable operators is quite interesting, but I have some reservations. First, I did not see any mention of the order of evaluation and determination of operator precedence. Secondly, the problem of mixed mode of operands also was not considered. For example,

```
COMPLEX a,b,c;
...
a = 2. * (a+ b*c);
```

would be considered a straightforward expression for complex arithmetic, but it contains binary operators of mixed type and the classic case of operator precedence (is it (a+b)*c or a+(b*c)?). If these problems are not resolved in a more complete set of specifications, I don't feel that the constructs are of much interest. It seems that you may end up putting UNIX's 'yacc' into the preprocessing phase, and this may be more of a challenge than you'd want to bargain for."

Mr. Evenden's points are well taken. First, I would argue that mixed mode arithmetic should not be supported. Thus, the above expression would be written using a cast:

```
COMPLEX a,b,c;
...
a = (COMPLEX)(2.) * (a+ b*c);
```

The problem involving precedence is more tricky. One answer is to give all user-defined operators equal precedence and to *require* parentheses to specify the order of evaluation. However, this would make user-defined operations more restrictive than operations on intrinsic types.

Mr. Evenden continued, "Two of your ideas I find to be plain 'fluff': automatic arrays and 'loop.' Dynamic allocation of memory is readily taken care of by calls to a memory allocation procedure . . . if you want to use 'loop' for cosmetic purposes, a define of 'for(;;)' or 'while(1)' does the job nicely!"

I have taken a lot of heat concerning "loop." The reason I suggested it is rather fundamental. The simplest structured loop is an unconditional loop, which can only be terminated with break. It appeared to me that this should be supported by the language internally. I realize that the form for(;;) does *exactly* what I want.

I also had specific reasons for suggesting variable length arrays. Algorithms often require variable size arrays, and it is often undesirable to declare an array that is "big enough for all supported applications." Furthermore, it seems more natural for beginners to specify array declaration in this way. Moreover, the operation would become independent of a specific runtime library feature, which could differ (in principle) between implementations.

Mr. Evenden also addressed the problem of variable length arguments: "The problem with variable arguments is quite nasty . . . I am not too keen on your method for solving the problem and would like to suggest an alternative approach. If the compiler would put the argument count of the argument stack at the top of the stack (as per your method) the programmer who needs this information can get it as follows:

```
func(arg1,arg2,...,argN)
{
        int s_size, *dummy;
        dummy = &arg1;
        s_size = dummy[-1];
}
```

Admittedly, this is clumsy and there should be a better way. My second suggestion is to provide that if the [function] ... name is used in the context of a simple integer, then that integer value will be located at the top of the argument stack ... [it] will contain the [argument] count. [The following example] illustrates the usage of this concept."

```
double   /* hypothetical routine to return minimum
value */
amin()   /* of a list of double precision numbers
*/
{
        double *list, min;

        if(amin <= 0)
                return(0.0); /* no args condition */

        list = (double *)(&amin + sizeof(int));

        for(min = *list++; --amin; list++)
                if(*list < min)
                        min = *list;

        return(min);     /* return the minimum */

}
```

I think this second idea has one problem. The name *amin* without parentheses is treated by C as a pointer to the function amin(). The problem is that a function really has basically three attributes: its address, the number of arguments, and the starting location for the arguments. To access these other attributes, you could add two pseudo-functions analogous to the return() statement. These pseudo-functions are illustrated in the following example, which is a rewrite of Mr. Evenden's last example.

```
double    /* hypothetical routine to return minimum
value */
amin()    /* of a list of double precision numbers
*/
{
        double *list, min;

        if(noargs() == 0)
                return(0.0); /* no args condition */
        list = (double *)(addrof() + sizeof(int));

        for(min = *list++; --amin; list++)
                if(*list < min)
                        min = *list;

        return(min);     /* return the minimum */

}
```

In this example, noargs() returns the number of arguments that a function has received, whereas addrof() returns the starting address (as a pointer to characters). The pseudo-functions return the information about the function they reside in. The mechanism is therefore unambiguous and should be practical.

In conclusion, Bob Desinger of Cupertino, California, noted that a much better approach to improving C was suggested in the Bell Labs Technical Memorandum "The C++ Programming Language." According to Desinger, it offers the following (including examples):

- User-defined data types (such as complex numbers)
- Operator overloading (such as defining +)
- Argument checking for functions [for example, for printf()]

I have yet to see a copy of this memorandum, but I recommend that interested readers look for it.

Part 7

WISH LISTS

This section includes some of the shorter (mainly unrelated) subjects that appeared in columns. These subjects often include valuable insights about C and programming in general. Others are just pragmatic ideas.

Programming Philosophy

John A. Grosberg of Scottsdale, Arizona, wrote an interesting letter concerning programming style and philosophy. He wrote his letter after reading the August 1984 column, which included a short listing by Alex Cameron (see Listing 3-1, discussed in Part 2). Mr. Grosberg wrote, "Your column... caught my attention, particularly the short listing of Mr. Alex Cameron's routines to automatically allocate I/O buffers.... I am writing to present a few ideas on program structure, and I will use his listing as an example. This is not an attack on his application or on the style he used in his listing; I assume that there were reasons for the form chosen. But my perfectionism was provoked by that listing, and the more I read it, the more I wanted to write. One important principle of program design is that the structure of the program (I will use *program, routine,* and *function* interchangeably for this discussion) should reflect the structure of the problem. This sounds nice, but what does it mean? Without guidelines it is almost a theological principle, over which well-meaning people could argue loud and long and never come to agreement. The reason for this is that the 'structure of the problem' depends on your viewpoint; that is, it is relative to the observer... the program's structure reflects the way we are thinking about the problem."

Since the way we write programs is based on our viewpoint, Mr. Grosberg suggested a set of standard reference points: "In mechanical drafting, there are three standard orthogonal viewpoints that are used to describe most objects. They are called 'front,' 'side,' and 'top' views of the object. The structure of the physical object inheres in the spatial relationships of its elements, and these must be captured in the drawing.

"In software, an important aspect of structure is the temporal relationships among the elements. The two primary temporal relationships are sequence and frequency, and these relationships should be captured in the code. If one action occurs before another in time (sequence), then the first should precede the second in the code. If an action occurs the same number of times (frequency) as another, then they should be in the same (logical) block of code."

Mr. Grosberg's recommendations are practical, and this type of coding technique could only improve maintainability of software. He continued, "Expanding on the concept of temporal relationships as expressed in code, consider that on any single execution of a program, an element of that program may be executed once, more than once, or less than once [that is, not executed]. If the element executes once and only once per program execution (sequence), it should be simply listed in sequence where it belongs. If the element executes more than once per execution (repetition), it should appear once in a loop. If the element executes less than once per program execution (alternation), it should appear once in a program branch statement. Finally, all elements that execute the same number of times should appear together in the listing."

Although these points seem obvious to me (and also to Mr. Grosberg), it is clear that they are not often followed. I cannot claim to have adhered to these principles in the past, but I plan to do so in the future. For those interested in pursuing the concepts further, he recommends *Practical LCP, A Direct Approach to Structured Programming*, by Albert C Gardner (McGraw-Hill, 1980). Mr. Grosberg has recoded Alex Cameron's listing to exemplify his comments; this code is presented in Listing 3-15. Concerning the code itself, he commented, "In Mr. Cameron's function 'sfopen,' the call to 'alloc' actually occurs only once per execution, but it is written three times in the code [sequence]. The 'return' occurs only once per execution, but is written 10 times [sequence]. The three main 'if' statements

```
if(*mode == 'x')
{
            ...
}
```

are written as if they occur sequentially, when in fact only one of them can occur per execution [alternation]. The structure of the code actually obscures the execution behavior of the function."

Mr. Grosberg did not claim to have perfectly embodied his comments in Listing 3-15. He just created it (untested) to illustrate his remarks. I find his ideas worthwhile.

Controlling Size of Intrinsic Data Types

John M. Gamble of Batavia, Ohio, wrote, "I am very glad you printed this column [August 1984] (I ranked it number one for the month) because it inspired me to jot down my own wish list. It is only one wish long, but it is something I have longed for, for some time."

Mr. Gamble's wish is for a way to more precisely control the sizes of intrinsic data types in C. For example, integers can have different sizes on different machines. He continued, "The size of the various types (int, char, long, etc.) vary too much from machine to machine. However, I don't think that forcing a size to a type (a la Plum Hall) is the answer (besides, I hate the baby words Plum uses to define them). Instead, I think that another 'storage class specifier' (see *The C Programming Language,* page 192) like typedef could be defined. I'm going to call it 'sizetype.' Sizetype would be used just like typedef, but what is declared is the size of the storage class. For example, we could define a type small this way:

```
sizetype   u8   small;
```

The letter *u* is optional and stands for 'unsigned.' Thus a variable of type small is unsigned and eight bits long. Another example would be:

```
sizetype   16   hexsize;
```

which would guarantee that variables of type hexsize are sixteen bits long."

I am enthusiastic about Mr. Gamble's suggestion. It would enhance portability of C code. Anyone who has moved between microcomputers and minis is aware that there can be significant problems when moving from machines with signed or unsigned characters. Integer length differences are also annoying. Mr. Gamble added, "Use of the sizetype declaration would guarantee portability between machines (which currently is a problem). It also means that only one more reserved word is added, instead of the many that would be needed to define a type for every conceivable integer length. If the sizeof operator could be altered to return fractions, we could use sizetype to define bit lengths that are not multiples of eight. On the other hand, I notice that the *sizeof* operation on a bit-field structure is not defined in *The C Programming Language,* so maybe it is just up to the person who writes the compiler."

Floating Point Improvements

Gerald Evenden wrote about C floating-point deficiencies: "Most of my criticisms [of C] are minor except for one: evaluation of all floating-point data elements in double precision. When two type float values are joined by a binary operator, I fail to see any reason why we should pay the costly runtime premium of double precision evaluation! Of course, conversion of *float* function arguments to *double* is equally strange and pointless. I suspect floating-point arithmetic was one of the last features added to the language and got shortchanged in the final stages of the development of C. If the people at Bell Labs have any excuse for this peculiar handling of floating point by C, I'd sure like to hear it! Hopefully, some . . . readers may also have comments."

Mr. Evenden has hit on an important point. Not only is the conversion of *float* to *double* expensive, programming can get messy when dealing with pointers and arrays. For example, if a program needs a large number of floats (in an array), it is difficult to use with a function that expects pointers to *double*. I see no reason for using arrays of double precision numbers for many applications. Yet to simplify programming logic, memory must often be wasted (by a factor of two) for floating-point arrays. On systems such as the 8086/8087, the actual cost for single/double precision operations is the same, but conversions and other effects are still cause for grief.

Mr. Evenden continued, "I have given some thought to what would be required to make C's floating point behave in a more traditional manner, and I have come to the conclusion that upward compatibility of a new compiler might not be possible as far as floating-point syntax is involved. Obviously, the 'standard' library routines will have to be changed ('printf' will need '%E' and '%e') ... functions returning floating-point values will have to be in two precisions (sqrt() and dsqrt(), for example)."

Variable Formats in printf()

I'd like to change gears and consider an aspect of printf format strings. Consistent with previous discussions, I remind the readers that this is a discussion relevant to the C library and not the compiler.

A typical printf() call might look as follows:

```
float number;
...
printf("%7.3e\n",number);
```

In certain cases, you might wish to vary the format dynamically. One way to accomplish this is as follows:

```
float number;
...
char fmt_string[100];   /* make format string here */
char format[10];        /* format contained here */
strcpy(format,"7.3");   /* copy a specific format */
...
sprintf(fmt_string,"%%%sf",format); /* make format string */
printf(fmt_string,number);  /* print number in format */
```

The format string in the sprintf() is "%%%sf." The first two percent signs place a single output percent in fmt_string. The %s causes the string format (containing "7.3") to go into fmt_string. Finally, the letter *f* is interpreted literally and is sent to fmt_string. The point of giving this example is to show how cumbersome the operation can be. Now I want to pose a simple solution to the problem.

To allow variable formats as part of a single printf(), you need a way to indicate an indirection. Then, printf() could use the current member of its argument list as a source for the format. This is illustrated as follows:

```
float number;
...
printf("%&s\n","7.3f",number);
```

The indirect format is &s, which tells printf() to take the first argument as a string and print it into the format string before proceeding. Thus, the ultimate format string is "%7.3f" as originally. Another possibility would be

```
float number;
float format = 7.3;
...
printf("%&f\n",format,number);
```

which demonstrates the range of choices allowed by indirect formats. To print an ampersand, the following sequence would be required:

```
printf("%&&");
```

Why would these be useful? Primarily, they allow programs to readily adapt to data variations. This could allow greater user selection, or, if extended to scanf(), greater ability to read and write "foreign" data files.

Conclusion

In conclusion, I'd like to quote Gerald Evenden one more time. Concerning future upgrades or modifications of C, Mr. Evenden wrote, "Some people criticize C as being a 'spartan' language, but I maintain that this spartan attribute is its principal and strongest feature... [C] is a real programmer's language, providing an excellent tool for doing everything from real time processing, to writing other compilers, to sophisticated scientific applications. If we ever make changes to C, we will have to be very careful to maintain this strong feature of the language."

I leave this quotation as my parting remark.

LISTING 3-1

```c
/*
** stdlib3.c -- standard I/O library
**
** Copyright 1984   A. Cameron
*/
#include "bdscio.h"
/*
**
**      Standard fopen
**
**          return fd on success, NULL on error       **
*/
sfopen(filename,mode)
char *filename;
char *mode;
{
        int fd;

        if (*mode == 'w')      /* write mode */
        {
                if (!(fd = alloc(BUFSIZ)))
                        return(NULL);
                else
                {
                        if (fcreat(filename,fd) == -1)
                        {
                                free(fd);
                                return(NULL);
                        }

                        return(fd);
                }

        }

        if (*mode == 'r')      /* read mode */
        {
                if (!(fd = alloc(BUFSIZ)))
                        return(NULL);
                else
                {
                        if (fopen(filename,fd) == -1)
                        {
                                free(fd);
                                return(NULL);
                        }
```

```
                                return(fd);
                        }
                }

                if (*mode == 'a')       /* append mode */
                {
                        if (!(fd = alloc(BUFSIZ)))
                                return(NULL);
                        else
                        {
                                if (fappend(filename,fd) == -1)
                                {
                                        free(fd);
                                        return(NULL);
                                }

                                return(fd);

                }

                return(NULL);   /* failure */

}
/*
**
**      Standard fclose
**
*/
sfclose(fd)
int fd;
{
        fputc(CPMEOF,fd);

        if (!(fclose(fd)))
        {
                free(fd);
                return(NULL);
        }

        return(ERROR);
}
```

LISTING 3-2

```c
/**********************************************************************
*                                                                     *
*       lsup.c                           created: 25-Mar-84           *
*                                                                     *
*       long pointer support for small memory model 8086 C compilers. *
*                                                                     *
*       version 1.00 as of 25-Mar-84                                  *
*                                                                     *
*       Copyright 1984 (c) Anthony Skjellum.                          *
*       All rights reserved.                                          *
*                                                                     *
*       This program may be freely distributed for all non-commercial *
*       purposes, but may not be sold.                                *
*                                                                     *
*       The routines contained here are designed to be portable to    *
*       a large variety of compilers.  Currently they have been tested*
*       with Aztec C86 v 1.05i only.                                  *
*                                                                     *
*       Modules comprising this package:                              *
*                                                                     *
*               lsup.c          this file.                            *
*               lsup.h          header/definition file.               *
*               _lsup.h         lower level header for this file      *
*               llsup.asm       assembly language support (compiler   *
*                               independent)                          *
*               llint.asm       compiler interface code   (compiler   *
*                               dependent)                            *
*                                                                     *
*       Subroutines included here:                                    *
*       (those marked with an asterisk are only included if compiler  *
*        used lacks some preprocessor support feature)                *
*                                                                     *
*                                                                     *
**********************************************************************/

#include "_lsup.h"              /* header with definitions */

/*
        Special routines: Included only if compiler lacks one of
        several features.
*/

/* lassign(dest,source): assignment of type LPTR to the left */

#ifndef MSUBST
```

```
lassign(dest,source)
LPTR dest;
LPTR source;
{
        dest._llong = source._llong;    /* assignment */
}


#endif


/*
        General purpose routines:
*/


/* llstrcpy(dest,src):  copy null terminated strings between long ptrs */

llstrcpy(dest,src)
LPTR *dest;
LPTR *src;
{
        char chr;                       /* temporary */

        while(1)                        /* loop */
        {
                chr = lchr(&src);       /* get   a character */
                l_stchr(&dest,chr);     /* store a character */

                linc(&dest);            /* increment destination ptr */
                linc(&src);             /* and source pointer */

                if(!chr)                /* we are done at eos */
                        break;
        }

}

/* debugging routines: */

lprint(lptr)
LPTR *lptr;
{
        printf("%lx",lptr->_llong);
}
```

LISTING 3-3

```
#include "_lsup.h"

/* place any special function specifications (defined in lsup.c) here: */
```

LISTING 3-4

```
/***********************************************************************
 *                                                                     *
 *      _lsup.h                  created: 25-Mar-84                    *
 *                                                                     *
 *      a component of lsup.c                                          *
 *                                                                     *
 *      version 1.00 as of 25-Mar-84                                   *
 *                                                                     *
 *      Copyright 1984 (c) Anthony Skjellum.                           *
 *      All rights reserved.                                           *
 *                                                                     *
 *      This program may be freely distributed for all non-commercial  *
 *      purposes, but may not be sold.                                 *
 *                                                                     *
 *      This is a header/definition file which must be included        *
 *      in any module which utilizes long pointers.                    *
 *                                                                     *
 ***********************************************************************/

/*
        compiler feature toggles:
        comment out any which don't apply to the compiler in use.
*/

#define MSUBST               /* macro substitution supported */

/* typedefs */

typedef struct __lword
{
        unsigned _addr;      /* address */
        unsigned _segm;      /* segment */
} LWORD;

typedef union __lptr
{
        long    _llong;      /* long format (for assignments) */
        char    _lstr[4];    /* character format */
        LWORD   _lword;      /* long-word format */
} LPTR;
```

```
/* constants */

/* macros */

/* lassign(destination,source): effect assignment of type LPTR */

#ifdef  MSUBST
#define lassign(d,s)    d._llong = s._llong;
#endif

/* function specifications: */

char lchr();
```

LISTING 3-5

```
;
; llsup.asm
;
; a component of lsup.c
;
; Copyright 1984 (c) A. Skjellum. All rights reserved.
;
; version of 25-Mar-84
; updated:   31-Mar-85 (used with MASM 1.0)
;
; This routine makes no assumptions about the behavior of the
; C compiler in use.
;
; all procedures are "near"
;
        dseg    segment para public 'data'
        dseg    ends

        cseg    segment para public 'code'
                assume  cs:cseg,ds:dseg

;
; linc:         increment a long pointer by 1 byte
;
; expects:      es:bx with long pointer to increment
; returns:      pointer incremented.
; consumes:     es, bx, f, ax
;
        public  linc
```

```
linc     proc    near
         inc     bx              ; increment low part of word
;        or      bx,bx           ; is it zero now? (NOT NEEDED --> inc set zf)
         jnz     linc_exit       ; no, we are done
         mov     ax,es
         add     ax,1000h        ; another 64k of paragraphs
         mov     es,ax           ; store back to es
linc_exit:
         ret                     ; return
linc     endp


;
; ldec:   decrement a long pointer by 1 byte
;
; expects:    es:bx with long pointer to decrement
; returns:    pointer decremented.
; consumes:   es, bx, f, ax
;
         public  ldec
ldec     proc    near
         or      bx,bx           ; zero currently ?
         pushf                   ; save condition (BUG FIX)
         dec     bx              ; decrement it
         popf                    ; restore condition (BUG FIX)
         jnz     ldec_exit       ; just decrement low end and exit...
         mov     ax,es           ; get segment register
         sub     ax,1000h        ; remove 64k of paragraphs
         mov     es,ax           ; store back to es
ldec_exit:
         ret                     ; return
ldec     endp


;
; ladd:   add a constant to a long pointer
;
; expects:    es:bx with long pointer's original value
;             ax with unsigned constant to be added
; returns:    pointer with constant added
; consumes:   es, bx, f, ax
;
         public  ladd
ladd     proc    near
         add     bx,ax           ; add in offset
         jnc     ladd_exit       ; no carry, so we are done.
         mov     ax,es
         add     ax,1000h        ; add 64k of paragraphs
         mov     es,ax           ; and store back to es
```

```
ladd_exit:
        ret
ladd    endp

;
; lsub:         subtract a constant from a long pointer
;
; expects:      es:bx with long pointer's original value
;               ax with unsigned constant to be subtracted
; returns:      pointer with constant subtracted
; consumes:     es, bx, f, ax
;
        public  lsub
lsub    proc    near
        sub     bx,ax           ; subtract offset
        jnb     lsub_exit       ; no borrow, so we are done.
        mov     ax,es
        sub     ax,1000h        ; subtract 64k of paragraphs
        mov     es,ax           ; and store back to es
lsub_exit:
        ret
lsub    endp

;
; lsum:         add a signed offset to a long pointer
;
; expects:      es:bx with long pointer
;               ax with signed offset
; returns:      pointer with constant added (signed)
; consumes:     es, bx, f, ax
;
        public  lsum
lsum    proc    near
        or      ax,ax           ; negative?
        js      lsum_neg
        call    ladd            ; do addition
        ret                     ; and exit
lsum_neg:
        and     ax,07fffh       ; and out sign flag
        jnz     lsum_neg_ok
        mov     ax,8000h        ; -32768 value (don't treat as 0)
lsum_neg_ok:
        call    lsub
        ret
lsum    endp

;
; lcopy:        copy from one long pointer to another,
```

```
;                up to 1024k bytes of data
;
; expects:       ds:si with src  address
;                es:di with dest address
;                ds:cx with length (dx is high order, cx is low order)
;
; returns:       block copied
;                ds, es intact
; consumes:      ax, cx, f
;
;
;       this routine uses a copy downward method, to produce
;       correct copying for overlapping regions
;
        public  lcopy
lcopy   proc    near
        ;
        ; convert dx into segment form:
        ;
        push    dx              ; save original form of dx
        push    cx              ; save low order of long count
        and     dx,15           ; smallest meaningful value
        xchg    dh,dl           ; switch upper and lower parts
        mov     cl,4
        shl     dh,cl           ; effect is shift left by 12 bits
        pop     cx              ; and recover low order of long count
        ;
        mov     ax,es
        add     ax,dx
        mov     es,ax
        mov     ax,ds
        add     ax,dx
        mov     ds,ax           ; gross adjustment of segments
        pop     dx              ; recover original form of dx
        ;
        add     di,cx           ; adjust dest. ptr to end of area
        jnc     no_dest_adj
        mov     ax,es
        add     ax,1000h        ; add offset
        mov     es,ax           ; and store back to segment register
no_dest_adj:
        ;
        ; do same work for source pointer:
        ;
        add     si,cx           ; do the addition
        jnc     no_mor_adj      ; no more adjustment needed if no carry
        mov     ax,ds
```

```
                add     ax,1000h            ; do the adjustment
                mov     ds,ax               ; and store back to ds
        ;
        ; at this stage:
        ;
        ;       es:di is at the last byte of the dest. area
        ;       ds:si is at the last byte of the src. area
        ;
no_mor_adj:
                std                         ; set direction flag for moves
lc_loop:
                or      si,si               ; is si zero ?
                lodsb                       ; get byte ds:[si], decrement si
                jnz     no_ds_adj           ; no need to adjust if non-zero at start
                mov     ax,ds
                sub     ax,1000h
                mov     ds,ax               ; adjust pointer for next load
no_ds_adj:
                or      di,di               ; is di zero ?
                stosb                       ; set byte es:[di] = al, decrement di
                jnz     no_es_adj           ; no need to adjust if non-zero at start
                mov     ax,es
                sub     ax,1000h
                mov     es,ax               ; adjust pointer for next store
no_es_adj:
                loop    lc_loop             ; copy whole block (--cx, jnz lc_loop)
                dec     dx                  ; work on outer loop
                or      dx,dx
                jnz     lc_loop             ; loop over dx counts too
        ;
        ; we are done
        ;
                inc     si
                inc     di                  ; restore to original calling values
                ret                         ; exit
lcopy           endp

cseg            ends
                end
```

LISTING 3-6

```
;
; llint.asm
;
; version of 25-Mar-84
```

```
;
; a component of lsup.c
;
; Copyright 1984 (c) A. Skjellum. All rights reserved.
;
; these routines are setup for Aztec C86 v 1.05i
;
; all procedures are "near"
;
        dseg    segment para public 'data'
        dseg    ends

        cseg    segment para public 'code'
                assume  cs:cseg,ds:dseg,es:dseg,ss:dseg

;
; Routines which do not merit calls to portable routines in llsup.asm
;


;
; ds = flptr(lptr,sptr)
; LPTR *lptr;
; char *sptr;
;
; form a long pointer from a "normal" ds relative short pointer (sptr)
; and store at lptr
;
; note: no portable segment (flptr) in llsup.asm since this
; is such a trivial routine.
;
; return value is also ds, should this prove useful
;
        public  flptr_
flptr_  proc    near
        mov     bx,sp           ; prepare for argument load
        mov     ax,4[bx]        ; get short pointer ds:ax
        mov     bx,2[bx]        ; get address where to store long pointer
        mov     [bx],ax         ; store low order
        mov     ax,ds
        mov     2[bx],ax        ; store high order
        ret                     ; return value is also ds
flptr_  endp


;
; the following four routines are examples of what can
; be done to supplement general routines with specific
```

```
; (more efficient ones).  Many more variations are
; possible than the two presented here.  They follow
; directly from this basic idea:
;
;
; char lchr(lptr)
; LPTR *lptr;
;
; return character pointed to by lptr
;
        public  lchr_
lchr_   proc    near
        mov     bx,sp           ; prepare for argument load
        push    ds              ; save ds register
        mov     bx,2[bx]        ; get address of lptr
        mov     ax,[bx]         ;
        mov     ds,2[bx]        ; begin forming pointer
        mov     bx,ax           ; ds:bx now is valid pointer
        sub     ax,ax           ; zero whole acc.
        mov     al,[bx]         ; get the character
        pop     ds
        ret                     ; exit with char in ax
lchr_   endp


;
; int lint(lptr)
; LPTR *lptr;
;
; return integer or unsigned pointed to by lptr
;
        public  lint_
lint_   proc    near
        mov     bx,sp           ; prepare for argument load
        push    ds              ; save ds register
        mov     bx,2[bx]        ; get address of lpr
        mov     ax,[bx]         ;
        mov     ds,2[bx]        ; begin forming pointer
        mov     bx,ax           ; ds:bx now is valid pointer
        mov     ax,[bx]         ; get the integer or unsigned
        pop     ds              ; recover old ds value
        ret                     ; and exit with char in ax
lint_   endp


;
; l_stchr(lptr,chr)
; LPTR *lptr;
; char chr;
```

;
; store character chr at address lptr
;
        public l_stchr_
l_stchr_ proc   near
        mov   bx,sp   ; prepare for argument load
        mov   cl,4[bx]   ; get character
        mov   bx,2[bx]   ; prepare for load of long pointer
        push   ds   ; save ds segment register
        mov   ax,[bx]   ;
        mov   ds,2[bx]   ; begin forming pointer
        mov   bx,ax   ; ds:bx now is valid pointer
        mov   [bx],cl   ; store byte
        pop   ds
        ret
l_stchr_ endp

;
; l_stint(lptr,val)
; LPTR *lptr;
; int val;
;
; store integer or unsigned at address lptr
;
        public l_stint_
l_stint_ proc   near
        mov   bx,sp   ; prepare for argument load
        mov   cx,4[bx]   ; get integer to store
        mov   bx,2[bx]   ; prepare to form ds:bx with correct
                                ; storage address
        push   ds   ; save current ds
        mov   ax,[bx]   ;
        mov   ds,2[bx]   ; begin forming pointer
        mov   bx,ax   ; ds:bx now is valid pointer
        mov   [bx],cx   ; store the integer
        pop   ds
        ret   ; exit
l_stint_ endp

;
; lload(dest,lptr,len)
; char *dest;
; LPTR *lptr;
; unsigned len;
;
; general purpose copy routine from long data storage to ds: relative
; storage

```
;
; we assume es = ds for Aztec C explicitly here
;
; due to convenient 8086 instructions, the portable function would
; consist merely of a "cld", "rep movsb" sequence followed by a return.
; Therefore, no portable lload is included in llsup.asm
;
        public  lload_
lload_  proc    near
        mov     bx,sp           ; prepare for argument load
        push    ds              ; save Aztec ds segment
        push    si
        push    di              ; save source and destination indices
        ;
        mov     cx,6[bx]        ; get length for move
        mov     di,2[bx]        ; es:di now has the destination address
        mov     bx,4[bx]        ; prepare to load long ptr
        mov     si,[bx]         ; get low order
        mov     ds,2[bx]        ; and then high order
        cld
        rep     movsb           ; do the move
        pop     di
        pop     si
        pop     ds
        ret
lload_  endp


;
; lstor(lptr,src,len)
; LPTR *lptr;
; char *src;
; unsigned len;
;
; Reverse of lload: this routine copies data from ds:src to lptr
; Once again, there is no llsup analog.
;
        public  lstor_
lstor_  proc    near
        mov     bx,sp           ; prepare for argument load
        push    es
        push    di
        push    si              ; save registers as required by Aztec C.
        mov     cx,6[bx]        ; get length of move
        mov     si,4[bx]        ; ds:si now contains source index
        mov     bx,2[bx]        ; prepare to form es:di
        mov     di,[bx]
```

```
        mov     es,2[bx]
        rep     movsb           ; move the data
        pop     si
        pop     di
        pop     es
        ret                     ; restore registers and exit
lstor_  endp

;
; --------------------------------------------------
;
; routines that call portable subroutines in llsup.asm
;
; --------------------------------------------------
;
; linc(lptr)
; LPTR *lptr;
;
; increment a long pointer by 1
;
        public  linc_
linc_   proc    near
        extrn   linc:near
        mov     bx,sp           ; prepare for argument load
        push    es              ; save es value from caller
        mov     bx,2[bx]
        push    bx              ; address where answer will go
        mov     es,2[bx]        ; get segment
        mov     bx,[bx]         ; and address
        call    linc            ; do the work
        pop     ax
        xchg    ax,bx
        mov     [bx],ax
        mov     2[bx],es        ; store the value
        pop     es              ; recover the old value
        ret                     ; and exit
linc_   endp


;
; ldec(lptr)
; LPTR *lptr;
;
; decrement a long pointer by 1
;
        public  ldec_
ldec_   proc    near
        extrn   ldec:near
```

```
        mov     bx,sp           ; prepare for argument load
        push    es              ; preserve es
        mov     bx,2[bx]        ; get address ds:bx
        push    bx              ; address where answer will go
        mov     ax,[bx]         ;
        mov     es,2[bx]
        mov     bx,ax
        call    ldec            ; do the decrement
        pop     ax
        xchg    ax,bx
        mov     [bx],ax
        mov     2[bx],es        ; store the value
        pop     es              ; recover it for sake of caller
        ret                     ; and then exit
ldec_   endp


;
; ladd(lptr,offset)
; LPTR *lptr;
; unsigned offset;
;
; add unsigned offset to a long pointer
;
        public  ladd_
ladd_   proc    near
        extrn   ladd:near
        mov     bx,sp           ; prepare for argument load
        push    es              ; save es value of caller
        mov     ax,4[bx]        ; get the offset to ax
        mov     bx,2[bx]
        push    bx              ; address where answer will go too.
        mov     cx,[bx]
        mov     es,2[bx]
        mov     bx,cx
        call    ladd            ; do the addition
        pop     ax
        xchg    ax,bx
        mov     [bx],ax
        mov     2[bx],es        ; store the value
        pop     es              ; recover old es value
        ret                     ; and then exit
ladd_   endp


;
; lsub(lptr,offset)
; LPTR *lptr;
; unsigned offset;
```

```
;
; subtract unsigned offset from a long pointer
;
        public  lsub_
lsub_   proc    near
        extrn   lsub:near
        mov     bx,sp           ; prepare for argument load
        push    es              ; preserve es
        mov     ax,4[bx]        ; get the offset
        mov     bx,2[bx]
        push    bx              ; store answer at this addr. too.
        mov     cx,[bx]
        mov     es,2[bx]
        mov     bx,cx
        call    lsub            ; do the subtraction
        pop     ax
        xchg    ax,bx
        mov     [bx],ax
        mov     2[bx],es        ; store the value
        pop     es              ; restore es
        ret                     ; and then exit
lsub_   endp


;
; lsum(lptr,offset)
; LPTR *lptr;
; int offset;
;
; add signed offset to a long pointer
;
        public  lsum_
lsum_   proc    near
        extrn   lsum:near
        mov     bx,sp           ; prepare for argument load
        push    es              ; preserve caller's es
        mov     ax,4[bx]        ; get the signed offset
        mov     bx,2[bx]
        push    bx
        mov     cx,[bx]
        mov     es,2[bx]
        mov     bx,cs
        call    lsum            ; do the signed addition
        pop     ax
        xchg    ax,bx
        mov     [bx],ax
        mov     2[bx],es        ; store the value
        pop     es              ;
```

```
        ret                     ; exit.
lsum_   endp

;
; lcopy(dest,src,len)
; LPTR *dest;
; LPTR *src;
; long len;       (treated as a long unsigned quantity)
;
;       copy from src to dest, len bytes.
;
; note this routine can be used to copy arbitrarily large chunks of memory
;
        public  lcopy_
lcopy_  proc    near
        extrn   lcopy:near
        mov     bx,sp           ; prepare for argument load
        push    ds
        push    es              ; save segment registers
        push    di
        push    si              ; save these registers for Aztec C
        ;
        mov     cx,6[bx]        ; get length (low order)
        mov     dx,8[bx]        ; high order of length
        mov     ax,2[bx]        ; get ds:ax as pointer to dest.
        xchg    ax,bx
        mov     di,[bx]
        mov     es,2[bx]
        mov     bx,ax
        mov     bx,4[bx]        ; get ds:bx as pointer for dest.
        mov     si,[bx]
        mov     ds,2[bx]        ; get long pointer
        ;
        call    lcopy
        ;
        pop     si
        pop     di
        pop     es
        pop     ds
        ret
lcopy_  endp


cseg    ends
        end
/*
```

LISTING 3-7

```
                env.c                       created: 25-Mar-84

        This package echoes the environment to the standard output.

        example of using long pointers with lsup package.

        This is set up to work with Aztec C.

        by Anthony Skjellum. (C) 1984. All rights reserved.
        Released for non-commercial purposes only.

        This program echoes the environment block to the console.
        In effect, this is the same as the DOS 2.0 SET command.
        Nevertheless, it illustrates the usefulness of long pointers.

        ---------------------------------------------

        The following changes were made to the $begin
        routine of the Aztec C 1.05i module calldos.asm:

                i) a new global variable called envseg was created

                        envseg_ segment word common 'cata'
                        $envdat dw 0
                        $envseg dw ?
                        envseg_ ends

               ii) On entry to $begin, when es contains the
                   program segment prefix (PSP), es:[2ch] contains
                   the segment address of the environment.  This
                   segment address is stored into the second word
                   of envseg_ (ie $envseg).

                   The environment may now be referred to through
                   the external LPTR envseg.

              iii) If DOS 2.0 allocation is to be used, be sure to
                   shrink the program size using the SETBLOCK function.
                   This must also be done in $begin where the psp,
                   ds, segments are both available.
*/

#include <stdio.h>
#include "lsup.h"         /* support for long pointers */

extern  LPTR envseg;      /* envseg is a structure of type LPTR */
```

```
main(argc,argv)
int argc;
char *argv[];
{
        char chr;
        int i;
        LPTR lptr;

        lassign(lptr,envseg); /* get long pointer to environment */

        while(1)        /* loop */
        {
                chr = lchr(&lptr);      /* get the next byte */

                if(!chr) /* we have hit the end of the environment */
                        break;

                while((chr = lchr(&lptr))) /* get characters of string */
                {
                        putchar(chr);   /* write them to console */
                        linc(&lptr);    /* increment pointer */
                }

                linc(&lptr);    /* pass the zero byte just encountered */

                putchar('\n');  /* add new line between entries */

        } /* end while(1) */
```

LISTING 3-8

```
        ;
        ; improvements to llsup routines by Bruce Komusin
        ; % Microworld
        ; L'Estoril
        ; 31 Ave. Princesse Grace
        ; Monte Carlo, Monaco
        ;
        ; these routines offer more temporal and byte-efficient
        ; code than those originally presented in llsup.asm
        ;
        ldec    proc    near
                or      bx,bx
                jz      ldec_2
                dec     bx
                ret
```

```
ldec_2    dec     bx
ldec_3    mov     ax,es
          sub     ax,1000h
          mov     es,ax
          ret
ldec      endp

lsub      proc    near
          sub     bx,ax
          jb      ldec_3
          ret
lsub      endp
```

LISTING 3-9

```
/*
        gpr.c                       created: 01-0ct-83

        general purpose utility routines for use with C to simplify
        user/program interaction.

        by Anthony Skjellum

        Copyright 1983, 1984, 1985 (c) Caltech.  All rights reserved.
        This subroutine library may be distributed freely and
        used for all non-commercial purposes but may not be sold.

        Routines:

                iinp():  integer input w/ prompt, range check + retry
                finp():  float   input w/ prompt, range check + retry
                sinp():  string  input w/ prompt
                cinq():  yes/no question processor w/ prompt + retry
                display(): display a file

        updated: 20-Jul-84
        updated: 31-Mar-85

        testing information: this code was tested with Aztec C 1.05j
        testing information: this code compiled okay under Lattice C 2.12
*/

#include <stdio.h>

/* Unix flag (used by display()) */
/*
```

```c
#define UNIX 1
*/
#ifndef UNIX
#define TEOF    26      /* ^Z */
#endif

/* general purpose subroutines: */

/* iinp(): integer input with range checking, prompt and retry */

iinp(prompt,cflag,low,high)
char *prompt;
char cflag;
int low;
int high;
{
        int ival;

        while(1)
        {
                printf("%s",prompt);
                if(scanf("%d",&ival) < 1)
                {
                        while(getchar() != '\n')
                                ;
                        continue;
                }
                if((!cflag)||(ival >= low)&&(ival <= high))
                        break;
                                /* no checking, or within bounds */

                printf("\nValue out of range, try again...\n");
        }

        return(ival); /* return the value */

} /* end iinp() */

/* finp(): floating point input with range checking, prompt and retry */

double finp(prompt,cflag,low,high)
char *prompt;
char cflag;
double low;
double high;
{
        double fval;
```

```
        while(1)
        {
                printf("%s",prompt);
                if(scanf("%lf",&fval) < 1)
                {
                        while(getchar() != '\n')
                                ;
                        continue;
                }

                if((!cflag)||(fval >= low)&&(fval <= high))
                        break;
                                /* no checking, or within bounds */

                printf("\nValue out of range, try again...\n");
        }

        return(fval); /* return the value */

} /* end finp() */

/* subroutine sinp(): input a string with prompt, length limit */

sinp(prompt,string,length)
char *prompt;
char *string;
int length;
{
        int len;                        /* length of actual string input */
        char chr;
        char *fgets();                  /* string input function */

        printf("%s",prompt);                    /* display the prompt */
        while(isspace(chr = getchar()))
                ;
        ungetc(chr,stdin);
        fgets(string,length,stdin);     /* input the string */

        if((len = strlen(string)))
                string[strlen(string)-1] = '\0';

        return(len);
} /* end sinp() */

/* subroutine cinq(): yes no question processor with prompt, retry */
```

```
cinq(prompt)
char *prompt;
{
        char chr;

        while(1)
        {
                printf("%s",prompt);

                do /* drain spurious 'white space' */
                {
                        chr = tolower(getchar()); /* use first char */
                }
                while(isspace(chr));
                if((chr == 'y')||(chr == 'n')) break;

                printf("\nRespond with Y or N, please try again...\n");
        }

        return((chr == 'y') ? 1 : 0);
}

/* display(): subroutine to print an ascii file on the console */

display(fname)
char *fname;
{
        char c;         /* character to output */
        FILE *disp;

        if((disp = fopen(fname,"r")) == NULL)
                return(-1);     /* can't open file */

        while((c = getc(disp)) != EOF) /* print the file */
        {
#ifndef UNIX
                if(c == TEOF) /* text end of file */
                        break;
#endif

                putchar((c & 127));     /* output each character less parity */
        }

        fclose(disp);   /* close the file */
        return(0);      /* successful completion */
}
```

LISTING 3-10

```
/*
        program:        rktest1.c
        created:        03-Nov-83
        by:             A. Skjellum

        Copyright 1983, 1984 (c) California Institute of Technology.
        All rights Reserved.  This program may be freely distributed
        for all non-commercial purposes but may not be sold.

        updated:        16-Nov-83
        purpose:        illustrate the use of rk4 program

        uses:           rk4.c

        summary:
                integrates the differential equation:

                y'(t) + y(t) = t + 1
                y(0) = 5.0.

                for which the exact solution:

                y(t) = t + 5exp(-t) is known.
*/

/* constants */

#define YZERO   5.0     /* initial value for y */
#define TSTART  0.0     /* starting time for integration */
#define TEND    10.0    /* ending time for integration */
#define STEPS   80      /* 40 steps in integration */

/* subroutines: */

/* exact(): returns exact solution value, given t */

double exact(t)
double t;
{
        extern double exp();    /* exponential function */

        if(t)
                return((t + YZERO*exp(-t)));
```

```c
        return(YZERO);
}

/* fn(t,y): return f(t,y) given t,y values */

double fn(t,y)
double t;
double y;
{
        /*
                differential equation is y' + y = t + 1

                therefore, f = t + 1 - y.

        */

        return(t + 1.0 - y);
}

/* solutn(): print solution step at console */

solutn(t,y)
double *t;      /* pointer to t value */
double *y;      /* pointer to y value */
{
        printf("t = %7.3e, y = %7.3e, y_exact = %7.3e, diff = %7.3e\n",
                *t,*y,exact(*t),*y - exact(*y));
}

/* main program: */

main()
{
        /* external declarations */

        double fn();    /* ensure that this is typed as double */

        /* local variables: */

        register int i;

        double yarray[STEPS],tarray[STEPS];
                /* integrated solution stored here */

        /* begin code: */
```

```
        printf("\n\nrktest1.c    as of 03-Nov-83\n\n");
        printf("Integrates: y' + y = 1 + t      for\n\n");
        printf("t = %7.3e to %7.3e, with %u steps\n\n",
                TSTART,TEND,STEPS);

        /*
                integrate the answer from t = 0 to t = 10 sec
                80 points.
        */

        rk4(fn,TSTART,TEND,STEPS,YZERO,tarray,yarray);
                    /* compute the answers */

        for(i=0;i<STEPS;i++)     /* print solution */
                solutn(tarray+i,yarray+i);

        printf("\n\nEnd of execution\n\n");
}
/*
        program:        rktest1.c
        created:        03-Nov-83
        by:             A. Skjellum

        Copyright 1983, 1984 (c) California Institute of Technology.
        All rights Reserved.  This program may be freely distributed
        for all non-commercial purposes but may not be sold.

        updated:        16-Nov-83
        purpose:        illustrate the use of rk4 program

        uses:           rk4.c

        summary:
                integrates the differential equation:

                y'(t) + y(t) = t + 1
                y(0) = 5.0.

                for which the exact solution:

                y(t) = t + 5exp(-t) is known.

*/

/* constants */
```

```c
#define YZERO   5.0     /* initial value for y */
#define TSTART  0.0     /* starting time for integration */
#define TEND    10.0    /* ending time for integration */
#define STEPS   80      /* 40 steps in integration */


/* subroutines: */

/* exact(): returns exact solution value, given t */

double exact(t)
double t;
{
        extern double exp();    /* exponential function */

        if(t)
                return((t + YZERO*exp(-t)));

        return(YZERO);
}

/* fn(t,y): return f(t,y) given t,y values */

double fn(t,y)
double t;
double y;
{
        /*
                differential equation is y' + y = t + 1

                therefore, f = t + 1 - y.

        */

        return(t + 1.0 - y);
}

/* solutn(): print solution step at console */

solutn(t,y)
double *t;      /* pointer to t value */
double *y;      /* pointer to y value */
{
        printf("t = %7.3e, y = %7.3e, y_exact = %7.3e, diff = %7.3e\n",
                *t,*y,exact(*t),*y - exact(*y));
}
```

```
/* main program: */

main()
{
        /* external declarations */

        double fn();    /* ensure that this is typed as double */

        /* local variables: */

        register int i;

        double yarray[STEPS],tarray[STEPS];
                /* integrated solution stored here */

        /* begin code: */

        printf("\n\nrktest1.c    as of 03-Nov-83\n\n");
        printf("Integrates: y' + y = 1 + t      for\n\n");
        printf("t = %7.3e to %7.3e, with %u steps\n\n',
                TSTART,TEND,STEPS);

        /*
                integrate the answer from t = 0 to t = 10 sec
                80 points.
        */

        rk4(fn,TSTART,TEND,STEPS,YZERO,tarray,yarray);
                        /* compute the answers */

        for(i=0;i<STEPS;i++)    /* print solution */
                solutn(tarray+i,yarray+i);

        printf("\n\nEnd of execution\n\n");
}
```

LISTING 3-11

```
/*
        Runge - Kutta order 4 Algorithm

        Creation date:  31-Oct-83
        Author:         Mike Roberts
```

```
                Copyright 1983, 1984 (c) California Institute of Technology.
                All rights Reserved.  This program may be freely distributed
                for all non-commercial purposes but may not be sold.

                This algorithm is described in detail on page 205 of
                Burden, Richard L.:  Numerical Analysis.

                To approximate the solution of the initial value problem
                        y'=f(t,y),   a<=t<=b, y(a)=alpha,
                at (N+1) equally spaced numbers in the interval [a,b]:
                INPUT endpoints a,b; integerg N; initial condition alpha.
                OUTPUT approximation w to y at the (N+1) values of t.

        Step 1:
                Set     h=(b-a)/N;
                        t=a;
                        w=alpha;
                Output (t,w).
        Step 2:
                For i=1,2,...,N do Steps 3-5:

                        Step 3:
                                Set     K1=hf(t,w);
                                        K2=hf(t+h/2,w+K1/2);
                                        K3=hf(t+h/2,w+k2/2);
                                        K4=hf(t+h,w+K3).
                        Step 4:
                                Set w=w+(K1+2K2+2K3+K4)/6;      (Compute w[i].)
                                    t=a+ih.                     (Compute t[i].)
                        Step 5:
                                Output (t,w).

        Step 6:
                Stop.

*/

#define FALSE 0
#define TRUE  1

rk4(function,a,b,n,alpha,t,w)

double (*function)();   /* function giving f(t,y) */
double a;               /* beginning of interval */
double b;               /* end of interval */
int n;                  /* number of steps in interval */
double alpha;           /* initial condition for y */
```

```
        double t[];             /* array for returning T[i] values */
        double w[];             /* array for returning W[i] values */
        {
                register int i; /* counter for integration steps */
                double h;       /* stepsize */
                double time;
                double yapprox; /* approximation for y value  */

                /*  STEP 1:  Initialization  */

                h = (b-a) / (double)n ;         /* Compute stepsize */
                time = a;                       /* Initialize time */
                yapprox = alpha;                /* Start with the approximation
                                                   equal to the initial value */

                for (i=0; i<n; i++)             /* Main integration loop */
                {
                        if(i)   /* if not first time, call the integrator */
                        rk4_1(function,h,time,&yapprox);

                                /* Pass the function pointer, the h, time, and
                                   yapprox values, and the pointers to
                                   the current positions in the T and W
                                   matrices */

                        time = a + h*(double)i; /* compute time */
                        t[i] = time;            /* also save it */
                        w[i] = yapprox;         /* store value for function */
                }
        }

/* This is the RK4 integrator portion.  It performs one step of the
        integration, and is called on each step from the RK4 loop.

        function = pointer to function to integrate
        h = stepsize
        time = current time location
        yapprox = current w (function approximation)

*/

rk4_1(function,h,time,yapprox)

double (*function)();           /* Pointer to function to integrate */
double h;                       /* Step size */
```

```
        double time;                    /* Current time step */
        double *yapprox;                 /* Current approximation of function */

{
        double k1, k2, k3, k4;  /* Temporary values in RK calculation */

        k1 = h * (*function)(time,*yapprox);      /* Evaluate first approx */
        k2 = h * (*function)(time+h/2.0, *yapprox+k1/2.0);
                                         /* Evaluate second approx */
        k3 = h * (*function)(time+h/2.0, *yapprox+k2/2.0);
                                         /* And the third */
        k4 = h * (*function)(time+h, *yapprox+k3);
                                         /* And the last one */

        *yapprox += (k1 + 2.0*(k2 + k3) + k4)/6.0; /* new approx */
}
```

LISTING 3-12

```
/*
        rk4n.c                  created: 07-Nov-83
        authors:                A. Skjellum,
                                M. Roberts

        updated:                14-Nov-83
                                by MJR

        Copyright 1983, 1984 (c) California Institute of Technology.
        All rights Reserved.  This program may be freely distributed
        for all non-commercial purposes but may not be sold.

        Purpose:
        integrate M first order differential equations

        y'[i] = f[i](t;y[j=1...M])

        M equations.

        algorithm:      see Burden, Faires, Reynolds, p. 239-240
                        also see p. 205

                        1. interval t = [a,b]
                        2. choose N > 0 as as partition of interval (N steps)
                        3. define step size h = (b-a)/N.
                        4. Initial conditions: (denote w[i,j] as approxes to y's)
```

```
                w[i,0] = alpha[i]
                means: ith w at time zero is set to initial value
                        alpha[i].

        5. Computing the w[i,j+1] from w[i,j] is done as follows:

                loop over i = 1 to M

                    compute k1[i] = h*f[i](t,w[1,j],...,w[M,j])

                end of loop

                loop over i = 1 to M

                    compute k2[i] = h*f[i](t+h/2,w[1,j]+.5*k1[1],...,
                                    w[M,j] + .5*k1[M])

                end of loop

                loop over i = 1 to M

                    compute k3[i] =h*f[i](t+h/2,w[1,j]+.5*k2[1],...,
                                    w[M,j] + .5*k2[M])

                end of loop

                loop over i = 1 to M

                    compute k4[i] =h*f[i](t+h,w[1,j]+k3[1],...,
                                    w[M,j] + k3[M])

                end of loop

                loop over i = 1 to M

                    w[i,j+1] = w[i,j] +
                              {k1[i] + 2*k2[i] + 2*k3[i] + k4[i]}/6

                end of loop

*/

double  (*rk_function)();
double  (*rk_source)();
double  (*rk_store)();
double  (*rk_kuttas)[4];
double  (*rk_comp[4])();                /* tells us how to form k's */
```

```c
/* functions called indirectly by k_calc()  */

double rk_1(n,j,i)        /* to provide compatibility with calling */
int n;
int j;
int i;
{
        return ((*rk_source)(j,n));
}

double rk_23(n,k,j,i)  /* N is in { 0...M } = argument number.
                          Since we have one argument to FN per equation,
                          N will indicate which we are currently being
                          asked to provide.  Same goes for other RK_x
                          functions below.  */
int n;
int k;
int j;
int i;
{
        return((*rk_source)(j,n) + .5*rk_kuttas[n][k]);
}

double rk_2(n,j,i)
int n;
int j;
int i;
{
        return(rk_23(n,0,j,i));
}

double rk_3(n,j,i)
int n;
int j;
int i;
{
        return(rk_23(n,1,j,i));
}

double rk_4(n,j,i)
int n;
int j;
int i;
{
        return((*rk_source)(j,n) + rk_kuttas[n][2]);
}
```

```c
/* Here's the integrator!!! */

double rk4n(function,wsource,wstore,m,a,b,n,alpha,t,kuttas)

double (*function)();   /* pointer to function which returns deriv info */
double (*wsource)();    /* source of w[i,j] values */
double (*wstore)();     /* function which stores w[i,j] values for us */
int m;                  /* number of equations */
double a;               /* start of interval */
double b;               /* end   of interval */
int n;                  /* number of points */
double alpha[];         /* array of initial values */
double t[];             /* array where we store times */
double kuttas[][4];     /* n x 4 kuttas (k1,k2,k3,k4 i=1,...m) */
{
        register int i; /* looping variable */
        register int j; /* looping variables */
        double time;
        double h = (b-a)/(double)n;    /* step size */

        double rk_k2(),rk_k3(),rk_k4(); /* include for emphasis */

        rk_function = function;

        rk_kuttas  = kuttas;
        rk_source  = wsource;
        rk_store   = wstore;

        rk_comp[0] = rk_1;
        rk_comp[1] = rk_2;
        rk_comp[2] = rk_3;
        rk_comp[3] = rk_4;

        /* First assign initial values  */

        for (i = 0;i < m;i++)
                (*rk_store)(0,i,alpha[i]);

        /* Now loop through the necessary loop, calculating
                each K value for each equation in each time step. */

        for(j = 0;j < n;j++)    /* n time steps */
        {
                time = a + h*(double)j; /* compute time */
                t[j] = time;            /* also save it */
```

```
                        rk4_1n(m,j,time,h);
        }
}

/* rk4_1n(): compute one solution step for n equations */

rk4_1n(m,j,time,h)
int m;
int j;                          /* time step we're working on */
double time;
double h;
{
        register int k; /* k calculation loop */
        register int i; /* m equations loop */
        double value;   /* temporary */

        for(k=0;k < 4;k++)      /* k compute loop */
                k_calc(m,k,j,time,h);

        for(i=0;i<m;i++)        /* compute new w[i,j]'s j fixed here */
        {
                value = (*rk_source)(j,i) + .166666667*(rk_kuttas[i][0] +
                        2.0*(rk_kuttas[i][1] + rk_kuttas[i][2])
                                + rk_kuttas[i][3]);
                                /* value for w[i,j] */
                (*rk_store)(j+1,i,value); /* save this hard got number */

        }
}

/* k_calc(): compute rk coefficients for fixed j */

k_calc(m,k,j,time,h)
int m;
int k;
int j;
double time;
double h;
{
        register int i;
        double tval;

        switch(k)
        {
                case 0:
                        tval = time;
                        break;
```

```
            case 1:
            case 2:
                    tval = time + .5*h;
                    break;
            case 3:
                    tval = time + h;
                    break;
    }

    for(i=0;i<m;i++)                   /*  used to be 1;<=m  */
    {
            rk_kuttas[i][k] = h*(*rk_function)(j,i,tval,rk_comp[k]);
    }
}
```

LISTING 3-13

```
/*
        program:        rkst1.c
        created:        03-Nov-83
        by:             A. Skjellum

        modified:       14-Nov-83
        by:             M. J. Roberts

        Copyright 1983, 1984 (c) California Institute of Technology.
        All rights Reserved.  This program may be free.y distributed
        for all non-commercial purposes but may not be sold.

        purpose:        illustrate the use of rk4n program

        uses:           rk4n() (rks.c)
        summary:
                integrates the differential equation:

                y'(t) + y(t) = t + 1
                y(0) = 5.0.

                for which the exact solution:

                y(t) = t + 5exp(-t) is known.

                Integrates the same equation as rktest1
                but using the more general equation solver,
                rk4n().  This run is exactly the same as for
                rktest1, except that, rather than trying to solve
```

exactly the same equation, we will solve a
"system" of one differential equation.

*/

/* constants */

```
#define SYSIZE  1       /* number of functions in system */
#define YZERO   5.0     /* initial value for y */
#define TSTART  0.0     /* starting time for integration */
#define TEND    10.0    /* ending time for integration */
#define STEPS   50      /* 50 steps in integration */
```

/* variables external to all functions */

```
double wvalue[STEPS+1][SYSIZE];
double yarray[STEPS+1][SYSIZE];
double tarray[STEPS];
        /* integrated solution stored here */
```

/* subroutines: */

/* exact(): returns exact solution value, given t */

```
double exact(t)
double t;
{
        extern double exp();    /* exponential function */

        return((t + YZERO*exp(-t)));
}
```

/* fn(j,i,t,y): return f(t,y) given t,y values */

```
double fn(j,i,t,y)
int j;
int i;
double t;
double (*y)();
{
        double a,b;             /* temporary storage space */

        /*
                differential equation is y' + y = t + 1

                therefore, y' = t + 1 - y.
```

```
                */

                a = (*y)(0,j,i);        /* calculate function
                                           Note that the ZERO was passed so as to
                                           allow the function to know which argument
                                           we are talking about - in this case,
                                           we only need one argument evaluated, so
                                           pass it 0 to indicate the first (zeroeth,
                                           actually) argument is to be calculated. */

                b = t + 1.0 - a;        /* and figure out the rest of it */
                return(b);
}

/* store():  the routine to store away the W values for later reference */

double store(row, col, value)
int row, col;           /* location to store the value */
double value;           /* the actual value to store */
{
        wvalue[row][col]=value;
        return (value);
}

/* source():  return the  W value referenced by input parameters   */

double source(row,col)
int row, col;           /* location to look up */

{
        return (wvalue[row][col]);
}

/* solutn(): print solution step at console */

solutn(j,i)
int j,i;        /* element numbers */
{
        double time;
        double ex;
        double approx;

        time  = tarray[j];
        ex    = exact(time);
        approx = source(j,i);
```

```c
          printf("t = %7.3e, y = %7.3e, y_exact = %7.3e, diff = %7.3e\n",
                 time,approx,ex,approx - ex);
}

/* main program: */

main()
{
        /* external declarations */

        double store(), source();

        double fn();    /* ensure that this is typed as double */

        /* local variables: */

        register int i,j;

        double init[1];         /* initial condition matrix */

        /* begin code: */

        printf("\n\nrktest1.c   as of 03-Nov-83\n\n");
        printf("Integrates: y' + y = 1 + t     for\n\n");
        printf("t = %7.3e to %7.3e, with %u steps\n\n",
                TSTART,TEND,STEPS);

        /*
                integrate the answer from t = 0 to t = 10 sec
                STEPS points.
        */

        init[0] = YZERO;        /* set up initial condition matrix */

        rk4n(fn,source,store,SYSIZE,TSTART,TEND,STEPS,init,tarray,yarray);
                        /* compute the answers for 1 function */

        /* Print out solution   */

        for(j=0;j<STEPS;j++)    /* print solution */
                solutn(j,0);

        printf("\n\nEnd of execution\n\n");
}
```

LISTING 3-14

```
/*
        program:        rkst2.c
        created:        03-Nov-83
        by:             A. Skjellum

        modified:       14-Nov-83
        by:             M. J. Roberts
        and:            5-Dec-83
        by:             M. J. Roberts

        modified:       25-Jul-84
        by:             A. Skjellum

        Copyright 1983, 1984 (c) California Institute of Technology.
        All rights Reserved.  This program may be freely distributed
        for all non-commercial purposes but may not be sold.

        purpose:        illustrate the use of RKS program
        update:         to test the rk4n() subroutine using a system
                        of two differential equations.

        uses:           rk4n() (rks.c)
        summary:

                        integrates the differential equation system:

                        u1'(t) = 8u2(t)             u1(0) = 10
                        u2'(t) = 2u1(t)             u2(0) = 7

                        for which the exact solution is known to be:

                        u1(t) = 12exp(4t) - 2exp(-4t)
                        u2(t) =  6exp(4t) +  exp(-4t)

*/

/* constants */

#define SYSIZE  2       /* number of functions in system */
#define Y1ZERO  10.0    /* initial value for first equation */
#define Y2ZERO  7.0     /* initial value for other equation */
#define TSTART  0.0     /* starting time for integration */
#define TEND    1.0     /* ending time for integration */
#define STEPS   50      /* 50 steps in integration */

/* variables external to all functions */
```

```c
        double wvalue[STEPS+1][SYSIZE];
        double yarray[STEPS+1][SYSIZE],tarray[STEPS];
                /* integrated solution stored here */

/* subroutines: */

/* exact(): returns exact solution value, given t */

double exact(n,t)
int n;          /* which equation is it? 0 or 1? */
double t;

{
        extern double exp();    /* exponential function */

        /* This must find solutions for both U1 and U2.  The
                exact solutions are given in the header comments to
                this program, above. */

        switch (n)
        {
                case 0:
                        return(12*exp(4*t) - 2*exp(-4*t));
                case 1:
                        return( 6*exp(4*t) +   exp(-4*t));
}       }

/* fn(j,i,t,y):  return f(t,y) given t,y values */

double fn(j,i,t,y)
int j;
int i;
double t;
double (*y)();
{
        switch (i)
        {
                case 0:
                        /*  u1'(t) = 8 * u2(t)  */
                        return(8*(*y)(1,j,i));

                case 1:
                        /*  u2'(t) = 2 * u1(t) */
                        return(2*(*y)(0,j,i));
        }
}
```

```c
/* store():  the routine to store away the W values for later reference */

double store(row, col, value)
int row, col;           /* location to store the value */
double value;           /* the actual value to store  */
{
        wvalue[row][col]=value;
        return (value);
}

/* source():  return the  W value referenced by input parameters  */

double source(row,col)
int row, col;           /* location to look up */

{
        return (wvalue[row][col]);
}

/* solutn(): print solution step at console */

solutn(j,i)
int j,i;        /* element numbers */
{
        printf("\nt=%7.3e, y%1d=%7.3e, y%1d_exact=%7.3e, diff=%7.3e",
                tarray[j],i,source(j,i),i,exact(i,tarray[j]),
                source(j,i) - exact(i,tarray[j]));
}

/* main program: */

main()
{
        /* external declarations */

        double store(), source();

        double fn();    /* ensure that this is typed as double */

        /* local variables: */

        register int i,j;

        double init[SYSIZE];            /* initial condition matrix */

        /* begin code: */
```

```
            printf("\n\nrkst2.c     as of 25-Jul-84\n\n");
            printf("       Integrates the differential equation system:\n\n");
            printf("         u1'(t) = 8u2(t)              u1(0) = 10\n");
            printf("         u2'(t) = 2u1(t)              u2(0) = 7\n");
            printf("       for which the exact solution is known to be:\n\n");
            printf("         u1(t) = 12exp(4t) - 2exp(-4t)\n");
            printf("         u2(t) =  6exp(4t) +  exp(-4t)\n\n");
            printf("       for     t = %7.3e to %7.3e, with %u steps\n\n",
                   TSTART,TEND,STEPS);

            /*
                    integrate the answer from t = 0 to t = 10 sec
                    STEPS points.
            */

            init[0] = Y1ZERO;        /* set up initial condition matrix */
            init[1] = Y2ZERO;

            rk4n(fn,source,store,SYSIZE,TSTART,TEND,STEPS,init,tarray,yarray);
                            /* compute the answers for 1 function */

            /* Print out solutions  */

            for(i=0;i<SYSIZE;i++)
                    for(j=0;j<STEPS;j++)     /* print solution */
                            solutn(j,i);

            printf("\n\nEnd of execution\n\n");
    }
```

LISTING 3-15

```
    /*
            Revised <untested> version of "sfopen."  The original
            version was written by A. Cameron and published in Dr. Dobb's
            Journal, August 1984 issue.

            This revision is to illustrate the design principle that
            the structure of a program should reflect the behavior of
            the program (a corollary of the principle that the structure
            of a solution should reflect the structure of the problem)

            The focus of this example is that the execution sequence
            and execution frequency are primary elements of problem
            structure and should be mirrored in the code.
```

```
            by: John A. Grosberg

            [relevant for BDS C]
*/

#define NULL    0
#define BUFSIZ  256
#define TRUE    1
#define ERR     -1

sfopen(filename, mode)
char *filename;
char *mode;
{
        int fd,
            err;

        if (fd = alloc(BUFSIZ))
        {
                switch(*mode)
                {
                        case 'w':                       /* write mode */
                                err = (fcreat(filename,fd) == ERR);
                                break;
                        case 'r':                       /* read  mode */
                                err = (fopen(filename,fd) == ERR);
                                break;
                        case 'a':                       /* append mode */
                                err = (fappend(filename,fd) == ERR);
                                break;
                        default:                        /* invalid mode */
                                err = TRUE;
                                break;
                }

                if (err)
                {
                        free(fd);
                        fd = NULL;
                }
        }
        else                                    /* alloc failure */
        {
                fd = NULL;                      /* redundant */
        }

        return(fd);
}
```

4
HOW COMPILERS WORK

by Allen Holub

The chapter originally appeared in DDJ #107 (September 1985) as a "C Chest" column.

Before looking at Jim Hendrix's version of the Small C compiler, some general compiler theory may be useful. In the interest of clarity I'll reduce the problem from the recognition of a real computer language to a small arithmetic expression analyzer. The techniques used for one are applicable to the other. This expression analyzer will take as input an ASCII string representing an arithmetic expression. Only numbers, parentheses, and the operators + − / * are legal. The analyzer returns the result of the evaluation. For example, if you give it the string "(3+1)*2" the analyzer returns the number 8. The routine is simpleminded, but the point of this exercise is to understand compilers, not to analyze complicated expressions.

Anatomy of a Compiler

Every compiler has three functionally distinct parts. These parts are often combined, but it's best to look at them as separate functions. The first part of the compiler is a *token* recognizer. A token is some collection of ASCII characters from the input stream that are meaningful to the compiler when taken as a group. That is, a program can be seen as a collection of tokens, each of which is made up of one or more sequential ASCII characters. For example, in C the ASCII character ; is a token; similarly, the keyword *while* is a token. The matter is complicated by operators such as +, ++, and +=, all of which are single tokens. A token is a sort of programming atom, an indivisible part of the language (you can't say *wh ile*), and a token recognizer is a subroutine that, when called, returns the next token from the input stream. Usually tokens are represented internally as an enumerated type or as

139

a set of integer values corresponding to #defines in a header file somewhere, and the token recognizer returns this integer value. Small-C doesn't do this, though. Rather, various subroutines within the compiler retrieve the tokens from input one at a time as they are needed.

The second part of the compiler, and the part that does most of the work, is the *parser*. The verb *to parse* retains its meaning when applied to compilers: "to resolve (a sentence, etc.) into its component parts of speech and describe them grammatically."[1] For a compiler, replace the word *sentence* with *program*. Computer languages may be described by means of a formal grammar (see below), and the parser breaks up a program into its component parts and interprets the parts in a larger, grammatical context. That is, a parser organizes the tokens in such a way that the compiler can generate code conveniently.

A good (though not practical) way to look at the process is as the creation of a *parse tree*. For example, the expression "(a−b)*(c−d)" can be organized into the tree shown in Figure 4-1.

Figure 4-1. A parse tree for (a-b)*(c-d)

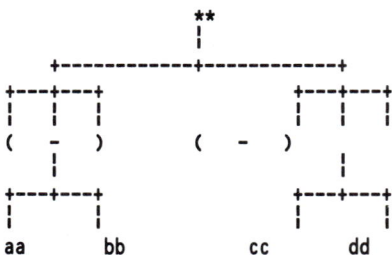

The third part of the compiler, the code generator, traverses the parse tree in an orderly way, generating code according to certain rules. For example, if you do a *post order* traversal of the tree shown in Figure 4-1 (visit the left node, middle node, right node, and then the root, recursively) the tokens will be read in the following order:

```
( a b - ) ( c d - ) *
```

Now, the expression may be evaluated by applying the following rules to each token in the tree as it is visited:

1. If the token is a parenthesis, do nothing.

2. If the token is a variable (a,b,c or d), push the variable onto a stack.

3. If the token is a minus (−), pop two items off the stack, subtract them, and push the result.

4. If the token is an asterisk (*), pop two items off the stack, multiply them, and push the result.

When you're done parsing (traversing the tree), the answer will be on the top of the stack. Owners of Hewlett-Packard calculators are familiar with the process. In a real compiler, the actual rule applied will be some function of the type of token found and the position of that token in the parse tree.

There are several flavors of parsers.[2] Most compilers use table-driven parsers. It's easier to automate compiler creation with table driven parsers, and they're also more efficient. The Unix utility YACC (Yet Another Compiler Compiler), when given a formal description of a programming language, creates a set of tables that can be used by a generic table-driven parser.[3] Similarly, LEX (LEXical analyzer) can output a C program that recognizes tokens.[4]

Unfortunately, most public domain compilers don't use the more sophisticated table-driven methods (and Small-C is no exception). These compilers use a parsing method known as *recursive descent*. Recursive descent parsers are easier to understand than their table-driven cousins. However, they have several disadvantages. They are inherently inefficient, using large amounts of stack space, and they have to be built by hand. To change a table-driven compiler you need only to change the table; to change the way a recursive descent compiler works, you have to change the compiler itself, so maintenance is a problem with recursive descent compilers.

Grammars: Representing Computer Languages

The best way to start writing a program is to reduce the problem to some sort of symbolic form. Pseudo-code, flowcharts, and Warnier-Orr diagrams are all examples of this kind of symbolic reduction. Compilers are no exception to this process. When writing a compiler, you start by representing the programming language to be compiled in a formal, symbolic format called a *grammar*. Any programming language can be described by several grammars. The type of parser you're going to use will determine which of these is correct for your application. The most useful notation used for grammars is the Backus-Naur Format (abbreviated BNF), which I introduce below.

To create an expression analyzer, you need to start with a grammar. The first question to ask is: What exactly is an expression? You'll remember from the third grade that an expression is composed of factors. A factor by itself (that is, a single number) is an expression, as are two factors separated by an operator. BNF representations of these two rules are:

```
<expression> ::= <factor>

<expression> ::= <factor> <operator> <factor>
```

You can save some typing by using the vertical bar to represent *or*:

```
<expression> ::=   <factor>
                 | <factor> <operator> <factor>
```

Note in these definitions that no element of the BNF definition of the <expression> is a real symbol (one that can be found in the input stream). That is, <factor> and <operator> both have to be defined further before they can be related to a real program. Symbols such as <factor> that need further definition are called *nonterminal* symbols. Symbols that *can* be found in the input are called *terminal* symbols. The four terminal symbols that can be operators are + − / *. A BNF rule for <operator> is:

```
<operator> ::= + | - | * | /
```

Defining a factor is a little harder. A factor can be a number, but it can also be another expression (as in a+b−d: "a+b" is one factor and "d" is the second factor). A BNF definition of factor is:

```
<factor> ::=   <number> | <expression>
```

The only symbol yet to be defined is <number>. Since a number is an easy thing for the token recognizer to find, you can cheat a little and define <number> in English. The entire grammar is shown in Figure 4-2.

Figure 4-2. A simple expression recognition grammar

```
1. <expression> ::=   <factor>
                    | <factor> <operator> <factor>
2. <operator>   ::= + | - | * | /
3. <factor>     ::=   <number> | <expression>
4. <number>     ::=   A string of ASCII characters
                      in the range 0 to 9.
```

Notice that every nonterminal used at of a ::= is also defined to the left, and that no terminal symbols are found to the left of a ::=. To test the grammar, plug in an example: 1+2. Both 1 and 2 are <number>s; so you can replace them with the equivalent nonterminal symbols by using rule 4:

```
        1    +    2
   <number> + <number>
```

According to rule 3, a single number is also a factor, so you can do another replacement:

```
   <number> + <number>
   <factor> + <factor>
```

The + can be evaluated using rule 2:

```
<factor>         +      <factor>
<factor> <operator> <factor>
```

And finally, by using rule 1, you can replace the above with a single <expression>:

```
<factor> <operator> <factor>
        <expression>
```

So you can reduce 1+2 to an <expression> using the rules of the grammar. Therefore, you can conclude that 1 + 2 is a legal expression in this grammar.

What if there's an error in the expression? Let's try to parse "1+*." You can apply rules 3 and 6 to yield

```
<number> <operator> <operator>
```

and then apply rule 4 to get:

```
<factor> <operator> <operator>
```

But there is no rule you can apply to reduce this any further, so you can conclude that 1+* is not an expression as defined by this grammar.

Parsing with a Grammar

A parser, then, can be seen as a program that reduces a collection of input tokens to a single nonterminal. We have "parsed" the expression 1 + 2. To turn a parser into a real compiler, you need to make it do something active, too, to generate code. So, you can associate an action rule with each grammatical rule. This grammar, slightly shuffled around and with action rules added, is shown in Figure 4-3.

Every time you apply a grammatical rule, you must also perform the action specified in the equivalent action rule. For example, 1+2, parsed with the grammar in Figure 4-3, is shown in Figure 4-4.

A somewhat more involved example is given in Figure 4-5. You can see how the process works. If the action rules had generated the code necessary to perform the operation, rather than doing the operation itself, you would have a compiler.

As you've probably noticed, the grammar just defined isn't very useful. It would be nice to have at least parentheses and negative numbers and be able to negate an entire expression (such as −(17*11)). You may also notice in the above examples that the expression is parsed left to right, so you

Figure 4-3. Adding actions to the grammar

Grammar:

1. <expression> ::= <factor>
2. <expression> ::= <factor> <operator> <factor>
3. <operator>   ::= + | - | * | /
4. <factor>   ::= <number>
5. <factor>   ::= <expression>
6. <number>   ::= Any string of ASCII characters
                    in the range 0 to 9.

Action rules:

1. Do nothing.
2. Pop two objects off the stack, apply the operator remembered in rule 3, and then push the result.
3. Remember the operator for rule 2.
4. Push the number onto the stack.
5. Do nothing.
6. Translate the ASCII string into a number.

can make all possible substitutions as you parse. A more realistic grammar makes its substitutions in a somewhat more complex way, and the grammar has to reflect this complexity. A grammar has to be organized so that the parser can always tell what rule to apply based on the current input symbol, and the current rule being processed. A better expression-recognizing grammar is given in Figure 4-6. This grammar is used in the actual program.[5]

A Recursive Descent Parser

The best way to see how a parser works is to look at one. Before discussing the parser, I want to describe how the program is organized. The actual subroutines in the parser are highly recursive. As such, they use up a lot of stack space as they work. Because of this stack usage, you'd want to pass as few parameters as possible to the subroutines (because all these parameters take up stack space).

Figure 4-4. Parsing 1+2 using grammar in Figure 4-3

			rule	action
1	+	2		
<number>	+	2	6	Translate ASCII to int
<factor>	+	2	4	Push 1
<factor>	+	<number>	6	Translate ASCII to int
<factor>	+	<factor>	4	Push 2
<factor> <operator> <factor>			3	Remember the +
<expression>			2	Pop the 1 & 2, apply + and push the result.

Figure 4-5. Parsing 1 + 2 - 3

	Apply rule	Action
1 + 2 - 3	-	Start here
\<number> + 2 - 3	6	Translate "1" to int
\<factor> + 2 - 3	4	Push 1
\<factor> \<operator> 2 - 3	3	Remember +
\<factor> \<operator> \<number> - 3	6	Translate "2" to int
\<factor> \<operator> \<factor> - 3	4	Push 2
\<expression> - 3	2	Pop two numbers, apply + and push result.
\<factor> - 3	1	Do nothing.
\<factor> \<operator> 3	3	Remember -
\<factor> \<operator> \<number>	6	Translate "3" to int
\<factor> \<operator> \<factor>	4	Push 3
\<expression>	2	Pop two numbers off the stack, subtract and push the result.

Figure 4-6. A more realistic expression-recognizing grammar

```
<expr>     ::=   <factor>                (1)
             |   <factor> * <expr>       (2)
             |   <factor> / <expr>       (3)
             |   <factor> + <expr>       (4)
             |   <factor> - <expr>       (5)

<factor>   ::=    ( <expr> )             (6)
             |   -( <expr> )             (7)
             |    <constant>             (8)
             |   -<constant>             (9)

<constant> ::=   A string of ASCII characters
                 in the range 0 to 9.
```

So, you make global those variables that would normally be passed to the subroutines as arguments. However, this practice introduces new problems. In C, all nonstatic global variables are shared between all modules in a program. But the expression parser is probably going to be a library routine, and you don't want it to interfere with the normal workings of the rest of a program. Moreover, you don't want the programmer to have to remember that certain globals are used by a particular library routine and can't be used anywhere else. So, you make the globals static, and also make static those subroutines that are used only internally. Now, however, you need some way to initialize the static globals from outside the parser module. You do this initialization with the "access routine" starting on line 84 of the listing (the only externally accessible subroutine in the module). This access routine (called parse()) does nothing but initialize the globals and then call expr() to do the work. Another organizational concern is the main() routine in lines 34-79. The primary purpose of main() is to test parse(), thus the #ifdef/#endif on lines 32 and 81. DEBUG is not #defined when you compile for inclusion in a library. The main() routine given is moderately useful in its own right. You can enter the expression from the command line ("expr 17/(2*12)") or you can just type expr and then enter expressions as the program prompts you—sort of a rudimentary desk calculator.

Moving back to parsers, there are a few things to notice about the grammar in Figure 4-6. First, the left-most symbol following the ::= is always either a terminal or the same nonterminal for all rules. That is, all rules associated with <expr> have <factor> as their left-most symbol. The left-most symbol of all <factor> rules is either a terminal, (or −, or the nonterminal <constant>. The left-most symbol of a constant has to be an ASCII digit. This property of the grammar is required by the parser so that it can know what rule to apply in a given situation. For example, when evaluating an <expr>, the parser will always apply a rule associated with <factor> first.

A second property of the grammar is that the definitions for <expr> and <factor> are recursive. An <expr> is defined in terms of other <expr>s. The recursion in <factor> is two levels deep. A <factor> is defined in terms of an <expr>, which is in turn defined in terms of a <factor>. The recursion in the grammar suggests that you can also use recursion in a parser that implements the grammar.

So, given an appropriate grammar, you can translate that grammar directly into a parser. In the program given here, all nonterminal symbols in the grammar have an equivalent subroutine with the same name. The routine for <expr> starts on line 104, <factor> on line 124, and <constant> on line 155.

Looking again at the grammar in Figure 4-6, you'll see that the first thing done in all the <expr> rules (1-5) is to look for a <factor>. Similarly, the first thing the subroutine expr() does is call the subroutine factor() (line 108). Looking back at the grammar, the next thing <expr> does is look for a terminal symbol (either a * / + − or a null string). The equivalent code is the switch on lines 110-117. The default case takes care of the null terminal (rule 1). The recursive evaluation of <expr> in rules 2-5 is also done in the switch. On line 119 expr() returns the evaluated expression.

Factor() is somewhat more complex. It first checks (on lines 128-132) for the leading minus sign required by rules 7 and 9. After stripping off the minus, rules 6 and 7 become identical, similarly rules 8 and 9 are identical once the minus is gone. So, factor() now decides which rule to process by looking for a leading parenthesis (line 134). If it doesn't find the parenthesis, rule 8 is processed (line 135) by calling the subroutine constant(), otherwise rule 6 is processed by skipping past the parenthesis and then calling expr() (lines 138-139). You can also do some error checking here by looking for a close parenthesis when expr() returns (lines 143-147).

The final part of the parser is the routine constant() on lines 155-169. This routine is essentially atoi(), but it advances the string pointer past the end of a number and flags an error if a number isn't found.

Note that in this program (and in the Small-C Compiler) the three functional parts of the compiler are merged. There is no explicit token recognizer; rather, each routine is responsible for advancing the global string pointer (Str) past the token being processed. Similarly, the code generation part of the compiler is integrated into the parser. In our example, code generation is replaced by the various return statements. In a real compiler the routine factor() would generate code to push a value onto a runtime stack rather than return a value. The switch on lines 110 to 117 would be replaced by something like:

```
switch( *Str )
{
case '+':
        Str++;
        expr();
        codegen(1);

case '-':
        Str++;
        expr();
        codegen(2);

/* etc. */
}
```

Since the code to push one number onto the stack is generated in factor(), the first number will be pushed by the factor() call on line 108. By the time expr() returns, the code to push the second number will have been generated (by the factor() call inside expr()). The call to codegen(1) inside the switch generates the code needed to pop two numbers off the stack, add them together, and push the result. The codegen(2) call behaves similarly, but it subtracts rather than adds.

That's the bulk of the problem. A better understanding of what's going on will help when you try to sort out the workings of Small-C itself.

Notes

1. The *Compact Edition of the Oxford English Dictionary* (Oxford: Oxford University Press, 1971), p. 2083.

2. A good short description of table-driven parsing techniques can be found in Dr. Henry A. Seymour, "An Introduction to Parsing," *Dr. Dobb's Journal*, #98 (December 1984), pp. 78–86. A more in-depth look at the subject, and at compiler design in general, can be found in Alfred V. Aho, Ravi Sethi, and Jeffrey D. Ullman, *Compilers: Principles, Techniques, Tools* (Reading, Mass.: Addison-Wesley, 1985); and P.M.Lewis, D.J.Rosenkrantz and R.E. Stearns, *Compiler Design Theory* (Reading, Mass.: Addison-Wesley, 1976).

3. See Axel T. Schreiner and H. George Friedman, Jr., *Introduction to Compiler Construction with Unix* (Englewood Cliffs: Prentice-Hall, 1985) and Stephen C.

Johnson, "Yacc: Yet Another Compiler-Compiler," *Unix Programmer's Manual*, Vol. 2 (New York: Holt, Rinehart and Winston, 1979), pp. 353–387.

4. See Schreiner and Friedman, *loc. cit.*, and M. E. Lesk and E. Schmidt, "Lex - A Lexical Analyzer Generator," *Unix Programmer's Manual*, Vol. 2, pp. 388–400.

5. A grammar for the C language is in B.W. Kernighan & D.B. Ritchie, *The C Programming Language* (Englewood Cliffs, N.J.: Prentice-Hall, 1978), pp. 214–219.

LISTING 4-1

```
 1: #include <stdio.h>
 2:
 3: /* EXPR.C:  (C) Copyright 1985, Allen I. Holub.  All rights reserved
 4:  *
 5:  *      Evaluate an expression pointed to by str. Expressions evaluate
 6:  *      right to left unless parenthesis are present. Valid operators are
 7:  *      * + - / for multiply add, subtract and divide. The expression must
 8:  *      be formed from the character set { 0123456789+-*()/ }. White
 9:  *      space is not allowed.
10:  *
11:  *      <expr>     ::=    <factor>
12:  *                     | <factor> * <expr>
13:  *                     | <factor> / <expr>
14:  *                     | <factor> + <expr>
15:  *                     | <factor> - <expr>
16:  *
17:  *      <factor>   ::=    ( <expr> )
18:  *                     | -( <expr> )
19:  *                     | <constant>
20:  *                     | -<constant>
21:  *
22:  *      <constant> ::=  A string of ASCII chars in the range '0'-'9'.
23:  *
24:  *------------------------------------------------------------------
25:  * Global variables:
26:  */
27:
28: static  char    *Str ;  /* Current position in string being parsed */
29: static  int     Error ; /* # of errors found so far                */
30:
31: /*----------------------------------------------------------------*/
32: #ifdef DEBUG
33:
34: main(argc, argv)
35: char    **argv;
36: {
37:         /*      Routine to exercise the expression parser. If an
38:          *      expression is given on the command line it is
39:          *      evaluated and the result is printed, otherwise
40:          *      expressions are fetched from stdin (one per line)
41:          *      and evaluated. The program will return -1 to the
42:          *      shell on a syntax error, 0 if it's in interactive
43:          *      mode, otherwise it returns the result of the
44:          *      evaluation.
45:          */
46:
47:         char buf[133], *bp = buf ;
```

```
48:        int err, rval;
49:
50:        if( argc > 2 )
51:        {
52:                fprintf(stderr, "Usage: expr [<expression>]");
53:                exit( -1 );
54:        }
55:
56:        if( argc > 1 )
57:        {
58:                rval = parse( argv[1], &err );
59:                printf(err ? "*** ERROR ***" : "%d", rval );
60:                exit( rval );
61:        }
62:
63:        printf("Enter expression or <CR> to exit program\n");
64:
65:        while( 1 )
66:        {
67:                printf("? ");
68:
69:                if( gets(buf) == NULL || !*buf )
70:                        exit(0);
71:
72:                rval = parse(buf, &err);
73:
74:                if( err )
75:                        printf("*** ERROR ***\n");
76:                else
77:                        printf("%s = %d\n", buf, rval);
78:        }
79: }
80:
81: #endif
82: /*----------------------------------------------------------------*/
83:
84: int    parse( expression, err )
85: char   *expression;
86: int       *err;
87: {
88:        /* Return the value of "expression" or 0 if any errors were
89:         * found in the string. "*Err" is set to the number of errors.
90:         * "Parse" is the "access routine" for expr(). By using it you
91:         * need not know about any of the global vars used by expr().
92:         */
93:
94:        register int    rval;
95:
96:        Error = 0;
```

```
 97:            Str  = expression;
 98:            rval = expr();
 99:            return( (*err = Error) ? 0 : rval );
100: }
101:
102: /*----------------------------------------------------------------*/
103:
104: static int expr()
105: {
106:            int    lval;
107:
108:            lval = factor();
109:
110:            switch (*Str)
111:            {
112:            case '+':  Str++;    lval += expr();      break;
113:            case '-':  Str++;    lval -= expr();      break;
114:            case '*':  Str++;    lval *= expr();      break;
115:            case '/':  Str++;    lval /= expr();      break;
116:            default :                                 break;
117:            }
118:
119:            return( lval );
120: }
121:
122: /*----------------------------------------------------------------*/
123:
124: static int factor()
125: {
126:            int    rval = 0 , sign = 1 ;
127:
128:            if ( *Str == '-' )
129:            {
130:                    sign = -1 ;
131:                    Str++;
132:            }
133:
134:            if ( *Str != '(' )
135:                    rval = constant();
136:            else
137:            {
138:                    Str++;
139:                    rval = expr();
140:
141:                    if ( *Str == ')' )
142:                            Str++;
143:                    else
144:                    {
145:                            printf("Mis-matched parenthesis\n");
```

```
146:                         Error++  ;
147:                 }
148:         }
149:
150:         return (rval * sign);
151: }
152:
153: /*----------------------------------------------------------------*/
154:
155: static int constant()
156: {
157:         int     rval = 0 ;
158:
159:         if( !isdigit( *Str ))
160:                 Error++;
161:
162:         while ( *Str && isdigit(*Str) )
163:         {
164:                 rval = (rval * 10) + (*Str - '0') ;
165:                 Str++;
166:         }
167:
168:         return( rval );
169: }
```

5
THE SMALL-C COMPILER

by J. E. Hendrix

This chapter originally appeared in DDJ #74 and #75 (December 1982 and January 1983). Small-C version 2 has since been adapted to CP/M and designated version 2.1 (see "A New Library for Small-C" in this volume). The listings printed here are of the new version. The text of this article has been altered to accommodate this change. Most notably, the section on the standard I/O library has been eliminated, since it would have been redundant.

    Ron Cain stirred up considerable interest when he demonstrated ("A Small-C Compiler for the 8080s," see DDJ #45 or excerpt in this volume) how effective even a small compiler can be. Many people were inspired to adapt his compiler to their systems. My own implementation resulted in Small-VM ("Small VM, Nucleus of a Portable Software Development System," DDJ #61), which interfaces the compiler, and programs compiled by it, to North Star DOS. The Small-Shell command processor ("Small-Shell: Part 2 of a North Star VOS," DDJ #63) further enhanced this environment, giving it even more of a Unix flavor.
    I immediately used the compiler to create a set of utility programs based on the ones presented in the book *Software Tools* by B. W. Kernighan and P. J. Plauger. The original compiler was more than adequate for the task and clearly superior to the RATFOR language used in the book. But it was a bare-bones compiler, literally begging for improvement. It seemed too that a little effort devoted to code optimizing might yield valuable benefits. So, with encouragement from Ron Cain and the Doctor, I set out to produce a second version. Listing 5-1 contains the results.
    I am indebted to Ron Cain, who presented the original compiler for all to do with as they pleased and who provided much invaluable guidance for this project. Neal Block of Fountain Valley, California, was also very helpful in providing many specific suggestions relating to performance, generalizing the compiler for use on machines of various word lengths, and suggesting approaches to

implement the new control structures. I hope before long to see him come forth with an assembler and linking loader written especially for Small-C. Finally, Dr. James Van Zandt of Nashua, New Hampshire, suggested replacing the serial table searches with hash searches, resulting in greatly improved speed.

Differences

This version of the compiler differs from the original one in the following respects:

1. Code optimization has been added. Programs are now typically 15 to 30 percent smaller than before.
2. Data initialization is supported for global variables, arrays, and pointers. Uninitialized objects default to binary zero.
3. Constant expressions are now evaluated at compile time. They may also be used as array dimensions, data initializers, and in "case" statements.
4. The #ifdef, #ifndef, #else, and #endif statements are supported with nesting.
5. The "extern" storage class is supported for global variable, array, pointer, and function declarations. The effect is to declare them as external references to the assembler.
6. It has a mechanism for passing an argument count to called functions.
7. It supports the following new statements:
   a. for
   b. do/while
   c. switch/case/default
   d. goto
8. It permits lists of expressions.
9. It supports the following assignment operators:
   !=, ^=, &=, +=, -=, *=, /=, %=, >>=, and <<=
10. It supports the logical operators || and &&. Testing proceeds left to right and ceases when the outcome is known.
11. The logical operators ~ and ! are supported.
12. Local variables are now local to the block rather than the whole function.
13. The backslash escape sequences for character and string constants have been added (per my letter in *DDJ* #56, p. 6).
14. I made several changes to accommodate my assembler.
    a. Lowercase names are converted to uppercase before being placed into the symbol table. Lowercase and uppercase symbols are thus synonymous. This feature is optional.
    b. Header and trailer code is automatically added to the output, enabling multifile programs to be compiled and assembled separately (see DDJ #61 for details).
    c. Tabs are no longer generated in the output file.
15. The original compiler would generate a cascade of spurious error messages, following a proper error message. I have eliminated these by snuffing all but

the first one in a simple statement; in practice this works well since one diagnostic is usually enough to make you evaluate an entire simple statement.

16. The following fixes have been applied:
    a. The left- and right-shift routines of the arithmetic and logical library have been modified so that a shift of zero bits properly returns the original value (letter from James L. Colvin, Jr., in DDJ #52, pp. 7, 37).
    b. Arguments no longer have to be typed in the same order as they appear in the function header (P.L. Woods, "Small-C: An Implementer's Notes and a Bug Corrected," DDJ #52, p. 20). A flaw in this patch has been corrected (my letter in DDJ #56, p. 6).
    c. In its original form Small-C did not always properly scale values involved in address arithmetic. I described this problem and gave the solution in "Small-C Expression Analyzer" (DDJ #62).
    d. The function symname no longer accepts symbols longer than 8 characters.
    e. The global integer lastst is now zeroed at the beginning of each function so null functions always generate a return.
    f. Comments terminated by */ at the beginning of a line are now handled correctly (my letter in DDJ #56, p. 6).

17. Literals are now dumped at the end of each function, permitting a smaller literal queue. Globals are defined at the point of their declaration, eliminating the function dumpglb.

18. A hash search is used on the macro table and the global part of the symbol table. The improvement in speed is considerable.

New Features Explained

The following comments describe some of the new features in greater detail:

Code Optimizing

Machine-independent optimizing is done by changing the expression analyzer, and machine-dependent optimizing is done by including an optional output (peephole) optimizer.

Machine-independent optimizing uses the following techniques:

1. Expressions, or partial expressions, that result in a constant value generate only a single immediate load instruction.
2. After code has been generated for the right side of a binary operator, if the secondary register was not used, the precautionary push/pop of the left-side value is changed to a swap. But if the left-side value is a constant, it is loaded directly into the secondary register instead.
3. Constants being added to or subtracted from integer pointers or array names are doubled at compile time rather than execution time.

4. No testing code is generated for if(const), while(const), and for(...; const; ...) statements. The compiler does not bother to delete code controlled by these statements when const is zero since that situation is most likely a program error; the #ifdef and #ifndef should be used to eliminate conditional code at compile time.

5. Tests against zero (for example, "while(i >= 0)," "if(abc() == 0)," and so on) result in special inline code that is smaller and faster than the standard procedure of loading zero, performing a library call, then testing the returned value for 1 or 0.

6. Zero subscripts generate no code for adding to the array address or pointer value.

7. Local variables are allocated all at one time when the first executable statement in a block is encountered. Declarations are not allowed after that point except within inner blocks.

8. Unnecessary jumps around statements controlled by an else are avoided. This is the case when a return or goto precedes the else.

9. The function modstk now generates two swaps to preserve the primary register only on a return with an expression.

Machine-dependent optimizing is done by two functions, putstk and peephole. Putstk now generates MOV A,L/STAX D rather than CALL CCPCHAR. Peephole is the output optimizer mentioned earlier. A staging buffer is used to hold the code generated by an expression. When the buffer is flushed, peephole scrutinizes the output, making changes as it sees fit. The output optimizer is a compile time option, since some may view this as something better suited to a separate utility program. I found it irresistible, however, to piggyback this simple function onto the compiler; it makes for faster and easier optimized compiles.

Peephole employs two techniques. First, integers being retrieved from the top of the stack are obtained with a POP H/PUSH H sequence rather than the usual LXI H,O/DAD SP/CALL CCGINT sequence. Integers next to the top of the stack are retrieved with a POP B/POP H/PUSH H/PUSH B sequence. If an XCHG follows the retrieve sequence, then the desired operand is popped directly into the DE register pair. These techniques result in smaller, faster code; they are always effective if the compiler contains peephole.

The second technique involves replacing commonly occurring sequences of commands with calls to new entry points in the runtime library (Listing 5-3). This technique reduces program size at the expense of speed; it must be requested at run time to be effective.

Passing Argument Counts

When a function is called, a count of the number of arguments being passed is placed in the accumulator. This takes only 2 bytes. To retrieve the count, the called function simply assigns to a variable the value returned by the function CCARGC (uppercase). This must be done first in the function, since other operations may call certain runtime library routines that destroy the accumulator. CCARGC is a new entry point in the runtime library; it simply redefines CCSXT, which moves A to HL sign extended. That allows 127 arguments before going berserk. For obvious reasons, the compiler does not generate code to load an argument count for calls to CCARGC. Since many programs do not use the argument count feature, the compiler skips it in programs containing the statement "#define NOCCARGC" (uppercase). This reduces program size and run time.

Data Initialization

You can initialize global variables, array elements, and pointers just as in full C, except that symbols may not be used as initializers. When not initialized, globals default to zero. An equal sign must introduce initializers.

You may use constant expressions to initialize variables or array elements only. If the size of an array is not given, it is determined by the number of initializers present. Character constants with backslash escape sequences are permitted. When multiple initializers are present, they must be enclosed in braces and separated by commas. If too few initializers are given, trailing elements are set to zero. If too many initializers are given, an error message is issued.

You may use a quoted character string to initialize only character arrays and pointers. In this case a terminating zero byte is automatically generated. An array name references the first byte and a pointer contains the address of the first byte. If no array size is given, it is set to the length of the string plus one. If the string is longer than the stated size, the size is increased to match the string.

One negative side effect of the zero default is that very large arrays generate many "DB 0,0,0,..." or "DW 0,0,0,..." statements in the output. If this proves to be a problem in practice, you could set up a runtime option to sidestep the zero default.

Local Declarations

The original compiler would accept local declarations anywhere within a function, and duplicate declarations produced errors. This version requires local declarations to appear first within a block and permits multiple declarations of the same symbol. The local part of the symbol table is now searched in reverse order so as to see the latest occurrence of a variable first. Upon leaving a block, the nonlabel declarations occurring within it are stripped from the symbol table. Local declarations may not contain initializers.

Goto Statement

I included this statement with some reluctance. I see no compelling need for it, and I shudder to think of how easily its abuse camouflages the logic of a program. Occasionally, however, there are situations where it can prevent code redundancy without obscuring the logic. I included the goto largely because it is expected and also because it can prove invaluable when converting existing programs to Small-C.

There is one restriction on the use of the goto statement. Since local variables may be declared within any block, the compiler cannot know the level of the stack pointer at target labels that have not yet been defined, so it cannot adjust the stack pointer before the branch. I could not find an efficient method of solving this dilemma, so I chose to make block-locals (other than at the start of a function) and goto statements mutually exclusive within a given function.

Extern Storage Class

The extern storage class may be specified with global declarations only. If the LINK option (see Installation below) is effective, such objects are defined as external references to the assembler and other globals are defined as entry points. If LINK is not effective, extern globals are not defined to the assembler and other globals are defined but not as entry points. If int or char is not specified following extern, then int is assumed.

Invoking the Compiler

Three types of runtime parameters may be given—filenames, redirection specifications, and switches. The operating environment handles redirection specifications without passing them to the program.

By default, Small-C obtains its input from the standard input file (stdin). If a list of filenames is given on the command line, then instead of reading stdin, Small-C reads the named files in the order listed. Any nonswitch parameter is taken for a filename. Output always goes to the standard output file (stdout).

Switches are preceded by a hyphen. The -M switch allows you to MONITOR progress by having the compiler write each function header line to the console. This switch is useful for isolating errors to the functions containing them.

The -A switch causes the ALARM (control-G to the console) to sound when an error is reported.

The -P switch causes the compiler to PAUSE after reporting each error. A carriage-return from the keyboard continues processing.

The -L# switch (# is a file descriptor in the range 1-9) instructs Small-C to LIST the source code on the file indicated. If file descriptor 1 (stdout) is specified, the listing is mixed with the normal output. In this case a semicolon precedes each line of source code. No listing is produced if the switch is not given.

Machine-independent and pop/push optimizing (described earlier) are always performed. The -O switch causes the output OPTIMIZER to further reduce program size at the expense of execution speed.

The -B# switch exists only if the compiler will not be used with a linking loader (see Installation below); that is, program parts will be combined at assembly time rather than load time. It causes label numbering to BEGIN following the value #. If # is zero (default) a complete program is being compiled. In this case, header and trailer code, designed to link the program with its environment, is appended to the program. A value of 1 means the first of a multipart program is being compiled; header code only will be appended. A value between 1 and 9000 identifies an intermediate part; in this case no code is appended to the output. A value of 9000 means the last part is being compiled; trailer code only will be appended. Values for # must be chosen to prevent clashes with labels generated in other parts of the program.

The null switch "-" or any undefined switch causes the compiler to exit after displaying the help line:

```
usage: CC [file]... [-M] [-A] [-P] [-L#] [-O] [-B#]
```

Installation

You may compile this version of Small-C using the original compiler. First, however, you need to make the following changes to your present compiler (if not already done).

1. Apply the fixes mentioned earlier (item 16 under Differences). You may omit fixes c, d, and e.
2. Install the change that allows the compiler to properly handle backslash escape sequences (DDJ #56, p. 6).
3. Make whatever changes are required by your runtime environment. Be sure your system supports the Standard I/O Library functions fgets, fputs, and fputc (Listing 5-2). All input and output is through these functions.

Note: The original compiler, in several instances, performed a "logical and" of 127 with a source byte. I have removed these operations, preferring to let the input routine do it (if required at all).

4. Prepare a temporary copy of the new compiler as input to the first (using your present updated compiler) of two compiles. This is done by deleting lines from the new compiler that cannot be handled by the present one or that are not desirable for your installation.

Conditional compilation statements (#ifdef, #ifndef, #else, and #endif) are present in the source files to document which lines should be deleted and which ones should be retained. For the first compile, they must be deleted along with all inappropriate lines. Once a usable compiler has been generated, the temporary source files should be discarded and the newly generated compiler must be used to produce a second version from the full source files. This second compile (phase 2) is required because it will include statements that could not be compiled by the original compiler (phase 1).

Several symbols are defined in the cc.def file for the purpose of controlling compiler options. If the action taken by the compiler is inappropriate when any of these symbols is defined, that symbol should be deleted or commented out. These symbols are described below.

DYNAMIC compiles statements that dynamically allocate memory for various tables and arrays within the compiler. If DYNAMIC is not defined, the tables and arrays are compiled directly into the compiler. This symbol also controls statements that call CCAVAIL, whose primary purpose is to return the amount of free memory remaining, but is used here to verify that the machine stack and allocated memory do not overlap; the run aborts in that case. If serial table searching is used with dynamic memory allocation, then each new entry to the global symbol table is allocated separately. The table may grow until it overlaps the machine stack, producing an allocation error.

LINK implies that compiler output will be used with a relocatable assembler and linking loader. It compiles statements for declaring "extern" globals as external references and all other globals as entry points. In this case, multipart programs cannot be combined at assembly time and the beginning label option (-B# switch) is not available.

COL causes labels in the output to be terminated by a colon.

UPPER compiles statements that cause symbols placed into the symbol table to be converted to uppercase. If your assembler does not require this, then disable the definition of UPPER.

SEPARATE implies that the compiler is to be compiled in parts rather than all at once. In this case, separate compile runs should be directed to each of the files cc1.c, cc2.c, cc3.c, and cc4.c. These, in turn, include subordinate files; for example, cc11.c, cc12.c, and cc13.c (for part 1). If this symbol is missing, then cc1.c includes all the subordinate files, and the files cc2.c, cc3.c, and cc4.c are not used.

NOCCARGC is a runtime option that tells the compiler not to generate code for passing argument counts to called functions. This results in smaller, faster programs when it is known that there will be no calls to the runtime routine CCARGC.

Four symbols permit you to determine which, if any, of the new language statements are to be supported by the compiler. You may have to leave them out to make the compiler small enough to compile itself in one gulp on a 48K machine.

STDO controls the do statement. STFOR controls the for statement. STSWITCH controls the switch, case, and default statements. STGOTO controls the goto statement. These defines also associate a numeric value with each statement; the compiler uses this to determine if the last statement in a function is a return.

OPTIMIZE causes the peephole optimizer to be included.

Availability

This version of Small-C is copyrighted; nevertheless, it is available to the general public for use without formal restrictions. Take it, use it, copy it, modify it, and give it away as you please. However, be sure to preserve the copyright notices. I am distributing Small-C under the user-supported concept, so if you obtain a "free" copy and find it useful, send a registration form and $20 to the author. You must obtain written permission to sell Small-C for more than your actual cost for media, packaging, and postage.

LISTING 5-1

FILE:STDIO.H

```
/*
** STDIO.H -- Standard Small-C Definitions
**
** Copyright 1984  L. E. Payne and J. E. Hendrix
*/
#define stdin    0
#define stdout   1
#define stderr   2
#define ERR    (-2)
#define EOF    (-1)
#define YES      1
#define NO       0
#define NULL     0
#define CR      13
#define LF      10
#define BELL     7
#define SPACE   ' '
#define NEWLINE LF       /*23*/ /*45*/
```

FILE:CC.DEF

```
/*
** Small-C Compiler Version 2.1
**
** Copyright 1982, 1983 J. E. Hendrix
**
** Version 2.0 -> 2.1 Change Record
**     (primed numbers keyed to text)
** 01' fix bogus label generated by "continue" within "switch"
**     (A. Macpherson)
** 02' fix problem of "peephole" missing end of staging buffer
**     (E. Payne & A. Macpherson)
** 03' permit (*func)() syntax for functions as arguments
**     (E. Payne)
** 04  change spelling of "heir" to "hier"
** 05  change spelling of "plunge" to "plnge"
** 06  always compile function "upper"
** 07' allow smaller NAMEMAX/NAMESIZE w/o truncating keywords
**     (E. Payne)
** 08' disallow local declarations inside "switch" statements
** 09' make "outdec" handle the constant 32768 properly
** 10  change CCALLOC() to calloc()
** 11  change CCAVAIL() to avail()
** 12  change CCPOLL() to poll()
** 13' install (*func)() syntax
** 14' correct extraneous operand fetch in expressions
**     like (i+5)();
```

```
** 15' make expressions like (&ia[...] - &ia[...]) scale
**     properly to give the number of objects lying between
** 16' eliminate "DW 0" generated by "int (*func)();"
** 17' "fclose" should return NULL or ERR like UNIX
** 18' "fflush" should return NULL or EOF like UNIX
** 19' "fgets" should return the newline like UNIX
** 20' remove redundant loop from "inline" (E. Payne)
** 21  rename functions (e.g., or(), and(),
**     ret(), call(), etc.) to avoid M80 reserved words
** 22  shorten CCDDPDPI and CCDDPDPC to 6 characters
**     to satisfy L80 and LIB
** 23' use NEWLINE symbol for newline value
** 24' fix pstr() end-of-line problem
**     (A. Macpherson & M. Grundy)
** 25' allocate space for local pointer declared as ptr[]
**     (A. Macpherson)
** 26' make primary() recognize expression strings
**     (A. Macpherson)
** 27  alter code generation for M80, L80
** 28' use double colon to declare entry points
** 29  employ standard functions isalpha(), isdigit(),
**     and toupper()
** 30' drop bad optimizing case from peephole(),
**     per Paul West (DDJ #81)
** 31' supply argument for avail() to abort on stack
**     overflow
** 32' prevent preprocess() from taking newline as
**     white space
** 33' always declare "_link" external in LINK mode
**     to force loading of required library functions
** 34' restrict doubling of constants operating on
**     integer addresses to add and subtract operators
** 35' use XRA A to pass an argument count of zero
**     per Paul West (DDJ #81)
** 36' improve indirect function calls per Paul West (DDJ #81)
** 37' automatically declare undeclared functions to be
**     external
** 38  drop support of sequential macro and global table
**     searching
** 39' provide a default extension of .C to input file
**     names, and assume an output .MAC file if stdout
**     has not been redirected to a disk file
** 40  drop support of parameter prompting and drop
**     CMD_LINE
** 41  drop external function declarations from
**     cc1.c, cc2.c, cc3.c, and cc4.c
** 42' begin execution at main() rather than first function
** 43  drop tabs from the output
** 44  always compile calls to poll() in the compiler
```

```
** 45' use LF as newline character instead of CR
** 47' accept #include "...." or <....> constructs
** 48' show even #asm input in the listing and prevent an
**     extra ";" at the end of the output from commenting
**     out the first EXT
** 49' correct double spacing in the output during
**     #asm ... #endasm intervals
** 50' correct lingering problem with correctly performing
**     operand fetches for indirect function calls
** 51' correct bad syntax in trailer() if LINK not defined
** 52' init locptr before first function so something like
**     "int ia[x];" where x is not #defined won't hang
** 53' generate error on attempt to declare pointer arrays
** 54' generate "EXT _link" only if "main()" is defined
** 55' eliminate redundant code generated at the end of a
**     compound statement
** 56  change system global names from leading _ to U to
**     accommodate users with pre 3.44 MACRO-80 packages
** 57  modify fflush() so that it will not attempt to flush
**     the auxiliary buffer unless fd is opened for output
** 58' properly initialize auxiliary buffering controls so
**     that i/o will work properly after an fd has been
**     closed and reopened
** 59' don't ignore ! while optimizing if(!(i==0)) ..., etc.
** 60  fix lexcmp() so it doesn't return 0 for "Happy" and "hello"
** 61' enlarge MACNBR & MACQSIZE
** 62' correct FREAD.C and FWRITE.C so that fread() and fwrite() will
**     return the number of "items" written rather than "bytes"
**     and make write() more efficient
** 63' make _putsec(), in CSYSLIB, realize that it is not necessarily at
**     end of file, preventing it from padding an old sector with 1A bytes
** 64' fix the expression analyzer so the operators += and -= in
**     expressions like i += p (where p is a pointer) will not erroneously
**     assign to p
** 65' fix Uparse(),in CSYSLIB, so i/o redirection will work properly
**     under CP/M-Plus (from Frank Hayes)
*/


/*
** compile options
*/
#define NOCCARGC /* no argument counts */
#define SEPARATE /* compile separately */
#define OPTIMIZE /* compile output optimizer */
#define DYNAMIC  /* allocate memory dynamically */
#define COL      /* terminate labels with a colon */
/* #define UPPER    /* force symbols to upper case */
```

```
#define LINK        /* will use with linking loader */

/*
** machine dependent parameters
*/
#define BPW     2   /* bytes per word */
#define LBPW    1   /* log2(BPW) */
#define SBPC    1   /* stack bytes per character */
#define ERRCODE 7   /* op sys return code */

/*
** symbol table format
*/
#define IDENT   0
#define TYPE    1
#define CLASS   2
#define OFFSET  3
#define NAME    5
#define OFFSIZE (NAME-OFFSET)
#define SYMAVG  10
#define SYMMAX  14

/*
** symbol table parameters
*/
#define NUMLOCS   25
#define STARTLOC  symtab
#define ENDLOC    (symtab+(NUMLOCS*SYMAVG))
#define NUMGLBS   200
#define STARTGLB  ENDLOC
#define ENDGLB    (ENDLOC+((NUMGLBS-1)*SYMMAX))
#define SYMTBSZ   3050  /* NUMLOCS*SYMAVG + NUMGLBS*SYMMAX */

/*
** System wide name size (for symbols)
*/
#define NAMESIZE 9
#define NAMEMAX  8

/*
** possible entries for "IDENT"
*/
#define LABEL    0
#define VARIABLE 1
#define ARRAY    2
#define POINTER  3
#define FUNCTION 4

/*
```

```
** possible entries for "TYPE"
**     low order 2 bits make type unique within length
**     high order bits give length of object
*/
/*      LABEL   0 */
#define CCHAR   (1<<2)
#define CINT    (BPW<<2)

/*
** possible entries for "CLASS"
*/
/*      LABEL   0 */
#define STATIC    1
#define AUTOMATIC 2
#define EXTERNAL  3
#define AUTOEXT   4           /*37*/

/*
** "switch" table
*/

#define SWSIZ   (2*BPW)
#define SWTABSZ (60*SWSIZ)

/*
** "while" statement queue
*/
#define WQTABSZ 30
#define WQSIZ   3
#define WQMAX   (wq+WQTABSZ-WQSIZ)

/*
** entry offsets in while queue
*/
#define WQSP    0
#define WQLOOP  1
#define WQEXIT  2

/*
** literal pool
*/
#define LITABSZ 800
#define LITMAX  (LITABSZ-1)

/*
** input line
*/
#define LINEMAX  127
#define LINESIZE 128
```

```
/*
** output staging buffer size
*/
#define STAGESIZE   800
#define STAGELIMIT  (STAGESIZE-1)

/*
** macro (define) pool
*/
#define MACNBR    130             /*61*/
#define MACNSIZE  (MACNBR*(NAMESIZE+2))
#define MACNEND   (macn+MACNSIZE)
#define MACQSIZE  (MACNBR*7)      /*61*/
#define MACMAX    (MACQSIZE-1)

/*
** statement types
*/
#define STIF      1
#define STWHILE   2
#define STRETURN  3
#define STBREAK   4
#define STCONT    5
#define STASM     6
#define STEXPR    7
#define STDO      8 /* compile "do" logic */
#define STFOR     9 /* compile "for" logic */
#define STSWITCH 10 /* compile "switch/case/default" logic */
#define STCASE   11
#define STDEF    12
#define STGOTO   13 /* compile "goto" logic */
#define STLABEL  14 /*55*/
```

---- **FILE: CC1.C**

```
/*
** Small-C Compiler Version 2.1
**
** Copyright 1982, 1983 J. E. Hendrix
**
** Part 1
*/
#include stdio.h
#include cc.def

/*
** miscellaneous storage
*/
char
#ifdef OPTIMIZE
```

```
    optimize, /* optimize output of staging buffer */
#endif
    alarm,    /* audible alarm on errors? */
    monitor,  /* monitor function headers? */
    pause,    /* pause for operator on errors? */
#ifdef DYNAMIC
    *stage,   /* output staging buffer */
    *symtab,  /* symbol table */
    *litq,    /* literal pool */
    *macn,    /* macro name buffer */
    *macq,    /* macro string buffer */
    *pline,   /* parsing buffer */
    *mline,   /* macro buffer */
#else
    stage[STAGESIZE],
    symtab[SYMTBSZ],
    litq[LITABSZ],
    macn[MACNSIZE],
    macq[MACQSIZE],
    pline[LINESIZE],
    mline[LINESIZE],
    swq[SWTABSZ],
#endif
    *line,    /* points to pline or mline */
    *lptr,    /* ptr to either */
    *glbptr,  /* ptrs to next entries */
    *locptr,  /* ptr to next local symbol */
    *stagenext,/* next addr in stage */
    *stagelast,/* last addr in stage */
    quote[2], /* literal string for '"' */
    *cptr,    /* work ptrs to any char buffer */
    *cptr2,
    *cptr3,
    msname[NAMESIZE], /* macro symbol name array */
    ssname[NAMESIZE]; /* static symbol name array */
int
#ifdef STGOTO
    nogo,     /* > 0 disables goto statements */
    noloc,    /* > 0 disables block locals */
#endif
    op[16],   /* function addresses of binary operators */
    op2[16],  /* same for unsigned operators */
    opindex,  /* index to matched operator */
    opsize,   /* size of operator in bytes */
    swactive, /* true inside a switch */
    swdefault,/* default label #, else 0 */
    *swnext,  /* address of next entry */
    *swend,   /* address of last table entry */
#ifdef DYNAMIC
```

```
  *wq,        /* while queue */
#else
  wq[WQTABSZ],
#endif
  argcs,      /* static argc */
  *argvs,     /* static argv */
  *wqptr,     /* ptr to next entry */
  litptr,     /* ptr to next entry */
  macptr,     /* macro buffer index */
  pptr,       /* ptr to parsing buffer */
  oper,       /* address of binary operator function */
  ch,         /* current character of line being scannec */
  nch,        /* next character of line being scanned */
  declared,   /* # of local bytes declared, else -1 when done */
  iflevel,    /* #if... nest level */
  skiplevel,  /* level at which #if... skipping started */
  func1,      /* true for first function */
  nxtlab,     /* next avail label # */
  litlab,     /* label # assigned to literal pool */
  beglab,     /* beginning label -- first function */
  csp,        /* compiler relative stk ptr */
  argstk,     /* function arg sp */
  argtop,
  ncmp,       /* # open compound statements */
  errflag,    /* non-zero after 1st error in statement */
  eof,        /* set non-zero on final input eof */
  input,      /* fd # for input file */
  input2,     /* fd # for "include" file */
  output,     /* fd # for output file */
  files,      /* non-zero if file list specified on cmd line */
  filearg,    /* cur file arg index */
  glbflag,    /* non-zero if internal globals */
  ctext,      /* non-zero to intermix c-source */
  ccode,      /* non-zero while parsing c-code */
              /* zero when passing assembly code */
  listfp,     /* file pointer to list device */
  lastst,     /* last executed statement type */
  *iptr;      /* work ptr to any int buffer */

#include cc11.c
#include cc12.c
#include cc13.c

#ifndef SEPARATE
#include cc21.c
#include cc22.c
#include cc31.c
#include cc32.c
#include cc33.c
```

```
#include cc41.c
#include cc42.c
#endif
```

FILE:CC11.C

```
/*
** execution begins here
*/
main(argc, argv) int argc, *argv; {
  argcs=argc;
  argvs=argv;
#ifdef DYNAMIC
  swnext=calloc(SWTABSZ, 1);
  swend=swnext+((SWTABSZ-SWSIZ)>>1);
  stage=calloc(STAGESIZE, 1);
  stagelast=stage+STAGELIMIT;
  wq=calloc(WQTABSZ, BPW);
  litq=calloc(LITABSZ, 1);
  macn=calloc(MACNSIZE, 1);
                               /*10*/
  macq=calloc(MACQSIZE, 1);
  pline=calloc(LINESIZE, 1);
  mline=calloc(LINESIZE, 1);
#else
  swend=(swnext=swq)+SWTABSZ-SWSIZ;
  stagelast=stage+STAGELIMIT;
#endif
  swactive=         /* not in switch */
  stagenext=        /* direct output mode */
  iflevel=          /* #if... nesting level = 0 */
  skiplevel=        /* #if... not encountered */
  macptr=           /* clear the macro pool */
  csp =             /* stack ptr (relative) */
  errflag=          /* not skipping errors till ";" */
  eof=              /* not eof yet */
  ncmp=             /* not in compound statement */
  files=
  filearg=
  quote[1]=0;
  func1=            /* first function */
  ccode=1;          /* enable preprocessing */
  wqptr=wq;         /* clear while queue */
  quote[0]='"';     /* fake a quote literal */
  input=input2=EOF;
  ask();            /* get user options */
  openfile();       /* and initial input file */
  preprocess();     /* fetch first line */
#ifdef DYNAMIC
  symtab=calloc((NUMLOCS*SYMAVG + NUMGLBS*SYMMAX), 1);
```

```
#endif
                            /*10*/
  locptr=STARTLOC;          /*52*/
  glbptr=STARTGLB;
  glbflag=1;
  ctext=0;
  header();           /* intro code */
  setops();           /* set values in op arrays */
  parse();            /* process ALL input */
  outside();          /* verify outside any function */
  trailer();          /* follow-up code */
  fclose(output);
  }

/*
** process all input text
**
** At this level, only static declarations,
**      defines, includes and function
**      definitions are legal...
*/
parse() {
  while (eof==0) {
    if(amatch("extern", 6))   dodeclare(EXTERNAL);
    else if(dodeclare(STATIC));
    else if(match("#asm"))    doasm();
    else if(match("#include"))doinclude();
    else if(match("#define")) addmac();
    else                      newfunc();
    blanks();       /* force eof if pending */
    }
  }

/*
** dump the literal pool
*/
dumplits(size) int size; {
  int j, k;
  k=0;
  while (k<litptr) {
    poll(1); /* allow program interruption */
    defstorage(size);
    j=10;
    while(j--) {
      outdec(getint(litq+k, size));
      k=k+size;
      if ((j==0)|(k>=litptr)) {
        nl();
        break;
```

```
          }
        outbyte(',');
        }
      }
    }

/*
** dump zeroes for default initial values
*/
dumpzero(size, count) int size, count; {
  int j;
  while (count > 0) {
    poll(1); /* allow program interruption */
    defstorage(size);
    j=30;
    while(j--) {
      outdec(0);
      if ((--count <= 0)|(j==0)) {
        nl();
        break;
        }
      outbyte(',');
      }
    }
  }

/*
** verify compile ends outside any function
*/
outside()  {
  if (ncmp) error("no closing bracket");
  }

/*
** get run options
*/
ask() {
  int i;
  i=listfp=nxtlab=0;
  output=stdout;
#ifdef OPTIMIZE
  optimize=
#endif
  alarm=monitor=pause=NO;
  line=mline;
  while(getarg(++i, line, LINESIZE, argcs, argvs)!=EOF) {
    if(line[0]!='-') continue;
    if((toupper(line[1])=='L')&(isdigit(line[2]))&(line[3]<=' ')) {
      listfp=line[2]-'0';
```

```
            continue;
            }
        if(line[2]<=' ') {
          if(toupper(line[1])=='A') {
            alarm=YES;
            continue;
            }
          if(toupper(line[1])=='M') {
            monitor=YES;
            continue;
            }
#ifdef OPTIMIZE
          if(toupper(line[1])=='O') {
            optimize=YES;
            continue;
            }
#endif
          if(toupper(line[1])=='P') {
            pause=YES;
            continue;
            }
          }
#ifndef LINK
        if(toupper(line[1])=='B') {
          bump(0); bump(2);
          if(number(&nxtlab)) continue;
          }
#endif
        sout("usage: cc [file]... [-m] [-a] [-p] [-l#]", stderr);
#ifdef OPTIMIZE
        sout(" [-o]", stderr);
#endif
#ifndef LINK
        sout(" [-b#]", stderr);
#endif
        sout(NEWLINE, stderr);                          /*23*/
        abort(ERRCODE);
        }
    }

/*
** input and output file opens
*/
openfile() {            /* entire function revised *//*39*/
  char outfn[15];
  int i, j, ext;
  input=EOF;
  while(getarg(++filearg, pline, LINESIZE, argcs, argvs)!=EOF) {
    if(pline[0]=='-') continue;
```

```
      ext = NO;
      i = -1;
      j = 0;
      while(pline[++i]) {
        if(pline[i] == '.') {
          ext = YES;
          break;
          }
        if(j < 10) outfn[j++] = pline[i];
        }
      if(!ext) {
        strcpy(pline + i, ".C");
        }
      input = mustopen(pline, "r");
      if(!files && isatty(stdout)) {
        strcpy(outfn + j, ".MAC");
        output = mustopen(outfn, "w");
        }
      files=YES;
      kill();
      return;
      }
    if(files++) eof=YES;
    else input=stdin;
    kill();
    }

/*
** open a file with error checking
*/
mustopen(fn, mode) char *fn, *mode; {           /*39*/
  int fd;
  if(fd = fopen(fn, mode)) return fd;
  sout("open error on ", stderr);
  lout(fn, stderr);
  abort(ERRCODE);
  }

setops() {
  op2[00]=        op[00]= ffor;    /* heir5 */
  op2[01]=        op[01]= ffxor;   /* heir6 */
  op2[02]=        op[02]= ffand;   /* heir7 */
  op2[03]=        op[03]= ffeq;    /* heir8 */
  op2[04]=        op[04]= ffne;
  op2[05]=ule;    op[05]= ffle;    /* heir9 */
  op2[06]=uge;    op[06]= ffge;
  op2[07]=ult;    op[07]= fflt;
  op2[08]=ugt;    op[08]= ffgt;
  op2[09]=        op[09]= ffasr;   /* heir10 */
```

```
    op2[10]=      op[10]= ffasl;
    op2[11]=      op[11]= ffadd;    /* heir11 */
    op2[12]=      op[12]= ffsub;
    op2[13]=      op[13]=ffmult;    /* heir12 */
    op2[14]=      op[14]= ffdiv;
    op2[15]=      op[15]= ffmod;
    }
```

─── FILE:CC12.C

```
/*
** open an include file
*/
doinclude() {
  char *cp;                                          /*47*/
  blanks();            /* skip over to name */
  switch (*lptr) {                                   /*47*/
    case '"': case '<': cp = ++lptr;                 /*47*/
    while(*cp) {                                     /*47*/
      switch(*cp) {case '"': case '>': *cp=NULL;}    /*47*/
      ++cp;                                          /*47*/
      }                                              /*47*/
    }                                                /*47*/
  if((input2=fopen(lptr,"r"))==NULL) {
    input2=EOF;
    error("open failure on include file");
    }
  kill();        /* clear rest of line */
      /* so next read will come from */
      /* new file (if open) */
  }

/*
** test for global declarations
*/
dodeclare(class) int class; {
  if(amatch("char",4)) {
    declglb(CCHAR, class);
    ns();
    return 1;
    }
  else if((amatch("int",3))|(class==EXTERNAL)) {
    declglb(CINT, class);
    ns();
    return 1;
    }
  return 0;
  }

/*
```

```
** declare a static variable
*/
declglb(type, class)  int type, class; {
  int k, j;
  while(1) {
    if(endst()) return;      /* do line */
    if(match("(*")!match("*")) {              /*03*/
      j=POINTER;
      k=0;
      }
    else {
      j=VARIABLE;
      k=1;
      }
    if (symname(ssname, YES)==0) illname();
    if(findglb(ssname)) multidef(ssname);
    if(match(")")) ;         /*03*/
    if(match("()")) j=FUNCTION;
    else if (match("[")) {
      paerror(j);            /*53*/
      k=needsub();    /* get size */
      j=ARRAY;    /* !0=array */
      }
    if(class==EXTERNAL) external(ssname);
    else if(j!=FUNCTION) j=initials(type>>2, j, k);    /*16*/
    addsym(ssname, j, type, k, &glbptr, class);
    if (match(",")==0) return; /* more? */
    }
  }

/*
** declare local variables
*/
declloc(typ)  int typ; {
  int k,j;
  if(swactive) error("not allowed in switch");       /*08*/
#ifdef STGOTO
  if(noloc) error("not allowed with goto");
#endif
  if(declared < 0) error("must declare first in block");
  while(1) {
    while(1) {
      if(endst()) return;
      if(match("*")) j=POINTER;
      else           j=VARIABLE;
      if (symname(ssname, YES)==0) illname();
      /* no multidef check, block-locals are together */
      k=BPW;
      if (match("[")) {
```

```
            paerror(j);                /*53*/
            if(k=needsub()) {          /*25*/
              j=ARRAY;
              if(typ==CINT)k=k<<LBPW;
              }
            else {j=POINTER; k=BPW;}   /*25*/
            }
                                       /*14*/
        else if((typ==CCHAR)&(j==VARIABLE)) k=SBPC;
        declared = declared + k;
        addsym(ssname, j, typ, csp - declared, &locptr, AUTOMATIC);
        break;
        }
    if (match(",")==0) return;
    }
  }

/*
** test for pointer array (unsupported)
*/
paerror(j) int j; {
  if(j==POINTER) error("no pointer arrays");    /*53*/
  }

/*
** initialize global objects
*/
initials(size, ident, dim) int size, ident, dim; {
  int savedim;
  litptr=0;
  if(dim==0) dim = -1;
  savedim=dim;
  entry();
  if(match("=")) {
    if(match("{")) {
      while(dim) {
        init(size, ident, &dim);
        if(match(",")==0) break;
        }
      needtoken("}");
      }
    else init(size, ident, &dim);
    }
  if((dim == -1)&(dim==savedim)) {
     stowlit(0, size=BPW);
     ident=POINTER;
     }
  dumplits(size);
  dumpzero(size, dim);
```

```
    return ident;
    }

/*
** evaluate one initializer
*/
init(size, ident, dim) int size, ident, *dim; {
  int value;
  if(qstr(&value)) {
    if((ident==VARIABLE)|(size!=1))
      error("must assign to char pointer or array");
    *dim = *dim - (litptr - value);
    if(ident==POINTER) point();
    }
  else if(constexpr(&value)) {
    if(ident==POINTER) error("cannot assign to pointer");
    stowlit(value, size);
    *dim = *dim - 1;
    }
  }

/*
** get required array size
*/
needsub() {
  int val;
  if(match("]")) return 0; /* null size */
  if (constexpr(&val)==0) val=1;
  if (val<0) {
    error("negative size illegal");
    val = -val;
    }
  needtoken("]");      /* force single dimension */
  return val;          /* and return size */
  }


/*
** begin a function
**
** called from "parse" and tries to make a function
** out of the following text
**
** Patched per P.L. Woods (DDJ #52)
*/
newfunc() {
  char *ptr;
#ifdef STGOTO
  nogo    =            /* enable goto statements */
```

```
  noloc = 0;           /* enable block-local declarations */
#endif
  lastst=               /* no statement yet */
  litptr=0;             /* clear lit pool */
  litlab=getlabel();    /* label next lit pool */
  locptr=STARTLOC;      /* clear local variables */
  if(monitor) lout(line, stderr);
  if (symname(ssname, YES)==0) {
    error("illegal function or declaration");
    kill(); /* invalidate line */
    return;
    }
  if(func1) {
    postlabel(beglab);
    func1=0;
    }
  if(ptr=findglb(ssname)) {      /* already in symbol table ? */
    if(ptr[IDENT]!=FUNCTION)       multidef(ssname);
    else if(ptr[OFFSET]==FUNCTION) multidef(ssname);
    else {                       /*37*/
      /* earlier assumed to be a function */
      ptr[OFFSET]=FUNCTION;
      ptr[CLASS]=STATIC;         /*37*/
      }                          /*37*/
    }
  else
    addsym(ssname, FUNCTION, CINT, FUNCTION, &glbptr, STATIC);
  if(match("(")==0) error("no open paren");
  entry();
  locptr=STARTLOC;
  argstk=0;              /* init arg count */
  while(match(")")==0) { /* then count args */
    /* any legal name bumps arg count */
    if(symname(ssname, YES)) {
      if(findloc(ssname)) multidef(ssname);
      else {
        addsym(ssname, 0, 0, argstk, &locptr, AUTOMATIC);
        argstk=argstk+BPW;
        }
      }
    else {error("illegal argument name");junk();}
    blanks();
    /* if not closing paren, should be comma */
    if(streq(lptr,")")==0) {
      if(match(",")==0) error("no comma");
      }
    if(endst()) break;
    }
  csp=0;       /* preset stack ptr */
```

```
      argtop=argstk;
      while(argstk) {
        /* now let user declare what types of things */
        /*     those arguments were */
        if(amatch("char",4))     {doargs(CCHAR);ns();}
        else if(amatch("int",3)) {doargs(CINT);ns();}
        else {error("wrong number of arguments");break;}
        }
/*55*/
      statement();
#ifdef STGOTO
      if(lastst != STRETURN && lastst != STGOTO) ffret();
#else
      if(lastst != STRETURN) ffret();
#endif
/*55*/
      if(litptr) {
        printlabel(litlab);
        col();
        dumplits(1); /* dump literals */
        }
      }

/*
** declare argument types
**
** called from "newfunc" this routine adds an entry in the
** local symbol table for each named argument
**
** rewritten per P.L. Woods (DDJ #52)
*/
doargs(t) int t; {
  int j, legalname;
  char c, *argptr;
  while(1) {
    if(argstk==0) return; /* no arguments */
    if(match("(*")|match("*")) j=POINTER;  else j=VARIABLE; /*03*/
    if((legalname=symname(ssname, YES))==0) illname();
    if(match(")")) ;             /*03*/
    if(match("()")) ;            /*03*/
    if(match("[")) {
      paerror(j);                /*53*/
      while(inbyte()!=']') if(endst()) break;/* skip "[...]" */
      j=POINTER; /* add entry as pointer */
      }
    if(legalname) {
      if(argptr=findloc(ssname)) {
        /* add details of type and address */
        argptr[IDENT]=j;
```

```
          argptr[TYPE]=t;
          putint(argtop-getint(argptr+OFFSET, OFFSIZE), argptr+OFFSET, OFFSIZE);
          }
        else error("not an argument");
        }
      argstk=argstk-BPW;          /* cnt down */
      if(endst())return;
      if(match(",")==0) error("no comma");
      }
   }
```

FILE:CC13.C

```
/*
** statement parser
**
** called whenever syntax requires a statement
**  this routine performs that statement
**  and returns a number telling which one
*/
statement() {
  if ((ch==0) & (eof)) return;
  else if(amatch("char",4))  {declloc(CCHAR);ns();}
  else if(amatch("int",3))   {declloc(CINT);ns();}
  else {
    if(declared >= 0) {
#ifdef STGOTO
      if(ncmp > 1) nogo=declared; /* disable goto if any */
#endif
      csp=modstk(csp - declared, NO);
      declared = -1;
      }
    if(match("{"))            compound();
    else if(amatch("if",2))   {doif();lastst=STIF;}
    else if(amatch("while",5)) {dowhile();lastst=STWHILE;}
#ifdef STDO
    else if(amatch("do",2))   {dodo();lastst=STDO;}
#endif
#ifdef STFOR
    else if(amatch("for",3))  {dofor();lastst=STFOR;}
#endif
#ifdef STSWITCH
    else if(amatch("switch",6)) {doswitch();lastst=STSWITCH;}
    else if(amatch("case",4))   {docase();lastst=STCASE;}
    else if(amatch("default",7)) {dodefault();lastst=STDEF;}
#endif
#ifdef STGOTO
    else if(amatch("goto", 4))  {dogoto(); lastst=STGOTO;}
    else if(dolabel())          lastst=STLABEL;      /*55*/
#endif
```

```
      else if(amatch("return",6))   {doreturn();ns();lastst=STRETURN;}
      else if(amatch("break",5))    {dobreak();ns();lastst=STBREAK;}
      else if(amatch("continue",8)){docont();ns();lastst=STCONT;}
      else if(match(";"))           errflag=0;
      else if(match("#asm"))        {doasm();lastst=STASM;}
      else                          {doexpr();ns();lastst=STEXPR;}
      }
  return lastst;
  }

/*
** semicolon enforcer
**
** called whenever syntax requires a semicolon
*/
ns() {
  if(match(";")==0) error("no semicolon");
  else errflag=0;
  }

compound()  {
  int savcsp;
  char *savloc;
  savcsp=csp;
  savloc=locptr;
  declared=0;    /* may now declare local variables */
  ++ncmp;        /* new level open */
  while (match("}")==0)
    if(eof) {
      error("no final }");
      break;
      }
    else statement();    /* do one */
  --ncmp;                /* close current level */
/*55*/
#ifdef STGOTO
  if(lastst != STRETURN && lastst != STGOTO)
#else
  if(lastst != STRETURN)
#endif
    modstk(savcsp, NO); /* delete local variable space */
  csp=savcsp;
/*55*/
#ifdef STGOTO
  cptr=savloc;           /* retain labels */
  while(cptr < locptr) {
    cptr2=nextsym(cptr);
    if(cptr[IDENT] == LABEL) {
      while(cptr < cptr2) *savloc++ = *cptr++;
```

```
      }
    else cptr=cptr2;
    }
#endif
  locptr=savloc;          /* delete local symbols */
  declared = -1;          /* may not declare variables */
  }

doif() {
  int flab1,flab2;
  flab1=getlabel(); /* get label for false branch */
  test(flab1, YES); /* get expression, and branch false */
  statement();      /* if true, do a statement */
  if (amatch("else",4)==0) {      /* if...else ? */
    /* simple "if"...print false label */
    postlabel(flab1);
    return;         /* and exit */
    }
  flab2=getlabel();
#ifdef STGOTO
  if((lastst != STRETURN)&(lastst != STGOTO)) jump(flab2);
#else
  if(lastst != STRETURN) jump(flab2);
#endif
  postlabel(flab1); /* print false label */
  statement();      /* and do "else" clause */
  postlabel(flab2); /* print true label */
  }

doexpr() {
  int const, val;
  char *before, *start;
  while(1) {
    setstage(&before, &start);
    expression(&const, &val);
    clearstage(before, start);
    if(ch != ',') break;
    bump(1);
    }
  }

dowhile() {
  int wq[4];                /* allocate local queue */
  addwhile(wq);             /* add entry to queue for "break" */
  postlabel(wq[WQLOOP]);    /* loop label */
  test(wq[WQEXIT], YES);    /* see if true */
  statement();              /* if so, do a statement */
  jump(wq[WQLOOP]);         /* loop to label */
  postlabel(wq[WQEXIT]);    /* exit label */
```

```
      delwhile();          /* delete queue entry */
    }
#ifdef STDO
dodo() {
  int wq[4], top;
  addwhile(wq);
  postlabel(top=getlabel());
  statement();
  needtoken("while");
  postlabel(wq[WQLOOP]);
  test(wq[WQEXIT], YES);
  jump(top);
  postlabel(wq[WQEXIT]);
  delwhile();
  ns();
  }
#endif

#ifdef STFOR
dofor() {
  int wq[4], lab1, lab2;
  addwhile(wq);
  lab1=getlabel();
  lab2=getlabel();
  needtoken("(");
  if(match(";")==0) {
    doexpr();           /* expr 1 */
    ns();
    }
  postlabel(lab1);
  if(match(";")==0) {
    test(wq[WQEXIT], NO); /* expr 2 */
    ns();
    }
  jump(lab2);
  postlabel(wq[WQLOOP]);
  if(match(")")==0) {
    doexpr();           /* expr 3 */
    needtoken(")");
    }
  jump(lab1);
  postlabel(lab2);
  statement();
  jump(wq[WQLOOP]);
  postlabel(wq[WQEXIT]);
  delwhile();
  }
#endif
```

```
#ifdef STSWITCH
doswitch() {
  int wq[4], endlab, swact, swdef, *swnex, *swptr;
  swact=swactive;
  swdef=swdefault;
  swnex=swptr=swnext;
  addwhile(wq);
  *(wqptr + WQLOOP - WQSIZ) = 0;                    /*01*/
  needtoken("(");
  doexpr();     /* evaluate switch expression */
  needtoken(")");
  swdefault=0;
  swactive=1;
  jump(endlab=getlabel());
  statement();  /* cases, etc. */
  jump(wq[WQEXIT]);
  postlabel(endlab);
  sw();         /* match cases */
  while(swptr < swnext) {
    defstorage(CINT>>2);
    printlabel(*swptr++);   /* case label */
    outbyte(',');
    outdec(*swptr++);       /* case value */
    nl();
    }
  defstorage(CINT>>2);
  outdec(0);
  nl();
  if(swdefault) jump(swdefault);
  postlabel(wq[WQEXIT]);
  delwhile();
  swnext=swnex;
  swdefault=swdef;
  swactive=swact;
  }

docase() {
  if(swactive==0) error("not in switch");
  if(swnext > swend) {
    error("too many cases");
    return;
    }
  postlabel(*swnext++ = getlabel());
  constexpr(swnext++);
  needtoken(":");
  }

dodefault() {
  if(swactive) {
```

```
      if(swdefault) error("multiple defaults");
      }
    else error("not in switch");
    needtoken(":");
    postlabel(swdefault=getlabel());
    }
#endif

#ifdef STGOTO
dogoto() {
  if(nogo > 0) error("not allowed with block-locals");
  else noloc = 1;
  if(symname(ssname, YES)) jump(addlabel());
  else error("bad label");
  ns();
  }

dolabel() {
  char *savelptr;
  blanks();
  savelptr=lptr;
  if(symname(ssname, YES)) {
    if(gch()==':') {
      postlabel(addlabel());
      return 1;
      }
    else bump(savelptr-lptr);
    }
  return 0;
  }

addlabel() {
  if(cptr=findloc(ssname)) {
    if(cptr[IDENT]!=LABEL) error("not a label");
    }
  else cptr=addsym(ssname, LABEL, LABEL, getlabel(), &locptr, LABEL);
  return (getint(cptr+OFFSET, OFFSIZE));
  }
#endif

doreturn() {
  if(endst()==0) {
    doexpr();
    modstk(0, YES);
    }
  else modstk(0, NO);
  ffret();
  }
```

```
dobreak()  {
  int *ptr;
  if ((ptr=readwhile(wqptr))==0) return;      /*01*/
  modstk((ptr[WQSP]), NO);
  jump(ptr[WQEXIT]);
  }

docont()  {
  int *ptr;
  ptr = wqptr;                                /*01*/
  while (1) {                                 /*01*/
    if ((ptr=readwhile(ptr))==0) return;      /*01*/
    if (ptr[WQLOOP]) break;                   /*01*/
    }                                         /*01*/
  modstk((ptr[WQSP]), NO);
  jump(ptr[WQLOOP]);
  }

doasm()  {
  ccode=0;                 /* mark mode as "asm" */
  while (1) {
    inline();
    if (match("#endasm")) break;
    if(eof)break;
    sout(line, output);              /*49*/
    }
  kill();
  ccode=1;
  }
```

FILE:CC2.C

```
/*
** Small-C Compiler Version 2.1
**
** Copyright 1982, 1983 J. E. Hendrix
**
** Part 2
*/
#include stdio.h
#include cc.def

extern char
#ifdef DYNAMIC
 *symtab,
 *stage,
 *macn,
 *macq,
 *pline,
 *mline,
```

```
#else
  symtab[SYMTBSZ],
  stage[STAGESIZE],
  macn[MACNSIZE],
  macq[MACQSIZE],
  pline[LINESIZE],
  mline[LINESIZE],
#endif
#ifdef OPTIMIZE
  optimize,
#endif
  alarm, *glbptr, *line, *lptr, *cptr, *cptr2, *cptr3,
 *locptr, msname[NAMESIZE], pause, quote[2],
 *stagelast, *stagenext;
extern int
#ifdef DYNAMIC
  *wq,
#else
  wq[WQTABSZ],
#endif
  ccode, ch, csp, eof, errflag, iflevel,
  input, input2, listfp, macptr, nch,
  nxtlab, op[16], opindex, opsize, output, pptr,
  skiplevel, *wqptr;

#include cc21.c
#include cc22.c
```

FILE:CC21.C

```
junk() {
  if(an(inbyte())) while(an(ch)) gch();
  else while(an(ch)==0) {
    if(ch==0) break;
    gch();
    }
  blanks();
  }

endst() {
  blanks();
  return ((streq(lptr,";")¦(ch==0)));
  }

illname() {
  error("illegal symbol");
  junk();
  }
```

```
multidef(sname)  char *sname; {
  error("already defined");
  }

needtoken(str)  char *str; {
  if (match(str)==0) error("missing token");
  }

needlval() {
  error("must be lvalue");
  }

findglb(sname)  char *sname; {
  if(search(sname, STARTGLB, SYMMAX, ENDGLB, NUMGLBS, NAME))
    return cptr;
  return 0;
  }

findloc(sname)  char *sname; {
  cptr = locptr - 1;  /* search backward for block locals */
  while(cptr > STARTLOC) {
    cptr = cptr - *cptr;
    if(astreq(sname, cptr, NAMEMAX)) return (cptr - NAME);
    cptr = cptr - NAME - 1;
    }
  return 0;
  }

addsym(sname, id, typ, value, lgptrptr, class)
  char *sname, id, typ;  int value, *lgptrptr, class; {
  if(lgptrptr == &glbptr) {
    if(cptr2=findglb(sname)) return cptr2;
    if(cptr==0) {
      error("global symbol table overflow");
      return 0;
      }
    }
  else {
    if(locptr > (ENDLOC-SYMMAX)) {
      error("local symbol table overflow");
      abort(ERRCODE);
      }
    cptr = *lgptrptr;
    }
  cptr[IDENT]=id;
  cptr[TYPE]=typ;
  cptr[CLASS]=class;
  putint(value, cptr+OFFSET, OFFSIZE);
  cptr3 = cptr2 = cptr + NAME;
```

```
    while(an(*sname)) *cptr2++ = *sname++;
    if(lgptrptr == &locptr) {
      *cptr2 = cptr2 - cptr3;          /* set length */
      *lgptrptr = ++cptr2;
      }
    return cptr;
    }

nextsym(entry) char *entry; {
  entry = entry + NAME;
  while(*entry++ >= ' '); /* find length byte */
  return entry;
  }

/*
** get integer of length len from address addr
** (byte sequence set by "putint")
*/
getint(addr, len) char *addr; int len; {
  int i;
  i = *(addr + --len);  /* high order byte sign extended */
  while(len--) i = (i << 8) | *(addr+len)&255;
  return i;
  }

/*
** put integer i of length len into address addr
** (low byte first)
*/
putint(i, addr, len) char *addr; int i, len; {
  while(len--) {
    *addr++ = i;
    i = i>>8;
    }
  }

/*
** test if next input string is legal symbol name
*/
symname(sname, ucase) char *sname; int ucase; {
  int k;char c;
  blanks();
  if(alpha(ch)==0) return (*sname=0);     /*19*/
  k=0;
  while(an(ch)) {
#ifdef UPPER
    if(ucase)
      sname[k]=toupper(gch());
    else
```

```
#endif
      sname[k]=gch();
    if(k<NAMEMAX) ++k;
    }
  sname[k]=0;
  return 1;
  }

/*
** return next avail internal label number
*/
getlabel() {
  return(++nxtlab);
  }

/*
** post a label in the program
*/
postlabel(label) int label; {
  printlabel(label);
  col();
  nl();
  }

/*
** print specified number as a label
*/
printlabel(label)  int label; {
  outstr("CC");
  outdec(label);
  }

/*
** test if c is alphabetic
*/
alpha(c)  char c; {
  return (isalpha(c) || c=='_');
  }

/*
** test if given character is alphanumeric
*/
an(c)  char c; {
  return (alpha(c) || isdigit(c));
  }

addwhile(ptr)  int ptr[]; {
  int k;
  ptr[WQSP]=csp;            /* and stk ptr */
```

```
    ptr[WQLOOP]=getlabel();   /* and looping label */
    ptr[WQEXIT]=getlabel();   /* and exit label */
    if (wqptr==WQMAX) {
      error("too many active loops");
      abort(ERRCODE);
      }
    k=0;
    while (k<WQSIZ) *wqptr++ = ptr[k++];
    }

  delwhile() {
    if (wqptr > wq) wqptr=wqptr-WQSIZ;               /*01*/
    }

  readwhile(ptr) int *ptr; {                         /*01*/
    if (ptr <= wq) {                                 /*01*/
      error("out of context");                       /*01*/
      return 0;
      }
    else return (ptr-WQSIZ);                         /*01*/
   }

  white() {
  #ifdef DYNAMIC
    /* test for stack/prog overlap at deepest nesting */
    /* primary -> symname -> blanks -> white */
    avail(YES);  /* abort on stack overflow */   /*31*/
  #endif
    return (*lptr<= ' ' && *lptr!=NULL);           /*19*/
    }

  gch() {
    int c;
    if(c=ch) bump(1);
    return c;
    }

  bump(n) int n; {
    if(n) lptr=lptr+n;
    else  lptr=line;
    if(ch=nch = *lptr) nch = *(lptr+1);
    }

  kill() {
    *line=0;
    bump(0);
    }

  inbyte()  {
```

```
  while(ch==0) {
    if (eof) return 0;
    preprocess();
    }
  return gch();
  }

inline() {            /* numerous revisions */      /*20*/
  int k,unit;
  poll(1);   /* allow operator interruption */
  if (input==EOF) openfile();
  if(eof) return;
  if((unit=input2)==EOF) unit=input;
  if(fgets(line, LINEMAX, unit)==NULL) {
    fclose(unit);
    if(input2!=EOF) input2=EOF;
    else input=EOF;
    *line=NULL;
    }
  else if(listfp) {                       /*48*/
    if(listfp==output) cout(';', output); /*48*/
    sout(line, listfp);        /*19*/ /*48*/
    }                                     /*48*/
  bump(0);
  }
```

FILE:CC22.C

```
ifline() {
  while(1) {
    inline();
    if(eof) return;
    if(match("#ifdef")) {
      ++iflevel;
      if(skiplevel) continue;
      symname(msname, NO);          /*19*/
      if(search(msname, macn, NAMESIZE+2, MACNEND, MACNBR, 0)==0)
                                    /*19*/
        skiplevel=iflevel;
      continue;
      }
    if(match("#ifndef")) {
      ++iflevel;
      if(skiplevel) continue;
      symname(msname, NO);          /*19*/
      if(search(msname, macn, NAMESIZE+2, MACNEND, MACNBR, 0))
                                    /*19*/
        skiplevel=iflevel;
      continue;
      }
```

```
    if(match("#else")) {
      if(iflevel) {
        if(skiplevel==iflevel) skiplevel=0;
        else if(skiplevel==0)  skiplevel=iflevel;
        }
      else noiferr();
      continue;
      }
    if(match("#endif")) {
      if(iflevel) {
        if(skiplevel==iflevel) skiplevel=0;
        --iflevel;
        }
      else noiferr();
      continue;
      }
    if(skiplevel) continue;
                                            /*48*/
    if(ch==0) continue;
    break;
    }
  }

keepch(c)   char c; {
  if(pptr<LINEMAX) pline[++pptr]=c;
  }

preprocess() {
  int k;
  char c;
  if(ccode) {
    line=mline;
    ifline();
    if(eof) return;
    }
  else {
    line=pline;
    inline();
    return;
    }
  pptr = -1;
  while(ch != NEWLINE && ch) {            /*23,32*/
    if(white()) {
      keepch(' ');
      while(white()) gch();
      }
    else if(ch=='"') {
      keepch(ch);
      gch();
```

```
    while((ch!='"')|((*(lptr-1)==92)&(*(lptr-2)!=92))) {
      if(ch==0) {
        error("no quote");
        break;
        }
      keepch(gch());
      }
    gch();
    keepch('"');
    }
  else if(ch==39) {
    keepch(39);
    gch();
    while((ch!=39)|((*(lptr-1)==92)&(*(lptr-2)!=92))) {
      if(ch==0) {
        error("no apostrophe");
        break;
        }
      keepch(gch());
      }
    gch();
    keepch(39);
    }
  else if((ch=='/')&(nch=='*')) {
    bump(2);
    while(((ch=='*')&(nch=='/'))==0) {
      if(ch) bump(1);
      else {
        ifline();
        if(eof) break;
        }
      }
    bump(2);
    }
  else if(an(ch)) {
    k=0;
    while((an(ch)) & (k<NAMEMAX)) {          /*07*/
      msname[k++]=ch;                         /*07*/
      gch();
      }
    msname[k]=0;
    if(search(msname, macn, NAMESIZE+2, MACNEND, MACNBR, 0)) {
      k=getint(cptr+NAMESIZE, 2);
      while(c=macq[k++]) keepch(c);
      while(an(ch)) gch();                    /*07*/
      }
    else {
      k=0;
      while(c=msname[k++]) keepch(c);
```

```
          }
        }
      else keepch(gch());
      }
    if(pptr>=LINEMAX) error("line too long");
    keepch(0);
    line=pline;
    bump(0);
    }

  noiferr() {
    error("no matching #if...");
    errflag=0;
    }

  addmac() {
    int k;
    if(symname(msname, NO)==0) {
      illname();
      kill();
      return;
      }
    k=0;
    if(search(msname, macn, NAMESIZE+2, MACNEND, MACNBR, 0)==0) {
      if(cptr2=cptr) while(*cptr2++ = msname[k++]);
      else {
        error("macro name table full");
        return;
        }
      }
    putint(macptr, cptr+NAMESIZE, 2);
    while(white()) gch();
    while(putmac(gch()));
    if(macptr>=MACMAX) {
      error("macro string queue full"); abort(ERRCODE);
      }
    }

  putmac(c)   char c; {
    macq[macptr]=c;
    if(macptr<MACMAX) ++macptr;
    return c;
    }

  /*
  ** search for symbol match
  ** on return cptr points to slot found or empty slot
  */
  search(sname, buf, len, end, max, off)
```

```
     char *sname, *buf, *end;  int len, max, off; {
  cptr=cptr2=buf+((hash(sname)%(max-1))*len);
  while(*cptr != 0) {
    if(astreq(sname, cptr+off, NAMEMAX)) return 1;
    if((cptr=cptr+len) >= end) cptr=buf;
    if(cptr == cptr2) return (cptr=0);
    }
  return 0;
  }

hash(sname) char *sname; {
  int i, c;
  i=0;
  while(c = *sname++) i=(i<<1)+c;
  return i;
  }

setstage(before, start) int *before, *start; {
  if((*before=stagenext)==0) stagenext=stage;
  *start=stagenext;
  }

clearstage(before, start) char *before, *start; {
  *stagenext=0;
  if(stagenext=before) return;
  if(start) {
#ifdef OPTIMIZE
    peephole(start);
#else
    sout(start, output);
#endif
    }
  }

outdec(number)  int number; {
  int k,zs;
  char c, *q, *r;                                 /*09*/
  zs = 0;
  k=10000;
  if (number<0) {
    number=(-number);
    outbyte('-');
    }
  while (k>=1) {
    q=0; r=number;                                /*09*/
    while(r >= k) {++q; r -= k;}                  /*09*/
    c = q + '0';                                  /*09*/
    if ((c!='0')|(k==1)|(zs)) {
      zs=1;
```

```
      outbyte(c);
      }
    number=r;                                           /*09*/
    k=k/10;
    }
  }

ol(ptr)  char ptr[]; {
  ot(ptr);
  nl();
  }

ot(ptr) char ptr[]; {
  outstr(ptr);
  }

outstr(ptr) char ptr[]; {
  poll(1); /* allow program interruption */
  /* must work with symbol table names terminated by length */
  while(*ptr >= ' ') outbyte(*ptr++);
  }

outbyte(c) char c; {
  if(stagenext) {
    if(stagenext==stagelast) {
      error("staging buffer overflow");
      return 0;
      }
    else *stagenext++ = c;
    }
  else cout(c,output);
  return c;
  }

cout(c, fd) char c; int fd; {
  if(fputc(c, fd)==EOF) xout();
  }

sout(string, fd) char *string; int fd; {
  if(fputs(string, fd)==EOF) xout();
  }

lout(line, fd) char *line; int fd; {
  sout(line, fd);
  cout(NEWLINE, fd);                                    /*23*/
  }

xout() {
  fputs("output error", stderr);                        /*23*/
```

```
  abort(ERRCODE);
  }

nl() {
  outbyte(NEWLINE);                                         /*23*/
  }

col() {
#ifdef COL
  outbyte(':');
#endif
  }

error(msg) char msg[]; {
  if(errflag) return; else errflag=1;
  lout(line, stderr);
  errout(msg, stderr);
  if(alarm) fputc(7, stderr);
  if(pause) while(fgetc(stderr)!=NEWLINE);                  /*23*/
  if(listfp>0) errout(msg, listfp);
  }

errout(msg, fp) char msg[]; int fp; {
  int k; k=line+2;
  while(k++ <= lptr) cout(' ', fp);
  lout("/\\", fp);
  sout("**** ", fp); lout(msg, fp);
  }

streq(str1,str2)  char str1[],str2[]; {
  int k;
  k=0;
  while (str2[k]) {
    if ((str1[k])!=(str2[k])) return 0;
    ++k;
    }
  return k;
  }

astreq(str1,str2,len)  char str1[],str2[];int len; {
  int k;
  k=0;
  while (k<len) {
    if ((str1[k])!=(str2[k]))break;
    /*
    ** must detect end of symbol table names terminated by
    ** symbol length in binary
    */
    if(str1[k] < ' ') break;
```

```
    if(str2[k] < ' ') break;
    ++k;
    }
  if (an(str1[k]))return 0;
  if (an(str2[k]))return 0;
  return k;
 }

match(lit)  char *lit; {
  int k;
  blanks();
  if (k=streq(lptr,lit)) {
    bump(k);
    return 1;
    }
  return 0;
  }

amatch(lit,len)  char *lit;int len; {
  int k;
  blanks();
  if (k=astreq(lptr,lit,len)) {
    bump(k);
    while(an(ch)) inbyte();
    return 1;
    }
  return 0;
 }

nextop(list) char *list; {
  char op[4];
  opindex=0;
  blanks();
  while(1) {
    opsize=0;
    while(*list > ' ') op[opsize++] = *list++;
    op[opsize]=0;
    if(opsize=streq(lptr, op))
      if((*(lptr+opsize) != '=')&
        (*(lptr+opsize) != *(lptr+opsize-1)))
          return 1;
    if(*list) {
      ++list;
      ++opindex;
      }
    else return 0;
    }
  }
```

```
blanks() {
  while(1) {
    while(ch) {
      if(white()) gch();
      else return;
      }
    if(line==mline) return;
    preprocess();
    if(eof)break;
    }
  }
```

---- FILE:CC3.C

```
/*
** Small-C Compiler Version 2.1
**
** Copyright 1982, 1983 J. E. Hendrix
**
** Part 3
*/
#include stdio.h
#include cc.def

extern char
#ifdef DYNAMIC
 *stage,
 *litq,
#else
  stage[STAGESIZE],
  litq[LITABSZ],
#endif
 *glbptr, *lptr, ssname[NAMESIZE], quote[2], *stagenext;
extern int
  ch, csp, litlab, litptr, nch, op[16], op2[16],
  oper, opindex, opsize;

#include cc31.c
#include cc32.c
#include cc33.c
```

---- FILE:CC31.C

```
/*
** lval[0] - symbol table address, else 0 for constant
** lval[1] - type of indirect obj to fetch, else 0 for static
** lval[2] - type of pointer or array, else 0 for all other
** lval[3] - true if constant expression
** lval[4] - value of constant expression (+ auxiliary uses)
** lval[5] - true if secondary register altered
** lval[6] - function address of highest/last binary operator
```

```
** lval[7] - stage address of "oper 0" code, else 0
*/

/*
** skim over terms adjoining || and && operators
*/
skim(opstr, testfunc, dropval, endval, hier, lval)
  char *opstr;
  int (*testfunc)(), dropval, endval, (*hier)(), lval[]; { /*13*/
  int k, hits, droplab, endlab;
  hits=0;
  while(1) {
    k=plnge1(hier, lval);
    if(nextop(opstr)) {
      bump(opsize);
      if(hits==0) {
        hits=1;
        droplab=getlabel();
        }
      dropout(k, testfunc, droplab, lval);
      }
    else if(hits) {
      dropout(k, testfunc, droplab, lval);
      const(endval);
      jump(endlab=getlabel());
      postlabel(droplab);
      const(dropval);
      postlabel(endlab);
      lval[1]=lval[2]=lval[3]=lval[4]=lval[7]=0;  /*50*/
      return 0;
      }
    else return k;
    }
  }

/*
** test for early dropout from || or && evaluations
*/
dropout(k, testfunc, exit1, lval)
  int k, (*testfunc)(), exit1, lval[]; {              /*13*/
  if(k) rvalue(lval);
  else if(lval[3]) const(lval[4]);
  (*testfunc)(exit1); /* jumps on false */            /*13*/
  }

/*
** plunge to a lower level
*/
plnge(opstr, opoff, hier, lval)
```

```
  char *opstr;
  int opoff, (*hier)(), lval[]; {                   /*13*/
  int k, lval2[8];
  k=plnge1(hier, lval);
  if(nextop(opstr)==0) return k;
  if(k) rvalue(lval);
  while(1) {
    if(nextop(opstr)) {
      bump(opsize);
      opindex=opindex+opoff;
      plnge2(op[opindex], op2[opindex], hier, lval, lval2);
      }
    else return 0;
    }
  }

/*
** unary plunge to lower level
*/
plnge1(hier, lval) int (*hier)(), lval[]; {         /*13*/
  char *before, *start;
  int k;
  setstage(&before, &start);
  k=(*hier)(lval);                                  /*13*/
  if(lval[3]) clearstage(before,0);  /* load constant later */
  return k;
  }

/*
** binary plunge to lower level
*/
plnge2(oper, oper2, hier, lval, lval2)
  int (*oper)(),(*oper2)(),(*hier)(),lval[],lval2[]; {  /*13*/
  char *before, *start;
  setstage(&before, &start);
  lval[5]=1;          /* flag secondary register used */
  lval[7]=0;          /* flag as not "... oper 0" syntax */
  if(lval[3]) {       /* constant on left side not yet loaded */
    if(plnge1(hier, lval2)) rvalue(lval2);
    if(lval[4]==0) lval[7]=stagenext;
    const2(lval[4]<<dbltest(oper, lval2, lval)); /*34*/
    }
  else {              /* non-constant on left side */
    push();
    if(plnge1(hier, lval2)) rvalue(lval2);
    if(lval2[3]) {    /* constant on right side */
      if(lval2[4]==0) lval[7]=start;
      if(oper==ffadd) { /* may test other commutative operators */
```

```
      csp=csp+2;
      clearstage(before, 0);
      const2(lval2[4]<<dbltest(oper, lval, lval2)); /*34*/
                              /* load secondary */
      }
    else {
      const(lval2[4]<<dbltest(oper, lval, lval2)); /*34*/
                              /* load primary */
      smartpop(lval2, start);
      }
    }
  else {              /* non-constants on both sides */
    smartpop(lval2, start);
                                              /*34*/
    if(dbltest(oper, lval,lval2)) doublereg(); /*34*/
    if(dbltest(oper, lval2,lval)) {            /*34*/
      swap();
      doublereg();
      if(oper==ffsub) swap();
      }
                                              /*34*/
    }
  }
if(oper) {
  if(lval[3]=lval[3]&lval2[3]) {
    lval[4]=calc(lval[4], oper, lval2[4]);
    clearstage(before, 0);
    lval[5]=0;
    }
  else {
    if((lval[2]==0)&(lval2[2]==0)) {
      (*oper)();                                /*13*/
      lval[6]=oper;   /* identify the operator */
      }
    else {
      (*oper2)();                               /*13*/
      lval[6]=oper2;  /* identify the operator */
      }
    }
  if(oper==ffsub) {
    if((lval[2]==CINT)&(lval2[2]==CINT)) {
      swap();
      const(1);
      ffasr();   /** div by 2 **/
      }
    }
  if((oper==ffsub)|(oper==ffadd)) result(lval, lval2);
  }
}
```

```
calc(left, oper, right) int left, (*oper)(), right; {    /*13*/
        if(oper ==   ffor) return (left  | right);
   else if(oper == ffxor) return (left  ^ right);
   else if(oper == ffand) return (left  & right);
   else if(oper ==   ffeq) return (left == right);
   else if(oper ==   ffne) return (left != right);
   else if(oper ==   ffle) return (left <= right);
   else if(oper ==   ffge) return (left >= right);
   else if(oper ==   fflt) return (left <  right);
   else if(oper ==   ffgt) return (left >  right);
   else if(oper ==  ffasr) return (left >> right);
   else if(oper ==  ffasl) return (left << right);
   else if(oper ==  ffadd) return (left +  right);
   else if(oper ==  ffsub) return (left -  right);
   else if(oper ==ffmult) return (left *  right);
   else if(oper ==  ffdiv) return (left /  right);
   else if(oper ==  ffmod) return (left %  right);
   else return 0;
   }

expression(const, val) int *const, *val; {
  int lval[8];
  if(hier1(lval)) rvalue(lval);
  if(lval[3]) {
    *const=1;
    *val=lval[4];
    }
  else *const=0;
  }

hier1(lval)  int lval[]; {
  int k,lval2[8], lval3[2], oper;                /*64*/
  k=plnge1(hier3, lval);
  if(lval[3]) const(lval[4]);
        if(match("|="))  oper=ffor;
   else if(match("^="))  oper=ffxor;
   else if(match("&="))  oper=ffand;
   else if(match("+="))  oper=ffadd;
   else if(match("-="))  oper=ffsub;
   else if(match("*="))  oper=ffmult;
   else if(match("/="))  oper=ffdiv;
   else if(match("%="))  oper=ffmod;
   else if(match(">>=")) oper=ffasr;
   else if(match("<<=")) oper=ffasl;
   else if(match("="))   oper=0;
   else return k;
   if(k==0) {
     needlval();
     return 0;
```

```
    }
  lval3[0] = lval[0];                                    /*64*/
  lval3[1] = lval[1];
  if(lval[1]) {
    if(oper) {
      push();
      rvalue(lval);
      }
    plnge2(oper, oper, hier1, lval, lval2);
    if(oper) pop();
    }
  else {
    if(oper) {
      rvalue(lval);
      plnge2(oper, oper, hier1, lval, lval2);
      }
    else {
      if(hier1(lval2)) rvalue(lval2);
      lval[5]=lval2[5];
      }
    }
  store(lval3);                                          /*64*/
  return 0;
  }

hier3(lval)   int lval[]; {
  return skim("||", eq0, 1, 0, hier4, lval);
  }

hier4(lval)   int lval[]; {
  return skim("&&", ne0, 0, 1, hier5, lval);
  }

hier5(lval)   int lval[]; {
  return plnge("|", 0, hier6, lval);
  }

hier6(lval)   int lval[]; {
  return plnge("^", 1, hier7, lval);
  }

hier7(lval)   int lval[]; {
  return plnge("&", 2, hier8, lval);
  }

hier8(lval)   int lval[]; {
  return plnge("== !=", 3, hier9, lval);
  }
```

```
hier9(lval)  int lval[]; {
  return plnge("<= >= < >", 5, hier10, lval);
  }

hier10(lval)  int lval[]; {
  return plnge(">> <<", 9, hier11, lval);
  }

hier11(lval)  int lval[]; {
  return plnge("+ -", 11, hier12, lval);
  }

hier12(lval)  int lval[]; {
  return plnge("* / %", 13, hier13, lval);
  }
```

FILE:CC32.C

```
hier13(lval)  int lval[]; {
  int k;
  char *ptr;
  if(match("++")) {                    /* ++lval */
    if(hier13(lval)==0) {
      needlval();
      return 0;
      }
    step(inc, lval);
    return 0;
    }
  else if(match("--")) {               /* --lval */
    if(hier13(lval)==0) {
      needlval();
      return 0;
      }
    step(dec, lval);
    return 0;
    }
  else if (match("~")) {               /* ~ */
    if(hier13(lval)) rvalue(lval);
    com();
    lval[4] = ~lval[4];
    return (lval[7]=0);     /*59*/
    }
  else if (match("!")) {               /* ! */
    if(hier13(lval)) rvalue(lval);
    lneg();
    lval[4] = !lval[4];
    return (lval[7]=0);     /*59*/
    }
  else if (match("-")) {               /* unary - */
```

```
    if(hier13(lval)) rvalue(lval);
    neg();
    lval[4] = -lval[4];
    return (lval[7]=0);       /*59*/
    }
  else if(match("*")) {                /* unary * */
    if(hier13(lval)) rvalue(lval);
    if(ptr=lval[0])lval[1]=ptr[TYPE];
    else lval[1]=CINT;
    lval[2]=0;  /* flag as not pointer or array */
    lval[3]=0;  /* flag as not constant */
    lval[4]=1;  /* omit rvalue() on func call */ /*50*/
    lval[7]=0;                /*59*/
    return 1;
    }
  else if(match("&")) {                /* unary & */
    if(hier13(lval)==0) {
      error("illegal address");
      return 0;
      }
    ptr=lval[0];
    lval[2]=ptr[TYPE];
    if(lval[1]) return 0;
    /* global & non-array */
    address(ptr);
    lval[1]=ptr[TYPE];
    return 0;
    }
  else {
    k=hier14(lval);
    if(match("++")) {               /* lval++ */
      if(k==0) {
        needlval();
        return 0;
        }
      step(inc, lval);
      dec(lval[2]>>2);
      return 0;
      }
    else if(match("--")) {          /* lval-- */
      if(k==0) {
        needlval();
        return 0;
        }
      step(dec, lval);
      inc(lval[2]>>2);
      return 0;
      }
    else return k;
```

```
      }
   }

hier14(lval)  int *lval; {
   int k, const, val, lval2[8];
   char *ptr, *before, *start;
   k=primary(lval);
   ptr=lval[0];
   blanks();
   if((ch=='[')|(ch=='(')) {
      lval[5]=1;     /* secondary register will be used */
      while(1) {
         if(match("[")) {                    /* [subscript] */
            if(ptr==0) {
               error("can't subscript");
               junk();
               needtoken("]");
               return 0;
               }
            else if(ptr[IDENT]==POINTER)rvalue(lval);
            else if(ptr[IDENT]!=ARRAY) {
               error("can't subscript");
               k=0;
               }
            setstage(&before, &start);
            lval2[3]=0;
            plnge2(0, 0, hier1, lval2, lval2); /* lval2 deadend */
            needtoken("]");
            if(lval2[3]) {
               clearstage(before, 0);
               if(lval2[4]) {
                  if(ptr[TYPE]==CINT) const2(lval2[4]<<LBPW);
                  else                const2(lval2[4]);
                  ffadd();
                  }
               }
            else {
               if(ptr[TYPE]==CINT) doublereg();
               ffadd();
               }
            lval[2]=0;                                       /*15*/
            lval[1]=ptr[TYPE];
            k=1;
            }
         else if(match("(")) {               /* function(...) */
            if(ptr==0) callfunction(0);
            else if(ptr[IDENT]!=FUNCTION) {
               if(k && !lval[4]) rvalue(lval);  /*13*//*14*//*50*/
               callfunction(0);
```

```
              }
          else callfunction(ptr);
          k=lval[0]=lval[3]=lval[4]=0;      /*50*/
          }
        else return k;
        }
      }
  if(ptr==0) return k;
  if(ptr[IDENT]==FUNCTION) {
    address(ptr);
    lval[0]=0;                              /*14*/
    return 0;
    }
  return k;
  }

primary(lval)  int *lval; {
  char *ptr, sname[NAMESIZE];               /*19*/
  int k;
  if(match("(")) {              /* (expression,...) */
    do k=hier1(lval); while(match(","));    /*26*/
    needtoken(")");
    return k;
    }
  putint(0, lval, 8<<LBPW); /* clear lval array */
  if(symname(sname, YES)) {                 /*19*/
      if(ptr=findloc(sname)) {              /*19*/
#ifdef STGOTO
        if(ptr[IDENT]==LABEL) {
          experr();
          return 0;
          }
#endif
        getloc(ptr);
        lval[0]=ptr;
        lval[1]=ptr[TYPE];
        if(ptr[IDENT]==POINTER) {
          lval[1]=CINT;
          lval[2]=ptr[TYPE];
          }
        if(ptr[IDENT]==ARRAY) {
          lval[2]=ptr[TYPE];
          return 0;
          }
        else return 1;
        }
     if(ptr=findglb(sname))                 /*19*/
       if(ptr[IDENT]!=FUNCTION) {
         lval[0]=ptr;
```

```
              lval[1]=0;
              if(ptr[IDENT]!=ARRAY) {
                if(ptr[IDENT]==POINTER) lval[2]=ptr[TYPE];
                return 1;
                }
              address(ptr);
              lval[1]=lval[2]=ptr[TYPE];
              return 0;
              }
        ptr=addsym(sname,FUNCTION,CINT,0,&glbptr,AUTOEXT);
                                              /*19*//*37*/
        lval[0]=ptr;
        lval[1]=0;
        return 0;
        }
    if(constant(lval)==0) experr();
    return 0;
    }

experr() {
  error("invalid expression");
  const(0);
  junk();
  }

callfunction(ptr)   char *ptr; { /* symbol table entry or 0 */
  int nargs, const, val;
  nargs=0;
  blanks();                /* already saw open paren */
                                          /*36*/
  while(streq(lptr,")")==0) {
    if(endst()) break;
    if(ptr) {                         /*36*/
      expression(&const, &val);       /*36*/
      push();                         /*36*/
      }                               /*36*/
    else {                            /*36*/
      push();                         /*36*/
      expression(&const, &val);       /*36*/
      swapstk();                      /*36*/
      }                               /*36*/
    nargs=nargs+BPW;      /* count args*BPW */
    if (match(",")==0) break;
    }
  needtoken(")");
  if(streq(ptr+NAME, "CCARGC")==0) loadargc(nargs>>LBPW);
  if(ptr) ffcall(ptr+NAME);
  else callstk();
  csp=modstk(csp+nargs, YES);
```

}

FILE:CC33.C

```
/*
** true if val1 -> int pointer or int array and val2 not ptr or array
*/
dbltest(oper, val1, val2) int (*oper)(), val1[], val2[]; {   /*34*/
  if((oper!=ffadd) && (oper!=ffsub)) return 0;               /*34*/
  if(val1[2]!=CINT) return 0;
  if(val2[2]) return 0;
  return 1;
  }

/*
** determine type of binary operation
*/
result(lval, lval2) int lval[], lval2[]; {
  if((lval[2]!=0)&(lval2[2]!=0)) {
    lval[2]=0;
    }
  else if(lval2[2]) {
    lval[0]=lval2[0];
    lval[1]=lval2[1];
    lval[2]=lval2[2];
    }
  }

step(oper, lval) int (*oper)(), lval[]; {                    /*13*/
  if(lval[1]) {
    if(lval[5]) {
      push();
      rvalue(lval);
      (*oper)(lval[2]>>2);                                   /*13*/
      pop();
      store(lval);
      return;
      }
    else {
      move();
      lval[5]=1;
      }
    }
  rvalue(lval);
  (*oper)(lval[2]>>2);                                       /*13*/
  store(lval);
  }

store(lval)  int lval[]; {
  if(lval[1]) putstk(lval);
```

```
    else        putmem(lval);
    }

rvalue(lval) int lval[]; {
  if ((lval[0]!=0)&(lval[1]==0)) getmem(lval);
  else                           indirect(lval);
  }

test(label, parens)  int label, parens; {
  int lval[8];
  char *before, *start;
  if(parens) needtoken("(");
  while(1) {
    setstage(&before, &start);
    if(hier1(lval)) rvalue(lval);
    if(match(",")) clearstage(before, start);
    else break;
    }
  if(parens) needtoken(")");
  if(lval[3]) {  /* constant expression */
    clearstage(before, 0);
    if(lval[4]) return;
    jump(label);
    return;
    }
  if(lval[7]) {  /* stage address of "oper 0" code */
    oper=lval[6];/* operator function address */
         if((oper==ffeq)!
             (oper==ule)) zerojump(eq0, label, lval);
    else if((oper==ffne)!
             (oper==ugt)) zerojump(ne0, label, lval);
    else if (oper==ffgt) zerojump(gt0, label, lval);
    else if (oper==ffge) zerojump(ge0, label, lval);
    else if (oper==uge)  clearstage(lval[7],0);
    else if (oper==fflt) zerojump(lt0, label, lval);
    else if (oper==ult)  zerojump(ult0, label, lval);
    else if (oper==ffle) zerojump(le0, label, lval);
    else                 testjump(label);
    }
  else testjump(label);
  clearstage(before, start);
  }

constexpr(val) int *val; {
  int const;
  char *before, *start;
  setstage(&before, &start);
  expression(&const, val);
  clearstage(before, 0);  /* scratch generated code */
```

```
  if(const==0) error("must be constant expression");
  return const;
  }

const(val) int val; {
  immed();
  outdec(val);
  nl();
  }

const2(val) int val; {
  immed2();
  outdec(val);
  nl();
  }

constant(lval)  int lval[]; {
  lval=lval+3;
  *lval=1;         /* assume it will be a constant */
  if (number(++lval)) immed();
  else if (pstr(lval)) immed();
  else if (qstr(lval)) {
    *(lval-1)=0; /* nope, it's a string address */
    immed();
    printlabel(litlab);
    outbyte('+');
    }
  else return 0;
  outdec(*lval);
  nl();
  return 1;
  }

number(val)  int val[]; {
  int k, minus;
  k=minus=0;
  while(1) {
    if(match("+")) ;
    else if(match("-")) minus=1;
    else break;
    }
  if(isdigit(ch)==0)return 0;
  while (isdigit(ch)) k=k*10+(inbyte()-'0');
  if (minus) k=(-k);
  val[0]=k;
  return 1;
  }

address(ptr) char *ptr; {
```

```
    immed();
    outstr(ptr+NAME);
    nl();
    }

  pstr(val)   int val[]; {
    int k;
    k=0;
    if (match("'")==0) return 0;
    while(ch!=39)    k=(k&255)*256 + (litchar()&255);
    gch();                                                    /*24*/
    val[0]=k;
    return 1;
    }

  qstr(val)   int val[]; {
    char c;
    if (match(quote)==0) return 0;
    val[0]=litptr;
    while (ch!='"') {
      if(ch==0) break;
      stowlit(litchar(), 1);
      }
    gch();
    litq[litptr++]=0;
    return 1;
    }

  stowlit(value, size) int value, size; {
    if((litptr+size) >= LITMAX) {
      error("literal queue overflow"); abort(ERRCODE);
      }
    putint(value, litq+litptr, size);
    litptr=litptr+size;
    }

/*
** return current literal char & bump lptr
*/
litchar() {
  int i, oct;
  if((ch!=92)!(nch==0)) return gch();
  gch();
  if(ch=='n') {gch(); return NEWLINE;}          /*23*/
  if(ch=='t') {gch(); return  9;} /* HT */
  if(ch=='b') {gch(); return  8;} /* BS */
  if(ch=='f') {gch(); return 12;} /* FF */
  i=3; oct=0;
  while(((i--)>0)&(ch>='0')&(ch<='7')) oct=(oct<<3)+gch()-'0';
```

```
     if(i==2) return gch(); else return oct;
     }
```

── FILE:CC4.C

```
  /*
  ** Small-C Compiler Version 2.1
  **
  ** Copyright 1982, 1983 J. E. Hendrix
  **
  ** Part 4
  */
  #include stdio.h
  #include cc.def

  extern char
   *macn,
   *cptr, *symtab,              /*37*/
  #ifdef OPTIMIZE
   optimize,
  #endif
   *stagenext, ssname[NAMESIZE];
  extern int
   beglab,  csp, output;

  #include cc41.c
  #include cc42.c
```

── FILE:CC41.C

```
  /*
  ** print all assembler info before any code is generated
  */
  header() {
    beglab=getlabel();
                                 /*42*/
    }

  /*
  ** print any assembler stuff needed at the end
  */
  trailer() {
  #ifndef LINK
     if((beglab == 1)|(beglab > 9000)) {         /*51*/
       /* implementation dependent trailer code goes here */
       }
  #else
     char *ptr;               /*54*/
     cptr=STARTGLB;                                   /*37*/
     while(cptr<ENDGLB) {                             /*37*/
       if(cptr[IDENT]==FUNCTION && cptr[CLASS]==AUTOEXT)  /*37*/
```

```
      external(cptr+NAME);                          /*37*/
    cptr+=SYMMAX;                                   /*37*/
    }                                               /*37*/
#ifdef UPPER
  if((ptr=findglb("MAIN")) && (ptr[OFFSET]==FUNCTION)) /*54*/
#else
  if((ptr=findglb("main")) && (ptr[OFFSET]==FUNCTION)) /*54*/
#endif
    external("Ulink");  /* link to library functions *//*33*/
#endif
  ol("END");
  }

/*
** load # args before function call
*/
loadargc(val) int val; {
  if(search("NOCCARGC", macn, NAMESIZE+2, MACNEND, MACNBR, 0)==0) {
    if(val) {                   /*35*/
      ot("MVI A,");
      outdec(val);
      nl();
      }                         /*35*/
    else ol("XRA A");           /*35*/
    }
  }

/*
** declare entry point
*/
entry() {
  outstr(ssname);
  col();
#ifdef LINK
  col();                        /*28*/
#endif
  nl();
  }

/*
** declare external reference
*/
external(name) char *name; {
#ifdef LINK
  ot("EXT ");
  ol(name);
#endif
  }
```

```
/*
** fetch object indirect to primary register
*/
indirect(lval) int lval[]; {
  if(lval[1]==CCHAR) ffcall("CCGCHAR##");
  else               ffcall("CCGINT##");
  }

/*
** fetch a static memory cell into primary register
*/
getmem(lval)  int lval[]; {
  char *sym;
  sym=lval[0];
  if((sym[IDENT]!=POINTER)&(sym[TYPE]==CCHAR)) {
    ot("LDA ");
    outstr(sym+NAME);
    nl();
    ffcall("CCSXT##");
    }
  else {
    ot("LHLD ");
    outstr(sym+NAME);
    nl();
    }
  }

/*
** fetch addr of the specified symbol into primary register
*/
getloc(sym)  char *sym; {
  const(getint(sym+OFFSET, OFFSIZE)-csp);
  ol("DAD SP");
  }

/*
** store primary register into static cell
*/
putmem(lval)  int lval[]; {
  char *sym;
  sym=lval[0];
  if((sym[IDENT]!=POINTER)&(sym[TYPE]==CCHAR)) {
    ol("MOV A,L");
    ot("STA ");
    }
  else ot("SHLD ");
  outstr(sym+NAME);
  nl();
  }
```

```
/*
** put on the stack the type object in primary register
*/
putstk(lval) int lval[]; {
  if(lval[1]==CCHAR) {
    ol("MOV A,L");
    ol("STAX D");
    }
  else ffcall("CCPINT##");
  }

/*
** move primary register to secondary
*/
move() {
  ol("MOV D,H");
  ol("MOV E,L");
  }

/*
** swap primary and secondary registers
*/
swap() {
  ol("XCHG;;");   /* peephole() uses trailing ";;" */
  }

/*
** partial instruction to get immediate value
** into the primary register
*/
immed() {
  ot("LXI H,");
  }

/*
** partial instruction to get immediate operand
** into secondary register
*/
immed2() {
  ot("LXI D,");
  }

/*
** push primary register onto stack
*/
push() {
  ol("PUSH H");
  csp=csp-BPW;
  }
```

```c
/*
** unpush or pop as required
*/
smartpop(lval, start) int lval[]; char *start; {
  if(lval[5])  pop(); /* secondary was used */
  else unpush(start);
  }

/*
** replace a push with a swap
*/
unpush(dest) char *dest; {
  int i;
  char *sour;
  sour="XCHG;;";  /* peephole() uses trailing ";;" */
  while(*sour) *dest++ = *sour++;
  sour=stagenext;
  while(--sour > dest) { /* adjust stack references */
    if(streq(sour,"DAD SP")) {
      --sour;
      i=BPW;
      while(isdigit(*(--sour))) {
        if((*sour = *sour-i) < '0') {
          *sour = *sour+10;
          i=1;
          }
        else i=0;
        }
      }
    }
  csp=csp+BPW;
  }

/*
** pop stack to the secondary register
*/
pop() {
  ol("POP D");
  csp=csp+BPW;
  }

/*
** swap primary register and stack
*/
swapstk() {
  ol("XTHL");
  }

/*
```

```
** process switch statement
*/
sw() {
  ffcall("CCSWITCH##");
  }

/*
** call specified subroutine name
*/
ffcall(sname)  char *sname; {
  ot("CALL ");
  outstr(sname);
  nl();
  }

/*
** return from subroutine
*/
ffret() {
  ol("RET");
  }

/*
** perform subroutine call to value on stack
*/
callstk() {
  ffcall("CCDCAL##");                    /*36*/
  }

/*
** jump to internal label number
*/
jump(label)  int label; {
  ot("JMP ");
  printlabel(label);
  nl();
  }

/*
** test primary register and jump if false
*/
testjump(label)  int label; {
  ol("MOV A,H");
  ol("ORA L");
  ot("JZ ");
  printlabel(label);
  nl();
  }
```

```c
/*
** test primary register against zero and jump if false
*/
zerojump(oper, label, lval) int (*oper)(), label, lval[]; { /*13*/
  clearstage(lval[7], 0);  /* purge conventional code */
  (*oper)(label);                                           /*13*/
  }

/*
** define storage according to size
*/
defstorage(size) int size; {
  if(size==1) ot("DB ");
  else        ot("DW ");
  }

/*
** point to following object(s)
*/
point() {
  ol("DW $+2");
  }

/*
** modify stack pointer to value given
*/
modstk(newsp, save)  int newsp, save; {
  int k;
  k=newsp-csp;
  if(k==0)return newsp;
  if(k>=0) {
    if(k<7) {
      if(k&1) {
        ol("INX SP");
        k--;
        }
      while(k) {
        ol("POP B");
        k=k-BPW;
        }
      return newsp;
      }
    }
  if(k<0) {
    if(k>-7) {
      if(k&1) {
        ol("DCX SP");
        k++;
        }
```

```
      while(k) {
        ol("PUSH B");
        k=k+BPW;
        }
      return newsp;
      }
    }
  if(save) swap();
  const(k);
  ol("DAD SP");
  ol("SPHL");
  if(save) swap();
  return newsp;
  }

/*
** double primary register
*/
doublereg() {ol("DAD H");}
```

FILE:CC42.C

```
/*
** add primary and secondary registers (result in primary)
*/
ffadd() {ol("DAD D");}

/*
** subtract primary from secondary register (result in primary)
*/
ffsub() {ffcall("CCSUB##");}

/*
** multiply primary and secondary registers (result in primary)
*/
ffmult() {ffcall("CCMULT##");}

/*
** divide secondary by primary register
** (quotient in primary, remainder in secondary)
*/
ffdiv() {ffcall("CCDIV##");}

/*
** remainder of secondary/primary
** (remainder in primary, quotient in secondary)
*/
ffmod() {ffdiv();swap();}

/*
```

```
** inclusive "or" primary and secondary registers
** (result in primary)
*/
ffor() {ffcall("CCOR##");}

/*
** exclusive "or" the primary and secondary registers
** (result in primary)
*/
ffxor() {ffcall("CCXOR##");}

/*
** "and" primary and secondary registers
** (result in primary)
*/
ffand() {ffcall("CCAND##");}

/*
** logical negation of primary register
*/
lneg() {ffcall("CCLNEG##");}

/*
** arithmetic shift right secondary register
** number of bits given in primary register
** (result in primary)
*/
ffasr() {ffcall("CCASR##");}

/*
** arithmetic shift left secondary register
** number of bits given in primary register
** (result in primary)
*/
ffasl() {ffcall("CCASL##");}

/*
** two's complement primary register
*/
neg() {ffcall("CCNEG##");}

/*
** one's complement primary register
*/
com() {ffcall("CCCOM##");}

/*
** increment primary register by one object of whatever size
*/
```

```
inc(n) int n; {
  while(1) {
    ol("INX H");
    if(--n < 1) break;
    }
  }

/*
** decrement primary register by one object of whatever size
*/
dec(n) int n; {
  while(1) {
    ol("DCX H");
    if(--n < 1) break;
    }
  }

/*
** test for equal to
*/
ffeq()  {ffcall("CCEQ##");}

/*
** test for equal to zero
*/
eq0(label) int label; {
  ol("MOV A,H");
  ol("ORA L");
  ot("JNZ ");
  printlabel(label);
  nl();
  }

/*
** test for not equal to
*/
ffne()  {ffcall("CCNE##");}

/*
** test for not equal to zero
*/
ne0(label) int label; {
  ol("MOV A,H");
  ol("ORA L");
  ot("JZ ");
  printlabel(label);
  nl();
  }
```

```c
/*
** test for less than (signed)
*/
fflt()   {ffcall("CCLT##");}

/*
** test for less than to zero
*/
lt0(label) int label; {
  ol("XRA A");
  ol("ORA H");
  ot("JP ");
  printlabel(label);
  nl();
  }

/*
** test for less than or equal to (signed)
*/
ffle()   {ffcall("CCLE##");}

/*
** test for less than or equal to zero
*/
le0(label) int label; {
  ol("MOV A,H");
  ol("ORA L");
  ol("JZ $+8");
  ol("XRA A");
  ol("ORA H");
  ot("JP ");
  printlabel(label);
  nl();
  }

/*
** test for greater than (signed)
*/
ffgt()   {ffcall("CCGT##");}

/*
** test for greater than to zero
*/
gt0(label) int label; {
  ol("XRA A");
  ol("ORA H");
  ot("JM ");
  printlabel(label);
  nl();
```

```
  ol("ORA L");
  ot("JZ ");
  printlabel(label);
  nl();
  }

/*
** test for greater than or equal to (signed)
*/
ffge()  {ffcall("CCGE##");}

/*
** test for greater than or equal to zero
*/
ge0(label) int label; {
  ol("XRA A");
  ol("ORA H");
  ot("JM ");
  printlabel(label);
  nl();
  }

/*
** test for less than (unsigned)
*/
ult()  {ffcall("CCULT##");}

/*
** test for less than to zero (unsigned)
*/
ult0(label) int label; {
  ot("JMP ");
  printlabel(label);
  nl();
  }

/*
** test for less than or equal to (unsigned)
*/
ule()  {ffcall("CCULE##");}

/*
** test for greater than (unsigned)
*/
ugt()  {ffcall("CCUGT##");}

/*
** test for greater than or equal to (unsigned)
*/
```

```
uge() {ffcall("CCUGE##");}

#ifdef OPTIMIZE
peephole(ptr) char *ptr; {
  while(*ptr) {
    if(streq(ptr,"LXI H,0\nDAD SP\nCALL CCGINT##")) {
      if(streq(ptr+29, "XCHG;;")) {pp2();ptr=ptr+36;}
      else                        {pp1();ptr=ptr+29;}
    }
    else if(streq(ptr,"LXI H,2\nDAD SP\nCALL CCGINT##")) {
      if(streq(ptr+29, "XCHG;;")) {pp3(pp2);ptr=ptr+36;}
      else                        {pp3(pp1);ptr=ptr+29;}
    }
    else if(optimize) {
      if(streq(ptr, "DAD SP\nCALL CCGINT##")) {
        ol("CALL CCDSGI##");
        ptr=ptr+21;
      }
      else if(streq(ptr, "DAD D\nCALL CCGINT##")) {
        ol("CALL CCDDGI##");
        ptr=ptr+20;
      }
      else if(streq(ptr, "DAD SP\nCALL CCGCHAR##")) {
        ol("CALL CCDSGC##");
        ptr=ptr+22;
      }
      else if(streq(ptr, "DAD D\nCALL CCGCHAR##")) {
        ol("CALL CCDDGC##");
        ptr=ptr+21;
      }
      else if(streq(ptr,
"DAD SP\nMOV D,H\nMOV E,L\nCALL CCGINT##\nINX H\nCALL CCPINT##")) {
        ol("CALL CCINCI##");
        ptr=ptr+57;
      }
      else if(streq(ptr,
"DAD SP\nMOV D,H\nMOV E,L\nCALL CCGINT##\nDCX H\nCALL CCPINT##")) {
        ol("CALL CCDECI##");
        ptr=ptr+57;
      }
      else if(streq(ptr,
"DAD SP\nMOV D,H\nMOV E,L\nCALL CCGCHAR##\nINX H\nMOV A,L\nSTAX D")) {
        ol("CALL CCINCC##");
        ptr=ptr+59;
      }
      else if(streq(ptr,
"DAD SP\nMOV D,H\nMOV E,L\nCALL CCGCHAR##\nDCX H\nMOV A,L\nSTAX D")) {
        ol("CALL CCDECC##");
        ptr=ptr+59;
```

```
      }
    else if(streq(ptr, "DAD D\nPOP D\nCALL CCPINT##")) {
      ol("CALL CDPDPI##");
      ptr=ptr+26;
      }
    else if(streq(ptr, "DAD D\nPOP D\nMOV A,L\nSTAX D")) {
      ol("CALL CDPDPC##");
      ptr=ptr+27;
      }
    else if(streq(ptr, "POP D\nCALL CCPINT##")) {
      ol("CALL CCPDPI##");
      ptr=ptr+20;
      }
                                                    /*30*/
    /* additional optimizing logic goes here */
    else cout(*ptr++, output);
      }
    else cout(*ptr++, output);
    }
  }

pp1() {
  ol("POP H");
  ol("PUSH H");
  }

pp2() {
  ol("POP D");
  ol("PUSH D");
  }

pp3(pp) int (*pp)(); {                              /*13*/
  ol("POP B");
  (*pp)();                                          /*13*/
  ol("PUSH B");
  }
#endif
```

6
A NEW LIBRARY FOR SMALL-C

by James Hendrix and Ernest Payne

This chapter first appeared in DDJ #91 and #92 (May and June 1984). The library has since been revised. The listings printed here are of the new version, and the text of the article has been altered to accommodate the changes.

Small-C Version 2, by James Hendrix (in this volume), presented a meager function library that failed to stress compatibility with the Unix libraries. Readers quickly pointed out that shortcoming, and several people have gone on to develop their own "standard" libraries.

This chapter describes one such library that was developed jointly by the authors. It was implemented under CP/M 2.2 and provides full support for the Small-C compiler and programs it compiles. Virtually all the Unix functions that apply to foreign environments have been included. Naturally, standard files, with I/O redirection, and Unix-style command-line argument passing is supported. We chose the MACRO-80 package, from Microsoft, for the project.

Other than the arithmetic and logical library (a load module in this library), which remains essentially as Ron Cain presented it in 1980 (see "A Small-C Compiler for the 8080s," DDJ #45 or excerpt in this volume), only about 20 lines of assembly language code exist in this implementation. That makes even the low-level system functions much easier to understand, and to adapt to other environments.

We made some changes in the compiler itself with this implementation, so it has been redesignated version 2.1. Except for the library, the differences from version 2 are minor, so we only mention them in passing. They are:

1. To reduce command-line clutter, a filename in the command line (not a redirection specification) causes the compiler to output to a file having the same name but with an extension of MAC. The default input file extension is C. If more than one file is specified, they are compiled into a single program bearing the name of the first file. If no filename is given, input and output are done on the standard

input and output files, as before, and redirection may be used to change the default console assignments.

2. Undeclared functions are automatically declared to be external.

3. The syntax (*func)() for declaring pointers to functions and for calling such functions is now accepted.

4. To accommodate the MACRO-80 package, the code generating logic was changed and some functions were renamed both to avoid clashes with reserved symbols and because external names are limited to six characters.

5. Fixes and enhancements reported in DDJ by Andrew Macpherson of East Sussex, England, and Paul West of Ann Arbor, Michigan, have been applied. Several other minor fixes have been applied.

6. Calls to nonstandard functions have been replaced by standard library calls.

The Small-C Handbook by J. E. Hendrix (Reston Publishing Company, 1984) fully documents, from the user's point of view, the Small-C language and compiler, including this library. Most of the material in the section User Functions is borrowed from the book.

Library Organization

Generally, each library function is compiled and assembled separately and is then kept in a library of relocatable object modules, which we call CLIB.REL. Some functions that share common code, or are otherwise related, are grouped into a single module. Examples are printf and fprintf, and the low-level system functions found in the module CSYSLIB. At link time, L80 is directed to search CLIB.REL to resolve external references. Everything needed to support the program under CP/M is loaded and linked into the resulting COM file. Modules that are not referenced are not loaded. The minimum set of functions loaded comes to 5.5K bytes.

Since L80 does not scan backwards to find a module, the library is organized so that backward references only involve modules that are known to be loaded. Otherwise, it is arranged alphabetically. The compiler always generates an external reference to _link, which contains just

```
_link::~ext~_main
       end
```

This occurs first in the library and forces the loading of CSYSLIB, which follows. The last module in the library is CALL, the arithmetic and logical library. It is loaded last in order to establish the location of the beginning of free memory.

System Functions

The low-level system functions in the source file CSYSLIB.C are shown in Listing 6-1. The names of these functions and their global variables formerly began with the underscore character to avoid clashes with user-written function and variable names. But we found that older versions of MACRO-80 would not accept such names as external references. So the letter U, meaning "underscore," was substituted. Throughout this article the underscore still appears, although the listings that postdate the article contain the letter U.

Program Initiation and Termination

The last part of CALL contains the following code:

```
_end:   lhld    6               ;get bdos address
        sphl                    ;use for base of stack
        lxi     h,_end          ;get start of free memory
        shld    _memptr##       ;use for memory allocation
        jmp     _main##         ;parse command line, execute program
        end     _end
```

The label _end designates the end of the program and the beginning of free memory. As indicated by the last line, this is also where program execution begins. (L80 plants a jump to this address at the beginning of the user program.) This logic is executed once, and then its memory space becomes available for use by the program. The label _end (1) sets SP to the base of BDOS, thus overlaying the CCP, (2) sets _memptr to the beginning of free memory, and (3) jumps to _main (in CSYSLIB.C) to prepare for execution of the program.

The function _parse() is called by _main() to perform command-line parsing and I/O redirection. It first copies the CP/M command line into a dynamically allocated buffer and then scans it, calling _field() to isolate arguments and _redirect() to alter the assignments of stdin and stdout (appending is supported). If a redirection open fails, the program aborts after displaying the letter R for redirection error. Finally, argc and argv are pushed onto the stack and main() is called to start program execution. On return, exit() is called with a zero argument signifying successful completion. Of course, the program could call exit() directly and pass whatever error code it wishes. The error code, if it is nonzero, is written as a byte to the console. Any open files are closed and a warm start is performed.

The BDOS Interface

A bare-bones BDOS interface is provided as a function called _bdos(). It takes two arguments—first the function code to be placed in the C register, then the value to be placed in the DE register pair before calling address 5. On return, HL (the primary register for Small-C) receives the CP/M return code from the A register. This simple interface is sufficient to support the library functions. A more complete BDOS interface was described by Terje Bolstad (see "CP/M BDOS and BIOS Calls for C" in this volume). His ideas could be applied here to provide more flexibility, if that is desirable.

Memory Management

Memory is allocated in unlinked, contiguous blocks beginning at the end of the program. Each call to _alloc() allocates one block of zeroed or uninitialized memory, depending on the value of the second argument. The standard functions malloc() and calloc() call _alloc(). Memory may be deallocated by calling free() or cfree(). But care must be taken to deallocate memory in the reverse order from which it was allocated. Deallocating memory simply places a new value in _memptr and everything above that address is considered free. A function called avail() may be called to find out how much memory lies between _memptr and the stack pointer. If there is a program/stack overlap, avail() will either return zero or abort the program after displaying the letter M for memory error, as requested. Malloc() and calloc() abort this way if sufficient memory is not available.

File Management

Low-level Unix functions identify files by means of small integer values called file descriptors. By contrast, the Unix Standard I/O Library uses a pointer to a file control structure. Our library uses the file descriptor approach throughout, even though it includes functions from the Standard I/O Library. The impact of this difference is negligible if you restrict file references to the values returned by the function fopen() and the symbols stdin, stdout, and stderr (defined in the header file STDIO.H in Listing 6-1 as 0, 1, and 2, respectively). The symbol MAXFILES in CLIB.DEF determines how many files may be opened simultaneously. Seven integer arrays are dimensioned according to that value. They are:

_status[MAXFILES]	This is a bit-encoded status word indicating whether a file is open on the corresponding file descriptor; zero implies a closed condition. Separate bits authorize reading and writing, and there are bits for end-of-file and error conditions.
_device[MAXFILES]	This contains a nonzero code designating one of the CP/M logical devices when a nondisk file is opened on the corresponding file descriptor.

_fcbptr[MAXFILES]	When a disk file is first opened on a file descriptor, a standard CP/M file control block is dynamically allocated and its address is kept here. When the file is closed, the FCB is saved for reuse. Recall that the memory allocation scheme is too primitive to allow indiscriminate freeing of memory. Likewise, the program must not free memory that was allocated before a disk file is opened.
_bufptr[MAXFILES]	As with the FCB, a buffer is allocated when a disk file is opened; its address is kept here. Buffers, also, are saved when a file is closed.
_chrpos[MAXFILES]	This is an offset to the next byte to be obtained from the corresponding buffer. NOTE: The current sector of a file is maintained in the random record number field in the FCB itself, and only random CP/M reads and writes are performed.
_dirty[MAXFILES]	A nonzero value here indicates that the corresponding buffer contains new data that need to be written to disk.
_nextc[MAXFILES]	A character that has been pushed back into a file by ungetc() is kept here. The value EOF (defined in STDIO.H), since it cannot be pushed back, indicates an empty bucket.

There is no attempt to save space in these arrays, since Small-C generates significantly more code to access character values than integers. Since these arrays are small, more space would be tied up in code than would be saved by making some of them character arrays.

The function _mode() is used extensively to verify both that a file descriptor has a legal value and that the indicated file is open. If the file descriptor is valid the status of its file is returned, otherwise zero is returned.

The function _open() is called by both fopen() and freopen(). It tries to open a file on a designated file descriptor. It verifies that the first character of the mode argument is *r* (read), *w* (write), or *a* (append). If the filename is CON:, LST:, PUN:, or RDR:, it simply assigns the indicated logical device to the file descriptor and returns. Otherwise, if necessary, it allocates an FCB and a buffer for the file. It then calls _newfcb() to (1) validate the filename, (2) force it to uppercase, and (3) initialize the FCB. Finally, it calls _bdos() to open the file. In the case of read mode, the first sector (128-byte CP/M record) of the file is automatically read into the buffer. In the case of write mode, if the file already exists it is first deleted and a new one is created. In the case of append mode, if the file does not exist a new one is created. If the file does exist it is opened, then positioned at the beginning of the last block, and then read to end-of-file by repeatedly calling fgetc(). If a control-Z signals end-of-file, _chrpos is adjusted to begin writing at that position. Note that although this approach avoids reading the entire file, a character stream file is presumed and embedded control-Z characters may be missed. If + follows the mode character (for example, r+), an update mode is implied, and _status is set to allow both reading and writing. This new feature of Unix/C is documented by C. D. Perez in *A Guide to the C Library for Unix Users*. Apparently, under Unix/C, you must call fseek() or rewind() when switching between read and write operations. However, our library permits unrestricted switching between reads and writes; each operation begins with the byte following the last one transferred. Since Small-C does not yet support long integers, we do not support fseek(). Instead, cseek() provides a seek to CP/M record boundaries.

When a read detects end-of-file, the EOF bit in _status is set, thereby disabling further reads. Writes are permitted, however. The EOF bit is cleared by a successful seek or rewind operation. Opening a file in write or append mode automatically sets the EOF bit. You may extend a file either by opening in append mode or by opening in read-update mode, reading to end-of-file, and then writing.

Unix performs only binary file transfers, and the end of a file is maintained as a pointer in the directory structure. It is up to the device drivers to translate between the newline character and the carriage-return, line-feed sequence. This scheme cannot be followed under CP/M, however. First, there is no place in the CP/M file directory to store an end-of-file pointer. Then, in order to maintain ASCII file compatibility with other CP/M software, control-Z must be used to signal end-of-file, and the newline character must be translated into a carriage-return, line-feed sequence on output and vice versa on input. Therefore, it was necessary to choose a means of discriminating between byte stream (binary) and character stream (ASCII) operations. It would not have violated the intent of the C developers to specify different, non-Unix open modes for this purpose. But we preferred to retain the standard open modes and distinguish between the I/O functions instead. In our library, calls to read(), fread(), write(), and fwrite() give binary transfers. All other calls (for example, getc(), fgets(), and so on) give ASCII transfers. This makes Small-C programs upward compatible with Unix without changing the open modes.

Note that binary reads detect end-of-file only at the end of the last sector in a file. This is necessarily inconsistent with Unix, which can tie the end of a file to the byte.

Diagrammed in Figure 6-1 are the principal functions involved in I/O transfers. Lines connecting the function names illustrate the possible flow of control. All input/output requests pass through either _read() or _write(). These perform only binary data transfers, one byte at a time. The logic for character stream operations is in fgetc() and fputc() which, in turn, are called by the other character stream functions.

The functions _conin() and _conout() perform console communication. CP/M Direct Console I/O is used for all console communication. On output, this gives full control of the console device to the program. It also allows the program to reliably poll the console (by means of the function poll()) for operator input while writing data to the console. Had conventional console I/O been

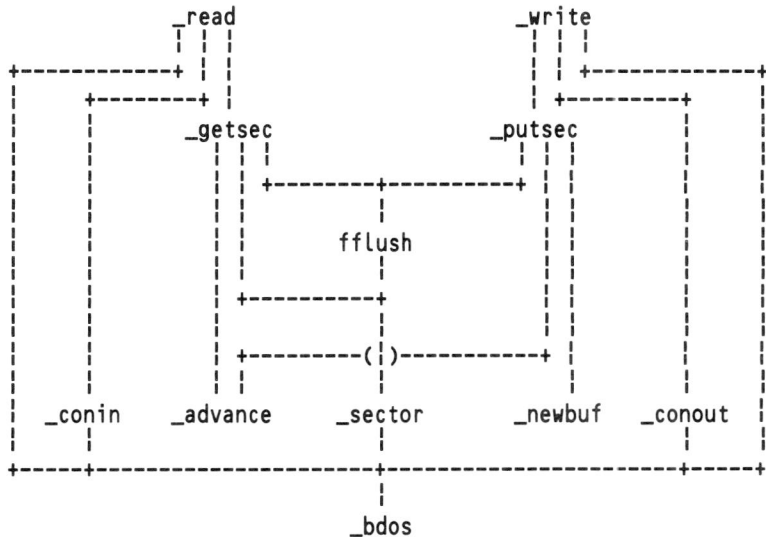

Figure 6-1. Data transfer flow of control

used, CP/M would also poll for control characters, making it a matter of chance who would get an input character. A consequence of this choice is that the customary keyboard input services (echo, rubout, and so on) had to be built into _conin() and fgets(). But, as a look at these functions will show, the cost was modest.

As their names imply, _getsec() and _putsec() transfer a sector of data between a buffer and the disk. They are called when buffers become empty or full. Getting a sector involves first flushing the buffer to disk if it contains new data. Next, the random record number (RRN) of the FCB is advanced by calling _advance(). Finally, the data is transferred by calling _sector() (which calls _bdos()). The end-of-file status is set if the attempt fails.

Writing a sector differs from reading by more than the direction of the data flow. The order of calls to _sector() and _advance() are reversed, since the RRN now describes the position in the file where the newly filled buffer should go. After transferring the data, _newbuf() is called to pad the buffer with control-Z characters in anticipation of further _write() calls.

A change to the original getsec() allowed the reading of disk directories. A directory is made to look like an ASCII file of filenames, one to a line. A directory is indicated by a drive specifier without a filename. For example, the specifier B: indicates the directory on drive B. X: indicates the default directory. Fopen() and freopen() accept these "directory" names just like any other name. Directory names may also be used when redirecting the standard input file. Directory files can only be read; writing produces an error. Isatty() answers YES to directory files, cseek() returns EOF, fflush() does nothing, and ungetc() works as usual. This feature takes up .3K bytes, which can be eliminated by deleting #define DIR in CSYSLIB.C before compiling it. We have dropped the original function dir() in favor of this more generalized (and Unix-like) approach.

User Functions

Listing 6-2 shows the source code for the user-level functions. Most of them are patterned after Unix counterparts. However, some are unique to this library and are designated as Small-C functions. Several symbols, which are defined in STDIO.H, are mentioned. They are:

```
#define stdin   0   /* fd for standard input file */
#define stdout  1   /* fd for standard output file */
#define stderr  2   /* fd for standard error file */
#define ERR    -2   /* error condition return value */
#define EOF    -1   /* end-of-file return value */
#define NULL    0   /* value of a null character */
```

In addition, the abbreviation fd refers to a file descriptor.

Input/Output Functions

```
fopen (name, mode)   char *name, *mode;
```

This function attempts to open the file indicated by the null-terminated character string at name. Mode points to a string indicating the use for which the file is to be opened. The values for mode are *r* (read), *w* (write), and *a* (append).

Read mode opens an existing file for input. Write mode either creates a new file or opens an old file and truncates it so writing will start at the beginning of the file. Append mode allows writing that begins at the end of an existing file or the beginning of a new one.

In addition, there are modes that allow file updating (both reading and writing). They are r+ (update read), w+ (update write), and a+ (update append).

These modes are the same as their nonupdate counterparts in terms of their effect at open time, but they allow switching between read() and write() modes by interleaving calls to input and output functions. Unless the program performs a seek or rewind operation, the next read or write operation begins at the point where the previous one finished. If the attempt to open a file is successful, fopen() returns an fd value for the open file; otherwise it returns NULL. That fd is then used in subsequent input/output function calls to identify the file. Only the standard files may be used without first calling fopen().

```
freopen (name, mode, fd) char *name, *mode; int fd;
```

This function closes the previously opened file indicated by fd and opens a new one whose name is in the null-terminated character string at name. Mode points to a character string indicating the open mode (same as for fopen). It returns the original value of fd on success or NULL on a failure to close the old file or to open the new one. Note, however, that since the fd for the standard input file is zero, there is no way to distinguish success from failure in that case.

```
fclose (fd)   int fd;
```

This function closes the specified file. If any new data is being held in the file's buffer, it is first written to disk. It returns NULL on success, or a nonzero value on error.

```
fgetc (fd)   int fd;   (alias getc)
```

This function returns the next character from the file indicated by *fd*. If no more characters remain in the file or an error condition occurs, it returns EOF. The end of the file is detected by an occurrence of the implementation-standard end-of-file character or the physical end of the file.

```
ungetc (c, fd)   char c;  int fd;
```

This function logically (not physically) pushes the character *c* back into the file indicated by *fd*. The next read from that file will retrieve that character first. Only one character at a time may be held in waiting. This function returns the character itself on success, or EOF if a previously pushed character is being held or if *c* has the value of EOF. You cannot push EOF into a file. Performing a seek or rewind operation on a file causes a pushed character to be forgotten.

```
getchar ()
```

This function is equivalent to fgetc (stdin).

```
fgets (str, sz, fd)   char *str; int sz, fd;
```

This function reads up to *sz-1* characters into memory from the file indicated by *fd*, starting at the address indicated by *str*. Input is terminated after transferring a newline character. A null character is appended after the newline or in the last position if newline is not found. Fgets() returns *str* for success, otherwise NULL for end-of-file or an error.

```
fread (ptr, sz, cnt, fd)   char *ptr; int sz, cnt, fd;
```

This function reads, from the file indicated by *fd*, *cnt* items of data *sz* bytes in length into memory starting at the address indicated by *ptr*. A count of the actual number of items read is returned to the caller. This might be less than *cnt* if the end of the file was encountered. This function performs a binary transfer; it does not convert carriage-return, line-feed sequences into newline characters and it has no special regard for end-of-file bytes. It recognizes only the physical end of the file. You should call feof() to determine when the data is exhausted, and ferror() to detect error conditions.

```
read (fd, ptr, cnt) int fd, cnt; char *ptr;
```

This function reads, from the file indicated by *fd*, *cnt* bytes of data into memory starting at the address indicated by *ptr*. A count of the actual number of bytes read is returned to the caller. This might be less than *cnt* if the end of the file was encountered. This function performs a binary transfer; it does not convert carriage-return, line-feed sequences into newline characters and it has no special regard for end-of-file bytes. It only recognizes the physical end of the file. You should call feof() to determine for sure when the data is exhausted, and ferror() to detect error conditions.

```
gets (str)   char *str;
```

This function reads characters into memory from stdin starting at the address indicated by str. Input is terminated when a newline character is encountered, but the newline itself is not transferred. A null character terminates the input string. Gets() returns str for success, otherwise NULL for end-of-file or an error. Since this function may transfer any amount of data, you must check the size of the input string to verify that it has not gone beyond its allotted space.

```
feof (fd) int fd;
```

This function returns a nonzero value if the file designated by fd has reached its end. Otherwise, it returns NULL.

```
ferror (fd) int fd;
```

This function returns a nonzero value if the file designated by fd has encountered an error condition since it was opened. Otherwise, it returns NULL.

```
clearerr (fd) int fd;
```

This function clears the error status for the file indicated by fd.

```
fputc (c, fd)   char c; int fd; (alias putc)
```

This function writes the character *c* to the file indicated by fd. It returns the character itself on success, otherwise EOF. If c is a new line, then a carriage-return, line-feed pair is written.

    putchar (c)   char c;

This function is equivalent to fputc (c, stdout).

    fputs (str, fd)   char *str; int fd;

This function writes characters beginning at the address indicated by *str* to the file indicated by *fd*. Each successive character is written until a null byte is found. The null byte is not written and a newline character is not appended.

    puts (str)   char *str;

This function works like fputs (str, stdout) except that it appends a new line to the output.

    fwrite (ptr, sz, cnt, fd) char *ptr; int sz, cnt, fd;

This function writes, to the file indicated by *fd*, *cnt* items of data *sz* bytes long from memory starting at the address indicated by *ptr*. It returns a count of the number of items written. An error condition may cause the number of items written to be less than *cnt*. You should call ferror() to verify error conditions, however. This function performs a binary transfer; it does not convert newline characters into carriage-return, line-feed sequences.

    write (fd, ptr, cnt) int fd, cnt; char *ptr;

This function writes, to the file indicated by *fd*, *cnt* bytes of data from memory starting at the address indicated by *ptr*. It returns a count of the number of bytes written. An error condition may cause the number of items written to be less than *cnt*. You should call ferror() to verify error conditions. however. This function performs a binary transfer; it does not convert newline characters into carriage-return, line-feed sequences.

    fflush (fd)   int fd;

This function forces any system-buffered changes out to the file. Ordinarily, data written to a disk file is held in a memory buffer until (1) the buffer becomes full, (2) the buffer space is needed to hold a different sector of data from the disk, or (3) a close of the file is performed. Fclose() calls this function. Fflush() returns NULL on success or EOF on error.

    cseek (fd, offset, from) int fd, offset, from;

This Small-C function positions the file indicated by *fd* to the beginning of the 128-byte record that is *offset* positions from the first record, current record, or end of file depending on whether *from* is 0, 1, or 2 respectively. Subsequent reads and writes proceed from that point. It returns NULL for success, otherwise EOF.

```
rewind (fd) int fd;
```

This function positions the file indicated by *fd* to its beginning. It is equivalent to a seek to the first byte of the file. It returns NULL on success, otherwise EOF.

```
ctell (fd) int fd;
```

This Small-C function returns the position of the current record of the file indicated by *fd*. The returned value is the offset of the current 128-byte record with respect to the first record of the file. If *fd* is not assigned to a disk file, -1 is returned.

```
unlink (name)   char *name; (alias delete)
```

This function deletes the file indicated by the null-terminated character string at *name*. It returns NULL on success, otherwise ERR.

```
rename (old, new) char *old, *new;
```

This Small-C function changes the name of the file specified by *old* to the name indicated by *new*. It returns NULL on success, otherwise ERR.

```
auxbuf (fd, size) int fd, size;
```

This Small-C function allocates an auxiliary buffer of *size* bytes for *fd*. It returns zero on success and ERR on failure, *fd* must be open, and *size* must be greater than zero and less than the amount of free memory. If *fd* is a device, the buffer is allocated but ignored. Extra buffering is useful in reducing disk head movement or drive switching during sequential operations. Once an auxiliary buffer is allocated it sticks for the duration of program execution, even if *fd* is closed. Calling this function a second time for the same *fd* returns ERR, but otherwise has no effect. Alternating read and write operations or performing seeks will produce unpredictable results. Ungetc() will operate normally, however. Ordinarily, it is counterproductive to allocate auxiliary buffers to both input and output files.

```
iscons (fd) int fd;
```

This Small-C function returns a nonzero value if *fd* is assigned to the console, otherwise NULL.

```
isatty (fd) int fd;
```

This function returns a nonzero value if *fd* is assigned to a device rather than a disk file, otherwise NULL.

Formatted Input/Output Functions

```
printf(str, arg1, arg2, ...) char *str;
```

This function writes to the standard output file a formatted character string consisting of the null-terminated character array at *str* laced at specified points with the character-string equivalents of the arguments

```
arg1, arg2 ...
```

It returns a count of the total number of characters written. The string at *str* is called a control string. It is required, but the other arguments are optional. The control string contains ordinary characters and groups of characters called conversion specifications. Each conversion specification informs printf() how to convert the corresponding argument into a character string for output. The converted argument replaces its conversion specification in the output. The character % signals the start of a conversion specification, and one of the letters b, c, d, o, s, u, or x ends it.

Between these may be found, in the order listed and with no intervening blanks, a minus sign (-), a decimal integer constant (nnn), and/or a decimal fraction (.mmm). These subfields are all optional. In fact, you frequently see conversion specifications with none of them. The minus sign indicates that the string, produced by applying a specified conversion to its argument, is to be left-adjusted in its field in the output.

The decimal integer indicates the minimum width of that field (in characters). If more space is needed it will be used, but at least the number of positions indicated will be generated. The decimal fraction is used where the argument being converted is itself a character string (more correctly, the address of a character string). In this case the decimal fraction indicates how many characters maximum to take from the string. If there is no decimal fraction in the specification, then all of the string is used.

The terminating letter indicates the type of conversion to be applied to the argument. It may be one of the following:

- b The argument should be considered an unsigned integer and converted to *binary* format for output. No leading zeroes are generated. This specification is unique to Small-C and should be used with that in mind.

- c This argument should be output as a *character* without any conversion. In that case, the high-order byte will be ignored.

- d The argument should be considered a signed integer and converted to a (possibly signed) *decimal* digit string for output. No leading zeroes are generated. The sign is the left-most character; it is blank for positive and "-" for negative.

o   The argument should be considered an unsigned integer and converted to *octal* format for output. No leading zeroes are generated.

s   The argument is the address of a null-terminated character *string* that should be output as is but subject to the justification, minimum width, and maximum size specifications indicated.

u   The argument should be considered an *unsigned* integer and converted to an unsigned decimal character string for output. No leading zeroes are generated.

x   The argument should be considered an unsigned integer and converted to *hexadecimal* format for output. No leading zeroes are generated.

If % is followed by anything other than a valid specification, it is ignored and the next character is written without change. So %% writes %.

Printf() scans the control string from left to right sending everything to stdout until it finds a % character. It then evaluates the following conversion specification and applies it to the first argument (following the control string). The resultant string is written to stdout. It then resumes writing data from the control string until it finds another conversion specification; it applies that one to the second argument. The procedure continues until the control string is exhausted. The result is a formatted output message consisting of both literal and variable data.

```
fprintf(fd, str, arg1, arg2, ...) int fd; char *str;
```

This function works like printf() except that output goes to the file indicated by *fd*.

```
scanf(str, arg1, arg2, ...) char *str;
```

This function reads a series of fields from the standard input file, converts them to internal format according to conversion specifications contained in the control string *str*, and stores them at the locations indicated by the arguments:

```
arg1, arg2, ...
```

It returns a count of the number of fields read. A field in the input stream is a contiguous string of graphic characters. It ends with the next white-space character (blank, tab, or newline) or, if its conversion specification indicates a maximum field width, it ends when the field width is exhausted. A field normally begins with the first graphic character after the previous field; that is, leading white space is skipped. Since the newline character is skipped while searching for the next field, scanf() reads as many input lines as required to satisfy the number of conversion specifications in its control string. Each of the arguments following the control string must yield an address value.

The control string contains conversion specifications and white space (which is ignored). Each conversion specification informs scanf() how to convert the corresponding field into interal format, and each argument following *str* indicates the address where the corresponding converted field is to be stored. The character % signals the start of a conversion specification and one of the letters b, c, d, o, s, u, or x ends it.

Between these may be found, with no intervening blanks, an asterisk and/or a decimal integer constant. These subfields are both optional. In fact, conversion specifications frequently include neither of them. The asterisk indicates that the corresponding field in the input stream is to be skipped. Skip specifications do not have corresponding arguments. The numeric field indicates the maximum field width in characters. If present, it causes the field to be terminated when the indicated number of characters has been scanned, even if no white space is found. However, if a white-space character is found before the field width is exhausted, the field is terminated at that point.

The terminating letter indicates the type of conversion to be applied to the field. It may be one of the following:

- b The field should be considered a *binary* integer and converted to an integer value. The corresponding argument should be an integer address. Leading zeroes are ignored. This specification is unique to Small-C and should be used with that in mind.

- c The field should be accepted as a single *character* without any conversion. This specification inhibits the normal skip over white-space characters. The argument for such a field should be a character address.

- d The input field should be considered a (possibly signed) *decimal* integer and converted into an integer value. The corresponding argument should be an integer address. Leading zeroes are ignored.

- o The field should be considered an *octal* integer and converted to an integer value. The corresponding argument should be an integer address. Leading zeroes are ignored.

- s The field should be considered a character *string* and stored with a null terminator at the character address indicated by its argument. There must be enough space at that address to hold the string and its terminator. Remember, you can specify a maximum field width to prevent overflow. The specification %1s will read the next graphic character, whereas %c will read the next character, whatever it is.

- u The field should be considered an *unsigned* decimal integer and converted to an integer value. The corresponding argument should be an integer address. Leading zeroes are ignored. This specification is unique to Small-C and should be used with that in mind.

- x The field should be considered a *hexadecimal* number and converted to an integer value. The corresponding argument should be an integer address. Leading zeroes or a leading 0x or 0X will be ignored.

Scanf() scans the control string from left to right, processing input fields until the control string is exhausted or a field is found that does not match its conversion specification. If the value returned by scanf() is less than the number of conversion specifications, an error has occurred or the end of the input file has been reached. EOF is returned if no fields are processed because end-of-file has been reached.

```
fscanf(fd, str, arg1, arg2, ...) int fd; char *str;
```

This function works like scanf() except that the input is taken from the file indicated by *fd*.

Format Conversion Functions

```
atoi(str) char *str;
```

This function converts the decimal number represented by the string at *str* to an integer, and returns its value. Leading white space is skipped and an optional sign (+ or -) may precede the left-most digit. The first non-numeric character terminates the conversion.

```
atoib(str, base) char *str; int base;
```

This Small-C function converts the unsigned integer of radix *base* represented by the string at *str* to an integer, and returns its value. Leading white space is skipped. The first non-numeric character terminates the conversion.

```
itoa(nbr, str) int nbr; char *str;
```

This function converts the number *nbr* to its decimal character-string representation at *str*. The result is left-justified at *str* with a leading minus sign if *nbr* is negative. A null character terminates the string, which must be large enough to hold the result.

```
itoab(nbr, str, base) int nbr; char *str; int base;
```

This Small-C function converts the unsigned integer *nbr* to its character-srting representation at *str* in radix *base*. The result is left-justified at *str*. A null character terminates the string, which must be large enough to hold the result.

```
dtoi(str, nbr) char *str; int *nbr;
```

This Small-C function converts the (possibly) signed decimal number in the character string at *str* to an integer at *nbr* and returns the length of the numeric field found. The conversion stops when it finds the end of the string or any illegal numeric character. Working with 16-bit integers, a leading sign and five digits at most will be used. Dtoi() returns ERR if the absolute value of the number exceeds 32767.

```
otoi(str, nbr) char *str; int *nbr;
```

This Small-C function converts the octal number in the character string at *str* to an integer at *nbr* and returns the length of the octal field found. It stops when it encounters a non-octal digit in *str*. Working with 16-bit integers, six digits at most will be used. An octal number larger than 177777 causes otoi() to return ERR.

```
utoi(str, nbr) char *str; int *nbr;
```

This Small-C function converts the unsigned decimal number represented by the character string at *str* to an integer at *nbr* and returns the length of the numeric field found. It stops when it encounters the end of the string or any nondecimal character. Working with 16-bit integers, five digits at most will be used. A number larger than 65535 causes utoi() to return ERR.

```
xtoi(str, nbr) char *str; int *nbr;
```

This Small-C function converts the hexadecimal number in the character string at *str* to an integer at *nbr* and returns the length of the hexadecimal field found. It stops when it encounters a nonhexadecimal digit in *str*. Working with 16-bit integers, four digits at most will be used. If more digits are present, xtoi() returns ERR.

```
itod(nbr, str, sz) int nbr, sz; char *str;
```

This Small-C function converts *nbr* to a signed (if negative) character string at *str*. The result is right-justified and blank-filled in *str*. The sign and possibly high order digits are truncated if the destination string is too small. It returns *str*. *Sz* indicates the length of the string. If *sz* is greater than zero, a null byte is placed at str[sz-1]. If *sz* is zero, a search for the first null byte following *str* locates the end of the string. If *sz* is less than zero, all *sz* characters of *str* are used including the last one.

```
itoo(nbr, str, sz) int nbr, sz; char *str;
```

This Small-C function converts *nbr* to an octal character string at *str*. The result is right-justified and blank-filled in the destination string. High order digits are truncated if the destination string is too small. It returns str. Sz indicates the length of the string. If *sz* is greater than zero, a null byte is placed at str[sz-1]. If *sz* is zero, a search for the first null byte following *str* locates the end of the string. If *sz* is less than zero, all *sz* characters of *str* are used including the last one.

```
itou(nbr, str, sz) int nbr, sz; char *str;
```

This Small-C function converts *nbr* to an unsigned decimal character string at *str*. It works like itod() except that the high order bit of *nbr* is taken for a magnitude bit.

```
itox(nbr, str, sz) int nbr, sz; char *str;
```

This Small-C function converts *nbr* to a hexadecimal character string at *str*. The result is right-justified and blank-filled in the destination string. High order digits are truncated if the destination string is too small. It returns *str*. *Sz* indicates the length of the string. If *sz* is greater than zero, a null byte is placed at str[sz-1]. If *sz* is zero, a search for the first null byte following *str* locates the end of the string. If *sz* is less than zero, all *sz* characters of *str* are used including the last one.

String Handling Functions

```
left(str) char *str;
```

This Small-C function left-adjusts the character string at *str*. Starting with the first non-blank character and proceeding through the null terminator, the string is moved to the address indicated by *str*.

```
pad (str, ch, n) char *str, ch; int n;
```

This Small-C function fills the string at *str* with *n* occurrences of the character *ch*.

```
reverse(str) char *str;
```

This function reverses the order of the characters in the null terminated string at *str*.

```
strcat(dest, sour) char *dest, *sour;
```

This function appends the string at *sour* to the end of the string at *dest*. The null character at the end of *dest* is replaced by the leading character of *sour*. A null character terminates the new *dest* string. The space reserved for *dest* must be large enough to hold the result. This function returns *dest*.

```
strncat(dest, sour, n) char *dest, *sour; int n;
```

This function works like strcat() except that a maximum of *n* characters from the source string will be transferred to the destination string.

```
strcmp(str1, str2)  char *str1, *str2;
```

This function returns an integer less than, equal to, or greater than zero depending on whether the string at *str1* is less than, equal to, or greater than the string at *str2*. Character-by-character comparisons are made starting at the left end of the strings until a difference is found. Comparison is based on the numeric values of the characters. *Str2* is considered less than *str1* if *str2* is equal to but shorter than *str1*, and vice versa.

    lexcmp(str1, str2) char *str1, *str2;

This Small-C function works like strcmp() except that a lexicographical comparison is used. For meaningful results, only characters in the ASCII character set (0 - 127 decimal) should appear in the strings. Alphabetics are compared in dictionary order, with uppercase letters matching their lowercase equivalents. Special characters precede the alphabetics and are themselves preceded by the control characters, except DEL, which compares highest.

    strncmp(str1, str2, n) char *str1, *str2; int n;

This function works like strcmp() except that a maximum of *n* characters are compared.

    strcpy(dest, sour) char *dest, *sour;

This function copies the string at *sour* to *dest*. *Dest* is returned. The space at *dest* must be large enough to hold the string at *sour*.

    strncpy(dest, sour, n) char *dest, *sour; int n;

This function works like strcpy() except that *n* characters are placed in the destination string regardless of the length of the source string. If the source string is too short, null padding occurs. If it is too long, it is truncated in *dest*. A null character follows the last character placed in the destination string.

    strlen(str) char *str;

This function returns a count of the number of characters in the string at *str*. It does not count the null character that terminates the string.

    strchr(str, c) char *str, c;

This function returns a pointer to the first occurrence of the character *c* in the string at *str*. It returns NULL if the character is not found. Searching ends with the first null character.

    strrchr(str, c) char *str, c;

This function works like strchr() except that the right-most occurrence of the character is sought.

Character Classification Functions

The following functions determine whether a character belongs to a designated class of characters. They return true (nonzero) if it does and false (zero) if it does not.

```
isalnum(c) char c;
```

This function determines if *c* is alphanumeric (A-Z, a-z, or 0-9).

```
isalpha(c) char c;
```

This function determines if *c* is alphabetic (A-Z or a-z).

```
isascii(c) char c;
```

This function determines if *c* is an ASCII character (decimal values 0-127).

```
iscntrl(c) char c;
```

This function determines if *c* is a control character (ASCII codes 0-31 or 127).

```
isdigit(c) char c;
```

This function determines if *c* is a digit (0-9).

```
isgraph(c) char c;
```

This function determines if *c* is a graphic symbol (ASCII codes 33-126).

```
islower(c) char c;
```

This function determines if *c* is a lowercase letter (ASCII codes 97-122).

```
isprint(c) char c;
```

This function determines if *c* is a printable character (ASCII codes 32-126). Spaces are considered printable.

```
ispunct(c) char c;
```

This function determines if *c* is a punctuation character (all ASCII codes except control characters and alphanumeric characters).

`isspace(c) char c;`

This function determines if c is a white-space character (ASCII SP, HT, VT, CR, LF, or FF).

`isupper(c) char c;`

This function determines if c is an uppercase letter (ASCII codes 65-90).

`isxdigit(c) char c;`

This function determines if c is a hexadecimal digit (0-9, A-F, or a-f).

`lexorder(c1, c2) char c1, c2;`

This Small-C function returns an integer less than, equal to, or greater than zero depending on whether c1 is less than, equal to, or greater than c2 lexicographically. For meaningful results, only characters in the ASCII character set (0 - 127 decimal) should be passed. Alphabetics are compared in dictionary order, with uppercase letters matching their lowercase equivalents. Special characters precede the alphabetics and are themselves preceded by the control characters, except DEL, which compares highest.

Character Translation Functions

`toascii(c) char c;`

This function returns the ASCII equivalent of c. In systems that use the ASCII character set, it merely returns c unchanged. This function makes it possible to use the properties of the ASCII code set without introducing implementation dependencies into programs.

`tolower(c) char c;`

This function returns the lowercase equivalent of c if c is an uppercase letter; otherwise, it returns c unchanged.

`toupper(c) char c;`

This function returns the uppercase equivalent of c if c is a lowercase letter; otherwise, it returns c unchanged.

Mathematical Functions

    abs(nbr)   int nbr;

This function returns the absolute value of *nbr*.

    sign(nbr)   int nbr;

This function returns -1, 0, or +1 depending on whether *nbr* is less than, equal to, or greater than zero.

Program-Control Functions

    calloc(nbr, sz) int nbr, sz;

This function allocates nbr*sz bytes of zeroed memory. It returns the address of the memory block on success, otherwise zero.

    malloc(nbr) int nbr;

This function allocates *nbr* bytes of uninitialized memory. It returns the address of the memory block on success, otherwise zero.

    avail(abort) int abort;

This Small-C function returns the number of bytes of free memory available between the program and the stack. It also checks to see if the stack overlaps allocated memory; if so and if abort is not zero, the program is aborted and the console displays the letter *M* to indicate that a memory error has occurred. However, if abort is zero, avail() returns zero to the caller. This function makes it possible to make full use of all available memory. However, care should be taken to leave enough space for the stack to use.

    free(addr) char *addr; (alias cfree)

This function frees up a block of allocated memory beginning at *addr*. It returns *addr* on success, otherwise NULL. It is necessary to free memory in the reverse order from which it was allocated. Freeing memory that was allocated before opening a file should be avoided, since the open function dynamically allocates buffer and FCB space. You should not assume that closing a file relinquishes its space.

    getarg(nbr, str, sz, argc, argv) char *str;
                int nbr, sz, argc, *argv;

This Small-C function locates the command-line argument indicated by *nbr*, moves it (null-terminated) to the string *str* of maximum size *sz*, and returns the length of the field obtained. *Argc* and *argv* must be the same values provided to the function main() when the program is started. If *nbr* is zero, the program name is requested. If it is one, the first argument following the program name is requested, and so on. CP/M does not deliver the program name to a program, so an asterisk is substituted in its place. If no argument corresponds to *nbr*, getarg() puts a null byte at *str* and returns EOF.

```
poll(pause) int pause;
```

This Small-C function polls the console for operator input. If no input is pending, zero is returned. If a character is waiting, the value of pause determines what happens. If pause is zero, the character is returned immediately. If pause is not zero and the character is a control-*S*, there is a pause in program execution; when the next character is entered from the keyboard, zero is returned to the caller. If the character is a control-C, program execution is terminated. All other characters are returned to the caller immediately.

```
exit(errcode)   int errcode;              (alias abort)
```

This function closes all open files and returns to the operating system. If errcode is not zero, it is written to the console; a program that exits with a control-*G* (bell), for instance, would sound the console beeper.

Conclusion

No doubt the Small-C compiler and its library will continue to develop as more people with access to the source code take an interest in it and report their developments. Some obvious areas for improvement in the library are:

1. Achieving a better memory allocation scheme that would permit allocation and deallocation operations to be performed in any order.

2. Adapting this implementation to other CPUs and operating systems; this library should be especially portable to other environments because it is written in C and, to the authors at least, the logic is easy to follow.

3. Improving the efficiency. No doubt there are many ways in which this code can be made smaller and faster. We hope, however, that these efforts would not obscure the simplicity and transparency of logic.

We would like to express our appreciation to Ron Cain, who started the ball rolling in 1980, and to *Dr. Dobb's Journal* for its continued support of Small-C.

Availability

This version of the Small-C library is copyrighted; nevertheless, it is available to the general public for use without formal restrictions. Take it, use it, copy it, modify it, and give it away as you please. However, be sure to preserve the copyright notices. I am distributing Small-C with this library under the user-supported concept, so if you obtain a "free" copy and find it useful, send a registration form and $20 to the author. You must obtain written permission to sell Small-C or its library for more than your actual cost for media, packaging, and postage.

LISTING 6-1

FILE:STDIO.H

```
/*
** STDIO.H -- Standard Small-C Definitions
**
** Copyright 1984   L. E. Payne and J. E. Hendrix
*/
#define stdin    0
#define stdout   1
#define stderr   2
#define ERR     (-2)
#define EOF     (-1)
#define YES      1
#define NO       0
#define NULL     0
#define CR      13
#define LF      10
#define BELL     7
#define SPACE   ' '
#define NEWLINE LF        /*23*/ /*45*/
```

FILE:CLIB.DEF

```
/*
** CLIB.DEF -- Definitions for Small-C library functions.
**
** Copyright 1983   L. E. Payne and J. E. Hendrix
**
** Credits:
** 1) This library of Small-C functions was produced
**    jointly by:
**
**    Ernest Payne
**    1331 W. Whispering Hills Drive
**    Tucson, AZ   85704
**
**    and
**
**    James E. Hendrix
**    Box 8378
**    University, MS   38677-8378
**
** 2) The function Ubdos() is an adaption of
**    Gene Cotton's work reported by Ron Cain (DDJ #48).
**
** 3) The functions Uparse(), Ufield(), and Uredirect()
**    are a revision of Jan-Henrik Johansson's setarg()
**    (DDJ #74), and getarg() is a modification of his
**    revision of James Hendrix' function (DDJ #75).
```

```
**
** 4) The standard C functions were obtained from
**    "A Guide to the C Library for UNIX Users"
**    by C. D. Perez of Bell Laboratories.
**
*/

/*
** Definition of CP/M FCB and additional parameters
*/
#define FCBSIZE    36   /* size of file control block */
#define DRIVE       0   /* CP/M drive designator offset */
#define NAMEOFF     1   /* CP/M file name offset */
#define NAMEOFF2   16   /* CP/M 2nd file name offset */
#define NAMESIZE    8   /* CP/M file name size */
#define TYPEOFF     9   /* CP/M file type offset */
#define TYPESIZE    3   /* CP/M file type size */
#define NTSIZE     11   /* CP/M file name & type size */
#define RRNOFF     33   /* CP/M random record number offset */
#define CPMEOF     26   /* CP/M end-of-file byte */
#define BUFSIZE   128   /* size of I/O buffer */
#define MAXFILES   10   /* maximum open files */
/*
** CP/M function calls
*/
#define CLOFIL     16   /* close file */
#define DCONIO      6   /* direct console i/o */
#define DELFIL     19   /* delete file */
#define FNDFIL     17   /* find first occurrence of a file */
#define FNDNXT     18   /* find next occurrence of a file */
#define GETPOS     36   /* get number of current sector */
#define GOCPM      00   /* go to CP/M */
#define LSTOUT     05   /* list output */
#define MAKFIL     22   /* make file */
#define OPNFIL     15   /* open file */
#define POSEND     35   /* position file to end */
#define PUNOUT     04   /* punch output */
#define RENAME     23   /* rename file */
#define RDRND      33   /* read sector randomly */
#define RDRINP     03   /* reader input */
#define SETDMA     26   /* set dma */
#define WRTRND     40   /* write sector randomly */
/*
** Device codes
*/
#define CPMCON DCONIO /* console */
#define CPMRDR RDRINP /* reader  */
#define CPMPUN PUNOUT /* punch   */
#define CPMLST LSTOUT /* list    */
```

```
/*
** File status bits
*/
#define RDBIT     1   /* open for read */
#define WRTBIT    2   /* open for write */
#define EOFBIT    4   /* eof condition */
#define ERRBIT    8   /* error condition */
/*
** ASCII characters
*/
#define ABORT   3
#define RUB     8
#define PAUSE  19
#define WIPE   24
#define DEL   127
```

---------- **FILE:CSYSLIB.C**

```
/*
** CSYSLIB -- System-Level Library Functions
**
** Copyright 1984  L. E. Payne and J. E. Hendrix
*/

#include stdio.h
#include clib.def
#define NOCCARGC      /* no argument count passing */
#define DIR           /* compile directory option */

/*
****************** System Variables ********************
*/

int
 *Uauxsz,            /* addr of Uxsize[] in AUXBUF */
  Uauxin,            /* addr of Uxinit() in AUXBUF */      /*58*/
  Uauxrd,            /* addr of Uxread() in AUXBUF */
  Uauxwt,            /* addr of Uxwrite() in AUXBUF */
  Uauxfl,            /* addr of Uxflush() in AUXBUF */

  Ucnt=1,            /* arg count for main */
  Uvec[20],          /* arg vectors for main */

  Ustatus[MAXFILES] = {RDBIT, WRTBIT, RDBIT|WRTBIT},
                     /* status of respective file */
  Udevice[MAXFILES] = {CPMCON, CPMCON, CPMCON},
                     /* non-disk device assignments */
  Unextc[MAXFILES]  = {EOF, EOF, EOF},
                     /* pigeonhole for ungetc bytes */
  Ufcbptr[MAXFILES], /* FCB pointers for open files */
```

```
  Ubufptr[MAXFILES], /* buffer pointers for files */
  Uchrpos[MAXFILES], /* character position in buffer */
  Udirty[MAXFILES];  /* "true" if changed buffer */

char
 *Umemptr,           /* pointer to free memory. */
  Uarg1[]="*";       /* first arg for main */

/*
*************** System-Level Functions *****************
*/

/*
** -- Process Command Line, Execute main(), and Exit to CP/M
*/
Umain() {
  Uparse();
  main(Ucnt,Uvec);
  exit(0);
  }

/*
** Parse command line and setup argc and argv.
*/
Uparse() {
  char *count, *ptr;
  count = 128;   /* CP/M command buffer address */
  ptr = Ualloc((count = *count&255)+1, YES);       /*65*/
  strncpy(ptr, 129, count);                        /*65*/
  Uvec[0]=Uarg1;                            /* first arg = "*" */
  while (*ptr) {
    if(isspace(*ptr)) {++ptr; continue;}
    switch(*ptr) {
      case '<': ptr = Uredirect(ptr, "r", stdin);
                continue;
      case '>': if(*(ptr+1) == '>')
                    ptr = Uredirect(ptr+1, "a", stdout);
                else ptr = Uredirect(ptr,   "w", stdout);
                continue;
      default:  if(Ucnt < 20) Uvec[Ucnt++] = ptr;
                ptr = Ufield(ptr);
      }
    }
  }

/*
** Isolate next command-line field.
*/
Ufield(ptr) char *ptr; {
```

```
  while(*ptr) {
    if(isspace(*ptr)) {
      *ptr = NULL;
      return (++ptr);
      }
    ++ptr;
    }
  return (ptr);
  }

/*
** Redirect stdin or stdout.
*/
Uredirect(ptr, mode, std)  char *ptr, *mode; int std; {
  char *fn;
  fn = ++ptr;
  ptr = Ufield(ptr);
  if(Uopen(fn, mode, std)==ERR) exit('R');
  return (ptr);
  }

/*
** ------------ File Open
*/

/*
** Open file on specified fd.
*/
Uopen(fn, mode, fd) char *fn, *mode; int fd; {
  char *fcb;
  if(!strchr("rwa", *mode)) return (ERR);
  Unextc[fd] = EOF;
  if(Uauxin) Uauxin(fd);                    /*58*/
  if(strcmp(fn,"CON:")==0) {
    Udevice[fd]=CPMCON; Ustatus[fd]=RDBIT|WRTBIT; return (fd);
    }
  if(strcmp(fn,"RDR:")==0) {
    Udevice[fd]=CPMRDR; Ustatus[fd]=RDBIT;  return (fd);
    }
  if(strcmp(fn,"PUN:")==0) {
    Udevice[fd]=CPMPUN; Ustatus[fd]=WRTBIT; return (fd);
    }
  if(strcmp(fn,"LST:")==0) {
    Udevice[fd]=CPMLST; Ustatus[fd]=WRTBIT; return (fd);
    }
  if(fcb = Ufcbptr[fd]) pad(fcb, NULL, FCBSIZE);
  else {
    if((fcb = Ufcbptr[fd] = Ualloc(FCBSIZE, YES)) == NULL
         || (Ubufptr[fd] = Ualloc(BUFSIZE, YES)) == NULL)
```

```
        return (ERR);
      }
    pad(Ubufptr[fd], CPMEOF, BUFSIZE);
    Udirty[fd] = Udevice[fd] = Uchrpos[fd] = 0;
#ifdef DIR
    if(fn[1] == ':' && fn[2] == NULL) {   /* directory file */
      pad(fcb, NULL, FCBSIZE);
      pad(fcb+NAMEOFF, '?', NTSIZE);
      if(toupper(fn[0]) != 'X') *fcb = toupper(fn[0]) - 64;
      Uchrpos[fd] = BUFSIZE;
      Udevice[fd] = FNDFIL;
      Ustatus[fd] = RDBIT;
      return (fd);
      }
#endif
    if(!Unewfcb(fn,fcb)) return (ERR);
    switch(*mode) {
      case 'r': {
        if(Ubdos(OPNFIL,fcb)==255) return (ERR);
        Ustatus[fd] =  RDBIT;
        if(Usector(fd,  RDRND)) Useteof(fd);
        break;
        }
      case 'w': {
        if(Ubdos(FNDFIL,fcb)!=255) Ubdos(DELFIL,fcb);
      create:
        if(Ubdos(MAKFIL,fcb)==255) return (ERR);
        Ustatus[fd] = EOFBIT|WRTBIT;
        break;
        }
      default: {       /* append mode */
        if(Ubdos(OPNFIL,fcb)==255) goto create;
        Ustatus[fd] = RDBIT;
        cseek(fd, -1, 2);
        while(fgetc(fd)!=EOF) ;
        Ustatus[fd] = EOFBIT|WRTBIT;
        }
      }
    if(*(mode+1)=='+') Ustatus[fd] |= RDBIT|WRTBIT;
    return (fd);
    }

/*
** Create CP/M file control block from file name.
** Entry: fn = Legal CP/M file name (null terminated)
**             May be prefixed by letter of drive.
**        fcb = Pointer to memory space for CP/M fcb.
** Returns the pointer to the fcb.
*/
```

```
Unewfcb(fn, fcb) char *fn, *fcb; {
  char *fnptr;
  pad(fcb+1, SPACE, NTSIZE);
  if(*(fn + 1) == ':') {
    *fcb = toupper(*fn) - 64;
    fnptr = fn + 2;
    }
  else fnptr = fn;
  if(*fnptr == NULL) return (NO);
  fnptr = Uloadfn(fcb + NAMEOFF, fnptr, NAMESIZE);
  if(*fnptr == '.') ++fnptr;
  else if(*fnptr) return (NO);
  fnptr = Uloadfn(fcb + TYPEOFF, fnptr, TYPESIZE);
  if(*fnptr) return (NO);
  return (YES);
  }

/*
** Load into fcb and validate file name.
*/
Uloadfn(dest, sour, max) char *dest, *sour; int max; {
  while(*sour && !strchr("<>.,;:=?*[]", *sour)) {
    if(max--) *dest++ = toupper(*sour++);
    else break;
    }
  return (sour);
  }

/*
** ----------- File Input
*/

/*
** Binary-stream input of one byte from fd.
*/
Uread(fd) int fd; {
  char *bufloc;
  int ch;
  switch (Umode(fd)) {
    default: Useterr(fd); return (EOF);
    case RDBIT:
    case RDBIT!WRTBIT:
    }
  if((ch = Unextc[fd]) != EOF) {
    Unextc[fd] = EOF;
    return (ch);
    }
  switch(Udevice[fd]) {
    /* PUN & LST can't occur since they are write moce */
```

```c
      case CPMCON: return (Uconin());
      case CPMRDR: return (Ubdos(RDRINP,NULL));
      default:
          if(Uauxsz && Uauxsz[fd]) return (Uauxrd(fd));
          if(Uchrpos[fd]>=BUFSIZE && !Ugetsec(fd))
            return (EOF);
          bufloc = Ubufptr[fd] + Uchrpos[fd]++;
          return (*bufloc);
    }
  }

/*
** Console character input.
*/
Uconin() {
  int ch;
  while(!(ch = Ubdos(DCONIO, 255))) ;
  switch(ch) {
    case ABORT: exit(0);
    case    LF:
    case    CR: Uconout(LF); return (Uconout(CR));
    case    DEL: ch = RUB;
       default: if(ch < 32) { Uconout('^'); Uconout(ch+64);}
                else Uconout(ch);
                return (ch);
    }
  }

/*
** Read one sector from fd.
*/
Ugetsec(fd) int fd; {
#ifdef DIR
  if(Udevice[fd]) {         /* directory file */
    char *bp, *name, *type, *end;
    Ubdos(SETDMA, 128);
    if((name = Ubdos(Udevice[fd], Ufcbptr[fd])) == 255) {
      Useteof(fd);
      return (NO);
      }
    Udevice[fd] = FNDNXT;
    name = (name << 5) + (128 + NAMEOFF);
    type = name + NAMESIZE;
    end = name + NTSIZE;
    bp = Ubufptr[fd] + BUFSIZE;
    *--bp = CR;
    while(--end >= name) { /* put filename at end of buffer */
      if(*end == SPACE) continue;
      *--bp = *end;
```

```
      if(end == type) *--bp = '.';
      }
    Uchrpos[fd] = bp - Ubufptr[fd];
    return (YES);
    }
#endif
  if(fflush(fd)) return (NO);
  Uadvance(fd);
  if(Usector(fd, RDRND)) {
    pad(Ubufptr[fd], CPMEOF, BUFSIZE);
    Useteof(fd);
    return (NO);
    }
  return (YES);
  }

/*
** ------------ File Output
*/

/*
** Binary-Stream output of one byte to fd.
*/
Uwrite(ch, fd) int ch, fd; {
  char *bufloc;
  switch (Umode(fd)) {
    default: Useterr(fd); return (EOF);
    case WRTBIT:
    case WRTBIT|RDBIT:
    case WRTBIT|EOFBIT:
    case WRTBIT|EOFBIT|RDBIT:
    }
  switch(Udevice[fd]) {
    /* RDR can't occur since it is read mode */
    case CPMCON: return (Uconout(ch));
    case CPMPUN:
    case CPMLST: Ubdos(Udevice[fd], ch);
                 break;
    default:
      if(Uauxsz && Uauxsz[fd]) return (Uauxwt(ch, fd));
      if(Uchrpos[fd]>=BUFSIZE && !Uputsec(fd)) return (EOF);
      bufloc = Ubufptr[fd] + Uchrpos[fd]++;
      *bufloc = ch;
      Udirty[fd] = YES;
    }
  return (ch);
  }

/*
```

```
/*
** Console character output.
*/
Uconout(ch) int ch; {
  Ubdos(DCONIO, ch);
  return (ch);
  }

/*
** Write one sector to fd.
*/
Uputsec(fd) int fd; {
  if(fflush(fd)) return (NO);
  Uadvance(fd);
  if(Ustatus[fd]&EOFBIT || Usector(fd, RDRND))    /*63*/
    pad(Ubufptr[fd], CPMEOF, BUFSIZE);
  return (YES);
  }

/*
** ------------ Buffer Service
*/

/*
** Advance to next sector.
*/
Uadvance(fd) int fd; {
  int *rrn;
  rrn = Ufcbptr[fd] + RRNOFF;
  ++(*rrn);
  Uchrpos[fd] = 0;
  }

/*
** Sector I/O.
*/
Usector(fd, func) int fd, func; {
  int error;
  Ubdos(SETDMA, Ubufptr[fd]);
  error = Ubdos(func, Ufcbptr[fd]);
  Ubdos(SETDMA, 128);
  Udirty[fd] = NO;
  return (error);
  }

/*
** ------------ File Status
*/

/*
```

```
/*
** Return fd's open mode, else NULL.
*/
Umode(fd) char *fd; {
  if(fd < MAXFILES) return (Ustatus[fd]);
  return (NULL);
  }

/*
** Set eof status for fd and
** disable future i/o unless writing is allowed.
*/
Useteof(fd) int fd; {
  Ustatus[fd] |= EOFBIT;
  }

/*
** Clear eof status for fd.
*/
Uclreof(fd) int fd; {
  Ustatus[fd] &= ~EOFBIT;
  }

/*
** Set error status for fd.
*/
Useterr(fd) int fd; {
  Ustatus[fd] |= ERRBIT;
  }

/*
** ------------ Memory Allocation
*/

/*
** Allocate n bytes of (possibly zeroed) memory.
** Entry: n = Size of the items in bytes.
**    clear = "true" if clearing is desired.
** Returns the address of the allocated block of memory
** or NULL if the requested amount of space is not available.
*/
Ualloc(n, clear) char *n; int clear; {
  char *oldptr;
  if(n < avail(YES)) {
    if(clear) pad(Umemptr, NULL, n);
    oldptr = Umemptr;
    Umemptr += n;
    return (oldptr);
    }
  return (NULL);
```

```
        }
/*
** ------------ CP/M Interface
*/

/*
** Issue CP/M function and return result.
** Entry: c  = CP/M function code (register C)
**        de = CP/M parameter (register DE or E)
** Returns the CP/M return code (register A)
*/
Ubdos(c,de) int c,de; {
#asm
        pop     h       ;hold return address
        pop     d       ;load CP/M function parameter
        pop     b       ;load CP/M function number
        push    b       ;restore
        push    d       ;  the
        push    h       ;    stack
        call    5       ;call bdos
        mvi     h,0     ;
        mov     l,a     ;return the CP/M response
#endasm
   }
```

LISTING 6-2

FILE: ABS.C

```
/*
** abs -- returns absolute value of nbr
*/
abs(nbr)  int nbr; {
  if (nbr < 0) return (-nbr);
  return (nbr);
  }
```

FILE: ATOI.C

```
#define NOCCARGC   /* no argument count passing */
/*
** atoi(s) - convert s to integer.
*/
atoi(s) char *s; {
  int sign, n;
  while(isspace(*s)) ++s;
  sign = 1;
  switch(*s) {
    case '-': sign = -1;
    case '+': ++s;
    }
```

```
    n = 0;
    while(isdigit(*s)) n = 10 * n + *s++ - '0';
    return (sign * n);
    }
```

---FILE: ATOIB.C

```
#define NOCCARGC  /* no argument count passing */
/*
** atoib(s,b) - Convert s to "unsigned" integer in base b.
**              NOTE: This is a non-standard function.
*/
atoib(s, b) char *s; int b; {
  int n, digit;
  n = 0;
  while(isspace(*s)) ++s;
  while((digit = (127 & *s++)) >= '0') {
    if(digit >= 'a')      digit -= 87;
    else if(digit >= 'A') digit -= 55;
    else                  digit -= '0';
    if(digit >= b) break;
    n = b * n + digit;
    }
  return (n);
  }
```

---FILE: AUXBUF.C

```
#define NOCCARGC  /* no argument count passing */
#include stdio.h
#include clib.def
extern int *Uauxsz, Uauxin, Uauxrd, Uauxwt, Uauxfl,   /*58*/
           Ustatus[];
/*
** This module is loaded with a program only if auxbuf()
** is called.  It links to Uopen(), Uread(), Uwrite(), and
** fflush() through Uauxsz, Uauxin, Uauxrd, Uauxwt, and Uauxfl
** in CSYSLIB.  This technique reduces the overhead for
** programs which don't use auxiliary buffering.  Presumably,
** if there is enough memory for extra buffering, there is
** room to spare for this overhead too.  A bug in some
** versions of Small-C between 2.0 and 2.1 may cause the calls
** to Uauxrd, Uauxwt, and Uauxfl in Uread(), Uwrite(), and
** fflush(), respectively, to produce bad code.  The current
** compiler corrects the problem.
*/
int
  Uxsize[MAXFILES],   /* size of buffer */
  Uxaddr[MAXFILES],   /* aux buffer address */
  Uxnext[MAXFILES],   /* address of next byte in buffer */
  Uxend[MAXFILES],    /* address of end-of-data in buffer */
```

```
  Uxeof[MAXFILES];    /* true if current buffer ends file */
/*
** auxbuf -- allocate an auxiliary input buffer for fd
**    fd = file descriptor of an open file
**    size = size of buffer to be allocated
** Returns NULL on success, else ERR.
** Note: Ungetc() still works.
**       A 2nd call returns ERR, but has no effect.
**       If fd is a device, buffer is allocated but ignored.
**       Buffer stays allocated when fd is closed.
**       Do not mix reads and writes or perform seeks on fd.
*/
auxbuf(fd, size) int fd; char *size; {    /* fake unsigned */
  if(!Umode(fd) || !size || avail(NO) < size  || Uxsize[fd])
    return (ERR);
  Uxaddr[fd] = malloc(size); Uxinit(fd);                    /*58*/
  Uauxin = Uxinit;  /* tell Uopen() where Uxinit() is */ /*58*/
  Uauxrd = Uxread;  /* tell Uread() where Uxread() is */
  Uauxwt = Uxwrite; /* tell Uwrite() where Uxwrite() is */
  Uauxsz = Uxsize;  /* tell both where Uxsize[] is */
  Uauxfl = Uxflush; /* tell fflush() where Uxflush() is */
  Uxsize[fd] = size; /* tell Uread() that fd has aux buf */
  return (NULL);
  }

/*
** Initialize aux buffer controls
*/
Uxinit(fd) int fd; {                                       /*58*/
  Uxnext[fd] = Uxend[fd] = Uxaddr[fd];
  Uxeof[fd] = NO;
  }

/*
** Fill buffer if necessary, and return next byte.
*/
Uxread(fd) int fd; {
  char *ptr;
  while(YES) {
    ptr = Uxnext[fd];
    if(ptr < Uxend[fd]) {++Uxnext[fd]; return (*ptr);}
    if(Uxeof[fd]) {Useteof(fd); return (EOF);}
    Uauxsz = NULL;            /* avoid recursive loop */
    Uxend[fd] = Uxaddr[fd]
             + read(fd, Uxnext[fd]=Uxaddr[fd], Uxsize[fd]);
    Uauxsz = Uxsize;          /* restore Uauxsz */
    if(feof(fd)) {Uxeof[fd] = YES; Uclreof(fd);}
    }
  }
```

```
/*
** Empty buffer if necessary, and store ch in buffer.
*/
Uxwrite(ch, fd) int ch, fd; {
  char *ptr;
  while(YES) {
    ptr = Uxnext[fd];
    if(ptr < (Uxaddr[fd] + Uxsize[fd]))
      {*ptr = ch; ++Uxnext[fd]; return (ch);}
    if(Uxflush(fd)) return (EOF);
    }
  }

/*
** Flush aux buffer to file.
*/
Uxflush(fd) int fd; {
  int i, j;
  i = Uxnext[fd] - Uxaddr[fd];
  Uauxsz = NULL;   /* avoid recursive loop */
  j = write(fd, Uxnext[fd]=Uxaddr[fd], i);
  Uauxsz = Uxsize; /* restore Uauxsz */
  if(i != j) return (EOF);
  return (NULL);
  }
```

─── **FILE:AVAIL.C**

```
#define NOCCARGC  /* no argument count passing */
extern char *Umemptr;
/*
** Return the number of bytes of available memory.
** In case of a stack overflow condition, if 'abort'
** is non-zero the program aborts with an 'S' clue,
** otherwise zero is returned.
*/
avail(abort) int abort; {
  char x;
  if(&x < Umemptr) {
    if(abort) exit('M');
    return (0);
    }
  return (&x - Umemptr);
  }
```

─── **FILE:CALL.MAC**

```
;
;----- CALL: Small-C arithmetic and logical library
;
CCDCAL::
```

```
        PCHL
;
CCDDGC::
        DAD     D
        JMP     CCGCHAR
;
CCDSGC::
        INX     H
        INX     H
        DAD     SP
;
;FETCH A SINGLE BYTE FROM THE ADDRESS IN HL AND SIGN INTO HL
CCGCHAR::
        MOV     A,M
;
;PUT THE ACCUM INTO HL AND SIGN EXTEND THROUGH H.
CCARGC::
CCSXT::
        MOV     L,A
        RLC
        SBB     A
        MOV     H,A
        RET
;
CCDDGI::
        DAD     D
        JMP     CCGINT
;
CCDSGI::
        INX     H
        INX     H
        DAD     SP
;
;FETCH A FULL 16-BIT INTEGER FROM THE ADDRESS IN HL INTO HL
CCGINT::
        MOV     A,M
        INX     H
        MOV     H,M
        MOV     L,A
        RET
;
CCDECC::
        INX     H
        INX     H
        DAD     SP
        MOV     D,H
        MOV     E,L
        CALL    CCGCHAR
        DCX     H
```

```
            MOV     A,L
            STAX    D
            RET
;
CCINCC::
            INX     H
            INX     H
            DAD     SP
            MOV     D,H
            MOV     E,L
            CALL    CCGCHAR
            INX     H
            MOV     A,L
            STAX    D
            RET
;
CDPDPC::
            DAD     D
CCPDPC::
            POP     B       ;RET ADDR
            POP     D
            PUSH    B
;
;STORE A SINGLE BYTE FROM HL AT THE ADDRESS IN DE
CCPCHAR::
PCHAR:      MOV     A,L
            STAX    D
            RET
;
CCDECI::
            INX     H
            INX     H
            DAD     SP
            MOV     D,H
            MOV     E,L
            CALL    CCGINT
            DCX     H
            JMP     CCPINT
;
CCINCI::
            INX     H
            INX     H
            DAD     SP
            MOV     D,H
            MOV     E,L
            CALL    CCGINT
            INX     H
            JMP     CCPINT
;
```

```
CDPDPI::
        DAD     D
CCPDPI::
        POP     B       ;RET ADDR
        POP     D
        PUSH    B
;
;STORE A 16-BIT INTEGER IN HL AT THE ADDRESS IN DE
CCPINT::
PINT:   MOV     A,L
        STAX    D
        INX     D
        MOV     A,H
        STAX    D
        RET
;
;INCLUSIVE "OR" HL AND DE INTO HL
CCOR::
        MOV     A,L
        ORA     E
        MOV     L,A
        MOV     A,H
        ORA     D
        MOV     H,A
        RET
;
;EXCLUSIVE "OR" HL AND DE INTO HL
CCXOR::
        MOV     A,L
        XRA     E
        MOV     L,A
        MOV     A,H
        XRA     D
        MOV     H,A
        RET
;
;"AND" HL AND DE INTO HL
CCAND::
        MOV     A,L
        ANA     E
        MOV     L,A
        MOV     A,H
        ANA     D
        MOV     H,A
        RET
;
;IN ALL THE FOLLOWING COMPARE ROUTINES, HL IS SET TO 1 IF THE
;   CONDITION IS TRUE, OTHERWISE IT IS SET TO 0 (ZERO).
;
```

```
;TEST IF HL = DE
;
CCEQ::
        CALL    CCCMP
        RZ
        DCX     H
        RET
;
;TEST IF DE != HL
CCNE::
        CALL    CCCMP
        RNZ
        DCX     H
        RET
;
;TEST IF DE > HL (SIGNED)
CCGT::
        XCHG
        CALL    CCCMP
        RC
        DCX     H
        RET
;
;TEST IF DE <= HL (SIGNED)
CCLE::
        CALL    CCCMP
        RZ
        RC
        DCX     H
        RET
;
;TEST IF DE >= HL (SIGNED)
CCGE::
        CALL    CCCMP
        RNC
        DCX     H
        RET
;
;TEST IF DE < HL (SIGNED)
CCLT::
        CALL    CCCMP
        RC
        DCX     H
        RET
;
;COMMON ROUTINE TO PERFORM A SIGNED COMPARE OF DE AND HL
; THIS ROUTINE PERFORMS DE - HL AND SETS THE CONDITIONS:
; CARRY REFLECTS SIGN OF DIFFERENCE (SET MEANS DE < HL)
; ZERO/NON-ZERO SET ACCORDING TO EQUALITY.
```

```
CCCMP::
        MOV     A,H         ;INVERT SIGN OF HL
        XRI     80H
        MOV     H,A
        MOV     A,D         ;INVERT SIGN OF DE
        XRI     80H
        CMP     H           ;COMPARE MSBS
        JNZ     CCCMP1      ;DONE IF NEQ
        MOV     A,E         ;COMPARE LSBS
        CMP     L
CCCMP1: LXI     H,1         ;PRESET TRUE COND
        RET
;
;TEST IF DE >= HL (UNSIGNED)
CCUGE::
        CALL    CCUCMP
        RNC
        DCX     H
        RET
;
;TEST IF DE < HL (UNSIGNED)
CCULT::
        CALL    CCUCMP
        RC
        DCX     H
        RET
;
;TEST IF DE > HL (UNSIGNED)
CCUGT::
        XCHG
        CALL    CCUCMP
        RC
        DCX     H
        RET
;
;TEST IF DE <= HL (UNSIGNED)
CCULE::
        CALL    CCUCMP
        RZ
        RC
        DCX     H
        RET
;
;COMMON ROUTINE TO PERFORM UNSIGNED COMPARE
; CARRY SET IF DE < HL
; ZERO/NONZERO SET ACCORDINGLY
CCUCMP::
        MOV     A,D
        CMP     H
```

```
                JNZ     UCMP1
                MOV     A,E
                CMP     L
        UCMP1:  LXI     H,1
                RET
;
;SHIFT DE ARITHMETICALLY RIGHT BY HL AND RETURN IN HL
CCASR::
                XCHG
                DCR     E
                RM
                MOV     A,H
                RAL
                MOV     A,H
                RAR
                MOV     H,A
                MOV     A,L
                RAR
                MOV     L,A
                JMP     CCASR+1
;
;SHIFT DE ARITHMETICALLY LEFT BY HL AND RETURN IN HL
CCASL::
                XCHG
                DCR     E
                RM
                DAD     H
                JMP     CCASL+1
;
;SUBTRACT HL FROM DE AND RETURN IN HL
CCSUB::
                MOV     A,E
                SUB     L
                MOV     L,A
                MOV     A,D
                SBB     H
                MOV     H,A
                RET
;
;FORM THE TWO'S COMPLEMENT OF HL
CCNEG::
                CALL    CCCOM
                INX     H
                RET
;
;FORM THE ONE'S COMPLEMENT OF HL
CCCOM::
                MOV     A,H
                CMA
```

```
                MOV     H,A
                MOV     A,L
                CMA
                MOV     L,A
                RET
;
;MULTIPLY DE BY HL AND RETURN IN HL (SIGNED MULTIPLY)
CCMULT::
MULT:           MOV     B,H
                MOV     C,L
                LXI     H,0
MULT1:          MOV     A,C
                RRC
                JNC     MULT2
                DAD     D
MULT2:          XRA     A
                MOV     A,B
                RAR
                MOV     B,A
                MOV     A,C
                RAR
                MOV     C,A
                ORA     B
                RZ
                XRA     A
                MOV     A,E
                RAL
                MOV     E,A
                MOV     A,D
                RAL
                MOV     D,A
                ORA     E
                RZ
                JMP     MULT1
;
;DIVIDE DE BY HL AND RETURN QUOTIENT IN HL, REMAINDER IN DE (SIGNED DIVIDE)
CCDIV::
DIV:            MOV     B,H
                MOV     C,L
                MOV     A,D
                XRA     B
                PUSH    PSW
                MOV     A,D
                ORA     A
                CM      CCDENEG
                MOV     A,B
                ORA     A
                CM      CCBCNEG
                MVI     A,16
```

```
          PUSH      PSW
          XCHG
          LXI       D,0
CCDIV1:   DAD       H
          CALL      CCRDEL
          JZ        CCDIV2
          CALL      CCCMPBCDE
          JM        CCDIV2
          MOV       A,L
          ORI       1
          MOV       L,A
          MOV       A,E
          SUB       C
          MOV       E,A
          MOV       A,D
          SBB       B
          MOV       D,A
CCDIV2:   POP       PSW
          DCR       A
          JZ        CCDIV3
          PUSH      PSW
          JMP       CCDIV1
CCDIV3:   POP       PSW
          RP
          CALL      CCDENEG
          XCHG
          CALL      CCDENEG
          XCHG
          RET
;
;NEGATE THE INTEGER IN DE (INTERNAL ROUTINE)
CCDENEG:  MOV       A,D
          CMA
          MOV       D,A
          MOV       A,E
          CMA
          MOV       E,A
          INX       D
          RET
;
;NEGATE THE INTEGER IN BC (INTERNAL ROUTINE)
CCBCNEG:  MOV       A,B
          CMA
          MOV       B,A
          MOV       A,C
          CMA
          MOV       C,A
          INX       B
          RET
```

```
;
;ROTATE DE LEFT ONE BIT (INTERNAL ROUTINE)
CCRDEL: MOV     A,E
        RAL
        MOV     E,A
        MOV     A,D
        RAL
        MOV     D,A
        ORA     E
        RET
;
;COMPARE BC TO DE (INTERNAL ROUTINE)
CCCMPBCDE: MOV  A,E
        SUB     C
        MOV     A,D
        SBB     B
        RET
;
;LOGICAL NEGATION
CCLNEG::
        MOV     A,H
        ORA     L
        JNZ     $+6
        MVI     L,1
        RET
        LXI     H,0
        RET
;
; EXECUTE "SWITCH" STATEMENT
;
;   HL = SWITCH VALUE
; (SP) -> SWITCH TABLE
;           DW ADDR1, VALUE1
;           DW ADDR2, VALUE2
;           ...
;           DW 0
;         [JMP default]
;           continuation
;
CCSWITCH::
        XCHG            ;DE = SWITCH VALUE
        POP     H       ;HL -> SWITCH TABLE
SWLOOP: MOV     C,M
        INX     H
        MOV     B,M     ;BC -> CASE ADDR, ELSE 0
        INX     H
        MOV     A,B
        ORA     C
        JZ      SWEND   ;DEFAULT OR CONTINUATION CODE
```

```
        MOV     A,M
        INX     H
        CMP     E
        MOV     A,M
        INX     H
        JNZ     SWLOOP
        CMP     D
        JNZ     SWLOOP
        MOV     H,B     ;CASE MATCHED
        MOV     L,C
SWEND:  PCHL
;
Uend:   lhld    6               ;get bdos address
        sphl                    ;use for base of stack
        lxi     h,Uend          ;get start of free memory
        shld    Umemptr##       ;use for memory allocation
        jmp     Umain##         ;parse command line, execute program
        end     Uend
```

---FILE:CALLOC.C

```
#define NOCCARGC   /* no argument count passing */
#include stdio.h
/*
** Cleared-memory allocation of n items of size bytes.
** n    = Number of items to allocate space for.
** size = Size of the items in bytes.
** Returns the address of the allocated block,
** else NULL for failure.
*/
calloc(n, size) char *n, *size; {
  return (Ualloc(n*size, YES));
  }
```

---FILE:CLEARERR.C

```
#define NOCCARGC   /* no arg count passing */
#include stdio.h
#include clib.def
extern int Ustatus[];
/*
** Clear error status for fd.
*/
clearerr(fd) int fd; {
  if(Umode(fd)) Ustatus[fd] &= ~ERRBIT;
  }
```

---FILE:CSEEK.C

```
#define NOCCARGC   /* no argument count passing */
#include stdio.h
#include clib.def
```

```
  extern int Ufcbptr[], Uchrpos[], Unextc[];
  /*
  ** Position fd to the 128-byte record indicated by
  ** "offset" relative to the point indicated by "base."
  **
  **      BASE    OFFSET-RELATIVE-TO
  **       0      first record
  **       1      current record
  **       2      end of file (last record + 1)
  **
  ** Returns NULL on success, else EOF.
  */
  cseek(fd, offset, base) int fd, offset, base; {
    int oldrrn, *rrn;
    if(!Umode(fd) || isatty(fd) || fflush(fd)) return (EOF);
    rrn = Ufcbptr[fd] + RRNOFF;
    oldrrn = *rrn;
    switch (base) {
      case 2: Ubdos(POSEND, Ufcbptr[fd]);
      case 1: *rrn += offset;
              break;
      case 0: *rrn = offset;
              break;
      default: return (EOF);
      }
    if(Usector(fd, RDRND)) {
      *rrn = oldrrn;
      return (EOF);
      }
    Uchrpos[fd] = 0;
    Unextc[fd] = EOF;
    Uclreof(fd);
    return (NULL);
    }
```

FILE:CTELL.C

```
  #define NOCCARGC  /* no arg count passing */
  #include stdio.h
  #include clib.def
  extern int Ufcbptr[], Uchrpos[];
  /*
  ** Return offset to current 128-byte record.
  */
  ctell(fd) int fd; {
    int *rrn;
    if(!Umode(fd) || isatty(fd)) return (-1);
    rrn=Ufcbptr[fd]+RRNOFF;
    return (*rrn);
    }
```

```
/*
** Return offset to next character in current buffer.
*/
ctellc(fd) int fd; {
  return (Uchrpos[fd]);
  }
```

─────────────────────────────────────── FILE:DTOI.C

```
#define NOCCARGC   /* no argument count passing */
#include stdio.h
/*
** dtoi -- convert signed decimal string to integer nbr
**         returns field length, else ERR on error
*/
dtoi(decstr, nbr)  char *decstr;  int *nbr; {
  int len, s;
  if((*decstr)=='-') {s=1; ++decstr;} else s=0;
  if((len=utoi(decstr, nbr))<0) return ERR;
  if(*nbr<0) return ERR;
  if(s) {*nbr = -*nbr; return ++len;} else return len;
  }
```

─────────────────────────────────────── FILE:EXIT.C

```
#define NOCCARGC   /* no argument count passing */
#include stdio.h
#include clib.def
/*
** Close all open files and exit to CP/M.
** Entry: errcode = Character to be sent to stderr.
** Returns to CP/M rather than the caller.
*/
exit(errcode) char errcode; {
  int fd;
  if(errcode) Uconout(errcode);
  for(fd=0; fd < MAXFILES; fclose(fd++));
  Ubdos(GOCPM,NULL);
  }
#asm
abort   equ     exit
        entry   abort
#endasm
```

─────────────────────────────────────── FILE:FCLOSE.C

```
#define NOCCARGC   /* no argument count passing */
#include stdio.h
#include clib.def
/*
** Close fd
** Entry: fd = File descriptor for file to be closed.
```

```
** Returns NULL for success, otherwise ERR
*/
extern int Ufcbptr[], Ustatus[], Udevice[];
fclose(fd) int fd; {
  if(!Umode(fd)) return (ERR);
  if(!isatty(fd)) {
    if(fflush(fd) || Ubdos(CLOFIL,Ufcbptr[fd])==255)
      return (ERR);
    }
  return (Ustatus[fd]=Udevice[fd]=NULL);
  }
```

── **FILE:FEOF.C**

```
#define NOCCARGC   /* no argument count passing */
#include clib.def
extern int Ustatus[];
/*
** Test for end-of-file status.
** Entry: fd = file descriptor
** Returns non-zero if fd is at eof, else zero.
*/
feof(fd) int fd; {
  return (Ustatus[fd] & EOFBIT);
  }
```

── **FILE:FERROR.C**

```
#define NOCCARGC   /* no arg count passing */
#include stdio.h
#include clib.def
extern Ustatus[];
/*
** Test for error status on fd.
*/
ferror(fd) int fd; {
  return (Ustatus[fd] & ERRBIT);
  }
```

── **FILE:FFLUSH.C**

```
#define NOCCARGC   /* no argument count passing */
#include stdio.h
#include clib.def
extern int Udirty[], *Uauxsz, Uauxfl;
/*
** Write buffer for fd if it has changes.
** Entry: fd = File descriptor of pertinent file.
** Returns NULL on success, otherwise EOF.
** Returns NULL if file is opened for input only
**         or if it is not a disk file.
*/
```

```
fflush(fd) int fd; {
  if(Umode(fd) & WRTBIT) {
    if((Uauxsz && Uauxsz[fd] && Uauxfl(fd)) ||
       (!isatty(fd) && Udirty[fd] && Usector(fd, WRTRND))) {
      Useterr(fd);
      return (ERR);
      }
    }
  return (NULL);
  }
```

---------- FILE:FGETC.C

```
#define NOCCARGC  /* no argument count passing */
#include stdio.h
#include clib.def
extern int Uchrpos[];
/*
** Character-stream input of one character from fd.
** Entry: fd = File descriptor of pertinent file.
** Returns the next character on success, else EOF.
*/
fgetc(fd) int fd; {
  int ch;
  while(1) {
    switch(ch = Uread(fd)) {
      default:   return (ch);
      case CPMEOF: switch(Uchrpos[fd]) {
                     default: --Uchrpos[fd];
                     case 0:
                     case BUFSIZE:
                     }
                   Useteof(fd);
                   return (EOF);
      case CR:     return ('\n');
      case LF:     /* NOTE: Uconin() maps LF -> CR */
      }
    }
  }
#asm
getc  equ    fgetc
      entry  getc
#endasm
```

---------- FILE:FGETS.C

```
#define NOCCARGC  /* no arg count passing */
#include stdio.h
#include clib.def
/*
** Gets an entire string (including its newline
```

```
** terminator) or size-1 characters, whichever comes
** first. The input is terminated by a null character.
** Entry: str  = Pointer to destination buffer.
**        size = Size of the destination buffer.
**        fd   = File descriptor of pertinent file.
** Returns str on success, else NULL.
*/
fgets(str, size, fd) char *str; int size, fd; {
  return (Ugets(str, size, fd, 1));
  }

/*
** Gets an entire string from stdin (excluding its newline
** terminator) or size-1 characters, whichever comes
** first. The input is terminated by a null character.
** The user buffer must be large enough to hold the data.
** Entry: str  = Pointer to destination buffer.
** Returns str on success, else NULL.
*/
gets(str) char *str; {
  return (Ugets(str, 32767, stdin, 0));
  }

Ugets(str, size, fd, nl) char *str; int size, fd, nl; {
  int backup;
  char *next;
  next = str;
  while(--size > 0) {
    switch (*next = fgetc(fd)) {
      case  EOF: *next = NULL;
                 if(next == str) return (NULL);
                 return (str);
      case '\n': *(next + nl) = NULL;
                 return (str);
      case  RUB: if(next > str) backup = 1; else backup = 0;
                 goto backout;
      case WIPE: backup = next - str;
         backout:
                 if(iscons(fd)) {
                   fputs("\b \b\b \b", stderr);
                   ++size;
                   while(backup--) {
                     fputs("\b \b", stderr);
                     if(*--next < 32) fputs("\b \b", stderr);
                     ++size;
                     }
                   continue;
                   }
      default: ++next;
```

```
      }
    }
  *next = NULL;
  return (str);
  }
```

---FILE:FOPEN.C

```
#define NOCCARGC    /* no arg count passing */
#include stdio.h
#include clib.def
/*
** Open file indicated by fn.
** Entry: fn   = Null-terminated CP/M file name.
**               May be prefixed by letter of dirve.
**               May be just CON:, RDR:, PUN:, or LST:.
** ;     mode = "a"  - append
**              "r"  - read
**              "w"  - write
**              "a+" - append update
**              "r+" - read   update
**              "w+" - write  update
** Returns a file descriptor on success, else NULL.
*/
fopen(fn, mode) char *fn, *mode; {
  int fd;
  fd = 0; /* skip stdin (= error return) */
  while(++fd < MAXFILES) {
    if(Umode(fd) == NULL) {
      if(Uopen(fn, mode, fd)!=ERR) return (fd);
      break;
      }
    }
  return (NULL);
  }
```

---FILE:FPRINTF.C

```
#define NOCCARGC
/*
** Yes, that is correct.  Although these functions use an
** argument count, they do not call functions which need one.
*/
#include stdio.h
/*
** fprintf(fd, ctlstring, arg, arg, ...) - Formatted print.
** Operates as described by Kernighan & Ritchie.
** b, c, d, o, s, u, and x specifications are supported.
** Note: b (binary) is a non-standard extension.
*/
fprintf(argc) int argc; {
```

```c
  int *nxtarg;
  nxtarg = CCARGC() + &argc;
  return(Uprint(*(--nxtarg), --nxtarg));
  }

/*
** printf(ctlstring, arg, arg, ...) - Formatted print.
** Operates as described by Kernighan & Ritchie.
** b, c, d, o, s, u, and x specifications are supported.
** Note: b (binary) is a non-standard extension.
*/
printf(argc) int argc; {
  return(Uprint(stdout, CCARGC() + &argc - 1));
  }

/*
** Uprint(fd, ctlstring, arg, arg, ...)
** Called by fprintf() and printf().
*/
Uprint(fd, nxtarg) int fd, *nxtarg; {
  int  arg, left, pad, cc, len, maxchr, width;
  char *ctl, *sptr, str[17];
  cc = 0;
  ctl = *nxtarg--;
  while(*ctl) {
    if(*ctl!='%') {fputc(*ctl++, fd); ++cc; continue;}
    else ++ctl;
    if(*ctl=='%') {fputc(*ctl++, fd); ++cc; continue;}
    if(*ctl=='-') {left = 1; ++ctl;} else left = 0;
    if(*ctl=='0') pad = '0'; else pad = ' ';
    if(isdigit(*ctl)) {
      width = atoi(ctl++);
      while(isdigit(*ctl)) ++ctl;
      }
    else width = 0;
    if(*ctl=='.') {
      maxchr = atoi(++ctl);
      while(isdigit(*ctl)) ++ctl;
      }
    else maxchr = 0;
    arg = *nxtarg--;
    sptr = str;
    switch(*ctl++) {
      case 'c': str[0] = arg; str[1] = NULL; break;
      case 's': sptr = arg;        break;
      case 'd': itoa(arg,str);     break;
      case 'b': itoab(arg,str,2);  break;
      case 'o': itoab(arg,str,8);  break;
      case 'u': itoab(arg,str,10); break;
```

```
        case 'x': itoab(arg,str,16); break;
        default:  return (cc);
        }
    len = strlen(sptr);
    if(maxchr && maxchr<len) len = maxchr;
    if(width>len) width = width - len; else width = 0;
    if(!left) while(width--) {fputc(pad,fd); ++cc;}
    while(len--) {fputc(*sptr++,fd); ++cc; }
    if(left) while(width--) {fputc(pad,fd); ++cc;}
    }
  return(cc);
  }
```

---FILE:FPUTC.C

```
#define NOCCARGC   /* no arg count passing */
#include stdio.h
#include clib.def
extern int Ustatus[];
/*
** Character-stream output of a character to fd.
** Entry: ch = Character to write.
**        fd = File descriptor of pertinent file.
** Returns character written on success, else EOF.
*/
fputc(ch, fd) int ch, fd; {
  switch(ch) {
    case EOF:  Uwrite(CPMEOF, fd); break;
    case '\n': Uwrite(CR, fd); Uwrite(LF, fd); break;
    default:   Uwrite(ch, fd);
    }
  if(Ustatus[fd] & ERRBIT) return (EOF);
  return (ch);
  }
#asm
putc  equ   fputc
      entry putc
#endasm
```

---FILE:FPUTS.C

```
#define NOCCARGC   /* no arg count passing */
#include stdio.h
#include clib.def
/*
** Write a string to fd.
** Entry: string = Pointer to null-terminated string.
**        fd     = File descriptor of pertinent file.
*/
fputs(string,fd) char *string; int fd; {
  while(*string)
```

```
      fputc(*string++,fd) ;
    }
```

FILE:FREAD.C

```
#define NOCCARGC   /* no argument count passing */
#include clib.def
extern int Ustatus[];
/*
** Item-stream read from fd.
** Entry: buf = address of target buffer
**        sz = size of items in bytes
**        n = number of items to read
**        fd = file descriptor
** Returns a count of the items actually read.
** Use feof() and ferror() to determine file status.
*/
fread(buf, sz, n, fd) char *buf; int sz, n, fd; {
  return (read(fd, buf, n*sz)/sz);    /*62*/
  }

/*
** Binary-stream read from fd.
** Entry:  fd = file descriptor
**        buf = address of target buffer
**        n = number of bytes to read
** Returns a count of the bytes actually read.
** Use feof() and ferror() to determine file status.
*/
read(fd, buf, n) int fd, n; char *buf; {
  char *cnt;   /* fake unsigned */
  cnt = 0;
  while(n--) {
    *buf++ = Uread(fd);
    if(Ustatus[fd] & (ERRBIT | EOFBIT)) break;
    ++cnt;
    }
  return (cnt);
  }
```

FILE:FREE.C

```
#define NOCCARGC   /* no argument count passing */
extern char *Umemptr;
/*
** free(ptr) - Free previously allocated memory block.
** Memory must be freed in the reverse order from which
** it was allocated.
** ptr    = Value returned by calloc() or malloc().
** Returns ptr if successful or NULL otherwise.
*/
```

```
free(ptr) char *ptr; {
  return (Umemptr = ptr);
  }
#asm
cfree   equ     free
        entry   cfree
#endasm
```

FILE:FREOPEN.C

```
#define NOCCARGC  /* no argument count passing */
#include stdio.h
/*
** Close previously opened fd and reopen it.
** Entry: fn   = Null-terminated CP/M file name.
**              May be prefixed by letter of drive.
**              May be just CON:, RDR:, PUN:, or LST:.
**        mode = "a"  - append
**               "r"  - read
**               "w"  - write
**               "a+" - append update
**               "r+" - read   update
**               "w+" - write  update
**        fd   = File descriptor of pertinent file.
** Returns the original fd on success, else NULL.
*/
freopen(fn, mode, fd) char *fn, *mode; int fd; {
  if(fclose(fd)) return (NULL);
  if(Uopen(fn, mode, fd)==ERR) return (NULL);
  return (fd);
  }
```

FILE:FSCANF.C

```
#define NOCCARGC  /* no argument count passing */
/*
** Yes, that is correct.  Although these functions use an
** argument count, they do not call functions which need one.
*/
#include stdio.h
/*
** fscanf(fd, ctlstring, arg, arg, ...) - Formatted read.
** Operates as described by Kernighan & Ritchie.
** b, c, d, o, s, u, and x specifications are supported.
** Note: b (binary) is a non-standard extension.
*/
fscanf(argc) int argc; {
  int *nxtarg;
  nxtarg = CCARGC() + &argc;
  return (Uscan(*(--nxtarg), --nxtarg));
  }
```

```
/*
** scanf(ctlstring, arg, arg, ...) - Formatted read.
** Operates as described by Kernighan & Ritchie.
** b, c, d, o, s, u, and x specifications are supported.
** Note: b (binary) is a non-standard extension.
*/
scanf(argc) int argc; {
  return (Uscan(stdin, CCARGC() + &argc - 1));
  }

/*
** Uscan(fd, ctlstring, arg, arg, ...) - Formatted read.
** Called by fscanf() and scanf().
*/
Uscan(fd,nxtarg) int fd, *nxtarg; {
  char *carg, *ctl, *unsigned;
  int *narg, wast, ac, width, ch, cnv, base, ovfl, sign;
  ac = 0;
  ctl = *nxtarg--;
  while(*ctl) {
    if(isspace(*ctl)) {++ctl; continue;}
    if(*ctl++ != '%') continue;
    if(*ctl == '*') {narg = carg = &wast; ++ctl;}
    else            narg = carg = *nxtarg--;
    ctl += utoi(ctl, &width);
    if(!width) width = 32767;
    if(!(cnv = *ctl++)) break;
    while(isspace(ch = fgetc(fd))) ;
    if(ch == EOF) {if(ac) break; else return(EOF);}
    ungetc(ch,fd);
    switch(cnv) {
      case 'c':
        *carg = fgetc(fd);
        break;
      case 's':
        while(width--) {
          if((*carg = fgetc(fd)) == EOF) break;
          if(isspace(*carg)) break;
          if(carg != &wast) ++carg;
          }
        *carg = 0;
        break;
      default:
        switch(cnv) {
          case 'b': base =  2; sign = 1; ovfl = 32767; break;
          case 'd': base = 10; sign = 0; ovfl =  3276; break;
          case 'o': base =  8; sign = 1; ovfl =  8191; break;
          case 'u': base = 10; sign = 1; ovfl =  6553; break;
          case 'x': base = 16; sign = 1; ovfl =  4095; break;
```

```
          default:  return (ac);
          }
        *narg = unsigned = 0;
        while(width-- && !isspace(ch=fgetc(fd)) && ch.=EOF) {
          if(!sign)
            if(ch == '-') {sign = -1; continue;}
            else sign = 1;
          if(ch < '0') return (ac);
          if(ch >= 'a')       ch -= 87;
          else if(ch >= 'A')  ch -= 55;
          else                ch -= '0';
          if(ch >= base || unsigned > ovfl) return (ac);
          unsigned = unsigned * base + ch;
          }
        *narg = sign * unsigned;
      }
    ++ac;
    }
  return (ac);
  }
```

FILE:FWRITE.C

```
#define NOCCARGC   /* no argument count passing */
#include clib.def
extern int Ustatus[];
/*
** Item-stream write to fd.
** Entry: buf = address of source buffer
**        sz = size of items in bytes
**        n = number of items to write
**        fd = file descriptor
** Returns a count of the items actually written or
** zero if an error occurred.
** May use ferror(), as always, to detect errors.
*/
fwrite(buf, sz, n, fd) char *buf; int sz, n, fd; {      /*62*/
  if(write(fd, buf, n*sz) == -1) return (0);
  return (n);
  }

/*
** Binary-stream write to fd.
** Entry: fd = file descriptor
**        buf = address of source buffer
**        n = number of bytes to write
** Returns a count of the bytes actually written or
** -1 if an error occurred.
** May use ferror(), as always, to detect errors.
*/
```

```
write(fd, buf, n) int fd, n; char *buf; {    /*62*/
  char *cnt;  /* fake unsigned */
  cnt = n;
  while(cnt--) {
    Uwrite(*buf++, fd);
    if(Ustatus[fd] & ERRBIT) return (-1);
    }
  return (n);
  }
```

FILE:GETARG.C

```
#define NOCCARGC  /* no argument count passing */
#include stdio.h
/*
** Get command line argument.
** Entry: n    = Number of the argument.
**        s    = Destination string pointer.
**        size = Size of destination string.
**        argc = Argument count from main().
**        argv = Argument vector(s) from main().
** Returns number of characters moved on success,
** else EOF.
*/
getarg(n,s,size,argc,argv)
  int n; char *s; int size, argc, argv[]; {
  char *str;
  int i;
  if(n < 0 | n >= argc) {
    *s = NULL;
    return EOF;
    }
  i = 0;
  str=argv[n];
  while(i<size) {
    if((s[i]=str[i])==NULL) break;
    ++i;
    }
  s[i]=NULL;
  return i;
  }
```

FILE:GETCHAR.C

```
#define NOCCARGC  /* no argument count passing */
#include stdio.h
/*
** Get next character from standard input.
*/
getchar() {
  return (fgetc(stdin));
```

```
                }
```

---------- FILE:ISALNUM.C

```c
/*
** return 'true' if c is alphanumeric
*/
isalnum(c) int c; {
  return ((c<='z' && c>='a') ||
          (c<='Z' && c>='A') ||
          (c<='9' && c>='0'));
  }
```

---------- FILE:ISALPHA.C

```c
/*
** return 'true' if c is alphabetic
*/
isalpha(c) int c; {
  return ((c<='z' && c>='a') || (c<='Z' && c>='A'));
  }
```

---------- FILE:ASASCII.C

```c
/*
** return 'true' if c is an ASCII character (0-127)
*/
isascii(c) char *c; {
  /* c is a simulated unsigned integer */
  return (c <= 127);
  }
```

---------- FILE:ISATTY.C

```c
extern int Udevice[];
/*
** Return "true" if fd is a device, else "false"
*/
isatty(fd) int fd; {
  return (Udevice[fd]);
  }
```

---------- FILE:ISCNTRL.C

```c
/*
** return 'true' if c is a control character
** (0-31 or 127)
*/
iscntrl(c) char *c; {
  /* c is a simulated unsigned integer */
  return ((c <= 31) || (c == 127));
  }
```

---FILE:ISCONS.C

```
#include stdio.h
#include clib.def
extern int Udevice[];
/*
** Determine if fd is the console.
*/
iscons(fd) int fd; {
  return (Udevice[fd] == CPMCON);
  }
```

---FILE:ISDIGIT.C

```
/*
** return 'true' if c is a decimal digit
*/
isdigit(c) int c; {
  return (c<='9' && c>='0');
  }
```

---FILE:ISGRAPH.C

```
/*
** return 'true' if c is a graphic character
** (33-126)
*/
isgraph(c) int c; {
  return (c>=33 && c<=126);
  }
```

---FILE:ISLOWER.C

```
/*
** return 'true' if c is lower-case alphabetic
*/
islower(c) int c; {
  return (c<='z' && c>='a');
  }
```

---FILE:ISPRINT.C

```
/*
** return 'true' if c is a printable character
** (32-126)
*/
isprint(c) int c; {
  return (c>=32 && c<=126);
  }
```

---FILE:ISPUNCT.C

```
#define NOCCARGC   /* no argument count passing */
/*
** return 'true' if c is a punctuation character
```

```
** (all but control and alphanumeric)
*/
ispunct(c) int c; {
  return (!isalnum(c) && !iscntrl(c));
  }
```

─────────────────────────────────────── FILE:ISSPACE.C
```
/*
** return 'true' if c is a white-space character
*/
isspace(c) int c; {
  /* first check gives quick exit in most cases */
  return(c<=' ' && (c==' ' || (c<=13 && c>=9)));
  }
```

─────────────────────────────────────── FILE:ISUPPER.C
```
/*
** return 'true' if c is upper-case alphabetic
*/
isupper(c) int c; {
  return (c<='Z' && c>='A');
  }
```

─────────────────────────────────────── FILE:ISXDIGIT.C
```
/*
** return 'true' if c is a hexadecimal digit
** (0-9, A-F, or a-f)
*/
isxdigit(c) int c; {
  return ((c<='f' && c>='a') ||
          (c<='F' && c>='A') ||
          (c<='9' && c>='0'));
  }
```

─────────────────────────────────────── FILE:ITOA.C
```
#define NOCCARGC  /* no argument count passing */
/*
** itoa(n,s) - Convert n to characters in s
*/
itoa(n, s) char *s; int n; {
  int sign;
  char *ptr;
  ptr = s;
  if ((sign = n) < 0) /* record sign */
    n = -n;       /* make n positive */
  do {  /* generate digits in reverse order */
    *ptr++ = n % 10 + '0';  /* get next digit */
    } while ((n = n / 10) > 0);        /* delete it */
  if (sign < 0) *ptr++ = '-';
```

```
  *ptr = '\0';
  reverse(s);
}
```

FILE:ITOAB.C

```
#define NOCCARGC   /* no argument count passing */
/*
** itoab(n,s,b) - Convert "unsigned" n to characters in s using base b.
**               NOTE: This is a non-standard function.
*/
itoab(n, s, b) int n; char *s; int b; {
  char *ptr;
  int lowbit;
  ptr = s;
  b >>= 1;
  do {
    lowbit = n & 1;
    n = (n >> 1) & 32767;
    *ptr = ((n % b) << 1) + lowbit;
    if(*ptr < 10) *ptr += '0'; else *ptr += 55;
    ++ptr;
    } while(n /= b);
  *ptr = 0;
  reverse (s);
}
```

FILE:ITOD.C

```
#include stdio.h
/*
** itod -- convert nbr to signed decimal string of width sz
**         right adjusted, blank filled; returns str
**
**         if sz > 0 terminate with null byte
**         if sz = 0 find end of string
**         if sz < 0 use last byte for data
*/
itod(nbr, str, sz)  int nbr;  char str[];  int sz;  {
  char sgn;
  if(nbr<0) {nbr = -nbr; sgn='-';}
  else sgn=' ';
  if(sz>0) str[--sz]=NULL;
  else if(sz<0) sz = -sz;
  else while(str[sz]!=NULL) ++sz;
  while(sz) {
    str[--sz]=(nbr%10+'0');
    if((nbr=nbr/10)==0) break;
    }
  if(sz) str[--sz]=sgn;
  while(sz>0) str[--sz]=' ';
```

```
    return str;
  }
```

---FILE:ITOO.C

```
/*
** itoo -- converts nbr to octal string of length sz
**         right adjusted and blank filled, returns str
**
**         if sz > 0 terminate with null byte
**         if sz = 0 find end of string
**         if sz < 0 use last byte for data
*/
itoo(nbr, str, sz)  int nbr;  char str[];  int sz;  {
  int digit;
  if(sz>0) str[--sz]=0;
  else if(sz<0) sz = -sz;
  else while(str[sz]!=0) ++sz;
  while(sz) {
    digit=nbr&7; nbr=(nbr>>3)&8191;
    str[--sz]=digit+48;
    if(nbr==0) break;
    }
  while(sz) str[--sz]=' ';
  return str;
  }
```

---FILE:ITOU.C

```
#include stdio.h
/*
** itou -- convert nbr to unsigned decimal string of width sz
**         right adjusted, blank filled; returns str
**
**         if sz > 0 terminate with null byte
**         if sz = 0 find end of string
**         if sz < 0 use last byte for data
*/
itou(nbr, str, sz)  int nbr;  char str[];  int sz;  {
  int lowbit;
  if(sz>0) str[--sz]=NULL;
  else if(sz<0) sz = -sz;
  else while(str[sz]!=NULL) ++sz;
  while(sz) {
    lowbit=nbr&1;
    nbr=(nbr>>1)&32767;  /* divide by 2 */
    str[--sz]=((nbr%5)<<1)+lowbit+'0';
    if((nbr=nbr/5)==0) break;
    }
  while(sz) str[--sz]=' ';
  return str;
```

}

FILE:ITOX.C

```
/*
** itox -- converts nbr to hex string of length sz
**         right adjusted and blank filled, returns str
**
**         if sz > 0 terminate with null byte
**         if sz = 0 find end of string
**         if sz < 0 use last byte for data
*/
itox(nbr, str, sz)  int nbr;  char str[];  int sz;  {
  int digit, offset;
  if(sz>0) str[--sz]=0;
  else if(sz<0) sz = -sz;
  else while(str[sz]!=0) ++sz;
  while(sz) {
    digit=nbr&15; nbr=(nbr>>4)&4095;
    if(digit<10) offset=48; else offset=55;
    str[--sz]=digit+offset;
    if(nbr==0) break;
    }
  while(sz) str[--sz]=' ';
  return str;
  }
```

FILE:LEFT.C

```
/*
** left -- left adjust and null terminate a string
*/
left(str) char *str; {
  char *str2;
  str2=str;
  while(*str2==' ') ++str2;
  while(*str++ = *str2++);
  }
```

FILE:LEXCMP.C

```
#define NOCCARGC   /* no argument count passing */
/*
** lexcmp(s, t) - Return a number <0, 0, or >0
**                as s is <, =, or > t.
*/
lexcmp(s, t) char *s, *t; {
  while(lexorder(*s, *t) == 0)
    if(*s++) ++t;
    else return (0);
  return (lexorder(*s, *t));
  }
```

```
/*
** lexorder(c1, c2)
**
** Return a negative, zero, or positive number if
** c1 is less than, equal to, or greater than c2,
** based on a lexicographical (dictionary order)
** collating sequence.
**
*/
char Ulex[128] = {
    /**** NUL - / ****/
     0,  1,  2,  3,  4,  5,  6,  7,  8,  9,
    10, 11, 12, 13, 14, 15, 16, 17, 18, 19,
    20, 21, 22, 23, 24, 25, 26, 27, 28, 29,
    30, 31, 32, 33, 34, 35, 36, 37, 38, 39,
    40, 41, 42, 43, 44, 45, 46, 47,
    /**** 0-9 ****/
    65, 66, 67, 68, 69, 70, 71, 72, 73, 74,
    /****  : ; < = > ? @ ****/
    48, 49, 50, 51, 52, 53, 54,
    /**** A-Z ****/
    75, 76, 77, 78, 79, 80, 81, 82, 83, 84, 85, 86, 87,
    88, 89, 90, 91, 92, 93, 94, 95, 96, 97, 98, 99,100,
    /**** [ \ ] ^ U ****/
    55, 56, 57, 58, 59, 60,
    /**** a-z ****/
    75, 76, 77, 78, 79, 80, 81, 82, 83, 84, 85, 86, 87,
    88, 89, 90, 91, 92, 93, 94, 95, 96, 97, 98, 99,100,
    /**** { | } ~ ****/
    61, 62, 63, 64,
    /**** DEL ****/
    101
    };

lexorder(c1, c2) char c1, c2; {
  return(Ulex[c1] - Ulex[c2]);
  }
```

FILE:LINK.MAC

```
Ulink:: ext Umain
        end
```

FILE:MALLOC.C

```
#define NOCCARGC   /* no argument count passing */
#include stdio.h
/*
** Memory allocation of size bytes.
** size  = Size of the block in bytes.
** Returns the address of the allocated block,
```

```
**  else NULL for failure.
*/
malloc(size) char *size; {
  return (Ualloc(size, NO));
  }
```

FILE:OTOI.C

```
#include stdio.h
/*
** otoi -- convert unsigned octal string to integer nbr
**         returns field size, else ERR on error
*/
otoi(octstr, nbr) char *octstr; int *nbr; {
  int d,t; d=0;
  *nbr=0;
  while((*octstr>='0')&(*octstr<='7')) {
    t=*nbr;
    t=(t<<3) + (*octstr++ - '0');
    if ((t>=0)&(*nbr<0)) return ERR;
    d++; *nbr=t;
    }
  return d;
  }
```

FILE:PAD.C

```
#define NOCCARGC   /* no argument count passing */
/*
** Place n occurrences of ch at dest.
*/
pad(dest, ch, n) char *dest, *n; int ch; {
  /* n is a fake unsigned integer */
  while(n--) *dest++ = ch;
  }
```

FILE:POLL.C

```
#define NOCCARGC   /* no argument count passing */
#include stdio.h
#include clib.def
/*
** Poll for console input or interruption
*/
poll(pause) int pause; {
  int i;
  i = Ubdos(DCONIO, 255);
  if(pause) {
    if(i == PAUSE) {
      while(!(i = Ubdos(DCONIO, 255))) ;
      if(i == ABORT) exit(0);
      return (0);
```

```
          }
      if(i == ABORT) exit(0);
      }
    return (i);
    }
```

—— FILE:PUTCHAR.C

```
#define NOCCARGC   /* no argument count passing */
#include stdio.h
/*
** Write character to standard output.
*/
putchar(ch) int ch; {
  return (fputc(ch, stdout));
  }
```

—— FILE:PUTS.C

```
#define NOCCARGC   /* no argument count passing */
#include stdio.h
/*
** Write string to standard output.
*/
puts(string) char *string; {
  fputs(string, stdout);
  fputc('\n', stdout);
  }
```

——— FILE:RENAME.C

```
#define NOCCARGC   /* no argument count passing */
#include stdio.h
#include clib.def
/*
** Rename a file.
**   from = address of old filename.
**     to = address of new filename.
**   Returns NULL on success, else ERR.
*/
rename(from, to) char *from, *to; {
  char fcb[FCBSIZE];
  pad(fcb, NULL, FCBSIZE);
  if(!Unewfcb(to, fcb) || Ubdos(OPNFIL, fcb) != 255) {
    Ubdos(CLOFIL, fcb);
    return (ERR);
    }
  if(Unewfcb(from, fcb) &&
     Unewfcb(to, fcb+NAMEOFF2) &&
     Ubdos(RENAME, fcb) != 255)
    return (NULL);
  return (ERR);
```

```
                                                              FILE:REVERSE.C
#define NOCCARGC   /* no argument count passing */
/*
** reverse string in place
*/
reverse(s) char *s; {
  char *j;
  int c;
  j = s + strlen(s) - 1;
  while(s < j) {
    c = *s;
    *s++ = *j;
    *j-- = c;
    }
  }
```

```
                                                              FILE:REWIND.C
#define NOCCARGC   /* no argument count passing */
/*
** Rewind file to beginning.
*/
rewind(fd) int fd; {
  return(cseek(fd, 0, 0));
  }
```

```
                                                              FILE:SIGN.C
/*
** sign -- return -1, 0, +1 depending on the sign of nbr
*/
sign(nbr)  int nbr; {
  if(nbr>0) return 1;
  if(nbr==0) return 0;
  return -1;
  }
```

```
                                                              FILE:STRCAT.C
/*
** concatenate t to end of s
** s must be large enough
*/
strcat(s, t) char *s, *t; {
  char *d;
  d = s;
  --s;
  while (*++s) ;
  while (*s++ = *t++) ;
  return(d);
```

}

FILE:STRCHR.C

```
/*
** return pointer to 1st occurrence of c in str, else 0
*/
strchr(str, c) char *str, c; {
  while(*str) {
    if(*str == c) return (str);
    ++str;
    }
  return (0);
  }
```

FILE:STRCMP.C

```
/*
** return <0,   0,   >0 aUording to
**       s<t, s=t, s>t
*/
strcmp(s, t) char *s, *t; {
  while(*s == *t) {
    if(*s == 0) return (0);
    ++s; ++t;
    }
  return (*s - *t);
  }
```

FILE:STRCPY.C

```
/*
** copy t to s
*/
strcpy(s, t) char *s, *t; {
  char *d;
  d = s;
  while (*s++ = *t++) ;
  return(d);
  }
```

FILE:STRLEN.C

```
/*
** return length of s
*/
strlen(s) char *s; {
  char *t;
  t = s - 1;
  while (*++t) ;
  return (t - s);
  }
```

———————————————————————————————— FILE:STRCAT.C

```
/*
** concatenate n bytes max from t to end of s
** s must be large enough
*/
strncat(s, t, n) char *s, *t; int n; {
  char *d;
  d = s;
  --s;
  while(*++s) ;
  while(n--) {
    if(*s++ = *t++) continue;
    return(d);
    }
  *s = 0;
  return(d);
  }
```

———————————————————————————————— FILE:STRNCMP.C

```
/*
** strncmp(s,t,n) - Compares two strings for at most n
**                  characters and returns an integer
**                  >0, =0, or <0 as s is >t, =t, or <t.
*/
strncmp(s, t, n) char *s, *t; int n; {
  while(n && *s==*t) {
    if (*s == 0) return (0);
    ++s; ++t; --n;
    }
  if(n) return (*s - *t);
  return (0);
  }
```

———————————————————————————————— FILE:STRNCPY.C

```
/*
** copy n characters from sour to dest (null padding)
*/
strncpy(dest, sour, n) char *dest, *sour; int n; {
  char *d;
  d = dest;
  while(n-- > 0) {
    if(*d++ = *sour++) continue;
    while(n-- > 0) *d++ = 0;
    }
  *d = 0;
  return (dest);
  }
```

```
/*
** strrchr(s,c) - Search s for rightmost occurrence of c.
** s      = Pointer to string to be searched.
** c      = Character to search for.
** Returns pointer to rightmost c or NULL.
*/
strrchr(s, c) char *s, c; {
  char *ptr;
  ptr = 0;
  while(*s) {
    if(*s==c) ptr = s;
    ++s;
    }
  return (ptr);
  }
```

FILE:TOASCII.C

```
/*
** return ASCII equivalent of c
*/
toascii(c) int c; {
  return (c);
  }
```

FILE:TOLOWER.C

```
/*
** return lowercase of c if uppercase, else c
*/
tolower(c) int c; {
  if(c<='Z' && c>='A') return (c+32);
  return (c);
  }
```

FILE:TOUPPER.C

```
/*
** return uppercase of c if it is lowercase, else c
*/
toupper(c) int c; {
  if(c<='z' && c>='a') return (c-32);
  return (c);
  }
```

FILE:UNGETC.C

```
#define NOCCARGC   /* no argument count passing */
#include stdio.h
extern Unextc[];
/*
** Put c back into file fd.
```

```
** Entry:  c = character to put back
**        fd = file descriptor
** Returns c if successful, else EOF.
*/
ungetc(c, fd) int c, fd; {
  if(!Umode(fd) || Unextc[fd]!=EOF || c==EOF) return (EOF);
  return (Unextc[fd] = c);
  }
```

――――――――――――――――――――――――――――――― **FILE:UNLINK.C**

```
#define NOCCARGC   /* no arg count passing */
#include stdio.h
#include clib.def
/*
** Unlink (delete) the named file.
** Entry: fn = Null-terminated CP/M file name.
**             May be prefixed by letter of drive.
** Returns NULL on success, else ERR.
*/
unlink(fn) char *fn; {
  char fcb[FCBSIZE];
  pad(fcb, NULL, FCBSIZE);
  if(Unewfcb(fn, fcb) && Ubdos(DELFIL, fcb) != 255)
    return (NULL);
  return (ERR);
  }
#asm
delete   equ    unlink
         entry  delete
#endasm
```

――――――――――――――――――――――――――――――― **FILE:UTOI.C**

```
#include stdio.h
/*
** utoi -- convert unsigned decimal string to integer nbr
**         returns field size, else ERR on error
*/
utoi(decstr, nbr)  char *decstr;  int *nbr;  {
  int d,t; d=0;
  *nbr=0;
  while((*decstr>='0')&(*decstr<='9')) {
    t=*nbr;t=(10*t) + (*decstr++ - '0');
    if ((t>=0)&(*nbr<0)) return ERR;
    d++; *nbr=t;
    }
  return d;
  }
```

```
#include stdio.h
/*
** xtoi -- convert hex string to integer nbr
**         returns field size, else ERR on error
*/
xtoi(hexstr, nbr)  char *hexstr;  int *nbr;  {
  int d,t; d=0;
  *nbr=0;
  while(1)
    {
    if((*hexstr>='0')&(*hexstr<='9')) t=48;
    else if((*hexstr>='A')&(*hexstr<='F')) t=55;
    else if((*hexstr>='a')&(*hexstr<='f')) t=87;
    else break;
    if(d<4) ++d; else return ERR;
    *nbr=*nbr<<4;
    *nbr=*nbr+(*hexstr++)-t;
    }
  return d;
  }
```

7
SMALL-MAC: AN ASSEMBLER FOR SMALL-C

by J. E. Hendrix

This chapter was adapted from the Small-Mac manual.

Small-Mac is a macro assembler designed primarily for use on the 8080/Z80 machines under CP/M. It was created as a companion for the Small-C compiler (see "Small-C Version 2" in this volume). As such, it was designed to appeal to Small-C users by stressing simplicity, portability, adaptability, and educational value. Program size and execution speed were considered less important than these primary goals. Therefore, like the compiler, Small-Mac was written in Small-C and is being distributed in both source and object formats.

The salient features of the Small-Mac package are:

- Ease of use
- Simplified macro facility
- C-language expression operators
- Descriptive error messages
- Object file visibility
- Externally defined machine instruction table.

The following programs are included in the Small-Mac package:

MAC	macro assembler
LNK	linkage editor
LGO	load-and-go loader
LIB	library manager
CMIT	CPU configuration utility
DREL	dump relocatable files

MAC is a two-pass, table driven, relocatable, macro assembler. It "learns" the target machine from a machine instruction table (MIT), that is created with a text editor and compiled with the CMIT configuration utility. Small-Mac generates relocatable object modules in the 8-bit Microsoft format, and is invoked with a simple command syntax. Listing 7-1 contains the source code for MAC.

LNK is the Small-Mac linkage editor. It combines object modules with modules from libraries into a complete executable program. The default output is a standard .COM file. However, it can generate a load-and-go (.LGO) file for execution at any desired address. Listing 7-2 contains the source code for LNK.

LGO loads and optionally executes .LGO files. It is most useful for loading system extensions after you have booted the operating system. Listing 7-3 contains the source code for LGO.

LIB builds, maintains, and lists the contents of LNK compatible libraries. This facility enables you to assemble modules that are common to various programs, gather them into a single library, and then have LNK search the library for just those modules needed by the program being linked. Listing 7-4 contains the source code for LIB.

CMIT compiles machine instruction tables, lists them, and optionally configures the assembler with the resulting object table. This approach to defining the machine instructions to the assembler provides a great deal of flexibility in adapting the assembler to different CPUs and in creating specialized instruction sets without incurring the overhead of macro processing. Listing 7-5 contains the source code for CMIT.

DREL produces a formatted dump of .REL and .LIB files. This makes it possible to study the contents of these files even though they are structured as a continuous stream of bit fields. Listing 7-6 contains the source code for DREL.

Listing 7-7 contains the source code for functions common to several of these programs.

System Requirements

The implementation of the Small-Mac package runs on 8080/8085/Z80 machines using the CP/M-80 operating system. You should have two diskette drives and at least 56K of memory.

Concepts and Facilities

Source Files

Source lines have a free field format, with fields appearing in the following order on each line:

```
symbol/label    operation    operand    comment
```

Each field is optional, and null lines are ignored. Fields are separated by white space (spaces and tabs), except that comments are prefixed by a semicolon (;).

The Symbol/Label Field

A symbol consists of a contiguous sequence of letters, digits, and any of the special characters _ . $? or @. The first character must not be a digit. Uppercase and lowercase letters are equivalent. Symbols may be any length, but only the first eight characters are significant, and only six characters are used for declaring external references and entry points in object modules.

Labels in the symbol/label field are always terminated with a colon (:). They may appear alone or followed by an instruction and/or comments. The address assigned to the label is the address of the first byte of the next instruction or data item. Two colons following a label declare it to be an entry point. References to labels and nonlabel symbols *must not* be terminated with colons.

The Operation Field

If no label or symbol precedes an operation code (op-code) or assembler directive (pseudo-op), then the operation field may begin in the first character position. The pseudo-ops are defined within the assembler, but the machine instruction op-codes are defined in an external machine instruction table, which is compiled into internal format and placed into the assembler by the configuration utility CMIT.

The Operand Field

Operands and/or operand locations (memory addresses or register names) are specified in the operand field.

Symbols in the operand field must either be defined elsewhere or be declared to be external. This is done by terminating them with a pair of number signs (#) or by using the EXT directive.

The dollar sign $ may be used in the operand field as an implied reference to the address of the current instruction.

Memory references and numeric values may be written as expressions. Small-Mac expression operators are a subset of those in the C language and follow the same precedence and grouping rules. This gives the C/assembly programmer just one set of rules to learn. For more about expressions, see Expressions below.

Comments

Comments may appear as the last field on any line. A semicolon (;) introduces comments. A line may consist entirely of comments by specifying a semicolon as the first graphic character. White space is not necessary before a comment.

Object Files

There are two kinds of Small-Mac object files: modules and libraries. Modules are created by the assembler and always have a .REL filename extension. Libraries are created by the library manager and consist of a pair of files: the library itself (.LIB extension) and an index into the library (.NDX extension).

Small-Mac object modules are relocatable and follow the 8-bit Microsoft format. This is a bit field format intended to reduce the size of object files. There is no byte alignment except at the beginning of a module. The bit fields are listed in Table 7-1.

The order of the items in a module is:

1. program name
2. entry symbols (unordered)
3. program area size
4. body of module
    absolute items
    program-relative items
    external reference increments
    set location counter items
5. list (in alphanumeric sequence) of
    external reference chains
    entry points
6. end of program
7. end of file

A library is just the concatenation of a collection of modules, except that there is only one end-of-file item. A library index is merely a series of 16-bit word pairs pointing to the beginning of each module in the library. The first word specifies the 128-byte block and the second the byte in the block. Both begin at zero.

Program-relative items may be addresses, data, or chain pointers. The end of a chain is indicated by an absolute item of value zero. All external references to a particular entry point are chained together so that the linker may find them and replace (resolve) them with the address of the matching entry point. If an external reference is included in an expression so that the result is an offset (negative or positive) from the reference, then an "external reference increment" item immediately precedes the chain link. This is added after resolving

Table 7-1.
Bit Fields in Small-Mac Modules

LINK ITEM FORMAT	DESCRIPTION	USED?
0 <8-bits>	absolute item	YES
1000000 lll <string>	entry symbol	YES
1000001 lll <string>	select common block	NO
1000010 lll <string>	program name	YES
1000011 lll <string>	library to search	NO
1000100 lll <string>	extension link item	NO
1000101 tt <16-bits> lll <string>	common area size	NO
1000110 tt <16-bits> lll <string>	external reference chain	YES
1000111 tt <16-bits> lll <string>	entry point	YES
1001000 tt <16-bits>	external reference decr.	NO
1001001 tt <16-bits>	external reference incr.	YES
1001010 tt <16-bits>	data area size	NO
1001011 tt <16-bits>	set location counter	YES
1001100 tt <16-bits>	location counter chain	NO
1001101 tt <16-bits>	program area size	YES
1001110 tt <16-bits>	end of module	YES
1001111	end of file	YES
101 <16-bits>	program relative item	YES
110 <16-bits>	data relative item	NO
111 <16-bits>	common relative item	NO

The lll field occupies 3 bits and specifies the string length. The tt field occupies 2 bits and specifies the type of 16-bit field that follows. The type codes are:

CODE	MEANING	USED?
00	absolute	YES
01	program relative	YES
10	data relative	NO
11	common relative	NO

the reference. The "increment" item has no effect on the loading location counter. Small-Mac assembler listings show both the chain pointer and the increment value.

Machine Instructions

As mentioned above, machine instructions are defined in an external machine instruction table (MIT). This is an ASCII file that specifies the operation mnemonics, the operand syntax, and the object code for each machine instruction. The configuration utility CMIT compiles the table into internal format, then optionally lists it and/or plants a copy of it in the assembler.

This approach to defining the machine instructions makes it much easier to adapt the assembler to other CPUs. It also makes it easy to create specialized instruction sets that are readily assembled without the overhead of macro processing.

Listings 7-8 and 7-9 show the machine instruction tables for the 8080 and Z80 processors, respectively. Each line consists of three fields: object, mnemonic, and operand. White space separates the fields.

Expression specifiers may appear in the operand and object fields. They indicate where in the operand syntax an expression may appear, and where in the object code the corresponding expression value is to be placed. Also specified is the size of the object value (one or two bytes), and whether or not it is a PC (program counter) relative value. Expression specifiers consist of the lowercase letter x or p and (in the object field) a digit indicating the number of bytes (one or two). The letter x indicates an ordinary expression value, and the letter p indicates a PC-relative value. Except for these specifiers, all other letters in the mnemonic and operand fields must be uppercase.

In the compiled MIT, 16 bits are used to describe the format of the object code. Each code byte takes one bit in the format word, and each expression takes 3 bits. Therefore, any combination of code bytes and expressions may be generated as long as the number of format bits used does not exceed 16.

Underscore characters are used between object components for legibility. The code bytes and expression values are generated in the order specified in the object field. If more than one expression is specified, the assembler places them in the object file in the same order as they appear in the operand field.

To match an instruction to an entry in the MIT, the assembler performs a hash search for the mnemonic and then a serial search for the correct operand variant. The serial search proceeds in the order of the variants in the MIT. This works quite well for 8080 assembly language but rather poorly for the Z80, which has an obscene number of variants of some mnemonics (for example, LD). If you have an idea of the relative frequency of use of the operand variants, you may rearrange the order of the MIT to improve search time. But be warned that you *must* keep all the variants of a given mnemonic together.

The use of vertical bars ¦ in the MIT operand field is a space-saving device that is effective because of the redundancy of operand variants in most instruction sets and the tendency of CPU architects to assign object codes sequentially. The vertical bar separates operand variants specified on the same line. In such cases, the object byte that immediately precedes the first expression or comes last if there is no expression is understood to apply to the first variant. For each subsequent variant on the line, that byte is incremented by one. The other object bytes remain the same.

If you plan to alter an MIT, it is most important that you understand how the assembler matches an expression with an expression specifier in the MIT operand field. For a detailed understanding, see the function match() in the file MIT.C. Once the instruction mnemonic is found in the MIT, match() is called to attempt a match on the correct operand variant. It compares characters from left to right, treating uppercase and lowercase the same. If a mismatch occurs that variant fails; if a match occurs then the next pair of characters is compared. When an x or p is found in the MIT operand field, the string beginning with the current instruction character is skipped until a comma or an unmatched right parenthesis is encountered. Unmatched, in this case, means unmatched while skipping the expression string.

For instance, if the instruction "LD A,((a+b)/2)" is being matched with "LD A,(x)" then the second right parenthesis terminates the expression skipping because only the first right parenthesis is matched in the skipping process. So the string "(a+b)/2" is taken as the expression. This part of the instruction is extracted from the source line during the matching process and placed in a separate buffer for subsequent analysis.

Now, what would happen if the instruction "LD A,(x)" appeared in the MIT before "LD A,(HL)" while the instruction "LD A,(HL)" was being assembled? That's right, "HL" would be taken for an expression and the instruction would erroneously match "LD A,(x)". Therefore, take care to place such variants after any other variant that could match it. Incidentally, this error would no doubt produce an assembly error message.

Assembler Directives

Small-Mac supports the assembler instructions (pseudo-ops) listed in Table 7-2. This release of Small-Mac does not provide repeat pseudo-ops or conditional assembly.

Table 7-2.
Pseudo-ops Supported by Small-Mac

SYNTAX	FUNCTION
[label] DW value[,value[,...]]	define words
[label] DB value[,value[,...]]	define bytes
[label] DS expr	define storage
[label] EXT symbol[,symbol[,...]]	declare external references
symbol SET expr	set symbol to expr
symbol EQU expr	equate symbol to expr
[label] ORG expr	set location counter to expr
[label] END [expr]	end of source file (expr gives starting address)
symbol MACRO	begin a macro definition
ENDM	end a macro definition
[label] macroname [par[,par[,...]]]	call (expand) the named macro

In the pseudo-ops listed in Table 7-2, brackets enclose optional elements. The term *value* stands for either an expression or a character string. Character strings are enclosed in either apostrophes (') or quotes ("). If you want an occurrence of the delimiter within the string, code two successive delimiters. The term *expr* stands for an expression.

```
[label] DW    value[,value[,...]]
```

Define Words: For each value in the operand field, the assembler reserves one word containing that value. If a label is specified, it assumes the address of the first word.

[label] DB   value[,value[,...]]

Define Bytes: For each value in the operand field, the assembler reserves one byte containing that value. Each value must be absolute. If a label is specified, it assumes the address of the first byte.

[label] DS   expr

Define Storage: The number of bytes of memory specified by the expression are reserved. They have no predictable value. The expression must yield an absolute value. If a label is specified, it assumes the address of the first byte.

[label] EXT symbol[,symbol[,...]]

Declare External References: Each symbol is declared to be external. If a label is given, it assumes the address of the next instruction or data byte in the program. Note that declaring a symbol external is sufficient to cause the module containing it as an entry point to be loaded with the program by the linker. It need not actually be referenced.

symbol   SET expr

Set Symbol Value: This pseudo-op "sets" the symbol to the value of the expression. The same symbol may be reset later by other SET pseudo-ops. Once a value is given to a symbol, it may be used in expressions.

symbol   EQU expr

Equate Symbol to Value: This pseudo-op "equates" the symbol to the value of the expression. The same symbol may not be used with SET or EQU again. Once a value is given to a symbol, it may be used in expressions.

[label] ORG expr

Set Location Counter Origin: This pseudo-op sets the origin for the assembler location counter. Small-Mac only allows forward movement of the location counter. This prevents programmers from overlapping old code with new and confusing the linker as it attempts to resolve external reference chains.

[label] END [expr]

End of Source File: This pseudo-op designates the end of a source file. It is required, and it must be the last line of each source file. If a label is present, it assumes the program-relative address of the byte following the last byte assembled. If an expression is given, it must evaluate to a program-relative value, that the assembler takes as the starting address of the program. Only one starting address should be specified when a program is assembled from more than one source file. However, if more than one is given, the assembler will take the last one processed. If no starting address is given, execution will begin at the first instruction of the program.

The starting address, if any, is included in the output object file. When the linker builds an executable program from several modules, it inserts in front of the program a jump to the starting address. If it encounters more than one module with a starting address, it uses the last one.

```
symbol   MACRO
```

Begin a Macro Definition: This pseudo-op signals the beginning of a macro definition. The symbol is required and gives the name of the macro. For more on macro processing, see The Macro Facility below.

```
ENDM
```

End a Macro Definition: This pseudo-op signals the end of a macro definition.

```
[label] macroname [par[,par[,...]]]
```

Call a Macro: This pseudo-op is used to call (or expand) a macro. The label is optional. If given, it assumes the program-relative address of the first byte of the macro expansion. *Macroname* is the name given to the macro. Actual parameters are supplied in a comma-separated list in the operand field. Parameters are merely character sequences that replace corresponding substitution sentinels in the macro body. If spaces, commas, or semicolons are in a parameter, it must be delimited by quotes (") or apostrophes ('). Delimiters within such strings are written as two successive delimiters. Missing parameters are taken as null strings. Two successive commas indicate a missing parameter. A parameter is also missing if the parameter list does not go far enough to include it.

Expressions

Expressions may appear in the operand field of certain machine instructions or pseudo-ops. For the proper placement of expressions in machine instructions, see the machine instruction tables in Listings 7-8 and 7-9. Expression evaluation always produces a 16-bit binary value. If the expression appears in the operand field of an instruction, its value is placed in the object file. If the instruction requires less than 16 bits, high order bits are truncated. Expressions in the DW and DB pseudo-ops likewise produce values in the object file.

Relocation Rules

The value of an expression is either absolute or program relative, depending on whether and how symbols are used.

Program-relative items in an object file are converted to absolute by the linker once it has determined the absolute address at which the module will reside, whereas absolute items are loaded without change.

Recall that a label always has a program-relative value; that is, it assumes the program-relative address of the next assembled item in the program. But a numeric constant is absolute. The relocation attribute of an expression depends on the attributes of its primary terms and the way they are combined. Table 7-3 illustrates the rules for determining the relocation attribute of expressions.

Table 7-3.
Rules for Determining the Relocation Attribute of Expressions

COMBINATION	RESULT
abs ? abs	abs
abs + rel	rel
abs ? rel	error
rel + abs	rel
rel - abs	rel
rel - rel	abs
rel == rel	abs
rel < rel	abs
rel <= rel	abs
rel != rel	abs
rel > rel	abs
rel >= rel	abs
rel ? rel	error

A question mark in the list stands for any operator other than the ones explicitly shown for each combination of left- and right-hand attributes.

Ordinarily, only 16-bit object fields take relocatable expressions. However, a relocatable expression may appear for a PC-relative field; that is, a field containing a signed offset that is added by the CPU to the program counter to obtain the effective address. The Z80 JR (jump relative) instruction is an example of PC-relative addressing. In such cases MAC takes the expression as the target address. It subtracts the location counter and the instruction length from the expression, converting it an absolute offset from the following instruction. But if the expression evaluates to an absolute value, MAC assumes the programmer means to give an offset from the current instruction; it therefore subtracts only the instruction length to account for the fact that the CPU applies the offset after advancing the PC.

Numbers

Numbers must be integer values. They are assumed to be decimal unless followed immediately by O or Q (specifies octal), or H (specifies hexadecimal).

The first character of a number must be a decimal digit. A leading zero may be needed to make hexadecimal numbers conform to this rule. Numbers are converted to 16-bit values and then combined with the rest of the expression (if any).

Symbols

Symbols in an expression must either be defined elsewhere or be declared external. A symbol appearing in the operand field may be terminated with a pair of number signs (#), declaring it to be an external reference. The EXT directive also declares symbols to be external. External symbols have the program-relative attribute. Symbols defined with the SET and EQU pseudo-ops are assigned the relocation attribute of the expressions in their operand fields.

Operators

Small-Mac expression operators are a subset of those in the C language and follow the same precedence and grouping rules. They are listed in Table 7-4.

Operators with the highest precedence are at the top, and all operators in the same box in Table 7-4 have the same precedence. Arrows indicate the direction of grouping. You may use parentheses to control grouping. Any number of nesting levels is permitted.

The Current Instruction Address

You may use the dollar sign $ as an implied label for the address of the current instruction. It has the program-relative attribute.

The Macro Facility

Source lines located between the MACRO and ENDM pseudo-ops constitute the body of a macro. They are stashed away in a buffer during pass one

Table 7-4.
Small-Mac Expression Operators

!	logical NOT	<-
~	one's complement	<-
-	unary minus	<-
*	multiplication	->
/	division	->
%	modulo (remainder)	->
+	addition	->
-	subtraction	->
<<	shift left	->
>>	shift right	->
<	less than	->
<=	less than or equal	->
>	greater than	->
>=	greater than or equal	->
==	equal	->
!=	not equal	->
&	bitwise AND	->
^	bitwise exclusive OR	->
|	bitwise inclusive OR	->
&&	logical AND	->
||	logical OR	->

of the assembly process. The occurrence of a macro name in the operation field causes the body of the named macro to be inserted at that point in the program. This is called a macro "expansion" or macro "call." The first term comes from the fact that a single instruction is "expanded" into a whole set of instructions. The second term comes by analogy to subroutine calls. Indeed, macros are also known as "open" or "inline" subroutines. Macro calls must follow their definitions in the source file.

Nesting of macro definitions and macro calls is not allowed. If more than one macro definition has the same name, only the first one is used.

Parameter Substitution

Parameters may be specified with each macro call to tailor the expanded code to the circumstances peculiar to the call. Simply place ?1 in the body of the macro where the first actual parameter should go, ?2 for the second and ?0 for the tenth and final one. At most, ten parameters are allowed. Parameters in a macro call are identified by position and are separated by commas. Successive commas or missing trailing parameters produce a null substitution; that is, the substitution sentinel (for example, ?3) corresponding to a null parameter is squeezed out of the expanded text. If you desire a ? in the expanded text, code ?? in the macro body. Quotes or apostrophes may delimit an actual parameter containing spaces. An occurrence of the delimiter within the string is achieved by giving two successive delimiters.

Parameter substitution is performed without regard to context. Therefore, substitutions occur within quoted strings, comments, and even symbols and mnemonics. You can use this simple concept to your advantage.

Local Labels

Ten labels that are local to each macro expansion may be specified in the macro body as @0 through @9. The first such label encountered by the assembler and its references will appear in the expanded text as @1, the second as @2, and so on. The sequence continues to increase throughout the program so that every such label and its references is guaranteed to be unique. This avoids "redundant definition" errors when the same macro is called repeatedly.

The Load-and-Go Facility

At times it is desirable to develop programs that run at addresses other than the standard CP/M TPA address. Frequently such programs are special device drivers or other BIOS extensions that should usually be invoked whenever a cold start is performed. Small-Mac includes a special load-and-go loader, LGO, for such purposes. LGO loads and optionally transfers control to programs that are created by LNK with a special load-and-go format.

The -G# switch requests LNK to generate a load-and-go program. The number sign (#) stands for the hexadecimal address at which the program is to execute. Load-and-go files contain a return instruction at the beginning so that attempts to invoke them as ordinary CP/M commands (by renaming the filename extensions) will fail gracefully. Following the return are words specifying the load address, the length in bytes, and the starting address. This information is used by LGO to load precisely the right number of bytes at the right address and to (optionally) begin execution at the right place.

It is the programmer's responsibility to ensure that this creates no problems during subsequent operation of the operating system. Refer to your CP/M manuals for the proper techniques.

The User Interface

The command to invoke a Small-Mac program consists of (1) the program name with optional drive designator in standard CP/M format, (2) redirection specifications for standard output files, and (3) switches used to control the action of the program.

Standard Input and Output Files

Small-Mac programs support Unix-like redirectable "standard" files. A standard file is a file that is automatically opened upon program execution. By default, the "standard input" file is assigned to the keyboard and the "standard output" file is assigned to the screen.

You may direct the standard input file away from the keyboard by placing a < in the command line followed by the new source. This may be a filename (complete with extension and optional drive specifier), or a logical device such as RDR:.

Likewise, you may direct the standard output file away from the screen by placing a > in the command line. When standard output is redirected by >> (for example, >>FILE3), the output is appended to whatever data was already in the named file. If the file does not already exist, it is created and >> is no different than >.

Both redirection specifications may be given simultaneously in any position following the program name in the command line.

Take care not to assign both input and output to the same file; the result will be a corrupted file.

Small-Mac programs use standard input only for keyboard response to error messages, so there should be no need to redirect it. Standard output is used for listings and error messages, so by default these go to the screen.

Command Line Parameters

Switches consist of a hyphen followed immediately by one or two letters and, perhaps, a numeric value. Switch letters are chosen to have mnemonic value. Except for LIB, all the Small-Mac programs allow switches to appear in any position after the program name. LIB takes only one switch, and it must come first in the command line.

Small-Mac programs take nonswitch parameters as filenames. The order in which they are listed can make a difference. See the individual program descriptions below for details.

Usage Messages

To aid in remembering the various switches and parameters used with Small-Mac programs, the console displays a usage message whenever a Small-Mac program is invoked with a null or undefined switch. If you need help remembering how to invoke a program, just enter the program's name followed by an isolated hyphen. Usage messages indicate the syntax of the commands that invoke Small-Mac programs; they have the form

```
Usage: <program> <switch>... <file>...
```

where <program> is the program name, <switch> is a switch, and <file> is a filename. The < and > characters are not part of the syntax. They only indicate that a generic term is enclosed.

Redirection specifications are not shown in usage messages since they are common to all programs; their presence can be assumed.

Square brackets appear in usage messages to indicate fields that are optional. The brackets are not part of the command.

Programs take default actions when an optional switch is missing. These actions are chosen to be the most usual ones, so that switches are usually needed only in exceptional cases. LIB is an exception, since it must always be told what to do.

The ellipsis appears in usage messages to indicate that a given type of field may occur more than once in the command. The ellipsis itself is not a part of the command.

Words or combinations of words are used as generic names for specific types of parameters. For example, the term *source* stands for an assembler input file.

Error Handling

All Small-Mac programs send error messages to the standard output file. If a fatal error is reported, the program aborts with an audible alarm. If possible, the program runs to completion before aborting. However, some errors (for example, command line errors) may cause immediate program termination.

Two errors are caught by the Small-C runtime system rather than the program:

1. R, Redirection specification error, which indicates an attempt to redirect standard input to come from a nonexistent file. This should not occur, since there is no reason to redirect Small-Mac standard input files.
2. M, Memory allocation error, which indicates that an attempt was made to allocate more memory than was available.

Program Control

You may interrupt any of the programs in the Small-Mac package while they are running. To make a program pause temporarily, enter a control-S from the keyboard. Another keystroke continues program execution. To abort a program, enter control-C.

USING SMALL-MAC PROGRAMS

MAC: The Small-Mac Assembler

```
Usage: MAC [-L] [-NM] [-P] [-S#] [object] source...
-L         Generate an assembly listing
-NM        No macro processing
-P         Pause on errors
-S#        Set the symbol table for # symbols maximum
object     Name of the object file
source...  Names of the source files
```

Description

Source Files

You must specify at least one source file in the command line. If more than one is given, they will be assembled into a single object module in the order given. You may include a drive specifier with the source filenames to direct the assembler to specific drives. If no drive is indicated, the default drive is assumed. If a source file cannot be found, MAC aborts with an error message. The default and only allowed source filename extension is MAC.

The Object File

You may specify one object file. If none is given, the object code goes into a file on the default drive bearing the same name as the first source file, but with a REL extension. You may include a drive specifier with the object filename to direct the output to a specific drive. If no drive is indicated, the default drive is assumed. The object filename must have a REL extension to distinguish it from the source files. The module name in the object file is taken from the first six characters of the object filename.

The Assembly Listing

An assembly listing will be produced only if you include the -L switch in the command line. The listing and any error messages are sent to the standard output file and, therefore, go to the screen unless redirected.

Error messages follow the line in the listing to which they apply. However, if no listing is being generated, each erroneous source line is printed before its error message(s).

The listing output is paginated for printing on 11-inch high pages. You should use either a wide printer or a compressed print mode for assembly listings.

Each line in the listing contains (left to right):

- The source line number in decimal
- The current location counter value in hexadecimal
- The hexadecimal object code generated by the current source line
- The source line

Program relocatable items in the object column are flagged with an apostrophe. Other items are absolute. If the object code will not fit in the allotted space, overflow lines are printed.

A sorted dump of the symbol table is produced at the end of the listing. Each line shows the symbol value, relocation attribute flag, symbol, and symbol type. Symbol types are indicated with the following suffixes:

```
:         label
::        entry point
##        external reference
```

The Macro Override

You may specify the -NM switch, meaning "no macros," if macro processing is not required. This speeds up the assembler by about 13 percent. Macro processing is *not* needed for programs generated by the Small-C compiler.

Error Pauses

The -P switch causes MAC to pause after displaying the errors for each line. It waits until a carriage return is received from the keyboard.

Symbol Table Size

The -S# switch sets the size of the symbol table. The number sign stands for an unsigned decimal integer, indicating the maximum number of symbols that the table will hold. Since performance degrades as the symbol table approaches capacity, leave some unused space in the table. The default table size is 500 symbols.

Whatever memory is left over after allocating the symbol table is used for macro buffer space. The larger the symbol table, the less space remains for macro definitions; the smaller the symbol table, the more space remains for macro definitions.

If you need to assemble programs with approximately 400 symbols or more, use -S# to increase the size of the symbol table. On the other hand, if you get a "Macro Buffer Overflow" error, try decreasing the symbol table size.

Examples

COMMAND	DESCRIPTION
MAC PROG	Assemble PROG.MAC, generating PROG.REL on the default drive. Do not produce a listing and do not pause on errors.
MAC PROG PROG2 -L -P	Assemble PROG.MAC and PROG2.MAC, generating PROG.REL on the default drive. Produce a listing on the screen and pause on errors.
MAC P1 P2 P3 B:P.REL -NM	Assemble P1.MAC, P2.MAC, and P3.MAC, generating P.REL on drive B. Do not produce a listing, do not pause on errors, and do not perform macro processing.
MAC PROG -L >LST:	Assemble PROG.MAC, generating PROG.REL on the default drive. Produce a listing on the LST device and do not pause on errors.

Normal Messages

MESSAGE	EXPLANATION
Waiting...	MAC is waiting for a carriage return from the keyboard.

Error Messages

MESSAGE	EXPLANATION
Backward Movement	An ORG would move the assembly location counter backward.
Bad Data	A DW or DB specifies improper data.
Bad Expression	An improper expression is in the operand field.
Bad Label	An improper label is in the symbol/label field.
Bad Operation	A mnemonic cannot be found in the machine instruction table.
Bad Parameter	A macro call specifies too many parameters.
Bad Symbol	An improper symbol has been found.
xxxxxxxx - Can't Open	The named file cannot be opened.
Close Error	A file cannot be closed properly.
Invalid Extension	A command-line file specification contains an improper extension.
Macro Buffer Overflow	The macro text buffer has overflowed.
Missing END	An input file lacks the END pseudo-op.
Missing ENDM	The end of a source file was encountered while within a macro definition.
Redundant Definition	The same symbol appears more than once in the symbol/label field. Only the SET pseudo-op is permitted to redefine symbols, and then only the ones it defined originally.
Relocation Error	An 8-bit field has evaluated to a program-relative value or the expression on an END pseudo-op is not program relative.
Symbol Table Overflow	No more symbols will fit into the symbol table.
xxxxxxxx - Too Long	The command line contains a filename that is too long.
Undefined Symbol	The operand field contains a reference to an undefined symbol.
Write Error in REL File	An output error has occurred in the object file. Most likely the output disk drive has run out of space.

LNK: Small-Mac Linkage Editor

```
Usage: LNK [-B] [-G#] [-M] program [module/library...]
```

-B	Linking a BIG program. Reserve all of memory for the symbol table and buffer program text entirely on disk.
-G#	Output a LGO file for execution at address #.
-M	Monitor linking activity.
program	A file specifier for the program being linked.

module/library... A list of zero or more module (.REL) and/or library (.LIB) files.

Description

Functional Description

LNK performs three primary tasks: it combines separately assembled modules into a single program, resolves external references, and adds the base address of each module to all the program-relative items contained within it, thereby converting them to absolute values.

This work is done in two phases. First, it scans the command line to look for module and library names. Each module that is named in the command line is read into a loading buffer behind the previous module. As each module is being loaded, a temporary list of pointers to program relative items is written into a "reference" file (.R$) for use in phase two. Also, entry points and external references are loaded into a symbol table for use in resolving external references.

The symbol table is structured as two linked lists arranged in alphanumeric order—one for external references and one for entry points. Each symbol table entry contains a chain pointer, the name of the symbol, and a 16-bit address. In the case of an entry point, the value is just the entry point address. But in the case of an external reference it is the address of the head of a chain of references to that symbol. LNK resolves an external reference by replacing every link in its chain with the value of the matching entry point.

After loading each module, LNK attempts to resolve all external references that match entry points in the new module. As each external reference is resolved, its place in the symbol table is reclaimed for future use. New external references use up reclaimed space before the table is extended. Entry points must remain in the table in case they are referenced by upcoming modules.

When LNK encounters a filename with a .LIB extension it assumes it to be a library. In that case a search is made for library members (modules) that contain entry points matching yet unresolved external references. This search is facilitated by the fact that every entry point contained in a module is listed near the beginning of the module. If no match is found, the module is skipped. To speed up the skipping process, an index file (.NDX) is used to obtain the location of the beginning of the next module. LNK seeks directly to the next module without reading through the unwanted one. When the scan is finished, the library is rescanned to resolve backward references. This is repeated until no more modules are loaded, at which time LNK continues scanning the command line for further modules and/or libraries.

Note that merely declaring a symbol to be external will cause its module to be loaded. It need not actually be referenced.

When the command line is exhausted, LNK enters phase two. It closes the reference file and reopens it for input. It then begins writing the buffered object code to the output file (either .COM or .LGO). As it proceeds, it compares the address of each item to the current address from the reference file. On each match, a relative item has been found, so LNK adds an offset value, making it an absolute value. The next reference address is read and the process continues. To reduce head movement during phase two, additional buffering is used for the reference file.

The -B Switch. Normally, LNK attempts to use all available memory for buffering program text (object) and for the symbol table. However, there may not be enough memory for LNK, its symbol table, and the program being loaded. When LNK sees that a module about to be loaded will not fit in main memory, it overflows into a temporary file with an extension of ".O$". Processing then continues as before, except that subsequent modules are placed into the overflow file. This slows down the loading process significantly, but it occurs only on larger programs.

The low end of memory is used for program text and the high end for the symbol table. As processing continues, each grows in the direction of the other. Overflow occurs when the next module to be loaded would overlap an imaginary cushion of 200 entries at the end of the symbol table. Even after overflowing to disk, the symbol table may overflow when the cushion is exhausted. At that point, LNK aborts with the message "Must Specify -B Switch." When you invoke LNK with the -B switch, LNK overflows immediately to disk, leaving all available memory for the symbol table. This should permit the linking of programs of any size.

The Load-and-Go Switch. The -G# switch causes LNK to output a .LGO file instead of a .COM file. The address at which the program will run is specified by the hexadecimal number represented by #. The LGO loader must be used to load and/or execute the program.

The Monitor Switch. The -M switch causes LNK to monitor its loading and linking activities. It produces on the standard output file a list of modules loaded, their sizes, and their load addresses (both program-relative and absolute).

Program and Module Names. At least one module (.REL file) name must be specified. A filename without an extension is taken as a module name. The first module determines the name of the output program. Subsequent modules are loaded with and linked to the "program" module, but have no influence on the program name. If an extension is given to a module name, it must be .REL. If a drive designator (for example, B:) is specified, it is used for finding the input file. However, the output file always goes onto the default drive.

Library Names. Libraries are identified by specifying the .LIB extension, that must be specified with the filename. A drive designator may be given to specify where the library and its index are to be found. LNK requires the presence of an index file on the same drive bearing the same name, but with a .NDX extension.

The library C.LIB contains the standard Small-C runtime functions. Whenever you link a Small-C program, you must specify C.LIB.

The Special Module END. To facilitate the linking of Small-C programs, LNK is sensitive to the module name END. That module in C.LIB must always be loaded last. This is because it contains statements that initialize the beginning of free memory before the program begins execution. When LNK would load a module by that name, it passes it by, and at the end of phase one goes back and loads it last. If LNK were to see more than one module named END, it would load only the last one.

This feature may be useful when you construct private libraries.

Special Note

Compile LNK only with Small-C 2.1 (edit level 63) or later. Edit 63 fixes CSYSLIB so that when it overflows a buffer while writing into a file, it no longer assumes that it is at the end of the file. This prevents it from padding a sector with 1A (hex) in the middle of a file when random access is being used.

Examples:

COMMAND	COMMENT
LNK PROG -GE000	Load PROG.REL, yielding PROG.LGO for execution at address E000.
LNK P1 P2 C.LIB	Link P1.REL, P2.REL, and any required modules from C.LIB, yielding P1.COM for execution as a standard CP/M command.
LNK -B -M >LST: ABC C.LIB	Link ABC.REL and any required modules from C.LIB, yielding ABC.COM. ABC is very big, so load it entirely to disk, leaving all of available memory for the symbol table. Monitor the linking process on the LST device.

Normal Messages

MESSAGE	EXPLANATION
xxxx Bytes at yyyy zzzz mmmmmm	Module mmmmmm of length xxxx is loaded at relative address yyyy (absolute zzzz). This appears only when -M is specified.

xxxx Byte Buffer	The amount of memory available for the symbol table and the object buffer is xxxx. This appears only when -M is specified.
xxxx Bytes (hex)	The size of the program in hexadecimal is xxxx.
xxxxx Bytes (dec)	The size of the program in decimal is xxxxx.
xxxx Overflow Point	The relative address of the first module to overflow is xxxx. This appears only if LNK is compiled with the DEBUG symbol and -M is specified.
Resolving xxxxxx to yyyy	LNK is starting to resolve external reference xxxxxx with head of chain at yyyy. This appears only if LNK is compiled with the DEBUG symbol and -M is specified.
Start in xxxxxx	A starting address was specified for module xxxxxx.

Error Messages

MESSAGE	EXPLANATION
Abnormal End of REL File	The end of a module or library has been reached without finding a proper end-of-file item.
xxxxxxxx - Can't Open	The named file cannot be opened.
Close Error	A file cannot be closed properly.
Corrupt Library or Index	A seek error has occurred while attempting to locate the next module in a library.
Corrupt Module	An unrecognizable link item has been found in a module or library member.
Error Reading xxxxxxxx	An I/O error has occurred while reading the named file.
Error Writing xxxxxxxx	An error has occurred while writing the named file. Mostly likely this means that the disk ran out of space.
Invalid Extension	A command-line file specification contains an improper extension.
Must Specify -B Switch	There is not enough free memory to contain both the symbol table and program text. Rerun LNK specifying the -B switch.
Premature End of Index	The index for a library contains too few entries.
Redundant: xxxxxx	The named symbol occurs more than once as an entry point.
Seek Error in xxxxxxxx	A seek error occurred while attempting to find a relative item in the overflow file. This could be caused by a problem with the overflow file, or a logic flaw in LNK.
xxxxxxxx - Too Long	The command line contains a filename that is too long.
Unresolved: xxxxxx	No entry point was found to match the named external reference.

Unsupported Link Item	An input module contains a recognizable but unsupported Microsoft link item.

LGO: Small-Mac Load-and-Go Loader

```
Usage: LGO [-G] [-M] program

-G        Execute program after loading.
-M        Monitor the load address, size, and starting
          address.
program   File specifier for the program being loaded
```

Description

LGO is a very simple loader designed to load .LGO files at their designated addresses and optionally begin execution. Its primary purpose is to permit the convenient installation of operating system extensions at cold start time.

When the -G# switch is used with LNK, it outputs a special .LGO file instead of the usual .COM file. Load-and-go files have the following format:

ITEM	BYTES
RET instruction	1
starting address	2
base address	2
program size	2
object text	<size>

The RET instruction serves two purposes. It identifies the file as having the load-and-go format and it produces a graceful exit in case someone were to rename the file to a .COM extension and then attempt to execute it as a CP/M command.

The base address and size tell LGO exactly where to load the program and how many bytes to load. Only the indicated number of bytes are loaded. That number is reported by LNK when the .LGO file is created. Always verify that .LGO programs will fit exactly where they are expected to go.

You should also consult the CP/M documentation and the documentation for your particular implementation of CP/M to learn how CP/M manages its TPA (temporary program area). If you place a .LGO program above CP/M, there will be no problem. However, if you place it below the CCP at the top end of the TPA, you must write your program to adjust the address at location 0006 to refer to the beginning of your program, which in turn must contain a jump to the address in BDOS that originally existed at location 0006. This will cause CP/M to operate normally with a reduced TPA, leaving your program intact even as normal programs are executed in the TPA.

You cannot place a permanent program at the low end of the TPA, and you certainly cannot allow one to overlap LGO while it is executing in the TPA as a normal CP/M command. LGO is written in Small-C; therefore, its normal stack is located at the high end of the TPA. So, in order to make the top of the TPA available for loading programs, LGO moves its own stack to the first 256 bytes following itself.

When LGO is executed, a program name must be specified in the command line. If an extension is given, it must be .LGO.

LGO performs the following functions:

- Opens the named file
- Verifies that it has the load-and-go format
- Reads the initial parameters
- Loads the indicated number of bytes at the indicated address
- If -G was specified, it transfers control to the starting address.

Examples:

COMMAND	COMMENT
LGO DRIVER -G	Load DRIVER.LGO at the appropriate address and begin execution.
LGO PROG -M	Load PROG.LGO, display the loading address, size, and starting address on the screen, then exit to CP/M.
LGO ABC	Load ABC.LGO, and exit to CP/M.

Error Messages

MESSAGE	EXPLANATION
xxxxxxxx - Can't Open	The named file cannot be opened.
Error Reading xxxxxxxx	An I/O error occurred while reading the indicated file.
Invalid Extension	A command-line file specification contains an improper extension.
Invalid LGO Format	The named file is not a true load-and-go file.
xxxxxxxx - Too Long	The command line contains a filename that is too long.

LIB: — Small-Mac Library Manager

```
Usage: LIB -{DPTUX}[A] library [module...]

-D      Delete named modules
```

-P[A]	Print named or all (-PA) modules
-T[A]	Print a table of contents of named or all (-TA) modules
-U	Update (add/replace) named module
-X[A]	Extract named or all (-XA) modules

Description

LIB is used to maintain libraries of relocatable object modules (library members). Each member has exactly the same format as a freestanding object module (.REL file). Each library consists of a concatenation of object modules in a file that has a .LIB extension. An index file (.NDX) must accompany each library. The index file contains a series of word pairs, each specifying the address of the first byte of a member within the library. The first word indicates the block and the second the byte within the block. LNK and LIB use this information to seek directly to the next library member. LIB maintains libraries in alphanumeric order.

When LIB is invoked, the first parameter must be a switch indicating the function to be performed. This must be followed by the name of the library in question. The library name may have the extension .LIB (which is assumed as the default), but no other. A drive designator may be given to indicate where the library is to be found.

Whenever LIB creates or modifies a library, it outputs on the same drive a new library with an extension of .L$ and a new index with an extension of .N$. Then, upon successful completion, it deletes the original library and index and renames the new files with permanent extensions.

The -D and -U commands require a list of member names to be operated upon. The other commands may operate on either a list of members or all members. The list can be supplied three ways: it may be given in the command line following the library name, entered from the console, or obtained from a file of names. If names appear in the command line, they are taken as the list. Otherwise LIB obtains the names from the standard input file. If standard input has been redirected to a disk file, LIB reads the file, obtaining one name per line. However, if standard input has not been redirected, LIB prompts for each name to be entered from the keyboard. A null response (carriage return only) signals the end of the list.

The -P, -T, and -X commands operate on every member in the library if the name list is empty; that is, no names appear in the command line and a null reply is given to the first prompt, or the file to which standard input has been redirected is empty. If you want to avoid the prompt and do not wish to supply a null file, simply append the letter A to the switch, giving -PA, -TA, or -XA.

Name lists may appear in any order.

Member names are only six characters long. However, a filename may be eight characters long (excluding drive designator and extension). The name list may specify names of up to eight characters. Such names are truncated to six characters when referencing library modules. However, the -U command will use all eight characters when looking for freestanding modules to copy into a library. The -X command uses only six characters when it creates freestanding modules. When names will be truncated, LIB lists them on the screen and asks whether or not to proceed.

Deleting Members

The -D switch causes LIB to delete specific members from an existing library. Each member to be deleted must be specified in the name list.

Printing Library Members

The -P switch causes LIB to print the contents of selected modules. Specified members are printed with program (module) name, program size, entry points, external references, and the end of program sentinel. To save space, object text is not shown. DREL can be used to see the complete contents of a module.

Printing a Table of Contents

The -T switch causes LIB to print a table of contents; that is, a list of member names. This is an eight-column list in alphanumeric order going left to right, top to bottom.

Creating or Updating a Library

The -U switch causes LIB to update (that is, add and replace) named members. For each name specified, a stand-alone module is copied into the new library. If a module of the same name is in the old library, it is replaced. Before proceeding with the update operation, each named file is sought on disk. If any are not found, LIB asks whether to proceed.

If the named library does not exist, a null library is created and the operation proceeds as usual.

Extracting Library Members

The -X command causes LIB to copy the named members from the library into stand-alone files. Each file is placed on the default drive with a .REL extension.

Examples:

COMMAND	COMMENT
LIB -U M ABC DEF HIJ	Update M.LIB (and M.NDX) with ABC.REL, DEF.REL, and HIJ.REL.
LIB -X MY	Extract members from MY.LIB. Accept member names from the keyboard. If the first response is null, all members are to be extracted.
LIB -D MY <ABC.LST	Delete from MY.LIB (and MY.NDX) the members that are named in the file ABC.LST.
LIB -P M GETREL	Print the member GETREL from M.LIB.
LIB -TA C	List the entire table of contents of C.LIB.

Normal Messages

MESSAGE	EXPLANATION
Added xxxxxx	The indicated member has been added to the library.
Created xxxxxx	The indicated file has been created as a stand-alone module.
Creating New Library	The named library did not exist, so a new library by that name is being created.
Continue?	Should LIB continue or quit?
Deleted xxxxxx	The indicated member has been deleted from the library.
Module Name: xxxxxx	Prompt for the next module name.
Replaced xxxxxx	The indicated member has been replaced in the library.

Error Messages

MESSAGE	EXPLANATION
xxxxxxx - Can't Find - Ignored	The named file cannot be found and will be ignored.
xxxxxxx - Can't Open	The named file cannot be opened.
Can't Rename Files	The commanded operation is complete, but the new files cannot be renamed to permanent extensions.
Close Error	A file cannot be closed properly.
Corrupt Library or Index	An index-directed seek did not locate the beginning of a member.
Delete by Name Only	Specific members were not named for a delete operation.
xxxxxxx - Duplicate Name - Ignored	The same member name was specified more than once.

Error Reading Index	An I/O error occurred while reading the index file.
Error Writing New Index	An I/O error occurred while writing the new index file. Most likely this means that the disk is full.
xxxxxxxx - Extension Forced to xxx	A filename extension was specified. LIB will ignore it and use .REL instead.
Invalid Extension	A command-line file specification contains an improper extension.
xxxxxxxx - Invalid Format - Ignored	An invalid filename format was specified. It will be ignored.
Limited Stack Space	LIB is operating with limited stack space. It may malfunction. A larger TPA is needed.
Memory Overflow	LIB cannot proceed because there is not enough memory.
Premature End of Index	The end of the index file was reached before the end of the library.
Too Many Modules Specified	LIB cannot handle the number of member names specified. Lib will take at most 200 module names. Multiple LIB runs can be made or LIB can be recompiled with a larger value assigned to the symbol MAXMODS.
xxxxxx Was Not in Library	The indicated member was not found in the library.
xxxxxxxx - Will be Truncated to xxxxxx	The indicated name will be truncated as shown.
xxxxxxxx - Too Long	The command line contains a filename that is too long.

CMIT: Small-Mac Configuration Utility (Compile Machine Instruction Tables)

```
Usage: CMIT [-C] [-L] [table] [mac]

-C      Configure the executable assembler with the indicated or
        default machine instruction table.
-L      List the compiled machine instruction table.
table   The name of the machine instruction table file in source format
        (default 8080.MIT).
mac     Assembler .COM file (default MAC.COM).
```

Description

CMIT is used to compile machine instruction tables (MITs) from external source format into internal format. Listings 7-8 and 7-9 show the two machine instruction tables supplied with Small-Mac.

Once a table has been compiled, it is printed and/or copied into the executable assembler, thereby configuring it to a specific CPU.

After you have compiled and linked a new MAC.COM, you must configure it by running CMIT before you may execute it. You may reconfigure a previously configured MAC.COM anytime.

CMIT produces its listings from the object table. It reads the source table a second time and looks up each instruction in the internal MIT using the same functions the assembler uses. CMIT then lists each instruction, showing the source, the number of looks needed to find it in the internal MIT, and the object code that will be generated when the instruction is assembled.

Whenever a new MIT is created, you must carefully check its listing to verify that it will generate the correct object code.

The -C Switch

The -C switch causes CMIT to configure an executable assembler with the compiled MIT.

The -L Switch

The -L switch causes CMIT to list the compiled table on the standard output file. The output may therefore be redirected to a printer, disk file, or whatever.

If no switches are given, -L is assumed. However, if any switches are given, only requested actions are taken.

Naming the Machine Instruction Table

If no MIT source file is named, then 8080.MIT (on the default drive) is assumed. A filename without an extension or with an extension of .MIT designates a different MIT source file. You may give a drive specifier.

Naming the Target Assembler

If no executable assembler file is named, MAC.COM on the default drive is assumed. A filename with an extension of .COM designates a different copy of the assembler. You may give a drive specifier.

Examples:

COMMAND	COMMENT
CMIT	Compile 8080.MIT (from the default drive) and list the resulting table.

Small-Mac: An Assembler for Small-C

CMIT -C	Compile 8080.MIT (from the default drive) and place a copy in MAC.COM (also on the default drive).
CMIT Z80 B:MAC.COM	Compile Z80.MIT (from the default drive) and place a copy in B:MAC.COM.

Normal Messages

MESSAGE	EXPLANATION
Buffer Space Used nnnnn	The indicated number of bytes of buffer space was actually used for the internal MIT.
Operation Codes nnnnn	The indicated number of unique operation codes (mnemonics) were compiled.

Error Messages

MESSAGE	EXPLANATION
xxxxxxxx - Write Error	A I/O error occurred while writing into the indicated file. Most likely the disk is full.
Bad Expression Specifier	An illegal expression specifier was found in the source file.
Bad Hex Byte	An illegal hexadecimal byte value was found in the source file.
Can't Find Instruction in MIT	While verifying the object table, CMIT could not find an instruction mnemonic Most likely, this indicates a program error in CMIT.
Can't Find Operand	While verifying the object table, CMIT could not find an instruction operand. Most likely, instructions having the same mnemonic were separated in the source file.
xxxxxxxx - Can't Open	The named file cannot be opened.
Can't Rewind MIT File	The source file will not rewind.
Close Error	A file cannot be closed properly.
Invalid Extension	A command-line file specification contains an improper extension.
MIT Buffer Overflow	Insufficient space was allowed in the internal MIT buffer. This can be corrected by increasing the value assigned to MIBUFSZ in MAC.H, then recompiling both CMIT and MAC.
xxxxxxxx MIT is nnnnn Bytes but Should be nnnnn	The size of the internal MIT in the indicated executable assembler and in CMIT.COM are not the same. This can be corrected by verifying that MAC.H contains the correct values for MICOUNT, MIBUFSZ, and MIOPNDS, then recompiling both CMIT and MAC.

MIT Mnemonic Overflow	Insufficient space was allowed in the internal MIT for hashing mnemonics. This can be corrected by increasing the value assigned to MICOUNT in MAC.H, then recompiling both CMIT and MAC.
MIT Operand Overflow	Insufficient space was allowed in the internal MIT for operands. This can be corrected by increasing the value assigned to MIOPNDS in MAC.H, then recompiling both CMIT and MAC.
xxxxxxx - Too Long	The command line contains a filename that is too long.

DREL: Dump Relocatable Object Files

    Usage: DREL

Description

DREL produces a formatted listing of the contents of an object file. It dumps either stand-alone modules or libraries. Output goes to the standard output file and, therefore, may be redirected to a printer, disk file, or whatever.

No command line switches are accepted. You are prompted for each file to be dumped. If a file cannot be found, you are prompted for another input file. Filenames must include extensions. Drive specifiers may be given. A null response to the prompt signals DREL to quit.

Example:

```
library/module name: TEST.REL

- program: TEST
 prog size: 008E'
   load at: 0064'
0064 0085' 05 00 EB CE 05 88 89 CD 0085' CD 008A' C3
0074 10 00 21 0089' 21 10 00 3A 00 00 3A 0005+ 007D'
0082 3A FFFB+ 0080' 01 32 03 34 05 36 07 38 09
 ext chain: 0083' EREF
- end prog: 0000
- end file

library/module name:
```

The first column of the body of the module is the program relative address of the first byte shown to the right.

Items with no suffix are absolute. Items with an apostrophe (') suffix are program-relative items. Items with a plus sign (+) suffix are offsets, which LNK adds to the following external reference after it has been resolved. Therefore, such items do not occupy space in the program and do not cause the location counter to advance. This must be taken into account when locating items in a dump. EREF is an external reference with head of chain at 0083 hex. Try following the chain.

The "load at" item was generated by an ORG or DS pseudo-op.

The absolute value of 0000 on the "end prog" item indicates that no starting address was specified.

Availability

Small-Mac is copyrighted; however, it is available to the general public for use without formal restrictions. Take it, use it, copy it, modify it, and give it away as you please. However, be sure to preserve the copyright notices. I am distributing Small-Mac as user-supported software, so if you obtained a "free" copy and find it useful, send a registration form and $20 to the author. You must obtain written permission to sell Small-Mac for more than your actual cost for media, packaging, and postage.

LISTING 7-1

```
                                                              FILE: MAC.C
/*
** MAC.C -- Small-Mac Assembler -- Part 1: Mainline and Macro Functions
**
**              Copyright 1985 J. E. Hendrix
**
** Usage: MAC [-L] [-NM] [-P] [-S#] [object] source...
**
** -L       Generate an assembly listing on the standard output file.
**
** -NM      No macro processing.  This speeds up the assembler somewhat.
**          Macro processing is NOT needed for Small-C 2.1 output files.
**
** -P       Pause on errors waiting for an operator response of CR.
**
** -S#      Set symbol table size to accept # symbols.
**
** object   Name of the object file to be output.  It must have a REL
**          extension to be recognized as the output file.  A drive
**          specifier is allowed.  If not specified, the object code
**          will go into a file (on the default drive) bearing the same
**          name as the first source file, but with a REL extension.
**
** source... Names of the source files to be assembled. The default, and
**          only allowed, extension is MAC. A drive specifier is allowed.
**          The named files will be assembled as one file concatenated
**          in the order given.
**
**          NOTE: The module name in the REL file will be taken from
**          the first 6 characters of the object filename.
*/
#include <stdio.h>
#include "notice.h"
#include "mac.h"
#include "rel.h"
#include "mit.h"
#define NOCCARGC

/*
** symbol table
*/
int
  stmax = STMAX,              /* maximum symbols */
  stn,                        /* number of symbols loaded */
  *stp;                       /* symbol table pointer arrar */
char
  *st,                        /* symbol table buffer */
  *stend,                     /* end of symbol table */
```

```
  *stptr,                    /* st entry pointer */
  stsym[MAXLAB+1];           /* temporary symbol space */

/*
** macro definition table
*/
char
  *mt,                       /* macro table buffer */
  *mtprev,                   /* previous mt entry */
  *mtnext,                   /* next available mt byte */
  *mtend,                    /* end of macro table */
  *mtptr;                    /* mt entry pointer */

int
  pass = 1,                  /* which pass? */
  badsym,                    /* bad symbol? */
  gotep,                     /* have an entry point? */
  gotxr,                     /* have an external reference? */
  gotlabel,                  /* have a label? */
  gotnam,                    /* have a name? */
  eom,                       /* end of module? */
  endv,                      /* END value */
  endt,                      /* END type */
  err,                       /* error? */
  lerr,                      /* line error flags */
  loc,                       /* location counter */
  lin,                       /* line counter */
  srcfd,                     /* source file fd */
  list,                      /* generate a listing? */
  lline,                     /* listing line, force 1st page heading */
  part1,                     /* part 1 of listing line printed? */
  ccnt,                      /* count of code characters printed */
  lpage,                     /* listing page */
  pause,                     /* pause on errors? */
  looks,                     /* number of looks to find instruction */
  macros = YES,              /* macro processing? */
  mlnext,                    /* next macro label to assign */
  mlnbr[10],                 /* macro label numbers */
  mpptr[10],                 /* macro parameter pointers */
  defmode,                   /* macro definition mode */
  expmode;                   /* macro expansion mode */

char
  *ep,                       /* expression pointer */
  *lp,                       /* line pointer */
  line[MAXLINE],             /* source line */
  *prior,                    /* prior ext ref in chain */
  srcfn[MAXFN+4],            /* source filename */
  objfn[MAXFN+4];            /* object filename */
```

```c
main(argc, argv) int argc, *argv; {
  fputs("Small-Mac Assembler, ", stderr); fputs(VERSION, stderr);
  fputs(CRIGHT1, stderr);
  getsw(argc, argv);            /* get command line switches */
  pass1(argc, argv);            /* build symbol table */
  pass2(argc, argv);            /* generate object code */
  if(err) abort(7);             /* sound the alarm */
  }

/*
** pass one
*/
pass1(argc, argv) int argc, *argv; {
  int max;
  st = calloc(STBUFSZ,   1);    /* allocate zeroed symbol table */
  stp = calloc(stmax, INTSZ);
  stend = st + STBUFSZ;         /* remember end of table */
  max = avail(YES);             /* how much available? */
  max -= STACK + (MAXOPEN * OHDOPEN);  /* calculate how much */
  mt = mtnext = calloc(max, 1); /* allocate space */
  mtend = mt + max - MAXLINE;   /* note end of macro buffer */
  dopass(argc, argv);           /* do pass 1 */
  }

/*
** pass two
*/
pass2(argc, argv) int argc, *argv; {
  int i;
  outrel = open(objfn, "w");    /* open object file */
  putname();                    /* declare module name */
  putent();                     /* declare entry points */
  putsz();                      /* declare program size */
  pass = 2;                     /* signal pass 2 */
  dopass(argc, argv);           /* do pass 2 */
  putexs();                     /* declare ep and xr symbols */
  putend();                     /* declare end of program */
  if(ferror(outrel)) err = YES;
  close(outrel);                /* close object file */
  }

/*
** process passes 1 and 2
*/
dopass(argc, argv) int argc, *argv; {
  int mop;
  int i;
  mlnext = lpage = i = lin = loc = 0;  /* reset everything */
  lline = 100;                  /* force page heading */
```

```
while(getarg(++i, srcfn, MAXFN, argc, argv) != EOF) {
  if(srcfn[0] == '-') continue;
  if(extend(srcfn, SRCEXT, OBJEXT)) continue;
  srcfd = open(srcfn, "r");         /* open source file */
  eom = NO;                         /* not end of module */
  goto input;
  while(YES) {
    poll(YES);
    ++lin; lerr = 0;                /* bump line counter & zero errors */
    part1 = NO;                     /* part 1 of .ine not listed */
    begline();                      /* begin a listing line */
    if(macros == NO) {
      dolabel();                    /* do label and find next field */
      if(!domach()) doasm();        /* machine or assembler instr? */
    }
    else {
      lp = line;
      lp = getsym(lp, NO);
      if(!(mop = macop()) && gotnam) {/* 2nd field a token? */
        lp = skip(1, line);         /* no, try first */
        mop = macop();
      }
      if(defmode) {                 /* definition mode */
        if(mop == ENDM) defmode = NO;
        if(pass == 1) putmac();     /* put line in macro table */
      }
      else {                        /* copy or expansion mode */
        if(mop == CALL) {           /* enter expansion mode */
          expmode = YES;
          putparm();                /* save parameters */
          dolabel();                /* process label */
        }
        else if(mop == MACRO) {     /* enter definition mode */
          defmode = YES;
          if(pass == 1) newmac();   /* init new macro in table */
        }
        else if(mop == ENDM) {      /* leave expansion mode */
          expmode = NO;
        }
        else {
          if(expmode) replace();
          dolabel();                /* do label and find next field */
          if(!domach()) doasm();    /* machine or assembler instr? */
        }
      }
    }
    endline();                      /* end a listing line */
    if(pass == 2) gripe();          /* gripe about errors */
    if(expmode) getmac();           /* fetch next macro line */
```

```
      else {
        input:
        if(eom) break;
        if(!fgets(line, MAXLINE, srcfd)) error("- Missing END");
        }
      }
    if(defmode) {err = YES; puts("- Missing ENDM");}
    close(srcfd);                       /* close source file */
    }
  }
/*
** can line take more?
*/
cantake(i, need) int i, need; {
  return (i < (MAXLINE - 3) - need);
  }

/*
** get a line from the macro buffer
*/
getmac() {
  char *cp; cp = line;
  while(*cp++ = *mtptr++) ;
  }

/*
** get switches from command line
*/
getsw(argc, argv) int argc, *argv; {
  char arg[MAXFN+4]; int i, j, len;
  i = 0;
  while(getarg(++i, arg, MAXFN, argc, argv) != EOF) {
    if(arg[0] == '-') {
          if(toupper(arg[1]) == 'L') list = YES;
      else if(toupper(arg[1]) == 'P') pause = YES;
      else if(toupper(arg[1]) == 'N' &&
              toupper(arg[2]) == 'M') macros = NO;
      else if(toupper(arg[1]) == 'S') {
        len = utoi(arg + 2, &j);
        if(len > 0 && !arg[len + 2]) stmax = j;
        else usage();
        }
      else usage();
      }
    else {
      if(extend(arg, OBJEXT, OBJEXT) || !*objfn) {
        if(arg[1] == ':') j = 2; else j = 0;
        strcpy(objfn, arg + j);
```

```
          }
        }
      }
    }
/*
** recognize macro operation
*/
macop() {
  if(fldcmp(lp, "ENDM" ) == 0) return (ENDM);
  if(fldcmp(lp, "MACRO") == 0) return (MACRO);
  if(!expmode && !defmode && mtfind()) return (CALL);
  return (NO);
  }

/*
** test for macro buffer overflow
*/
macover(ptr) char *ptr; {
  if(ptr > mtend) error("- Macro Buffer Overflow");
  }

/*
** find stsym in macro table
** return true if found, else false
** leave mtptr pointing to body of desired macro
*/
mtfind() {
  if(atend(*lp) == 0) {
    mtptr = mt;
    do {
      if(fldcmp(lp, mtptr + MTNAM) == 0) {
        mtptr += MTNAM;
        mtptr += strlen(mtptr) + 1;
        return (YES);
        }
      mtptr = getint(mtptr);
      } while(mtptr);
    }
  return (NO);
  }

/*
** establish new macro
*/
newmac() {
  int i; i = 0;
  if(!gotnam || badsym) symerr();
  else {
```

```c
    macover(mtnext);
    if(mtprev) putint(mtprev, mtnext);
    mtprev = mtnext;
    putint(mtnext, 0);
    mtnext += INTSZ;
    while(*mtnext++ = stsym[i++]) ;
    }
  }

/*
** put a line in the macro buffer
*/
putmac() {
  char *cp; cp = line;
  macover(mtnext);              /* will buffer take it? */
  while(*mtnext++ = *cp++) ;    /* copy everything */
  }

/*
** save macro call parameters in macro buffer
** and reset macro labels
*/
putparm() {
  int i, dlm; char *cp;
  i = -1; cp = mtnext;
  lp = skip(2, lp);                    /* skip to parameters */
  while(++i < 10) {
    mlnbr[i] = 0;                      /* null macro label nbr */
    while(isspace(*lp)) ++lp;
    if(atend(*lp) || *lp == ',') mpptr[i] = 0;
    else {
      macover(cp);
      mpptr[i] = cp;
      while(!atend(*lp) && *lp != ',') {
        if(*lp == '\"' || *lp == '\'') {          /* string? */
          dlm = *lp;
          while(!atend(*++lp)) {
            if(*lp == dlm && *++lp != dlm) break;
            *cp++ = *lp;
            }
          }
        else *cp++ = *lp++;
        }
      *cp++ = NULL;
      }
    if(*lp == ',') ++lp;
    }
  if(!atend(*lp)) parerr();
  }
```

```
/*
** replace parameters
*/
replace() {
  char lin[MAXLINE]; int ndx;
  char *cp, *cp2;    int i;
  strcpy(lin, line); cp = lin; i = 0;
  do {
    if(*cp == '?') {                        /* substitution marker? */
      if(isdigit(*++cp)) {                  /* parameter substitution? */
        ndx = *cp++ - '0' - 1;              /* which one? */
        if(ndx < 0) ndx = 9;                /* make 0 mean 10 */
        if(cp2 = mpptr[ndx]) {              /* got parameter? */
          while(*cp2)                       /* yes, copy it */
            if(cantake(i, 1)) line[i++] = *cp2++;
          }
        continue;
        }
      }
    if(*cp == '@') {                        /* label substitution? */
      if(cantake(i, 1)) line[i++] = '@';    /* insert label prefix */
      if(isdigit(*++cp)) {                  /* which one? */
        ndx = *cp++ - '0';
        if(!mlnbr[ndx]) mlnbr[ndx] = ++mlnext; /* need new label number? */
        if(cantake(i, 5)) {
          left(itou(mlnbr[ndx], line + i, 5)); /* insert label number */
          while(line[i]) ++i;               /* bypass label number */
          }
        continue;
        }
      }
    if(cantake(i, 1)) line[i++] = *cp++;
    else {
      line[i++] = '\n';
      break;
      }
    } while(*cp);
  line[i] = NULL;
  }

/*
** abort with a usage message
*/
usage() {
  error("Usage: MAC [-L] [-NM] [-P] [-S#] [object] source...");
  }
```

FILE: MAC2.C

```
/*
```

```
**  MAC2.C -- Small-Mac Assembler -- Part 2: Pass 1 and 2 Functions
**
**              Copyright 1985 J. E. Hendrix
*/
#include <stdio.h>
#include "mac.h"
#include "rel.h"
#include "ext.h"
#define NOCCARGC

extern int iloc;                        /* instr location */

/*
** add a new symbol to the symbol table
*/
addsym() {
  char *dest, *sour;
  if(*stptr) error("- Symbol Table Overflow");
  stp[stn++] = stptr;                   /* set symbol pointer */
  dest = stptr; sour = stsym;
  while(*dest++ = toupper(*sour++));
  }

/*
** determine if an assembler instruction
*/
aifind() {
  char *cp; cp = lp;
  while(isgraph(*lp)) ++lp;
  while(isspace(*lp)) ++lp;
       if(fldcmp(cp, "DW")  == 0) return (DW);
  else if(fldcmp(cp, "DB")  == 0) return (DB);
  else if(fldcmp(cp, "DS")  == 0) return (DS);
  else if(fldcmp(cp, "EXT") == 0) return (EX);
  else if(fldcmp(cp, "SET") == 0) return (SET);
  else if(fldcmp(cp, "EQU") == 0) return (EQU);
  else if(fldcmp(cp, "ORG") == 0) return (ORG);
  else if(fldcmp(cp, "END") == 0) return (END);
  return (ERR);
  }

/*
** begin a line in the listing
*/
begline() {
  char str[6];
  if(pass == 2 && list) {
    if(begpage()) {
      puts("line  loc ----object----  source"); puts("");
```

```c
        lline += 2;
        }
      itou(lin, str, 5); fputs(str, stdout);
      itox(loc, str, 6); fputs(str, stdout);
      putchar(' '); ccnt = 0; ++lline;
      }
  }

/*
** begin a page?
*/
begpage() {
  char str[4];
  if(lline >= 58) {
    lline = 2;
    ++lpage;
    if(lpage > 1) puts("\n\n\n\n\n\n\n");
    fputs("file: ", stdout); fputs(srcfn, stdout);
    itou(lpage, str, 4);
    fputs("     page: ", stdout); puts(str); puts("");
    return (YES);
    }
  return (NO);
  }


/*
** detect assembler instruction and process it
*/
doasm() {
  int j;
  if(atend(*lp) && (!stsym[0] || gotlabel)) return;
  if((j = aifind()) == ERR) {       /* lp -> 2nd field or end */
    lp = skip(1, line);             /* lp -> 1st field */
    j = aifind();
    stsym[0] = NULL;                /* declare nc symbol */
    }
  switch(j) {
    case  EX: doext();        return;
    case  DW: dodat(INTSZ);   return;
    case  DB: dodat(1);       return;
    case  DS: doloc(YES);     return;
    case ORG: doloc(NO);      return;
    case SET: doval(SETBIT);  return;
    case EQU: doval(0);       return;
    case END: doend();        return;
    }
  oprerr();
  }
```

```
/*
** define data (DB & DW)
*/
dodat(sz) int sz; {
  int dlm;
  while(!atend(*lp)) {
    if(isspace(*lp) || *lp == ',') ++lp;
    else if(*lp == '\"' || *lp == '\'') {        /* string? */
      dlm = *lp;
      while(!atend(*++lp)) {
        if(*lp == dlm && *++lp != dlm) break;
        if(pass == 2) {field = *lp; genabs(sz);}
        else loc += sz;
        }
      }
    else {                                        /* expression? */
      ep = lp;
      expr(&field, &type);
      lp = ep;
      if(pass == 2) {
        type &= RELBITS;
        if(type == ABS) genabs(sz);
        else {
          if(sz == 1) {relerr(); genabs(1);}      /* 1-byte relocatable? */
          else genrel();                          /* output relocatable item */
          }
        }
      else loc += sz;
      }
    }
  }

/*
** process END instruction
*/
doend() {
  eom = YES;                                      /* flag end of module */
  onexpr();
  if((type & RELBITS) == PREL) {
    endt = PREL;
    endv = field;
    }
  else if(field) relerr();
  }

/*
** define external reference (EXT)
*/
doext() {
```

```
  while(!atend(*lp)) {
    while(isspace(*lp) || *lp == ',') {++lp; continue;}
    lp = getsym(lp, NO);                    /* fetch the next symbol */
    if(badsym) {symerr(); continue;}        /* symbol error */
    else if(stfind()) {                     /* already in table? */
      if(stptr[STFLAG] & (LABBIT|EQUBIT|SETBIT)) {rederr(); continue;}
      }
    else addsym();                          /* not yet defined */
    if(pass == 1) stptr[STFLAG] |= XRBIT|ABS;  /* 1st ext ref is ABS 0 */
    }
  }

/*
** detect label and stow it away
*/
dolabel() {
  lp = skip(1, line);                       /* locate first field */
  lp = getsym(lp, NO);                      /* fetch a symbol */
  if(gotlabel) {                            /* got a label */
    if(badsym) {laberr(); return;}
    if(stfind()) {                          /* already ir table */
      if(pass == 1) {
        if(stptr[STFLAG] & (LABBIT|EQUBIT|SETBIT|XRBIT))
          {rederr(); return;}
        }
      else if(stptr[STFLAG] & (LABBIT2|EQUBIT|SETBIT|XRBIT))
        {rederr(); return;}
      else stptr[STFLAG] |= LABBIT2;
      }
    else addsym();                          /* not defined, stow it */
    if(pass == 1) {
      putint(stptr + STVALUE, loc);         /* value */
      if(gotep)                             /* flags */
          stptr[STFLAG] = LABBIT|PREL|EPBIT;
      else stptr[STFLAG] = LABBIT|PREL;
      }
    }
  }

/*
** set location counter (ORG, DS)
*/
doloc(bump) int bump; {
  if(onexpr()) {
    if(bump) field = loc += field;
    else if(loc <= field) loc = field;
    else bakerr();
    if(pass == 2) {item = SETLC; type = PREL; putrel();}
    }
```

```
    }

/*
** detect machine instruction and process it
*/
domach() {
  char *fmt, *cp;
  if(gotlabel) cp = lp;
  else         cp = skip(1, line);      /* backup if no label */
  if(fmt = find(cp)) {                  /* machine instruction? */
    fmt += INTSZ;                       /* locate format byte in mit */
    if(pass == 2) domac2(fmt);          /* do pass 2 processing */
    else loc += (*fmt & 3) + 1;         /* bump location counter */
    return (YES);
    }
  return (NO);                          /* may be pseudo-op */
  }

/*
** detect machine instruction and generate object code
*/
domac2(ptr) char *ptr; {
  int format, len, ilen, pcr, t, v, opcode, holding;
  format = getint(ptr++);               /* ptr is now 1 byte early */
  len = ilen = (format & 7) + 1;
  format >>= 3;                         /* first code/expr bit */
  iloc = loc;                           /* preserve istr loc for $ */
  holding = NO;
  ep = expbuf;                          /* set ep for expr() */
  while(len-- > 0) {                    /* for each byte of code */
    if(format & 1) {                    /* expression */
      if(holding) {
        holding = NO;
        field = opcode + opadj;         /* adjust last byte before expr */
        opadj = 0;
        genabs(1);
        }
      expr(&v, &t);                     /* evaluate next expression */
      format >>= 1;                     /* pc relative bit */
      if(format & 1) {
        if((t & RELBITS) == PREL) {
          v -= ilen + iloc;             /* calc offset from this instr */
          t = (t & ~RELBITS) + ABS;     /* now abs, may be 1 byte */
          }
        else v -= ilen;                 /* adjust offset from this instr */
        pcr = YES;                      /* remember it's pc relative */
        }
      else pcr = NO;
      format >>= 1;                     /* size bit */
```

```
      if(format & 1) {                   /* 2-byte expr */
        if(t & XRBIT) {                  /* ext ref */
          if(v) {                        /* must offset from ext ref */
            item = XPOFF;
            type = ABS;
            field = v;
            listcode(2, "+ ");           /* list offset */
            putrel();                    /* write 2-byte offset */
            }
          field = prior;                 /* will link to prior ref */
          }
        else field = v;                  /* expr value */
        if((t & RELBITS) == ABS)
            genabs(2);                   /* write 2 absolute bytes */
        else genrel();                   /* write 2 relocatable bytes */
        --len;
        }
      else {                             /* 1-byte expr */
        if((t & RELBITS) == PREL)
          relerr();                      /* 1 byte can't be relocatable */
        if(pcr && (v > 127 || v < -128))
          rngerr();                      /* range error */
        field = v;                       /* expr value */
        genabs(1);                       /* write 1 absolute byte */
        }
      }
    else {                               /* code byte */
      if(holding) {
        field = opcode;                  /* don't adjust, not last byte */
        genabs(1);                       /* write prior code byte */
        }
      opcode = *++ptr & 255;             /* hold this one, may be more */
      holding = YES;
      }
    format >>= 1;
    }
  if(holding) {
    field = opcode + opadj;
    genabs(1);                           /* write last code byte */
    }
  }

/*
** define a symbol value (SET, EQU)
*/
doval(set) int set; {
  char *ptr; int found;
  if(!stsym[0] || badsym || gotlabel) {nerr(); return;}
  if((found = stfind()) == 0) addsym();       /* not defined */
```

```
    ptr = stptr;                             /* preserve stptr */
    onexpr();                                /* evaluate expression */
    if(pass == 1 || set) {
      if(found == 0 || ptr[STFLAG] & set) {
        putint(ptr + STVALUE, field);        /* value */
        ptr[STFLAG] = set|type;              /* flags */
        }
      else rederr();
      }
    else if(ptr[STFLAG] & (LABBIT|EQUBIT|SETBIT|XRBIT)) rederr();
    else ptr[STFLAG] |= EQUBIT;
    if(pass == 2) {                          /* list value */
      if((ptr[STFLAG] & RELBITS) == PREL)
           listcode(2, "' =");
      else listcode(2, "  =");
      }
    }

/*
** end a line in the listing
*/
endline() {
  char *cp; int col; col = 0;
  if(pass == 2 && list) {
    if(part1) puts("");
    else {
      part1 = YES;
      while(ccnt++ < 16) putchar(' ');
      cp = line;
      while(*cp) {
        if(*cp != '\t') {++col; putchar(*cp++);}
        else {do putchar(' '); while(++col % 8); ++cp;}
        }
      }
    }
  }

/*
** generate an absolute value of sz bytes
*/
genabs(sz) int sz; {
  listcode(sz, " ");
  loc += sz;                                 /* bump location counter */
  item = ABS;
  while(sz--) {putrel(); field >>= 8;}
  }

/*
** generate a relocatable item
```

```
*/
genrel() {
  listcode(2, "' ");
  loc += 2;                    /* bump location counter */
  item = PREL;
  putrel();                    /* write 2-byte relocatable item */
  }

/*
** gripe about errors in a line
*/
gripe() {
  if(lerr) {
    if(!list) outerr(line);
    if(lerr &    1) outerr("- Backward Movement\n");
    if(lerr &    2) outerr("- Bad Number\n");
    if(lerr &    4) outerr("- Bad Expression\n");
    if(lerr &    8) outerr("- Bad Label\n");
    if(lerr &   16) outerr("- Bad Operation\n");
    if(lerr &   32) outerr("- Redundant Definition\n");
    if(lerr &   64) outerr("- Bad Symbol\n");
    if(lerr &  128) outerr("- Relocation Error\n");
    if(lerr &  256) outerr("- Undefined Symbol\n");
    if(lerr &  512) outerr("- Bad Parameter\n");
    if(lerr & 1024) outerr("- Range Error\n");
    if(pause) wait();
    outerr("\n");
    err = YES;
    }
  }

bakerr() {lerr |=    1;}
numerr() {lerr |=    2;}
experr() {lerr |=    4;}
laberr() {lerr |=    8;}
oprerr() {lerr |=   16;}
rederr() {lerr |=   32;}
symerr() {lerr |=   64;}
relerr() {lerr |=  128;}
underr() {lerr |=  256;}
parerr() {lerr |=  512;}
rngerr() {lerr |= 1024;}

/*
** list a code item
*/
listcode(sz, suff) int sz; char suff[]; {
  int i; char str[3];
  if(list) {
```

```
      i = sz + sz + strlen(suff);
      if((ccnt + i) > 16) {endline(); begline();}
      while(sz--) {
        if(sz) itox((field >> 8) & 255, str, 3);
        else   itox(field & 255, str, 3);
        if(*str == ' ') *str = '0';
        fputs(str, stdout);
        }
      fputs(suff, stdout);
      ccnt += i;
      }
  }

/*
** output an error line
*/
outerr(str) char *str; {
  begpage(); fputs(str, stdout); ++lline;
  }

/*
** require one expression only
*/
onexpr() {
  ep = lp;
  expr(&field, &type);
  if(atend(*ep)) return (YES);
  experr();
  return (NO);
  }

/*
** output end of program and file
*/
putend() {
  item = EPROG; type = endt; field = endv; putrel();
  item = EFILE; type = ABS;  field = 0;    putrel();
  }

/*
** output entry points
*/
putent() {
  char *cp;
  cp = st;
  while(cp < stend) {
    poll(YES);
    if(*cp) {
      if(cp[STFLAG] & EPBIT) {            /* entry point */
```

```
          item = ENAME;
          strncpy(symbol, cp, MAXSYM + 1);
          putrel();
          }
        }
      cp += STENTRY;
      }
  }

/*
** output entry point or external reference
*/
putex(cp, i) char *cp; int i; {
  item = i;
  type = cp[STFLAG] & RELBITS;
  field = getint(cp + STVALUE);
  strncpy(symbol, cp, MAXSYM + 1);
  putrel();
  }

/*
** output ent pnt and ext ref symbols
*/
putexs() {
  int i; char *cp;
  ccnt = 0;                          /* init for show() */
  shell(0, stn - 1);                 /* sort the symbols */
  if(list && !begpage()) {++lline; puts("");}
  for(i = 0; i < stn; ++i) {
    poll(YES);
    cp = stp[i];
    if(list) show(cp);
    if(cp[STFLAG] & XRBIT) putex(cp, XCHAIN);
    if(cp[STFLAG] & EPBIT) putex(cp, EPOINT);
    }
  puts("");
  }

/*
** output module name
*/
putname() {
  int i, j;
  item = PNAME;
  if(objfn[1] == ':') i = 2; else i = 0;
    = 0;
  while(objfn[i] && objfn[i] != '.' && j < MAXSYM)
    symbol[j++] = objfn[i++];
  symbol[j] = NULL;
```

```
    putrel();
    }

/*
** output program size
*/
putsz() {
  item = PSIZE;
  type = PREL;
  field = loc;
  putrel();
  }

/*
** shell sort the symbols
*/
shell(l, u) int l, u; {
  int gap, i, j, k, jg;
  gap = (u - l + 1) >> 1;
  while(gap > 0) {
    i = gap + l;
    while(i <= u) {
      j = i++ - gap;
      while(j >= l) {
        jg = j + gap;
        if(strcmp(stp[j], stp[jg]) <= 0) break;
        k = stp[jg]; stp[jg] = stp[j]; stp[j] = k;
        j -= gap;
        }
      }
    gap >>= 1;
    }
  }

/*
** show a symbol
*/
show(cp) char *cp; {
  char str[5];
  begpage();
  itox(getint(cp + STVALUE), str, 5); fputs(str, stdout);
  if((cp[STFLAG] & RELBITS) == PREL) fputs("' ", stdout);
  else fputs("  ", stdout);
  fputs(cp, stdout);
  ccnt += 6 + strlen(cp);
  if(cp[STFLAG] & LABBIT) {putchar(':'); ++ccnt;}
  if(cp[STFLAG] & EPBIT)  {putchar(':'); ++ccnt;}
  if(cp[STFLAG] & XRBIT)  {fputs("##", stdout); ccnt += 2;}
  if(ccnt < 60)
```

```c
      while(ccnt % 20) {putchar(' '); ++ccnt;}
    else {puts(""); ++lline; ccnt = 0;}
    }

/*
** find stsym in symbol table
** leave stptr pointing to desired or null entry
** return true if found, else false
*/
stfind() {
  char *start;
  stptr = start = st + hash(stsym, stmax) * STENTRY;
  while(*stptr) {
    if(strcmp(stsym, stptr) == 0) return (YES);
    if((stptr += STENTRY) >= stend) stptr = st;
    if(stptr == start) break;
    }
  return (NO);
  }
```

FILE: MAC3.C

```c
/*
** MAC3.C -- Small-Mac Assembler -- Part 3: Expression Analyzer
**
**                 Copyright 1985 J. E. Hendrix
**
*/
#include <stdio.h>
#include "mac.h"
#include "rel.h"
#include "ext.h"

#define NOCCARGC         /* no argument count passing */

#define OR     1         /* | */
#define XOR    2         /* ^ */
#define AND    3         /* & */
#define EQ     4         /* == */
#define NE     5         /* != */
#define LE     6         /* <= */
#define GE     7         /* >= */
#define LT     8         /* < */
#define GT     9         /* > */
#define RSH   10         /* >> */
#define LSH   11         /* << */
#define PLUS  12         /* + */
#define MINUS 13         /* - */
#define MULT  14         /* * */
```

```
#define DIV    15           /* / */
#define MOD    16           /* % */
#define CPL    17           /* ~ */
#define NOT    18           /* ! */
#define LPN    19           /* ( */
#define RPN    20           /* ) */
#define LOC    21           /* $ */
#define SYM    22           /* symbol */
#define NUM    23           /* number */
#define EOE    24           /* end of expr */

int
  number,                   /* value of numeric token */
  iloc,                     /* instruction location */
  ct;                       /* current token */

int                         /* operators by precedence level */
  l1ops[] = {OR, NULL},
  l2ops[] = {XOR, NULL},
  l3ops[] = {AND, NULL},
  l4ops[] = {EQ, NE, NULL},
  l5ops[] = {LE, GE, LT, GT, NULL},
  l6ops[] = {LSH, RSH, NULL},
  l7ops[] = {PLUS, MINUS, NULL},
  l8ops[] = {MULT, DIV, MOD, NULL};

/*
** evaluate the next expression at ep
** caller must set ep
*/
expr(value, type) int *value, *type; {
  ct = NULL;                              /* no current token */
  if(token(EOE)) {
    *value = 0; *type = ABS;              /* null expression */
    return;
    }
  if(!level1(value, type) || ct != EOE) experr();
  }

level1(v, t) int *v, *t; {return (down(l1ops, level2, v, t));}
level2(v, t) int *v, *t; {return (down(l2ops, level3, v, t));}
level3(v, t) int *v, *t; {return (down(l3ops, level4, v, t));}
level4(v, t) int *v, *t; {return (down(l4ops, level5, v, t));}
level5(v, t) int *v, *t; {return (down(l5ops, level6, v, t));}
level6(v, t) int *v, *t; {return (down(l6ops, level7, v, t));}
level7(v, t) int *v, *t; {return (down(l7ops, level8, v, t));}
level8(v, t) int *v, *t; {return (down(l8ops, unary,  v, t));}

unary(v, t) int *v, *t; {
```

```
  if(token(CPL)) {                        /* ~ */
    if(!unary(v, t)) return (NO);
    *v = ~*v;
    goto check;
    }
  else if(token(NOT)) {                   /* ! */
    if(!unary(v ,t)) return (NO);
    *v = !*v;
    goto check;
    }
  else if(token(MINUS)) {                 /* - */
    if(!unary(v, t)) return (NO);
    *v = -*v;
  check:
    if(*t & RELBITS) relerr();            /* can't be relocatable */
    *t &= ~RELBITS;                       /* force ABS */
    return (YES);                         /* lie about it */
    }
  else return (primary(v, t));
  }

primary(v, t) int *v, *t; {
  int ok;
  if(token(LPN)) {                        /* ( */
    ok = level1(v, t);
    if(token(RPN)) return(ok);
    return (NO);
    }
  *t = ABS; *v = 0;                       /* defaults */
  if(token(NUM)) {                        /* number */
    *v = number;
    return (YES);
    }
  else if(token(LOC)) {                   /* $ */
    *v = iloc;
    *t = PREL;
    return (YES);
    }
  else {
    if(token(SYM)) {                      /* symbol */
      if(stfind()) {
        *t = stptr[STFLAG];
        if(!(stptr[STFLAG] & XRBIT)) {
          if(gotxr) rederr();
          *v = getint(stptr + STVALUE);
          }
        else goto doxr;                   /* ext ref */
        }
      else if(gotxr) {                    /* define new ext ref */
```

```
            addsym();                             /* symbol */
            *t = XRBIT|ABS;                       /* 1st ext ref is ABS 0 */
            doxr:
            prior = getint(stptr + STVALUE);      /* save prior ptr */
            putint(stptr + STVALUE, loc);         /* this becomes prev */
            stptr[STFLAG] |= XRBIT|PREL;          /* ext ref is relative */
            }
         else underr();                           /* undefined */
         return (YES);
         }
      }
   return (NO);
   }

/*
** drop to a lower level
*/
down(ops, level, v, t) int *ops, (*level)(), *v, *t; {
   int *op;
   if(!(*level)(v, t)) return (NO);
   op = --ops;
   while(*++op) {
     if(token(*op)) {
       if(!down2(*op, level, v, t)) return (NO);
       if(token(EOE)) return (YES);
       op = ops;
       }
     }
   return (YES);
   }

/*
** binary drop to a lower level
*/
down2(oper, level, v, t) int oper, (*level)(), *v, *t; {
   int ok, vr, tr, tl;
   ok = (*level)(&vr, &tr);
   *v = binary(*v, oper, vr);                    /* apply operator */
   tl = *t & RELBITS;
   *t = (*t | tr) & ~RELBITS;     /* merge flag bits & default to ABS */
   tr &= RELBITS;
   if(tl == ABS) {
     if(tr == ABS) return (ok);                  /* abs <oper> abs */
     else {                                      /* abs <oper> rel */
       if(oper == PLUS) {*t |= PREL; return (ok);}
       return (NO);
       }
     }
   else {                                        /* rel <oper> abs */
```

```c
    if(tr == ABS) {
      switch(oper) {
        case PLUS: case MINUS:
        *t |= PREL;
        return (ok);
        }
      return (NO);
      }
    else {                                      /* rel <oper> rel */
      switch(oper) {
        case MINUS:
        case EQ: case LT: case LE:
        case NE: case GT: case GE:
        return (ok);
        }
      return (NO);
      }
    }
  }

/*
** apply a binary operator
*/
binary(left, oper, right) int left, oper, right; {
  switch(oper) {
    case OR:    return (left | right);
    case XOR:   return (left ^ right);
    case AND:   return (left & right);
    case EQ:    return (left == right);
    case NE:    return (left != right);
    case LE:    return (left <= right);
    case GE:    return (left >= right);
    case LT:    return (left < right);
    case GT:    return (left > right);
    case RSH:   return (left >> right);
    case LSH:   return (left << right);
    case PLUS:  return (left + right);
    case MINUS: return (left - right);
    case MULT:  return (left * right);
    case DIV:   return (left / right);
    case MOD:   return (left % right);
    }
  return (NULL);
  }

/*
** scan for next token
*/
token(want) int want; {
```

```
  int len;
  if(ct) return (found(want, ct));        /* already have a token */
  while(isspace(*ep)) ++ep;
  switch(*ep++) {
    case '|': return (found(want, OR));
    case '^': return (found(want, XOR));
    case '&': return (found(want, AND));
    case '+': return (found(want, PLUS));
    case '-': return (found(want, MINUS));
    case '*': return (found(want, MULT));
    case '/': return (found(want, DIV));
    case '%': return (found(want, MOD));
    case '~': return (found(want, CPL));
    case '(': return (found(want, LPN));
    case ')': return (found(want, RPN));
    case '$': return (found(want, LOC));
    case ',': return (found(want, EOE));
    case '!': if(*ep++ == '=') return (found(want, NE));  --ep;
                               return (found(want, NOT));
    case '<': if(*ep++ == '=') return (found(want, LE));  --ep;
              if(*ep++ == '<') return (found(want, LSH)); --ep;
                               return (found(want, LT));
    case '>': if(*ep++ == '=') return (found(want, GE));  --ep;
              if(*ep++ == '>') return (found(want, RSH)); --ep;
                               return (found(want, GT));
    case '=': if(*ep++ == '=') return (found(want, EQ));  --ep;
  }
  --ep;
  ep = getsym(ep, YES); if(stsym[0]) {return (found(want, SYM));}
  if(len = getnum(ep))     {ep += len; return (found(want, NUM));}
  if(atend(*ep))                       return (found(want, EOE));
  return (NO);
}

/*
** what was found?
*/
found(want, have) int want, have; {
  ct = have;                            /* new current token */
  if(ct == want) {                      /* was it sought? */
    if(ct != EOE) ct = NULL;            /* yes, pass it by */
    return (YES);                       /* caller has a hit */
  }
  return (NO);                          /* sorry, no hit */
}

/*
** get hex, dec, or oct number as binary value in number
** return length of field processed, else zero
```

```
*/
getnum(at) char *at; {
  int bump, len; char *end, *cp;
  cp = at;
  if((*cp == '\'' || *cp == '"') && *cp == cp[2]) {    /* quoted char */
    number = cp[1] & 255;
    return (3);
    }
  switch(*cp) {
    case '0': case '1': case '2': case '3': case '4':
    case '5': case '6': case '7': case '8': case '9':
    end = cp;
    bump = 1;
    while(YES) {
      switch(toupper(*end)) {
        default: if(isxdigit(*end)) {++end; continue;}
                 bump = 0;
                 len = utoi(cp, &number); break;
        case 'Q':
        case 'O': len = otoi(cp, &number); break;
        case 'H': len = xtoi(cp, &number); break;
        }
      break;
      }
    if(len != (end - cp)) numerr();    /* bad number */
    return ((end - at) + bump);
    }
  return (0);  }

/*
** get a symbol into stsym
*/
getsym(at, ref) char *at; int ref; {
  int j;
  j = badsym = gotep = gotxr = gotlabel = 0;
  if(!isdigit(*at)) {
    while(YES) {
      switch(toupper(*at)) {
        case '#':
          if(ref) {gotxr = YES; if(*++at == '#') ++at; break;}
        default:
          if(ref) break;
          badsym = YES;
        case 'A': case 'B': case 'C': case 'D': case 'E':
        case 'F': case 'G': case 'H': case 'I': case 'J':
        case 'K': case 'L': case 'M': case 'N': case 'O':
        case 'P': case 'Q': case 'R': case 'S': case 'T':
        case 'U': case 'V': case 'W': case 'X': case 'Y': case 'Z':
        case '0': case '1': case '2': case '3': case '4':
```

```
          case '5': case '6': cape '7': case '8': case '9':
          case '_': case '.': case '$': case '?': case '@':
            if(j < MAXLAB) stsym[j++] = toupper(*at);
            ++at;
            continue;
          case ':':
            gotlabel = YES;
            if(*++at == ':') {gotep = YES; ++at;}
          case ' ': case '\t': case '\n':
          case ',': case NULL: case COMMENT:
          }
        while(isspace(*at)) ++at;
        break;
      }
    }
  stsym[j] = NULL;
  if(stsym[0] && !gotlabel) gotnam = YES; else gotnam = NO;
  return (at);
  }
```

LISTING 7-2

FILE:LNK.C

```
/*
** LNK.C -- Small-Mac Linkage Editor
**
**                    Copyright 1985 J. E. Hendrix
**
** Usage: LNK [-B] [-G#] [-M] program [module/library...]
**
** -B                A BIG program is being linked, so use all
**                   of free memory for the symbol table and load the
**                   program to disk entirely.  This is slower but it
**                   gets the job done.
**
** -G#               Make program absolute at address # (hex) and
**                   output as "program.LGO" instead of "program.COM".
**
** -M                Monitor linking activity.
**
** program           A file specifier for the program being linked.
**                   The default, and only allowed, extension is REL.
**
** module/library... A list of zero or more module (.REL) and/or
**                   library (.LIB) files.  Each module is linked to
**                   the program and the libraries are searched for
**                   just those modules which satisfy one or more
```

```
**                       unresolved external references.
**
** NOTE: Merely declaring a symbol to be external will cause
** it's module to be loaded.  It need not actually be referenced.
**
** NOTE: The symbol TMNAME is defined to be the name of the
** terminal module; i.e., the module which must be loaded last
** of all.  That module contains special code which identifies
** the physical end of the program and the beginning of free
** memory.  The linker is sensitive to its name and waits until
** all other modules are loaded before loading the terminal module.
**
** The absence of an extension, or a .REL extension, identifies a module;
** whereas, a .LIB extension identifies a library.  If necessary, a
** library is rescanned to resolve backward external references between
** modules within the library. Module files and libraries are processed
** in the order in which they occur in the command line.
**
** Drive Designators (e.g. B:):
**    - allowed with module and library names
**    - program drive designator locates the input .REL file
**    - output goes to the default drive
**
** Filename Extensions:
**    - must specify .LIB with library name
**    - standard extensions are:
**
**      .REL = relocatable object module
**      .LIB = library of object modules
**      .NDX = index to library (not user specified)
**      .COM = CP/M command file (default output)
**      .LGO = load-and-go file (-G# output)
**      .O$  = temporary overflow file
**      .R$  = temporary reference file
**
** Enter control-S to pause and control-C to abort.
**
** NOTE: Compile only with Small-C 2.1 (edit level 63) or later.
** Edit 63 fixes CSYSLIB so that when it overflows a buffer while
** writing into a file it will no longer assume that it is at the
** end of the file.  This prevents it from padding a sector with
** 1A (hex) in the middle of a file when random access is being used.
*/
#include <stdio.h>
#include "notice.h"
#include "rel.h"

#define NODEBUG             /* don't compile debug displays */
#define NOCCARGC            /* don't pass arg counts to functions */
```

```
#define NAMESIZE    15
#define MAXFIL      10
#define STACK       512         /* allow for stack space */
#define AUXBUF      2048        /* aux buffer for reference file */
#define MAXOPEN     4           /* maximum files opened */
#define OHDOPEN     164         /* memery overhead per open file */
#define COMBASE     259         /* 0100H + 3 */
#define RET         201         /* RET instruction (0C9H) */
#define JMP         195         /* JMP instruction (0C3H) */
#define RES         -1          /* value of resolved ext ref */
#define XRPLUS      -2          /* ext-ref-plus-offset flag */
#define TMNAME      "END"       /* terminal module name */
#define MODEXT      ".REL"
#define LIBEXT      ".LIB"
#define NDXEXT      ".NDX"
#define COMEXT      ".COM"
#define LGOEXT      ".LGO"
#define OFLEXT      ".O$"
#define REFEXT      ".R$"

/*
** symbol table definitions
*/
#define NXT     0               /* next-entry pointer */
#define VAL     2               /* offset value */
#define SYM     4               /* symbol */
#define SSZ (SYM+MAXSYM+1)      /* size of table entry */
#define HIGH 127                /* high-value byte */
#define CUSHION  (200*SSZ)      /* reserved for table at overflow point */
char high[] = {HIGH,0};         /* high-value symbol */

/*
** global variables
*/
char
    *xr,                        /* external reference */
    *nxt,                       /* next in ext ref chain */
    *ep,                        /* entry point */
    *buffer,                    /* beginning of code buffer */
    *bnext,                     /* next byte in code buffer */
    *sfree,                     /* head of freed entry list */
    *snext,                     /* next symbol table entry */
    *cloc,                      /* location counter */
    *cmod,                      /* module location */
    *cbase,                     /* base address */
    *csize,                     /* program size (fake unsigned) */
    *goloc,                     /* go location */
    *cdisk,                     /* disk overflow location */
    *epfirst,                   /* first entry point */
```

```
  *epprev,                 /* previous entry point */
  *epnext,                 /* next entry point */
  *xrfirst,                /* first external reference */
  *xrprev,                 /* previous external reference */
  *xrnext,                 /* next external reference */
  modname[MAXSYM+1],       /* name of current module */
  infn   [NAMESIZE],       /* input filename */
  ndxfn  [NAMESIZE],       /* index filename */
  tmfn   [NAMESIZE],       /* terminal-module library name */
  csfn   [NAMESIZE],       /* code seg filename */
  crfn   [NAMESIZE],       /* code rel filename */
  outfn  [NAMESIZE];       /* output filename */

int
  lgo,             /* load-and-go format? */
  monitor,         /* monitor activity? */
  instr,           /* instruction to plant at 0000 */
  addr,            /* start address */
  ref,             /* reference to program relative item */
  big,             /* linking a big program? */
  xrplus,          /* value of offset for next ext ref */
  xrpflag=XRPLUS,  /* value of xrplus flag */
  ndxfd,           /* index fd */
  inblock,         /* block of next library member */
  inbyte,          /* byte in block of next library member */
  tmblock,         /* block of terminal module in tmfn */
  tmbyte,          /* byte of terminal module in tmblock */
  csfd,            /* code segment fd */
  crfd,            /* code relative index fd */
  outfd;           /* output fd */

extern int Uchrpos[];        /* lives in CSYSLIB */

main(argc,argv) int argc, argv[]; {
  fputs("Small-Mac Linkage Editor, ", stderr); fputs(VERSION, stderr);
  fputs(CRIGHT1, stderr);
  getsw(argc, argv);         /* fetch and remember switches */
  getmem();                  /* acquire maximum memory buffer */
  phase1(argc, argv);        /* load and link */
  if(!okay()) abort(7);      /* quit early */
  phase2();                  /* generate final output */
  }

/*
** get as much memory as possible for symbol table
*/
getmem() {
  char sz[8];
  int max;
```

```
  max = avail(YES);                  /* how much available? */
  max -= STACK + AUXBUF + (MAXOPEN * OHDOPEN);
  buffer = bnext = malloc(max);      /* allocate space */
  snext  = buffer + (max - SSZ);     /* first entry */
  sfree  = 0;                        /* no reusable entries yet */
#ifdef DEBUG
  if(monitor) {itou(max, sz, 8); puts2(sz, " Byte Buffer");}
#endif
  newtbl(&epfirst);                  /* set low and high ent pts */
  newtbl(&xrfirst);                  /* set low and high ext refs */
  }

/*
** get next module name
*/
getname() {
  if(getrel() == PNAME) {
    strcpy(modname, symbol);
    return (YES);
    }
  if(item == EFILE) return (NO);
  error2(infn, " - Corrupted");
  }

/*
** read next entry from library index file
*/
getndx() {
  if(read(ndxfd, &inblock, 2) != 2 ||  /* next block */
     read(ndxfd, &inbyte, 2) != 2) {   /* next byte in block */
    error2("- Error Reading ", infn);
    }
  }

/*
** get switches from command line
*/
getsw(argc, argv) int argc, *argv; {
  char arg[NAMESIZE];
  int argnbr, b, len;
  argnbr = 0;
  while(getarg(++argnbr, arg, NAMESIZE, argc, argv) != EOF) {
    if(arg[0] != '-') continue;                    /* skip file names */
    if(toupper(arg[1]) == 'G') {
      lgo = YES;
      len = xtoi(arg + 2, &b);
      if(len >= 0 && !arg[len + 2]) cbase = b; else usage();
      }
    else if(toupper(arg[1]) == 'B') big = YES;
```

```
      else if(toupper(arg[1]) == 'M') monitor = YES;
      else usage();
      }
  }

/*
** is symbol an unresolved ext ref?
** on return of true, xrnext -> matching xr entry
*/
isunres() {
  int i;
  xrnext = getint(xrfirst);
  while(xrnext) {
    if((i = strcmp(symbol, xrnext + SYM)) < 0) return (NO);
    if(i == 0)  return (YES);
    xrnext = getint(xrnext);
    }
  return (NO);
  }

/*
** link external references to entry points
*/
link() {
  int cspg, csch;
  cspg = ctell(csfd);                    /* remember temp file position */
  csch = ctellc(csfd);
  xrnext = getint(xrprev = xrfirst);     /* first external reference */
  epnext = getint(epfirst);              /* first entry point */
  while(YES) {
    if(strcmp(xrnext + SYM, epnext + SYM) > 0) {       /* xr > ep */
      epnext = getint(epnext);
      continue;
      }
    if(strcmp(xrnext + SYM, epnext + SYM) < 0) {       /* xr < ep */
      xrnext = getint(xrprev = xrnext);
      continue;
      }
    if(*(xrnext + SYM) != HIGH) {                      /* xr = ep */
      resolve();                         /* resolve this ext ref */
      putint(xrprev, getint(xrnext));    /* delink from xr chain */
      putint(xrnext, sfree);             /* link to prev freed entry */
      sfree = xrnext;                    /* make first freed entry */
      xrnext = getint(xrprev);           /* advance to next ext ref */
      continue;                          /* same ext ref in diff modules? */
      }
    break;
    }
  cseek(csfd, cspg, 0);                  /* restore temp file position */
```

```
  Uchrpos[csfd] = csch;
  }

/*
** load a module
*/
load() {
  char str[8];
  epprev = epfirst;                  /* start at the very beginning */
  xrprev = xrfirst;
  do {
    poll(YES);
    switch(getrel()) {
      case  DSIZE: if(!field) break;
         default: error("- Unsupported Link Item");
      case    ERR: error("- Corrupt Module");
      case  EPROG: if(type == PREL) {
                     puts2("Start In ", modname);
                     goloc = field + cmod;
                   }
      case  ENAME: break;            /* bypass enames */
      case XCHAIN: newsym(&xrprev, "xr");
                   break;
      case EPOINT: newsym(&epprev, "ep");
                   break;
      case  PSIZE: cmod = cloc;
                   if(monitor) {
                     itox(field, str, 8);
                     fputs(str, stdout); fputs(" Bytes at", stdout);
                     itox(cloc,  str, 6);
                     fputs(str, stdout); fputs("'", stdout);
                     itox(cloc+cbase, str, 6);
                     fputs(str, stdout); puts2(" ", modname);
                   }
                   if(!csfd &&
                      (big || (bnext + field) > (snext - CUSHION))) {
                     cdisk = cloc;             /* disk overflow point */
                     csfd = open(csfn, "w+");  /* open overflow file */
#ifdef DEBUG
                     if(monitor) {
                       itox(cdisk, str, 8); puts2(str, " Overflow Point");
                     }
#endif
                   }
                   break;
      case  SETLC: field = field + cmod;
                   while(cloc < field) {      /* adj loc ctr */
                     if(csfd) write(csfd, "\0", 1);
                     else *bnext++ = 0;
```

```
                            ++cloc;
                            }
                            break;
        case    XPOFF:  write(crfd, &xrpflag, 2);          /* flag xr plus */
                        write(crfd, &field, 2);            /* xr offset */
                        break;
        case    PREL:   field = field + cmod;
                        if(csfd) write(csfd, &field, 2);   /* put on disk */
                        else {                             /* put in memory */
                          putint(bnext, field);
                          bnext += 2;
                          }
                        write(crfd, &cloc, 2);             /* reference for pass 2 */
                        cloc += 2;
                        break;
        case    ABS:    if(csfd) write(csfd, &field, 1);   /* put on disk */
                        else *bnext++ = field;             /* put in memory */
                        ++cloc;
                        break;
        }
    } while(item != EPROG);
  }

/*
** create new file specifier from an old one
*/
newfn(dest, sour, ext) char *dest, *sour, *ext; {
  if(sour[1] == ':' && strcmp(ext, NDXEXT)) sour += 2;
  while(*sour && *sour != '.') *dest++ = *sour++;
  strcpy(dest, ext);
  }

/*
** store new symbol table entry
** they arrive in alphanumeric order
*/
newsym(prev, ts) int *prev; char *ts; {
  char at[8], *cp, *new;
  if(new = sfree) sfree = getint(sfree);                   /* use old entry */
  else {
    new = snext;
    if((snext -= SSZ) < bnext) error("- Must Specify -B Switch");
    }
  cp = *prev;
  while(strcmp(symbol, cp + SYM) >= 0) {                   /* find position */
    *prev = cp;
    cp = getint(cp);
    }
  putint(new, cp);                                         /* point new entry ahead */
```

```
      putint(*prev, new);                /* point prev entry here */
      *prev = new;                       /* this becomes prev entry */
      if(type == PREL) field = field + cmod;/* adjust for module location */
      putint(new + VAL, field);          /* load value */
      strcpy(new + SYM, symbol);         /* load symbol */
#ifdef DEBUG
      if(monitor) {
        itox(getint(new + VAL), at, 8);
        fputs(at, stdout); fputs(" ", stdout);
        fputs(ts, stdout); fputs(" ", stdout);
        puts(symbol);
        }
#endif
      }

   /*
   ** initial table entries
   */
   newtbl(low) int *low; {
     *low = snext;                       /* always points to low entry */
     strcpy(snext + SYM, "");            /* store low symbol */
     putint(snext, snext - SSZ);         /* link to next (high) symbol */
     snext -= SSZ;                       /* now point to next entry */
     strcpy(snext + SYM, high);          /* store high symbol */
     putint(snext, 0);                   /* end of chain */
     snext -= SSZ;                       /* bump to next entry */
     }

   /*
   ** get next module name
   */
   nxtmod() {
     getndx();                           /* get location and */
     seek();                             /* go straight to next member */
     return (getname());
     }

   /*
   ** report the outcome and decide whether to quit
   */
   okay() {
     int err; char *eplast;
     err = eplast = 0;
     xrnext = getint(xrfirst);           /* first external reference */
     epnext = getint(epfirst);           /* first entry point */
     while(YES) {
       poll(YES);
       if(strcmp(xrnext + SYM, epnext + SYM) > 0) {        /* ext > ent */
         if(epnext == eplast) {
```

```
          puts2("- Redundant: ", xrnext + SYM);
          err = YES;
          }
        eplast = epnext;
        epnext = getint(epnext);
        continue;
        }
      if(strcmp(xrnext + SYM, epnext + SYM) < 0) {       /* ext < ent */
        puts2("- Unresolved: ", xrnext + SYM);
        err = YES;
        xrnext = getint(xrnext);
        continue;
        }
      if(*(xrnext + SYM) != HIGH) {                      /* ext = ent */
        xrnext = getint(xrnext);
        continue;                /* same ext ref in diff modules? */
        }
      break;
      }
  if(err) return (NO);
  return (YES);
  }

/*
** load input files and library members
*/
phase1(argc, argv) int argc, *argv; {
  char sz[8];
  int i, lib, eof;
  eof = EOF;
  cdisk = -1;                          /* high value for pointer */
  if(lgo) instr = RET;                 /* load and go format */
  else {instr = JMP; cbase = COMBASE;} /* COM file format */
  i = 0;
  while(getarg(++i, infn, NAMESIZE, argc, argv) != EOF) {
    if(infn[0] == '-') continue;       /* skip switches */
    if(extend(infn, MODEXT, LIBEXT))
        lib = YES;
    else lib = NO;
    if(!*outfn) {                      /* first file name */
      if(lgo) newfn(outfn, infn, LGOEXT);
      else    newfn(outfn, infn, COMEXT);
      newfn(csfn, infn, OFLEXT);
      newfn(crfn, infn, REFEXT);
      crfd = open(crfn, "w+");         /* open refererce file */
      auxbuf(crfd, AUXBUF);  /* extra buffering lowers head movement */
      }
    if(lib) search();   /* search library if unresolved ext refs */
    else {
```

```
      inrel = open(infn, "r");         /* must open */
      getname();                       /* program name */
      load();                          /* load module */
      link();                          /* link previous modules */
      close(inrel);                    /* must close */
      }
   }
  if(!*outfn) usage();
  if(*tmfn) {                          /* must get terminal module */
    inrel = open(tmfn, "r");
    inblock = tmblock; inbyte = tmbyte;
    seek(); getname(); load(); link();
    close(inrel);
    }
  csize = cloc;
  if(ferror(crfd)) error2("- Error Writing ", crfn);
  write(crfd, &eof, 2);
  rewind(crfd);
  if(ferror(csfd)) error2("- Error Writing ", csfn);
  rewind(csfd);
  itox(csize, sz, 8); puts2(sz, " Bytes (hex)");
  itou(csize, sz, 8); puts2(sz, " Bytes (dec)");
  }

/*
** generate absolute output in COM or LGO format
**
** COM format: JMP <start> <program>
**
** LGO format: RET <start> <prog-base> <prog-size> <program>
*/
phase2() {
  char at[5];
  outfd = open(outfn, "w");
  write(outfd, &instr, 1);       /* plant first instruction */
  addr = cbase + goloc;
  write(outfd, &addr, 2);        /* with its address */
  if(lgo) {
    write(outfd, &cbase, 2);     /* where to load for execution */
    write(outfd, &csize, 2);     /* how many bytes to load */
    }
  cloc = -1;                     /* allow efficient pre-increment */
  readref();                     /* get first reference */
  while(++cloc < csize) {        /* while more code */
    if(cloc != ref) {            /* not relative reference */
      if(cloc < cdisk)
        field = *(cloc + buffer);
      else read(csfd, &field, 1);
      write(outfd, &field, 1);   /* copy one byte as is */
```

```
        continue;
        }
      if(cloc < cdisk)           /* get next 2-byte re.ative item */
        field = getint(cloc + buffer);
      else read(csfd, &field, 2);
      field = field + cbase;     /* make absolute */
      if(xrplus) {
        field += xrplus;         /* apply offset */
        xrplus = 0;
        }
      write(outfd, &field, 2);   /* copy 2 bytes adjusted */
      readref();                 /* get next reference */
      ++cloc;                    /* need additional increment */
      }
  if(ferror(outfd))  error2("- Error Writing ", outfn);
  close(outfd);
  if(csfd) {
    if(ferror(csfd)) error2("- Error Reading ", csfn);
    close(csfd);
    delete(csfn);
    }
  if(ferror(crfd))   error2("- Error Reading ", crfn);
  close(crfd);
  delete(crfn);
  }

/*
** read next reference
*/
readref() {
  read(crfd, &ref, 2);                       /* get next reference */
  if(ref == XRPLUS) {                        /* ext ref offset flag? */
    read(crfd, &xrplus, 2);                  /* yes, get cffset value */
    read(crfd, &ref, 2);                     /* then get reference */
    }
  }

/*
** resolve external references to a given symbol
*/
resolve() {
  char at[5];
  if(!(xr = getint(xrnext + VAL))) return;   /* head of ext ref chain */
  ep = getint(epnext + VAL);                 /* entry point address */
  do {
#ifdef DEBUG
    if(monitor) {
      poll(YES);
      fputs("Resolving ", stdout);
```

```c
            itox(xr, at, 5); fputs(at, stdout);
            fputs(" to ", stdout);
            itox(ep, at, 5); fputs(at, stdout);
            puts2(" ", xrnext + SYM);
            }
#endif
        if(xr < cdisk) {                            /* in memory */
          nxt = getint(xr + buffer);
          if(nxt == 0) ep += cbase;                 /* end of chain is absolute */
          putint(xr + buffer, ep);
          }
        else {                                      /* on disk */
          xrseek(xr - cdisk); read(csfd, &nxt, 2);
          if(nxt == 0) ep += cbase;                 /* end of chain is absolute */
          xrseek(xr - cdisk); write(csfd, &ep, 2);
          }
        } while(xr = nxt);
    }

/*
** search a library
*/
search() {
  int linked;
  linked = NO;
  newfn(ndxfn, infn, NDXEXT);
  ndxfd = open(ndxfn, "r");
  inrel = open(infn, "r");
  while(YES) {                                      /* rescan till done */
    while(nxtmod()) {
      if(strcmp(modname, TMNAME) == 0) {            /* will load this one last */
        strcpy(tmfn, infn);
        tmblock = inblock;
        tmbyte = inbyte;
        continue;
        }
      while(getrel() == ENAME) {
        poll(YES);
        if(isunres()) {                             /* unresolved reference? */
          load();                                   /* load module */
          link();                                   /* link to previous ones */
          linked = YES;
          break;
          }
        }
      }
    if(!linked) break;
    linked = NO;
    rewind(ndxfd);
```

```
      }
    close(ndxfd);
    close(inrel);
    }

/*
** seek to next member in old library
*/
seek() {
  if(inblock == EOF) error("- Premature End of Index");
  if(cseek(inrel, inblock, 0) == EOF)
    error("- Corrupt Library or Index");
  Uchrpos[inrel] = inbyte;
  inrem = 0;                    /* force getrel() to read a byte */
  }

/*
** abort with a usage message
*/
usage() {
  error("Usage: LNK [-B] [-G#] [-M] program [module/library...]");
  }

/*
** seek external reference
*/
xrseek(byte) int byte; {
  if(cseek(csfd, (byte >> 7) & 511, 0) == EOF)
    error2("- Seek Error in ", csfn);
  Uchrpos[csfd] = byte & 127;
  }
```

LISTING 7-3

FILE:LGO.C

```
/*
** LGO.C -- Small-Mac Load-and-Go Loader
**
**              Copyright 1985 J. E. Hendrix
**
** Usage: LGO [-G] [-M] program
**
** -G     Execute program after loading.
**
** -M     Monitor load address and size.
**
** "Program" is a file specifier for the program being loaded.
** Default, and only allowed, extension is LGO.
**
```

```c
** Enter control-S to pause and control-C to abort.
*/
#include <stdio.h>
#include "notice.h"

#define NOCCARGC            /* don't pass arg counts to functions */

#define NAMESIZE    15
#define STACK       256     /* allow for stack space */
#define RET         201     /* RET instruction */
#define LGOEXT      ".LGO"

/*
** global variables
*/
char
 *base,              /* base address */
 *start,             /* starting address */
  infn[NAMESIZE];    /* input filename */

int
  infd,              /* input fd */
  size,              /* program size */
  monitor,           /* monitor activity? */
  go;                /* execute? */

/*
** load program.LGO with format:
**
**          RET <start> <base> <size> <program>
*/
main(argc,argv) int argc, argv[]; {
  int i; char str[5];
  fputs("Small-Mac Load-and-Go Loader, ", stderr); fputs(VERSION, stderr);
  fputs(CRIGHT1, stderr);
  getsw(argc, argv);                        /* process switches */
  i = 0;
  while(getarg(++i, infn, NAMESIZE, argc, argv) != EOF) /* get fn */
    if(infn[0] != '-') {i = 0; break;}
  if(i) usage();
  extend(infn, LGOEXT, LGOEXT);
  infd = open(infn, "r");
  read(infd, &base, 1);
  if(base != RET) error("- Invalid LGO Format");
  read(infd, &start, 2);                    /* get starting address */
  read(infd, &base,  2);                    /* get base address */
  read(infd, &size,  2);                    /* get program size */
  if(monitor) {                             /* monitor? */
    fputs("From ",    stdout); itox(base,    str, 5); fputs(str, stdout);
```

```
      fputs(", To ",    stdout); itox(base+size, str, 5); fputs(str, stdout);
      fputs(", Size ",  stdout); itox(size,      str, 5); fputs(str, stdout);
      fputs(", Start ", stdout); itox(start,     str, 5); puts(str);
      }
  malloc(STACK);        /* new machine stack */
  malloc(1);            /* leaves new stack address in HL */
  #asm
  SPHL                  ; move stack
  LXI H,0               ; CP/M return
  PUSH H                ; re-stack CP/M return
  #endasm
  read(infd, base, size);                     /* load program */
  if(ferror(infd)) error2("- Error Reading ", infn);
  if(go) {              /* execute program? */
    start;              /* leaves starting address in HL */
    #asm
    PCHL                ; Jump to start address with
                        ; CP/M return on top of this stack.
    #endasm
    }
  exit(0);
  }

/*
** get switches from command line
*/
getsw(argc, argv) int argc, *argv; {
  char arg[NAMESIZE];
  int argnbr; argnbr = 0;
  while(getarg(++argnbr, arg, NAMESIZE, argc, argv) != EOF) {
    if(arg[0] != '-') continue;               /* skip file names */
    if(toupper(arg[1]) == 'G') go = YES;
    else if(toupper(arg[1]) == 'M') monitor = YES;
    else usage();
    }
  }

/*
** abort with a usage message
*/
usage() {
  error("Usage: LGO [-G] [-M] program");
  }
```

LISTING 7-4

FILE:LIB.C

```
/*
** LIB.C -- Small-Mac Library Manager
```

```
**
**                 Copyright 1985 J. E. Hendrix
**
** Usage: LIB -{DPTUX}[A] library [module...]
**
** -D     delete named modules
** -P[A]  print named, or all (-PA), modules on stdout
** -T[A]  table of contents of named, or all (-TA), files on stdout
** -U     update (adding/replace) named modules
**        (gets module names from stdin if not in command line)
** -X[A]  extract named, or all (-XA), modules
**
**        The A suffix obviates prompting stdin for module
**        names when none are in the command line.  This is handy for
**        eliminating operator intervention, especially in batch mode.
**        Ordinarily, when no modules are given in the command line,
**        LIB prompts the user (if stdin is not redirected) and
**        accepts one module name at a time from stdin.  If none
**        are given (CR response to first prompt) and the command
**        switch is -P, -T, or -X then all members of the library are
**        processed.
**
** Drive Designators (e.g. B:):
**     allowed with any library and module names
**     new library and index go on same drive as old
**     will default to the default drive
**
** Filename Extensions:
**     do NOT specify with library or module names
**     standard extensions are:
**
**     .REL = relocatable object module
**     .LIB = library of object modules
**     .NDX = index to library
**     .L$  = temporary new library
**     .N$  = temporary new index
**
** Enter control-S to pause and control-C to abort.
*/
#include <stdio.h>
#include "notice.h"
#include "rel.h"

#define NOCCARGC              /* no argument count passing */
#define NAMESIZE   15
#define MAXMODS    200
#define MODEXT     ".REL"
#define LIBEXT     ".LIB"
#define NDXEXT     ".NDX"
```

```c
#define L_EXT    ".L$"
#define N_EXT    ".N$"
#define HIGH     127           /* high-value byte */

char
  cmd[5],                      /* command switch */
  oldlib[NAMESIZE],            /* old library name */
  oldndx[NAMESIZE],            /* old index name */
  newlib[NAMESIZE],            /* new library name (temporary) */
  newndx[NAMESIZE],            /* new index name (temporary) */
 *modname;                     /* points to module name buffer */

int
 *mptr,                        /* module name pointers */
 *mdone,                       /* done with module? */
  modules,                     /* count of modules to process */
  all,                         /* process all members? */
  inndx,                       /* input index fd */
  outndx,                      /* output index fd */
  oldblock,                    /* block of next input member */
  oldbyte,                     /* byte in block of next input member */
  newblock,                    /* block of next output member */
  newbyte;                     /* byte in block of next output member */

int  item2, type2, field2, inrel2, inrem2, inch2;
char sym2[NAMESIZE];

main(argc,argv) int argc, argv[]; {
  fputs("Small-Mac Library Manager, ", stderr); fputs(VERSION, stderr);
  fputs(CRIGHT1, stderr);
  mptr  = calloc(MAXMODS, 2);   /* allocate zeroed memory */
  mdone = calloc(MAXMODS, 2);
  if(getarg(1, cmd, 5, argc, argv) == EOF) usage();
  cmd[1] = toupper(cmd[1]);
  cmd[2] = toupper(cmd[2]);
  if(cmd[0] != '-' || (cmd[2] && cmd[2] != 'A') || strlen(cmd) > 3) usage();
  if(getarg(2, oldlib, NAMESIZE, argc, argv) == EOF) usage();
  extend(oldlib, LIBEXT, LIBEXT);
  newfn(oldndx, oldlib, NDXEXT);
  newfn(newlib, oldlib, L_EXT);
  newfn(newndx, oldlib, N_EXT);
  getmods(argc, argv);          /* gather switches and module names */
  switch(cmd[1]) {
    case 'D': drop();    break;
    case 'T': table();   break;
    case 'U': update();  break;
    case 'X': extract(); break;
    case 'P': print();   break;
    default: usage();
```

```
      }
    }
/*
** add module to library
*/
addmod(name) char *name; {
  char *cp, nam[NAMESIZE];
  saverel();                       /* save REL variables */
  strcpy(nam, name); extend(nam, MODEXT, MODEXT);
  inrel = open(nam, "r");
  cpymod(NO);                      /* do not already have header */
  close(inrel);
  restrel();                       /* restore REL variables */
  strcpy(nam, name);
  if(nam[1] == ':') cp = nam + 2; else cp = nam;
  cp[MAXSYM] = NULL;
  }

/*
** close input library and index
*/
closein(mod1, mod2) char *mod1, *mod2 ; {
  close(inrel);
  close(inndx);
  }

/*
** close output library and index
*/
closeup(mod1, mod2) char *mod1, *mod2 ; {
  closein();
  endrel();
  close(outrel);
  putndx(newblock, newbyte);                /* index EFILE */
  putndx(EOF, EOF);                         /* terminate new index */
  close(outndx);
  movfil(newlib, oldlib);                   /* take original names */
  movfil(newndx, oldndx);
  }

/*
** compare module names ignoring drive designators
*/
cmpmod(mod1, mod2) char *mod1, *mod2; {
  char str1[NAMESIZE], str2[NAMESIZE];
  if(mod1[1] == ':') mod1 += 2; strncpy(str1, mod1, MAXSYM);
  if(mod2[1] == ':') mod2 += 2; strncpy(str2, mod2, MAXSYM);
  return (strcmp(str1, str2));
  }
```

```
/*
** copy one module from inrel to outrel
*/
cpymod(hdr) int hdr; {
  if(outndx) putndx(newblock, newbyte); /* must not be extracting */
  if(hdr && !putrel()) abort(7);        /* already have input header */
  do {
    poll(YES);
    if(getrel() == ERR || !putrel()) abort (7);
    } while(item != EPROG);
  fflush(outrel);                 /* must empty aux buf for ctell() */
  newblock = ctell(outrel);       /* remember for next member */
  newbyte = ctellc(outrel);
  if(newbyte == 128) {++newblock; newbyte = 0;}
  }

/*
** drop modules from library
*/
drop() {
  char mod[NAMESIZE];
  if(modules == 0) error("- Delete by Name Only");
  openup();
  while(nxtmod(mod)) {
    if(match(mod, NO)) {
      puts2("Deleted ", mod);
      continue;
      }
    cpymod(YES);
    }
  missing();
  closeup();
  }

/*
** terminate REL or LIB file
*/
endrel() {
  item = EFILE;
  field = 0;
  type = 0;
  if(!putrel()) abort(7);
  }

/*
** extract files from library
*/
extract() {
  char modnam[NAMESIZE];
```

```
    openin();
    while(nxtmod(modnam)) {
      if(match(modnam, YES)) {
        extend(modnam, MODEXT, MODEXT);
        outrel = open(modnam, "w");
        cpymod(YES);
        endrel();
        close(outrel);
        puts2("Created ", modnam);
        }
      }
    missing();
    closein();
    }

/*
** get module names
*/
getmods(argc, argv) int argc, argv[]; {
  char *cp, *mp, name[NAMESIZE], fn[NAMESIZE];
  int err, eof, arg, i, j;
  if(!(mp = modname = malloc(MAXMODS*10))) error("- Memory Overflow");
  if((j = avail(NO)) >= 0 && j < 512) {
    puts("- Limited Stack Space");
    err = YES;
    }
  all = YES;                   /* default to all modules */
  if(argc > 3) arg = 3;        /* get module names from command line */
  else {
    arg = 0;                   /* get module names from stdin */
    if(cmd[2] && (cmd[1] == 'P' || cmd[1] == 'T' || cmd[1] == 'X')) {
      modname[0] = HIGH;       /* high value */
      modname[1] = NULL;
      return;
      }
    }
  err = eof = NO;
  while(modules < MAXMODS-1) {
    poll(YES);
    if(arg) {
      if(getarg(arg++, name, NAMESIZE, argc, argv)==EOF) {eof = YES; break;}
      }
    else {
      if(!reqstr("Module Name: ", name, NAMESIZE)) {eof = YES; break;}
      }
    all = NO;                          /* do selected modules only */
    if(cp = strchr(name, '.')) {
      fputs(name, stdout); puts2(" - Extension Forced to ", MODEXT);
      *cp = NULL;
```

```
      err = YES;
      }
    if(cp = strchr(name, ':')) {
      if(cp == name+1) ++cp;              /* set up next check */
      else {
        puts2(name, " - Invalid Format - Ignored");
        goto ignore;
        }
      }
    else cp = name;                       /* set up next check */
    if(strlen(cp) > MAXSYM) {
      strcpy(fn, cp);
      fputs(fn, stdout);
      fn[MAXSYM] = NULL;
      puts2(" - Will be Truncated to ", fn);
      err = YES;       /* assembler does actual truncation */
      }
    if(cmd[1] == 'U') {                   /* REL file must exist */
      strcpy(fn, name); extend(fn, MODEXT, MODEXT);
      if(i = fopen(fn, "r")) fclose(i);
      else {
        puts2(name, " - Can't Find - Ignored");
        goto ignore;
        }
      }
    for(i = 0; i < modules; ++i) {        /* find place for module */
      if(cmpmod(mptr[i], name) > 0) {     /* shift others up */
        for(j = modules; j > i; --j) mptr[j] = mptr[j-1];
        break;
        }
      if(cmpmod(name, mptr[i]) == 0) {    /* already loaded */
        puts2(mp, " - Duplicate Name - Ignored");
        goto ignore;
        }
      }
    mptr[i] = mp;                         /* load modname pointer */
    strcpy(mp, name);                     /* load modname buffer */
    while(*mp++) ;                        /* scoot to next address */
    ++modules;                            /* bump number of modules */
    continue;

    ignore:
    err = YES;
    }
  mptr[modules] = mp;                     /* load terminal pointer */
  *mp++ = HIGH;                           /* high value */
  *mp   = NULL;
  if(!eof) error("- Too Many Modules Specified");
  if(err) {
```

```c
      fputs("\nContinue? ", stderr);
      fgets(name, NAMESIZE, stderr);
      if(toupper(*name) != 'Y') exit(7);
      }
   }

/*
** read an entry from the old index
*/
getndx() {
  if(read(inndx, &oldblock, 2) != 2 ||   /* next block */
     read(inndx, &oldbyte, 2) != 2)      /* next byte in block */
    error("- Error Reading Index");
  }

/*
** check if name matches module list
*/
match(name, quit) char *name; int quit; {
  int i, done;
  char *mp;
  if(all) return(YES);
  done = YES;
  for(i = 0; i < modules; ++i) {
    if(cmpmod(mptr[i], name) == 0) {
      mdone[i] = YES;
      return(YES);
      }
    if(!mdone[i]) done = NO;
    }
  if(quit && done) exit(0);
  return(NO);
  }

/*
** print "not in library" messages
*/
missing() {
  int i;
  for(i = 0; i < modules; ++i)
    if(!mdone[i]) puts2(mptr[i], " Was Not in Library");
  }

/*
** move file1 to file2
*/
movfil(file1, file2) char *file1, *file2; {
  unlink(file2);
  if(file2[1] == ':') file2 += 2;
```

```
    if(rename(file1, file2)) error("- Can't Rename Files");
    }

/*
** create new filename from old filename and specified extension
*/
newfn(dest, sour, ext) char *dest, *sour, *ext; {
  while(*sour && *sour != '.') *dest++ = *sour++;
  strcpy(dest, ext);
  }

/*
** get next module name
*/
nxtmod(name) char *name; {
  seek();                              /* go straight to next member */
  if(getrel() == PNAME) {
    strcpy(name, symbol);
    return (YES);
    }
  if(item == EFILE) {
    *name++ = HIGH;                    /* high value */
    *name   = NULL;
    return (NO);
    }
  error("- Corrupt Library or Index");
  }

/*
** open library and index for input
*/
openin() {
  while(!(inrel = fopen(oldlib, "r"))) {
    puts("\nCreating New Library");
    outrel = open(oldlib, "w");
    item = EFILE;
    putrel();
    close(outrel);
    outndx = open(oldndx, "w");
    putndx(0, 0);
    putndx(EOF, EOF);
    close(outndx);
    }
  inndx = open(oldndx, "r");
  }

/*
** open libraries and indices for updating
*/
```

```c
openup() {
  openin();
  outrel = open(newlib, "w");
  outndx = open(newndx, "w");
  auxbuf(outrel, 4096);
  }

/*
** print files from library
*/
print() {
  char modnam[NAMESIZE];
  openin();
  while(nxtmod(modnam)) {
    if(match(modnam, YES)) {
      while(YES) {
        poll(YES);
        if(item > ENAME) seerel();
        getrel();
        if(item == EPROG) break;
        }
      }
    }
  missing();
  closein();
  }


/*
** write an entry to the new index
*/
putndx(block, byte) int block, byte; {
  if(write(outndx, &block, 2) != 2 ||    /* next block to index */
    write(outndx, &byte, 2) != 2)        /* next byte in block to index */
    error("- Error Writing New Index");
  }

/*
** restore REL variables
*/
restrel() {
  item    = item2;
  type    = type2;
  field   = field2;
  strcpy(symbol, sym2);
  inrel   = inrel2;
  inchunk = inch2;
  inrem   = inrem2;
  }
```

```c
/*
** save REL variables
*/
saverel() {
  item2  = item;
  type2  = type;
  field2 = field;
  strcpy(sym2, symbol);
  inrel2 = inrel;
  inch2  = inchunk;
  inrem2 = inrem;
  inrem  = 0;             /* force getrel() to read a byte */
  }


/*
** seek to next member in old library
*/
extern int Uchrpos[];          /* lives in CSYSLIB */
seek() {
  getndx();
  if(oldblock == EOF) error("- Premature End of Index");
  if(cseek(inrel, oldblock, 0) == EOF)
    error("- Corrupt Library or Index");
  Uchrpos[inrel] = oldbyte;
  inrem = 0;             /* force getrel() to read a byte */
  }


/*
** print table of contents
*/
table() {
  char name[NAMESIZE]; int i, j;
  openin();
  puts("");
  i = 0;
  while(nxtmod(name)) {
    poll(YES);
    if(match(name, YES)) {
      fputs(name, stdout);
      j = 9 - strlen(name);
      while(j--) putchar(' ');
      if (!(++i % 8)) puts("");
      }
    }
  puts("");
  missing();
  closein();
  }
```

```
/*
** update (add and replace) modules in alphanumeric order
*/
update() {
  char mod[NAMESIZE]; int m;
  openup();
  m = 0;                            /* first in module list */
  nxtmod(mod);                      /* first in old library */
  while(YES) {
    if(cmpmod(mptr[m], mod) > 0) {  /* module > member */
      cpymod(YES);                  /* copy rest of member */
      nxtmod(mod);                  /* next in old library */
      continue;
      }
    if(cmpmod(mptr[m], mod) < 0) {  /* module < member */
      addmod(mptr[m]);              /* add new module */
      puts2("   Added ", mptr[m]);
      ++m;                          /* next in module list */
      continu;
      }
    if(*mod != HIGH) {              /* equal and not at end */
      addmod(mptr[m]);              /* add new module */
      ++m;                          /* next in module list */
      puts2("Replaced ", mod);
      nxtmod(mod);                  /* next in old library */
      continue;
      }
    break;
    }
  closeup();
  }

/*
** abort with a usage message
*/
usage() {
  error("Usage: LIB -{DPTUX}[A] library [module...]");
  }
```

LISTING 7-5

FILE:CMIT.C

```
/*
** CMIT.C -- Machine Instruction Table Compiler
**
**              Small-Mac Assembler Configuration Utility
**
**                   Copyright 1985 J. E. Hendrix
**
```

```
** Usage: CMIT [-C] [-L] [table] [mac]
**
** -C    Configure the executable assembler (MAC.COM) with the indicated,
**       or default, machine instructin table.
**
** -L    List the compiled machine instruction table.
**
** table The name of the machine instruction table file in source
**       format (default 8080.MIT).  The default and only allowed
**       filename extension is MIT.  A drive specifier is allowed.
**
** mac   Assembler COM file (default MAC.COM).  Must have COM extension
**       to be recognized as such.  Need specify only if not o the
**       default drive or has a different name.
**
**       NOTE: if no switches are given, -L is assumed.  If any switches
**       are given, only those actions so specified are taken.
**
**       NOTE: After compiling and linking a new MAC.COM, it must be
**       configured by running this program before it may be executed.
**       A previously configured MAC.COM may be reconfigured at any time.
*/
#include <stdio.h>
#include "mac.h"        /* must be included first */
#include "mit.h"
#include "notice.h"

#define COMEXT ".COM"
#define MITEXT ".MIT"

char
  macfn[MAXFN] = "MAC.COM",   /* default assembler filename */
  mitfn[MAXFN] = "8080.MIT";  /* default mit filename */
int
  con,          /* configure? */
  list,         /* list? */
  looks;        /* number of looks to find it */

main(argc, argv) int argc, *argv; {
  char str[MAXFN];
  fputs("Small-Mac MIT Compiler, ", stderr); fputs(VERSION, stderr);
  fputs(CRIGHT1, stderr);
  getsw(argc, argv);            /* fetch and remember switches, etc. */
  load();
  if(list) print();
  if(con) config();
  }

/*
```

```
**  configure assembler with machine instruction table
*/
extern int Uchrpos[];
config() {
  int fd, sz;
  fd = open(macfn, "r+");              /* must exist */
  Uchrpos[fd] = 3;                     /* seek to mitable word */
  read(fd, &sz, INTSZ);                /* read table size */
  if(sz != mitable) {
    printf("%s MIT is %u Bytes but Should be %u\n", macfn, sz, mitable);
    abort(7);
    }
  write(fd, &mitable + 1, mitable);
  if(ferror(fd)) error2(macfn, " - Write Error");
  close(fd);
  }

/*
**  get switches from command line
*/
getsw(argc, argv) int argc, *argv; {
  char arg[MAXFN];
  int i, b, len;
  i = 0;
  while(getarg(++i, arg, MAXFN, argc, argv) != EOF) {
    if(arg[0] == '-') {
      if(toupper(arg[1]) == 'C')       con = YES;
      else if(toupper(arg[1]) == 'L')  list = YES;
      else usage();
      }
    else {
      if(extend(arg, MITEXT, COMEXT))
          strcpy(macfn, arg);
      else strcpy(mitfn, arg);
      }
    }
  if(!con) list = YES;
  }

/*
**  load table from diskette
*/
load() {
  char str[MAXLINE], *mitend, *vptr, *last, *ptr, *cp;
  int fd, top, bits, byte, ilen, h, i, j,
      opnd[MIOPNDS], opnds, et, *fptr;
  fd = open(mitfn, "r");
  ptr = mitbuf;
  mitend = mitbuf + (MIBUFSZ - MAXLINE);
```

```
opnds = 0;
while(fgets(str, MAXLINE, fd)) {            /* load operand fields */
  poll(YES);
  cp = skip(3, str);                        /* skip to operand field */
  if(!isgraph(*cp)) continue;               /* no operand to load */
  for(j = 0; j < opnds; ++j)                /* already have it? */
    if(fldcmp(cp, opnd[j]) == 0) break;
  if(j < opnds) continue;
  if(ptr > mitend) goto mitovr1;
  opnd[opnds++] = ptr;                      /* temp operand ptr */
  if(opnds == MIOPNDS) error2(str, "- MIT Operand Overflow");
  while(isgraph(*ptr = *cp++)) ++ptr;       /* copy operand field */
  *ptr++ = NULL;
  }
if(rewind(fd)) error("- Can't Rewind MIT File");/* 2nd pass */
last = ptr; *last = NULL;
top = 0;
while(fgets(str, MAXLINE, fd)) {            /* load mnemonics, etc. */
  poll(YES);
  if(ptr > mitend)   {mitovr1: error2(str, "- MIT Buffer Overflow");}
  if(top >= MICOUNT) error("- MIT Mnemonic Overflow");
  cp = skip(2, str);                        /* skip to mnemonic field */
  if(fldcmp(cp, last)) {                    /* new mnemonic */
    *ptr++ = 0;                             /* terminate prior instr */
    mitptr[top++] = last = ptr;             /* mnemonic ptr */
    while(isgraph(*ptr = *cp++)) ++ptr;     /* copy mnemonic field */
    *ptr++ = NULL;
    }
  vptr = ptr++; *vptr = 2*INTSZ;            /* vlen field */
  cp = skip(3, str);                        /* locate operand */
  if(isgraph(*cp)) {                        /* has an operand field */
    for(j = 0; j < opnds; ++j)
      if(fldcmp(cp, opnd[j]) == 0) break;
    if(j == opnds) error2(str, "- Can't Find Operand");
    putint(ptr, opnd[j]);
    }
  else putint(ptr, 0);                      /* has no operand */
  ptr += INTSZ;
  fptr = ptr; ptr += INTSZ; *fptr = 0;      /* fmt field */
  bits = 13;
  ilen = -1;
  cp = skip(1, str);                        /* code field */
  while(isgraph(*cp)) {
    if(islower(*cp)) {                      /* x1, x2, etc. */
      et = *cp++;                           /* expr type */
      bits -= 3; *fptr = ((*fptr >> 3) & 8191) + 8192;
      switch(*cp) {
        default: error2(str, "- Bad Expression Specifier");
        case '2': *fptr += 32768; ilen += 2; break;
```

```
            case '1': ++ilen;
            }
          if(et == 'p') *fptr += 16384;          /* pc relative expr */
          ++cp;
          continue;
          }
        if(isxdigit(*cp)) {
          if((j = xtoi(cp, &byte)) > 2) error2(str, "- Bad Hex Byte");
          cp += j;
          *ptr++ = byte; *vptr += 1;
          --bits; *fptr = ((*fptr >> 1) & 32767);
          ++ilen;
          continue;
          }
        ++cp;                                    /* bump past field separator */
        }
      *fptr >>= bits;                            /* right adjust format byte */
      *fptr |= ilen & 7;                         /* and insert instr length */
      }
    *ptr++ = 0;                                  /* terminate prior instr */
    printf("  Operation Codes %5u\n", top);
    printf("Buffer Space Used %5u\n", ptr - mitbuf);
    for(i = 0; i < MICOUNT; ++i)                 /* init hash indices */
      mitndx[i] = mitnxt[i] = EOF;
    for(i = 0; i < top; ++i) {                   /* create hash indices - pass 1 */
      poll(YES);
      h = hash(mitptr[i], MICOUNT);
      if(mitndx[h] == EOF) {
        mitndx[h] = i;
        }
      }
    for(i = j = 0; i < top; ++i) {               /* create hash indices - pass 2 */
      poll(YES);
      h = hash(mitptr[i], MICOUNT);
      if(mitndx[h] != i) {
        while(mitndx[j] != EOF) ++j;             /* must be empty slot */
        mitndx[j] = i;
        while(mitnxt[h] != EOF) h = mitnxt[h];
        mitnxt[h] = j;
        }
      }
    close(fd);
    }

/*
** print compiled machine instruction table
*/
print() {
```

```
int i ,k, bak, fd, fmt, len, opcode, holding;
char lin[MAXLINE], inst[MAXLINE], *ptr, *vptr, *cp;
fd = open(mitfn, "r");
while(fgets(lin, MAXLINE, fd)) {
  poll(YES);
  i = 0; cp = skip(2, lin);
  while(isgraph(inst[i++] = *cp++)) ;
  if(inst[i-1] == '\n') inst[i-1] = ' ';
  bak = i;
  cp = skip(3, lin);
  do {
    i = bak;
    while(isgraph(*cp) && *cp != ANOTHER) inst[i++] = *cp++;
    inst[i] = 0;
    if(*cp == ANOTHER) ++cp;
    printf("%-15s ", inst);            /* mnemonic */
    if(!(ptr = find(inst)))
      error("- Can't Find Instruction in MIT");
    printf(" (%2u looks) ", looks);
    ptr += INTSZ;
    fmt = getint(ptr);                 /* ptr -> first code byte */
    ptr += INTSZ;
    len = (fmt & 7) + 1;
    fmt >>= 3;
    holding = NO;
    while(len-- > 0) {                 /* for each byte of code */
      if(fmt & 1) {                    /* expression */
        if(holding) {
          opcode += opadj;
          opadj = 0;
          holding = NO;
          printf(" %2x", opcode);
          }
        fmt >>= 1;
        switch(fmt & 3) {
          case 0: printf(" x1"); break;            /* 1-byte */
          case 1: printf(" p1"); break;            /* 1-byte pc rel */
          case 2: printf(" x2"); --len; break;     /* 2-byte */
          case 3: printf(" p2"); --len; break;     /* 2-byte pc rel */
          }
        fmt >>= 1;
        }
      else {                                       /* code byte */
        if(holding) printf(" %2x", opcode);
        opcode = *ptr++ & 255;
        holding = YES;
        }
      fmt >>= 1;
      }
```

```
      if(holding) {
        opcode += opadj;
        printf(" %2x", opcode);
        }
      puts("");
      } while(*cp > ' ');
    }
  close(fd);
  }

/*
** abort with a usage message
*/
usage() {
  error("Usage: CMIT [-C] [-L] [table] [mac]");
  }
```

LISTING 7-6

FILE:DREL.C

```
/*
** DREL.C -- dump REL or LIB file
**
**           Copyright 1985 J. E. Hendrix
**
** No command line switches are accepted.  The user is prompted
** for each file to be dumped.  Output goes to the standard
** output file and is, therefore, redirectable to any output
** device or to a disk file.  If an input file cannot be found
** the user is prompted for another input file.  File names must
** be given, complete with extensions.  Drive specifiers may be
** given.
*/
#include <stdio.h>
#include "notice.h"
#include "mac.h"
#include "rel.h"

main() {
  char fn[MAXFN];
  fputs("Small-Mac REL/LIB Dump Utility, ", stderr); fputs(VERSION, stderr);
  fputs(CRIGHT1, stderr);
  while(YES) {
    if(!reqstr("Library/Module Name: ", fn, MAXFN)) exit();
    if(!(inrel = fopen(fn, "r"))) continue;
    do {
      poll(YES);                        /* poll for user interrupt */
      if(getrel() == ERR) abort(7);     /* get next REL item */
      seerel();                         /* display it */
```

```
      } while(item != EFILE);
    fclose(inrel);
    }
  }
```

LISTING 7-7

---FILE:STDIO.H

```
/*
** STDIO.H -- Standard Small-C Definitions
**
** Copyright 1984  L. E. Payne and J. E. Hendrix
*/
#define stdin    0
#define stdout   1
#define stderr   2
#define ERR     (-2)
#define EOF     (-1)
#define YES      1
#define NO       0
#define NULL     0
#define CR      13
#define LF      10
#define BELL     7
#define SPACE   ' '
#define NEWLINE LF         /*23*/ /*45*/
```

---FILE:MAC.H

```
/*
** miscellaneous definitions
*/
#define MAXFN     15          /* max file name space */
#define INTSZ      2          /* integer size in bytes */
#define COMMENT   ';'         /* comment delimiter */
#define ANOTHER   '!'         /* another operand option */
#define MAXLINE   81          /* length of source line */
#define MICOUNT  150          /* machine instruction hash space */
#define MIOPNDS  300          /* maximum unique operand formats */
#define MIBUFSZ 4600          /* mit syntax space */
#define OBJEXT   ".REL"       /* object file extension */
#define SRCEXT   ".MAC"       /* source file extension */
#define MAXLAB     8          /* maximum label characters used */
#define STACK   1024          /* reserved for stack space */
#define OHDOPEN  164          /* overhead bytes per open file */
#define MAXOPEN    2          /* maximum open files */

/*
** symbol table
*/
```

```
#define STMAX    500                      /* maximum lables allowed */
#define STVALUE  (MAXLAB + 1)             /* offset to value field */
#define STFLAG   (STVALUE + INTSZ)        /* offset to flag byte */
#define STENTRY  (STFLAG + 1)             /* st entry size */
#define STBUFSZ  (stmax * STENTRY)        /* st buffer size */
#define LABBIT2  128                      /* label flag (pass 2) */
#define LABBIT   64                       /* label flag */
#define EQUBIT   32                       /* EQU flag (pass 2) */
#define SETBIT   16                       /* SET flag */
#define XRBIT    8                        /* external-reference flag */
#define EPBIT    4                        /* entry-point flag */
#define RELBITS  3                        /* relative bits (ABS, PREL) */

/*
** macro table
*/
#define MTNXT    0                        /* pointer to next macro */
#define MTNAM    INTSZ                    /* macro name */

/*
** assembler instruction codes
*/
#define DW     1
#define DB     2
#define DS     3
#define EX     4
#define SET    5
#define EQU    6
#define ORG    7
#define END    8
#define MACRO  9
#define ENDM   10
#define CALL   11
```

---FILE:EXT.H

```
extern int
  pass, badsym, gotep, gotxr, gotlabel, gotnam, opadj,
  hashval, loc, lin, err, endv, endt, lerr, srcfd, eom,
  list, lline, part1, ccnt, lpage, pause, looks, mitable,
  mitndx[], mitnxt[], mitptr[], stmax, stn, *stp;

extern char
  *ep, *lp, *prior, *mt, *mtnext, *mtend, line[],
  expbuf[], srcfn[], objfn[],
  *st, *stend, *stptr, stsym[], mitbuf[];
```

---FILE:MIT.H

```
/*
** machine instruction table
```

```
*/
int
  mitable = 3*INTSZ*MICOUNT+MIBUFSZ,   /* mit size signature */
  mitndx[MICOUNT],                     /* mit indices (hash -> which) */
  mitnxt[MICOUNT],                     /* mit synonym chain */
  mitptr[MICOUNT];                     /* mnemonic syntax ptrs */
char
  mitbuf[MIBUFSZ];                     /* instruction syntax buffer */

extern int                             /* reside in mit.c */
  opadj,                               /* operation code adjustment */
  hashval;                             /* global hash value for speed */
```

───────────────────────────────────── **FILE:REL.H**

```
/*
** rel.h -- header for REL file processing
*/

                    /* item-type codes */

#define ABS      0   /* absolute item */
#define PREL     1   /* program (code) relative item */
#define DREL     2   /* data relative item */
#define CREL     3   /* common relative item */

#define ENAME    4   /* entry name */
#define CNAME    5   /* common block name */
#define PNAME    6   /* program name */
#define LNAME    7   /* library name */
#define EXT      8   /* extension link-item */

#define CSIZE    9   /* common size & name */
#define XCHAIN  10   /* external-reference-chain head & name */
#define EPOINT  11   /* entry point location & name */

#define XMOFF   12   /* external - offset */
#define XPOFF   13   /* external + offset */
#define DSIZE   14   /* data area size */
#define SETLC   15   /* set location counter for loading */
#define CHAIN   16   /* chain address (fill chain with loc ctr) */
#define PSIZE   17   /* program (code) size */
#define EPROG   18   /* end of program */
#define EFILE   19   /* end of file */

#define MAXSYM   6   /* maximum symbol length allowed in REL file */
#define ONES    -1   /* all one bits */

                    /* common variables */
extern int
```

```
  inrel,            /* file descriptor for input REL file */
  inrem,            /* remaining bits in inchunk */
  inchunk,          /* current chunk from REL file */
  outrel,           /* file descriptor for output REL file */
  outrem,           /* remaining bits in outchunk */
  outchunk,         /* current chunk for REL file */
  item,             /* current item code */
  type,             /* type field */
  field;            /* current bit field */
extern char
  symbol[9];        /* current string */
```

———————————————————————————————— FILE:EXTEND.C

```
/*
** if fn has no extension, extend it with ext1
** if fn has an extension, require it to match ext1 or ext2
** return true if fn's extension matches ext2, else false
*/
#include <stdio.h>
#include "mac.h"
#define NOCCARGC
extend(fn, ext1, ext2) char *fn, *ext1, *ext2; {
  char *cp;
  if(cp = strchr(fn, '.')) {
    if(strcmp(cp, ext2) == 0) return (YES);
    if(strcmp(cp, ext1) == 0) return (NO);
    puts2(fn, " - invalid extension");
    abort(7);
    }
  if(strlen(fn) > MAXFN-4) error2(fn, " - Too Long");
  strcat(fn, ext1);
  return (NO);
  }
```

———————————————————————————————— FILE:FILE.C

```
/*
** file related functions
*/
#define NOCCARGC
open(name, mode) char *name, *mode; {
  int fd;
  if(fd = fopen(name, mode)) return(fd);
  cant(name);
  }
close(fd) int fd; {
  if(fclose(fd)) error("Close Error");
  }
```

———————————————————————————————— FILE:GETREL.C

```
/*
```

```
**  getrel -- read a relocatable-object file
*/
#include <stdio.h>
#include "rel.h"
#include "mac.h"
/*

**  get next REL item
**  return item code on success, ERR on error
**  on successful return:
**      item = item code
**      type = type of field
**      field = value of field
**   symbol = symbol name
*/
getrel() {
  if(!getbits(1)) return (ERR);        /* get 1 bit */
  if(field == 0) {                      /* absolute item */
    if(!getbits(8)) return (ERR);      /* get next 8 bits */
    return (type = item = ABS);        /* absolute item */
    }
  if(!getbits(2)) return (ERR);        /* get next 2 bits */
  switch(type = item = field) {
    case 0: return (getspec());        /* special link item */
    case 1:                             /* program relative item */
    case 2:                             /* data relative item */
    case 3:                             /* common relative item */
    }
  if(getfld() == ERR) return (ERR);    /* get next 16 bits */
  return (item);                        /* relative items */
  }

getspec() {                             /* get next special item */
  if(!getbits(4)) return (ERR);        /* get next 4 bits */
  type = ABS;                           /* default type */
  item = field + 4;
  switch(field) {
    case 0:                             /* entry symbol */
    case 1:                             /* select common block */
    case 2:                             /* program name */
    case 3:                             /* request library search */
    case 4:                             /* extension link items */
      if(getsym() == ERR) return (ERR);
      break;
    case 5:                             /* define common size */
    case 6:                             /* head of external reference chain */
    case 7:                             /* define entry point */
      if(gettyp() == ERR || getfld() == ERR || getsym() == ERR) return (ERR);
      break;
```

```
      case 8:                              /* external - offset */
      case 9:                              /* external + offset */
      case 10:                             /* size of data area */
      case 11:                             /* set loading location counter */
      case 12:                             /* chain addr (fill chain with lc) */
      case 13:                             /* size of program */
        if(gettyp() == ERR || getfld() == ERR) return (ERR);
        break;
      case 14:                             /* end of program */
        if(gettyp() == ERR || getfld() == ERR) return (ERR);
        inrem = 0;                         /* force byte boundary */
        break;
      case 15:                             /* end of file */
        inrem = 0;                         /* force byte boundary */
    }
    return (item);
  }

gettyp() {
  if(!getbits(2)) return (ERR);            /* get 2-bit field type */
  return (type = field);
}

getfld() {                                 /* get type and value of field */
  int low;
  if(!getbits(8)) return (ERR);            /* get first 8 bits */
  low = field;                             /* save as low order byte */
  if(!getbits(8)) return (ERR);            /* get next 8 bits */
  field = (field << 8) | low;              /* combine high & low bytes */
  return (item);
}

getsym() {                                 /* get symbol */
  int i, save; char *cp;
  cp = symbol;
  save = field;                            /* save field */
  if(!getbits(3)) return (ERR);            /* get 3-bit symbol length */
  i = field;                               /* capture symbol length */
  while(i--) {
    if(!getbits(8)) return (ERR);          /* get next byte */
    *cp++ = field;
  }
  *cp = NULL;                              /* terminate symbol */
  field = save;                            /* restore field */
  return (item);
}

/*
** get next n bits from REL file into "field"
```

```
** return true on success, false on error
*/
getbits(n) int n; {
  int get;
  field = 0;                                   /* in·tialize result */
  while(n) {                                   /* more bits to fetch */
    if(inrem == 0) {                           /* need another chunk */
      if(read(inrel, &inchunk, 1) != 1) {      /* get next bit cluster */
        fputs("\n\7- Abnormal End of REL File\n", stdout);
        return (NO);                           /* fa·lure */
        }
      inrem = 8;                               /* 8 bits remain */
      }
    if(n > inrem) get = inrem; else get = n;   /* how many from this chunk */
    n     -= get;                              /* decrement bits needed */
    inrem -= get;                              /* decr remaining bits */
    field = (field << get) +
            ((inchunk >> inrem) & ~(ONES << get));
    }
  return (YES);                                /* success */
  }
```

---- FILE:INT.C

```
/*
** integer manipulation
*/
#define NOCCARGC
getint(a) int *a; {return (*a);}        /* get integer from address a */
putint(a, i) int *a, i; {*a = i;}       /* put integer i at address a */
```

---- FILE:MESS.C

```
/*
** mess.c -- message functions
*/
#include <stdio.h>
#define NOCCARGC
puts2(str1, str2) char *str1, *str2; {
  fputs(str1, stdout);
  puts(str2);
  }
cant(str) char *str; {
  error2(str, " - Can't Open");
  }
error2(str1, str2) char *str1, *str2; {
  fputs(str1, stdout);
  error(str2);
  }
error(str) char *str; {
  puts(str);
```

```
    abort(7);
}
```

---FILE: MIT.C

```
/*
** mit.c -- machine instruction table functions
**
**              mitndx[]        mitptr[]        mitnxt[]
**
**              ,--,--,         ,--,--,         ,--,--,
**              |  |  |         |  |  |         |  |  | <-+
** hash ->      |--|--|    ->   |--|--|         |--|--|   |
**              |  |  |         |  |  |         |  |  |--+
**              |  |  |         |  |  |         |  |  |
**              `--'--'         `--'--'         `--'--'
**                                 |
**                                 V
**                              mnemonic     variant...
**                                              |
**                              ,--,...00   vlen  optr     fmt    obj...
**                                              |
**                                          ,--, ,--,--, ,--,--, ,--,...
**          format bits (<-)                `--' `--'--' `--'--' `--'
**          3-bit instr length (-1)             |
**          field types                         V
**              0 = obj byte                operand pattern
**            001 = 8-bit expr
**            011 = 8-bit pc rel expr           ,--,...00
**            101 = 16-bit expr                 `--'
**            111 = 16-bit pc rel expr
**
*/
#include <stdio.h>
#include "mac.h"                /* must be included first */
/*
#define NOCCARGC
*/
int
  opadj,                        /* operation code adjustment */
  hashval;                      /* global hash value for speed */
char
  expbuf[MAXLINE];              /* buffer for operand expressions */

extern int
  mitable,                      /* machine instruction table (size) */
  mitndx[],                     /* mit indices (hash -> which) */
  mitnxt[],                     /* mit synonym chain */
  mitptr[];                     /* mnemonic syntax ptrs */

extern char
  mitbuf[];                     /* instruction syntax buffer */
```

```
extern int
  looks;                    /* number of looks to find it */

hash(ptr, cnt) char *ptr; int cnt; {          /* calculate hash value */
  hashval = 0;
  while(*ptr > ' ' && atend(*ptr) == 0)
    hashval = (hashval << 1) + toupper(*ptr++);
  return (hashval % cnt);
  }

find(inst) char *inst; {                /* search for instr in mit */
  char *mit;
  int h, ndx;
  looks = 0;
  ndx = mitndx[h = hash(inst, MICOUNT)];      /* calc hash index */
  while(ndx != EOF) {
    ++looks;
    if(fldcmp(inst, mit = mitptr[ndx]) == 0) {  /* mnemonic matches */
      inst = skip(2, inst);             /* instr operand field */
      mit += strlen(mit) + 1;           /* first variant */
      while(*mit++) {                   /* another variant? */
        ++looks;
        if(match(inst, getint(mit))) return (mit);
        mit += *(mit - 1);              /* next variant */
        }
      return (0);
      }
    if((h = mitnxt[h]) == EOF) return (0);
    ndx = mitndx[h];
    }
  return (0);
  }
match(inst, mit) char *inst, *mit; {          /* match operands to mit */
  char *backup, *exp; int nest;
  opadj = 0;
  backup = inst;
  if(mit == 0) {
    if(atend(*inst)) return (YES);
    return (NO);
    }
  exp = expbuf;                         /* init expr buffer */
  while(YES) {
    while(isspace(*inst)) ++inst;
    while(isspace(*mit)) ++mit;
    if(atend(*inst)) {
      if(atend(*mit) || *mit == ANOTHER) return (YES);
      goto next;
      }
    if(atend(*mit)) return (NO);
```

```
      if(islower(*mit)) {                  /* expression */
        ++mit;                             /* bump past x or y */
        nest = 0;
        while(!atend(*inst)) {             /* bypass expression */
          if(*inst == ',') break;
          if(*inst == ')' && nest == 0) break;
          switch(*inst) {
            case '(': ++nest; break;
            case ')': --nest;
          }
          *exp++ = *inst++;                /* extract expressions */
        }
        *exp++ = ','; *exp = NULL;         /* terminate expression */
        continue;
      }
      if(lexorder(*inst++, *mit++)) {
        next:
        while(*mit) {
          if(*mit == ANOTHER) {            /* end of syntax for this try */
            ++opadj;                       /* bump opcode adjustment */
            ++mit; inst = backup;          /* setup next try */
            exp = expbuf;                  /* reset expr buffer pointer */
            break;
          }
          ++mit;
        }
        if(atend(*mit)) return (NO);
      }
    }
  }
```

FILE:PUTREL.C

```
/*
** putrel -- write a relocatable-object file
*/
#include <stdio.h>
#include "rel.h"
#include "mac.h"
/*
** put next REL item
** return true on success, false on error
** on call:
**    item  = item code
**    type  = type of field
**    field = value of field
**    symbol = symbol name
*/
putrel() {
  switch(item) {
```

```
    case ABS:
      if(!putbits(0, 1) || !putbits(field, 8)) return (NO);
      return (YES);
    case PREL: case DREL: case CREL:
      if(!putbits(1, 1) || !putbits(item, 2) || !putfld()) return (NO);
      return (YES);
    }
  if(!putbits(4, 3) || !putbits(item-4, 4)) return (NO);
  switch(item) {
    case CSIZE: case XCHAIN: case EPOINT:
      if(!putbits(type, 2) || !putfld()) return (NO);
    case ENAME: case CNAME: case PNAME: case LNAME: case EXT:
      if(!putsym()) return (NO);
      return (YES);
    case XMOFF: case XPOFF: case DSIZE:
    case SETLC: case CHAIN: case PSIZE:
      if(!putbits(type, 2) || !putfld()) return (NO);
      return (YES);
    case EPROG:
      if(!putbits(type, 2) || !putfld()) return (NO);
    case EFILE:
      if(outrem < 8 && !putbits(0, outrem)) return (NO);/* finish byte */
      return (YES);
    }
  return (NO);
  }
puttyp() {
  if(putbits(type, 2)) return (YES);     /* put 2-bit field type */
  return (NO);
  }
putfld() {                               /* put low then high byte */
  if(putbits(field, 8) && putbits(field >> 8, 8)) return (YES);
  return (NO);
  }
putsym() {                               /* put symbol */
  int i; char *cp;
  if((i = strlen(symbol)) > MAXSYM) i = MAXSYM; /* enforce max length */
  if(!putbits(i, 3)) return (NO);        /* put 3-bit symbol length */
  cp = symbol;
  while(i--) {
    if(!putbits(*cp++, 8)) return (NO); /* put next byte */
    }
  return (YES);
  }

/*
** put next n bits from fld into REL file
** return true on success, false on error
*/
```

```
putbits(fld, n) int fld, n; {
  int put;
  while(n) {                                      /* more bits to put */
    if(n > outrem) put = outrem; else put = n;    /* how many for this chunk */
    outchunk = (outchunk << put) +
               ((fld >> (n-put)) & ~(ONES << put));
    n      -= put;                                /* decrement bits to put */
    outrem -= put;                                /* decr remaining bits */
    if(outrem == 0) {                             /* need another chunk */
      if(write(outrel, &outchunk, 1) != 1) {      /* put next bit cluster */
        fputs("\n\7- Write Error in REL File\n", stdout);
        return (NO);                              /* failure */
      }
      outrem = 8;                                 /* 8 bits remain */
    }
  }
  return (YES);                                   /* success */
}
```

── FILE:REL.C

```
/*
** rel.c -- common data for REL file processing
*/
                    /* common variables */
int
 inrel,             /* file descriptor for input REL file */
 inrem = 0,         /* remaining bits in input chunk */
 inchunk,           /* current chunk from REL file */
 outrel,            /* file descriptor for output REL file */
 outrem = 8,        /* remaining bits in output chunk */
 outchunk,          /* current chunk for REL file */
 item,              /* current item code */
 type,              /* type field */
 field;             /* current bit field */
char
 symbol[9];         /* current string */
```

── FILE:REQ.C

```
/*
** req.c -- request user input
*/
#include <stdio.h>

reqnbr(prompt, nbr) char prompt[]; int *nbr; {    /* request number */
  char str[20];
  int sz;
  if(iscons(stdin)) {
    puts(" ");
    fputs(prompt, stdout);
```

```
    }
  getstr(str, 20);
  if((sz = utoi(str, nbr)) < 0 || str[sz]) return (NO);
  return (YES);
  }
reqstr(prompt, str, sz) char prompt[], *str; int sz; {  /* request string */
  if(iscons(stdin)) {
    puts(" ");
    fputs(prompt, stdout);
    }
  getstr(str, sz);
  return (*str);                        /* null name returns false */
  }
getstr(str, sz) char *str; int sz; {    /* get string from user */
  char *cp;
  fgets(str, sz, stdin);
  if(iscons(stdin) && !iscons(stdout))
     fputs(str, stdout);                /* echo */
  cp = str;
  while(*cp) {                          /* trim ctl chars & make uc */
    if(*cp == '\n') break;
    if(isprint(*str = toupper(*cp++))) ++str;
    }
  *str = NULL;
  }
```

FILE:SCAN.C

```
/*
** scanning functions
*/
#include <stdio.h>
#include "mac.h"
#define NOCCARGC
atend(ch) int ch; {                     /* is ch at end of line? */
  switch(ch) {
    case COMMENT: case NULL: case '\n': return (YES);
    }
  return (NO);
  }
fldcmp(s, t) char *s, *t; {             /* compare fields in a line */
  while(lexorder(*s, *t) == 0) {
    if(!isgraph(*s)) return (0);
    ++s; ++t;
    }
  if((isspace(*s) || atend(*s)) &&
     (isspace(*t) || atend(*t))) return (0);
  return (*s - *t);
  }
skip(n, str) int n; char str[]; {       /* find nth non-blank field in str */
```

```
      char *cp; cp = str;
      while(isspace(*cp)) ++cp;
      while(--n) {
        while(isgraph(*cp)) ++cp;
        while(isspace(*cp)) ++cp;
        }
      return (cp);
      }
```

---------- FILE:SEEREL.C

```
/*
** seerel -- show REL items
*/
#include <stdio.h>
#include "rel.h"
int lc, width;
/*
** display REL item
** on call:
**     item = item code
**     type = type of field
**    field = value of field
**   symbol = symbol name
*/
seerel() {
  char str[6]; int tmp;
  switch(item) {
    case    ABS: see8(field, ' '); lc += 1; newlin(NO); return;
    case   PREL:
    case   DREL:
    case   CREL: see16(); lc += 2; newlin(NO); return;
    case  XMOFF:
    case  XPOFF: tmp = type; type = item; see16();
                 type = tmp; newlin(NO); return;
    case  ENAME: seenam("      entry: ", NO); goto eol;
    case  CNAME: seenam("     common: ", NO); goto eol;
    case  PNAME: fputc('\n', stdout);
                 seenam("-   program: ", NO);
                 lc = 0;
                 goto eol;
    case  LNAME: seenam("    library: ", NO); goto eol;
    case    EXT: fputs("extension link item\n", stdout); return;

    case  CSIZE: seenam(" common sz: ", YES); goto eol;
    case XCHAIN: seenam(" ext chain: ", YES); goto eol;
    case EPOINT: seenam("  entry pt: ", YES); goto eol;

    case  DSIZE: fputs(" data size: ", stdout); goto fld;
    case  SETLC: fputs("   load at: ", stdout); lc = field; goto fld;
```

```
    case   CHAIN: fputs(" ld chn at: ", stdout); goto fld;
    case   PSIZE: fputs(" prog size: ", stdout); goto fld;
    case   EPROG: fputs("- end prog: ", stdout); goto fld;
    case   EFILE: fputs("- end file", stdout);   goto eol;
        fld: see16();
        eol: newlin(YES);
            return;
    }
  itou(item, str, 6); fputs(str,  stdout);
  fputs(" is an Unknown Item Code\n", stdout);
  }
see8(value, suff) int value, suff; {   /* display 8-bits */
  char str[5];
  if(width == 0 && item < CREL) {      /* need loc ctr pref */
    itox(lc, str, 5);
    outz(str);                         /* output loc ctr */
    fputc(' ', stdout);                /* output spacer */
    }
  itox(value & 255, str, 3);           /* convert to hex string */
  outz(str);                           /* output hex byte */
  if(suff) fputc(suff, stdout);        /* output suffix? */
  ++width;                             /* bump line width */
  }


see16() {                              /* display field */
  see8(field >> 8, 0);                 /* display high byte  */
  see8(field, xtype());                /* display low byte & type */
  fputc(' ', stdout);                  /* output spacer */
  }
seenam(pref, val) char *pref; int val; {/* display symbol */
  newlin(YES);
  width = 1;                           /* avoid address prefix */
  fputs(pref,   stdout);
  if(val) see16();                     /* output a value */
  fputs(symbol,  stdout);
  }
xtype() {
  switch(type) {
    case    ABS: return(' ');
    case   PREL: return('\'');
    case   DREL: return('\"');
    case   CREL: return('~');
    case  XPOFF: return('+');
    case  XMOFF: return('-');
    }
  return('?');
  }
```

```
newlin(nl) int nl; {                    /* decide about new line */
  if(width > 15 || (nl && width)) {
    fputc('\n', stdout);
    width = 0;
    }
  }

outz(str) char *str; {                  /* zero fill and output str */
  char *cp;
  cp = str;
  while(*cp == ' ') *cp++ = '0';        /* supply leading zeroes */
  fputs(str, stdout);
  }
```

―――――――――――――――――――――――――――――――――――――― FILE: WAIT.C

```
#include <stdio.h>
#define NOCCARGC
/*
** wait.c -- wait for operator response
*/
wait() {                    /* wait for user before clearing the message */
  fputs("\nWaiting...", stderr);
  fgetc(stderr);
  }
```

LISTING 7-8

8080 Machine Instruction Table

```
CE_x1   ACI  x
88      ADC  B|C|D|E|H|L|M|A
80      ADD  B|C|D|E|H|L|M|A
C6_x1   ADI  x
A0      ANA  B|C|D|E|H|L|M|A
E6_x1   ANI  x
CD_x2   CALL x
DC_x2   CC   x
FC_x2   CM   x
2F      CMA
3F      CMC
B8      CMP  B|C|D|E|H|L|M|A
D4_x2   CNC  x
C4_x2   CNZ  x
F4_x2   CP   x
EC_x2   CPE  x
FE_x1   CPI  x
E4_x2   CPO  x
CC_x2   CZ   x
```

```
27      DAA
39      DAD SP
19      DAD D
29      DAD H
09      DAD B
3D      DCR A
05      DCR B
0D      DCR C
15      DCR D
1D      DCR E
25      DCR H
2D      DCR L
35      DCR M
0B      DCX B
1B      DCX D
2B      DCX H
3B      DCX SP
F3      DI
FB      EI
76      HLT
DB_x1   IN x
3C      INR A
04      INR B
0C      INR C
14      INR D
1C      INR E
24      INR H
2C      INR L
34      INR M
03      INX B
13      INX D
23      INX H
33      INX SP
DA_x2   JC x
FA_x2   JM x
C3_x2   JMP x
D2_x2   JNC x
C2_x2   JNZ x
F2_x2   JP x
EA_x2   JPE x
E2_x2   JPO x
CA_x2   JZ x
3A_x2   LDA x
0A      LDAX B
1A      LDAX D
2A_x2   LHLD x
21_x2   LXI H,x
11_x2   LXI D,x
31_x2   LXI SP,x
```

```
01_x2  LXI  B,x
7C     MOV  A,H|A,L|A,M|A,A
54     MOV  D,H|D,L|D,M|D,A
5D     MOV  E,L|E,M|E,A
78     MOV  A,B|A,C|A,D|A,E
40     MOV  B,B|B,C|B,D|B,E|B,H|B,L|B,M|B,A
48     MOV  C,B|C,C|C,D|C,E|C,H|C,L|C,M|C,A
50     MOV  D,B|D,C|D,D|D,E
58     MOV  E,B|E,C|E,D|E,E|E,H
60     MOV  H,B|H,C|H,D|H,E|H,H|H,L|H,M|H,A
68     MOV  L,B|L,C|L,D|L,E|L,H|L,L|L,M|L,A
77     MOV  M,A
70     MOV  M,B|M,C|M,D|M,E|M,H|M,L
3E_x1  MVI  A,x
06_x1  MVI  B,x
0E_x1  MVI  C,x
16_x1  MVI  D,x
1E_x1  MVI  E,x
26_x1  MVI  H,x
2E_x1  MVI  L,x
36_x1  MVI  M,x
00     NOP
B5     ORA  L|M|A
B0     ORA  B|C|D|E|H
F6_x1  ORI  x
D3_x1  OUT  x
E9     PCHL
C1     POP  B
D1     POP  D
E1     POP  H
F1     POP  PSW
E5     PUSH H
D5     PUSH D
C5     PUSH B
F5     PUSH PSW
17     RAL
1F     RAR
D8     RC
C9     RET
20     RIM
07     RLC
F8     RM
D0     RNC
C0     RNZ
F0     RP
E8     RPE
E0     RPO
0F     RRC
C7     RST 0
```

```
D7       RST 16
DF       RST 24
E7       RST 32
EF       RST 40
F7       RST 48
FF       RST 56
CF       RST 8
C8       RZ
98       SBB B¦C¦D¦E¦H¦L¦M¦A
DE_x1    SBI x
22_x2    SHLD x
30       SIM
F9       SPHL
32_x2    STA x
02       STAX B
12       STAX D
37       STC
90       SUB B¦C¦D¦E¦H¦L¦M¦A
D6_x1    SUI x
EB       XCHG
A8       XRA B¦C¦D¦E¦H¦L¦M¦A
EE_x1    XRI x
E3       XTHL
```

LISTING 7-9

```
Z80 Macine Instruction Table
DD_8E_x1    ADC A,(IX+x)
FD_8E_x1    ADC A,(IY+x)
88          ADC A,B¦A,C¦A,D¦A,E¦A,H¦A,L¦A,(HL)¦A,A
CE_x1       ADC A,x
ED_4A       ADC HL,BC
ED_5A       ADC HL,DE
ED_6A       ADC HL,HL
ED_7A       ADC HL,SP
DD_86_x1    ADD A,(IX+x)
FD_86_x1    ADD A,(IY+x)
80          ADD A,B¦A,C¦A,D¦A,E¦A,H¦A,L¦A,(HL)¦A,A
C6_x1       ADD A,x
09          ADD HL,BC
19          ADD HL,DE
29          ADD HL,HL
39          ADD HL,SP
DD_09       ADD IX,BC
DD_19       ADD IX,DE
DD_29       ADD IX,IX
DD_39       ADD IX,SP
FD_09       ADD IY,BC
FD_19       ADD IY,DE
```

```
FD_29          ADD IY,IY
FD_39          ADD IY,SP
DD_A6_x1       AND (IX+x)
FD_A6_x1       AND (IY+x)
A0             AND B|C|D|E|H|L|(HL)|A
E6_x1          AND x
DD_CB_x1_46    BIT 0,(IX+x)
FD_CB_x1_46    BIT 0,(IY+x)
CB_40          BIT 0,B|0,C|0,D|0,E|0,H|0,L|0,(HL)|0,A
DD_CB_x1_4E    BIT 1,(IX+x)
FD_CB_x1_4E    BIT 1,(IY+x)
CB_48          BIT 1,B|1,C|1,D|1,E|1,H|1,L|1,(HL)|1,A
DD_CB_x1_56    BIT 2,(IX+x)
FD_CB_x1_56    BIT 2,(IY+x)
CB_50          BIT 2,B|2,C|2,D|2,E|2,H|2,L|2,(HL)|2,A
DD_CB_x1_5E    BIT 3,(IX+x)
FD_CB_x1_5E    BIT 3,(IY+x)
CB_58          BIT 3,B|3,C|3,D|3,E|3,H|3,L|3,(HL)|3,A
DD_CB_x1_66    BIT 4,(IX+x)
FD_CB_x1_66    BIT 4,(IY+x)
CB_60          BIT 4,B|4,C|4,D|4,E|4,H|4,L|4,(HL)|4,A
DD_CB_x1_6E    BIT 5,(IX+x)
FD_CB_x1_6E    BIT 5,(IY+x)
CB_68          BIT 5,B|5,C|5,D|5,E|5,H|5,L|5,(HL)|5,A
DD_CB_x1_76    BIT 6,(IX+x)
FD_CB_x1_76    BIT 6,(IY+x)
CB_70          BIT 6,B|6,C|6,D|6,E|6,H|6,L|6,(HL)|6,A
DD_CB_x1_7E    BIT 7,(IX+x)
FD_CB_x1_7E    BIT 7,(IY+x)
CB_78          BIT 7,B|7,C|7,D|7,E|7,H|7,L|7,(HL)|7,A
DC_x2          CALL C,x
FC_x2          CALL M,x
D4_x2          CALL NC,x
C4_x2          CALL NZ,x
F4_x2          CALL P,x
EC_x2          CALL PE,x
E4_x2          CALL PO,x
CC_x2          CALL Z,x|x
3F             CCF
DD_BE_x1       CP (IX+x)
FD_BE_x1       CP (IY+x)
B8             CP B|C|D|E|H|L|(HL)|A
FE_x1          CP x
ED_A9          CPD
ED_B9          CPDR
ED_A1          CPI
ED_B1          CPIR
2F             CPL
27             DAA
```

35	DEC (HL)
DD_35_x1	DEC (IX+x)
FD_35_x1	DEC (IY+x)
3D	DEC A
05	DEC B
0B	DEC BC
0D	DEC C
15	DEC D
1B	DEC DE
1D	DEC E
25	DEC H
2B	DEC HL
DD_2B	DEC IX
FD_2B	DEC IY
2D	DEC L
3B	DEC SP
F3	DI
10_p1	DJNZ p
FB	EI
E3	EX (SP),HL
DD_E3	EX (SP),IX
FD_E3	EX (SP),IY
08	EX AF,AF'
EB	EX DE,HL
D9	EXX
76	HALT
ED_46	IM 0
ED_56	IM 1
ED_5E	IM 2
ED_78	IN A,(C)
DB_x1	IN A,(x)
ED_40	IN B,(C)
ED_48	IN C,(C)
ED_50	IN D,(C)
ED_58	IN E,(C)
ED_60	IN H,(C)
ED_68	IN L,(C)
DD_34_x1	INC (IX+x)
FD_34_x1	INC (IY+x)
3C	INC A
03	INC BC¦B
0C	INC C
13	INC DE¦D
1C	INC E
23	INC HL¦H
DD_23	INC IX
FD_23	INC IY
2C	INC L
33	INC SP¦(HL)

ED_AA	IND
ED_BA	INDR
ED_A2	INI
ED_B2	INIR
E9	JP (HL)
DD_E9	JP (IX)
FD_E9	JP (IY)
DA_x2	JP C,x
FA_x2	JP M,x
D2_x2	JP NC,x
C2_x2	JP NZ,x|x
F2_x2	JP P,x
EA_x2	JP PE,x
E2_x2	JP PO,x
CA_x2	JP Z,x
38_p1	JR C,p
30_p1	JR NC,p
20_p1	JR NZ,p
18_p1	JR p
28_p1	JR Z,p
02	LD (BC),A
12	LD (DE),A
77	LD (HL),A
70	LD (HL),B¦(HL),C¦(HL),D¦(HL),E¦(HL),H¦(HL),L
36_x1	LD (HL),x
DD_77_x1	LD (IX+x),A
DD_70_x1	LD (IX+x),B¦(IX+x),C¦(IX+x),D
DD_73_x1	LD (IX+x),E¦(IX+x),H¦(IX+x),L
DD_36_x1_x1	LD (IX+x),x
FD_77_x1	LD (IY+x),A
FD_70_x1	LD (IY+x),B¦(IY+x),C¦(IY+x),D
FD_73_x1	LD (IY+x),E¦(IY+x),H¦(IY+x),L
FD_36_x1_x1	LD (IY+x),x
ED_43_x2	LD (x),BC
ED_53_x2	LD (x),DE
22_x2	LD (x),HL
DD_22_x2	LD (x),IX
FD_22_x2	LD (x),IY
ED_73_x2	LD (x),SP
0A	LD A,(BC)
1A	LD A,(DE)
DD_7E_x1	LD A,(IX+x)
FD_7E_x1	LD A,(IY+x)
78	LD A,B¦A,C¦A,D¦A,E¦A,H¦A,L¦A,(HL)¦A,A
ED_57	LD A,I
ED_5F	LD A,R
3A_x2	LD A,(x)
3E_x1	LD A,x
DD_46_x1	LD B,(IX+x)

```
FD_46_x1    LD B,(IY+x)
40          LD B,B|B,C|B,D|B,E|B,H|B,L|B,(HL)|B,A
06_x1       LD B,x
ED_4B_x2    LD BC,(x)
01_x2       LD BC,x
DD_4E_x1    LD C,(IX+x)
FD_4E_x1    LD C,(IY+x)
48          LD C,B|C,C|C,D|C,E|C,H|C,L|C,(HL)|C,A
0E_x1       LD C,x
DD_56_x1    LD D,(IX+x)
FD_56_x1    LD D,(IY+x)
50          LD D,B|D,C|D,D|D,E|D,H|D,L|D,(HL)|D,A
16_x1       LD D,x
12          LD (DE),A
ED_5B_x2    LD DE,(x)
11_x2       LD DE,x
DD_5E_x1    LD E,(IX+x)
FD_5E_x1    LD E,(IY+x)
58          LD E,B|E,C|E,D|E,E|E,H|E,L|E,(HL)|E,A
1E_x1       LD E,x
DD_66_x1    LD H,(IX+x)
FD_66_x1    LD H,(IY+x)
60          LD H,B|H,C|H,D|H,E|H,H|H,L|H,(HL)|H,A
26_x1       LD H,x
2A_x2       LD HL,(x)
ED_47       LD I,A
DD_2A_x2    LD IX,(x)
DD_21_x2    LD IX,x
FD_2A_x2    LD IY,(x)
FD_21_x2    LD IY,x
DD_6E_x1    LD L,(IX+x)
FD_6E_x1    LD L,(IY+x)
68          LD L,B|L,C|L,D|L,E|L,H|L,L|L,(HL)|L,A
2E_x1       LD L,x
ED_4F       LD R,A
F9          LD SP,HL
DD_F9       LD SP,IX
FD_F9       LD SP,IY
ED_7B_x2    LD SP,(x)
31_x2       LD SP,x|(x),A
ED_A8       LDD
ED_B8       LDDR
ED_A0       LDI
ED_B0       LDIR
ED_44       NEG
00          NOP
DD_B6_x1    OR (IX+x)
FD_B6_x1    OR (IY+x)
B0          OR B|C|D|E|H|L|(HL)|A
```

```
F6_x1        OR x
ED_BB        OTDR
ED_B3        OTIR
ED_79        OUT (C),A
ED_41        OUT (C),B
ED_49        OUT (C),C
ED_51        OUT (C),D
ED_59        OUT (C),E
ED_61        OUT (C),H
ED_69        OUT (C),L
D3_x1        OUT (x),A
ED_AB        OUTD
ED_A3        OUTI
F1           POP AF
C1           POP BC
D1           POP DE
E1           POP HL
DD_E1        POP IX
FD_E1        POP IY
F5           PUSH AF
C5           PUSH BC
D5           PUSH DE
E5           PUSH HL
DD_E5        PUSH IX
FD_E5        PUSH IY
DD_CB_x1_86  RES 0,(IX+x)
FD_CB_x1_86  RES 0,(IY+x)
CB_80        RES 0,B|0,C|0,D|0,E|0,H|0,L|0,(HL)|0,A
DD_CB_x1_8E  RES 1,(IX+x)
FD_CB_x1_8E  RES 1,(IY+x)
CB_88        RES 1,B|1,C|1,D|1,E|1,H|1,L|1,(HL)|1,A
DD_CB_x1_96  RES 2,(IX+x)
FD_CB_x1_96  RES 2,(IY+x)
CB_90        RES 2,B|2,C|2,D|2,E|2,H|2,L|2,(HL)|2,A
DD_CB_x1_9E  RES 3,(IX+x)
FD_CB_x1_9E  RES 3,(IY+x)
CB_98        RES 3,B|3,C|3,D|3,E|3,H|3,L|3,(HL)|3,A
DD_CB_x1_A6  RES 4,(IX+x)
FD_CB_x1_A6  RES 4,(IY+x)
CB_A0        RES 4,B|4,C|4,D|4,E|4,H|4,L|4,(HL)|4,A
DD_CB_x1_AE  RES 5,(IX+x)
FD_CB_x1_AE  RES 5,(IY+x)
CB_A8        RES 5,B|5,C|5,D|5,E|5,H|5,L|5,(HL)|5,A
DD_CB_x1_B6  RES 6,(IX+x)
FD_CB_x1_B6  RES 6,(IY+x)
CB_B0        RES 6,B|6,C|6,D|6,E|6,H|6,L|6,(HL)|6,A
DD_CB_x1_BE  RES 7,(IX+x)
FD_CB_x1_BE  RES 7,(IY+x)
CB_B8        RES 7,B|7,C|7,D|7,E|7,H|7,L|7,(HL)|7,A
```

```
C9           RET
D8           RET C
F8           RET M
D0           RET NC
C0           RET NZ
F0           RET P
E8           RET PE
E0           RET PO
C8           RET Z
ED_4D        RETI
ED_45        RETN
DD_CB_x1_16  RL (IX+x)
FD_CB_x1_16  RL (IY+x)
CB_10        RL B¦C¦D¦E¦H¦L¦(HL)¦A
17           RLA
DD_CB_x1_06  RLC (IX+x)
FD_CB_x1_06  RLC (IY+x)
CB_00        RLC B¦C¦D¦E¦H¦L¦(HL)¦A
07           RLCA
ED_6F        RLD
DD_CB_x1_1E  RR (IX+x)
FD_CB_x1_1E  RR (IY+x)
CB_18        RR B¦C¦D¦E¦H¦L¦(HL)¦A
DD_CB_x1_0E  RRC (IX+x)
FD_CB_x1_0E  RRC (IY+x)
CB_08        RRC B¦C¦D¦E¦H¦L¦(HL)¦A
0F           RRCA
ED_67        RRD
1F           RRA
C7           RST 0
C7           RST 00H
CF           RST 08H
C7           RST 0H
D7           RST 10H
D7           RST 16
DF           RST 18H
E7           RST 20H
DF           RST 24
EF           RST 28H
F7           RST 30H
E7           RST 32
FF           RST 38H
EF           RST 40
F7           RST 48
FF           RST 56
CF           RST 8
CF           RST 8H
DD_9E_x1     SBC A,(IX+x)
FD_9E_x1     SBC A,(IY+x)
```

```
98            SBC A,B│A,C│A,D│A,E│A,H│A,L│A,(HL)│A,A
DE_x1         SBC A,x
ED_42         SBC HL,BC
ED_52         SBC HL,DE
ED_62         SBC HL,HL
ED_72         SBC HL,SP
37            SCF
DD_CB_x1_C6   SET 0,(IX+x)
FD_CB_x1_C6   SET 0,(IY+x)
CB_C0         SET 0,B│0,C│0,D│0,E│0,H│0,L│0,(HL)│0,A
DD_CB_x1_CE   SET 1,(IX+x)
FD_CB_x1_CE   SET 1,(IY+x)
CB_C8         SET 1,B│1,C│1,D│1,E│1,H│1,L│1,(HL)│1,A
DD_CB_x1_D6   SET 2,(IX+x)
FD_CB_x1_D6   SET 2,(IY+x)
CB_D0         SET 2,B│2,C│2,D│2,E│2,H│2,L│2,(HL)│2,A
DD_CB_x1_DE   SET 3,(IX+x)
FD_CB_x1_DE   SET 3,(IY+x)
CB_D8         SET 3,B│3,C│3,D│3,E│3,H│3,L│3,(HL)│3,A
DD_CB_x1_E6   SET 4,(IX+x)
FD_CB_x1_E6   SET 4,(IY+x)
CB_E0         SET 4,B│4,C│4,D│4,E│4,H│4,L│4,(HL)│4,A
DD_CB_x1_EE   SET 5,(IX+x)
FD_CB_x1_EE   SET 5,(IY+x)
CB_E8         SET 5,B│5,C│5,D│5,E│5,H│5,L│5,(HL)│5,A
DD_CB_x1_F6   SET 6,(IX+x)
FD_CB_x1_F6   SET 6,(IY+x)
CB_F0         SET 6,B│6,C│6,D│6,E│6,H│6,L│6,(HL)│6,A
DD_CB_x1_FE   SET 7,(IX+x)
FD_CB_x1_FE   SET 7,(IY+x)
CB_F8         SET 7,B│7,C│7,D│7,E│7,H│7,L│7,(HL)│7,A
DD_CB_x1_26   SLA (IX+x)
FD_CB_x1_26   SLA (IY+x)
CB_20         SLA B│C│D│E│H│L│(HL)│A
DD_CB_x1_2E   SRA (IX+x)
FD_CB_x1_2E   SRA (IY+x)
CB_28         SRA B│C│D│E│H│L│(HL)│A
DD_CB_x1_3E   SRL (IX+x)
FD_CB_x1_3E   SRL (IY+x)
CB_38         SRL B│C│D│E│H│L│(HL)│A
DD_96_x1      SUB A,(IX+x)
FD_96_x1      SUB A,(IY+x)
90_           SUB A,B│A,C│A,D│A,E│A,H│A,L│A,(HL)│A,A
D6_x1         SUB x
DD_AE_x1      XOR (IX+x)
FD_AE_x1      XOR (IY+x)
A8            XOR B│C│D│E│H│L│(HL)│A
EE_x1         XOR x
```

8
P: A SMALL-C PREPROCESSOR

by Axel T. Schreiner

This chapter originally appeared in DDJ #93 (July 1984).

Jim Hendrix's Small-C compiler (see "Small-C Version 2" in this volume) supports some of the preprocessor commands that are usually available in C systems: a symbolic name can be defined for an arbitrary text, which is then inserted whenever the name appears in the source program. This facility is most frequently used to give meaningful names to various important constants in a program, but it can also be used to give C programs the appearance (almost) of Pascal programs, to substitute one function name for another, and so on. Hendrix's compiler also supports one level of file inclusion, although with a somewhat nonstandard syntax, and it supports conditional compilation based on whether certain symbolic names have been defined.

Such a preprocessor is an important tool in its own right. It can be combined with other language processors and assemblers as well. It also becomes considerably more flexible if text substitution can be parameterized (that is, if macro calls can have arguments and if file inclusion is performed to arbitrary depth). If the preprocessor additionally eliminates C-style comments and translates C-style constants to decimal notation, it simplifies the compiler's job significantly and at the same time obtains a uniform approach to constant notation, commenting conventions, and file inclusion.

The program described in this chapter, *p* (Listing 8-1), is such an independent preprocessor. It is written in Small-C and supports all the features of the regular C preprocessor described by Kernighan and Ritchie (*The C Programming Language*, Prentice-Hall, 1978) with the exception of an *if* preprocessor statement with a constant expression argument.

Features

p is based on a runtime support that passes arguments to the main program; it expects to be called as follows:

    p (option)... (inputfile (outputfile))

If no files are explicitly specified, *p* reads from "standard input" and writes to "standard output" (the runtime support presumably makes those connections as well). If the runtime support would normally connect to the terminal, it is simple to test certain features through input from the terminal, or to see the results of a preprocessor run directly at the terminal.

You may specify options in any order, and they are generally cumulative. The following options are available:

```
-d name(=value)     define a symbolic name
-e                  suppress position stamps
-i drive            search for file inclusion
-u name             undefine a symbolic name
-v                  verbose -- for debugging
```

You may define symbolic names when *p* is called. This is convenient for maintaining various versions of a program. The name *cpm* is predefined by *p*. You can undo this (in particular) using the option to undefine a name. To permit a compiler to emit error messages referencing the original source files, *p* creates a position stamp (that is, a line starting with # and containing a decimal line number and, if known, a filename, whenever this is necessary for correct sequencing of output lines. Hendrix's Small-C compiler cannot handle these position stamps; therefore, they can be suppressed.

CP/M identifies files by name and disk drive. Therefore, *p* searches *include* files on various disks: first on the disk of the input file (which may be the currently selected disk) and last on the currently selected disk. In between, *p* may optionally search other disk drives, if appropriate options have been specified. The search proceeds from right to left over the -i options.

The options are clearly patterned after the Unix system. The main program expects to receive pointers to the various options as a vector, argv. The number of such options, including (theoretically) the program name as first option, is also passed as an integer, argc. *p* is tolerant enough to accept the parameter of an option (such as an *include* drive) as part of the option or as a separate, immediately following option. Options, however, must precede the filenames.

Once started, *p* reads the input file and writes the output file. C-style comments (arbitrary texts enclosed in /* and */ sequences) are replaced by single blanks. Next, preprocessor command lines are processed. Then, in regular text lines, macro calls (appearances of defined names, possibly followed by a list of arguments in parentheses) are replaced. Replacement text is surrounded by blanks and is reprocessed for further macro calls. Recursion may happen, but reprocessing is aborted after a few attempts with an appropriate message.

Input lines, as well as output lines, may be arbitrarily long. You may optionally continue input lines over several source lines by placing a backslash before the end of the source line to be continued. C is free format, but preprocessing is line oriented; continuation should be necessary (and come in handy) only for preprocessor command lines, macro calls, and very long strings. Macro calls and strings must be fully contained within one (possibly continued) input line.

A macro call is not recognized within a comment, a preprocessor command line, a string, or a character constant. The replacement text is surrounded by blanks. You cannot use two adjacent macro calls to create another macro call from their replacement text.

If you define a macro with parameters, the macro call consists of the macro name and a list of arguments, separated by commas and enclosed by parentheses. Although the left parenthesis must immediately follow the macro name in the definition, it need not in the call. The call, however, must be completely contained on one input line to avoid rather sticky questions about whether a macro should be redefined inside its call, and so on. A macro argument is an arbitrary text and may even contain a comma within balanced parentheses, a string, or a character constant. The text is substituted wherever the corresponding parameter appears in the macro definition, even within a string. No blanks are forced around the argument text. There must be exactly as many arguments as there are defined parameters.

p removes leading white space from the output lines and converts constants to decimal notation. These "features" can easily be removed. They do impair the general applicability of the program, but they overcome certain problems in Hendrix's compiler while significantly shortening the output file.

The following constant notations are accepted and are converted to (signed) decimal representation:

```
digits              decimal constant
Odigits             octal constant (digits 0..7)
Oxdigits or         hexadecimal constant
OXdigits            (digits 0..9, a..f, A..F)
'c'                 character constant
```

Clearly, no blank may separate the base prefix from the actual constant. Character constants may be escaped; escape sequences consist of a backslash character followed by other characters. The following escapes are recognized:

```
b                   backspace
f                   form feed
n                   newline (line feed)
r                   return
t                   tab
'                   single quote
```

```
"           double quote
\           backslash itself
d           octal, up to three digits 0..7
```

Character constants are converted to decimal notation. This is reasonable for C programs, but it might cause problems elsewhere.

Preprocessor command lines begin with a # symbol. White space may follow, and then a keyword must be distinguishable. Depending on the keyword, there may be parameters; the rest of a command line can be quite arbitrary. The following commands are supported:

```
define      name replacement-text
define      name(name,...) replacement-text

undef       name

ifdef       name
ifndef      name
else
endif

include     "filename"
include     <filename>

line        linenumber filename
```

define is used to define a symbolic name for an arbitrary replacement text. You can parameterize the replacement text. The parameter names are local to each definition, and unfortunately no test exists to determine whether two parameter names within one definition are one and the same. Names follow C conventions: they must start in a letter or underscore, can contain letters, digits, or underscores, and can be arbitrarily long.

Redefinition is possible but provokes a message. You can use *undef* to remove a definition, and there is no complaint if the relevant name was never defined.

ifdef is fulfilled if the specified name is currently defined; *ifndef* is fulfilled if it is not. In either case, subsequent input lines (including preprocessor commands) are processed or skipped depending on the condition. *else* reverses the current value of the condition, and *endif* terminates the construct. You can nest these constructs to any depth. You should use *else* only once per construct, but this is not checked. Each *else* reverses the current state of things.

include causes file inclusion. The filename should follow CP/M conventions. If it does not contain an explicit disk drive specification, the file is searched on the list of drives beginning with the input file drive and ending with the currently selected drive. If the filename is enclosed in angle brackets rather than double quotes, the first drive on the list is skipped. (Normally, brackets are used to designate public *include* files, presumably residing on the currently selected disk and not on the disk of the input file.)

You can nest *include* to any depth, assuming the runtime support for this program is reasonable. Once the end of an included file is reached, processing continues after the *include* command causing the file inclusion. If a file cannot be opened or found, a message is printed, but processing continues.

The *line* command is intended for program generators. For purposes of diagnostics and position stamps in the output file, *p* accepts a line number and optionally a filename from the *line* command.

Other lines starting in # are processed as if they were text. Thus, *p* passes through such things as "asm" and "endasm," provided these lines are not modified by macro expansions. Position stamps from a previous run of *p* would also be passed through again.

Implementation

The task of preprocessing can be nicely structured into four problems, each solved essentially by a single C function:

```
take care of start options, initialize
while (there is another line)
    if (after removing comments, there is something &&
        after observing commands, there is something)
        preprocess the text line
```

main() takes care of start options and initialization. getline() collects a nonblank line and takes care of line continuation. comment() eliminates comments, which may extend over several lines, and removes leading white space. command() knows whether you are currently skipping in observance of some *if* construct; if you are, command() pretends that a command was actually found, so the the input line is not processed further. If there is a preprocessor command, command() recognizes and executes it. If the current line is regular text, process() takes care of macro expansion and output.

getline() collects input characters into a buffer until a newline character or end of file is found. If there is a backslash followed by a newline, both characters are ignored (but source lines are counted). If there is an end of file following a backslash, getline() complains. At end of file, getline() attempts to pop the stack of open input files. getline() returns once there is a nonblank input line, or if the end of the initial input file is reached. Non-ASCII characters are not accepted as input to simplify subsequent processing.

For input and output, two buffers must be maintained and should be able to grow more or less without limit. The rebuff() routine, which is called with a full buffer, handles this. It reallocates the buffer and recopies the information. Clearly, no other pointers into the buffer should exist at that point.

The comment() algorithm is simple: copy everything until /*, then quit copying (and reporting that there is text material) until */ is found. Matters are complicated slightly by strings, (invalid) character constants, and backslashes. The problem is handled with the state variable *cmode*, which maintains the current context—comment, string, character constant—across calls. Again, comment() suppresses blank lines as well as initial white space.

command() deals with preprocessor commands in all those line buffers that comment() did not prevent from being passed on. Calls to the symbol table management routines handle command processing. *if* constructs are implemented through two variables: *iflevel*, which counts the current nesting depth of these constructs, and *skip*, which is usually and initially zero, indicating that text should be processed. If text should be ignored, due to some *if* or *else*, skip is set to the value of *iflevel* at which skipping should terminate. If you are skipping and reach *else* or *endif* at the proper level, you are done; *skip* reverts to zero.

There should really be only one *else* per *if*. Enforcing this would require a stack indicating at each *iflevel* if you have already seen *else*. I felt this was not really necessary; consequently (as in Hendrix's compiler) multiple occurrences of *else* are allowed.

line and *include* require a certain amount of data processing. The syntax must be verified, and the relevant information must be stacked. There are stacks of open file pointers, filenames, and last line numbers. All the stacks are handled by push routines, which return the address of a new element linked before the stack. The result of push, therefore, must always be assigned back to the stack top pointer, which is passed as an argument. A common pop() routine handles removal of unwanted elements. A string stack is also used to hold the *include* prefixes passed as options.

process() does the actual work if a line is ever passed to it. The *line* buffer is scanned and copied to the *oline* buffer. The outmacro(), outnumber(), outdelim(), and out() routines are called to manage processing of a macro call, a numerical constant, a string or character constant, and a simple character, respectively. As long as a macro was actually expanded in a pass over *line*, the two buffers are interchanged and processing is repeated until either no more expansion is performed or a count runs out (to prevent infinite recursion). output() takes care of emitting position stamps and the processed text.

Finding names in the symbol table and undefining them is quite simple: the symbol table is represented with a one-way linked list of entries, each containing a pointer to the string defining the symbol and the symbol name itself. If the symbol is a parameterized macro, the name is followed by a left parenthesis and a (binary) parameter count. find() must take care to match names correctly. If a symbol definition is parameterized, the value contains (binary) parameter numbers in place of the original parameter names. Each parameter number takes just one byte and is flagged in the high bit, since all other text is ASCII.

The symbol table can employ a hashing mechanism. If the symbolic name HASH is undefined, the symbol table consists of a single linear list. If the name is defined, it must be as a power of 2, designating how many such linear lists should be kept. In this case, each name is first converted to a number indicating which of the lists should be used. This simple mechanism and a rather naive hash function in find() cut preprocessing time by about 20 percent.

define() does a significant amount of text processing to prepare a parameterized macro definition. marknm() has usually separated the macro header from the macro value within the line buffer. ismacro() and isname() make sure that the macro header uses only appropriate symbols and the proper arrangements of commas and parentheses. ismacro() prepares yet another string stack of parameter names. define() then removes leading and trailing white space from the value and replaces parameter names by flagged numbers. Finally, you must guard against redefinitions and store the result. A redefinition is flagged only if it is truly different; therefore, header files can usually be read several times without complaint.

outmacro() also does a large amount of text processing. If the macro is parameterized, markarg() is used to flag the text arguments in the input buffer and to prepare a stack of pointers to these argument values. This task, too, is complicated by the usual potential assortment of parentheses and string delimiters. Once the argument list is collected, it is a simple matter (possibly handled with outarg()) to emit the macro definition with the argument texts in place.

Installation

Getting *p* to run on your system might be a bit tricky. There is a bootstrap problem—*p* uses features supported only by *p* and not by Hendrix's compiler—and there is a problem concerning the runtime support.

Overcoming the bootstrap problem is simple. You should replace double quotes as a character constant by the value 34 (my Small-C compiler got confused in certain places until I did this). You need to replace all constants your compiler does not support (for example, the definitions of PARM and PARMNO and the values for *base* in the routine outnumber()). You might have to replace the character constants in the routine outdelim() if your compiler does not yet support those escape sequences. Finally, you have to play preprocessor for those macros that are parameterized. (Yes, it was not nice to use those, but I did want to show how parameterized macros can be used to clarify data types.)

The runtime support is quite a different matter. Although I agree with Jim Hendrix that these matters ought to be standardized, I would like to program on my CP/M system at home just as I do on the Unix systems at the office (*p* can be compiled with the C compiler on Unix version 7). I have actually made a runtime support that looks like the standard libraries available with Unix version 7 and above, is based on CP/M, and supports all BIOS and BDOS calls from Small-C.

I have had access to Chapter 17 of Hendrix's *Small-C Handbook* (Reston Publishing Company, 1984), describing his runtime support. Although I did not have access to the runtime support itself and therefore could not test it, I believe that installing *p* should be simple. The following probably should be done:

```
FILE         should be defined as int
_drive()     needs to access BDOS function 25
_narg()      is supported by the compiler
index()      is Hendrix's strrchr()
itod()       can be coded using Hendrix's itod()
```

I process the arguments to main() directly. Depending on the actual implementation, you might have to use Hendrix's function getarg().

I am assuming that the storage allocator, calloc()/cfree(), supports random order release of memory. The code in Listing 8-2 may be useful to those wishing to add such random order release to the Hendrix-Payne library published in this book.

Meanwhile, you should probably consult Kernighan and Ritchie's book to learn about all the routines mentioned "extern" at the beginning of the program. Most of them are simple to construct. It is essential, however, that you provide multiple open files so arbitrary nesting of file inclusion is possible. You also need a memory allocator, calloc() and cfree(), that reuses available space and is reasonably stable. I am using a scheme where memory above the load module and below the stack is managed by a list of words, each word pointing to the next. The low bit in each such word indicates if the area past that word and up to the next one is allocated or free. Kernighan and Ritchie mention, and Unix supports, routines to classify characters. This is most easily implemented as a 128-byte table with each byte classifying the corresponding character as special, uppercase or lowercase, numeric, hexadecimal, white space, punctuation, or control character. The routines are then simple masking operations that can now be provided as macros.

Part of this work was done during a sabbatical spent at the University of Illinois; in particular, the Small-C system was obtained from UseNet.

LISTING 8-1

```
/*
 *      contributed by A. T. Schreiner
 *                     Sektion Informatik
 *                     University of Ulm
 *                     West Germany
 *
 */


/*
 *      p -- Small-C preprocessor
 *      ats 6/83
 */

/*
 *      define...
 *
 *      verbose         to support -v for debugging
 */
char usage[] =
#ifdef  verbose
        "p [-d n[=v]] [-e] [-i d:] [-u n] [-v] [in [out]]",
        vflag;          /* set by -v */
#else
        "p [-d n[=v]] [-e] [-i d:] [-u n] [in [out]]";
#endif

                        /* command names:                */
#define DEFINE  1       /* # define name text            */
                        /* # define name(name,...) text  */
#define ELSE    2       /* # else                        */
#define ENDIF   3       /* # endif                       */
#define IFDEF   4       /* # ifdef name                  */
#define IFNDEF  5       /* # ifndef name                 */
#define INCLUDE 6       /* # include "file"              */
                        /* # include <file>              */
#define LINE    7       /* # line number name            */
#define UNDEF   8       /* # undef name                  */
#define DEFAULT 0       /* any others passed on          */

/*
 *      "FEATURES":
 *
 *              Macro calls must be fully contained on one source
 *              line -- all lines can be continued with \, however.
 *
```

```
 *              Recursive definitions are not detected as such.
 *              p' will report as per NEST.
 *
 *              #else can be used (to reverse the current
 *              #if condition) arbitrarily often.
 */

#include <stdio.h>

/*
 *      i/o header file

#define FILE     ???    type to represent files (used as FILE*)
#define stdin    ???    pre-opened standard input file
#define stdout   ???    pre-opened standard output file
#define stderr   ???    pre-opened diagnostic output file
#define NULL     0      null pointer, false
#define EOF      ???    end of file indication

 */

#include <ctype.h>

/*
 *      character classification macros header file
 *
 *      isascii(i)      i is ASCII character
 *      isalnum(c)      c is letter or digit
 *      isalpha(c)      c is letter
 *      isdigit(c)      c is digit
 *      islower(c)      c is lower case letter
 *      isspace(c)      c is white space
 *      isupper(c)      c is upper case letter
 *      isxdigit(c)     c is base 16 digit
 *
 *      i can be any integer, isascii(c) must be true for c
 */

#define INCR    80      /* line buffer increment */
#define HASH    128     /* hash table size (power of 2) */
#define NEST    10      /* limit for reprocessing - -1 is "infinite" */

                        /* cmode states */
#define CMcmt   1       /* in comment */
#define CMstr   2       /* in string */
#define CMchr   3       /* in character constant */

#define PARM    0x80    /* flag macro parameter number */
#define PARMNO  0x7f    /* extract parameter number */
```

P: A SMALL-C PREPROCESSOR

```
/*
 *      special data types
 */

#define LIST        int             /* list of word or string values */
#define l_next(x)   (*(x))          /* -> next element */
#define l_word(x)   ((x)[1])        /* word value */
#define l_str(x)    ((x)+1)         /* -> string value */
#define sz_WORD     4               /* size of word list element */
#define sz_STR(s)   (3+strlen(s))   /* size of string list element */
#define SYMBOL      int             /* list of symbol table elements */
#define s_next(x)   (*(x))          /* -> next element */
#define s_val(x)    ((x)[1])        /* -> defined value */
#define s_name(x)   ((x)+2)         /* -> name */
#define sz_SYM(n)   (5+strlen(n))   /* size of symbol table element */

/*
 *      runtime support routines
 */

extern  _drive(),       /* BDOS function 25: current drive number */
        _narg(),        /* number of arguments passed in this call */
        calloc(),       /* (n,l) return NULL or -> n elements of length l */
        cfree(),        /* (p) free area at p, returned by calloc() */
        exit(),         /* terminate program execution */
        fclose(),       /* (f) close file described by f */
        fgetc(),        /* (f) return EOF or next character from file f */
        fopen(),        /* (n,m) return NULL or descriptor for file "n"
                            opened to read (m == "r"), write ("w"),
                            or append ("a") */
        fputc(),        /* (c,f) write c on file f, return EOF or c */
        fputs(),        /* (s,f) write string s on file f */
        freopen(),      /* (n,m,f) like fopen(), but close and reuse f */
        index(),        /* (s,c) find c in string s, return NULL or -> to it.
                            '\0' is always found */
        itod(),         /* (i) return -> (static) string with i in decimal */
        strcmp(),       /* (a,b) <, ==, > 0 as string a is <, ==, > string b */
        strcpy(),       /* (a,b) copy string b to string a */
        strlen(),       /* (s) return number of characters in string s */
        strncmp(),      /* (a,b,n) like strcmp(), but for n bytes at most */
        strncpy();      /* (a,b,n) like strcpy(), but for n bytes at most */

/*
 *      global data
 */

int     parmno,         /* current number of parameters */
        linelen,        /* current maximum usable length */
        olinelen,
```

```
        lineno,         /* current line number */
        olineno,
        iflevel,        /* depth of open #if */
        skip;           /* non-0: iflevel to skip to */

char    eflag,          /* set by -e: prevent position stamps */
        cmode,          /* comment() mode */
        *line,          /* dynamic input line buffer */
        *lp,            /* current position in line */
        *oline,         /* dynamic output line buffer */
        *olp;           /* current position in oline */

LIST    *drive,         /* include prefixes */
        *filenms,       /* open file names */
        *files,         /* open file pointers */
        *lines,         /* line numbers */
        *parms;         /* parameters */

SYMBOL  *symbol;        /* list of symbol table elements */
#ifdef  HASH            /* hash feature (optional) */
                        /* symbol set by find() to -> hashtab at s */
int     hashtab[HASH];  /* really SYMBOL *: begin of chains */
#endif

FILE    *infile;        /* current input file */

main(argc, argv)
        int argc;
        int *argv;
{       char *cp, *vp;
#ifdef  verbose
        LIST *ip;
#endif

        /* current drive is last include prefix */
        vp = "a:";
        *vp += _drive();
        drive = pushs(drive, vp);

        /* predefine "cpm" */
        define("cpm", "");

        /* process arguments, values may be joined or separate */
        while (--argc)
        {       cp = *++argv;
                if (*cp != '-')
                        break;
                switch (cp[1]) {
```

```
            case 'd':
                if (*(cp += 2))
                        ;
                else if (--argc == 0)
                        goto error;
                else
                        cp = *++argv;
                if (vp = index(cp, '='))
                        *vp++ = '\0';
                else
                        vp = "";
                define(cp, vp);
                break;
            case 'e':
                eflag = 1;
                break;
            case 'i':
                /* explicit prefixes in order right to left */
                if (*(cp += 2))
                        ;
                else if (--argc == 0)
                        goto error;
                else
                        cp = *++argv;
                drive = pushs(drive, cp);
                break;
            case 'u':
                if (*(cp += 2))
                        ;
                else if (--argc == 0)
                        goto error;
                else
                        cp = *++argv;
                undefine(cp);
                break;
#ifdef verbose
            case 'v':
                vflag = 1;
                break;
#endif
            default:
                goto error;
            }
        }


        /* input file drive is first include prefix */
        vp = "a:";
        *vp += _drive();
```

```c
            /* allow input and output files */
            switch (argc) {
            case 2:         /* use input, drive(input), output */
            case 1:         /* use input, drive(input) */
                    if (cp[1] == ':')
                    {       vp = "?:";
                            *vp = cp[0];
                    }
                    if (freopen(*argv, "r", stdin) == NULL)
                    {       where("cannot read", *argv);
                            exit();
                    }
                    filenms = pushs(filenms, *argv);
#ifdef verbose
                    if (vflag)
                            where("reading");
#endif
                    if (--argc)
                    {       if (freopen(*++argv, "w", stdout) == NULL)
                            {       filenms = NULL;
                                    where("cannot write", *argv);
                                    exit();
                            }
#ifdef verbose
                            if (vflag)
                                    where("writing", *argv);
#endif
                    }
            case 0:         /* use stdin, current drive */
                    break;
            default:
error:              where(usage);
                    exit();
            }

            /* set first include prefix */
            drive = pushs(drive, vp);

#ifdef verbose
            if (vflag)
            {       for (ip = drive; ip; ip = l_next(ip))
                            where("drive", l_str(ip));
            }
#endif

            /* start reading on stdin */
            infile = stdin;

            /* allocate first buffers */
```

```
        if ((line = calloc(INCR, 1)) == NULL
           || (oline = calloc(INCR, 1)) == NULL)
        {       where("no room");
                exit();
        }
        olinelen = linelen = INCR;

        /* make sure, we first get a position stamp */
        olineno = lineno - 3;

        /* main loop */
        while (getline())
                if (! comment() && ! command())
                        process();
}

getline()              /* line = complete line, ascii */
                       /* return false on EOF */
{       int c;         /* current character */

        /* move to lp, concatenating continued lines */
        for (lp = line; ; )
        {       switch (c = fgetc(infile)) {
                case '\\':
                        switch (c = fgetc(infile)) {
                        case EOF:
                                where("trailing \\");
                        case '\n':
                                ++lineno;
                                continue;
                        }
                        in('\\');
                default:
                        if (! isascii(c))
                                where("illegal character");
                        else
                                in(c);
                        continue;
                case EOF:
                        ++ lineno;
                        if (lp != line)
                                break;
                        else if (files)
                        {       fclose(infile);
#ifdef  verbose
                                if (vflag)
                                        where("end include");
#endif
                                infile = pop(&files);
```

```
                                lineno = pop(&lines);
                                olineno = lineno - 3; /* stamp! */
                                pop(&filenms);
                                continue;
                        }
                        return 0;
                case '\n':
                        ++lineno;
                        if (lp == line)
                                continue;
                }
                break;  /* got a nonempty line */
        }
        *lp = '\0';
#ifdef   verbose
        if (vflag)
                where("getline", line);
#endif
        return 1;
}

comment()                  /* line = line w/out comments, lead white space */
                           /* return true if comment line */
{       char c;

        /* move from olp to lp, eliminating comments */
        for (lp = olp = line; ; )
        {       switch (c = *olp++) {
                case '\\':
                        if (cmode != CMstr && cmode != CMchr)
                                break;
                        in(c);
                        if (c = *olp++)
                                break;
                case '\0':
                        if (cmode == CMstr)
                        {       if (! skip)
                                        where("unbalanced \"");
                                in('\"');
                                cmode = 0;
                        }
                        else if (cmode == CMchr)
                        {       if (! skip)
                                        where("unbalanced \'");
                                in('\'');
                                cmode = 0;
                        }
                        *lp = '\0';
        #ifdef   verbose
```

```
                            if (vflag)
                                    where("comment", line);
#endif
                            return lp == line;
                    case '/':
                            if (cmode == 0 && *olp == '*')
                            {       cmode = CMcmt;
                                    ++olp;
                                    if (lp != line)
                                            in(' ');
                                    continue;
                            }
                            break;
                    case '*':
                            if (cmode == CMcmt && *olp == '/')
                            {       cmode = 0;
                                    ++olp;
                                    continue;
                            }
                            break;
                    case '"':
                            switch (cmode) {
                            case 0:
                                    cmode = CMstr;
                                    break;
                            case CMstr:
                                    cmode = 0;
                            }
                            break;
                    case '\'':
                            switch (cmode) {
                            case 0:
                                    cmode = CMchr;
                                    break;
                            case CMchr:
                                    cmode = 0;
                            }
                    }
                    if (cmode != CMcmt && (! isspace(c) || lp != line))
                            in(c);
            }
}

command()               /* process commands */
                        /* return true if done (i.e., to skip) */
{       int k;
        LIST *dp;
        FILE *fp;
        char *cp;
```

```
/*
 *      #if algorithm
 *
 *      skip    if non-zero, knows #if-level to which to skip;
 *              while skipping, comment() is executed, but not process().
 *
 *      iflevel current nesting depth of #if;
 *              counted even while skipping (of course).
 *
 *      #else   if skipping to current #if-level, stop skipping;
 *              if not skipping, start skipping to current level.
 *
 *      In order to limit #else to at most one per #if, we
 *      would need a stack; why bother??
 */

        if (*line != '#' || (k = kind(&lp)) == DEFAULT)
                return skip;

        /* process the command */
        switch (k) {
        case DEFINE:
                if (! skip)
                        define(lp, marknm(lp));
                break;
        case ELSE:
                if (! skip && iflevel == 0)
                        where("#else without #if");
                else if (skip == iflevel)
                        skip = 0;
                else if (skip == 0)
                        skip = iflevel;
                break;
        case ENDIF:
                if (! skip && iflevel == 0)
                        where("#endif without #if");
                else
                {       if (skip == iflevel)
                                skip = 0;
                        --iflevel;
                }
                break;
        case IFDEF:
        case IFNDEF:
                ++iflevel;
                if (! skip)
                {       marknm(lp);
                        if (isname(lp,""))
                                if (find(lp))
```

```
                                    {       if (k == IFNDEF)
                                                    skip = iflevel;
                                    }
                                    else
                                    {       if (k == IFDEF)
                                                    skip = iflevel;
                                    }
                        }
                        break;
                case INCLUDE:
                        if (! skip)
                                if (! markfl(lp))
                                        where("#include?");
                                else if (lp[2] == ':')
                                {       ++lp;
                                        if (fp = fopen(lp, "r"))
                                        {
pushfile:                                       files = pushw(files, infile);
                                                lines = pushw(lines, lineno);
                                                lineno = 0;
                                                olineno = lineno - 3; /* stamp ! */
                                                filenms = pushs(filenms, lp);
                                                infile = fp;
#ifdef  verbose
                                                if (vflag)
                                                        where("including", lp);
#endif
                                        }
                                        else
                                                where("cannot open include file", lp);
                                }
                                else
                                {       dp = drive;
                                        if (*lp == '<')
                                                dp = l_next(dp);
                                        *lp-- = ':';
                                        for (; dp; dp = l_next(dp))
                                        {       *lp = *l_str(dp);
                                                if (fp = fopen(lp, "r"))
                                                        goto pushfile;
                                        }
                                        where("cannot find include file", lp+2);
                                }
                        break;
                case LINE:
                        if (! skip)
                        {       if (isdigit(*lp))
                                {       for (k = *lp - '0'; isdigit(*++lp); )
                                                k = k*10 + *lp-'0';
```

```
                            while (isspace(*lp))
                                    ++lp;
                            cp = lp;
                            while (*lp && ! isspace(*lp))
                                    ++lp;
                            if (lp != cp)
                            {       *lp = '\0';
                                    lineno = k;
                                    if (filenms)
                                            pop(&filenms);
                                    filenms = pushs(filenms, cp);
                                    break;
                            }
                    }
                    where("#line?");
                }
                break;
        case UNDEF:
                if (! skip)
                {       marknm(lp);
                        undefine(lp);
                }
        }
        return 1;
}

process()               /* process regular input line */
{       char expand;    /* reprocess flag */
        char c;         /* current input character */
        SYMBOL *sp;     /* -> found symbol */
        char *name;     /* -> begin of name */
        int i;
        int nest;

        /* expand one buffer into the other */
        nest = NEST+1;
        do
        {       lp = line;
                *(olp = oline) = '\0';
                expand = 0;
                while(c = *lp++)
                        if (isalpha(c) || c == '_')
                        {       name = out(c);
                                while ((c = *lp) && (isalnum(c) || c == '_'))
                                {       out(c);
                                        ++lp;
                                }
                                if (sp = find(name))
                                {       expand = 1;
```

P: A SMALL-C PREPROCESSOR

```
                                        outmacro(name, sp);
                                }
                        }
                        else if (isdigit(c))
                                lp = outnumber(--lp);
                        else if (c == '\'' || c == 34)
                                lp = outdelim(--lp);
                        else
                                out(c);
                /* if something changed, flip buffers */
                if (expand)
                {       lp = line;
                        line = oline;
                        oline = lp;
                        i = linelen;
                        linelen = olinelen;
                        olinelen = i;
                }
        } while (expand && --nest);
        if (expand)
                where("#define nested too deep");
        output(oline);
}

/*
 *      symbol table routines
 */

define(s, v)            /* #define s v */
        char *s;        /* name of symbol ?? */
        char *v;        /* value */
{       SYMBOL *r;
        int f;
        char *cp, *p, c, *name;

        if (! ismacro(s))
                return;

        /* prune and parametrize value */
        while (isspace(*v))
                ++v;
        if (*v)
        {       for (cp = v + strlen(v); cp != v; )
                        if (! isspace(*--cp))
                                break;
                        else
                                *cp = '\0';
                /* if we have parameters, replace names by positions */
                if (parmno)
```

```
                    {       p = cp = v;
                            while (c = *cp++)
                                    if (isalpha(c) || c == '_')
                                    {       *(name = p++) = c;
                                            while ((c = *cp)
                                                    && (isalnum(c) || c == '_'))
                                            {       *p++ = c;
                                                    ++cp;
                                            }
                                            if (f = findparm(name, p-name))
                                            {       *(p = name) = f | PARM;
                                                    ++p;
                                            }
                                    }
                                    else
                                    {       *p++ = c;
                                            /* name as trailer of a constant?? */
                                            if (c == '0'
                                                    && (*cp == 'x' || *cp == 'X'))
                                                    do
                                                            *p++ = *cp++;
                                                    while (isxdigit(*cp));
                                            else if (isdigit(c))
                                                    while (isdigit(*cp))
                                                            *p++ = *cp++;
                                            else if (c == '\\')
                                                    if (*cp)
                                                            *p++ = *cp++;
                                    }
                            *p = '\0';
                    }
            }

            /* check if (different) redefinition */
            if (r = find(s))
            {       if (strcmp(s_val(r), v) != 0)
                            where("redefining", s);
                    undefine(s);    /* parmno may change */
#ifdef verbose
                    if (vflag)
                            fputs("redefine ", stderr);
#endif
            }

            /* if parametrized, save count */
            if (parmno)
            {       cp = s + strlen(s);
                    *cp = '(';
                    *++cp = parmno;
```

```
                *++cp = '\0';
        }


        /* ready to make new entry */
        if ((r = calloc(sz_SYM(s), 1)) == NULL)
        {       where("no room");
                exit();
        }
        else
        {
#ifdef  HASH    /* find() sets symbol -> hashtab at s */
                s_next(r) = *symbol;
                *symbol = r;
#else
                s_next(r) = symbol;
                symbol = r;
#endif
                s_val(r) = NULL;
                strcpy(s_name(r), s);
#ifdef  verbose
                if (vflag)
                        fputs("define ", stderr);
#endif
        }


        /* save new value */
        if ((s_val(r) = calloc(strlen(v)+1, 1)) == NUL_)
        {       where("no room");
                exit();
        }
        strcpy(s_val(r), v);
#ifdef  verbose
        if (vflag)
        {       fputs(s, stderr);
                fputc(' ', stderr);
                fputs(s_val(r), stderr);
                fputc('\n', stderr);
        }
#endif
}

undefine(s)             /* #undef s */
        char *s;        /* name of symbol ?? */
{       SYMBOL *r, *p;

        if (isname(s, "") && (r = find(s)))
        {       cfree(s_val(r));
```

```
                /* need to unlink symbol descriptor from chain */
#ifdef  HASH    /* find() sets symbol -> hashtab at s */
                if (r == *symbol)
                        *symbol = s_next(*symbol);
                else
                {       for (p = *symbol;
#else
                if (r == symbol)
                        symbol = s_next(symbol);
                else
                {       for (p = symbol;
#endif
                                        s_next(p) != r; p = s_next(p))
                                ;
                        s_next(p) = s_next(r);
                }
                cfree(r);
#ifdef  verbose
                if (vflag)
                        where("undefine", s);
#endif
        }
}

find(s)                 /* locate s in symbol table */
                        /* return NULL or -> entry */
        char *s;        /* name to find */
{       SYMBOL *r;
        char *sp, *rp, c;
#ifdef  HASH
        int h;

        /* symbol table chains start in hashtab[] */
        /* compute hash address as sum of letters */
        for (h = 0, sp = s; c = *sp; ++sp)
                h += c;
        symbol = hashtab + (h & (HASH-1));

        /* run down the chain */
        for (r = *symbol;
#else
        /* symbol table chain is one linear list */
        /* run down the chain */
        for (r = symbol;
#endif
                        r; r = s_next(r))
        {       for (sp = s, rp = s_name(r); (c = *sp) && *rp == c; ++sp, ++rp)
                        ;
                if (c == '\0' && (*rp == '\0' || *rp == '('))
```

P: A SMALL-C PREPROCESSOR

```
                              return r;
            }
            return NULL;
}

findparm(s, l)          /* return 0 or parameter number */
        char *s;        /* -> begin of possible parameter name */
        int l;          /* length of name */
{       int f;
        LIST *p;

        for (f = 0, p = parms; p; ++f, p = l_next(p))
                if (strncmp(l_str(p), s, l) == 0)
                        return parmno - f;
        return 0;
}

isname(s,d)             /* true, if s is a name */
                        /* return -> delimeter or NULL */
        char *s;        /* -> begin of name */
        char *d;        /* chars in which name may also end */
{       char *cp, c;

        for (cp = s; index(d, c = *cp) == NULL; ++cp)
                if (! isalnum(c) && c != '_')
                        goto error;
        if (cp == s || isdigit(*s))
        {
error:          where("illegal name", s);
                return NULL;
        }
        return cp;      /* return -> delimeter */
}

ismacro(s)              /* true, if s is a macro header */
        char *s;        /* -> begin of name or header */
{       char *cp, c;
        while (parms)   /* free old parameter list */
                pop(&parms);
        parmno = 0;
        if ((s = isname(s, "(")) == NULL)
                return 0;
        if (*s)         /* we have a new macro */
        {       *s = '\0';      /* delimit name */
                do              /* and parse parameters */
                {       while (isspace(*++s))
                                ;
                        if (cp = isname(s, ",) \t"))
                        {       c = *cp;
```

```
                                        *cp = '\0';
                                        parms = pushs(parms, s);
                                        ++ parmno;
                                }
                                else
                                        return 0;
                                while (isspace(c))
                                        c = *++cp;
                                s = cp;
                        } while (c == ',');
                        if (c != ')')
                        {       where("illegal macro header");
                                return 0;
                        }
                }
                return 1;
        }

        marknm(s)               /* bypass and terminate macro header */
                                /* return -> value */
                char *s;        /* ->begin of name */
        {       char c;

                /* find white space or ( */
                while ((c = *s) && ! isspace(c) && c != '(')
                        ++s;

                /* if (, there must be names, white space and then ) */
                if (c == '(')
                {       while ((c = *++s) && c != ')')
                                ;
                        /* after ) there must be \0 or white space */
                        if (c && (s[1] == '\0' || isspace(s[1])))
                                ++s;
                }

                /* terminate in place of white space */
                if (*s)
                        *s++ = '\0';

                /* this is a rough draft -- see ismacro/isname */
                return s;
        }

        /*
         *      input and output routines
         */

        in(c)                   /* store incoming character */
```

```
                char c;         /* to be stored at lp */
        {
                *lp++ = c;
                if (lp >= line+linelen)
                        rebuff(&lp, &line, &linelen);
        }

        out(c)                  /* store a character, return -> stored char */
                char c;         /* to be stored at olp */
        {
                *olp++ = c;
                if (olp >= oline+olinelen)
                        rebuff(&olp, &oline, &olinelen);
                *olp = '\0';    /* maintain trailer */
                return olp-1;
        }

        rebuff(p, buf, len)     /* make buffer longer */
                int *p;         /* & current pointer */
                int *buf;       /* & buffer pointer */
                int *len;       /* & maximum length */
        {
                if ((*p = calloc(*len + INCR, 1)) == NULL)
                {       where("no room");
                        exit();
                }
                strncpy(*p, *buf, *len);
                cfree(*buf);
                *buf = *p;
                *p = *buf + *len;
                *len += INCR;
        }

        output(s)               /* write a string */
                char *s;        /* to write as a line */
        {
                /* synchronize output linecount */
                if (! eflag && ++olineno != lineno)
                {       if (++olineno != lineno)
                        {       fputc('#', stdout);
                                fputs(itod(olineno = lineno), stdout);
                                if (filenms)
                                {       fputc(' ', stdout);
                                        fputs(l_str(filenms), stdout);
                                }
                        }
                        fputc('\n', stdout);
                }
```

```c
            /* emit string as a line */
            fputs(s, stdout);
            if (fputc('\n', stdout) == EOF)
            {       where("output file full");
                    exit();
            }
    }

    /*
     *      C constant processing:
     *
     *      digits          decimal
     *      Odigits         octal
     *      Oxdigits        hexadecimal
     *      'c'             character value (escapes ok)
     */

    outnumber(cp)           /* store a C constant in decimal */
                            /* return -> past it */
            char *cp;       /* -> constant text (digit) */
    {       char c, *p;
            int base;
            int i;

            base = 10;
            i = 0;
            if ((c = *cp) == '0')
            {       base = 010;
                    if ((c = *++cp) == 'x' || c == 'X')
                    {       base = 0x10;
                            c = *++cp;
                    }
            }
            for ( ; c; c = *++cp)
            {       if (isdigit(c))
                            c -= '0';
                    else if (isxdigit(c))
                            if (isupper(c))
                                    c -= 'A' - 10;
                            else
                                    c -= 'a' - 10;
                    else
                            break;
                    if (c < base)
                            i = i*base + c;
                    else
                            break;
            }
            for (p = itod(i); c = *p; ++p)
```

```
                        out(c);
            return cp;
}

outdelim(cp)            /* store a delimited string, return -> past trailer */
        char *cp;       /* -> delimeter */
{       char c, *p;

        if ((c = *cp) == '\"')
        {       out(c);
                while (c = *++cp)
                {       out(c);
                        if (c == '\"')
                                return cp+1;
                        if (c == '\\')
                                if (c = *++cp)
                                        out(c);
                                else
                                        break;
                }
        }
        else    /* it must be character constant */
                switch (c = *++cp) {
                case 0:
                case '\'':
                        goto error;
                case '\\':
                        switch (c = *++cp) {
                        case 'b':  c = '\b'; break;
                        case 'f':  c = '\f'; break;
                        case 'n':  c = '\n'; break;
                        case 'r':  c = '\r'; break;
                        case 't':  c = '\t';
                        case '\'':
                        case '\\':
                        case '\"':              break;
                        default:
                                if (! isdigit(c) || (c -= '0') > 7)
                                        goto error;
                                if (isdigit(cp[1]) && cp[1] <= '7')
                                {       c = (c << 3) + *++cp - '0';
                                        if (isdigit(cp[1]) && cp[1] <= '7')
                                                c = (c << 3) + *++cp - '0';
                                }
                        }
                default:
                        if (*++cp != '\'')
                        {
error:                          where("illegal character constant");
```

```
                        while (*cp && *cp != '\'')
                                ++cp;
                        if (*cp)
                                ++cp;
                        break;
                }
                for (p = itod(c); *p; ++p)
                        out(*p);
                out(' ');
                ++cp;
            }
        return cp;
}

/*
 *      macro processing
 */

outmacro(at, s)                 /* replace string by macro value */
        char *at;               /* replace from here on */
        SYMBOL *s;              /* using this definition */
{       char *vp, c;

        /* set output up for replacement */
        olp = at;

        /* force white space around replacement */
        if (olp > oline && (! isspace(olp[-1])))
                out(' ');

        /* if parametrized, collect arguments */
        if (vp = index(s_name(s), '('))
                markarg(*++vp);
        else
                parmno = 0;

        /* emit replacement */
        for (vp = s_val(s); c = *vp++; )
                if (c & PARM)
                        outarg(c & PARMNO);
                else
                        out(c);

        /* white space */
        out(' ');
}

markarg(n)                      /* mark and collect arguments */
        int n;                  /* number to find */
```

```
{       char c, cmode; /* cmode during argument collection only */
        int lpar;

        /* release parameter/argument list, if any */
        while (parms)
                pop(&parms);
        parmno = 0;

        /* find ( */
        while (isspace(c = *lp))
                ++lp;

        /* collect */
        if (c == '(')
        {       do
                {       parms = pushw(parms, ++lp);
                        ++ parmno;
                        lpar = cmode = 0;
                        for ( ; c = *lp; ++lp)
                        {       switch (c) {
                                case '(':
                                        if (cmode == 0)
                                                ++ lpar;
                                        continue;
                                case ',':
                                        if (cmode || lpar)
                                                continue;
                                        break;
                                case ')':
                                        if (cmode || lpar --)
                                                continue;
                                        break;
                                case '\'':
                                        switch (cmode) {
                                        case 0:
                                                cmode = CMchr;
                                        case CMstr:
                                                continue;
                                        }
                                        cmode = 0;
                                        continue;
                                case '\"':
                                        switch (cmode) {
                                        case 0:
                                                cmode = CMstr;
                                        case CMchr:
                                                continue;
                                        }
                                        cmode = 0;
```

```
                                continue;
                        case '\\':
                                if (*++lp == '\0')
                                        break;
                        default:
                                continue;
                        }
                        *lp = '\0';
                        break;
                }
        } while (c == ',');
        if (c == ')')
                ++lp;
        else
                where("incomplete macro call");
}

/* check and fill argument count */
if (parmno != n)
        where("wrong number of arguments");
for ( ; parmno < n; ++parmno)
        parms = pushw(parms, "");
}

outarg(i)                       /* emit argument */
        int i;                  /* number to emit */
{       LIST *p;
        char *cp, c;

        /* play double safe */
        if (i > parmno)
        {       where("outarg(>>)??");
                exit();
        }

        /* locate */
        for (i = parmno-i, p = parms; i && p; --i, p = l_next(p))
                ;
        if (p == NULL)
        {       where("outarg(NULL)??");
                exit();
        }

        /* emit, no white space */
        for (cp = l_word(p); c = *cp; ++cp)
                out(c);
}

/*
```

```
 *      stack routines
 */

pushw(l, w)             /* push word, return -> new list */
        LIST *l;        /* list */
        int w;          /* word to push */
{       LIST *r;

        if ((r = calloc(sz_WORD, 1)) == NULL)
        {       where("no room");
                exit();
        }
        l_next(r) = l;
        l_word(r) = w;
        return r;
}

pushs(l, s)             /* push string, return -> new list */
        LIST *l;        /* list */
        char *s;        /* string to push */
{       LIST *r;

        if ((r = calloc(sz_STR(s), 1)) == NULL)
        {       where("no room");
                exit();
        }
        l_next(r) = l;
        strcpy(l_str(r), s);
        return r;
}

pop(l)                  /* pop list, return word */
        LIST *l;        /* really **: list header */
{       LIST *r;
        int i;

        if (*l == NULL)
        {       where("pop(NULL)??");
                exit();
        }
        r = *l;         /* element to pop */
        i = l_word(r);  /* result */
        r = l_next(r);  /* following element */
        cfree(*l);
        *l = r;
        return i;       /* nonsense for a string list */
}

/*
```

```
 *      other utilities
 */

where(vararg)           /* error message writer */
        int vararg;     /* arbitrarily many strings */
{       int narg, *argv;

        narg = _narg();
        argv = &vararg;
        argv += narg;
        if (filenms)
        {       fputs(l_str(filenms), stderr);
                if (lineno)
                        fputs(", ", stderr);
                else
                        fputs(": ", stderr);
        }
        if (lineno)
        {       fputs("line ", stderr);
                fputs(itod(lineno), stderr);
                fputs(": ", stderr);
        }
        while (narg)
        {       fputs(*--argv, stderr);
                if (--narg)
                        fputc(' ', stderr);
        }
        fputc('\n', stderr);
}

kind(plp)               /* determine command */
                        /* move line pointer past it and white space */
        int *plp;       /* char**, -> line pointer; NULLed or advanced */
{       char *s;

        for (s = line+1; isspace(*s); ++s)
                ;
        if (*plp = cmd(s, "define"))    return DEFINE;
        if (*plp = cmd(s, "else"))      return ELSE;
        if (*plp = cmd(s, "endif"))     return ENDIF;
        if (*plp = cmd(s, "ifdef"))     return IFDEF;
        if (*plp = cmd(s, "ifndef"))    return IFNDEF;
        if (*plp = cmd(s, "include"))   return INCLUDE;
        if (*plp = cmd(s, "line"))      return LINE;
        if (*plp = cmd(s, "undef"))     return UNDEF;
        return DEFAULT; /* *plp is NULL */
}

cmd(l, c)               /* parse keyword */
```

```
                        /* return NULL or -> past it and white space */
        char *l;        /* -> begin of possible keyword */
        char *c;        /* -> keyword */
{
        /* compare *
        while (*l++ == *c++ && *c)
                ;
        if (*c)
                return 0;       /* incomplete keyword */
        if (*l == '\0')
                return l;       /* just keyword */
        if (! isspace(*l))
                return 0;       /* keyword plus trash */
        while (isspace(*++l))
                ;
        return l;               /* bypassed white space */
}

markfl(sp)              /* bypass and terminate file name */
                        /* return true if found */
        char *sp;       /* -> begin delimeter, " or < */
{       char s, *cp, c;

        if ((s = *(cp = sp)) && (s == '\"' || s == '<'))
                while (c = *++cp)
                        if (c == '\"' && s == '\"'
                            || c == '>' && s == '<')
                        {       *cp = '\0';
                                return cp-sp > 1;
                        }
        return 0;
}
```

Listing 8-2

```
/****
 ****   UN*X compatible dynamic memory allocation
 ****/

/*
 *      calloc  return pointer to vector of 0, or NULL
 *      cfree   free previously allocated area
 *
 *      The heap starts at _end and runs upward toward the stack.
 *      Each area in the heap is preceded by a word at an even address:
 *      a pointer chain runs from _end through these words to NULL:
 *      The low bit in each word is 1 if the following area is free.
 *      There is a blind, allocated element at the front of the chain.
 *
```

```
 *      BUG:    very unreasonable demands (e.g., wraparound)
 *              will corrupt memory.
 */

#define SLACK   1024    /* at least 1KB stack to be free */
#define NULL    0

word(wp)
        int *wp;
{
        return *wp;
}

char * calloc(n,len)
        int n;          /* number of elements */
        int len;        /* length of element */
{       int cell;       /* current allocation chain cell */
        char *p;        /* -> cell */
        char *np;       /* pointer in cell */
        int *ip, *wp;   /* for casting */

        len = (len*n + 1) & ~1;    /* even */
        if (len == 0)
                return NULL;
        for (ip = p = word(_end+1 & ~1) & ~1;
            np = (cell = *ip) & ~1;
            ip = p = np)
                if (cell & 1)                   /* lowbit == 1 means free */
                {       if ((n = np-p - 2) > len+2)
                        {       wp = p + len+2;
                                *wp = cell;
                                *ip = wp;
                        }
                        else if (n >= len)
                                *ip = np;
                        else
                                continue;
                        for (wp = p+2; len; len -= 2)
                                *wp++ = 0;
                        return p+2;
                }
        if ((wp = p + len+2) > &n - SLACK)
                return NULL;
        *ip = wp;
        *wp = NULL;
        for (wp = p+2; len; len -= 2)
                *wp++ = 0;
        return p+2;
}
```

```
cfree(fp)
            int *fp;         /* to be freed */
{           int *p, *np;

            --fp;                               /* to cell */
            for (p = _end+1 & ~1;
                np = word(p) & ~1;
                p = np)                         /* p-> previous cell */
                if (np == fp)                   /* fp-> cell to free */
                {       np = *fp;               /* np-> following cell */
                    if ((*fp & 1) || np == NULL)
                            break; /* he does not own it */
                    if (*p & 1)
                            if (*np & 1)
                                    *p = *np;
                            else if (*np == NULL)
                                    *p = NULL;
                            else
                            {       *p = np;
                                    *p |= 1;
                            }
                    else if (*np & 1)
                            *fp = *np;
                    else if (*np == NULL)
                            *fp = NULL;
                    else
                            *fp |= 1;
                    return;
                }
            fputs("cfree botch", stderr);
            exit();
}
```

9
GETARGS: A COMMAND-LINE ARGUMENT PROCESSOR

by Allen Holub

This chapter originally appeared in DDJ #103 (May 1985) as a "C Chest" column.

A command-line switch is an argument, usually preceded by a dash (–), that modifies the way that a program works. Just about every C program I write uses command-line switches, and all these programs have to process these switches one way or another. For a long time, I wrote a different little subroutine for each program, modifying the routine to deal with the idiosyncrasies of a particular program. After writing the same subroutine about a million times (and making the same off-by-one error with argc every time), I thought that there *had* to be a better way. All my processing routines were essentially the same in structure; only the names of the command-line switches were different. A general-purpose command-line processor was clearly what I needed.

Looking around in the literature for something that did the job, I found the Argum package, which appeared in Anthony Skjellum's C/Unix column in *DDJ* #70 (August 1982). The program was well-written and did what I needed, but it had several problems. First of all, it did a lot more than I needed, and the extra functions added extra code. Because this package was going to be included in every program I wrote, a reduction in scope seemed to be a good idea. Another related problem was the internal tables used by Argum. They were created at run time (as compared to compile time). This added both extra code and extra execution time to any program that used Argum. Finally, Argum had no convenient way to deal with errors on the command line. In view of these problems, I decided to write my own processor, a description of which follows. This is by far the most frequently used subroutine in my standard library.

Getargs( )

The command-line processor is actually a package of subroutines. Access to these routines is through a single procedure, called getargs(). The routines are table driven. In every program, you have to declare a table in which the various command-line switches are described. Getargs() removes the switches from the command line as it works. This means that position-sensitive arguments (for example, a switch that applies to all files that follow it on the command line, but not to any files that precede it) are not supported. I don't use this sort of switch very often and I got tired of having to skip past arguments that had already been processed to get to a filename. The arguments are evaluated left to right, so interaction between PROC type switches (see below) is possible.

When getargs() finds an error on the command line, it prints a list of all legal switches to stderr, along with a brief description of what those switches do and their default values. After it prints the error message, getargs() terminates the program with an exit(1) call. This closes any open files and returns to the operating system.

Command-Line Switch Formats

Command line switches all must take the form:

```
-<character>[<number>|<string>]
```

That is, all arguments start with a minus sign; each switch is identified by a single letter that follows the minus sign immediately (no intervening spaces); the letter may be followed by an optional number or string, again with no spaces between the character that serves as the switch identifier and the corresponding number or string. Switches may be combined, provided that the argument types allow this combination. For example, the command line

```
program -a -b123 -c
```

can also be written as

```
program -ab123c
```

However, if getargs() expects a string to follow the switch identifier character, then it assumes that the rest of the argument is part of the string. You have to be careful when combining string-type command-line switches with other types.

Using Getargs()

To use getargs() you must do two things: (1) set up a table to tell the routine what kind of command line switches to expect and (2) call the routine itself somewhere early in the main() module. The file getargs.h (Listing 9-1) contains the #defines and typedefs needed to create the command switch descriptor table. This table is an array of structures:

```
typedef struct
{
        unsigned        arg  : 7    ;
        unsigned        type : 4    ;
        int             *variable   ;
        char            *errmsg     ;
}
        ARG;
```

The arg field is a single character that identifies the switch on the command line. In the following descriptions this character is represented as <switch>. The type field may take any one of five values, all of which are #defined in getargs.h. The behavior of getargs() varies according to the value.
    INTEGER switches take the form:

```
-<switch> <number>
```

Numbers preceded by 0x are hex; by 0 without the x, octal. All others are decimal. The number is terminated by any character not legal in the indicated radix. Any characters that follow are assumed to be additional switches. The int sized variable pointed to by the variable field of the ARG structure is set to the value of <number>. If <number> isn't typed on the command line, *variable is set to 0.
    BOOLEAN switches cause some action based on the presence or absence of the indicated switch on the command line. If the switch is present, then the int pointed to by the variable field is set to 1, otherwise *variable is not modified.
    CHARACTER switches take the form:

```
-<switch> <character>
```

When the switch is found on the command line, then *variable is set to <character>.
    STRING switches take the form:

```
-<switch> <string>
```

When the switch is found on the command line, the character pointer pointed to by the variable field is set to point at a string consisting of all characters following (but not including) the <switch> character up to the end of the current argument (not to the end of the command line). In the case of combined switches in a single argument, the STRING argument must be the last one because all following characters will be considered part of <string>. When defining a STRING switch in the table, be sure to cast the variable into an integer pointer. See Listing 9-3, line 15, for an example.

PROC switches take the form:

```
-<switch> <anything>
```

They work like the STRING switch in that all characters following <switch> up to the end of the current argument are part of the <anything>. However, the variable field is a pointer to a subroutine that is called indirectly as soon as the switch is encountered on the command line. A pointer to <anything> is passed to this subroutine as a single argument. An example of such a subroutine is given in Listing 9-3, line 19. It is the responsibility of the called subroutine to parse <anything> as appropriate.

The errmsg field of the ARG structure is used to print an error message if an undefined switch is found. An example of the format is shown in Figure 9-1. This message was generated when the command line "argtest -x" was given to argtest.

Listing 9-3 is an example of how to use getargs(). Lines 5-9 are declarations of the objects that are used in the variable fields of the switch descriptor table. The initial values of these variables remain unchanged if the switch is not encountered on the command line at run time. The table itself, Argtab, is declared on lines 10-17. The main() routine calls getargs() on line 35. The rest of main() just prints the command line, both before and after the getargs() call, so you can see how getargs() strips processed switches out of argv.

Getargs() itself starts on line 98 of Listing 9-2. It is passed four arguments: argv, argc, a pointer to the switch descriptor table (tabp), and the size of this table in elements (not bytes). The routine returns a new value of argc, and argv is compressed (that is, all entries containing command-line switches are removed from it). The for loop on line 112 processes argv one element at a time. Nargv points into argv and strips processed switches. Nargv is initialized to point at argv[1] because argv[0] cannot possibly contain a command-line switch (it holds the program name). If no leading minus sign is found in the argument, *argv is copied to *nargv and both pointers are advanced. In addition, nargc (new argc) is incremented. If the argument does begin with a minus sign, it is processed as a command-line switch. In this case *argv is not copied to *nargv, and argv, but not nargv, is advanced. This effectively eliminates the argument containing the switch from the argv array.

Findarg() (Listing 9-2, line 44) is used by getargs() to see if an argument is in the table. It performs a linear search. Because the table is usually fairly small, it seemed as if the extra code needed for a binary search wasn't justified. Findarg() takes three arguments: c is the switch identifier character being searched for; tabp and tabsize are the same parameters as were passed to getargs().

Setarg() (Listing 9-2, line 9) is called when a command-line switch is found in the table. Argp is a pointer into the table, as returned from findarg(). Linep is a pointer into the argv entry that is being processed. Casts were used to make this routine as transportable as possible.

Pr_usage() (Listing 9-2, line 57) is used to print the error message shown in Figure 9-1 when an illegal command-line switch is found. It spins through the table, printing the current contents of the object pointed to by the variable field as well as the message given in the errmsg field.

Figure 9-1. Error output from program in Listing 9-3.

```
Illegal argument <x>. Legal arguments are:
-b         boolean argument     (value is FALSE)
-c<c>      character argument   (value is .)
-n<num>    integer argument     (value is 0)
-s<str>    string argument      (value is <doo wha>)
-p<str>    procedure argument
```

The final routine in the package is stoi() (for string to integer, Listing 9-4), which is used to process INTEGER switches. Stoi() is a fancy version of the standard library routine atoi() (described in B.W. Kernighan and D.W. Ritchie, *The C Programming Language* [Prentice-Hall, 1978], p. 58). Stoi() can handle numbers in base 8, 10, or 16. If code size is a real issue, you may want to remove the code that processes octal numbers (Listing 9-4, lines 45-53). Another major difference between stoi() and atoi() is that stoi() is passed a *pointer* to a character pointer. That is, it is passed the *address* of the pointer, which in turn points into the string to be processed. This extra level of indirection lets you modify the character pointer itself to point past the end of the number being processed. If you use atoi(), you have to go through the string twice, once to extract the number and once more to skip past the characters that represent that number.

Conclusion

Several additions could be made to getargs(), at the cost of an increase in complexity and code size.

A common command-line function is to open or close a file in a particular mode and to abort if the file cannot be opened. At present I'm doing this with a PROC type command-line switch, but you could add another argument type, whose variable field points to a FILE pointer. Alternately, variable could point to a structure that included the FILE pointer, an open mode, a pointer to an error processing routine, and a default filename.

Another nice feature would be to mark an argument if its presence is required on the command line. You could accomplish this by adding additional types (that is, REQ_INTEGER), or by adding another field to the structure. An error message would be printed if the argument wasn't found on the command line.

Getargs() depends on initializers to set default argument values. If your compiler doesn't support initializers, you can add a default value field to the structure.

I have violated my smallness rule by using stoi() to process numeric arguments. If you expect only decimal numbers, you may want to replace stoi() with atoi(). However, stoi() is a useful routine in its own right.

I'm sure you can think of other bells and whistles. I've been using getargs() for a couple years now and am satisfied with it in its existing state. Defining the way the command line looks and then getting switches from it is now a painless process.

Listing 9-1

```
 1: /*      Getargs.h     Typedefs and defines needed for getargs
 2:  */


 3: #define INTEGER       0
 4: #define BOOLEAN       1
 5: #define CHARACTER     2
 6: #define STRING        3
 7: #define PROC          4

 8: typedef struct
 9: {
10:         unsigned      arg  : 7 ;    /* Command line switch       */
11:         unsigned      type : 4 ;    /* variable type             */
12:         int           *variable ;   /* pointer to variable       */
13:         char          *errmsg   ;   /* pointer to error message  */
14: }
15: ARG;
```

LISTING 9-2

FILE:GETARGS.C

```
 1: /*     GETARGS.C     Command line argument processor for C programs
 2:  *
 3:  *          (C) Copyright 1985, Allen I. Holub.  All rights reserved.
 4:  *          This program may be copied for personal, non-profit use only.
 5:  */

 6: #include <stdio.h>
 7: #include <getargs.h>

 8: typedef int    (*PFI)();

 9: static char    *setarg( argp, linep )
10: ARG            *argp;
11: char           *linep;
12: {
13:         /*    Set an argument. argp points at the argument table entry
14:          *    corresponding to *linep. Return linep, updated to point
15:          *    past the argument being set.
16:          */

17:         ++linep;

18:         switch( argp->type )
19:         {
```

```
20:         case INTEGER:
21:                 *argp->variable = stoi( &linep );
22:                 break;

23:         case BOOLEAN:
24:                 *argp->variable = 1;
25:                 break;

26:         case CHARACTER:
27:                 *argp->variable = *linep++ ;
28:                 break;

29:         case STRING:
30:                 *(char **)argp->variable = linep ;
31:                 linep = "";
32:                 break;

33:         case PROC:
34:                 (* (PFI)(argp->variable) )( linep );
35:                 linep = "";
36:                 break;

37:         default:
38:                 fprintf(stdout,"INTERNAL ERROR: BAD ARGUMENT TYPE\n");
39:                 break;
40:         }

41:         return( linep );
42: }

43: /*----------------------------------------------------------------------*

44: static ARG      *findarg( c, tabp, tabsize )
45: int             c, tabsize;
46: ARG             *tabp;
47: {
48:         /*      Return pointer to argument table entry corresponding
49:          *      to c (or 0 if c isn't in table).
50:          */
51:
52:         for(; --tabsize >= 0 ; tabp++ )
53:                 if( tabp->arg == c )
54:                         return tabp;

55:         return 0;
56: }
```

```
57: static pr_usage( tabp, tabsize )
58: ARG      *tabp;
59: int      tabsize;
60: {
61:          /*      Print the argtab in the form:
62:           *              -<arg> <errmsg>     (value is <*variable>)
63:           */

64:          for(; --tabsize >= 0 ;  tabp++ )
65:          {
66:                  switch( tabp->type )
67:                  {
68:                  case INTEGER:
69:                          fprintf(stdout, "-%c<num> %-40s (value is ",
70:                                                  tabp->arg, tabp->errmsg);
71:                          fprintf(stdout, "%-5d)\n", *(tabp->variable) );
72:                          break;

73:                  case BOOLEAN:
74:                          fprintf(stdout,"-%c      %-40s (value is ",
75:                                                  tabp->arg, tabp->errmsg);
76:                          fprintf(stdout, "%-5s)\n", *(tabp->variable)
77:                                                  ? "TRUE": "FALSE");
78:                          break;

79:                  case CHARACTER:
80:                          fprintf(stdout, "-%c<c>   %-40s (value is ",
81:                                                  tabp->arg, tabp->errmsg);
82:                          fprintf(stdout, "%-5c)\n", *(tabp->variable) );
83:                          break;

84:                  case STRING:
85:                          fprintf(stdout, "-%c<str> %-40s (value is ",
86:                                                  tabp->arg, tabp->errmsg);
87:                          fprintf(stdout, "<%s>)\n",
88:                                                  *(char **)tabp->variable);
89:                          break;

90:                  case PROC:
91:                          fprintf(stdout, "-%c<str> %-40s\n",
92:                                                  tabp->arg, tabp->errmsg);
93:                          break;
94:                  }
95:          }
96: }
```

```
 97: #define ERRMSG  "Illegal argument <%c>.   Legal arguments are:\n\n"

 98: int     getargs(argc, argv, tabp, tabsize )
 99: int     argc, tabsize ;
100: char    **argv ;
101: ARG     *tabp  ;
102: {
103:        /* Process command line arguments. Stripping all command line
104:         * switches out of argv. Return a new argc. If an error is found
105:         * exit(1) is called (getargs won't return) and a usage message
106:         * is printed showing all arguments in the table.
107:         */

108:        register int    nargc      ;
109:        register char   **nargv, *p ;
110:        register ARG    *argp      ;

111:        nargc = 1 ;
112:        for(nargv = ++argv ; --argc > 0 ; argv++ )
113:        {
114:                if( **argv != '-' )
115:                {
116:                        *nargv++ = *argv ;
117:                        nargc++;
118:                }
119:                else
120:                {
121:                        p = (*argv) + 1 ;

122:                        while( *p )
123:                        {
124:                                if(argp = findarg(*p, tabp, tabsize))
125:                                        p = setarg( argp, p );
126:                                else
127:                                {
128:                                        fprintf(stdout, ERRMSG, *p );
129:                                        pr_usage( tabp, tabsize );
130:                                        exit( 1 );
131:                                }
132:                        }
133:                }
134:        }
135:        return nargc ;
136: }
```

Listing 9-3

———————————————————————————— **FILE: ARGTEST.C**

```
 1: /*      ARGTEST.C       Test program for getargs.
 2:  */

 3: #include <stdio.h>
 4: #include "getargs.h"

 5: int     boolarg = 0;                    /* Variables used by argtab */
 6: int     chararg = '.';
 7: int     intarg  = 0;
 8: char    *strarg  = "doo wha" ;
 9: extern  proc();

10: ARG     Argtab[]=
11: {
12:         { 'b',  BOOLEAN,    &boolarg,        "boolean argument"       },
13:         { 'c',  CHARACTER,  &chararg,        "character argument"     },
14:         { 'n',  INTEGER,    &intarg,         "integer argument"       },
15:         { 's',  STRING,     (int *)&strarg,  "string argument"        },
16:         { 'p',  PROC,       (int *)&proc,    "procedure argument"     }
17: };

18: #define TABSIZE ( sizeof(Argtab) / sizeof(ARG) )

19: proc( str )
20: char    *str;
21: {
22:         printf("Inside procedure called by -p command line switch, ");
23:         printf("string = <%s>\n", str );
24: }

25: main(argc, argv)
26: int     argc;
27: char    **argv;
28: {
29:         register int    i;

30:         printf("Argc == %d. ", argc);
31:         printf("Cmd line: argtest ");
32:         for( i = 1 ; i < argc ; printf("%s ", argv[i++]) )
33:                 ;
34:         printf("\n");

35:         argc = getargs( argc, argv, Argtab, TABSIZE) ;
36:         printf("Argc == %d. ", argc);
37:         printf("Cmd line: argtest ");
```

```
38:            for( i = 1 ; i < argc ; printf("%s ", argv[i++]) )
39:                    ;
40:            printf("\n");
41: }
```

Listing 9-4

── **FILE:STOI.C**

```
 1 /* STOI.C       More powerful version of atoi.
 2  *
 3  *       Copyright (C) 1985 by Allen  Holub.  All rights reserved.
 4  *       This program may be copied for personal, non-profit use only.
 5  */
 6
 7 #define islower(c)      ( 'a' <= (c) && (c) <= 'z' )
 8 #define toupper(c)      ( islower(c) ? (c) - ('a' - 'A') : (c) )
 9
10 int             stoi(instr)
11 register char   **instr;
12 {
13        /*     Convert string to integer. If string starts with 0x it is
14         *     interpreted as a hex number, else if it starts with a 0 it
15         *     is octal, else it is decimal. Conversion stops on encountering
16         *     the first character which is not a digit in the indicated
17         *     radix. *instr is updated to point past the end of the number.
18         */
19
20        register int    num = 0 ;
21        register char   *str    ;
22        int             sign = 1 ;
23
24        str = *instr;
25
26        while(*str == ' ' || *str == '\t' || *str == '\n' )
27                str++ ;
28
29        if( *str == '-' )
30        {
31                sign = -1 ;
32                str++;
33        }
34
35        if(*str == '0')
36        {
37                ++str;
38                if (*str == 'x' || *str == 'X')
39                {
40                        str++;
41                        while( ('0'<= *str && *str <= '9') ||
```

```
42                              ('a'<= *str && *str <= 'f') ||
43                              ('A'<= *str && *str <= 'F')  )
44                   {
45                         num *= 16;
46                         num += ('0'<= *str && *str <= '9') ?
47                                  *str - '0'                      :
48                                  toupper(*str) - 'A' + 10    ;
49                         str++;
50                   }
51             }
52             else
53             {
54                   while( '0' <= *str  &&  *str <= '7' )
55                   {
56                         num *= 8;
57                         num += *str++ - '0' ;
58                   }
59             }
60       }
61       else
62       {
63             while( '0' <= *str  &&  *str <= '9' )
64             {
65                   num *= 10;
66                   num += *str++ - '0' ;
67             }
68       }
69
70       *instr = str;
71       return( num * sign );
72 }
```

10
CROSS-REFERENCE GENERATOR IN C: A PROGRAM CONVERSION AID

by Jeff Taylor

This chapter originally appeared in DDJ #68 (June 1982).

Cross-reference listings are of little use to the person who wrote the program, so most such programs just gather dust on the back shelf. But those of us who do not own Apples or IBM PCs get much of our software by converting programs written for some other computer. Cross-reference listings save hours of debugging effort during conversion. When I started to convert Ron Cain's Small-C compiler (see "A Small-C Compiler for the 8080s," DDJ #45, excerpted in this volume) to my LSI-11, I hauled my program XREF off the back shelf where it had been resting. Ron's different coding style turned up a few errors in XREF that I had missed. More troublesome was the overflow of the symbol table. There wasn't enough memory with that symbol table organization. CREF, the program described in this article, is a test bed for a more compact symbol table organization. Eventually, I will fold this symbol table organization back into XREF.

CREF is written in C for the Unix 4.2 BSD compiler and runtime library. It accepts a list of filenames from the command line; if no filenames are present, input is taken from the standard input. The cross-reference listing is printed on the standard output. The listing consists of all filenames in #include statements, and all function, variable, and macro names in alphabetical order. Under each name is a list of files it appears in. To the right of each filename is a list of the lines in that file where the name appears.

The three-level hierarchy in the listing is reflected in the symbol table organization, as shown in Figure 10-1. At the top is the name table, next a file table for each name, and at the bottom, lists of line numbers for each name and file.

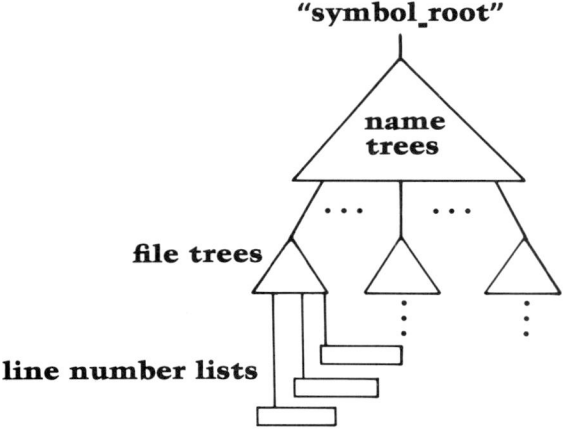

**Figure 10-1.
Symbol table organization.**

Each name entry is unique, and there is a file entry for each name in the file. This is where the symbol table was reorganized; how it was changed is explained later.

Binary search trees are used for the name and file symbol tables. Each entry contains the text for the symbol and pointers (possibly NULL) to the right and left descendents. A binary tree grows from the root down, with new entries added at the tips or leaves. The function lookup() finds the entry for a symbol, or if it is not present, where it should go. To search a binary search tree, start at the root and compare the symbol against the one stored in the entry. If it doesn't match, move to the left for symbols less than the entry, otherwise move to the right. Repeat until the symbol is found or a NULL pointer is encountered. If the symbol is not found, that NULL pointer is where it should be added. The tree is always kept in alphabetical order. The function tree_walk() traverses a binary tree in alphabetical order.

Both recursive and iterative implementations exist for lookup() and tree_walk(). Recursive code for recursive data structures is short, straightforward, and stack-intensive. The iterative version of tree_walk() is longer and not as readable. Instead of using C's built-in stack to keep track of the binary tree traversal, CREF uses an explicit stack. The algorithm is taken from *The Art of Computer Programming* by Donald Knuth (Addison-Wesley, 1968, volume 1, page 317). Instead of using a separate stack, the binary tree entries are turned into a stack, using the left fields to point to the next entry in the stack. Note that this destroys the binary tree.

The list of line numbers is kept in a circularly linked list. The pointer into the list points to the *last* line number. The initialization for the do . . . while loop in list_file() moves the pointer to the start of the list. Line numbers are added to the end of the list. A new line number is added to the list only if it is not already at the end of the list. This is adequate to keep duplicates out, unless a file is listed twice.

This symbol table organization works fine. For large programs, however, there is considerable redundancy. A separate copy of the filename is kept for each name in the file. Instead of keeping the text for a symbol in the entry, a pointer to the text is kept in the entry. A tree rooted at file_root keeps track of the text for all filenames to avoid duplicates. The same structure is kept for all binary trees. The code to manipulate binary trees is the same for all the trees.

CREF is intended for cross-referencing C programs. By changing the reserved word list and the code that skips over comments and quoted strings, you can adapt it to most other languages. I don't currently have any programs too large for CREF, but sooner or later they will come along. When that happens, I will get to try out a new data structure to store parts of the symbol table on disk. Sounds like a good way to learn about B-trees.

LISTING 10-1

```c
/* CREF - C cross-reference utility

   Author: Jeff Taylor, The Toolsmith (c) copyright 1982, 1985.
   Environment: C; UNIX 4.2 BSD.
   Algorithms:
     Modified algorithm T from "The Art of Computer Programming," Vol. 1,
         p. 317, by D.E. Knuth used in tree_walk().
   History:
     22 November 1982 - remove recursion from lookup().
     16 December 1982 - remove recursion from tree_walk().
     26 March 1985 - port to DECUS C.
     27 March 1985 - line # list made a circular queue: insert(), list_file().
         reserved word search changed to binary search: keyword().
     28 March 1985 - port to UNIX 4.2 BSD.
*/

#include <stdio.h>
#include <ctype.h>
#include "style.h"

#define lower(c)      (isupper(c) ? tolower(c) : (c))
#define streq(a, b)   (strcmp(a, b) == 0)
#define WIDTH   80    /* width of output device */

struct instance {
  struct instance *next;
  int line;
};
union ptr {
  struct node *files;
  struct instance *lines;
};
struct node {
  struct node *right, *left;
  union ptr p;
  char *name;
};

struct node *symbol_root = NULL;
struct node *file_root = NULL;
int line_count = 0;
#define ID 'a'       /* identifier */
#define INTEGER '0'  /* integer */

/**********************************
 *  Symbol Table handling routines  *
 **********************************/
```

```c
/* lookup - install name at or below root */
struct node **lookup(root, name)
register struct node **root;
register char *name;
{
  register int cond;

#ifdef RECURSIVE
  if (*root != NULL) {
    if ((cond = lexcmp(name, (*root)->name)) != 0)
      root = lookup((cond < 0) ? &(*root)->left, &(*root)->right, name);
  }
#else
  while (*root != NULL && (cond = lexcmp(name, (*root)->name)))
    root = (cond < 0) ? &(*root)->left : &(*root)->right;
#endif
  return (root);
}

/* add - insert entry for "name" in tree at "root" */
struct node *add(name)
char *name;
{
  char *malloc();
  register struct node *r;

  r = (struct node *) malloc(sizeof(struct node));
  r->left = r->right = NULL;   r->p.lines = NULL;
  r->name = name;
  return (r);
}

/* tree_walk - call 'ftn' for each node in inorder */
void tree_walk(root, ftn)
register struct node *root;
register void (*ftn)();
{
#ifdef RECURSIVE
  if (root != NULL) {
    tree_walk(root->left, ftn);
    (*ftn)(root);
    tree_walk(root->right, ftn);
  }
#else
  register struct node *stack, *tmp;

  stack = NULL;         /* stack initially empty */
  for ( ; ; ) {
    if (root != NULL) {
```

```c
        tmp = root;
        root = root->left;         /* move to left */
        tmp->left = stack; stack = tmp;  /* push tmp */
      } else if (stack != NULL) {  /* stack not empty */
        root = stack; stack = stack->left;       /* pop */
        (*ftn)(root);       /* visit node */
        root = root->right;        /* move right */
      } else        /* stack is empty */
        break;
  }
#endif
}

/* insert - add 'line_no' to the circular list, 'origin' */
struct instance *insert(origin, line_no)
register struct instance *origin;
int line_no;
{
  char *malloc();
  register struct instance *t;

  if (origin == NULL || origin->line != line_no) {
    t = (struct instance *) malloc(sizeof(struct instance));
    if (origin == NULL)
      origin = t;
    t->line = line_no;  t->next = origin->next;
    origin->next = t;
    origin = t;
  }
  return (origin);
}

/* use - log an occurrence of "name" in "file" at "line" */
void use(name, file, line)
char *name, *file;
int line;
{
  char *newcpy();
  register struct node **ft, **nt;

  if (*(nt = lookup(&symbol_root, name)) == NULL)
    *nt = add(newcpy(name));
  if (*(nt = lookup(&((*nt)->p.files), file)) == NULL) {
    if (*(ft = lookup(&file_root, file)) == NULL)
      *ft = add(newcpy(file));
    *nt = add((*ft)->name);
  }
  (*nt)->p.lines = insert((*nt)->p.lines, line);
}
```

```c
/* get_name - extract file name from line */
void get_name(line, file)
register char *line;
char *file;
{
  void copy_until();
  register char *delim;

  while (*line == ' ' || *line == '\t')
    ++line;
  if (*line != '\n') {  /* if none, use "file" as is */
    if (*line == '"') {
      delim = "\"\n";
      ++line;
    } else if (*line == '<') {
      delim = ">\n";
      ++line;
    } else
      delim = " \t\n";
    copy_until(file, line, delim);
  }
}

/* new_line - return pointer to the next line */
char *new_line()
{
  static char line[MAXLINE+1];

  ++line_count;
  return (fgets(line, MAXLINE, stdin));
}

/* white_space - tests for blanks, tabs and comments */
boolean white_space(s)
register char **s;
{
  if (**s == ' ' || **s == '\t')
    return (TRUE);
  if (**s == '/' && *(*s+1) == '*') {    /* comment */
    while (*++*s != '/') {
      while (*++*s != '*') {
        if (**s == EOS) {
          if ((*s = new_line()) != NULL)
            --*s;       /* because of pre-increment in inner while loop */
          else {
            fprintf(stderr, "unexpected EOF\n");
            return (FALSE);
          }
        }
      }
```

```c
      }
    }
    return (TRUE);
  }
  return (FALSE);
}

/* ishex - is 'c' a hexadecimal digit? */
boolean ishex(c)
register char c;
{
    return (('0' <= c && c <= '9') || ('a' <= c && c <= 'f'));
}
/* get_token - strip leading token from s */
char get_token(s, t)
register char **s, *t;
{
  char esc();
  register char class;

  while (white_space(s))
    ++*s;
  if (isalpha(**s) || **s == '_') {       /* identifier */
    class = ID;
    do
      *t++ = *(*s)++;
    while (isdigit(**s) || isalpha(**s) || **s == '_');
  } else if (**s == '\"' || **s == '\'') {      /* string or literal */
    class = **s;
    do {
      esc(s);
      ++*s;
      if (**s == EOS) {
        if ((*s = new_line()) == NULL)
          goto out;
      }
    } while (**s != class);
    ++*s;
  } else if (isdigit(**s)) {
    do {
      class = *++*s;
      class = lower(class);    /* n.b. lower() may be a macro */
    } while (ishex(class) || class == 'x' || class == 'l' || class == '.');
    class = INTEGER;
  } else {
    class = *(*s)++;
  }
out:
  *t = EOS;
```

```
    return (class);
}

static char *reserved[] = {"auto", "break", "case", "char", "continue",
    "default", "do", "double", "else", "extern", "float", "for", "goto",
    "if", "int", "long", "register", "return", "short", "sizeof", "static",
    "struct", "switch", "typedef", "union", "unsigned", "while", "void"};

/* keyword - is "s" a reserved word in C */
boolean keyword(s)
char *s;
{
  register int cond;    /* condition code of lexcmp() */
  register int mid;
  int hi, lo;

  /* binary search; reserved[] must be in alphabetica. order */
  lo = 0;  hi = sizeof(reserved) / sizeof(char *) - 1;
  while (lo <= hi) {
    mid = (hi + lo) / 2;
    if ((cond = lexcmp(s, reserved[mid])) == 0)
      return (TRUE);
    if (cond < 0)
      hi = mid - 1;
    else
      lo = mid + 1;
  }
  return (FALSE);
}

/* xref - cross reference */
void xref(file)
register char *file;
{
  int atoi();
  register char class;
  char *s, token[MAXLINE+1];

  line_count = 0;
  while ((s = new_line()) != NULL) {
    if ((class = get_token(&s, token)) != '#') {
      while (class != '\n') {
        if (class == ID && !keyword(token))
          use(token, file, line_count);
        class = get_token(&s, token);
      }
    } else if (get_token(&s, token) == ID) {
      if (streq(token, "include")) {
        get_name(s, token);
```

```c
          use(token, file, line_count);
        } else if (streq(token, "define")) {
          get_token(&s, token);
          use(token, file, line_count);
        } else if (streq(token, "ifdef") || streq(token, "ifndef")) {
          get_token(&s, token);
          use(token, file, line_count);
        } else if (streq(token, "line")) {
          if (get_token(&s, token) == INTEGER)
            line_count = atoi(token);
          else
            fprintf(stderr, "#line %s\n", token);
        } else
          ;          /* ignore #else, #endif, etc. */
      }
    }
  }

/* putp - output a partial line to stdout */
unsigned putp(s)
register char *s;
{
  register unsigned n;

  for (n = 0; *s != EOS; ++n)
    putchar(*s++);
  return (n);
}

/* list_file - print lines within a file */
void list_file(ft)
register struct node *ft;
{
  char *itoa();
  register unsigned b;
  register struct instance *it;
  char buf[5];

  b = putp("    ");
  b += putp(ft->name);
  /* print line numbers */
  it = ft->p.lines = ft->p.lines->next; /* move 'lines' to start */
  do {
    if (b == 0)
      b = putp("           ");     /* this and 2nd to last line must agree */
    b += putp("   ");
    b += itoa(it->line, buf) - buf;
    putp(buf);
    if (b > WIDTH - 8) {          /* leave a margin on right */
```

```
      putp("\n");
      b = 0;
    }
    it = it->next;
  } while (it != ft->p.lines);
  if (b > 6)     /* non-blank line */
    putp("\n");
}

/* print_xref - dump cross reference table to stdout */
void print_xref(nt)
struct node *nt;
{
  putp(nt->name); putp("\n");
  tree_walk(nt->p.files, list_file);
}

main(argc, argv)
register int argc;
register char **argv;
{
  FILE *freopen();

  if (argc <= 1)
    xref("<stdin>");
  else {
    while (--argc > 0) {
      if (freopen(*++argv, "r", stdin) == NULL)
        fprintf(stderr, "can't open %s\n", *argv);
      else
        xref(*argv);
    }
  }
  tree_walk(symbol_root, print_xref);
}
```

LISTING 10-2

```
/* esc() - escaped character processing.

   Author: Jeff Taylor, The Toolsmith (c) copyright 1985
   Environment: UNIX 4.2 BSD; CC compiler.
*/

#include "style.h"

#define ESCAPE   '\\'
```

```c
char real[] = "\t\f\n\010";
char symb[] = "tfnb";

/* esc - map string into escaped character if appropriate */
char esc(s)
register char **s;
{
  register int i;

  if (**s == ESCAPE && *(*s + 1) != EOS) {    /* not special at end */
    ++*s;
    for (i = 0; i < sizeof(symb) - 1; ++i) {
      if (symb[i] == **s)
        return (real[i]);
    }
  }
  return (**s);
}
/* lexcmp() - alphabetical comparison.

   Author: Jeff Taylor, The Toolsmith (c) copyright 1985.
   Environment: C; UNIX 4.2 BSD.
*/

#include <ctype.h>
#include "style.h"

#define lower(c)      (isupper(c) ? tolower(c) : (c))

/* lexcmp - alphabetical comparison, similiar to strcmp() */
int lexcmp(aa, bb)
char *aa, *bb;
{
  register char *a, *b;

  for (a = aa, b = bb;  ;a++, b++) {
    if (lower(*a) != lower(*b))
      return (lower(*a) - lower(*b));   /* unequal */
    if (*a == EOS)
      break;
  }
  for (a = aa, b = bb; ; a++, b++) {
    if (*a != *b)
      return (*a - *b); /* unequal */
    if (*a == EOS)
      break;
  }
  return (0);    /* equal */
}
```

LISTING 10-3

```c
/* String package - unsigned inset();  char *newcpy();

   Author: Jeff Taylor, The Toolsmith (c) copyright 1985.
   Environment: C; UNIX 4.2 BSD.
*/

#include "style.h"

/* copy_until - copy from 'src' to 'dst' until 'delimiters' */
void copy_until(dst, src, delimiters)
register char *dst, *src;
char *delimiters;
{
  register char *d;

  while (*src != EOS) {
    for (d = delimiters; *d != EOS; ++d) {
      if (*src == *d)
        goto out;
    }
    *dst++ = *src++;
  }
out:
  *dst = EOS;
}

/* itoa - integer to ASCII */
char *itoa(n, ascii)
register int n;
register char *ascii;
{
  register int power;

  if (n < 0) {
    n = -n;  *ascii++ = '-';
  }
  power = 1;
  while (n / power >= 10)
    power = power * 10;
  do {
    *ascii++ = (n / power) + '0';
    n = n % power;  power = power / 10;
  } while (power != 0);
  *ascii = EOS;
  return (ascii);
}
```

```c
/* newcpy - copy a string into newly allocated space */
char *newcpy(string)
char *string;
{
  char *malloc(), *strcpy();

  /* include terminating EOS */
  return (strcpy(malloc(strlen(string) + 1), string));
}
```

11
CC: A DRIVER FOR SMALL-C

by Axel T. Schreiner

This chapter originally appeared in DDJ #92 (June 1984).

Once you make extensive use of a programming system consisting of compiler, assembler, and linker, you find yourself either typing a lot of commands or using the CP/M SUBMIT facility quite a bit. The latter, however, is not very flexible. It unconditionally runs whatever commands the batch file dictates, and those, regardless of argument substitution, may be more or less than what you intended.

A language like C encourages separate compilation and program composition from various source files, and a combination like Jim Hendrix's Small-C compiler (see "Small-C Version 2" in this volume) and MicroSoft's relocating assembler and linking loader makes it quite attractive to compile as little as possible during program development. When you add a separate preprocessor for Small-C and attempt to eliminate intermediate files, you find yourself typing lots of (almost) identical commands each time you want to preprocess, compile, erase, assemble, erase, link, and so on.

cc (Listing 11-1) is a program patterned after Dennis Ritchie's *cc* command in the Unix system. It accepts options and file specifications and through CP/M's SUBMIT feature, arranges for the proper amount of preprocessing, compiling, assembly, and loading. Essentially, you type what files ought to be processed to construct a program, then *cc* prepares a SUBMIT file and persuades CP/M to execute it.

Features

cc is based on a runtime support that passes arguments to the main program. It expects to be called as follows:

    cc (option)... file...

You may specify options in any order, and they are generally cumulative. The following options are available:

```
-c              compile only: do not execute the
                linker
-p              preprocess only
-s              preprocess and compile only
-o filename     output of the linker is "filename"
```

Other options are passed on to the relevant processor, mostly to the Small-C preprocessor (see "p: A Small-C Preprocessor" in this volume). *p* accepts the following:

```
-d name(=value)  define a symbolic name
-e               suppress position stamps
-i drive         search for file inclusion
-u name          undefine a symbolic name
```

So that *p* can be used prior to Hendrix's compiler, the -e option is included automatically.

Files are passed on to the appropriate processors. The most general files are processed first. Intermediate files, named after the original source files, are erased once they are no longer needed; objects, however, are retained. In the absence of the -o option, the resulting load module is named after the first of the more general source files. The following filename extensions are used by *cc*:

```
.c      preprocessor source file
.i      compiler source file
.mac    macro assembler source file
.rel    linker source file or library
```

If an extension is not present or not recognizable, the file is passed only to the linker. It is thus quite simple to pass libraries. Files are passed to the linker within each source file category in the order specified; the more general source file category, however, is passed first. This rarely produces conflicts.

The options are clearly patterned after the Unix system. The main program expects to receive pointers to the various options as a vector, argv. The number of such options, including (theoretically) the program name as first option, is also passed as an integer, argc. Options must precede the filenames.

Examples:

A few sample calls might illustrate just what *cc* does. The first example constructs the *cc* command itself:

```
B>cc cc.c
```

On my system I have the shortest possible names for the language processors, and I keep most tools on disk a:. Here the following commands would be issued:

```
A>b:p -e b:cc.c >b:cc.i
A>c b:cc.i >b:cc.mac
A>era b:cc.i
A>m =b:cc
A>era b:cc.mac
A>l b:cc/n/e,b:cc,c/s
A>b:
```

Assume that submit.c is compiled separately:

```
B>cc -c submit.c
    A>b:p -e b:submit.c >b:submit.i
    A>c b:submit.i >b:submit.mac
    A>era b:submit.i
    A>m =b:submit
    A>era b:submit.mac
    A>b:
```

Subsequently, compile cc.c and link it as follows:

```
B>cc submit cc.c
    A>b:p -e b:cc.c >b:cc.i
    A>c b:cc.i >b:cc.mac
    A>era b:cc.i
    A>m =b:cc
    A>era b:cc.mac
    A>l b:cc/n/e,b:cc,submit,c/s
    A>b:
```

It should be clear why such a driver program might be generally useful—not only for Small-C.

Implementation

The system driver basically has the following structure:

```
Obtain and save options, initialize
Obtain, test, and save files
For each category of source files: run preprocessor,
compiler, assembler as required
Run linker as required
```

Most of this is accomplished by main(); one subroutine for each processor handles the problem of issuing the actual commands. This arrangement makes the system easy to adapt to other processors.

File and option lists must be circular so that they can be easily traversed in input order. Push routines maintain the lists. A list element consists of a pointer to the next list element, followed by the string that constitutes the actual value stored. The list header points to the last element entered, which in turn points to the first element, and the circular list continues to the last element again. The list need not be marked, since you always start at the list header and thus know when you have traversed the list once.

For reasons explained below, filenames must be fully specified. If an explicit drive name is not part of the file specification, pushf() adds the current drive name.

The kind() function analyzes a file specification to determine the source category based on the file extension. All "unknown" extensions are considered to be object specifications. This allows linker libraries to pass through correctly. All other files must be existing source files. To detect trivial errors early, kind() tests source files for existence by opening them for reading.

The most interesting aspect of *cc* clearly is its use of the CP/M SUBMIT feature. During a warm start on drive a:, the CP/M console command processor (CCP) checks if a file $$$.sub exists. If it does, it is expected to contain one CCP command line (preceded by its length) per CP/M sector. The CCP takes the *last* sector from the file, truncates the file by one sector, and issues the command.

To use this feature, you need to store all command lines as a stack and then write them, appropriately formatted, into the file. You must also take care that once the driver program exits, drive a: is selected and a warm start is performed.

The submit() function (Listing 11-2) handles all of this. If it is called with a string argument, it stacks the string (using a dynamic memory allocation function that is part of my runtime support). If it is called with a NULL argument, it writes the stack (that is, the commands in reverse order) into the file, forces the CCP to select drive a: (and user area 0) by clearing the byte at location 4, and terminates program execution through a warm start.

submit() issues a command to (re)select the current drive, so that once the batch stream is completely processed the current drive is selected again. Nevertheless, during batch execution drive a: must be selected. This is why pushf() fully specifies each file.

submit() actually appends to the end of the batch file processed by the CCP. This has a desirable effect in that submit() can be used from *within* a batch stream—something that is lacking in the CP/M SUBMIT utility. (It is not difficult to position a CP/M file to end of file, especially on a sector boundary.) A simple test program (Listing 11-3) demonstrates this feature:

```
B>x a 'b c' "'d e' f" g
a
    A>b:x b c
    b
        A>b:x c
        c
        A>a:
    A>b:x 'd e' f
    d e
        A>b:x f
        f
        A>a:
    A>b:x g
    g
    A>b:
```

Quotes and double quotes can be used to hide white space within command arguments. The output shown above has been indented to show the nesting of batch streams.

Installation

Getting *cc* to run on your system might be a bit tricky. Basically you need to decide where your processors and standard libraries reside and how they ought to be called. Also, *cc* relies on my own runtime support, which is heavily oriented toward the Unix environment.

You should probably consult Kernighan and Ritchie, *The C Programming Language* (Prentice-Hall, 1978), to learn about all the routines that are mentioned "extern" at the beginning of the program. Most of them are simple to construct. It is essential, however, that you provide a memory allocator, calloc(), that is reasonably stable. I am using a scheme where memory above the load module and below the stack is managed by a list of words, each word pointing to the next. The low bit in each such word indicates if the area past that word and up to the next one is allocated or free.

I have had access to Chapter 17 of J.E. Hendrix, *The Small-C Handbook* (Reston Publishing Company, 1984), describing his runtime support (see also "A New Library for Small-C" in this volume). Although I did not have access to the runtime support itself and therefore could not test it. I believe that installing *cc* should be simple. The following probably must be done:

```
FILE            should be defined as int
_drive()        needs to access BDOS function 25
fseek(..,10)    is Hendrix's cseek(..,2)
rindex()        is Hendrix's strrchr()
```

You can replace _bputchar() by storing the relevant characters in a buffer of length 128 and using Hendrix's write() to emit the buffer. The file pointer _cfp then is not needed.

I process the arguments to main() directly. Depending on the actual implementation, you might have to use Hendrix's function getarg(). I am assuming that the storage allocator, calloc()/cfree(), supports random order release of memory.

Two runtime routines perhaps deserve special mention:

    fseek(fp, 0, 10)

positions the file indicated by fp to the end of the last allocated CP/M sector. (In Unix the third argument for fseek() must be 0, 1, or 2, indicating positioning relative to the beginning of the file, the present position, and the end of the file. Additionally, I permit 8, 9, and 10, indicating sector positioning.)

    _bputchar(ch)

emits the character *ch* to the file currently indicated by _cfp *without* interpreting tab, return, or other characters. Since submit() must write CP/M sectors containing binary length information, use of this internal routine of the runtime support is necessary. _bputchar() returns EOF on end of file (that is, when the relevant disk overflows).

Deciding where your processors live and how they ought to be called is your own problem. I have a CP/M system with two 200K floppies; one of these (barely) contains Small-C, the MicroSoft assembler and linker, a text editor, and my runtime library. Unless I trade the text editor for the preprocessor, I have to call the preprocessor from the second disk.

Notice that the SUBMIT file must be on the a: disk, and that this disk must be selected while this file is processed. My processors therefore all reside on this disk, and there is enough room left over for the SUBMIT file.

Constructing the proper calls is relatively simple; if you use other systems, you may have to add a small amount of code to the program.

Part of this work was done during a sabbatical spent at the University of Illinois; in particular, the Small-C system was obtained from UseNet.

LISTING 11-1

```
/*
 *      Contributed by  A. T. Schreiner
 *                      Sektion Informatik
 *                      University of Ulm
 *                      West Germany
 *
 */

/*
 *      cc - Small-C compiler driver
 *      ats 5/83
 */

/*
 *      define...
 *
 *      c80     to drive Software Toolworks C80
 */

char    usage[] =
        "cc [-c|p|s] [-d n[=v]] [-e] [-i d:] [-o task] [-u n] files";

#define Csource 1               /* results of kind() */
#define Msource 2
#define Psource 3

#define Cfile   ".i"            /* for these extensions */
#define Pfile   ".c"
#define Mfile   ".mac"

#define C       "c"             /* for these processors */
#define P       "b:p"
#define M       "m"
#define L       "l"

#define CLIB    "c/s"           /* and this library search */

/*
 *      "FEATURES:"
 *
 *              If the same file name is specified with different
 *              extensions, the most general source is processed...
 *              ...and the others will fail, but be linked several times!
 */

#include <stdio.h>
```

```
/*
 *      i/o header file

#define FILE     ???      type to represent files (used as FILE*)
#define stdin    ???      pre-opened standard input file
#define stdout   ???      pre-opened standard output file
#define stderr   ???      pre-opened diagnostic output file
#define NULL     0        null pointer, false
#define EOF      ???      end of file indication

 */

/*
 *      special data type
 */

#define LIST        int              /* list of word or string values */
#define l_next(x)   (*(x))           /* -> next element */
#define l_str(x)    ((x)+1)          /* -> string value */
#define l_first(x)  (*(x)+2)         /* -> first string value in circular list */
#define sz_STR(s)   (3+strlen(s))    /* size of string list element */
#define sz_FILE(s)  (5+strlen(s))    /* size of file (+ drive) element */
/*
 *      runtime support routines
 */

extern  _drive(),        /* BDOS function 25: current drive number */
        calloc(),        /* (n,l) return NULL or -> n elements of length l */
        cfree(),         /* (p) free area at p, returned by calloc() */
        exit(),          /* terminate program execution */
        fputs(),         /* (s,f) write string s on file f */
        freopen(),       /* (n,m,f) return NULL or file descriptor f,
                            closed if necessary, and reopened to read
                            (m == "r"), write ("w"), or append ("a") */
        rindex(),        /* (s,c) find c in string s end to front, return
                            NULL or ->c in s; '\0' is always found */
        strcat(),        /* (a,b) copy string b beyond string a */
        strcmp(),        /* (a,b) <, ==, > 0 as string a is <, ==, > string b */
        strcpy(),        /* (a,b) copy string b to string a */
        strlen(),        /* (s) return number of characters in string s */
        submit();        /* (s) add string s to command list; (NULL) submit */

/*
 *      global data
 */

char    buf[126],         /* to submit (length unchecked...) */
        drive[] = "?:",   /* current drive name */
        pflag,            /* run only preprocessor */
```

```
        cflag,          /* run only compiler */
        sflag;          /* run assembler */

LIST    *task,          /* task name (-o option) only */
        *popt,          /* p option list */
        *parg,          /* p argument list */
        *carg,          /* c argument list */
        *marg,          /* m argument list */
        *larg;          /* l argument list */

main(argc, argv)
        int argc;
        int *argv;
{       char *cp;
        LIST *arg;

        /* remember current drive */
        drive[0] = _drive() + 'a';

        /* default preprocessor options */
        popt = pushs(popt, "-e");

        /* record options and flags */
        while (--argc)
        {       cp = *++argv;
                /* options must precede files */
                if (*cp != '-')
                        break;
                /* dispatch and record, accept values attached or separate */
                switch(cp[1]) {
                case 'c':               /* -c         run p c m */
                        cflag = 1;
                        break;
                case 'd':               /* -d n[=v]   p option */
                case 'i':               /* -i d:      p option */
                case 'u':               /* -u n       p option */
                        popt = pushs(popt, *argv);
                        if (cp[2])
                                break;
                        if (--argc == 0)
                                goto error;
                        popt = pushs(popt, *++argv);
                        break;
                case 'e':               /* -e         p option */
                        popt = pushs(popt, *argv);
                        break;
                case 'o':               /* -o task    name task image */
                        if (cp[2])
                                task = pushf(task, cp+2);
```

```c
                    else if (--argc == 0)
                            goto error;
                    else
                            task = pushf(task, *++argv);
                    break;
            case 'p':                       /* -p         run p */
                    pflag = 1;
                    break;
            case 's':                       /* -s         run p c */
                    sflag = 1;
                    break;
            default:
                    goto error;
            }
        }

        /* there must be at least one file */
        if (argc == 0)
        {
error:          fputs(usage, stderr);
                exit();
        }

        /* collect files on various lists */
        do
        {       switch(kind(*argv)) {
                case Psource:
                        parg = pushf(parg, *argv);
                        break;
                case Csource:
                        carg = pushf(carg, *argv);
                        break;
                case Msource:
                        marg = pushf(marg, *argv);
                        break;
                default:
                        larg = pushf(larg, *argv);
                }
                ++argv;
        } while (--argc);

        /* run files preprocessor -> compiler -> assembler */
        if (arg = parg)
                do
                {       arg = *arg;
                        run(P, popt, l_str(arg), Pfile, Cfile);
                        if (pflag)
                                continue;
                        run(C, NULL, l_str(arg), Cfile, Mfile);
```

```
                    erase(l_str(arg), Cfile);
                    if (sflag)
                            continue;
                    asm(l_str(arg));
                    erase(l_str(arg), Mfile);
            } while (arg != parg);
    if (pflag)
            goto done;

    /* run files compiler -> assembler */
    if (arg = carg)
            do
            {       arg = *arg;
                    run(C, NULL, l_str(arg), Cfile, Mfile);
                    if (sflag)
                            continue;
                    asm(l_str(arg));
                    erase(l_str(arg), Mfile);
            } while (arg != carg);
    if (sflag)
            goto done;

    /* run files assembler */
    if (arg = marg)
            do
            {       arg = *arg;
                    asm(l_str(arg));
            } while (arg != marg);
    if (cflag)
            goto done;

    /* run (MicroSoft) linker */
    /* L task/n/e, parg..., carg..., marg..., larg..., CLIB */
    /* note that we do not explicitly check the length of this command */

    strcpy(buf, L);
    strcat(buf, " ");

    /* decide on output file name */
    if (task)
            strcat(buf, l_str(task));
    else if (parg)
            strcat(buf, l_first(parg));
    else if (carg)
            strcat(buf, l_first(carg));
    else if (marg)
            strcat(buf, l_first(marg));
    else if (larg)
            strcat(buf, l_first(larg));
```

```
            else
            {       strcat(buf, drive);
                    strcat(buf, "task");
            }
            strcat(buf, "/n/e");

            /* add all modules */
            if (arg = parg)
                    do
                    {       arg = *arg;
                            strcat(buf, ",");
                            strcat(buf, l_str(arg));
                    } while (arg != parg);
            if (arg = carg)
                    do
                    {       arg = *arg;
                            strcat(buf, ",");
                            strcat(buf, l_str(arg));
                    } while (arg != carg);
            if (arg = marg)
                    do
                    {       arg = *arg;
                            strcat(buf, ",");
                            strcat(buf, l_str(arg));
                    } while (arg != marg);
            if (arg = larg)
                    do
                    {       arg = *arg;
                            strcat(buf, ",");
                            strcat(buf, l_str(arg));
                    } while (arg != larg);

            /* add smallC library and submit */
            strcat(buf, ",");
            strcat(buf, CLIB);
            submit(buf);

            /* submit the batch stream */
done:
            submit(NULL);
}

/*
 *      circular list routines
 */

pushs(l, s)                     /* attach string to list */
        LIST *l;                /* list */
        char *s;                /* string */
```

```
{       LIST *r;          /* new element */

        if ((r = calloc(sz_STR(s), 1)) == NULL)
        {       fputs("no room", stderr);
                exit();
        }
        strcpy(l_str(r), s);
        /* empty list: link first element to itself */
        if (l == NULL)
                return l_next(r) = r;
        /* nonempty list: tie element into it */
        l_next(r) = l_next(l);
        return l_next(l) = r;
}

pushf(l, f)               /* attach file name to list */
        LIST *l;          /* list */
        char *f;          /* file name */
{       LIST *r;          /* new element */

        if ((r = calloc(sz_FILE(f), 1)) == NULL)
        {       fputs("no room", stderr);
                exit();
        }
        if (f[1] != ':')         /* use current drive */
        {       strcpy(l_str(r), drive);
                strcat(l_str(r), f);
        }
        else                     /* explicit drive */
                strcpy(l_str(r), f);
        if (l == NULL)
                return l_next(r) = r;
        l_next(r) = l_next(l);
        return l_next(l) = r;
}

/*
 *      source file type analysis
 */

kind(f)                   /* determine type of source */
        char *f;          /* file name */
{       char *p;

        if (p = rindex(f, '.'))
                if (strcmp(p, Pfile) == 0)
                {       if (freopen(f, "r", stdin) == NULL)
                                goto badfile;
                        *p = '\0';
```

```c
                            return Psource;
                }
                else if (strcmp(p, Cfile) == 0)
                {       if (freopen(f, "r", stdin) == NULL)
                                goto badfile;
                        *p = '\0';
                        return Csource;
                }
                else if (strcmp(p, Mfile) == 0)
                {       if (freopen(f, "r", stdin) == NULL)
                                goto badfile;
                        *p = '\0';
                        return Msource;
                }
        return 0;
badfile:
        fputs("cannot open ", stderr);
        fputs(f, stderr);
        exit();
}

/*
 *      routines to produce command calls
 */

run(cmd, opt, fnm, in, out)     /* run smallC task */
                                /* cmd opt... fnm.in > fnm.out */
        char *cmd;              /* command name */
        LIST *opt;              /* option list */
        char *fnm;              /* file name to process */
        char *in;               /* input file extension */
        char *out;              /* output file extension */
{       LIST *p;

        strcpy(buf, cmd);
        if (p = opt)
                do
                {       p = l_next(p);
                        strcat(buf, " ");
                        strcat(buf, l_str(p));
                } while (p != opt);
        strcat(buf, " ");
        strcat(buf, fnm);
#ifndef c80
        strcat(buf, in);
        strcat(buf, " >");
        strcat(buf, fnm);
        strcat(buf, out);
#endif
```

```
                submit(buf);
        }

        asm(fnm)                /* run (MicroSoft) macro assembler */
                                /* M = fnm */
                char *fnm;      /* file name to process */
        {
                strcpy(buf, M);
                strcat(buf, " =");
                strcat(buf, fnm);
                submit(buf);
        }

        erase(fnm,ext)          /* erase intermediate file */
                                /* era fnm.ext */
                char *fnm;      /* file name */
                char *ext;      /* extension */
        {
                strcpy(buf, "era ");
                strcat(buf, fnm);
                strcat(buf, ext);
                submit(buf);
        }
```

LISTING 11-2

```
        /*
         *
         *      Contributed by A. T. Schreiner
         *
         */


        /*
         *      submit() -- submit commands to CP/M batch
         *      ats 5/83
         */

        #define DSKBYTE 4       /* BDOS/CCP selected disk, user# */

        /*
         *      needed from the i/o header file

        #define FILE    ???     type to represent files
        #define NULL    0       null pointer, false
        #define EOF     ???     end of file indication

         */
```

```
/*
 *      runtime support routines
 */

extern  _bputchar(),    /* (c) write char c uninterpreted to file *_cfp */
        _cfp,
        _drive(),       /* BDOS function 25: current drive number */
        calloc(),       /* (n,l) return NULL or -> n elements of length l */
        exit(),         /* terminate program execution */
        fclose(),       /* (f) close file described by f */
        fopen(),        /* (n,m) return NULL or descriptor for file "n"
                                 opened to append (m == "a") */
        fseek(),        /* (f,p,w) position f to byte or sector p
                                 measured according to w */
        strcpy(),       /* (a,b) copy string b to string a */
        strlen();       /* (s) return number of characters in string s */

/*
 *      global data
 */

int *_submit;           /* chain of submitted buffers */

submit(s)               /* add command to CP/M job stream */
        char * s;       /* command to submit */
{       FILE *fp;       /* need to use block i/o, NOT putc */
        char *cp;
        int *wp, i;

        /* if string argument, save it as a command */
        if (s)
        {       if (strlen(s) > 126)
                        return NULL;    /* too long */
                if ((wp = calloc(strlen(s)+2+2,1)) == NULL)
                        return NULL;    /* no room */
                *wp = _submit;
                _submit = wp;
                cp = _submit+1;

                *cp = strlen(s);        /* length byte */
                strcpy(cp+1, s);        /* text */
                return s;
        }

        /* if anything to submit, write it to a:$$$.sub */
        if (_submit)
        {       if ((fp = fopen("a:$$$.sub", "a")) == NULL)
                        return NULL;    /* cannot make batch file */
                if (fseek(fp, 0, 10) == -1)
```

```
                            goto error;
                _cfp = fp;              /* for _bputchar() */

                /* last command: reselect current drive */
                _bputchar(2);
                _bputchar(_drive()+'a');
                _bputchar(':');
                for (i = 3; i < 127; ++i)
                        _bputchar(0);
                /* check last byte in sector for overflow */
                if (_bputchar(0))
                        goto error;

                /* other commands from stack */
                do
                {
                        cp = _submit+1;
                        for (i = 0; i < 127; ++i)
                        {       _bputchar(*cp);
                                if (*cp)
                                        ++cp;
                        }
                        if (_bputchar(*cp) == EOF)
                        {
error:                          fclose(fp);
                                return NULL;    /* overflow */
                        }
                } while (_submit = *_submit);

                /* signal CCP to select a: and user 0 */
                cp = DSKBYTE;
                *cp = 0;
        }

        /* exit this program and perform warm start */
        exit();
}
```

LISTING 11-3

```
/*
 *
 *      Contributed by A. T. Schreiner
 *
 */

#include <stdio.h>
extern  strcpy(), strcat(), submit(), puts();
```

```
main(argc, argv)
        int argc;
        int *argv;
{       int i;
        char buf[128];

        switch (argc) {
        default:
                strcpy(buf, "b:x ");
                for (i=2; i<argc; ++i)
                {       strcpy(buf+4, argv[i]);
                        submit(buf);
                }
        case 2:
                puts(argv[1]);
        case 1:
        }
        if (submit(NULL) == NULL)
                puts("oops");
}
```

12
CP/M BDOS AND BIOS CALLS FOR C

by Terje Bolstad

This chapter originally appeared in DDJ #80 (June 1983).

If you want to write CP/M utilities in C, you will probably need facilities to access the BDOS (Basic Disk Operating System) and/or the BIOS (Basic Input/Output System). Many C compilers for CP/M do not include such functions, and several that exist have severe limitations, in that they may not return proper values in all cases.

The two functions bdos() and bios() described here will enable you to incorporate direct BDOS and/or BIOS calls in programs written in C. Please note that programs that call bdos() or bios() are not portable beyond CP/M and the 8080 and Z80 series CPUs.

Originally, bdos() and bios() were written for the C/80 compiler from The Software Toolworks, but they also work with other compilers that push arguments on the stack in a nonreversed order before calling a function. Such C compilers include Small-C and most of its derivatives. bdos() and bios() have been tested to work properly with both C/80 from The Software Toolworks and the CW/C compiler from The Code Works.

bdos()

The bdos() function sets machine register C to the function number specified in funct and sets the register pair DE to the value given in arg, and initiates a call to BDOS. The function number may be specified numerically or symbolically. No checking of the arguments is done.

If funct is RETVN (12), RETLV (24), GETAA (27), GETROV (29) or GETDPA (31), bdos() returns the value remaining in register pair HL on return from BDOS. For all other BDOS functions, bdos() returns the value in A, with sign extension. In this way, BDOS error (255 or FF(hex)) is returned as -1.

bios()

The bios() function sets machine register pair BC to the value given in arg1, and the register pair DE to the value given in arg2, and initiates the appropriate BIOS call by transferring control to the BIOS jump vector entry point specified in funct. This entry point may be specified numerically or symbolically. No checking of the arguments is done.

If funct is either SELDSK (9) or SECTRAN (16), bios() returns the value remaining in the HL register after execution of the BIOS call; otherwise it returns the value remaining in register A on return from BIOS, with sign extension.

Note that you must specify all three arguments in the bios() function. If you do not need the last one, you must set it to 0 or any other value.

Installation

You may type the source code in Listing 12-1 into a file called CPMCALL.C. To use bdos() or bios() in a C source file, you must #include "CPMCALL.C" in that file.

A simple example of how to use bdos() and bios() is shown in Listing 12-2. In this example, bdos() is used to get the current disk, and bios() is used to print it on the console. You may use this example to test that you have installed bdos() and bios() correctly on your system. When run, the program should write the uppercase character corresponding to the current (logged) disk drive on the console. Log onto different drives and check that the program writes out the correct letter.

Normally it is not advisable to do input/output via bios() or bdos() (as done with bios() in the example), if this can be done via other conventional C functions, such as putchar().

To make sure your program is compatible with code for other compilers that do offer the same functions (for example, SuperSoft's C compiler), you should refer symbolically to the bdos() and bios() function numbers (as shown in the example), and never use numbers directly. The reason for this is that other compilers may not use the same numerical values for bios() function numbers as used in this version of bios().

You may want to delete (or comment out) all the #define macros that you will not use, so that they will not occupy unnecessary space in the compiler's macro substitution table.

After compilation, bdos() and bios() will assemble under CP/M's ASM, The Software Toolworks's AS, and most other 8080 assemblers. You may assemble both functions for nonstandard versions of CP/M by changing the CPBASE equate from 0 to the required value.

If you should want to delete the bdos() function and make a separate function of bios() only, you need to include the CPBASE equate in front of the bios() assembly code.

To use bdos() and bios(), refer to the CP/M Interface Guide and the CP/M Alteration Guide.

A final warning: You should avoid direct CP/M calls whenever possible. Even though they enable you to do wonderful things in CP/M, they limit the portability of your programs.

The following code may be copied, used and distributed by anyone, commercially or otherwise, provided the contribution notice is included.

LISTING 12-1

```
/***************************************************
*                                                   *
*   CP/M BDOS- AND BIOS- CALLS FOR C/80             *
*                                                   *
*   Contributed by T. Bolstad, ELEKTROKONSULT AS    *
*   Konnerudgaten. 3, N-3000 Drammen, NORWAY.       *
*                                                   *
*   Date: January 17, 1983.                         *
*                                                   *
***************************************************/

/*   DEFINITION OF BDOS FUNCTIONS                    */

#define RESET    0    /*   SYSTEM RESET              */
#define CONSIN   1    /*   CONSOLE INPUT             */
#define CONSOUT  2    /*   CONSOLE OUTPUT            */
#define READIN   3    /*   READER INPUT              */
#define PUNOUT   4    /*   PUNCH OUTPUT              */
#define LISTOUT  5    /*   LIST OUTPUT               */
#define DIRCON   6    /*   DIRECT CONSOLE I/O        */
#define GETIOB   7    /*   GET I/O BYTE              */
#define SETIOB   8    /*   SET I/O BYTE              */
#define PRNTST   9    /*   PRINT STRING              */
#define READCB  10    /*   READ CONSOLE BUFFER       */
#define GETCST  11    /*   GET CONSOLE STATUS        */
#define RETVN   12    /*   RETURN VERSION NUMBER     */
#define RESDSK  13    /*   RESET DISK SYSTEM         */
#define SELDISK 14    /*   SELECT DISK               */
#define OPENF   15    /*   OPEN FILE                 */
#define CLOSEF  16    /*   CLOSE FILE                */
#define SRCHFF  17    /*   SEARCH FOR FIRST          */
#define SRCHFN  18    /*   SEARCH FOR NEXT           */
#define DELF    19    /*   DELETE FILE               */
#define RDSEQ   20    /*   READ SEQUENTIAL           */
#define WRSEQ   21    /*   WRITE SEQUENTIAL          */
#define MAKEF   22    /*   MAKE FILE                 */
#define RENF    23    /*   RENAME FILE               */
#define RETLV   24    /*   RETURN LOGIN VECTOR       */
#define RETCD   25    /*   RETURN CURRENT DISK       */
#define STDMA   26    /*   SET DMA ADDRESS           */
#define GETAA   27    /*   GET ALLOCATION ADDRESS    */
#define WPDSK   28    /*   WRITE PROTECT DISK        */
#define GETROV  29    /*   GET READ/ONLY VECTOR      */
#define SETFAT  30    /*   SET FILE ATTRIBUTES       */
#define GETDPA  31    /*   GET DISK PARAMETERS ADDRESS */
#define SGUC    32    /*   SET/GET USER CODE         */
#define RDRAN   33    /*   READ RANDOM               */
```

```
#define WRRAN    34    /* WRITE RANDOM               */
#define COMFS    35    /* COMPUTE FILE SIZE          */
#define SETRRC   36    /* SET RANDOM RECORD          */
#define RESDRV   37    /* RESET DRIVE                */
#define WRRZF    38    /* WRITE RANDOM WITH ZERO FILL */

bdos(funct,arg)        /* corresponds to bdos((BC),(DE)) */
int    funct,arg;

/* CALL EXAMPLE:   bdos(RETVN,0)
   BOTH ARGUMENTS MUST BE SPECIFIED !
   Values are returned IN HL.  BDOS errors
   are returned as -1.                              */

{
#asm
CPBASE  EQU     0         ;NORMAL 0-ORG'ED CP/M
CPNTRY  EQU     CPBASE+5  ;BDOS ENTRY

        POP     H         ;GET RETURN ADDRESS
        POP     D         ;GET ARG (INFORMATION ADDRESS)
        POP     B         ;GET FUNCTION NO.
        PUSH    B         ;RESTORE STACK
        PUSH    D
        PUSH    H

        PUSH    B         ;SAVE FUNCTION NO. ON STACK
        CALL    CPNTRY    ;BDOS CALL
        XCHG              ;SAVE HL IN DE
        MOV     L,A       ;SAVE A IN L
                          ;SIGN EXTENSION TO H:
        RLC               ; GET SIGN BIT INTO CY
        SBB     A         ; IF CY=0, RESULT AFTER SBB IS ZERO
                          ; IF CY=1, RESULT AFTER SBB IS -1 (IE ALL ONES)
        MOV     H,A       ; NOW A IS MOVED TO HL WITH SIGN EXTENSION
        POP     B         ;GET FUNCTION NO IN BC
        MOV     A,C       ;GET FUNCTION NO IN A

        CPI     12        ;WAS IT 'RETURN VERSION NUMBER' ?
        JZ      RETHL1
        CPI     24        ;RETURN LOGIN VECTOR ?
        JZ      RETHL1
        CPI     27        ;GET ALLOCATION ADDRESS ?
        JZ      RETHL1
        CPI     29        ;GET READ/ONLY VECTOR ?
        JZ      RETHL1
        CPI     31        ;GET DISK PARAMETER ADDRESS?
        JZ      RETHL1
        JMP     BDOSRET
```

```
RETHL1: XCHG
BDOSRET: RET              ;WITH RETURNED VALUE IN HL

#endasm
}

/*      DEFINITION OF BIOS FUNCTIONS      */

#define BOOT     0   /* COLD-BOOT              */
#define WBOOT    1   /* WARM-BOOT              */
#define CONST    2   /* CONSOLE STATUS         */
#define CONIN    3   /* CONSOLE INPUT          */
#define CONOUT   4   /* CONSOLE OUTPUT         */
#define LIST     5   /* LIST DEVICE            */
#define PUNCH    6   /* PUNCH                  */
#define READER   7   /* READER                 */
#define HOME     8   /* HOME DISK DRIVE HEAD   */
#define SELDSK   9   /* SELECT DISK DRIVE      */
#define SETTRK  10   /* SET TRACK              */
#define SETSEC  11   /* SET SECTOR             */
#define SETDMA  12   /* SET DMA ADDRESS        */
#define READ    13   /* READ ONE SECTOR        */
#define WRITE   14   /* WRITE ONE SECTOR       */
#define LISTST  15   /* LIST STATUS            */
#define SECTRAN 16   /* SECTOR TRANSLATION     */

bios(funct,arg1,arg2) /* corresponds to bios(function,(BC),(DE)) */
int funct,arg1,arg2;

/* CALL EXAMPLE:   bios(SETTRK,5,0)
ALL 3 ARGUMENTS MUST BE SPECIFIED, even though
the last one is only used by SELDSK and SECTRAN. */

{
#asm
        POP     D           ;RETURN ADDRESS
        POP     H           ;ARGUMENT 2
        SHLD    ARG2S       ;SAVE IT
        POP     B           ;ARGUMENT 1
        XCHG                ;GET RETURN ADDRESS INTO HL

        POP     D           ;FUNCTION NO.

        PUSH    D           ;RESTORE SP
        PUSH    B
        PUSH    B
        PUSH    H           ;RESTORE RETURN ADDRESS
```

CP/M BDOS AND BIOS Calls for C

```
            PUSH    D           ;SAVE FUNCTION NO. ON STACK

            LXI     H,0         ;CALCULATE OFFSET ADDRESS FROM FUNCTION:
            DAD     D           ; GET FUNCTION NO. (OFFSET) IN HL
            DAD     H           ; 2*OFFSET
            DAD     D           ; 3*OFFSET
            XCHG                ; SAVE OFFSET ADDRESS IN DE

            LHLD    CPBASE+1    ;GET POINTER TO BIOS WBOOT ENTRY
            DCX     H           ;DECREMENT TO
            DCX     H           ;  POINT TO
            DCX     H           ;    START OF BIOS ENTRY JUMP TABLE

            DAD     D           ;ADD OFFSET (RESULT IN HL)
            XCHG                ;GET RESULT IN DE
            LXI     H,RET1
            PUSH    H           ;SAVE RETURN ADDRESS ON STACK

            LHLD    ARG2S       ;GET ARGUMENT 2
            XCHG                ;GET ARGUMENT 2 INTO DE
                                ; AND BIOS FUNCTION ENTRY ADDRESS INTO HL


            PCHL                ;GO TO BIOS

RET1:       XCHG                ;SAVE HL IN DE
            MOV     L,A

            RLC                 ;GET SIGN BIT INTO CY
            SBB     A           ;IF CY=0, RESULT AFTER SUBB IS ZERO
                                ;IF CY=1, RESULT AFTER SUBB IS -1 (IE ALL ONES)
            MOV     H,A
            POP     B           ;GET BIOS FUNCTION NO. IN BC
            MOV     A,C
            CPI     9           ;SELECT DISK FUNCTION ?
            JZ      RETHL2
            CPI     16          ;SECTOR TRANSLATION FUNCTION ?
            JZ      RETHL2

            JMP     RETBIOS
RETHL2:     XCHG                ;RETURN VALUE IN HL
RETBIOS:    RET
ARG2S:      DS      2

#endasm
}
```

LISTING 12-2

```
#include "cpmcall.c"
main()
{
        bios(CONOUT,bdos(RETCD,0)+'A',0);     /* print current disk */
}
```

13
SMALL-TOOLS: PROGRAMS FOR TEXT PROCESSING

by J. E. Hendrix

This chapter was adapted from the Small-Tools manual.

Brian W. Kernighan and P. J. Plauger, in the book *Software Tools* (Addison-Wesley, 1976), describe a philosophy of computer programming in which programs are considered tools to be used for solving problems. Each program, or tool, is designed to work with the other tools. Each performs one of a set of functions needed to complete a task. Given a set of tools, you can combine them in various ways to achieve desired results.

The key to making the software-tools concept work is to have the output of each tool compatible with the input of all the other tools. The tools must be designed for flexible use; they must not make too many assumptions about the functions they perform. They should do something rational even when their operating parameters are unusual, since even unusual effects may be useful.

The chief advantage of this approach to program design is that a new program need not be developed, nor an old one modified, whenever a need arises that is slightly different from what is already being done. Familiarity with the tools at hand and a little imagination can often produce the solution to a new problem.

The Small-Tools Package

Small-Tools is a set of programs inspired by the ones described in the book *Software Tools*. The programs are especially designed for use with single-user microcomputer systems.

Their area of application is text processing—an area of high activity in virtually every line of work. Tasks for which they are suited include (but are not limited to):

- Writing letters, reports, articles, and books
- Checking for spelling errors
- Writing computer programs
- Creating forms and documents by answering questions
- Composing legal documents from prewritten material and/or answering prompts
- Maintaining mailing lists
- Printing personalized form letters individually or from a mailing list
- Addressing envelopes

Many other uses are possible, depending on your needs and imagination.

The Small-Tools Programs

The Small-Tools package (Table 13-1, see page 521) consists of programs designed to perform the following specific functions on text files:

- Editing
- Formatting
- Sorting
- Merging
- Listing
- Printing
- Searching
- Changing
- Transliterating
- Copying and concatenating
- Encrypting and decrypting
- Replacing spaces with tabs
- Replacing tabs with spaces
- Counting characters, words, or lines
- Selecting printer fonts

All the programs work with files of the same format, and you can use the output of any program as input to any other program. Alternatively, you may send the output of any program to the console, to a printer, or to any device attached to

Table 13-1.
Small-Tools Programs and Usage Messages

listing	program	description
1	CHANGE	replace occurrences of a pattern
2	COPY	copy one or more files into one
3	COUNT	count characters, words, and/or lines
4	CRYPT	encrypt or decrypt files
5	DETAB	replace tabs with equivalent blanks
6	EDIT	create or modify files
7	ENTAB	replace blanks with equivalent tabs
8	FIND	find lines containing a pattern
9	FONT	set printer fonts
10	FORMAT	format and print files
11	LIST	list a file in columns and pages
12	MERGE	merge two sorted files for unique, equal, or all lines
13	PRINT	print with page skips, headings, and line numbers
14	SORT	sort text lines ascending or descending on key field
15	TRANS	transliterate characters
16		header files and functions common to all the programs

program	usage message
CHANGE	pattern [replacement]
COUNT	[file] [-C¦-W¦-L]
COPY	[file]... [.?] [-B] [-NCR] [-NLF] [-T#,#]
CRYPT	key
DETAB	[#]... [+#]
EDIT	[file] [-V]
ENTAB	[#]... [+#]
FIND	[~]pattern
FONT	[device]
FORMAT	[mergefile] [-BC#] [-EC#] [-BP#] [-EP#] [-PO#] [-NP] [-T] [-I] [-U] [-S] [-BS#] [-NR]
LIST	[file] [-C#] [-PW#] [-PL#] [-NB] [-NN] [-NP]
MERGE	file [file] [-1¦-2¦-3¦-F]
PRINT	[file]... [.?] [-NN] [-NH¦-NS] [-LM#] [-BP#] [-EP#] [-P] [-NR]
SORT	[-C#¦-F#?] [-D] [-U] [-Tx] [-Q]
TRANS	[~]from [to]

the computer. Likewise, the input to any program may come from the console or any device connected to the computer.

Input may also come from disk directories. The special filenames A:, B:, and so on represent the directories on the indicated drives (X: is the default drive). A directory is made to look like an ASCII file of filenames, one per line. This facility makes it easy to select filenames from which you can build SUB-MIT files, for performing multifile operations.

Used in combination, these programs can perform a wide variety of tasks.

You may notice in the source code for some these programs the use of bitwise logical operators ¦ and & in places where their relational counterparts

|| and && would seem more appropriate. This is because these programs were originally developed under Small-C version 1, which did not support the relational operators.

System Requirements

This implementation of the Small-Tools package runs on 8080/8085/Z80 machines using the CP/M-80 operating system. You should have two disk drives and 56K of memory. Since these programs are written in Small-C and are distributed as source code, you must have the Small-C compiler (version 2.1 or later).

Small-Tools Concepts and Facilities

File Concepts

Every Small-Tools file has the same format. A file consists of a sequence of lines. If the file resides on disk, the last line is followed by an end-of-file byte of value 26 decimal (1A hex). In the case where a file ends with the last byte of a sector, however, the end-of-file byte is not written. If the file is assigned to an input/output device, such as a printer, no end-of-file byte is written either.

A line consists of a series of zero or more characters terminated by a two-character carriage-return, line-feed sequence. A line may contain, at most, 192 data characters besides the two terminating characters. When you enter data from the console, a line is automatically terminated after the 192nd character. When reading text files, most programs interrupt a line after the 192nd character and begin the next line with the following character.

If the output of a program is directed to a disk file and a file by the same name already exists, then it is overwritten. The text editor is an exception; it first renames an existing file to a .$$$ extension, then after a successful write operation it deletes the .$$$ file.

Most programs have one input file and one output file. These "standard" files may be directed to disk files or devices. Unless redirected, the standard input file is assigned to the keyboard and the standard output file is assigned to the screen. You may place input/output redirection specifications in the command line to alter these default assignments.

The redirection specification for standard input consists of the "less than" symbol < followed immediately by a filename (in regular CP/M format) or a logical device name (CON: or RDR:) or a directory name (A:, B:, ..., G:, X:). The character string <B:FILE3 redirects standard input to FILE3 on drive B, and <B: redirects it to the directory on drive B.

The redirection specification for standard output uses the "greater than" symbol > instead. Filenames or logical devices (CON:, LST:, or PUN:) may be used. Naturally, directory names cannot be used for output When standard output is redirected by a pair of symbols (for example, >>FILE3) then the output is appended to whatever data was already in the named file. If the file does not already exist it is created, and >> is no different than >.

Both redirection specifications may be given simultaneously and placed in any order and in any position following the program name in the command line.

Take care not to assign both the input and the output of a program to the same file; the result will be a corrupted file.

Command-Line Format

The command to invoke a Small-Tools program consists of (1) the program name with optional drive designator in standard CP/M format, (2) redirection specifications for standard input and output files, and (3) parameters used to control the action of the program. One or more spaces are used to separate the parts of a command; therefore, a parameter may not contain embedded spaces. An escape sequence (described later) may be used to specify spaces in parameters.

Redirection specifications are not seen by the programs, so they may appear in any position following the program name. The position of parameters, however, may be important. The CHANGE program, for instance, takes two parameters—a text pattern to look for in the input file and a character string that replaces all occurrences of the text pattern in the output file. The first parameter is taken for the search pattern and the second parameter is taken for the replacement string. They must be given in that order.

Note: To be effective, several of the programs need to accept lowercase letters in parameters. However, the CP/M CCP and SUBMIT program convert command lines to uppercase before passing them on to programs. Patches to allow lowercase characters are provided in the documentation on the distribution diskette. After you apply these patches, you can create lowercase filenames with the CP/M utilities. I recommend, however, that you use lowercase only to specify text patterns and replacement strings, since you might encounter problems with lowercase CP/M filenames. The Small-Tools programs, on the other hand, always convert filenames to uppercase, in keeping with the CP/M convention.

Command-Line Switches

A special class of command-line parameter, known as a *switch*, is often used to control peripheral or secondary effects of a program. Switches usually consist of a hyphen immediately followed by one or more letters and, in some cases, numeric values. For example, the switch -BP123 informs the print program to (b)egin output on (p)age (123). As the parentheses indicate, switches are designed to be easily remembered.

Switches may appear in any position after the program name. Only nonswitch parameters are sensitive to position, and that is only with respect to one another. Switches and redirection specifications may be freely spread among nonswitch parameters without affecting them.

Since switches are introduced by hyphens, you should avoid filenames that begin with a hyphen (such names given as nonswitch parameters would look like switches).

Usage Messages

To aid in remembering the various switches and parameters used with these programs, the console displays a usage message whenever you invoke a Small-Tools program with a null or undefined switch. If you need help remembering how to invoke a program, just enter the program's name followed by an isolated hyphen. Usage messages indicate the syntax of the command to invoke a program; they have the form

```
usage: <program> <parameter>... <switch>...
```

where <program> is the program name, <parameter> is a nonswitch parameter, <switch> is a switch, and the ellipses indicate that other occurrences may follow. Switches are always optional. Nonswitch parameters may or may not be optional, depending on the program.

Redirection specifications are not shown in usage messages since they are common to most programs and their presence can be assumed.

Square brackets [] appear in usage messages to indicate optional fields. The brackets are not part of the command. Programs take a default action when an optional field is missing. Normally switches are needed only in exceptional cases.

The ellipsis (...) appears in usage messages to indicate, as above, that a given type of field may occur more than once in the command. The ellipsis itself is not part of the command.

The vertical bar | is used to indicate alternate choices. In reading a usage message, you may imagine the vertical bar stands for the word *or*. Like the square bracket and the ellipsis, the vertical bar is not part of the command.

The number sign # stands for a decimal integer of one or more digits.

The question mark ? stands for any character or, in some cases, a string of characters. Numbers, letters, and special characters are legal.

Words or combinations of words are used as generic names for specific types of parameters. For example, the term *outfile* stands for an output filename, the word *pattern* stands for any legal search pattern, and so on.

Error Handling

All Small-Tools programs, except the editor, handle errors in the same way. When an error occurs, a message is sent to the console with an audible alarm and the program terminates.

If the problem is an invaid command line parameter, the usage message described above is sent to the console. Other errors result in other appropriate messages.

Two error messages are common to all Small-Tools programs. The message "output error" indicates that an error occurred while writing into an output disk file. The most probable cause is not enough space on the diskette to contain the data. Since this error is common to all programs, it is not listed with the individual program descriptions below. The other common error message is "<file>: can't open," which means that a file by the name <file> cannot be found on the diskette in question.

Two errors are caught by the runtime library rather than the program:

- R, Redirection specification error, which indicates an attempt to redirect standard input to come from a nonexistent file.
- M, Memory allocation error, which indicates that an attempt was made to allocate more memory than was available. This error should never occur.

Escape Sequences

Sometimes it is necessary to enter nonprintable characters or characters that ordinarily have special meaning. You can enter such characters from the keyboard by using the colon as an escape character. An escape character changes the meaning of the character that follows it.

Together, the escape character and the character following are seen as a single character by the program. The escape sequences are:

```
:b                      backspace
:n                      newline (carriage return)
:s                      space
:t                      tab
:<other character>      the actual character given
```

Some special characters known as metacharacters have special meaning when they appear in search patterns or replacement strings. You may use the <other character> escape sequence to force them to be seen as themselves in these contexts.

The colon, having a special use (escape character), must be escaped to be accepted as itself; thus, :: is taken for a single colon.

Provision is made for the space character, since if an actual space were included in a parameter, it would delimit the parameter.

Metacharacters

Certain characters assume special meanings when they appear in search patterns or replacement strings (Table 13-2). As a group, these characters are designated *metacharacters* (as opposed to ordinary characters). Since these metacharacters occasionally need to appear as ordinary characters in a search pattern or replacement string, they may, in such cases, be entered as escape sequences. All the Small-Tools programs use the metacharacter definitions found in the file TOOLS.H. You may change these metacharacter assignments to suit your fancy by changing that file before compiling the programs.

Search Patterns

Search patterns are used by the text editor and some other programs to identify selected character strings.

The simplest form of search pattern is a character string identical to the one sought.

Preceding the pattern with a grave accent (`` ` ``) specifies that the string must appear at the beginning of a line. The grave accent in any other position has no special meaning.

Terminating a pattern with an apostrophe (') specifies that the string being sought must occur at the end of a line. An apostrophe in any other position has no special meaning.

The following patterns illustrate the use of these metacharacters:

pattern	meaning
`` `abcd ``	the string "abcd" at the beginning of a line
xyz'	the string "xyz" at the end of a line
`` `xxx' ``	a line consisting of only "xxx"
ab'cd`e	the string "ab'cd`e" occurring anywhere in a line

A question mark **?** in a pattern matches any character in that position of a string. Thus, the pattern **f?？t** matches foot, feet, f it, and so on.

An asterisk (*****) causes a match on zero or more occurrences of the preceding character. An asterisk at the beginning of a pattern has no special meaning. The following examples illustrate the use of the asterisk.

pattern	matching strings
*abc	*abc
a*bc	bc, abc, aabc, aaabc, ...
aa*bc	abc, aabc, aaabc, aaaabc, ...
s?*p	sp, sxp, sleep, s12 xp, ...
the:s*man	theman, the man, the man, ...

Table 13-2.
Metacharacters and Their Special Meanings

symbol	name	use
:	colon	escape character
`	grave accent	matches the beginning of a line
'	apostrophe	matches the end of a line
?	question mark	matches any character
*	asterisk	matches zero or more occurrences of the preceding character
[	left bracket	introduces a character class definition
]	right bracket	terminates a character class definition
-	hyphen	indicates a range of characters in a character class definition
~	tilde	complements a character class definition
^	circumflex	in a replacement string, stands for the entire original string

You may specify that a character position in the pattern will match any one of a list (or class) of characters, but no others. To do this, simply enclose the list of characters in square brackets. For example, the pattern ab[15Q]z matches ab1z, ab5z, abQz, but not ab3z.

Since the set of decimal digits, lowercase letters, and uppercase letters are used frequently, and since they are such long lists, a shorthand method of specifying [012...9], [abc...z], and [ABC...Z] exists. You may place a hyphen between the first and last characters. Thus, the pattern a[0-9] matches a0, a1, and so on, and the pattern [A-Z][a-z]* matches A, Able, Zebra, and so on.

You need not specify the entire set of decimal digits nor all of the letters when the shorthand notation is used. You may give [5-7], [a-g], and so on. The only restrictions are that the lower-valued character must be listed in front of the hyphen. You may use the shorthand notation in a list of characters specifying a character class. Thus, [s12g5-7a-zA-Z$(] is a valid character class.

The hyphen (-) has special meaning only when it falls between characters in a character class definition. If it appears at either end of the definition or outside such a definition, it has no special meaning.

If the first character inside the left bracket is a tilde (~), it causes a match on any character except those listed.

It is important to think of the character class as a single character position.

If you need a literal **[** or **]** in a pattern, then escape it as **:[** or **:]**, respectively.

Console Input

Whenever you use the console keyboard for input, you may correct errors anytime before you press the carriage-return key. You may erase input characters in the reverse order from which you entered them; simply press the delete (DEL) or backspace (BS) key for each erasure. A backspace-space-backspace sequence is echoed to the console for each such erasure; if the console device is a video screen, this causes the disappearance of the last character in the line being entered. Printer devices simply back up one print position.

You may erase the entire line you are entering by pressing control-X.

The CP/M printer toggle (control-P) does not work with Small-C programs. It is generally not needed anyway, since program output can usually be redirected to LST: or PUN:.

You may command a Small-Tools program that is executing to pause or abort. A paused program simply stops in its tracks and waits to be resumed. A control-S character from the console pauses a program, and another one resumes it. This is handy when a program's output is going to the console screen too fast. You may alternately pause and resume program execution so that you may study the output before it scrolls off the screen. You can abort a running or paused program by entering control-C.

Anytime a program's standard input is assigned to the console keyboard (default condition), the program will continue to process input until a control-Z is entered. The control-Z is taken for an end-of-file indicator. No prompt is given to signal the operator that a program is waiting for input when standard input is directed to the keyboard; the program sits there waiting for data to process. The text editor is the only exception to this rule.

Header File

The file TOOLS.H is included into each Small-Tools program at compile time. It defines several system-wide parameters. As mentioned above, the metacharacters are defined there. Also the maximum size of text lines and the dimensions of the console screen and printer paper are defined. You may change any of these values to suit your particular needs. You should preview this file before starting to compile any Small-Tools programs.

Program Descriptions

CHANGE

```
CHANGE pattern [replacement]
```

Description

CHANGE copies the standard input file to the standard output file. In the process, it scans the text for occurrences of a pattern; a replacement string is substituted for each occurrence found.

The search pattern is given in the command line and is formed according to the rules described above. Full use of metacharacters and escape sequences is allowed.

The replacement string is any string of characters. Only two metacharacters have significance in a replacement string: the circumflex, which stands for the entire string that matched the pattern, and the colon, which is the escape character. If you desire an actual circumflex or colon, use an escape sequence to specify it.

If no replacement string is given, the null string is assumed; that is, strings matching the pattern are deleted.

A search pattern or replacement string may not exceed 48 characters in length. Only the first 48 characters of longer strings are used.

It is a good idea to make a trial run of CHANGE with output to the console before making the final run.

Previewing the effect of the run on the screen will verify whether or not you have specified the pattern and replacement strings correctly. Recall that you may cause the program to pause and resume by successively entering control-S; also, you may cause it to abort by entering a control-C.

Examples:

command	description
CHANGE <ABC eror error	Copy file ABC to the console, changing occurrences of "eror" to "error."
CHANGE <F1 >F2 `[0-9]*	Copy file F1 to file F2, deleting all leading numeric digits from each line.

Messages

message	explanation
pattern too long	The expanded internal form of the pattern is too large to fit into its reserved memory space.
replacement too long	The expanded internal form of the replacement string is too large to fit in its reserved memory space.

COUNT

```
COUNT [file] [-C!-W!-L]
```

Description

COUNT scans an input file, counting all characters, words, and lines. It then reports its findings to the standard output file. A nonswitch parameter in the command line is taken for a filename that is opened for input. If no such filename is given, input comes from the standard input file, which may be redirected.

If no switch is given in the command line, it reports

```
nnnnn characters
nnnnn words
nnnnn lines
```

where nnnnn is a number between 0 and 65535.

If one of the switches is given, COUNT reports a single number, indicating the number of characters (-C), words (-W), or lines (-L) found. If more than one switch is given, only the first one is used.

The carriage-return and line-feed characters that terminate each line are not included in the character count. To get the total number of bytes in the file, add to the character count two times the line count plus one for the end-of-file byte (if the result is not a multiple of 128).

A word is defined as any contiguous string of printable characters.

Examples:

command	**comment**
COUNT <REPORT	Display on the console the number of characters, words, and lines in the file named REPORT.
COUNT <FILE >WORDS -W	Place the number of words in the file FILE into the file WORDS.

Messages: none

COPY

```
COPY [file]... [.?] [-B] [-NCR] [-NLF] [-T#,#]
```

Description

COPY is a general-purpose file-copying program. It copies standard Small-Tools files as well as files of straight binary data in which the content of the file is totally unrestricted. If you designate more than one input file, all the files are concatenated into a single output file. You may also specify that any "#include ..." statements (in C programs) or ".so ..." formatting commands (in FORMAT text files) be replaced by the contents of the named files.

Files to be copied are listed in the command line in the order they are to be joined. If no filenames are given, the standard input file is used. Output always goes to the standard output file.

If #include and .so files are to be included into the output, then the special .? switch (described below) must be placed in the command line.

It is customary to create filenames consisting of two parts, the name proper and an extension to the name that designates the type of data in the file. Normally these parts are separated by a period. The symbol ? stands for a string of zero or more characters corresponding to the extension used with the files that are to be included in the copy process. If ? is null (an isolated period is given), then all referenced files are included. If ? is one or more characters long, then only the files whose extensions match ? are included in the copy process.

The -B switch designates that a binary copy is to occur; that is, a straight byte-for-byte copy without any attempt to include referenced files and no attempt to stop on end-of-file bytes within the files. Every byte of each input disk file is copied to the output. If input is coming from the console or an I/O port, a control-Z terminates the input. If the .? switch is given for a binary copy, the console displays the message "cannot include files during binary copy" and the run aborts.

In the absence of the -B switch or one of the switches that implies a binary copy operation, standard text files are assumed; in that case, the include function is allowed and copying of an input file terminates when an end-of-file byte is encountered.

The -NCR switch, meaning "no carriage return," indicates that any carriage-return characters occurring in the input files are to be stripped away. This switch implies a binary copy operation.

The -NLF switch, meaning "no line feeds," indicates that any line-feed characters occurring in the input files are to be stripped away. This switch also implies a binary copy operation.

The -T#,# switch may be used to translate all occurrences of a given character in the input files to another character. The first sharp sign stands for the decimal value of the character to be translated; the second one is the value it will become. This switch also implies a binary copy operation. The action of this switch occurs after the -NCR and -NLF switches, so characters translated to carriage returns or line feeds will not be stripped.

You may use these last three switches to convert between standard text files and foreign text files.

Example:

command	comment
COPY ABC DEF >XYZ .	Write into the file XYZ the contents of file ABC followed by DEF, replacing any "#include ..." or ".so ..." lines with the contents of the named files.

Messages

message	explanation
cannot include files during binary copy	The include switch was given with a switch implying a binary copy operation.

CRYPT

    CRYPT key

Description

CRYPT is used to encrypt and decrypt files of any type. Input to CRYPT comes from the standard input file and output goes to the standard output file.

A key, designated "key" in the command format above, is always required. It may be any string of one or more characters (80 maximum). CRYPT combines the key with the input file in a cyclic fashion, using the "exclusive or" function to produce the output file. Processing takes no account of the character set or the end-of-file byte in text files; it proceeds all the way through the file. Thus, you may encrypt any type of file.

Once a file has been encrypted, it is decrypted by processing the encrypted file a second time using the same key used for encryption; that is, two passes on a file using the same key return the file to its original form. You may achieve extra security by using multiple encryption. Processing a file two or more times with different keys of different lengths makes the encrypted file harder to decipher. Decrypting is just a matter of processing the encrypted file again with each key used to encrypt it; the order in which the keys are used is immaterial.

This program is intended for use on disk files; however, it may operate on data from the keyboard or from some I/O device connected to a port on the computer. In such cases processing stops when a control-Z is encountered. The control-Z does not appear in the output. Encrypted data is not printable; it produces strange results on a printer or video screen.

Examples:

command	comment
CRYPT <LIST >CLIST MAY	Encrypt the file LIST with the key MAY into the file CLIST
CRYPT <CLIST MAY	If this command follows the one above, it decrypts the file CLIST, sending the output to the console.

    Messages: none

DETAB

```
DETAB [#]... [+#]
```

Description

DETAB is used to replace tab characters in a standard text file with the proper number of blanks needed to make the file appear correctly on a device that does not handle tab characters.

Input comes from the standard input file, and output goes to the standard output file.

If no parameters are given in the command line, tab stops will be assumed to exist at every eight columns, beginning with column 9. If this default setting is not correct, you may specify a list of numbers in the command line. Each number specifies a column in which a tab stop must exist to make the input print normally on a device that does handle tabs. You may prefix the last number by a plus sign to indicate that tab stops are to be assumed every # columns after the last tab stop. If no unsigned numbers precede +#, the first tab stop is at # plus 1.

Example:

command	comment
DETAB <SOURCE >LST: 5 +3	Copy the file SOURCE (which contains tab characters intended for a typewriter-like device with tab stops at positions 5, 8, 11, and so on) to the device designated by logical device LST:.

Messages

message	explanation
tab stop beyond max line length	Attempt to define a tab stop beyond the end of the maximum size line.

EDIT

```
EDIT [file] [-V]
```

Description

EDIT is the Small-Tools text editor. It is used to create and modify standard text files. If a file is named in the command line, EDIT automatically reads the named file into the editing buffer and displays the first several lines on the console. The editing buffer starts out empty when no file is named. A sharp sign prompts you for a command.

If the **-v** switch is given in the command line, a **v** command is issued before anything else is done; it turns off automatic viewing of the buffer. This is desirable when using EDIT in a submit file.

EDIT obtains commands from the standard input file. It is possible, therefore, to create a file of edit commands, then invoke the editor with standard input redirected to that file. This is handy for standard editing functions, especially when you invoke the editor from a submit file.

When EDIT displays lines from the buffer, it sends the output to the standard output file. You may redirect this output to a file or some device other than the console. No useful reason comes to mind for redirecting standard output, however.

The Editing Buffer

EDIT is an in-memory editor; that is, the entire file being edited must fit into an editing buffer in the main memory of the computer. EDIT activity affects only the in-memory copy of the file; the text residing on the disk is not affected while editing activity is taking place. A write command must be issued to cause the buffer contents to be written to disk, either as a new file or replacing an existing file.

Since the text formatter, copy program, print program, and Small-C compiler support include statements, files too large to fit into memory can be segmented into smaller parts and then treated as single files when formatting, copying, printing, and compiling.

Whenever EDIT changes a line in the buffer, it creates a new version of the line. The original line is deleted logically, but continues to take up space in the buffer. The same is true of lines deleted. For this reason, it is possible to overflow the buffer when making a large number of changes to a file that by itself would fit into the buffer. In practice this seldom happens; however, when it does happen, a write command followed by an enter command causes the buffer to be reorganized, squeezing out dead lines.

Accessing Disk Files

Three commands are provided for transferring text between the buffer and files on disk. They are:

command	description
e [file]	enter a file into the buffer
r [file]	read a file into the buffer
w [file]	write a file from the buffer

As mentioned above, the enter command replaces the contents of the buffer with the contents of a file. The read command differs from the enter command in that it inserts the contents of a file into the buffer at a designated point. The write command, as mentioned above, transfers the contents of the buffer to a file; it leaves the buffer unaffected by the operation. All or part of the buffer may be sent to the file, but in every case the file contains only the text actually written.

When you are performing extensive editing operations, you should periodically issue the write command to save the current state of the buffer on disk. If you do not do this and the computer loses power or the editor is accidentally exited, the contents of the buffer will be lost. If you attempt to exit the editor (Quit command) but forget to write to disk first, the warning "didn't write to disk" will appear on the console and you will be prompted for another command. A second attempt to exit the editor will silently succeed even if you do not write to disk first. If the buffer contains no changes, no warning is given.

The Default Filename

The filename in the enter, read, and write commands is optional. EDIT remembers which file it is working with. If any of these commands is issued without a filename, EDIT assumes the remembered name. This reduces the chance of error in repeatedly naming the same file; it also reduces the number of keystrokes in the editing session.

Whenever an enter command specifies a filename, that name becomes the new default filename. The filename given with a read or write command becomes the new default filename only if none of these three commands has been issued since the start of the program.

The file command **f** [file] may be used either to display or set the default filename. When no name is given, it simply displays the default name. When a name is given, it becomes the new default name.

The Current Line

The *current line* is the line in the buffer that will be the target of the next command if that command is given without any line number(s). Usually the last line affected by a command becomes the current line for future commands. In some cases the first line affected becomes the current line. The description of each command tells how it affects the current line setting.

The Flag Column

The left-most column of the console display is not used for displaying text; it is reserved for the current line flag, an asterisk, and the command-prompt character, a sharp sign. The flag on the current line, keeps you aware of your position within the buffer.

Line Numbers

Most commands operate on a single line or a contiguous group of lines. To designate the target line(s), you may place one or more line numbers immediately before the command if the default line numbers would not be appropriate. When you specify multiple line numbers, separate them by a comma or a semicolon. The use of a semicolon causes the first number to become the current line before the second number is evaluated. If you specify more line numbers than the command requires, the right-most number(s) are used.

A line number always corresponds to the position of a line in the buffer: line 1 is always the first line in the buffer, line 253 is the 253rd line in the buffer. This means that line numbers change as editing takes place. If, for example, line 25 is deleted, then line 26 becomes 25, line 27 becomes 26, and so on. If a line is inserted before line 5, then line 5 becomes line 6, line 6 becomes line 7, and so on. This does not prove difficult to keep up with, however, since you may specify line numbers symbolically by using special characters and search patterns. You seldom specify actual numeric line numbers.

The line command l displays the number of the current line so that it may be used in a subsequent command. You may specify a period (.) or a vertical bar | in place of a line number. The period stands for the current line and the vertical bar stands for the last line in the buffer.

A line number may be expressed as a search pattern delimited with slashes or backslashes. The line number /abc/ is the number of the first line following the current line that contains the pattern abc. The line number \`func()\ is the number of the last line preceding the current line that contains the pattern func() at the beginning of the line.

You may specify line numbers as the sum or difference of line numbers; for example, the expression .+5 specifies the fifth line after the current line, and the expression |-213 specifies the 213th line before the last line. The expression /John Doe/-1 is the number of the line preceding the next line containing the pattern "John Doe." Any number of terms may appear in a line number expression. If the value on the left of the **+** or **-** sign is omitted, it defaults to "**.**". If the value on the right is omitted, it defaults to "**1**". Thus, the following expressions are valid:

.+12-5	is equivalent to	.+7
+5-2-11	is equivalent to	.-8
.+7+	is equivalent to	.+8
++++++++	is equivalent to	.+8
-----	is equivalent to	.-5

The following commands illustrate the use of line numbers:

1,!p	Print every line in the buffer.
1,.d	Delete every line from the beginning of the buffer through the current line.
\.1.\,/.12./p	Print all lines from the previous line containing the string "1." at its beginning through the next line containing "12." at its beginning.
.-2,.+2d	Delete the current line and two lines on either side.
+23	Make the 23rd line below the current line become the new current line.
-----	Make the 5th previous line become the new current line.
/abc/;.-1,.+1d	Find the next line containing "abc", make it the current line, and delete it and one line on each side of it.

Search Patterns

Search Patterns used with commands may be formed using all the facilities described above. When search patterns are used for line numbers, you may use only the delimiters / and \. When they appear in the substitute command or in the global or exclude prefixes, the first character after the command or prefix letter (s, g, or x) is used for the delimiter.

Whenever a search pattern is given, it becomes the new default pattern. The default pattern is referenced by the occurrence of two successive delimiters.

Edit Commands

In the command descriptions that follow, the line numbers in square brackets are the default line numbers. You may override them by supplying different line numbers in their places. If only one line number is given for a command that takes two, the number given is taken for both numbers. If more than the required number of line numbers are given, the right-most numbers are used.

The term *designated line(s)* in the command descriptions refers to the effective line numbers, whether default or explicitly given as numbers, symbols (. and !), search patterns (for example, /`abc/), or expressions composed of these and arithmetic operators (+ or -). The term *designated file* refers to the effective filename whether default or explicitly given.

In the command formats shown below, the square brackets are not part of the commands; they illustrate which parts of the commands are optional. The symbol <text> stands for zero or more lines of text terminated with a period by itself in column one. And the number sign # stands for a decimal integer.

The command letters may be designated in uppercase or lowercase. An optional print command (p) may be appended to the end of any command. This is useful when automatic viewing of the buffer is turned off and you wish to see the effect of a command without issuing a separate print command.

You can abort any iterative command, except Write, by pressing the Escape key. Furthermore, you can terminate the print and zip commands by pressing any key. (For a summary of edit commands, see Table 13-4.)

```
[.+1]          The null command simply sets the current line
               to the line number given.  If no line number is
               given, then the line following the current line
               becomes the new current line.  Thus a simple
               carriage return drops the current line down one
               place — a convenient way to browse.

[.]a           Append <text> after the designated line.
<text>         If the line number is 0, <text> is placed
               before the first line in the buffer.  Every
               character in <text> is taken literally; that is,
               no metacharacters or escape sequences are
               recognized.  Characters may be rubbed out, but
               only in the line currently being entered. (BS
               or DEL deletes the last character, and ^X
               deletes the entire line.) To correct prior
               lines, it is necessary to terminate the Append
               command.  A line consisting of just an
               isolated period terminates <text>, but is not
               a part of <text>.

[.,.]c         Change the designated line(s) to <text>.
<text>         Upon completion, the first line of <text>
               becomes the new current line.  A line
               consisting of just an isolated period
               terminates <text>, but is not a part of <text>.

[.,.]d         Delete designated line(s).
               The line following the last line deleted
               becomes the new current line.  When the last
               line in the buffer is deleted, the last
               remaining line becomes the current line.

e [file]       Enter the designated file into the buffer.
               Anything that might have been in the buffer
```

	before the command was issued is lost. If the buffer contains changes, the warning "didn't write to disk" is given and the command is ignored. A second attempt to enter new text will be successful. The first line of the buffer becomes the new current line.
f [file]	Display or set the default filename. If a filename is given, it becomes the new default filename. In either case, the effective default filename is displayed. This command also displays the number of unused bytes remaining in the edit buffer.
[.]i <text>	Insert <text> before the designated line. The last line of <text> becomes the new current line. Insert differs from Append only in the placement of <text>. A line consisting of just an isolated period terminates <text>, but is not a part of <text>.
[.,.+1]j	Join the designated lines into one line. The joined line becomes the new current line.
l	The current line number is displayed.
[.,.]m#	Move designated line(s) to follow line #. The last line moved becomes the new current line.
[.,.]p[#]	Print the designated line(s) on the console. If only the current line is designated, then the context surrounding the current line is also printed. The context of the line is the # lines above and below it. The default context is 7. Any time # is given, however, it becomes the new default context for future print operations. If the console device is a video screen, it is cleared before the printing commences. The last line printed becomes the new current line. However, if ESC aborts the printing, the current line is backed up by the context value.
q	Quit editing. Control is returned to the operating system. If the buffer contains changes, the warning "didn't write to disk" is given and the command is ignored. A second attempt to quit will be successful.
[.]r [file]	Read the designated file into the buffer. The new text is placed after the designated line. The last line read becomes the new current line. Line number 0 may be given to cause

	text to be inserted before the first line of the buffer.
[.,.]s/pat/rep/[g]	Substitute rep for first or all pat in line(s). If the global flag g appears after the command, all occurrences of the search pattern pat are replaced; otherwise, only the first occurrence in each line is replaced. A circumflex (^) appearing in the replacement string rep represents the entire string matching the search pattern. It may appear any number of times. Thus the command "s/abc/^-^-^/" yields "abc-abc-abc". The escape sequence :n appearing in the replacement string splits the line into separate lines at each such occurrence. The last line changed becomes the current line.
v	View the current line in context automatically. By default, whenever the buffer is altered or the current line is changed, the new current line is printed in its context. This action may be turned off and on by issuing the **v** command. Each v toggles it to the opposite state.
[1,¦]w [file]	Write designated lines to the designated file. If the target file does not exist, a new file is created. If it exists, it is first renamed to a .$$$ extension, then if the operation is successful the .$$$ file is deleted. If, by chance, a .$$$ version of the file already exists, it is retained and the original file is ovewritten directly. Then, after a successful operation, the .$$$ file is deleted. If a write error occurs, the probable cause is insufficient space on the diskette or in its directory. In such cases, an error message is issued, the editor continues to run, and the original file is retained with a .$$$ extension.
[.,¦]z	Zip through the edit buffer. The designated lines are printed on the screen until any key is pressed. This allows quick browsing through the buffer.

Two prefixes may be attached to any of the commands listed above except append, change, insert, and quit; they are:

[1,!]g/pat/command   The global prefix searches the designated
                      lines for lines containing the search pattern
                      pat. Each such line is then made the
                      current line and the command (incicated by the
                      word *command*) is executed. The cefault
                      pattern seen by the command is just the search
                      pattern in the prefix. The current line upon
                      completion is determined by the last iteration
                      of the command.

[1,!]x/pat/command   The exclude prefix operates exactly like the
                      global prefix, except that lines that do not
                      contain the pattern are selected for processing.

The commands used with the global and the exclude prefixes may have their own line numbers as usual; however, no intervening space or punctuation is allowed between the right-most pattern delimiter and the command.

Messages

message	explanation
didn't write to disk	Attempt to "enter" another file or delete the entire buffer before the changes in the buffer have been written to disk.
error	A command was not entered correctly or a line number was entered as a search string and the search failed.
memory overflow	The editing buffer in memcry cannot hold any more lines. This occurs while attempting to enter or read a file that will not fit cr attempting to make too many changes to a file already in memory.
open error	An attempt to open a file specified in an Enter or Read command failed because no such file exists on the diskette in question.
write error	An error occurred while writing into a disk file.

ENTAB

ENTAB [#]... [+#]

Description

ENTAB is used to replace blanks in a standard text file with tab characters. It exactly reverses the effect of DETAB.

Input comes from the standard input file, and output goes to the standard output file.

If no parameters are given in the command line, tab stops are assumed to exist at every eight columns, starting with column 9. If this default setting is not correct, you may specify a list of numbers in the command line. Each number specifies a column in which a tab stop exists. You may prefix the last number by a plus sign to indicate that tab stops occur every # columns after the previous tab stop. If no unsigned numbers precede +#, the first tab stop is at # plus 1.

Examples:

command	comment
ENTAB <ABC >DEF	Copy file ABC to DEF, replacing consecutive spaces with equivalent tabs, assuming tab stops at every 8 positions starting with 9.
ENTAB <XYZ >LST: 5 +3	Copy file XYZ to the LST: device that has tab stops set at positions 5, 8, 11, and so on.

Messages

message	explanation
tab stop beyond 192	Attempt to set a tab stop beyond the last position in the maximum size line.

FIND

```
FIND [~]pattern
```

Description

FIND copies the standard input file to the standard output file. In the process, it scans the text for occurrences of a search pattern. Only lines containing or not containing the search pattern are output; that is, FIND selects from a file just those lines containing a search pattern or just those lines not containing it.

The search pattern is given in the command line and is formed according to the rules described above. Full use of metacharacters and escape sequences is allowed.

If the pattern is prefixed by a tilde symbol (~), then lines not containing the pattern are output, otherwise lines containing the pattern are selected.

Examples:

command	comment
FIND <ABC `[~:s:t]	Display upon the console all lines in the file ABC that begin with a nonblank, nontab character.

SMALL-TOOLS: PROGRAMS FOR TEXT PROCESSING

    FIND <ABC >DEF `^`'   Copy file ABC to DEF, removing all null lines.

Messages

message	explanation
pattern too long	The expanded internal form of the pattern is too large to fit into its reserved memory space.

FONT

```
FONT [device]
```

Description

This program selects optional print fonts for a printer. In its distribution form, it selects from the options available on the Epson FX-80 printer. However, it is a simple program and can be modified easily to work with other printers.

    Without a file (or logical device) name in the command line, it sends its output to the LST: device.

    FONT presents the menu in Table 13-3 to the standard output file (defaults to screen) and waits for a response from the standard input file (defaults to the keyboard).

Table 13-3.
Select Epson FX Options

```
set    clear    mode
 1       2      condensed
 3       4      double strike
 5       6      elite
 7       8      emphasized
 9      10      enlarged
11      12      italics
13      14      pica
15      16      subscript
17      18      superscript
19      20      proportional
select...
```

A valid response is translated into the required sequence of control characters, and the menu is again presented for another selection. A null response (carriage return) exits the program. Provision is made for setting and clearing each option individually.

Example:

command	comment
FONT	Send output to the LST: device.
FONT PUN:	Send output to the PUN: device.

Messages: none

FORMAT

```
FORMAT [mergefile] [-BC#] [-EC#]
[-BP#] [-EP#] [-PO#] [-NP] [-NR]
[-T] [-I] [-U] [-S] [-BS#]
```

Description

FORMAT is the Small-Tools text formatter. It converts text files containing embedded commands into formatted documents ready for printing.

FORMAT obtains its primary input from the standard input file. Input may, therefore, be directed to come from disk files or the keyboard. Output goes to the standard output file, so it may be directed to go to a disk file, the console screen, or a printer.

You may also specify a second input file, the merge file. In that case, a copy of the primary input file is produced for each line in the merge file. You may break each line of the merge file into any number of fields by using a delimiter character (default !) between fields, but not at the ends of the line. You can reference these fields, in the primary file, by placing a number between two occurrences of the delimiter. For example, !3! appearing in the primary file refers to the third field in the current line of the merge file.

When FORMAT finds such a reference, it replaces it by the designated field from the current line of the merge file. The result is a customized copy of the document for each line of the merge file. The most obvious application of the merge feature is mailing-list processing, but other uses are possible.

Since it is often necessary to do just part of a print job, switches are provided to control the starting and stopping of output. The switch -BC12 means to begin on copy 12; -EC25 means to end on copy 25. Copy here refers to complete copies of the primary file, one for each line in the merge file. If these switches are given without a merge file, then the indicated number of copies of the primary file are produced. In such cases the -BC# switch is useless and, since it defaults to the value 1, it may be omitted, causing # in the -EC# switch to be the actual number of copies produced.

The switch -BP2 means to begin on page 2; -EP112 means to end on page 112. Pages here refer to formatted pages within a copy of the primary file. If the switches -BC13 and -BP2 are both given, printing begins with page 2 of copy 13, then continues for all pages of subsequent copies. If the switches -EC24 and -EP1 are both given, printing ends after page 1 of copy 24.

A *page offset* may be specified in the command line. The switch -PO5 tells FORMAT to shift odd-numbered pages five spaces to the right and even-numbered pages five spaces to the left. This provides a wide margin for binding material that will have printing on both sides of the paper.

By default, FORMAT will pause before printing each page of the document. It displays the message "set page # ..." and then waits for a response indicating that the next page is in place and the printer is ready. This gives you an opportunity to load the next sheet of paper. A control-N from the keyboard causes FORMAT to skip to the next page; it again issues the "set page # ..." message before proceeding. Any other response causes FORMAT to commence printing.

The switch -NP tells FORMAT to print with no pauses; that is, after an initial "ready printer . . ." prompt, printing continues without pauses between pages. This option is used with continuous forms.

The -NR switch tells FORMAT to negate the ready prompt. This is useful when FORMAT is used in a SUBMIT file that you wish to run without interruption.

Two modes are provided for controlling the method of handling Underline, Boldface, and Italicize commands. They are Epson (or dot-matrix) mode, and TTY (or dumb printer) mode. In Epson mode (the default mode), control-character sequences cause the printer to underline, boldface, and italicize with a minimum of head movement. Double width printing is also possible. In TTY mode (specified with the -T switch), underlining and boldfacing are done by multistriking; italicizing and double-wide printing are not done at all.

The -I switch causes underline commands to be treated as italic commands.

The -U command causes italic commands to be treated as underline commands.

The -S switch causes FORMAT to show in the output the names of files included with the ".so file" command. This helps identify file boundaries in draft copies of large documents.

The -BS# switch overrides the default number of boldface strikes used in TTY mode. The symbol # is the number of strikes to use.

Commands

Commands instructing FORMAT what to do are embedded in the text being processed. Every line beginning with a period (or other designated character) is taken as a command. Each command consists of two letters immediately following the period. The letters are chosen for mnemonic value and thus are not difficult to remember.

Most commands take optional numeric or character string parameters in the same line. One or more spaces separate the command from its value. You may specify commands in lowercase or uppercase letters.

Instead of a period, the command flag may be changed to another character by giving the command character command .cc ? where ? stands for the new command flag. You may use the command ?cc . later to return to the period for a command flag. Changing the command flag permits you to process text with a leading period in the lines.

Every command that takes a numeric value will accept it as either an absolute value or a relative value. If an unsigned number is given, it is taken for the new value. If a plus or minus sign prefixes the number, however, then it is added to or subtracted from the original value to arrive at the new value.

For example, if a section of text is to be indented four places, after which normal indenting is to be resumed, you may give:

```
.in +4
   .
   .
   .
.in -4
```

This arrangement permits you to make local formatting changes independently of global considerations. You may then place global specifications at the beginning of the file, where you can easily find and change them. For instance, you should not have to search throughout a file to find every occurrence of a command that may need changing when you wish to reprint an existing document with different margin settings.

The Page Layout

Pages produced by FORMAT have the format shown in Figure 13-1.

The dimensions that specify the page layout are specified as number of lines (vertical) and number of columns (horizontal). Each dimension is shown with its corresponding default value in parentheses.

Notice that the top and bottom margins are each five lines high. That is the effective size of the margins; actually, the default sizes for margins 1 and 4 are 1 and 9 respectively. The margins are equalized by setting the paper in the printer such that the first line of print, margin 1, starts about four lines down from the top edge of the paper. This is a natural setting for the top-of-page position of paper in a printer.

When you use continuous forms in the printer, you should usually specify the -NP switch. In that case, FORMAT prints without pausing between pages. The bottom margin skips over the perforations between pages, leaving equal margins at the top and the bottom.

Figure 13-1. Page layout in FORMAT.

```
 _____  .........................
|                           | : margin 1 (5 lines)    :
| xxxxxx header xxxxxxxx    |..........               :
|                           | : margin 2 (2 lines)    :
|                           |..........               :
| xxxxxxxxxxxxxxxxxxxxxx    |                         :
| xxxxxxxxxxxxxxxxxxxxxx    |                         :
| xxxxxxxxxxxxxxxxxxxxxx    |      page length        :
| xxxxxxxx body xxxxxxx     |         (66 lines)      :
| xxxxxxxxxxxxxxxxxxxxxx    |                         :
| xxxxxxxxxxxxxxxxxxxxxx    |                         :
| xxxxxxxxxxxxxxxxxxxxxx    |..........               :
|                           | : margin 3 (2 lines)    :
|                           |..........               :
| xxxxxxx footer xxxxxx     | : margin 4 (5 lines)    :
|_____|.........................:....
       :              :
       :              right margin (column 74)
       :
  left margin (column 11)
```

If you are using cut sheets, you must mount them individually in the printer, and you should not specify the -NP switch. In that case, FORMAT pauses between pages, waiting for each sheet to be loaded. The pause comes immediately after printing the footer. Printing resumes immediately with the header of the next page. Thus, it is up to you to remove the old page and insert the new one exactly where printing should resume.

The following commands permit you to override the default page layout values:

```
.m1 #     margin 1
.m2 #     margin 2
.m3 #     margin 3
.m4 #     margin 4
.pl #     page length
.lm #     left margin
.rm #     right margin
```

You may give these commands at any point in the text and they become effective at that point. Normally, however, you give them at the start of the file and leave them alone thereafter.

Note: If you specify the page length as zero (.pl 0), then the document is considered to be just one page of infinite length. In that case, formatting proceeds as usual, except that there will be no page breaks and no headers or footers. This is useful in formatting text for input to other programs.

Headers and Footers

Header and footer lines are optional. Unless you specifically requested them, they appear as blank lines within the first and fourth margins. Once specified, header and footer lines automatically appear at the proper place on every page. They remain in effect until you redefine them. Footers begin on the current page and headers begin on the following page.

Only one line is used for a header or footer. The header appears as the last line of the first margin, and the footer appears as the first line of the fourth margin. These margins must, therefore, be at least one line in size for the headers and footers to appear.

The .he [text] command is used to define a header consisting of the text, if any, following the command. The .fo [text] command, likewise, defines a footer. If no text is given, a null header or footer (that is, a blank line) is indicated.

FORMAT permits different headers and footers to be defined for odd- and even-numbered pages. Altogether there are six commands:

```
.he [text]     header
.oh [text]     odd-page header
.eh [text]     even-page header
.fo [text]     footer
.of [text]     odd-page footer
.ef [text]     even-page footer
```

Two characters have special meaning within headers and footers. The number sign # stands for the current page number. Whenever it appears in a header or footer, it is replaced by the number of the current page. You may use the slash / to break the text into sections that are equally spaced across the page from the left margin to the right margin. The slashes are replaced by approximately equal numbers of spaces such that the first character of text falls on the left margin and the last character falls on the right margin. Judicious use of slashes can produce centering of text, spreading of text, and one-sided justification.

You may obtain a simple footer consisting of a page number centered between and surrounded by hyphens with the command ".fo /- # -/".

Line Filling and Right-Margin Justifying

Unless told otherwise, FORMAT does not print a line in the body of a page until it has gathered enough words to fill a line; that is, words are gathered into one line until a word is encountered that would extend beyond the right margin. That word is held and becomes the first word of the next line. This action is called *line filling*. You may turn it off by the .nf command, meaning "no filling." You may turn it on again by the .fi command, meaning "fill." If FORMAT encounters contiguous spaces while gathering words, it ignores all but the first. Two blanks are placed after the period that terminates a sentence.

Another action taken automatically by FORMAT is to spread spaces between words in a line so that the last character of the last word falls exactly on the right margin. This action is called right-margin justification. It is turned off by the .nj command, meaning "no justifying." It may be turned on again by the .ju command, meaning "justify."

Sometimes it is important that a certain number of blanks appear at a given position within a line. Line filling and justification should not alter them. To give added control over such circumstances, the tilde (~) is used to represent a "pseudo" space. It is treated like any nonblank character for line filling and justification purposes; however, it is changed to a blank just before it is output.

If the tilde must appear as a tilde, then you may specify another character to take its place as the pseudo-blank character. The command .bc x causes x to become the pseudo-blank, and the command .bc ~ returns the tilde to its original status.

Line Breaks

Under certain conditions, while FORMAT is filling lines, it may print a line that is not yet full. This is called a line break. In such cases, no right-margin justifying takes place; that is, all excess blanks are to the right of the line.

One thing that causes a break is a blank line in the text. When FORMAT encounters a blank line, it prints the current line as is, then prints the blank line. This is an easy way to break text into paragraphs separated by double spacing.

Certain commands force a break to occur; they are:

```
.fi       fill
.nf       no filling
.ju       justify right margin
.nj       no justifying
.br       break
.sp #     space # lines
.bp #     begin page
.in #     indent # places
.lm #     set left margin to #
.ti #     temporary indent of # places
.ce #     center the next # lines
.sq #     squeeze margins # places each
.ne #     need # lines together
```

The last thing that causes a break is a line with one or more leading blanks. Such a line prints with its leading blanks in place; line filling and justification, if in force, are applied to such a line.

Page Breaks

As FORMAT processes text, it keeps track of how many lines have been placed on the current page. When no more lines will fit, margins 3 and 4, possibly including a footer, are printed and a new page is started. If FORMAT is pausing between pages (the default condition), you hear the audible alarm and see the message "set page # ..." where # is the new page number. In this case, the trailing lines of margin 4, following the footer, are not printed. This prevents the bottom edge of the page from flipping up over the print mechanism and possibly interfering with moving parts.

If continuous printing is in effect, FORMAT proceeds uninterrupted with the next page.

Page breaks may be forced at any point in the text by using the .bp # command, meaning begin page. If a number appears with the command, it sets the value of the new page number; otherwise, the new page is numbered one greater than the previous page.

The value of the page numbers is significant in three ways. First, the page number may be printed in headers and footers. Second, the page number determines the direction of page offsets. And last, the page number may determine the point in the document at which printing begins or ends.

Indenting

An indent is a number of spaces added to or taken away from the left margin. The default indent is zero. You may use the .in # command to set the indent value for subsequent lines. You may use the .ti # command to set a temporary indent for the following line only. This is handy for paragraph indention. The default value for # in both commands is zero.

The squeeze command .sq # is a special form of indent, causing FORMAT to indent inward from both margins # places. This is handy for highlighting notes. The default value for # is zero. Squeezed printing continues until FORMAT encounters a .sq or .sq 0. On the left margin, the effect of squeezing is added to the running indent and the temporary indent. A plus sign with # causes the current squeeze value to be increased by #. A minus sign has the opposite effect.

Centering

The command .ce # tells FORMAT to center the next # lines of text. The default value for # is one, so the command .ce centers just the following line. The command .ce 0 means to stop centering lines; it is handy when an indefinite number of lines are to be centered. First give .ce 1000 (or any number larger than needed but no greater than 32767) followed by the text to be centered; end with a .ce 0 command.

Centering is done between the left and right margins the indent value has no effect on centering.

Underlining

Text may be underlined by means of either of two underline commands. The command .ul # instructs FORMAT to underline the next # lines of input text; gaps between words are not underlined. The command .cu # is used for continuous underlining; that is, gaps between words are underlined. Special characters are not normally underlined; the continuous underline, however, does underline parentheses, brackets, braces, colons, and semicolons.

The .ul and .cu commands are mutually exclusive. Whenever one is given, it overrides the other in case the other one was in effect.

As with the centering command, you may specify that an indefinite number of lines be underlined by placing an arbitrarily large value on a .ul # or .cu # command. After the text to be underlined, you may use a .ul 0 or .cu 0 to terminate underlining. Another way to terminate underlining is to issue the .nu command, which means "no underline." Any one of these three commands can terminate either type of underlining.

FORMAT operates in either of two modes as far as underlining (and italicizing and boldfacing) is concerned. In Epson mode (the default) underlining is accomplished by generating the proper sequences of control characters before and after the text to be underlined; the printer (Epson or other dot-matrix) then underlines as it prints. In Teletype (switch -t) mode, underlining is accomplished by preceding each character to be underlined with an underscore, backspace sequence. Depending on the type of print mechanism you have, this mode can be pretty slow and can create a great deal of jerky, back-and-forth head motion.

The Note Command

The command . text causes text to be displayed on the console when the program encounters it. First the audible alarm is sounded, then the word *note:* is displayed, followed by the text in the command. The note line is ignored as far as text formatting is concerned. You may use notes to give the operator special instructions related to the handling of particular documents. For instance, you may place a note at the end of a text file, giving the operator instructions as to what to do next.

Erroneous Commands

Unrecognizable commands are treated as notes. They sound the alarm and appear on the console as notes, but are ignored as far as text formatting is concerned. This signals the operator that something is wrong and shows the questionable line. This happens if text to be formatted has a command flag (usually a period) in the first position of a line.

Operator Prompting

The .pr text command is used to prompt the operator for information to be manually entered at some point in the document. It sounds the alarm, then displays the word *enter:* followed by the text in the command. If the operator is to manually supply the date for a letter, for instance, then the command ".pr date" would be placed at the point in the text file where the date should appear. It must be on a line by itself, however, just like all formatting commands. When this command is encountered, the operator hears the alarm and sees "enter: date" on the console.

At that point the program begins taking lines of text from the keyboard. It is processed as if it were actually in the input file instead of the prompt command. Input is terminated, as with the text editor, by a line containing only a period. In the case illustrated above, only a single line of input would be given. This would be followed by a terminator line. The terminating period is ignored for text formatting purposes.

Formatting commands may be entered manually during a response to a prompt. Also, you may use the delete (DEL or RUB) and backspace (BS) keys to delete the last remaining character in the line currently being entered, and a control-X to delete the entire line being entered.

Text from Alternate Sources

It is often convenient to create and save segments of text that you can call up later for inclusion into various documents as they are being formatted. To do this, use the text editor to enter the text and save it on disk under some descriptive filename. Then place at the appropriate location in the calling document the command ".so file" meaning the named file is the source for text to be processed at this point. FORMAT will copy the entire contents of the named file into the input stream just as though it were in the main file.

This command is analogous to the prompt command except that the text comes from a file rather than from the keyboard.

The ".so file" command is handy for use in preparing legal documents (or whatever) composed largely of standard paragraphs. The text in the named file may contain embedded formatting commands, including the prompt command.

Line Spacing

By default, FORMAT generates single-spaced output. This may be changed by giving the .ls # command to change line spacing to # lines. A value of 2 gives double spacing; that is, one blank line between printed lines.

Occasionally, extra blank lines are desired at selected places in the document. The space command .sp # may be used to obtain them. The command .sp 11 causes a line break followed by 11 blank lines.

Another way to get the same effect is to enter eleven blank lines into the text. This approach is not desirable, however, when more than one blank line is needed, because it is difficult to tell how many blank lines will be generated by looking at the screen. Six blank lines look about like five.

Keeping Text Together

Two methods exist to prevent splitting sections of text between pages. Sometimes, a table or list should be printed intact on a single page. To guarantee enough space, you may issue the need command .ne #, meaning that # lines are needed for the text that immediately follows. If the current page contains enough space, no special action is taken. If, on the other hand, insufficient space remains, FORMAT forces a page break and the following text begins a new page.

The second method concerns avoiding orphan lines at the bottom of pages. The minimum paragraph space command .mp # determines the minimum number of lines that must remain in the body of a page before a new paragraph will be printed. If insufficient space remains, a new page is begun. The default value for this is 2. This value may be changed at any point in the text file.

FORMAT has no automatic means of preventing widow lines at the top of a page. After you have proofed the document, you may insert .ne # commands for this purpose.

Formatting Commands

Formatting commands (Table 13-5) are placed within the text files being processed. Each one resides on a line by itself. You may give commands in uppercase or lowercase letters.

The square brackets appearing in the following command descriptions are not actually a part of the commands; they only indicate that the enclosed field is optional. Number signs (#) stand for decimal numbers between 0 and 32767. Any numeric value may be preceded with a minus or plus sign. The effect of a sign is to cause the number to be taken as a change to an existing value rather than an absolute new value. For example, .lm 5 means to set the left margin to column 5; .lm +5 means to move the left margin to the right five places. The question mark stands for any printable character. The words *text* and *file* are generic terms representing a line of text and a filename, respectively.

The formatting commands follow in alphabetical order:

```
.bc ?      blank character
           Use ? for the new pseudo-blank character.  Occurrences
```

of ? in the text will be treated as nonblanks for line filling and right margin justifying purposes, but will be converted to spaces before being output.

.bf # boldface
Print the next # lines of source text in boldface. The default value for # is 1. The command .bf 0 terminates boldface printing.

.bp [#] begin page
Force a page break. If a number is given, it determines the number of the next page; otherwise, the current page number plus 1 is assumed.

.br break
Force a line break; that is, the line being filled is printed as is, without right margin justification, and a new line is started.

.cc ? command character
Use ? in the future for the character that identifies commands. Following commands must be prefixed by ? rather than the customary period.

.ce [#] center
Force a line break, then cause the next # lines of text to be centered. The default value for # is 1.

.cu [#] continuous underline
Underline the following # lines of text including the blank spaces between words. If # is zero, underlining is terminated. The default for # is 1.

.dw [#] double width
Print the next # lines of source text in double width characters. The default value for # is 1. The command .dw 0 terminates double width printing. Double width printing works only in Epson mode.

.ef [text] even-page footer
Use *text* as a footer on even-numbered pages beginning with the current page. If no text is given, the even-page footer becomes null; that is, a blank line prints.

.eh [text] even-page header
Use *text* as a header on even-numbered pages beginning with the next page. If no text is given, the even-page header becomes null; that is, a blank line is printed.

.fi fill
Force a line break, then start line filling with the following text. Line filling is the default mode of operation, so this command would be used to reinstate line filling after it had been turned off.

.fo [text]   footer
             Use *text* for a footer on all following pages beginning
             with the current page. If no text is given, suppress
             all footers beginning with the current page. Suppressed
             footers appear as blank lines.

.he [text]   header
             Use *text* for a header on all pages after the current
             page. If no text is given, suppress all headers after
             the current page. Suppressed headers appear as blank lines.

.in [#]   indent
             Force a line break, then indent the following text #
             places to the right of the left margin. If # is signed,
             however, the current indent value is to be changed by
             the indicated amount in the indicated direction (minus
             to the left, plus to the right). If the new indent
             value becomes negative, printing begins before the left
             margin. The default value for # is 0.

.it #   italicize
             Print the next # lines of source text in italics. The
             default value for # is 1. The command .it 0
             terminates italicized printing. In TTY mcde, this
             command is ignored (unless the -U switch causes it to
             be interpreted as an underline command).

.ju   justify
             Force a line break, then begin justifying the right
             margin on the following lines. Since the justify mode
             is the default condition, this command would be used to
             reinstate justifying after it had been turned off.

.lm [#]   left margin
             Force a page break, then use # to determine a new value
             for the left margin. The left margin is the column in
             which the first character of a line appears if no
             indenting is effective. The default value for # is 11.

.ls [#]   line spacing
             Use # to determine a new value for line spacing. The
             default value for # is 1.

.m1 [#]   margin 1
             Use # to determine the number of lines in margin 1, the
             top margin. The default value for # is 1. This command
             should precede the .pl # command.

.m2 [#]   margin 2
             Use # to determine the number of lines in margin 2, the
             margin between margin 1 and the body of the page. The
             default value for # is 2. This command should precede
             the .pl # command.

.m3 [#]   margin 3
            Use # to determine the number of lines in margin 3, the
            margin between the body of the page and margin 4. The
            default value for # is 2. This command should precede
            the .pl # command.

.m4 [#]   margin 4
            Use # to determine the number of lines in margin 4, the
            bottom margin. The default value for # is 9. This
            command should precede the .pl # command.

.mc ?   merge character
            Use ? as the field separator within lines of the merge
            file. Unless specified otherwise, the vertical bar is used.

.mp [#]   minimum paragraph space
            Use # to determine the number of lines that must be
            available in the page before beginning a new paragraph.
            If insufficient space remains on the page, force a page
            break before beginning a new paragraph. The default
            value for # is 2.

.ne [#]   need
            Force a line break, then ensure that at least # lines
            are available together. If insufficient space exists on
            the current page, force a page break. The default value
            for # is 0; that is, the command is ignored.

.nf   no filling
            Force a line break, then discontinue filling lines.
            This implies a cessation of right margin justification
            also. If justification is in effect, it will be
            reinstated when line filling is again resumed.

.nj   no justifying
            Force a line break, then discontinue right margin
            justifying. This command has no effect on line filling;
            it simply results in a ragged right margin.

.nu   no underlining
            Terminate underlining of text. If either normal or
            continuous underlining is in effect, it will be
            discontinued.

.of [text] odd-page footer
            Use *text* as a footer on odd-numbered pages beginning
            with the current page. If no text is given, the
            odd-page footer becomes null; a blank line prints for a
            null footer.

.oh [text] odd-page header
            Use *text* as a header on odd-numbered pages beginning
            with the next page. If no text is given, the odd-page

.pl [#]   page length
           Use # to determine the page length. The default value
           for # is 66. The minimum page length is the sum of the
           margins .m1, .m2, .m3, and .m4 plus 1. So these margins
           must be set before issuing this command.

.po [#]   page offset
           Use # to determine a new value for the page offset.
           Printing on odd-numbered pages is shifted right by this
           amount, and printing on even-numbered pages is shifted
           left. You may specify the same function by giving the
           -PO# switch in the command line that invokes format.
           The default value for # is 0.

.pr [text] prompt
           Prompt the operator for input. The audible alarm is
           sounded and the message "enter: text," where the word
           text stands for the text following the command, is
           displayed on the console. Input from the keyboard is
           then processed as though it were in the input stream in
           place of the prompt command. Input from the keyboard is
           terminated by entering a line containing just a period;
           the terminator line is ignored for text formatting purposes.

.rm [#]   right margin
           Use # to determine a new value for the right margin;
           that is, the column where the last character is printed
           when right margin justifying is in effect. The default
           value for # is 74.

.rs [#]   reserve space
           Reserve # lines of white space. If insufficient lines
           exist on the present page, force a page break and then
           skip over the required number of lines. At most one
           page may be reserved.

.so file   source
           Use the named file as the source of text at this point
           in the process. When no more text remains in the
           designated file, continue with the next line.

.sq [#]   squeeze
           Force a line break, then indent inward from both margins
           the number of places indicated by #. The default value
           for # is 0. The command .sq returns to normal
           printing. The command .sq +# adds to the existing squeeze
           value and .sq -# subtracts from it.

.sp [#]   space
           Force a line break, then skip # blank lines. The
           default value for # is 1.

.ti [#]   temporary indent
             Force a line break, then override the running indent
             value with # for only the next printed line. Subsequent
             printed lines will obey the running indent value. A
             plus or minus sign with # causes it to be added to or
             subtracted from the running indent value to obtain the
             temporary indent value. The default value for # is 0;
             that is, the command is ignored.

.ul [#]   underline
             Underline the following # lines of input text; spaces
             between words are not underlined. If # is 0,
             underlining is terminated. The default value for # is 1.

.. [text]   comment
             Two successive command characters identify a comment
             line that is to be ignored by FORMAT. You can
             temporarily deactivate a command by placing an extra
             command character before it.

Messages:

message	explanation
ready printer...	The operator should make sure paper is in the printer and it is ready to accept data from the computer, then press return or enter.
set page #	The operator should load the next page into the printer, make it ready, then press Return or Enter. (Control-N will skip to the next page.)
copy # ready printer	Prepare the printer for copy number #. (Control-N will skip to the next copy.)
page #	Informs the operator which page is being printed, so a restart on the last page printed will be possible.
enter: <description>	The operator should enter data, as described, from the keyboard then terminate input with a line containing only a period in position 1.
note: <line>	The displayed line is either an operator note, an unrecognizable formatting command, or a text line that inadvertently begins with a period (or other command flag).
error: <line>	The displayed line contains a formatting command with a numeric argument that cannot be evaluated.

LIST

             LIST [file] [-C#] [-PL#] [-PW#] [-NB] [-NN] [-NP]

Description

LIST copies an input file to the standard output file. If a file is named in the command line, it is taken for input; otherwise, the standard input file is assumed. It optionally numbers lines, arranges the output in multiple columns per output page, and pauses between pages. The primary intent of LIST is for listing text files on the console screen; however, you may use it directly or in combination with FORMAT or PRINT to produce line-numbered and/or multicolumn listings on the printer.

The -C# switch tells LIST how many columns are to be placed on each output page. The default column count is one.

LIST divides the page width by # to determine the width of each column. If a line of input is too long to fit in a column's width, it wraps around to the next line in the same column. Normally, all lines will be shorter than the column width; if a line is exactly the width of a column, however, a column overflow occurs before the end of the line is detected. This results in a blank line in the column. You may strip out blank lines by specifying the -NB switch, meaning no blanks.

The -PL# switch tells LIST the page length in lines. This is not the physical size of a page, but the number of lines LIST will place on a page. The default page length depends on whether or not the output is redirected to a disk file. If it is, then the length is computed as PTRHIGH-PTRSKIP-PTRHDR (the same as PRINT uses); otherwise, CRTHIGH-1 lines (one less than the length of the video screen) is assumed. These symbols are defined in TOOLS.H and can be changed to suit your requirements.

The -PW# switch tells LIST the page width in character positions. The default value for page width is also determined by whether or not the output is redirected to a disk file. If it is, then PTRWIDE-1 is assumed; otherwise, CRTWIDE-1 is assumed. These symbols are defined in TOOLS.H and can be changed to suit your requirements.

Unless LIST is told otherwise, it numbers input lines. The switch -NN, meaning "no numbers," negates line numbering. Line numbers reside right justified and blank-filled in a four-character field in the beginning of each column. If line numbering is suppressed, the full column width is used for text.

Unless told otherwise, LIST pauses between pages and awaits your response before proceeding. This is intended to give you time to study the contents of the screen before it is scrolled away. If output is to a printer it allows you to load cut sheets individually into the printer. To make LIST continue printing nonstop, specify the -NP switch, meaning "no pauses." In this case, LIST continues automatically from one page to the next without giving any blank lines between pages. The output is still organized into (possibly) multicolumn pages, but there is no break between the pages. When the output is redirected to a disk file, there are never pauses between pages. It is not necessary, in that case, to specify the -NP switch.

The last line of a page is at the bottom of the right-most column, and the first line of the next page is at the top of the left-most column.

If you desire page breaks before printing, then send the output to a temporary disk file and use that as input to PRINT. The default page length matches the PRINT program, so page breaks will fall in exactly the right places.

LIST is especially useful when listing short lines of text such as the one-word lines typically found in a dictionary file. It saves a great deal of paper and makes viewing on the console screen much easier, too.

Examples:

command	comment
LIST <ABC -C3	List on the console the contents of the file ABC in a 3-column format with line numbering and pausing with each screenful.
LIST <ABC >DEF -C8 -PW132 -NP	Copy file ABC into DEF, counting lines and placing them into an 8-column format on pages 132 columns wide. PRINT may then be used to print DEF with page breaks and page headers.

Messages

message	explanation
waiting...	LIST is waiting until the operator responds with Return or Enter before proceeding to list the next page.

MERGE

```
MERGE file [file] [-1|-2|-3|-F]
```

Description

MERGE takes two sorted text files, merges them, and outputs the result.

The input files must be sorted in ascending sequence on the entire line. Comparisons are made on a lexicographical basis; that is, uppercase and lowercase letters have equal value, and special characters compare lower than alphabetics.

Output may consist of the contents of both files, lines unique to the first file, or lines unique to the second file.

The first file named in the command file is known as the *first* file. The next file listed is the *second* file. If a second file is not listed, then the standard input file is assumed in its place. Of course, the standard input may be redirected to come from a disk file; in that case, the redirection specification (second file) may appear anywhere in the command line—even before the first file.

Unless specified otherwise, MERGE outputs the entire merged contents of the two input files. Matching lines in the two files will not be duplicated in the output, however.

If you specify the -1 switch, then the lines in the first file that do not match the second file are output; no lines from the second file survive.

If you specify the -2 switch, then the lines in the second file that do not match the first file are output; no lines from the first file survive.

If you specify the -3 switch, then lines common to both files are output. If multiple occurrences of identical lines exist in both files, then as many occurrences of the line will be output as exist in the file that has the least number of such lines.

The -F switch calls for a formatted output of all lines. The format places lines unique to the first file at the left-most margin. Lines unique to the second file are indented two places. Finally, lines common to both files are indented another two places. Prefixes of 1), 2), and 3) are attached to each of these columns of output to clearly identify the type of line, since it is possible for lines of only one type to be output.

Examples:

command	comment
MERGE ABC DEF -1	Merge files ABC and DEF, showing on the console only those lines in ABC not found in DEF.
MERGE ABC DEF -F >LST:	Merge files ABC and DEF, placing a formatted listing of all lines on logical device LST:.
MERGE ABC DEF >GHI	Merge files ABC and DEF, placing the combined contents of both into the file GHI.

Messages: none

PRINT

```
PRINT [file]... [.?] [-NN] [-NH|-NS] [-LM#] [-BP#] [-EP#]
      [-P] [-NR]
```

Description

PRINT copies one or more text files to the standard output file. If standard output is not redirected away from the console, it is closed and reopened on device LST:. So LST: is the default output for PRINT. It normally numbers the lines, breaks the output into pages of 56 lines each, and puts a heading at the top of each page showing the filename and page number. Default input is from the standard input file, which, as usual, may be redirected. If a list of filenames is given in the command line, they are printed in the order listed with a page break between each file. In this case, the standard input file is not used.

If so directed, PRINT will also copy included text. Inclusion statements for the C language (#include file) and for the Small-Tools text formatter (.so file) will be followed by the contents of the named file. In this case line numbering restarts at 1 for each included file, but continues uninterrupted for the primary file. Include statements may be nested to any desired level—limited only by available memory.

The parameters you may specify with PRINT are:

[file]...   Print the named files instead of standard input.

.[?]   Print included files with an extension of ? where ?, if
            present, is a string of 1 to 3 characters. If ? is
            null, all included files are printed.

-NN   No line numbering.

-NH   No page headings.

-NS   No page skips (and no headings).

-LM#   Left margin of # spaces. The default margin is 0 spaces.

-BP#   Begin printing on page #.

-EP#   End printing on page #.

-P   Pause at the end of each page. The default mode is
            continuous printing.

-NR   No "ready printer..." prompt.

Example:

command	comment
PRINT ABC DEF >PUN:	Print files ABC and DEF on logical device PUN: placing a header on each page and giving a page break between files.
PRINT SORT.C .C	Print SORT.C together with any .C files it includes. Output goes to LST:.

Messages

message	explanation
ready printer...	PRINT is waiting for you to load paper into the printer and make it ready to accept data from the computer.
page #	Tells which page is currently printing so that a restart will be possible.

SORT

SORT [-C#|-F#?] [-D] [-U] [-Tx] [-Q]

Description

SORT reads the standard input file, sorts it line-by-line, and writes the sorted data to the standard output file. It works only with standard text files; binary data may not be sorted. Files of any size are accepted.

If no sort key is specified, the entire line is taken for the sort key; that is, the comparing process starts with the first character of the two lines being compared and proceeds from left to right, comparing corresponding characters until a difference is detected. The line whose mismatched character is lower lexicographically is output first for ascending sorts, and last for descending sorts.

Uppercase letters are considered equal to their lowercase counterparts. Special characters have the same relative position with respect to each other as they have in the ASCII colating sequence, but they all precede the alphabetics; the ASCII DEL character (value 127 decimal) compares higher than any other character, however.

If one line is longer than the other and no difference is found by the time the end of the shorter line is reached, then the shorter line is considered "less than" the longer line.

The default sort sequence is ascending. However, if the descending switch -D appears in the command line, the sequence is reversed.

If only part of a line is to be used for comparison purposes, one of two switches may be used to indicate where the sort key is to be found. The column switch -C# informs SORT that the sort key begins in column # and continues to the end of the line. If # is larger than the number of characters in a line, then the sort key is considered to be null and such lines sort first in the ascending sequence.

The field switch -F#? tells SORT that the #th field in a line is to be used for the sort key. A field may have varying lengths in different lines and may start in different columns in different lines. Fields are defined by the presence of delimiter characters. SORT knows what the delimiter character is by looking at the first character in the switch following the field number. The first field is everything in a line up to, but not including, the first delimiter. The second field is everything between the first and second delimiters. The end of the line is an implied delimiter for the last field.

When two lines are being compared, the sort key fields will generally occur in different positions and have different lengths. The method of comparison is the same as for whole lines. If one field is shorter than the other and the two fields match up to the delimiter of the shorter field, then the shorter field is considered lower in the sorting sequence. If two delimiter characters appear back-to-back, then they delimit the null field between; that is, the zero-length field between counts as a field. If it is used as a sort key, it will be considered "less than" any field of nonzero length.

A special "white space" delimiter is assumed in cases where the delimiter character is not given in the switch; that is, ? is omitted. The white space delimiter consists of all nonprinting characters falling between fields of printable characters. Think of it as a "fat" delimiter. The white space delimiter, in a text file, separates words. Thus the switch -F5 tells SORT to use the fifth word of each line of a file as its sort key.

Since the output of SORT brings together identical lines (when no sort key is specified), SORT is a natural place to weed out unwanted duplicate lines. The unique switch -U instructs SORT to do just that. When this switch is specified, only unique lines are output. The matching process for uniqueness always considers the entire line, even though a sort key may have specified.

Since files larger than memory may be sorted, it is often necessary for SORT to use temporary work files on disk to hold parts of the input file that have been sorted while it proceeds to sort the remainder of its input. To meet this requirement, SORT automatically creates as many temporary files as it needs. When it reaches the end of the input, it merges the temporary files to write the final output. The temporary files are then deleted. The names of the work files are SORT01.$$$, SORT02.$$$, SORT03.$$$, and so on. If you interrupt a sort operation, these files may be left on disk; you should delete them when you find them.

Unless specified otherwise, temporary files are created on the default drive. The temporary switch -Tx (where x stands for a drive designator A-G) specifies a particular drive for temporary files.

SORT normally uses the Shell Sort algorithm for arranging lines in memory. A second algorithm, the Quick Sort, is also available. The quick switch -Q invokes the Quick Sort algorithm. The advantage of Quick Sort is faster sorting, but it does have some drawbacks. When the input is already in sequence, Quick Sort becomes much slower than the Shell Sort algorithm, and uses up more memory, sometimes causing a memory allocation error. When this happens, the console displays "M" and the run aborts.

Since most of the time in a sort run is spent in the input and output phases, the improved speed of the Quick Sort algorithm is no great advantage; however, it has been kept as an option for the future when it might be used on systems with large amounts of memory and/or fast hard disks.

Examples:

command
SORT <ABC >DEF -F5 |

comment
Sort file ABC on the 5th field separated by the character |, placing the output into the file DEF.

SORT <ABC -U

Sort the file ABC on whole lines, displaying only unique lines on the console.

Messages

message
file too large

explanation
The input file is too large to sort since it would require more than 99 temporary files (no problem with floppy disks).

TRANS

```
TRANS [~]from [to]
```

Description

TRANS copies the standard input file to the standard output, transliterating selected characters to new values. The *from* parameter is a list of the characters to be changed. No spaces may appear between the characters in the list. The parameter *to* is a list of the new values to be assumed by the characters designated in the *from* list. Occurrences of the first *from* character are changed to the first *to* character. Occurrences of the second *from* character are changed to the second *to* character, and so on.

Thus, the command "TRANS <FILE1 >FILE2 abc ABC" would copy FILE1 to FILE2, capitalizing the lowercase letters a, b, and c.

Note: Patches to the CCP and the SUBMIT utility are required to make them accept lowercase letters. They are documented on the distribution diskette.

To make it easier to specify all or part of the alphabet in a *from* or *to* list, just the first and last letter in a list of letters may be given and connected by a hyphen. This abbreviated notation represents all of the letters between. Thus, the command "TRANS <FILE1 >FILE2 a-z A-Z" would copy FILE1 to FILE2, transliterating all lowercase letters to uppercase. And the command "TRANS a-zA-Z A-Za-z <FILE1 >FILE2" would change all lowercase letters to uppercase and vice versa as it copies from FILE1 to FILE2. The command "TRANS <FILE1 a-c d-f >FILE2" would change a to d, b to e, and c to f as it copies FILE1 to FILE2.

Escape sequences may be used freely in the *from* and *to* lists. Since both of these lists would be terminated a space or tab character, these values must be specified in the lists as :s and :t, respectively. A colon must be given as two consecutive colons.

If the *to* list is longer than the *from* list, the unmatched characters at the end of the *to* list are ignored.

On the other hand, if the *to* list is shorter than the *from* list, TRANS operates in collapse mode. The *to* list is automatically extended to the length of the *from* list by repeating the last character of the *to* list. Then TRANS collapses all consecutive occurrences of that character in the output to a single occurrence. Suppose, for instance, you wanted to place every word in a document on a line by itself. The command "TRANS <DOC1 >DOC2 :s:t :n" would do the job. Spaces and tabs would both be changed to new-line characters, then consecutive runs of new lines would be collapsed to single occurrences of the new-line character. This prevents having blank lines in the output.

To repeat, TRANS collapses occurrences of the last character of the *to* list when the *to* list is shorter than the *from* list. Since this may be true while the *to* list contains more than one character, it is possible to translate some characters while translating and collapsing others.

In the special case where the *to* list is omitted altogether, characters matching the *from* list are deleted in the output.

Sometimes you may want to delete or collapse all but a selected set of characters. The tilde character (~), meaning not, may be prefixed to the *from* list to achieve this effect. The *from* list then becomes all but the characters listed.

Since an isolated hyphen following the program name in the command line is taken for a null switch (meaning that the usage message is to be displayed), to eliminate hyphens from a file, you must escape the hyphen in the command line.

Examples:

command	**comment**
TRANS <ABC >DEF ~[a-z][A-Z] :n	Copy file ABC to DEF, collapsing all nonalphabetic characters into newline characters (that is, eliminating everything but words and placing them one to a line).
TRANS <ABC ~:[:]{}()	Display on the console only the brackets, braces, and parentheses in the file ABC.

Messages

message	**explanation**
from-list too large	The internal expanded form of the *from* list is too large to fit into its reserved memory space.
to-list too large	The internal expanded form of the *to* list is too large to fit into its reserved memory space.

Installation

All the programs include the files STDIO.H and TOOLS.H at compile time. STDIO.H is supplied with the Small-C compiler and should be used without change by every Small-C program. TOOLS.H, however, is common only to the Small-Tools programs and may be changed to suit your particular requirements. It defines (1) the maximum length of a text line, (2) the character sequence that clears your CRT screen, (3) the sizes of your CRT screen and printer page, and (4) which characters serve as metacharacters. Make any needed changes to this file before starting to compile the programs. Your keyboard layout and the type of word processing you do will greatly affect the ease of use of the metacharacters. Give a lot of thought before changing them, and annotate the documentation according to your changes.

The source code for each program is in a file bearing the name of the program and having a .C extension. EDIT is broken into two parts: EDIT.C and EDIT2.C (which is included into EDIT.C at compile time). FORMAT is broken into three parts: FORMAT.C, FORMAT2.C, and FORMAT3.C. The latter two are included into FORMAT.C at compile time. The remaining .C files are common functions that are included in the programs. All the include statements in the programs assume that the included files are on the default drive. If you operate differently, then change the include statements in the programs before starting to compile them.

FONT is written for use with the Epson FX-80 printer. You should study its source code and modify it to work with your own printer.

Several of the programs take command-line arguments that are text patterns. Unfortunately, the standard CP/M command processor (CCP) forces the entire command line to uppercase, thus defeating your attempts to specify lowercase letters. Furthermore, SUBMIT.COM does the same thing. These deficiencies are easily corrected, however, with the following patches.

CCP patch to allow lowercase letters: using SYSGEN and DDT, get a copy of CP/M in memory and look for:

```
0130    CP    61
0132    RC
0133    CPI   7B
0135    RNC
0136    ANI   5F    <---
0138    RET
```

The indicated instruction should be at offset 136H within the CCP. Change the 5F at 137H to FF and rewrite CP/M back onto the system tracks.

SUBMIT.COM patch to allow lowercase letters: execute DDT on SUBMIT.COM. Look for the code:

```
0362   LDA   0675
0365   SUI   61
0367   CPI   1A
0369   JNC   0374
036C   LDA   0675
036F   ANI   5F    <---
0371   STA   0675
0374   LDA   0675
0377   RET
```

Change the 5F to FF, exit DDT and "SAVE 5 SUBMIT.COM".

These patches will permit you to fully utilize the features of the Small-Tools programs; however, you can also create filenames with lowercase names. Small-C programs always force filenames to uppercase, but PIP expects the CCP to do this. Sometimes PIP has trouble with lowercase filenames. For that reason, and because drive indicators and built-in commands must be uppercase, it is best to lock your terminal in uppercase except when entering a text pattern or working with the text editor. Switches passed to the Small-Tools programs may be uppercase or lowercase.

Availability

The Small-Tools programs are copyrighted; however, they are available to the general public for use without formal restrictions. Take them, use them, copy them, modify them, and give them away as you please. However, be sure to preserve the copyright notices. I am distributing the Small-Tools package under the user-supported concept, so if you obtain a "free" copy and find it useful, send a registration form and $20 to the author. You must obtain written permission to sell Small-Tools for more than your actual cost for media, packaging, and postage.

Table 13-4.
Reference List of Editing Commands

[.+1]	null command (implied print)

[.]a
    \<text>
    .
	append \<text> after line

[.,.]c
    \<text>
    .
	change line(s) to \<text>

[.,.]d	delete line(s)
e [file]	enter named or default file into buffer
f [file]	display or set default file name

[.]i
    \<text>
    .
	insert \<text> before line

[.,.+1]j	join lines into one line
l	display current line number
[.,.] m#	move line(s) to follow line #
[.,.]p[#]	print line(s) and set context to # lines
[.]r [file]	read named/default file into buffer after line
[.,.]s/pat/rep/[g]	substitute rep for 1st or all pat in line(s)
q	quit editing
v	turn automatic viewing off or on
[1,l]w [file]	write line(s) into named or default file
[.,l]z	zip through buffer until any key pressed

Command Prefixes

[1,¦]g/pat/	global search of lines containing pattern
[1,¦]x/pat/	global search of lines not containing pattern

Table 13-5.
Reference List of Formatting Commands

Command	Description
.bc ?	blank character (pseudo-blank)
.bf [1]	boldface
.bp [#+1]	begin page
.br	break
.ce [1]	center
.cc ?	command character
.cu [1]	continuous underline
.dw [1]	double wide characters
.ef [text]	even-page footer
.eh [text]	even-page header
.fi	fill
.fo [text]	footer
.he [text]	header
.in [0]	indent
.it [1]	italicize
.ju	justify right margin
.lm [11]	left margin
.ls [1]	line spacing
.m1 [1]	margin 1 (header in last line)
.m2 [2]	margin 2 (between m1 and body)
.m3 [2]	margin 3 (between body and m4)
.m4 [9]	margin 4 (footer in first line)
.mc ?	merge character (merge-file field delimiter)
.mp [2]	minimum paragraph space
.ne [0]	need space on one page
.nf	no filling
.nj	no justifying
.nu	no underline
.of [text]	odd-page footer
.oh [text]	odd-page header
.pl [66]	page length
.po [0]	page offset
.pr [text]	prompt
.rm [74]	right margin
.rs [0]	reserve space
.so file	source file for text
.sp [1]	space
.sq [0]	squeeze
.ti [0]	temporary indent
.ul [1]	underline (discontinuous)

LISTING 13-1

```c
/*
** change.c -- change occurrences of "from" to "to"
**
** Copyright 1982 J. E. Hendrix.  All rights reserved.
*/
#include <stdio.h>
#include "tools.h"
#define NOCCARGC
#define MAXARG 49
#define MAXLIN1 (MAXLINE+1)
char lin[MAXLIN1], new[MAXLIN1], pat[MAXPAT], sub[MAXPAT];
char arg[MAXARG];
int i, k, lastn, n;
main(argc, argv) int argc, *argv; {
  if((getarg(1, arg, MAXARG, argc, argv)==EOF)
   |((arg[0]=='-')&(arg[1]==0)))
    error("usage: CHANGE pattern [replacement]\n");
  if(makpat(arg, 0, NULL, pat)==ERR)
    error("pattern too long\n");
  if(getarg(2, arg, MAXARG, argc, argv)==EOF)
    arg[0]=NULL;
  if(maksub(arg, 0, NULL, sub)==ERR)
    error("replacement too long\n");
  auxbuf(stdin, 4096);   /** alloc aux buffer to stdin **/
  while(fgets(lin, MAXLIN1, stdin)!=NULL) {
    poll(YES);
    lastn = -1;
    i=0;   k=0;
    trim(lin);
    while(YES) {
      n=amatch(lin, i, pat);
      if((n>=0)&(lastn!=n)) {   /** replace matched text **/
        catsub(lin, i, n, sub, new, &k, MAXLIN1);
        lastn=n;
        }
      if(lin[i]==NULL) break;
      if((n==-1)|(n==i)) {      /** no match or null match **/
        addset(lin[i], new, &k, MAXLIN1);
        ++i;
        }
      else i=n;                 /** skip matched text **/
      }
    if(addset(NULL, new, &k, MAXLIN1)==NO) {
      k=MAXLIN1-1;
      addset(NULL, new, &k, MAXLIN1);
      sout("\7line truncated: ", stderr);
      lout(new, stderr);
```

```
      }
    lout(new, stdout);
    }
  fclose(stdout);
  }

#include "pat.c"
#include "maksub.c"
#include "catsub.c"
#include "index.c"
#include "error.c"
#include "out.c"
#include "trim.c"
```

LISTING 13-2

```
/*
** copy.c -- copy named files to standard output
**
** Copyright 1982 J. E. Hendrix.  All rights reserved.
*/
#include <stdio.h>
#include "tools.h"
#define NOCCARGC
#define MAXARG 12
int fin, i, j;
int status;
int binary, striplf, stripcr, from, to;
char name[MAXFN], inclext[MAXFN];
main(argc, argv) int argc, *argv; {
  auxbuf(stdout, 4096);
  doargs(argc, argv);
  if((binary==YES)&(inclext[0]!=NULL)) {
    fputs("cannot include files during binary copy", stderr);
    abort(7);
    }
  fin=99;
  i=0;
  while(getarg(++i, name, MAXFN, argc, argv)!=EOF) {
    if((name[0]=='-')|(name[0]==EXTMARK)) continue;
    if((fin=fopen(name, "r"))==NULL) cant(name);
    if(binary) bcopy(fin, stdout);
    else       fcopy(fin, stdout);     fclose(fin);
    }
  if(fin==99) {
    if(binary) bcopy(stdin, stdout);
    else       fcopy(stdin, stdout);
    }
```

```
    fclose(stdout);
  }

doargs(argc, argv) int argc, *argv; {
  int len;
  char arg[MAXARG], error;
  inclext[0]=from=to=NULL;
  binary=striplf=stripcr=error=NO;
  i=0;
  while(getarg(++i, arg, MAXARG, argc, argv)!=EOF) {
    if(arg[0]==EXTMARK) {
      j=0;
      while(inclext[j]=arg[j]) ++j;
      continue;
      }
    if(arg[0]!='-') continue;
    if(arg[2]==NULL) {
      if(same(arg[1], 'b')) binary=YES;
      else error=YES;
      }
    else if(arg[4]==NULL) {
      if(same(arg[1], 'n')) {
        if(same(arg[2], 'c') & same(arg[3], 'r'))
          stripcr=binary=YES;
        else if(same(arg[2], 'l') & same(arg[3], 'f'))
          striplf=binary=YES;
        else error=YES;
        }
      else error=YES;
      }
    else if(same(arg[1], 't')) {
      binary=YES;
      len=utoi(arg+2, &from);
      if((len<1)|(arg[len+2]!=',')) error=YES;
      else {
        j=len+3;
        len=utoi(arg+j, &to);
        if((len<1)|(arg[len+j]!=NULL)) error=YES;
        }
      }
    else error=YES;
    if(error) {
      fputs("usage: COPY [file]... [.?] [-B] [-NCR] [-NLF] [-T#,#]\n", stderr);
      abort(7);
      }
    }
  }

bcopy(in, out) int in, out; {
```

```
  char c[1];
  while(YES) {
    status=read(in, c, 1);
    if(status==0) break;
    if(isatty(in)&(c[0]==4)) break;
    if(status < 1) {
      fputs("input error\n", stderr);
      fclose(out);
      abort(7);
      }
    if((c[0]==CR)&(stripcr)) continue;
    if((c[0]==LF)&(striplf)) continue;
    if((from!=to)&((c[0]&255)==from)) c[0]=to;
    status=write(out, c, 1);
    if(status < 1) {
      fputs("output error\n", stderr);
      fclose(out);
      abort(7);
      }
    poll(YES);
    }
  }

fcopy(in, out) int in, out; {
  int i, loc, in2;
  char buf[MAXLINE+1], str[MAXLINE+1];
  while(fgets(buf, MAXLINE+1, in)!=NULL) {
    poll(YES);
    if(inclext[0]==NULL) {
      sout(buf, out);
      continue;
      }
    loc=0;
    getwrd(buf, &loc, str);
    if((lexcmp(str, "#include")!=0) &&
       (lexcmp(str, ".so")!=0)) {
      sout(buf, out);
      continue;
      }
    getwrd(buf, &loc, str);
    strip(str);
    i=0;
    while((str[i]!=EXTMARK) && str[i]) ++i;
    if(inclext[1] && lexcmp(str+i, inclext)) {
      sout(buf, out);
      continue;
      }
    if((in2=fopen(str, "r"))==NULL) cant(str);
    copy(in2, out);
```

```
      fclose(in2);
      }
  }

#include "out.c"
#include "cant.c"
#include "same.c"
#include "strip.c"
#include "getwrd.c"
```

LISTING 13-3

```
  /*
  ** count.c -- count characters, words, and/or lines
  **
  ** Copyright 1982 J. E. Hendrix.  All rights reserved.
  */
  #include <stdio.h>
  #include "tools.h"
  #define NOCCARGC
  char strc[6], strw[6], strl[6];
  main(argc, argv) int argc, *argv; {
    char arg[MAXFN], *nc, *nl, *nw;
    int c, f, i, fd, inword;
    fd=stdin;
    i=f=0;
    while(getarg(++i, arg, MAXFN, argc, argv) != EOF) {
      if(arg[0] != '-') {
        if((fd = fopen(arg, "r")) == 0) cant(arg);
        continue;
        }
      switch(f = tolower(arg[1])) {
        case 'c': case 'w': case 'l': continue;
        default:
          fputs("usage: COUNT [file] [-C|-W|-L]\n", stderr);
          abort(7);
        }
      }
    nc=nl=nw=0;
    inword=NO;
    while((c=fgetc(fd))!=EOF) {
      poll(YES);
      if(c=='\n') {
        ++nl;
        }
      else ++nc;
      if(isspace(c)) inword=NO;
      else if(inword==NO) {
```

```
        inword=YES;
        ++nw;
        }
      }
    itou(nc, strc, 6);
    itou(nw, strw, 6);
    itou(nl, strl, 6);
    switch(f) {
      case 'c': lout(strc, stdout); break;
      case 'w': lout(strw, stdout); break;
      case 'l': lout(strl, stdout); break;
      default:
        sout(strc, stdout); lout(" characters", stdout);
        sout(strw, stdout); lout(" words", stdout);
        sout(strl, stdout); lout(" lines", stdout);
      }
    fclose(stdout);
    }
#include "cant.c"
#include "out.c"
```

LISTING 13-4

```
/*
** crypt.c -- encrypt or decrypt ASCII or binary files
**
** Copyright 1982 J. E. Hendrix.  All rights reserved.
*/
#include <stdio.h>
#define NOCCARGC
#define MAXKEY 81
#define CTLZ   26
main(argc, argv) int argc, *argv; {
  char c, key[MAXKEY];
  int i, keylen;
  auxbuf(stdin, 4096);
  keylen=getarg(1, key, MAXKEY, argc, argv);
  if((keylen==EOF)|(key[0]=='-')) {
    fputs("usage: CRYPT key\n", stderr);
    abort(7);
    }
  i=1;
  while(read(stdin, &c, 1) > 0) {
    poll(YES);
    if(isatty(stdin) && (c==CTLZ)) break;
    c=c^key[i-1];
    if(write(stdout, &c, 1) !=1 ) {
      fputs("output error\n", stderr);
```

```
      abort(7);
      }
    i=(i%keylen)+1;
    }
  }
```

LISTING 13-5

```
/*
** detab.c -- convert tabs to equivalent blanks
**
** Copyright 1982 J. E. Hendrix.  All rights reserved.
*/
#include <stdio.h>
#include "tools.h"
#define NOCCARGC
#define MAXLIN1 (MAXLINE+1)
main(argc,argv) int argc, *argv; {
  char c, tabs[MAXLIN1];
  int col, i;
  auxbuf(stdin, 4096);
  if(settab(tabs, argc, argv)==ERR) {
    fputs("usage: DETAB [#]... [+#]\n", stderr);
    abort(7);
    }
  col=1;
  while((c=getchar())!=EOF) {
    poll(YES);
    if(c=='\t')
      while(YES) {
        cout(' ', stdout);
        ++col;
        if(tabpos(col, tabs)==YES) break;
        }
    else if(c=='\n') {
      cout('\n', stdout);
      col=1;
      }
    else {
      cout(c, stdout);
      ++col;
      }
    }
  fclose(stdout);
  }
#include "settab.c"
#include "tabpos.c"
#include "out.c"
```

LISTING 13-6

```c
/*
** edit.c -- edit text
**
** Copyright 1982 J. E. Hendrix.  All rights reserved.
*/
#include <stdio.h>
#include "tools.h"
#define NOCCARGC
#define OK 1
#define RESERVE 600
#define PREV 0
#define NEXT 2
#define MARK 4
#define TEXT 5
#define INTEGER 2
#define LONG 4
#define LINE0 0
#define NOSTATUS 0
#define CURLINE '.'
#define LASTLINE '!'
#define SCAN '/'
#define BACKSCAN '\\'
#define FORWARD 1
#define BACKWARD 0
#define PERIOD '.'
#define COMMA ','
#define SEMICOL ';'
#define PLUS '+'
#define MINUS '-'
#define BLANK ' '
#define TAB '\t'
#define ESC 27
#define PROMPT '#'
#define CLFLAG '*'

#define PRINT 'p'
#define LINE 'l'
#define GLOBAL 'g'
#define EXCLUDE 'x'
#define APPEND 'a'
#define CHANGE 'c'
#define DELETE 'd'
#define INSERT 'i'
#define JOIN 'j'
#define MOVE 'm'
#define SUBSTITUTE 's'
#define ENTER 'e'
```

```
#define FILE 'f'
#define READ 'r'
#define WRITE 'w'
#define QUIT 'q'
#define VIEW 'v'
#define ZIP 'z'

int
  line1,   /* first line number */
  line2,   /* second line number */
  nlines,  /* number of line numbers given */
  curln,   /* current line (value of dot) */
  lastln;  /* last line (value of $) */

char *buf;    /* buffer for pointers and text */
/*
** buf[k+0] PREV     (2 bytes)   previous line
** buf[k+2] NEXT     (2 bytes)   next line
** buf[k+4] MARK     (1 byte)    mark for global commands
** buf[k+5] TEXT
*/
int  lastbf;  /* last element used in buf */
char *txt,    /* text line for matching and output */
     *savfil, /* remembered file name */
     *file;
int
  scr,        /* scratch file id */
  scrend[2];  /* end of info on scratch file */
char *lin, *pat, *sub, updtflag, nbrstr[7];
int cursav, i, status, maxbuf, context, view;

main(argc, argv) int argc, *argv; {
  if(isatty(stdin)) view=1; else view=0;
  txt=malloc(MAXLINE);
  lin=malloc(MAXLINE);
  pat=malloc(MAXPAT);
  sub=malloc(MAXPAT);
  file=malloc(MAXFN);
  savfil=malloc(MAXFN);
  maxbuf=avail(YES)-RESERVE;
  if(maxbuf < 0) maxbuf=32767;
  buf=malloc(maxbuf);
  setbuf();
  updtflag=NO;
  pat[0]=savfil[0]=nbrstr[6]=NULL;
  context=7;
  i=0;
  while(getarg(++i, txt, MAXFN, argc, argv)!=EOF) {
    if(txt[0]=='-') {
```

```
          if(same(txt[1], 'v')&(txt[2]==NULL)) view = 1 - view;
          else {
            fputs("usage: EDIT [file] [-V]\n", stderr);
            abort(7);
            }
          }
        else scopy(txt, 0, savfil, 0);
        }
      if(*savfil) {
        if(enter(savfil)==ERR) {
          fputs("error\n", stderr);
          }
        }
      if(isatty(stdin))
        fputc(PROMPT, stderr);
      while(fgets(lin, MAXLINE, stdin)!=NULL) {
        poll(YES);
        trim(lin);
        i=0;
        cursav=curln;
        if(getlst()==OK) {
          if(ckglob()==OK)
            status=doglob();
          else if(status!= ERR)
            status=docmd(NO);
          /* else error, do nothing */
          }
        if(status==ERR) {
          fputs("\7error\n", stderr);
          curln=cursav;
          }
        else if(status==EOF) break;
        /* else OK, then loop */
        if(isatty(stdin)) fputc(PROMPT, stderr);
        }
      }

/*
** docmd -- handle all commands except globals
*/
docmd(glob) int glob; {
  int gflag, line3, pflag;
  pflag=NO;
  status=ERR;
  switch(tolower(lin[i])) {
    case APPEND:
      if(ckp(lin, i+1, &pflag)==OK)
        status=append(line2, glob);
      break;
```

```
case CHANGE:
  if(ckp(lin, i+1, &pflag)==OK) {
    if(defalt(curln, curln)==OK) {
      if((status=append(line2, glob))!=ERR) {
        kill(line1, line2);
        ++curln;
        }
      }
    }
  break;
case DELETE:
  if(ckp(lin, i+1, &pflag)==OK) {
    if(defalt(curln, curln)==OK) {
      kill(line1, line2);
      if(curln < lastln) curln=nextln(curln);
      }
    }
  break;
case INSERT:
  if(ckp(lin, i+1, &pflag)==OK)
    status=append(prevln(line2), glob);
  break;
case LINE:
  if(lin[i+1]==NULL) {
    itou(curln, nbrstr, 6);
    puts(nbrstr);
    status=OK;
    }
  break;
case JOIN:
  if(ckp(lin, i+1, &pflag)==OK) {
    if(defalt(curln, curln+1)==OK) {
      if((status=join(line1, line2))==OK) {
        curln=line2;
        if((status=inject(txt))==OK)
          kill(line1, line2);
          ++curln;
        }
      }
    }
  break;
case MOVE:
  ++i;
  if(getone(&line3)==EOF) status=ERR;
  if(status==OK) {
    if(ckp(lin, i, &pflag)==OK) {
      if(defalt(curln, curln)==OK) status=move(line3);
      }
    }
```

```
      break;
case SUBSTITUTE:
  ++i;
  if(optpat()==OK) {
    if(getrhs(lin, &i, sub, &gflag)==OK) {
      if(ckp(lin, i+1, &pflag)==OK) {
        if(defalt(curln, curln)==OK)
          status=subst(sub, gflag);
      }
    }
  }
  break;
case ENTER:
  if(chkupdt()==ERR) status=OK;
  else if(nlines==0) {
    if(getfn(lin, i, file, MAXFN)==OK) {
      scopy(file, 0, savfil, 0);
      clrbuf();
      setbuf();
      status=enter(file);
    }
  }
  break;
case FILE:
  if(nlines==0) {
    if(getfn(lin, i, file, MAXFN)==OK) {
      scopy(file, 0, savfil, 0);
      puts(savfil);
    }
    itou(maxbuf-lastbf, nbrstr, 6);
    puts(nbrstr);
    status=OK;
  }
  break;
case READ:
  if(getfn(lin, i, file, MAXFN)==OK)
    status=doread(line2, file);
  pflag=view;
  break;
case WRITE:
  if(getfn(lin, i, file, MAXFN)==OK) {
    if(defalt(1, lastln)==OK)
      status=dowrit(line1, line2, file);
  }
  break;
case ZIP:
  if(defalt(curln, lastln)==OK)
    status=doprnt(line1, line2, glob);
  break;
```

```
      case PRINT:
        if(defalt(curln, curln)==OK)
          status=doprnt(line1, line2, glob);
        break;
      case NULL:
        if((nlines==0)&(glob==NO)) line2=nextln(curln);
        if(view) status=doprnt(line2, line2, glob);
        else {
          curln=line2;
          status=OK;
          }
        break;
      case QUIT:
        if((lin[i+1]==NULL)&(nlines==0)&(glob==NO)) {
          if(chkupdt()==ERR) status=OK;
          else status=EOF;
          }
        break;
      case VIEW:
        view=1-view;
        status=OK;
      }
    /* else status is ERR */
    if(curln < 1) curln = nextln(0);
    if((status==OK)&(pflag==YES))
      status=doprnt(curln, curln, glob);
    return status;
    }

/*
** chkupdt -- warn if update not written to disk
*/
chkupdt() {
  if(updtflag) {
    fputs("didn't write to disk!\n", stderr);
    updtflag=NO;
    return ERR;
    }
  return OK;
  }

/*
** ctoi -- convert string at in[*i] to integer, bump *i
*/
ctoi(in, i) char in[]; int *i; {
  int dd, num;
  char *digits;
  digits="0123456789";
  while((in[*i]==BLANK)|(in[*i]==TAB)) *i = *i + 1;
```

```
    num=0;
    while(in[*i]!=NULL) {
      dd=index(digits, in[*i]);
      if(dd < 0) break;
      num = 10*num + dd;
      *i = *i + 1;
      }
    return num;
    }

/*
** skipbl -- skip blanks and tabs
*/
skipbl(lin, i) char lin[]; int *i; {
  while((lin[*i]==' ')|(lin[*i]=='\t')) *i = *i + 1;
  }

/*
** nextln -- get line after ln
*/
nextln(ln) int ln; {
  if(++ln > lastln) return 0;
  return ln;
  }

/*
** prevln -- get line before ln
*/
prevln(ln) int ln; {
  if(--ln < 0) return lastln;
  return ln;
  }

/*
** join -- put line1 thru line2 together into txt
*/
join(ln1, ln2) int ln1, ln2; {
  int i, j;
  j=0;
  while(ln1 <= ln2) {
    i=getind(ln1++)+TEXT;
    while(txt[j++]=buf[i++])
      if(j >= MAXLINE) return ERR;
    --j;
    }
  return OK;
  }

/*
```

```
** doread -- read "file" after "line"
*/
doread(line, file) int line; char file[]; {
  int fd, stat;
  if((fd=fopen(file, "r"))==NULL) {
    fputs("open ", stderr);
    return ERR;
    }
  curln=line;
  stat=input(fd);
  fclose(fd);
  return stat;
  }

/*
** getlst -- collect line numbers (if any) at lin[i], bump i
*/
getlst() {
  int num;
  line2=0;
  nlines=0;
  while(getone(&num)==OK) {
    line1=line2;
    line2=num;
    ++nlines;
    if((lin[i]!=COMMA)&(lin[i]!=SEMICOL)) break;
    if(lin[i]==SEMICOL) curln=num;
    ++i;
    }
  if(nlines>2) nlines=2;
  if(nlines==0) line2=curln;
  if(nlines<=1) line1=line2;
  if(status!=ERR) status=OK;
  return status;
  }

/*
** getone -- evaluate one line number expression
*/
getone(num) int *num; {
  int istart, mul, pnum;
  skipbl(lin, &i);
  istart=i;
  if((lin[i]==PLUS)|(lin[i]==MINUS)) *num=curln;
  else *num=0;
  if(getnum(num)==OK)
    while(YES) {
      skipbl(lin, &i);
      if((lin[i]!=PLUS)&(lin[i]!=MINUS)) {
```

```
              status=EOF;
              break;
              }
          if(lin[i]==PLUS) mul = 1;
          else mul = -1;
          ++i;
          skipbl(lin, &i);
          pnum=1;
          getnum(&pnum);
          *num = *num + mul*pnum;
          if(status==EOF) status=ERR;
          if(status!=OK) break;
          }
      if((*num<0)|(*num>lastln)) return (status=ERR);
      if(i<=istart) return (status=EOF);
      return (status=OK);
      }

#include "edit2.c"
#include "same.c"
#include "pat.c"
#include "buf.c"
#include "error.c"
#include "index.c"
#include "maksub.c"
#include "catsub.c"
#include "scopy.c"
#include "trim.c"

/*
** edit2.c -- edit part 2
*/

/*
** getnum -- convert one term to a line number
*/
getnum(pnum) int *pnum; {
  int stat;
  char *digits;
  digits="0123456789";
  stat=OK;
  if(index(digits, lin[i]) >= 0) {
    *pnum=ctoi(lin, &i);
    --i;   /** backup then bump at end **/
    }
  else if(lin[i]==CURLINE) *pnum=curln;
  else if(lin[i]==LASTLINE) *pnum=lastln;
  else if((lin[i]==SCAN)|(lin[i]==BACKSCAN)) {
    if(optpat()==ERR) stat=ERR;
```

```
    else if(lin[i]==SCAN) stat=ptscan(FORWARD, pnum);
    else stat=ptscan(BACKWARD, pnum);
    }
  else if((lin[i]==PLUS)|(lin[i]==MINUS)) --i;
  else stat=EOF;
  if(stat==OK) ++i;
  return (status=stat);
  }

/*
** optpat -- make pattern if specified at lin[i]
*/
optpat() {
  if(lin[i]==NULL) i = ERR;
  else if(lin[i+1]==NULL) i = ERR;
  else if(lin[i+1]==lin[i]) ++i;
  else i = makpat(lin, i+1, lin[i], pat);
  if(pat[0]==NULL) i = ERR;
  if(i==ERR) {
    pat[0]=NULL;
    return ERR;
    }
  return OK;
  }

/*
** ptscan -- scan for next occurrence of pattern
*/
ptscan(way, num) int way, *num; {
  *num=curln;
  while(YES) {
    if(poll(YES)==ESC) return (ERR);
    if(way==FORWARD) *num=nextln(*num);
    else *num=prevln(*num);
    if(match(buf+getind(*num)+TEXT, pat)==YES) return OK;
    if(*num==curln) break;
    }
  return ERR;
  }

/*
** ckglob -- if global prefix, mark lines to be affected
*/
ckglob() {
  int gflag, k, line;
  if((same(lin[i], GLOBAL)==NO)&(same(lin[i], EXCLUDE)==NO))
    return (status=EOF);
  if(same(lin[i], GLOBAL)) gflag=YES;
  else gflag=NO;
```

```
    ++i;
    if((optpat()==ERR)|(defalt(1, lastln)==ERR))
      return (status=ERR);
    ++i;
    line=line1;
    while(line<=line2) {
      if(poll(YES)==ESC) return (status=ERR);
      k=gettxt(line++);
      if(match(txt, pat)==gflag) buf[k+MARK]=YES;
      else buf[k+MARK]=NO;
      }
    line=nextln(line2);
    while(line!=line1) {
      if(poll(YES)==ESC) return (status=ERR);
      k=getind(line);
      buf[k+MARK]=NO;
      line=nextln(line);
      }
    return (status=OK);
    }

/*
** defalt -- set defaulted line numbers
*/
defalt(def1, def2) int def1, def2; {
  if(nlines==0) {
    line1=def1;
    line2=def2;
    }
  if((line1>line2)|(line1<=0)|(line2>lastln))
    return (status=ERR);
  return (status=OK);
  }

/*
** doglob -- do command at lin[i] on all marked lines
*/
doglob() {
  int count, istart, k, line;
  status=OK;
  count=0;
  line=line1;
  istart=i;
  while(YES) {
    if(poll(YES)==ESC) return (status=ERR);
    k=getind(line);
    if(buf[k+MARK]==YES) {
      buf[k+MARK]=NO;
      cursav=curln=line;
```

```
      i=istart;
      if(getlst()==OK) {
        if(docmd(YES)==OK) count=0;
        }
      }
    else {
      line=nextln(line);
      ++count;
      }
    if((count>lastln)|(status!=OK)) break;
    }
  return status;
  }

/*
** append -- append lines after ln
*/
append(ln, glob) int ln, glob; {
  int stat;
  if(glob==YES) return ERR;
  curln=ln;
  stat=NOSTATUS;
  while(stat==NOSTATUS) {
    fputc(' ', stderr);
    if(fgets(lin, MAXLINE, stdin)==NULL) stat=EOF;
    else {
      trim(lin);
      if((lin[0]==PERIOD)&(lin[1]==NULL)) stat=OK;
      else if(inject(lin)==ERR) stat=ERR;
      }
    }
  return stat;
  }

/*
** kill -- delete lines from through to
*/
kill(from, to) int from, to; {
  int k1, k2;
  if((from==1)&(to==lastln)) {
    setbuf();
    updtflag=NO;
    return (status=OK);
    }
  if(from<=0) return (status=ERR);
  k2=getind(nextln(to));
  k1=getind(prevln(from));
  /** leaves gotline & gotind below affected area **/
  lastln=lastln-(to-from+1);
```

```
    curln=prevln(from);
    relink(k1, k2, k1, k2);
    return (status=OK);
    }

/*
** ckp -- check for "p" after command
*/
ckp(lin, i, pflag) char lin[]; int i, *pflag; {
  if(same(lin[i], PRINT)) {
    *pflag=YES;
    ++i;
    }
  else *pflag=NO;
  if(view) *pflag=YES;
  if(lin[i]==NULL) status=OK;
  else status=ERR;
  return status;
  }


/*
** move -- move line1 through line2 after line3
*/
move(line3) int line3; {
  int k0, k1, k2, k3, k4, k5;
  if((line1<=0)|((line1<=line3)&(line3<=line2))) return ERR;
  k1=getind(line1);
  k2=getind(line2);
  k3=getind(nextln(line2));
  k0=getind(prevln(line1));
  /** leaves gotline & gotind below affected area **/
  relink(k0, k3, k0, k3);
  if(line3>line1) {
    curln=line3;
    line3=line3-(line2-line1+1);
    }
  else curln=line3+(line2-line1+1);
  k5=getind(nextln(line3));
  k4=getind(line3);
  /** leaves gotline & gotind below affected area **/
  relink(k4, k1, k2, k5);
  relink(k2, k5, k4, k1);
  return OK;
  }

/*
** getrhs -- get substitution string for "s" command
*/
getrhs(lin, i, sub, gflag) char lin[], sub[]; int *i, *gflag; {
```

```
    if(lin[*i]==NULL) return ERR;
    if(lin[*i+1]==NULL) return ERR;
    *i=maksub(lin, *i+1, lin[*i], sub);
    if(*i==ERR) return ERR;
    if(same(lin[*i+1], GLOBAL)) {
      *i = *i + 1;
      *gflag=YES;
      }
    else *gflag=NO;
    return OK;
    }

/*
** subst -- substitute "sub" for occurrences of pattern
*/
subst(sub, gflag) char sub[]; int gflag; {
  char new[MAXLINE];
  int j, k, lastn, line, n, subbed;
  if(line1<=0) return ERR;
  line=line1;
  while(line<=line2) {
    if(poll(YES)==ESC) return (ERR);
    j=0;
    subbed=NO;
    gettxt(line);
    lastn=-1;
    k=0;
    while(YES) {
      if((gflag==YES)|(subbed==NO)) n=amatch(txt, k, pat);
      else n=-1;
      if((n>=0)&(lastn!=n)) {     /** replace matched text **/
        subbed=YES;
        catsub(txt, k, n, sub, new, &j, MAXLINE);
        lastn=n;
        }
      if(txt[k]==NULL) break;
      if((n==-1)|(n==k)) {        /** no match or null match **/
        addset(txt[k], new, &j, MAXLINE);
        ++k;
        }
      else k=n;                   /** skip matched text **/
      }
    if(subbed==YES) {
      if(addset(NULL, new, &j, MAXLINE)==NO) return ERR;
      curln=prevln(line);
      if(inject(new)==ERR) {
        curln=line;
        return ERR;
        }
```

```
        kill(curln+1, curln+1);
        }
      ++line;
      }
    return OK;
    }

/*
** getfn -- get file name from lin[i]
*/
getfn(lin, i, file, max) char lin[], file[]; int i, max; {
  int j, k, stat;
  stat=ERR;
  if(lin[i+1]==BLANK) {
    j=i+2;   /** get new file name **/
    skipbl(lin, &j);
    k=0;
    while(file[k++]=lin[j++]) if(--max < 1) break;
    if((k > 1)&(max > 0)) stat=OK;
    }
  else if((lin[i+1]==NULL)&(savfil[0]!=NULL)) {
    scopy(savfil, 0, file, 0);
    stat=OK;
    }
  if((stat==OK)&(savfil[0]==NULL))
    scopy(file, 0, savfil, 0);  /** save if no old one **/
  return stat;
  }

/*
** dowrit -- write "from" through "to" into file
*/
dowrit(from, to, file) int from, to; char file[]; {
  char tmp[MAXFN], *ptr;
  int fd, line;

  strcpy(tmp, file);
  if((ptr = strchr(tmp, '.')) == 0) ptr = tmp + strlen(tmp);
  strcpy(ptr, ".$$$");
  rename(file, tmp);

  if((fd=fopen(file, "w"))==NULL) return ERR;
  line=from;
  while(line<=to) {
    fputs(buf+getind(line++)+TEXT, fd);
    if(fputc('\n', fd)==EOF) {
      fputs("write ", stderr);
      fclose(fd);
      return ERR;
```

```
      }
    }
  if(fclose(fd)) return ERR;
  unlink(tmp);
  updtflag=NO;
  return OK;
  }

/*
** doprnt -- print lines from through to
*/
doprnt(from, to, glob) int from, to, glob; {
  int j, k;
  char pref;
  if(from<=0) return OK;
  if(same(lin[i], PRINT)) {
    ++i;
    if((lin[i]>='0')&(lin[i]<='9')) {
      if(lin[i+1]==NULL) context=lin[i]-'0';
      else return ERR;
      }
    else if(lin[i]!=NULL) return ERR;
    }
  if((from==to)&(glob==NO)) {
    j=from-context;
    k=to+context;
    }
  else {
    j=from;
    k=to;
    }
  if(j < 1) j=1;
  if(k > lastln) k=lastln;
  if(glob==NO) fputs(CLEAR, stdout);
  while(j <= k) {
    if(poll(YES)) {
      /* underflow handled in docmd() */
      curln = j - context;
      return OK;
      }
    if((j==to)&(glob==NO)) pref=CLFLAG;
    else pref=' ';
    gettxt(j++);
    fputc(pref, stdout);
    fputs(txt, stdout);
    fputc('\n', stdout);
    }
  curln=to;
  return OK;
```

```
        }

/*
** enter -- enter a new file
*/
enter(name) char name[]; {
  int err;
  err=doread(0, name);
  if(view) doprnt(1, 1, NO);
  curln=1;
  updtflag=NO;
  return err;
  }
```

LISTING 13-7

```
/*
** entab.c -- replace blanks with tabs and blanks
**
** Copyright 1982 J. E. Hendrix.  All rights reserved.
*/
#include <stdio.h>
#include "tools.h"
#define NOCCARGC
#define MAXLIN1 (MAXLINE+1)
main(argc, argv) int argc, *argv; {
  char c, tabs[MAXLIN1];
  int col, newcol;
  auxbuf(stdin, 4096);
  if(settab(tabs, argc, argv)==ERR) {
    fputs("usage: ENTAB [#]... [+#]\n", stderr);
    abort(7);
    }
  col=1;
  while(YES) {
    poll(YES);
    newcol=col;
    while((c=getchar())==' ') {
      ++newcol;
      if(tabpos(newcol, tabs)==YES) {
        cout('\t', stdout);
        col=newcol;
        }
      }
    if(c=='\t') {
      while(tabpos(newcol, tabs)==NO) ++newcol;
      cout('\t', stdout);
      col=newcol;
```

```
      continue;
      }
    while(col<newcol) {
      cout(' ', stdout);
      ++col;
      }
    if(c==EOF) break;
    cout(c, stdout);
    if(c=='\n') col=1;
    else if(c=='\b') --col; /* ok if it goes neg */
    else ++col;
    }
  fclose(stdout);
  }
#include "settab.c"
#include "tabpos.c"
#include "out.c"
```

LISTING 13-8

```
/*
** find.c -- find patterns in text file
**
** Copyright 1982 J. E. Hendrix.  All rights reserved.
*/
#include <stdio.h>
#include "tools.h"
#define NOCCARGC
#define MAXARG 49
#define MAXLIN1 (MAXLINE+1)
char arg[MAXARG], lin[MAXLIN1], pat[MAXPAT];
int err, argi;
main(argc, argv) int argc, *argv; {
  auxbuf(stdin, 4096);
  err=NO;
  if((getarg(1, arg, MAXARG, argc, argv)==EOF)|(arg[0]=='-'))
    error("usage: FIND [~]pattern\n");
  if(arg[0]==NOT) argi=1; else argi=0;
  if(getpat(arg+argi, pat)==ERR) error("pattern too long\n");
  while(fgets(lin, MAXLIN1, stdin)!=NULL) {
    poll(YES);
    trim(lin);
    if(match(lin, pat)) {
      if(argi==0) lout(lin, stdout);
      }
    else if(argi==1) lout(lin, stdout);
    }
  fclose(stdout);
```

```
    }
getpat(arg, pat) char arg[], pat[]; {
    return(makpat(arg, 0, NULL, pat));
    }

#include "pat.c"
#include "error.c"
#include "index.c"
#include "out.c"
#include "trim.c"
```

LISTING 13-9

```
/*
** font.c -- choose FX printer font
*/
#include <stdio.h>
#include "tools.h"
#define NOCCARGC
char
   condensed[]={27, 15, 0},
  xcondensed[]={    18, 0},
   double[]={27, 'G', 0},
  xdouble[]={27, 'H', 0},
   elite[]={27, 'M', 0},
  xelite[]={27, 'P', 0},
   emphasized[]={27, 'E', 0},
  xemphasized[]={27, 'F', 0},
   enlarged[]={27, 'W', 49, 0},
  xenlarged[]={27, 'W', 48, 0},
   italics[]={27, '4', 0},
  xitalics[]={27, '5', 0},
   pica[]={27, 'P', 0},
  xpica[]={27, 'M', 0},
   subscript[]={27, 'S', 49, 0},
  xsubscript[]={27, 'T', 0},
   superscript[]={27, 'S', 48, 0},
  xsuperscript[]={27, 'T', 0},
   proportional[]={27, 'p', 49, 0},
  xproportional[]={27, 'p', 48, 0};
char str[15], *ptr="LST:";
int i, fd;
main(argc, argv) int argc, *argv; {
  if(getarg(1, str, 15, argc, argv) != EOF) ptr = str;
  if(*str == '-') {
    fputs("usage: FONT [device]", stderr);
    abort(7);
    }
```

```
   if((fd=fopen(ptr, "w")) == 0) cant(ptr);
   do {
     fputs(CLEAR, stdout);
     fputs("    Select Epson FX Option (RETURN to exit)\n\n", stdout);
     fputs("set  clear   mode\n\n", stdout);
     fputs(" 1     2     condensed       \n", stdout);
     fputs(" 3     4     double strike\n", stdout);
     fputs(" 5     6     elite\n", stdout);
     fputs(" 7     8     emphasized      \n", stdout);
     fputs(" 9    10     enlarged\n", stdout);
     fputs("11    12     italics\n", stdout);
     fputs("13    14     pica\n", stdout);
     fputs("15    16     subscript\n", stdout);
     fputs("17    18     superscript\n", stdout);
     fputs("19    20     proportional\n", stdout);
     fputs("\nselect... ", stdout);
     fgets(str, 10, stdin);
     ptr = str;
     while(*ptr) {
       if(*ptr == '\n') *ptr=NULL;
       ++ptr;
       }
     if(utoi(str, &i)) {
       switch(i) {
         case  1: {fputs( condensed, fd); break;}
         case  2: {fputs(xcondensed, fd); break;}
         case  3: {fputs( double, fd); break;}
         case  4: {fputs(xdouble, fd); break;}
         case  5: {fputs( elite, fd); break;}
         case  6: {fputs(xelite, fd); break;}
         case  7: {fputs( emphasized, fd); break;}
         case  8: {fputs(xemphasized, fd); break;}
         case  9: {fputs( enlarged, fd); break;}
         case 10: {fputs(xenlarged, fd); break;}
         case 11: {fputs( italics, fd); break;}
         case 12: {fputs(xitalics, fd); break;}
         case 13: {fputs( pica, fd); break;}
         case 14: {fputs(xpica, fd); break;}
         case 15: {fputs( subscript, fd); break;}
         case 16: {fputs(xsubscript, fd); break;}
         case 17: {fputs( superscript, fd); break;}
         case 18: {fputs(xsuperscript, fd); break;}
         case 19: {fputs( proportional, fd); break;}
         case 20: {fputs(xproportional, fd); break;}
         }
       }
     } while (*str);
  }
#include "cant.c"
```

LISTING 13-10

```c
/*
** format.c -- text formatter
**
** Copyrignt 1982 J. E. Hendrix.  All rights reserved.
*/

#include <stdio.h>
#include "tools.h"
#define NOCCARGC
#define KILL 14   /* control-N */
#define INSIZE 396
#define MAXOUT 579
#define COMMAND '.'
#define PAGENUM '#'
#define TTLDELIM '/'
#define MRGCHAR '|'
#define SUBCHAR '/'
#define SUPCHAR '\\'
#define BLANK '~'
#define DEFM1 1
#define DEFM2 2
#define DEFM3 2
#define DEFM4 9
/**** LM is effectively one greater ****/
#define DEFLM 9
#define DEFRM 73
#define DEFMP 2
#define PAGELEN 66
#define HUGE 32000
#define NDIM 5
#define NWIDTH 4

int
  ttymode, /* tty mode if YES */
  itsub,   /* italic subs for underlines */
  ulsub,   /* underline subs for italics */
  pass,    /* pass counter */
  fill,    /* fill if YES */
  just,    /* justify if YES */
  lsval,   /* line spacing */
  inval,   /* indent value */
  lmval,   /* left margin value */
  rmval,   /* right margin value */
  pagekill,/* kill page if YES */
  pospec,  /* page offset specification */
  poval,   /* page offset for current page */
  tival,   /* temporary indent */
```

```
        ceval,    /* number of lines to center */
        ulval,    /* number of lines to underline */
        bfval,    /* number of lines to boldface */
        itval,    /* number of lines to italicize */
        dwval,    /* number of lines to double-wide */
        dwact,    /* double-wide is active */
        bfstrikes, /* number of boldface strikes */
        cuact,    /* continuous underline active if > 0 */
        mpcnt,    /* lines printed since last .mp page break */
        mpval,    /* minimum lines required for paragraphs */
        sqval,    /* squeeze indents */
        bline,    /* blank line flag */
        curpag,   /* current page number */
        newpag,   /* next page number */
        lineno,   /* next line to be printed */
        plval,    /* page length in lines */
        m1val,    /* margin before and including header */
        m2val,    /* margin after header */
        m3val,    /* margin after last text line */
        m4val,    /* bottom margin including footer */
        bottom,   /* last live line on page */
        outp,     /* last character position in outbuf */
        outw,     /* width of text in outbuf */
        outwds,   /* number of words in outbuf */
        pause,    /* pause on page breaks if YES */
        ready,    /* prompt "ready printer..." if YES */
        show,     /* show source file names */
        begin,    /* beginning page to print */
        end,      /* ending page to print */
        bcopy,    /* beginning copy */
        ecopy,    /* ending copy */
        mrgfd,    /* merge file fd */
        sentend,  /* YES for plausible end of sentence */
        dir;      /* direction for spreading blanks */

char
        sbpref[]={27,'S',49,1},   /* nontty subscript prefix */
        sbsuff[]={27,'T', 1,0},   /* nontty subscript suffix */
        sppref[]={27,'S',48,1},   /* nontty superscript prefix */
        spsuff[]={27,'T', 1,0},   /* nontty superscript suffix */
        *ulon, *uloff,
        ulpref[]={27,'-',49,1},   /* nontty underline prefix */
        ulsuff[]={27,'-',48,1},   /* nontty underline suffix */
        *bfon, *bfoff,
        bfpref[]={27,'E',1,0},    /* nontty boldface prefix */
        bfsuff[]={27,'F',1,0},    /* nontty boldface suffix */
        *dson, *dsoff,
        dspref[]={27,'G',1,0},    /* nontty dbl strike prefix */
        dssuff[]={27,'H',1,0},    /* nontty dbl strike suffix */
```

```
        *iton, *itoff,
          itpref[]={27,'4',1,0},   /* nontty italics prefix */
          itsuff[]={27,'5',1,0},   /* nontty italics suffix */
        *dwon, *dwoff,
          dwpref[]={27,'W',49,1},  /* nontty dbl wide prefix */
          dwsuff[]={27,'W',48,1};  /* nontty dbl wide suffix */
     char
        cmd,      /* command character */
        mrg,      /* merge field delimiter */
        blank,    /* literal blank character */
       *ulskips,  /* specific characters to skip underlining */
       *oheader,  /* odd page header */
       *eheader,  /* even page header */
       *ofooter,  /* odd page footer */
       *efooter,  /* even page footer */
       *outbuf,   /* output buffer */
       *ttlbuf,   /* buffer for titles */
       *mrgbuf,   /* buffer for merged text */
       *inbuf,    /* input buffer */
       *wrdbuf,   /* space for one word */
       *nbrstr;   /* number string */

     main(argc, argv) int argc, *argv; {
       oheader=malloc((MAXLINE+1));
       eheader=malloc((MAXLINE+1));
       ofooter=malloc((MAXLINE+1));
       efooter=malloc((MAXLINE+1));
       mrgbuf=malloc((MAXLINE+1));
       outbuf=malloc(MAXOUT);
       ttlbuf=malloc(MAXOUT);
       wrdbuf=malloc(MAXOUT);
       inbuf=malloc(INSIZE);
       nbrstr=malloc(NDIM);
       nbrstr[NWIDTH]=NULL;
       doargs(argc, argv);
       mpcnt=99;
       pass=0;
       if(mrgfd) {
         while(fgets(mrgbuf, (MAXLINE+1), mrgfd) && (pass < ecopy)) {
           if(++pass < bcopy) continue;
           trim(mrgbuf);
           nextpass();
           }
         }
       else if(ecopy == HUGE) nextpass();
       else for(pass = bcopy; pass <= ecopy; ++pass) nextpass();
       fclose(stdout);
       }
```

```
/*
** nextpass -- make next pass on stdin text
*/
nextpass() {
  char c, str[6];
  init();
  if(mrgfd || ecopy != HUGE) {
    cseek(stdin, 0, 0);
    left(itod(pass, str, 6));
    fputs("copy ", stderr);
    fputs(str, stderr);
    fputs("   ", stderr);
    }
  c=NULL;
  if(((pass <= bcopy) || (pause==YES)) &&
     ready && isatty(stdout)) {
    fputs("ready printer... ", stderr);
    c=fgetc(stderr);
    }
  if(c!=KILL) {
    process(stdin);
    if((lineno > 0)|(outp > -1)) space(HUGE);
    }
  else fputc('\n', stderr);
  }

/*
** process -- process text from fd
*/
process(fd) int fd; {
  while(fgets(inbuf, INSIZE, fd)!=NULL) {
    poll(YES);
    trim(inbuf);
    if((fd==stderr)&(inbuf[0]==cmd)&(inbuf[1]==NULL))
      return;
    if(inbuf[0]==cmd) command(inbuf);
    else {
      if(merge()==NO) continue;
      text(inbuf);
      }
    }
  }

/*
** include -- process included text (nexting allowec)
*/
include() {
  int i, fd;
  char fname[INSIZE];
```

```
    i=0;
    while((inbuf[i]!=' ')&(inbuf[i]!=NULL)) ++i;
    getwrd(inbuf, &i, fname);
    if((fd=fopen(fname, "r"))==NULL) cant(fname);
    lout(fname, stderr);
    if(show) {
      brk();
      put(fname);
      brk();
    }
    process(fd);
    fclose(fd);
    }

/*
** prompt -- prompt operator for input
*/
prompt() {
  fputs("\7enter: ", stderr);
  fputs(inbuf+3, stderr);
  fputc('\n', stderr);
  process(stderr);
  }

/*
** init -- initialize parameters
*/
init() {
  cmd=COMMAND;
  mrg=MRGCHAR;
  blank=BLANK;
  sentend=NO;
  fill=just=YES;
  lsval=1;
  inval=tival=sqval=0;
  lmval=DEFLM;
  rmval=DEFRM;
  bfval=itval=ceval=ulval=cuact=0;
  curpag=0;
  newpag=1;
  lineno=0;
  mpval=DEFMP;
  bline=NO; /** prevents a blank first page **/
  plval=PAGELEN;
  m1val=DEFM1;
  m2val=DEFM2;
  m3val=DEFM3;
  m4val=DEFM4;
  bottom=plval-m3val-m4val;
```

```
  oheader[0]=eheader[0]=NULL;
  ofooter[0]=efooter[0]=NULL;
  outp=-1;
  outw=outwds=0;
  dir=0;
  }

/*
** command -- process commands
*/
command(buf) char buf[]; {
  int argtyp, spval, val;
  if(buf[1] == cmd) return;    /* comment */
  val=getval(buf, &argtyp);
  switch((toupper(buf[1]) << 8) + toupper(buf[2])) {
    default: {
      fputs("\7note: ", stderr);
      fputs(buf, stderr);
      fputc('\n', stderr);
      return;
      }
    case 'FI': {
      brk();
      fill=YES;
      break;
      }
    case 'NF': {
      brk();
      fill=NO;
      break;
      }
    case 'JU': {
      brk();
      just=YES;
      break;
      }
    case 'NJ': {
      brk();
      just=NO;
      break;
      }
    case 'BR':{
      brk();
      break;
      }
    case 'LS': {
      setvalue(&lsval, val, argtyp, 1, 1, HUGE);
      break;
      }
```

```c
      case 'HE': {
        gettl(buf, oheader);
        gettl(buf, eheader);
        break;
        }
      case 'OH': {
        gettl(buf, oheader);
        break;
        }
      case 'EH': {
        gettl(buf, eheader);
        break;
        }
      case 'FO': {
        gettl(buf, ofooter);
        gettl(buf, efooter);
        break;
        }
      case 'OF': {
        gettl(buf, ofooter);
        break;
        }
      case 'EF': {
        gettl(buf, efooter);
        break;
        }
      case 'SP': {
        setvalue(&spval, val, argtyp, 1, 0, HUGE);
        space(spval);
        bline=YES;
        break;
        }
      case 'BP': {
        if((lineno > 0)|(outp > -1)) space(HUGE);
        setvalue(&curpag, val, argtyp, newpag, -HUGE, HUGE);
        newpag=curpag;
        break;
        }
      case 'PL': {
        if(val==0) {
          lineno=1;
          plval=0;
          }
        else {
          setvalue(&plval, val, argtyp,
              PAGELEN, m1val+m2val+m3val+m4val+1, HUGE);
          bottom=plval-m3val-m4val;
          }
        break;
```

```
      }
case 'IN': {
  brk();
  setvalue(&inval, val, argtyp, 0, -lmval, rmval-lmval-1);
  break;
  }
case 'LM': {
  brk();
  setvalue(&lmval, val-1, argtyp, DEFLM, 0, rmval-1);
  break;
  }
case 'RM': {
  setvalue(&rmval, val, argtyp, DEFRM, lmval+1, HUGE);
  break;
  }
case 'TI': {
  brk();
  setvalue(&tival, val, argtyp, 0,
      -(lmval+inval), rmval-(lmval+inval)-1);
  break;
  }
case 'SQ': {
  brk();
  setvalue(&sqval, val, argtyp, 0, 0, HUGE);
  break;
  }
case 'CE': {
  brk();
  setvalue(&ceval, val, argtyp, 1, 0, HUGE);
  break;
  }
case 'BF': {
  setvalue(&bfval, val, argtyp, 1, 0, HUGE);
  ulval=0;
  break;
  }
case 'IT': {
  setvalue(&itval, val, argtyp, 1, 0, HUGE);
  break;
  }
case 'DW': {
  setvalue(&dwval, val, argtyp, 1, 0, HUGE);
  break;
  }
case 'UL': {
  setvalue(&ulval, val, argtyp, 1, 0, HUGE);
  cuact=0;
  ulskips=" ()[]{}\t\b,.;:?!_'\"";
  bfval=0;
```

```
      break;
      }
    case 'CU': {
      setvalue(&ulval, val, argtyp, 1, 0, HUGE);
      if(ulval==0) cuact=0;
      else cuact=1;      /* becomes 2 after next putwrd */
      if(ttymode) ulskips=" \t\b";
      else        ulskips= "\t\b";
      break;
      }
    case 'NU': {
      ulval=cuact=0;
      break;
      }
    case 'MP': {
      setvalue(&mpval, val, argtyp, DEFMP, 0, HUGE);
      break;
      }
    case 'NE': {
      if(((bottom-lineno) < val) & (lineno > 0))
        space(HUGE);
      break;
      }
    case 'RS': {
      if(((bottom-lineno) < val) & (lineno > 0))
        space(HUGE);
      space(val);
      break;
      }
    case 'SO': {
      include();
      break;
      }
    case 'PR': {
      prompt();
      break;
      }
    case 'CC': {
      val=0;
      getwrd(buf, &val, wrdbuf);
      if(getwrd(buf, &val, wrdbuf)==1) cmd=wrdbuf[0];
      break;
      }
    case 'MC': {
      val=0;
      getwrd(buf, &val, wrdbuf);
      if(getwrd(buf, &val, wrdbuf)==1) mrg=wrdbuf[0];
      break;
      }
```

```
      case 'BC': {
        val=0;
        getwrd(buf, &val, wrdbuf);
        if(getwrd(buf, &val, wrdbuf)==1) blank=wrdbuf[0];
        break;
        }
      case 'M1': {
        setvalue(&m1val, val, argtyp, DEFM1, 0, HUGE);
        break;
        }
      case 'M2': {
        setvalue(&m2val, val, argtyp, DEFM2, 0, HUGE);
        break;
        }
      case 'M3': {
        setvalue(&m3val, val, argtyp, DEFM3, 0, HUGE);
        bottom=plval-m3val-m4val;
        break;
        }
      case 'M4': {
        setvalue(&m4val, val, argtyp, DEFM4, 0, HUGE);
        bottom=plval-m3val-m4val;
        break;
        }
      case 'P0': {
        setvalue(&pospec, val, argtyp, 0, 0, HUGE);
        break;
        }
      }
  }

#include "format2.c"
#include "format3.c"
#include "scopy.c"
#include "getwrd.c"
#include "cant.c"
#include "page.c"
#include "index.c"
#include "same.c"
#include "trim.c"
#include "out.c"

/*
** format2.c -- text formatter part 2
*/

/*
** getval -- evaluate optional numeric argument
*/
```

```
getval(buf, argtyp) char buf[]; int *argtyp; {
  int i;
  i=0;
  while((buf[i]!=' ')&(buf[i]!='\t')&(buf[i]!=NULL)) ++i;
  skipbl(buf, &i);
  *argtyp=buf[i];
  if((*argtyp=='+')|(*argtyp=='-')) ++i;
  if(utoi(buf+i, &i) < 0) {
    fputs("\7error: ", stderr);
    fputs(inbuf, stderr);
    fputc('\n', stderr);
    return 0;
    }
  return i;
  }

/*
** skipbl -- skip blanks and tabs
*/
skipbl(lin, i) char lin[]; int *i; {
  while((lin[*i]==' ')|(lin[*i]=='\t')) *i = *i + 1;
  }

/*
** setvalue -- set parameter and check range
*/
setvalue(param, val, argtyp, defval, minval, maxval)
  int *param, val, argtyp, defval, minval, maxval; {
  if(argtyp==NULL) *param=defval;
  else if(argtyp=='+') *param=*param+val;
  else if(argtyp=='-') *param=*param-val;
  else *param=val;
  if(*param > maxval) *param=maxval;
  if(*param < minval) *param=minval;
  }

/*
** text -- process text lines
*/
text(inbuf) char inbuf[]; {
  int i;
  char c1, c2;
  if((inbuf[0]==' ')|(inbuf[0]==NULL)) leadbl(inbuf);
  if(bfval > 0) {
    bold(inbuf, wrdbuf, INSIZE);
    --bfval;
    }
  dwact = NO;
  if(dwval > 0) {
```

```
    if(!ttymode) {
      dwact = YES;
      double(inbuf, wrdbuf, INSIZE);
      }
    --dwval;
    }
  if(ulval > 0) {
    if(itsub) italic(inbuf, wrdbuf, INSIZE);
    else      underl(inbuf, wrdbuf, INSIZE);
    --ulval;
    }
  if(itval > 0) {
    if(ulsub) underl(inbuf, wrdbuf, INSIZE);
    else      italic(inbuf, wrdbuf, INSIZE);
    --itval;
    }
  supersub(inbuf, wrdbuf, INSIZE);
  if(ceval > 0) {
    center(inbuf);
    put(inbuf);
    --ceval;
    }
  else if(inbuf[0]==NULL) put(inbuf);
  else if(fill==NO) put(inbuf);
  else {
    i=0;
    wrdbuf[0]=' ';
    while(getwrd(inbuf, &i, wrdbuf+1) > 0) {
      if((sentend==YES)&(isupper(wrdbuf[1])==YES)&(wrdbuf[2]!='.'))
        putwrd(wrdbuf);   /** leading space **/
      else putwrd(wrdbuf+1);
      if(inbuf[i-1]=='"') {
        c1=inbuf[i-3];
        c2=inbuf[i-2];
        }
      else {
        c1=inbuf[i-2];
        c2=inbuf[i-1];
        }
      if((inbuf[i]!='\t')&(isupper(c1)==NO)&
         ((c2=='.')|(c2=='?')|(c2=='!'))) sentend=YES;
      else sentend=NO;
      }
    }
  if(ulval==0) cuact=0;
  }

/*
** format3.c -- text formatter part 3
```

```
        */

        /*
        ** put -- put out line with proper spacing and indenting
        */
        put(buf) char buf[]; {
          int i;
          if((buf[0]==NULL)|(buf[0]==' ')) bline=YES;
          else {
            if(((bottom-lineno+1) < (mpval*lsval)) &&
               (bline==YES) &&
               (mpcnt >= mpval)) {
              mpcnt=0;
              skip(bottom-lineno+1);
              lineno=bottom+1;   /* force footing */
              }
            bline=NO;
            }
          ++mpcnt;
          if(lineno>bottom) pfoot();
          if(lineno==0) phead();
          i=poval;   /** minus on odd pages **/
          while(++i <= (lmval+tival+inval+sqval))
            print(" ", NO);
          tival=0;
          print(buf, NO);
          if((lsval-1) < (bottom-lineno)) skip(lsval);
          else skip(bottom-lineno+1);
          if(plval > 0) lineno=lineno+lsval;
          if(lineno > bottom) pfoot();
          }

        /*
        ** print -- print output to stdout if not skipping pages
        */
        print(str, title) char *str; int title; {
          while(*str) {
            if(*str == 1) {
              if(!title) onoff(*(str-1));
              }
            else {
              /* skip output of control sequence terminator */
              if((plval==0)|((curpag >= begin)&(pagekill==NO))) {
                begin=1;   /** future copies begin on page 1 **/
                if(*str != blank) cout(*str, stdout);
                else cout(' ', stdout);
                }
              else if(*str == 27) {
                while(*str != 1) cout(*str++, stdout);
```

```
          continue;
          }
      }
    ++str;
    }
  }

/*
** onoff -- set and clear xxon and xxoff pointers
*/
onoff(ch) int ch; {
        if(ch == ulpref[2]) {ulon=ulpref; uloff=ulsuff;}
  else if(ch == ulsuff[2]) ulon=uloff=0;
  else if(ch == bfpref[1]) {bfon=bfpref; bfoff=bfsuff;}
  else if(ch == bfsuff[1]) bfon=bfoff=0;
  else if(ch == dspref[1]) {dson=dspref; dsoff=dssuff;}
  else if(ch == dssuff[1]) dson=dsoff=0;
  else if(ch == itpref[1]) {iton=itpref; itoff=itsuff;}
  else if(ch == itsuff[1]) iton=itoff=0;
  else if(ch == dwpref[1]) {dwon=dwpref; dwoff=dwsuff;}
  else if(ch == dwsuff[1]) dwon=dwoff=0;
  }

/*
** skip -- output n blank lines
*/
skip(n) int n; {
  while((n--) > 0) print("\n", NO);
  }

/*
** phead -- put out header
*/
phead() {
  pagekill=NO;
  if((curpag=newpag++) >= begin) {
    if(page(curpag, pause, sdout)==KILL) {
      pagekill=YES;
      fputc('\n', stderr);
      }
    }
  if(curpag%2) poval = -pospec;
  else poval = pospec;
  if(m1val > 0) {
    skip(m1val-1);
    if(curpag%2) puttl(oheader, curpag);
    else puttl(eheader, curpag);
    }
  skip(m2val);
```

```
    lineno=m1val+m2val+1;
    }

/*
** pfoot -- put out footer
*/
pfoot() {
  skip(m3val);
  if(m4val > 0) {
    if(curpag%2) puttl(ofooter, curpag);
    else puttl(efooter, curpag);
    }
  if((curpag >= end)&((ecopy==HUGE)|(ecopy==pass))) {
    fclose(stdout);
    exit(0);
    }
  if(pause==NO) skip(m4val-1);
  lineno=0;
  }

/*
** puttl -- put out title line with optional page number
*/
puttl(buf, pageno) char buf[]; int pageno; {
  char str[2];
  int i, j, k ,parts;
  str[1]=NULL;
  i=poval;  /** minus on odd pages **/
  while(++i <= lmval) print(" ", YES);
  parts=1;
  i=k=0;
  while(buf[i]!=NULL) {
    if(buf[i]==PAGENUM) {
      itod(pageno, nbrstr, - NWIDTH);
      j=0;
      while(nbrstr[j]==' ') ++j;
      while(j < NWIDTH) {
        if(k < (MAXOUT-1)) ttlbuf[k++]=nbrstr[j];
        ++j;
        }
      }
    else {
      if(buf[i]==TTLDELIM) ++parts;
      if(k < (MAXOUT-1)) ttlbuf[k++]=buf[i];
      }
    ++i;
    }
  ttlbuf[k]=NULL;
  spread(ttlbuf, k+1, MAXOUT, rmval-lmval-k, parts, TTLDELIM);
```

```
  /* disable running ul, it, dw, ds, or bf */
  if(uloff) print(uloff, YES);
  if(itoff) print(itoff, YES);
  if(dsoff) print(dsoff, YES);
  if(bfoff) print(bfoff, YES);
  if(dwoff) print(dwoff, YES);
  print(ttlbuf, YES);
  /* reenable running ul, it, dw, ds, or bf */
  if(ulon) print(ulon, YES);
  if(iton) print(iton, YES);
  if(dson) print(dson, YES);
  if(bfon) print(bfon, YES);
  if(dwon) print(dwon, YES);
  print("\n", YES);
  }

/*
** gettl -- copy title from buf to ttl
*/
gettl(buf, ttl) char *buf, *ttl; {
  int i;
  i=0;
  while((buf[i]!=' ')&(buf[i]!='\t')&(buf[i]!=NULL)) ++i;
  skipbl(buf, &i);
  if((buf[i]=='\'')¦(buf[i]=='"')) ++i; /** strip leacing quote **/
  buf=buf+i;
  while(*ttl++ = *buf++);
  }

/*
** space -- space n lines or to bottom
*/
space(n) int n; {
  brk();
  if(lineno > bottom) return;
  if(lineno==0) {
    phead();
    if(n==HUGE) return;
    }
  if(n < (bottom+1-lineno)) skip(n);
  else skip(bottom+1-lineno);
  if(plval > 0) lineno=lineno+n;
  if(lineno > bottom) pfoot();
  }

/*
** leadbl -- delete leading blanks, set tival
*/
leadbl(buf) char buf[]; {
```

```
      int i, j;
      brk();
      i=0;
      while(buf[i]==' ') ++i;
      if(buf[i]!=NULL) tival = tival + i;
      j=0;
      while(buf[j++]=buf[i++]);
      }

  /*
  ** width -- compute width of character string
  */
  width(buf) char *buf; {
    int wide;
    wide=0;
    while(*buf) {
      if(*buf==27) {
        while(*buf++ != 1) ;
        continue;
        }
      if(*buf == '\b') --wide;
      else if(*buf != '\n') {
        ++wide;
        if(dwact && !isspace(*buf)) ++wide;
        }
      ++buf;
      }
    return (wide);
    }

  /*
  ** brk -- end current filled line
  */
  brk() {
    if(outp > -1) {
      outbuf[outp]=NULL;
      outp=-1;
      put(outbuf);
      }
    outw=outwds=0;
    }

  /*
  ** putwrd -- put a word in outbuf (does margin justification)
  */
  putwrd(wrdbuf) char wrdbuf[]; {
    int last, llval, nextra, w, i;
    w=width(wrdbuf);
    last=strlen(wrdbuf)+outp+1;
```

```
  llval=rmval-lmval-tival-inval-(sqval<<1);
  if((outp > -1)&((outw+w > llval)¦(last >= MAXOUT))) {
    last=last-outp-1;
    if(just!=YES) nextra=0;
    else nextra=llval-outw+1;
    spread(outbuf, outp, MAXOUT, nextra, outwds, ' ');
    if((nextra > 0)&(outwds > 1)) outp=outp+nextra;
    brk();
    }
  if(outp > 0 && cuact > 1 && !itsub && ttymode)
    outbuf[outp]='_';
  else {
    ++outwds;
    if(cuact==1) cuact=2;
    }
  if((outp < 0)&(wrdbuf[0]==' ')) i=1; else i=0;
  scopy(wrdbuf+i, 0, outbuf, outp+1);
  outp=last-i;
  outbuf[outp]=' ';
  outw=outw+w+1-i;
  }

/*
** spread -- spread words to justify right margin
*/
spread(buf, outp, max, nextra, outwds, gapid)
  char buf[], gapid; int outp, max, nextra, outwds; {
  int i, j, nb, ne, nholes;
  if((nextra <= 0)¦(outwds <= 1)) return;
  dir=1-dir; /* reverse prev direction */
  ne=nextra;
  nholes=outwds-1;
  i=outp-1;
  if((max-2) < (i+ne)) j=max-2;
  else j=i+ne;
  while(i < j) {
    if(buf[i]==gapid) {
      buf[j]=' ';
      if(dir==0) nb=(ne-1)/nholes + 1;
      else nb=ne/nholes;
      ne=ne-nb;
      nholes=nholes-1;
      while((nb--) > 0)
        buf[--j]=' ';
      }
    else buf[j]=buf[i];
    --i;
    --j;
    }
```

```
        }

/*
** center -- center a line by setting tival
*/
center(buf) char buf[]; {
  int i, j;
  j = -lmval - inval - sqval;
  if((i=((rmval-lmval-width(buf))/2)-inval-sqval) < j)
      tival = j;
  else tival = i;
  }

/*
** underl -- underline a line
*/
underl(buf, tbuf, size) char buf[], tbuf[]; int size; {
  char c, *ptr;
  int prefixed, i, j;
  if(*buf == 0) return;
  if(!ttymode) prefixed=NO;
  else prefixed=9;   /* neither YES nor NO */
  i=j=0;
  while((buf[i]!=NULL)&(j<(size-2))) {
    c=buf[i++];
    if(index(ulskips, c) < 0) {
      if(prefixed==NO) {
        prefixed=YES;
        ptr=ulpref;
        while((tbuf[j++]=*ptr++) != 1) ;
        }
      else if(ttymode) {
        tbuf[j++]='_';
        tbuf[j++]='\b';
        }
      }
    else {
      if(prefixed==YES) {
        prefixed=NO;
        ptr=ulsuff;
        while((tbuf[j++]=*ptr++) != 1) ;
        }
      if(cuact>0 && fill==NO && c==' ' && ttymode) c='_';
      }
    tbuf[j++]=c;
    }
  if(prefixed==YES) {
    ptr=ulsuff;
    while((tbuf[j++]=*ptr++) != 1) ;
```

```
    }
  tbuf[j]=NULL;
  scopy(tbuf, 0, buf, 0);
  }

/*
** bold -- boldface a line
*/
bold(buf, tbuf, size) char buf[], tbuf[]; int size; {
  char *ptr;
  int c, i, j;
  if(*buf == 0) return;
  i=j=0;
  if(!ttymode) {
    ptr=bfpref;
    while((tbuf[j++]=*ptr++) != 1) ;
    ptr=dspref;
    while((tbuf[j++]=*ptr++) != 1) ;
    }
  while((buf[i]!=NULL)&(j<(size-2))) {
    c=tbuf[j++]=buf[i++]&255;
    if(ttymode && (c > ' ') && (c < 127)) {
      int i;
      i = bfstrikes;
      while (--i) {
        tbuf[j++]='\b';
        tbuf[j++]=c;
        }
      }
    }
  if(!ttymode) {
    ptr=bfsuff;
    while((tbuf[j++]=*ptr++) != 1) ;
    ptr=dssuff;
    while((tbuf[j++]=*ptr++) != 1) ;
    }
  tbuf[j]=NULL;
  scopy(tbuf, 0, buf, 0);
  }

/*
** italic -- italicize a line
*/
italic(buf, tbuf, size) char buf[], tbuf[]; int size; {
  char *ptr;
  int i, j;
  if(*buf == 0) return;
  if(ttymode) return;
  i=j=0;
```

```
    ptr=itpref;
    while((tbuf[j++]=*ptr++) != 1) ;
    ptr=bfpref;
    while((tbuf[j++]=*ptr++) != 1) ;
    while((buf[i]!=NULL)&(j<(size-2)))  tbuf[j++]=buf[i++];
    ptr=itsuff;
    while((tbuf[j++]=*ptr++) != 1) ;
    ptr=bfsuff;
    while((tbuf[j++]=*ptr++) != 1) ;
    tbuf[j]=NULL;
    scopy(tbuf, 0, buf, 0);
    }

/*
** double -- double-wide a line (nontty mode only)
*/
double(buf, tbuf, size) char buf[], tbuf[]; int size; {
    char *ptr;
    int space, i, j;
    if(!*buf || ttymode) return;
    space = YES;
    i = j = 0;
    while(buf[i] && j < (size-3)) {
        if(isspace(buf[i])) {
            if(!space) {
                ptr=dwsuff;
                while((tbuf[j++]=*ptr++) != 1) ;
                }
            space = YES;
            }
        else {
            if(space) {
                ptr=dwpref;
                while((tbuf[j++]=*ptr++) != 1) ;
                }
            space = NO;
            }
        tbuf[j++]=buf[i++];
        }
    if(!space) {
        ptr=dwsuff;
        while((tbuf[j++]=*ptr++) != 1) ;
        }
    tbuf[j]=NULL;
    scopy(tbuf, 0, buf, 0);
    }

/*
** supersub -- process super- & sub-scripts
```

```
*/
supersub(buf, tbuf, size) char buf[], tbuf[]; int size; {
  char *pref, *suff, *ptr;
  int i, j;
  if(!*buf) return;
  i = j = suff = 0;
  while(buf[i] && j < (size-3)) {
    if(isspace(buf[i]) && suff) {
      while((tbuf[j++] = *suff++) != 1) ;
      suff = 0;
      }
    if(buf[i] == SUBCHAR && buf[i+1] == SUBCHAR) {
      if(!ttymode) {
        if(suff) {ptr = suff;   suff = 0;}
        else     {ptr = sbpref; suff = sbsuff;}
        while((tbuf[j++] = *ptr++) != 1) ;
        }
      i += 2;
      }
    else if(buf[i] == SUPCHAR && buf[i+1] == SUPCHAR) {
      if(!ttymode) {
        if(suff) {ptr = suff;   suff = 0;}
        else     {ptr = sppref; suff = spsuff;}
        while((tbuf[j++] = *ptr++) != 1) ;
        }
      i += 2;
      }
    else tbuf[j++] = buf[i++];
    }
  if(suff) while((tbuf[j++] = *suff++) != 1) ;
  tbuf[j] = NULL;
  scopy(tbuf, 0, buf, 0);
  }

/*
** doargs -- process command line arguments
*/
doargs(argc, argv) int argc, *argv; {
  char arg[MAXFN];
  int i, err;
  show=err=ttymode=itsub=ulsub=NO;
  pause=ready=YES;
  bfstrikes=3;
  pospec=mrgfd=0;
  mrgbuf[0]=NULL;
  begin=bcopy=1;
  end=ecopy=HUGE;
  i=0;
  while(getarg(++i, arg, MAXFN, argc, argv)!=EOF) {
```

```c
if(arg[0]=='-') {
  if(same(arg[1], 'n') & same(arg[2], 'p')) {
    pause=NO;
    continue;
    }
  if(same(arg[1], 'n') & same(arg[2], 'r')) {
    ready=NO;
    continue;
    }
  if(same(arg[1], 's') & arg[2] == NULL) {
    show = YES;
    continue;
    }
  if(same(arg[1], 't') & arg[2]==NULL) { /** tty mode **/
    ttymode=YES;
    continue;
    }
  if(same(arg[1], 'i') & arg[2] == NULL) {
    /* italics replace underlines */
    itsub=YES;
    continue;
    }
  if(same(arg[1], 'u') & arg[2] == NULL) {
    /* underlines replace italics */
    ulsub=YES;
    continue;
    }
  if(same(arg[1], 'b')) {
    if(same(arg[2], 'p')) {  /** begin page # **/
      if(utoi(arg+3, &begin) > 0) continue;
      }
    else if(same(arg[2], 'c')) {  /** copy # **/
      if(utoi(arg+3, &bcopy) > 0) continue;
      }
    else if(same(arg[2], 's')) {  /** boldface strikes **/
      if(utoi(arg+3, &bfstrikes) > 0) continue;
      }
    }
  if(same(arg[1], 'e')) {   /** end **/
    if(same(arg[2], 'p')) {  /** page # **/
      if(utoi(arg+3, &end) > 0) continue;
      }
    else if(same(arg[2], 'c')) {  /** copy # **/
      if(utoi(arg+3, &ecopy) > 0) continue;
      }
    }
  if(same(arg[1], 'p') & same(arg[2], 'o')) {  /** page offset **/
    if(utoi(arg+3, &pospec) > 0) continue;
    }
```

```
        err=YES;
        }
      else {
        if((mrgfd=fopen(arg, "r"))==NULL) cant(arg);
        continue;
        }
      err=YES;
      }
    if(err==YES) {
      fputs("usage: FORMAT [mergefile] [-BC#] [-EC#]\n",stderr);
      fputs("       [-BP#] [-EP#] [-PO#] [-NP] [-NR]\n",stderr);
      fputs("       [-T] [-I] [-U] [-S] [-BS#]\n",stderr);
      abort(7);
      }
    }


/*
** merge -- merge fields from mrgbuf into inbuf
*/
merge() {
  int i, j, k, l, m, merged;
  if(mrgbuf[0]==NULL) return YES;
  scopy(inbuf, 0, ttlbuf, 0);
  merged=NO;
  i=j=0;
  while(inbuf[i]=ttlbuf[j++]) {
    if(inbuf[i++]==mrg) {
      if((l=utoi(ttlbuf+j, &k)) < 1) continue;
      if(ttlbuf[j+l]!=mrg) continue;
      --i;
      j=j+l+1;
      m=0;
      while(--k) {
        while(mrgbuf[m]) {
          if(mrgbuf[m++]==mrg) break;
          }
        }
      while((mrgbuf[m]!=NULL)&(mrgbuf[m]!=mrg)) {
        inbuf[i++]=mrgbuf[m++];
        if(i >= (INSIZE-1)) break;
        }
      merged=YES;
      }
    }
  if(merged==NO) return YES;
  i = -1;
  while(inbuf[++i]) {
    if((inbuf[i]!=' ')&(inbuf[i]!='\t')) return YES;
```

```
      }
    return NO;
    }
```

LISTING 13-11

```c
/*
** list.c -- list text in columns on pages
**
** Copyright 1982 J. E. Hendrix.  All rights reserved.
*/
#include <stdio.h>
#include "tools.h"
#define NOCCARGC
int
  fd,     /* file descriptor for input */
  eof,    /* end of file if YES */
  cols,   /* number of cols */
  cwidth, /* col width */
  pwidth, /* page width */
  plength,/* page length */
  blanks, /* blank lines processed if YES */
  numbers,/* number lines if > 0 */
  pause;  /* pause before each page if YES */
main(argc, argv) int argc, *argv; {
  if(!isatty(stdout)) {          /* set default dimensions */
    pause=NO;
    pwidth=PTRWIDE-1;
    plength=PTRHIGH-PTRSKIP-PTRHDR;  /* page body height */
    }
  else {
    pause=YES;
    pwidth=CRTWIDE-1;
    plength=CRTHIGH-1;                /* allow for prompts */
    }
  blanks=YES;
  eof=NO;
  cols=1;
  numbers=1;
  fd=stdin;
  doargs(argc, argv);
  cwidth=pwidth/cols;
  while(eof==NO) {
    if(pause) {
      fputs("waiting... ", stderr);
      fgetc(stderr);
      }
    eof=column(fd, stdout, cwidth, cols, plength, &numbers);
```

```
    }
  fclose(stdout);
  }
doargs(argc, argv) int argc, *argv; {
  int i, j, k, err;
  char arg[MAXFN];
  err=NO;
  i=0;
  while(getarg(++i, arg, MAXFN, argc, argv) != EOF) {
    if(arg[0] != '-') {
      if(!(fd=fopen(arg, "r"))) {err=YES; break;}
      continue;
      }
    if(same(arg[1], 'c')) {
      if((j=utoi(arg+2, &cols)) < 1) {err=YES; break;}
      if((cols < 1)|(arg[j+2] > ' ')) {err=YES; break;}
      continue;
      }
    if(same(arg[1], 'n')) {
      if(arg[3] <= ' ') {
        if(same(arg[2], 'b')) {
          blanks=NO;
          continue;
          }
        if(same(arg[2], 'p')) {
          pause=NO;
          continue;
          }
        if(same(arg[2], 'n')) {
          numbers=0;
          continue;
          }
        err=YES;
        }
      }
    if(same(arg[1], 'p')) {
      if((j=utoi(arg+3, &k)) > 0) {
        if((k > 0)&(arg[j+3] <= ' ')) {
          if(same(arg[2], 'l')) {
            plength=k;
            continue;
            }
          if(same(arg[2], 'w')) {
            pwidth=k;
            continue;
            }
          }
        }
      }
```

```
      err=YES;
      }
   if(err) {
      fputs("usage: LIST [file] [-C#] [-PW#] [-PL#] [-NB] [-NN] [-NP]\n",
            stderr);
      abort(7);
      }
   }
column(in, out, cwidth, cols, plength, number)
   int in, out, cwidth, cols, plength, *number; {
   int eof, lines, colcnt, lwidth, i, bufsz, linecnt;
   char *ptr, *stop, *eptr, *nexteptr, *buf, *bend;
   bufsz=cols*(cwidth+1)*plength;
   ptr=buf=malloc(bufsz);
   bend=buf+bufsz;
   eof=NO;
   while(ptr < bend) {
     poll(YES);
     if(*number) {
       i=4;
       itou(*number, ptr, -i);
       ptr[i++]=' ';
       }
     else i=0;
     if(fgets(ptr+i, cwidth+1-i, in)==NULL) {
       eof=YES;
       break;
       }
     trim(ptr+i);
     if((blanks==NO) && (ptr[i]==NULL)) continue;
     if(*number) ++(*number);
     ptr=ptr+cwidth+1;
     }
   stop=ptr;
   ptr=buf;
   lwidth=cols*(cwidth+1);
   lines=(stop-buf)/lwidth;
   if((stop-buf)%lwidth) ++lines;
   if(lines==0) return eof;
   linecnt=lines;
   while(linecnt--) {
     poll(YES);
     eptr=ptr;
     colcnt=cols;
     while(colcnt--) {
       sout(eptr, out);
       if((nexteptr=eptr+(lines*(cwidth+1))) >= stop) break;
       if(colcnt > 0) {
         if((i=strlen(eptr)) < cwidth) {
```

```
            i=cwidth-i;
            while(i--) cout(' ', out);
            }
          }
        eptr=nexteptr;
        }
      cout('\n', out);
      ptr=ptr+cwidth+1;
      }
    free(buf);
    return eof;
    }
#include "out.c"
#include "same.c"
#include "trim.c"
```

LISTING 13-12

```
/*
** merge.c -- compares two sorted text files
**
** Copyright 1982 J. E. Hednrix.  All rights reserved.
**
** switch 1 = lines in first file only
** switch 2 = lines in second file only
** switch 3 = lines in both files
** switch f = lines in both files formatted
**
**          stdin defaults for second file
*/
#include <stdio.h>
#include "tools.h"
#define NOCCARGC
int cmpr, fd1, fd2, i;
char *line1, *line2, column, arg[MAXFN];
main(argc, argv) int argc, *argv; {
  int error;
  column='0';
  fd1=fd2=stdin;
  line1=malloc(MAXLINE+1);
  line2=malloc(MAXLINE+1);
  error=NO;
  i=0;
  while(getarg(++i, arg, MAXFN, argc, argv)!=EOF) {
    if(arg[0]!='-') {
      if(fd1==stdin) {
        if((fd1=fopen(arg, "r"))==NULL) cant(arg);
        }
      else if(fd2==stdin) {
```

```
        if((fd2=fopen(arg, "r"))==NULL) cant(arg);
        }
      else error=YES;
      }
    else if(((arg[1] > '0')&(arg[1] < '4'))
          |(same(arg[1], 'f')))
      column=arg[1];
    else error=YES;
    }
  if((error)|(fd1==stdin)) {
    fputs("usage: MERGE file [file] [-1|-2|-3|-F]\n", stderr);
    abort(7);
    }
  auxbuf(fd1, 4096);
  auxbuf(fd2, 4096);
  getline(line1, fd1);
  getline(line2, fd2);
  while(YES) {
    poll(YES);
    cmpr=lexcmp(line1, line2);
    if(cmpr < 0) {
      if(same(column, 'f')) fout("1) ", line1);
      else if((column=='0')|(column=='1')) sout(line1, stdout);
      getline(line1, fd1);
      continue;
      }
    else if(cmpr > 0) {
      if(same(column, 'f')) fout(" 2) ", line2);
      else if((column=='0')|(column=='2')) sout(line2, stdout);
      getline(line2, fd2);
      continue;
      }
    if(line1[0] == 127) break;
    if(same(column, 'f'))   fout("    3) ", line1);
    else if((column=='0')|(column=='3')) sout(line1, stdout);
    getline(line1, fd1);
    getline(line2, fd2);
    }
  fclose(stdout);
  }

getline(line, fd) char *line; int fd; {
  if(fgets(line, MAXLINE+1, fd)==NULL) {
    line[0] = 127;
    line[1] = NULL;
    }
  }

/*
```

```
** fout -- formatted output of a line
*/
fout(header, data) char *header, *data; {
  sout(header, stdout);
  sout(data, stdout);
  }

#include "out.c"
#include "cant.c"
#include "same.c"
```

LISTING 13-13

```
/*
** print.c -- print files with optional page skips, headings,
**            and line numbers.
**
** Copyright 1982 J. E. Hendrix.  All rights reserved.
*/
#include <stdio.h>
#include "tools.h"
#define MARGIN1 0
#define MARGIN2 1
char name[MAXFN], inclext[MAXFN];
int
  i,
  fin,
  files,
  headings,
  skips,
  numbers,
  begin,
  end,
  ready,
  pause;
int lineno, pageno, margin;
main(argc, argv) int argc, *argv; {
  headings=skips=numbers=YES;
  doargs(argc, argv);
  if(iscons(stdout)) freopen("LST:", "w", stdout);
  if(ready && isatty(stdout)) {
    fputs("ready printer... ", stderr);
    fgetc(stderr);
    }
  files=NO;
  i=0;
  while(getarg(++i, name, MAXFN, argc, argv)!=EOF) {
    if((name[0]=='-')|(name[0]==EXTMARK)) continue;
```

```
    files=YES;
    fin=fopen(name, "r");
    if(fin==0) cant(name);
    pageno=lineno=0;
    fprnt(name, fin);
    fclose(fin);
    if((lineno > 0)&(skips)) skip(PTRHIGH-lineno);
    }
  if(files==NO) {
    pageno=lineno=0;
    fprnt("<stdin>", stdin);
    if((lineno > 0)&(skips)) skip(PTRHIGH-lineno);
    }
  fclose(stdout);
  exit(0);
  }

doargs(argc, argv) int argc, *argv; {
  int i, j;
  inclext[0]=NULL;
  begin=0;
  end=32767;
  ready=YES;
  pause=NO;
  margin=0;
  i=0;
  while(getarg(++i, name, MAXFN, argc, argv)!=EOF) {
    if(name[0]==EXTMARK) {
      j=0;
      while(inclext[j]=toupper(name[j])) ++j;
      continue;
      }
    if(name[0]!='-') continue;
    if((same(name[1], 'b'))&(same(name[2], 'p'))) {
      utoi(name+3, &begin);
      continue;
      }
    if((same(name[1], 'e'))&(same(name[2], 'p'))) {
      utoi(name+3, &end);
      continue;
      }
    if((same(name[1], 'l'))&(same(name[2], 'm'))) {
      utoi(name+3, &margin);
      continue;
      }
    if((same(name[1], 'n'))&(same(name[2], 'r'))) {
      ready=NO;
      continue;
      }
```

```
      if(same(name[1], 'p')) {
        pause=YES;
        continue;
        }
      if(same(name[1], 'n')) {
        if(same(name[2], 'h')) {headings=NO; continue;}
        if(same(name[2], 's')) {  skips=NO; continue;}
        if(same(name[2], 'n')) { numbers=NO; continue;}
        }
      fputs("usage: PRINT [file]... [.?] [-NN] [-NH|-NS]\n",
            stderr);
      fputs("       [-LM#] [-BP#] [-EP#] [-P] [-NR]\n", stderr);
      abort(7);
      }
  }

fprnt(name, fin)
  char name[]; int fin; {
  char line[MAXLINE+1], word[MAXLINE+1];
  int textline, fin2, i, temp;
  textline=0;
  while(fgets(line, MAXLINE+1, fin)!=NULL) {
    poll(YES);
    if((lineno==0)&(skips)) {
      if(++pageno > end) exit(0);
      if(pageno >= begin) {
        page(pageno, pause, stdout);
        skip(MARGIN1);
        if(headings) {
          temp=margin;
          while(temp--) printf(" ", 0);
          if(numbers) printf("       ", 0);
          printf("File: %s     Page: %d\n", name, pageno, 2);
          }
        else printf("\n",0);
        ++lineno;
        skip(MARGIN2);
        }
      lineno=lineno+MARGIN1+MARGIN2;
      }
    ++textline;
    ++lineno;
    if(pageno >= begin) {
      temp=margin;
      while(temp--) printf(" ", 0);
      if(numbers)
        printf("%5d %s", textline, line, 2);
      else printf("%s", line, 1);
      }
```

```
      if((lineno >= (PTRHIGH-PTRSKIP))&(skips)) {
        skip(PTRHIGH-lineno);
        lineno=0;
        }
      if(inclext[0]!=EXTMARK) continue;
      i=0;
      getwrd(line, &i, word);
      if((lexcmp(word, "#include")==0) ||
         (lexcmp(word, ".so")==0)) {
        if(getwrd(line, &i, word) >= MAXFN) cant(word);
        strip(word);
        i=0;
        while((word[i]!=EXTMARK) && (word[i])) ++i;
        if((inclext[1]) &&
           (lexcmp(word+i, inclext)!=0)) continue;
        if((fin2=fopen(word, "r"))==NULL) cant(word);
        fprnt(name, fin2);
        fclose(fin2);
        }
    }
  }

skip(n) int n; {
  int i;
  if(pageno < begin) return;
  i=0;
  while(++i <= n) {
    poll(YES);
    fputc('\n', stdout);
    }
  }
#include "cant.c"
#include "page.c"
#include "same.c"
#include "strip.c"
#include "getwrd.c"
```

LISTING 13-14

```
/*
** sort.c -- sort text lines
**
** Copyright 1982 J. E. Hendrix.  All rights reserved.
**
** Each line in the buffer is preceeded by a 1-byte offset to
** the sort key.  Line pointers designate the first data byte.
*/
#include <stdio.h>
```

```c
#include "tools.h"
#define NOCCARGC
#define SHELL 1
#define QUICK 2
#define WRTMODE 2
#define MAXRUNS 99
#define LOGPTR 20
#define AVGLIN 28
#define RESERVE 2000
#define MERGEORDER 5
char *linbuf, outnam[MAXFN], tmpdrv;
char lastline[MAXLINE+1];
char *maxbuf, *maxlin;  /**** fake unsigned int ****/
char tmpout[]="X:sort00.$$$";
char tmpinp[]="X:sort00.$$$";
char tmpdel[]="X:sort00.$$$";
char delim;
int  field;
int tmpfd[MERGEORDER], *linptr, nlines;
int low, lim, high, outfil, output, t, order, unique, typesort;
main(argc, argv) int argc, *argv; {
  lastline[0]=outnam[0]=0;
  tmpdrv='X';
  doargs(argc, argv);
  if(tmpdrv == 'X') {
    strcpy(tmpout, tmpout+2);
    strcpy(tmpinp, tmpinp+2);
    strcpy(tmpdel, tmpdel+2);
    }
  else tmpout[0]=tmpinp[0]=tmpdel[0]=tmpdrv;
  output=stdout;
  if((lim=avail(YES))<0) lim=32767;
  maxlin=(lim-RESERVE)/(2+AVGLIN);
  linptr=malloc(2*maxlin);
  if((lim=avail(YES))<0) lim=32767;
  maxbuf=lim - RESERVE;
  linbuf=malloc(maxbuf);

  high=0;
  while(YES) {
    if(++high >= MAXRUNS) {
      fputs("file too large\n", stderr);
      abort(7);
      }
    t=gtext();

    sort(0, nlines-1);

    if(high==1) {
```

```
      if(t==NULL) {
        outfil=output;
        ptext();
        fclose(outfil);
        exit(0);
        }
      }
    maketmp();
    ptext();
    fclose(outfil);
    if(t==NULL) break;
    }

/*
** Must deallocate in reverse order from allocation.
** Will allocate input tmp file buffers/FCBs over this space;
** these must not reach end of linbuf where output tmp file
** space was allocated, since that space stays with that fd.
*/
  free(linbuf);
  free(linptr);

  linptr=malloc(2*(MERGEORDER+1));
  linbuf=malloc(MERGEORDER*(MAXLINE+1));
  lastline[0]=0;
  low=1;
  while(low < high) {                   /*05*/
    lim=low+MERGEORDER-1;
    if(high < lim) lim=high;
    t=0;
    while(t <= (lim-low)) {
      bumptmp(tmpinp);
      if((tmpfd[t]=fopen(tmpinp, "r"))==NULL) cant(tmpinp);
      auxbuf(tmpfd[t++], 2048); /* redundant calls ignored */
      }
    if(lim==high) outfil=output;
    else maketmp();
    if(++high >= MAXRUNS) {
      fputs("file too large\n", stderr);
      abort(7);
      }
    merge(lim-low+1);
    fclose(outfil);
    t=0;
    while(t <= (lim-low)) {
      fclose(tmpfd[t++]);               /*02*/
      killtmp();
      }
    low=low+MERGEORDER;
```

```
      }
    }

  doargs(argc, argv)  int argc, *argv;  {
    char arg[MAXFN], c;
    int i, error, len;
    field=0;
    delim=NULL;      /** indicates column number in field **/
    order=1;
    typesort=SHELL;
    unique=error=NO;
    i=0;
    while(getarg(++i, arg, MAXFN, argc, argv)!=EOF) {
      c=arg[1];
      if(arg[0]!='-') error=YES;
      else if(same(c, 't') &&
              (toupper(arg[2]) > 'A') &&
              (toupper(arg[2]) < 'G') &&
              (arg[3]==NULL))
              tmpdrv=arg[2];
      else if(same(c, 'c')) {
        delim=NULL;
        if(arg[utoi(arg+2, &field)+2] != NULL) error=YES;
        if(field) --field;
        }
      else if(same(c, 'f')) {
        if(arg[(len=utoi(arg+2, &field))+2] > ' ') {
          delim=arg[len+2];
          if(arg[len+3] != NULL) error=YES;
          }
        else delim=' ';
        if(field) --field;
        field = -field;
        }
      else if(arg[2]!=NULL) error=YES;
      else if(same(c, 'd')) order=-1;
      else if(same(c, 'u')) unique=YES;
      else if(same(c, 'q')) typesort=QUICK;
      else error=YES;
      if(error) {
        fputs("usage: SORT [-C#¦-F#?] [-D] [-U] [-Tx] [-Q]\n",
              stderr);
        abort(7);
        }
      }
    }

gtext() {
  int len;
```

```
  char *lbp;
  lbp=1; /** leave space for first sort key offset **/
  nlines=0;
  while(YES) {
    poll(YES);
    if((len=readline(linbuf+lbp, stdin))==NULL) break;
    linptr[nlines++]=lbp;
    lbp=lbp+len;  /** has 2 bytes for NULL and next offset **/
    if(((lbp+1) >= (maxbuf-(MAXLINE+1)))||(nlines >= maxlin))
      break;
    }
  return len;
  }

ptext() {
  int i;
  char *lbp;
  i=0;
  while(i < nlines) {
    poll(YES);
    lbp=linbuf+linptr[i++];
    if(duptest(lbp)) continue;
    sout(lbp, outfil);
    }
  }

duptest(line) char *line; {
  int diff;
  if(!unique) return (NO);              /*03*/
  diff = lexcmp(lastline, line);
  strcpy(lastline, line);
  return (!diff);
  }

bumptmp(tmpname) char tmpname[]; {
  char *digit;
  digit = strchr(tmpname, '.') - 1;
  if(*digit == '9') {*digit = '0'; --digit;}
  ++*digit;
  }

maketmp() {
  bumptmp(tmpout);
  if((outfil=fopen(tmpout,"w"))==NULL) cant(tmpout);
  }

killtmp() {
  bumptmp(tmpdel);
  unlink(tmpdel);
```

```
    }
sort(lv, uv) int lv, uv; {
  if(typesort==QUICK) quick(lv, uv);
  else                shell(lv, uv);
  }
shell(lv, uv) int lv, uv; {
  int gap, i, j, jg;
  gap = (uv-lv+1) >> 1; /** divide by 2 **/
  while(gap > 0) {
    poll(YES);
    i = gap + lv;
    while(i <= uv) {
      j = i++ - gap;
      while(j >= lv) {
        jg = j + gap;
        if(compare(linptr[j], linptr[jg]) <= 0) break;
        exchange(j, jg);
        j = j - gap;
        }
      }
    gap = gap>>1; /** divide by 2 **/
    }
  }
quick(lv, uv) int lv, uv; {
  int i, j, pivlin;
  avail(YES);
  poll(YES);
  if(lv >= uv) return;   /** only one element **/
  i=lv-1;
  j=uv;
  pivlin=linptr[j];
  while(i < j) {
    ++i;
    while(compare(linptr[i], pivlin) < 0) ++i;
    --j;
    while(i < j) {
      if(compare(linptr[j], pivlin) > 0) --j;
      else break;
      }
    if(i < j) exchange(i, j);
    }
  j=uv;
  exchange(i, j);
  if((i-lv) < (uv-i)) {
    quick(lv, i-1);
    quick(i+1, uv);
```

```
      }
    else {
      quick(i+1, uv);
      quick(lv, i-1);
      }
    }

  compare(p1, p2) int p1, p2; {
    char *ptr1, *ptr2;
    ptr1 = linbuf + (p1 - 1); ptr1 = ptr1 + *ptr1;
    ptr2 = linbuf + (p2 - 1); ptr2 = ptr2 + *ptr2;
    while(lexorder(*++ptr1, *++ptr2) == 0)
      if((*ptr1 == NULL)||(delimit(*ptr1))) return 0;
    if(delimit(*ptr1)) return -order;
    if(delimit(*ptr2)) return  order;
    if(lexorder(*ptr1, *ptr2) > 0) return order;
    return -order;
    }

  delimit(c) char c; {
    if(c > delim)    return NO;
    if(delim == ' ') return YES;
    if(c < delim)    return NO;
    return YES;
    }

  exchange(i, j) int i, j; {
    int k
    k=linptr[i]; linptr[i]=linptr[j]; linptr[j]=k;
    }

  merge(nfiles) int nfiles; {
    int i, inf, lbp, lp1, nf;
    char *ptr;
    lbp=1; /* leave space for first sort key offset **/
    nf=i=0;
    while(i < nfiles) {    /** get one line from each file **/
      if(readline((linbuf+lbp), tmpfd[i++])!=NULL) {
        linptr[++nf]=lbp;
        lbp=lbp+(MAXLINE+1);
        }
      }

    sort(1, nf);    /** make initial heap **/ /*04*/

    while(nf > 0) {
      poll(YES);
      lp1=linptr[1];
      ptr=linbuf+lp1;
```

```
      if(duptest(ptr)==NO) sout(ptr, outfil);
      inf=(lp1/(MAXLINE+1)); /** compute file index **/
      if(readline((linbuf+lp1), tmpfd[inf])==NULL)
        linptr[1]=linptr[nf--];
      reheap(nf);
      }
  }

reheap(nf) int nf; {
  int i, j;
  i=1;
  while((j=(i<<1)) <= nf) {
    if(j < nf) {       /** find smaller child **/
      if(compare(linptr[j], linptr[j+1]) > 0) ++j;
      }
    if(compare(linptr[i], linptr[j]) <= 0) break;
    exchange(i, j);    /** percolate **/
    i=j;
    }
  }

/*
** readline -- read next line, set its sort key offset,
**             and return its length
*/
readline(str, fd) char *str; int fd; {
  int fld;
  char *ptr, *offset;
  if(fgets(str, MAXLINE+1, fd)==NULL) return NULL;
  ptr=offset=str-1;   /** location of offset field **/
  fld=field;
  if(delim) {          /** must search for field'th field **/
    *offset = -1;
    while(*(++ptr)) {
      if(fld < 0) {
        if(delim == ' ') {
          if((*ptr > ' ')&(*(ptr+1) <= ' ')) ++fld;
          }
        else if(*ptr == delim) ++fld;
        }
      else if((fld == 0)&((delim != ' ')|(*ptr > ' '))) {
        *offset=(ptr-str);
        fld=1;
        }
      }
    if (*offset == -1) *offset=(ptr-str); /** end of line **/
    }
  else {  /** field is the column number of the sort key **/
    while(*(++ptr));
```

```
      if(field < (ptr-str)) *offset=field;
      else                  *offset=(ptr-str);
      }
   return (ptr-str+2); /** includes NULL and next offset **/
   }

#include "out.c"
#include "cant.c"
#include "same.c"
```

LISTING 13-15

```
/*
** trans.c -- map characters
**
** Copyright 1982 J. E. Hendrix.  All rights reserved.
*/
#include <stdio.h>
#include "tools.h"
#define NOCCARGC
#define MAXARG 80
#define MAXSET 127
main(argc, argv) int argc, *argv; {
   char arg[MAXARG+1], c, from[MAXSET+1], to[MAXSET+1];
   int allbut, collap, i, lastto, error;
   auxbuf(stdin, 4096);
   error=NO;
   if(getarg(1, arg, MAXARG, argc, argv)==EOF) error=YES;
   if(((arg[0]=='-')&(arg[1]<=' '))|(error==YES)) {
      fputs("usage: TRANS [~]from [to]\n", stderr);
      abort(7);
      }
   if(arg[0]==NOT) {
      allbut=YES;
      if(makset(arg, 1, from, MAXSET)==NO)
         error("from-list too large");
      }
   else {
      allbut=NO;
      if(makset(arg, 0, from, MAXSET)==NO)
         error("from-list too large");
      }
   if(getarg(2, arg, MAXARG, argc, argv)==EOF) to[0]=NULL;
   else if(makset(arg, 0, to, MAXSET)==NO)
      error("to-list too large");
   lastto=strlen(to)-1;
   if((strlen(from)>(lastto+1))|(allbut==YES)) collap=YES;
   else collap=NO;
```

```
      while(1) {
        poll(YES);
        i=xindex(from, c=fgetc(stdin), allbut, lastto);
        if((collap==YES)&(i>=lastto)&(lastto>-1)) { /* collapse */
          if(fputc(to[lastto], stdout)==EOF)
            error("output error");
          while(1) {
            i=xindex(from, c=fgetc(stdin), allbut, lastto);
            if(i<lastto) break;
            }
          }
        if(c==EOF) break;
        if((i>-1)&(lastto>-1)) {            /* translate */
          if(fputc(to[i], stdout)==EOF)
            error("output error");
          }
        else if(i<0) {                      /* copy */
          if(fputc(c, stdout)==EOF)
            error("output error");
          }
        }                                   /* delete */
      fclose(stdout);
      }
#include "pat.c"
#include "error.c"
#include "index.c"
#include "xindex.c"
#include "makset.c"
```

LISTING 13-16

FILE: STDIO.H

```
/*
** STDIO.H -- Standard Small-C Definitions
**
** Copyright 1983  L. E. Payne and J. E. Hendrix
*/
#define stdin    0
#define stdout   1
#define stderr   2
#define ERR    (-2)
#define EOF    (-1)
#define YES      1
#define NO       0
#define NULL     0
#define CR      13
#define LF      10
#define BELL     7
#define SPACE   ' '
```

```
#define NEWLINE LF
```

FILE: **TOOLS.H**

```
/*
** Small-Tools definitions.
**
** The metacharacter definitions do not completely
** follow UNIX or the Software-Tools definitions.
**
** You may change anything to suit your preferences.
*/
#define MAXFN      15     /* max file name space */
#define EXTMARK    '.'    /* file extension mark */
#define MAXLINE    192    /* max text line space */

        /* WY-50, TV-920, HZ-1500, AD-VP */
#define CLEAR   "\33\53" /* screen erase */
#define CRTWIDE    80    /* screen width */
#define CRTHIGH    24    /* screen height */
#define PTRWIDE    80    /* page width */
#define PTRHIGH    66    /* page height */
#define PTRSKIP    8     /* page perforation skips */
#define PTRHDR     2     /* page header lines */

#define MAXPAT    257   /* max pattern in internal format */
#define CHAR      'c'   /* identifies a character */
#define BOL       ''    /* beginning of line */
#define EOL       '\''  /* end of line */
#define ANY       '?'   /* any character */
#define CCL       '['   /* begin character class */
#define NCCL      '~'   /* negation of character class */
#define CCLEND    ']'   /* end of character class */
#define CLOSURE   '*'   /* zero or more occurrences */
#define DITTO     '^'   /* whatever string matches pattern */
#define ESCAPE    ':'   /* escape character */
#define NOT       '~'   /* negation character */

#define DITCODE   -3
#define COUNT     1
#define PREVCL    2
#define START     3
#define CLOSIZE   4
```

FILE: **BUF.C**

```
/*
** buf.c -- buffer manipulation functions (memory version)
*/
int gotline, gotind;
char *bufptr;
```

```
/*
** clrbuf -- initialize for new file (stub)
*/
clrbuf() {
  return;
  }
/*
** getind -- locate line index in buf
*/
getind(ln) int ln; {
  int j;
  if((j=ln-gotline) > 0)
    while(j--) getint(gotind+NEXT, &gotind, INTEGER);
  else if(j < 0)
    while(j++) getint(gotind+PREV, &gotind, INTEGER);
  gotline=ln;
  return gotind;
  }
/*
** getint -- obtain integer or long from buf at offset
*/
getint(offset, dest, length) int offset, length; char *dest; {
  bufptr=buf+offset;
  while(length--)  *dest++ = *bufptr++;
  }
/*
** putint -- place integer or long into buf at offset
*/
putint(offset, source, length) int offset, length; char *source; {
  bufptr=buf+offset;
  while(length--) *bufptr++ = *source++;
  }
/*
** gettxt -- locate text for line and make available
*/
gettxt(line) int line; {
  int i, j, k;
  i=(k=getind(line)) + TEXT;
  j=0;
  while(txt[j++]=buf[i++]);
  return k;
  }
/*
** input -- input text from fd into buf
*/
input(fd) int fd; {
```

```
  int k3;
  while(YES) {
    if(poll(YES)==ESC) return ERR;
    k3=lastbf;
    if(fgets(buf + (lastbf += TEXT), MAXLINE, fd)) {
      lastbf += trim(buf+lastbf) + 1;
      inlink(k3);
      if((lastbf+MAXLINE) > maxbuf) {
        fputs("memory overflow ", stderr);
        return ERR;
        }
      }
    else break;
    }
  lastbf -= TEXT;
  return OK;
  }

/*
** inject -- put text from lin after curln
*/
inject(lin) char lin[]; {
  int i, k3;
  if(*lin==NULL) {
    *lin='\n';
    *(lin+1)=NULL;
    }
  i=0;
  while(lin[i]!=NULL) {
    k3=lastbf;
    lastbf=lastbf+TEXT;
    while(lin[i]!=NULL) {
      if(lin[i]=='\n') {
        ++i;
        break;
        }
      addset(lin[i++], buf, &lastbf, maxbuf);
      }
    if(addset(NULL, buf, &lastbf, maxbuf)==NO) {
      fputs("memory overflow ", stderr);
      return ERR;
      }
    inlink(k3);
    }
  return OK;
  }

/*
** inlink -- link injected line
```

```
*/
inlink(k3) int k3; {
  int k1, k2;
  k1=getind(curln);
  /** leaves gotline & gotind before affected area **/
  getint(k1+NEXT, &k2, INTEGER);
  relink(k1, k3, k3, k2);
  relink(k3, k2, k1, k3);
  ++curln;
  ++lastln;
  }

/*
** relink -- rewrite two half links
*/
relink(a, x, y, b) int a, x, y, b; {
  putint(x+PREV, &a, INTEGER);
  putint(y+NEXT, &b, INTEGER);
  updtflag=YES;
  }

/*
** setbuf -- initialize line storage buffer
*/
setbuf() {
  relink(LINE0, LINE0, LINE0, LINE0);
  lastbf=LINE0+TEXT;
  addset(NULL, buf, &lastbf, maxbuf);
  gotline=curln=lastln=0;
  gotind=LINE0;
  }
```

─── **FILE: CANT.C**

```
/*
** cant.c -- abort with "name: can't open" message
*/
cant(str) char *str; {
  fputs(str, stderr);
  fputs(": can't open\n", stderr);
  abort(7);
  }
```

─── **FILE: CATSUB.C**

```
/*
** catsub.c -- add replacement text to end of new
*/
catsub(lin, from, to, sub, new, k, maxnew)
  char lin[], new[], sub[];
  int from, to, *k, maxnew; {
```

```
  int i, j;
  i=0;
  while(sub[i]!=NULL) {
    if(sub[i]==DITCODE) {
      j=from;
      while(j < to) addset(lin[j++], new, k, maxnew);
      }
    else addset(sub[i], new, k, maxnew);
    ++i;
    }
  }
```

FILE: DIGIT.C

```
/*
** digit.c -- return YES if c is a decimal digit, else NO
*/
digit(c) char c; {
  if((c>='0')&(c<='9')) return YES;
  return NO;
  }
```

FILE: ERROR.C

```
/*
** error.c -- display message str and abort
*/
error(str) char *str; {
  fputs(str, stderr);
  fputc('\n', stderr);
  abort(7);
  }
```

FILE: GETWRD.C

```
/*
** getwrd.c -- get non-blank word from in[i] into out, incr i
*/
getwrd(in, i, out) char in[], out[]; int *i; {
  char c;  int j;
  while(isspace(in[*i])) ++*i;
  j=0;
  while(c=in[*i]) {
    if(isspace(c)) break;
    out[j++]=c;
    ++*i;
    }
  out[j]=NULL;
  return j;
  }
```

―― FILE: INDEX.C

```
/*
** index.c -- find character c in string str
*/
index(str, c) char str[], c; {
  int i;
  i=-1;
  while(str[++i]!=NULL) if(str[i]==c) return i;
  return -1;
  }
```

―― FILE: MAKSET.C

```
/*
** makset.c -- make array into a set
*/
makset(array, k, set, size) char array[], set[]; int k, size; {
  int i, j;
  i=k;
  j=0;
  filset(NULL, array, &i, set, &j, size);
  return addset(NULL, set, &j, size);
  }
```

―― FILE: MAKSUB.C

```
/*
** maksub.c -- make substitution string in sub
*/
maksub(arg, from, delim, sub) char arg[], sub[], delim; int from; {
  int i, j;
  j=0;
  i=from;
  while((arg[i]!=delim)&(arg[i]!=NULL)) {
    if(arg[i]==DITTO) addset(DITCODE, sub, &j, MAXPAT);
    else addset(esc(arg, &i), sub, &j, MAXPAT);
    ++i;
    }
  if(arg[i]!=delim) return ERR; /**** missing delimiter ****/
  if(addset(NULL, sub, &j, MAXPAT)==NO) return ERR; /** no room **/
  return i;
  }
```

―― FILE: OUT.C

```
/*
** out.c -- output to fd checking for errors
*/
cout(c, fd) char c; int fd; {
  if(fputc(c, fd)==EOF) xout();
  }
```

```
sout(string, fd) char *string; int fd; {
  if(fputs(string, fd)==EOF) xout();
  }

lout(line, fd) char *line; int fd; {
  sout(line, fd);
  cout('\n', fd);
  }

xout() {
  fputs("output error\n", stderr);
  abort(7);
  }
```

──────────────────────────────── FILE: PAGE.C

```
/*
** page.c -- tell stderr of new page and possibly pause
*/
page(pageno, pause, fd) int pageno, pause, fd; {
  int i;
  char str[6];
  str[5]=NULL;
  itod(pageno, str, 5);
  i=0;
  while(str[i]==' ') ++i;
  if((pause==YES)&&(pageno>1)&&isatty(fd)) {
    fputs("\7set page ", stderr);
    fputs(str+i, stderr);
    fputs("... ", stderr);
    return fgetc(stderr);
    }
  else {
    fputs("page ", stderr);
    fputs(str+i, stderr);
    fputc('\n', stderr);
    return NULL;
    }
  }
```

──────────────────────────────── FILE: PAT.C

```
/*
** pat.c -- pattern making and matching functions
*/

/*
** addset -- put c in set & increment j
*/
addset(c, set, j, maxsiz) char c, set[]; int *j, maxsiz; {
  if(*j >= maxsiz) return NO;
```

```
    set[*j]=c;
    *j = *j + 1;
    return YES;
    }

/*
** amatch -- look for match starting at lin[from]
*/
amatch(lin, from, pat) char lin[], pat[]; int from; {
  int i, j, offset, stack;
  stack = -1;
  offset=from;
  j=0;
  while(pat[j]!=NULL) {
    if(pat[j]==CLOSURE) {
      stack=j;
      j=j+CLOSIZE;
      i=offset;
      while(lin[i]!=NULL) {
        if(omatch(lin, &i, pat, j)==NO) break;
        }
      pat[stack+COUNT]=i-offset;
      pat[stack+START]=offset;
      offset=i;
      }
    else if(omatch(lin, &offset, pat, j)==NO) {
      while(stack >= 0) {
        if(pat[stack+COUNT] > 0) break;
        stack=pat[stack+PREVCL];
        }
      if(stack < 0) return -1;
      pat[stack+COUNT]=pat[stack+COUNT]-1;
      j=stack+CLOSIZE;
      offset=pat[stack+START]+pat[stack+COUNT];
      }
    j=j+patsiz(pat, j);
    }
  return offset;
  }

/*
** dodash -- expand array[i-1] - array[i+1] into set[j]...
*/
dodash(valid, array, i, set, j, maxset)
  char valid[], set[], array[]; int *i, *j, maxset; {
  int k, limit;
  *i = 1 + *i;
  *j = -1 + *j;
  limit=index(valid, esc(array, i));
```

```
      k=index(valid, set[*j]);
      while(k <= limit)
        addset(valid[k++], set, j, maxset);
    }

/*
** esc -- map array[i] into escaped char if appropriate
*/
esc(array, i) char array[]; int *i; {
  if(array[*i]!=ESCAPE) return array[*i];
  else if(array[ *i + 1]==NULL)    /* esc not special at end */
    return ESCAPE;
  else {
    *i= *i + 1;
    if(array[*i]=='n') return '\n';
    else if(array[*i]=='t') return '\t';
    else if(array[*i]=='b') return '\b';
    else if(array[*i]=='s') return ' ';
    else return array[*i];
    }
  }


/*
** filset -- expand set in array into set stopping at delim
*/
filset(delim, array, i, set, j, maxset)
  char delim, array[], set[]; int *i, *j, maxset; {
  char *digits, *lowalf, *upalf;
  digits="0123456789";
  lowalf="abcdefghijklmnopqrstuvwxyz";
  upalf="ABCDEFGHIJKLMNOPQRSTUVWXYZ";
  while((array[*i]!=delim)&(array[*i]!=NULL)) {
    if(array[*i]==ESCAPE)
      addset(esc(array, i), set, j, maxset);
    else if(array[*i]!='-')
      addset(array[*i], set, j, maxset);
    else if((j <= 0)|(array[*i+1]==NULL))    /* literal - */
      addset('-', set, j, maxset);
    else if(index(digits, set[*j -1]) > -1)
      dodash(digits, array, i, set, j, maxset);
    else if(index(lowalf, set[*j -1]) > -1)
      dodash(lowalf, array, i, set, j, maxset);
    else if(index(upalf, set[*j -1]) > -1)
      dodash(upalf, array, i, set, j, maxset);
    else addset('-', set, j, maxset);
    *i = *i + 1;
    }
  }
```

```
/*
** getccl -- expand char class at arg[i] into pat[j]
*/
getccl(arg, i, pat, j) char arg[], pat[]; int *i, *j; {
  int jstart;
  *i = *i + 1;  /**** skip over '[' in arg ****/
  if(arg[*i]==NOT) {
    addset(NCCL, pat, j, MAXPAT);
    *i = *i + 1;
    }
  else addset(CCL, pat, j, MAXPAT);
  jstart = *j;
  addset(0, pat, j, MAXPAT);  /**** leave room for count ****/
  filset(CCLEND, arg, i, pat, j, MAXPAT);
  pat[jstart] = *j - jstart - 1;
  if(arg[*i]==CCLEND) return YES;
  return ERR;
  }


/*
** locate -- look for c in char class at pat[offset]
*/
locate(c, pat, offset) char c, pat[]; int offset; {
  int i;
  /*
  ** size of class is at pat[offset], characters follow
  */
  i=offset+pat[offset];
  while( i > offset) {
    if(c==pat[i--]) return YES;
    }
  return NO;
  }


/*
** makpat -- make pattern from arg[from], end at delim
*/
makpat(arg, from, delim, pat) char arg[], delim, pat[]; int from; {
  int i, j, lastcl, lastj, lj;
  j=lastj=0;
  lastcl = -1;
  i=from;
  while((arg[i]!=delim)&(arg[i]!=NULL)) {
    lj=j;
    if(arg[i]==ANY) addset(ANY, pat, &j, MAXPAT);
    else if((arg[i]==BOL)&(i==from)) addset(BOL, pat, &j, MAXPAT);
    else if((arg[i]==EOL)&(arg[i+1]==delim)) addset(EOL, pat, &j, MAXPAT);
    else if(arg[i]==CCL) {
      if(getccl(arg, &i, pat, &j)==ERR) break;
```

```
      }
    else if((arg[i]==CLOSURE)&(i>from)) {
      lj=lastj;
      if((pat[lj]==BOL)|(pat[lj]==EOL)|(pat[lj]==CLOSURE)) break;
      lastcl=stclos(pat, &j, &lastj, lastcl);
      }
    else {
      addset(CHAR, pat, &j, MAXPAT);
      addset(esc(arg, &i), pat, &j, MAXPAT);
      }
    lastj=lj;
    ++i;
    }
  if((arg[i]!=delim)|(addset(NULL, pat, &j, MAXPAT)==NO)) return ERR;
  return i;
  }

/*
** match -- find match anywhere in line
*/
match(line, pattern) char line[], pattern[]; {
  int i;
  i=0;
  while(YES) {
    if(amatch(line, i, pattern) >= 0) return YES;
    if(line[i++]==NULL) return NO;
    }
  }

/*
** omatch -- try to match a single pattern at pat[j]
*/
omatch(lin, i, pat, j) char lin[], pat[]; int *i, j; {
  int bump;
  bump = -1;
  if(pat[j]==BOL) {
    if(*i==0) bump=0;
    }
  else if(pat[j]==EOL) {
    if(lin[*i]==NULL) bump=0;
    }
  else if(lin[*i]==NULL) return NO;
  else if(pat[j]==CHAR) {
    if(lin[*i]==pat[j+1]) bump=1;
    }
  else if(pat[j]==ANY) bump=1;
  else if(pat[j]==CCL) {
    if(locate(lin[*i], pat, j+1)==YES) bump=1;
    }
```

```
    else if(pat[j]==NCCL) {
      if(locate(lin[*i], pat, j+1)==NO) bump=1;
      }
    else error("in omatch: can't happen\n");
    if(bump >= 0) {
      *i = *i + bump;
      return YES;
      }
    return NO;
    }

/*
** patsiz -- returns size of entry at pat[n]
*/
patsiz(pat, n) char *pat; int n; {
  pat=pat+n;
  if(*pat==CHAR) return 2;
  else if((*pat==BOL)|(*pat==EOL)|(*pat==ANY)) return 1;
  else if((*pat==CCL)|(*pat==NCCL)) return (*(++pat)+2);
  else if(*pat==CLOSURE) return CLOSIZE;
  else error("in patsiz: can't happen\n");
  }

/*
** stclos -- insert closure entry at pat[j]
*/
stclos(pat, j, lastj, lastcl) char pat[]; int *j, *lastj, lastcl; {
  int jp, jt;
  jp = *j - 1;
  while(jp >= *lastj) {   /**** make hole for closure ****/
    jt = jp + CLOSIZE;
    addset(pat[jp--], pat, &jt, MAXPAT);
    }
  *j = *j + CLOSIZE;
  jp = *lastj;
  addset(CLOSURE, pat, lastj, MAXPAT);   /** CLOSURE **/
  addset(0, pat, lastj, MAXPAT);         /** COUNT **/
  addset(lastcl, pat, lastj, MAXPAT);    /** PREVCL **/
  addset(0, pat, lastj, MAXPAT);         /** START **/
  return jp;
  }
```

───────────────────────────────────── FILE: SAME.C

```
/*
** same -- YES if c same as lower case lc, else NO
**         c may be upper or lower case
*/
same(c, lc) char c, lc; {
  if((c >= 'A')&(c <= 'Z')) c = c + 32;
```

```
    if (c == lc) return YES;
    return NO;
    }
```

---- FILE: SCOPY.C

```
/*
** scopy -- copy from[i] to to[j]
*/
scopy(from, i, to, j) char *from, *to; int i, j; {
  from=from+i;
  to=to+j;
  while(*to++ = *from++);
  }
```

---- FILE: SETTAB.C

```
/*
** settab.c -- search command line for tab list possibly
**             terminated with an interval (+n) and set up
**             tabs[MAXLINE+1]
*/
#define DEFTAB 8
settab(tabs, argc, argv) char tabs[]; int argc, *argv; {
  int i, j, k;
  char parm[9];
  i=0;
  while(++i<MAXLINE) tabs[i]=NO;
  if((getarg(1, parm, 9, argc, argv))==EOF) {
    i=0;
    while(++i<MAXLINE)
    if((i%DEFTAB)==1) tabs[i]=YES;
    return YES;
    }
  i=0;
  j=1;
  while(getarg(++i, parm, 9, argc, argv)!=EOF) {
    if(utoi(parm, &k)) {
      if(k<=MAXLINE) {
        tabs[k]=YES;
        j=k;
        }
      else {
        fputs("tab stop beyond max line length\n", stderr);
        return ERR;
        }
      }
    else if(parm[0]=='+') {
      if(utoi((parm+1), &k))
        while((j=j+k)<=MAXLINE) tabs[j]=YES;
      }
```

```
    else return ERR;
    }
  return YES;
  }
```

---— FILE: STRIP.C

```
/*
** strip -- Strip <, >, and " from str.
*/
strip(str) char *str; {
  char *cp;
  cp = str - 1;
  while(*++cp = *str++) {
    switch(*cp) {
      case '<': case '>': case '"': --cp;
      }
    }
  }
```

---— FILE: TABPOS.C

```
/*
** tabpos.c -- return YES if col is a tab stop, else NO
*/
tabpos(col, tabs) int col; char tabs[]; {
  if(col>MAXLINE) return YES;
  else return tabs[col];
  }
```

---— FILE: TRIM.C

```
/*
** trim -- trim \n from str & return its length
*/
trim(str) char *str; {
  char *s;
  s = str - 1;
  while(*++s) ;  /* prefix ++ is faster */
  if((*--s == '\n') && (s >= str)) *s = NULL; else ++s;
  return (s - str);
  }
```

---— FILE: XINDEX.C

```
/*
** xindex.c -- invert condition returned by index
*/
xindex(array, c, allbut, lastto) char array[], c; int allbut, lastto; {
  if(c==EOF) return -1;
  else if(allbut==NO) return index(array, c);
  else if(index(array, c)>-1) return -1;
  else return lastto+1;
  }
```

14
GREP.C: A GENERALIZED, REGULAR EXPRESSION PARSER IN C

by Allen Holub

This article originally appeared in DDJ #96 (October 1984).

Grep is the Unix pattern finder: it goes into a file or group of files and finds text patterns matching a symbolic regular expression. Grep is surprisingly useful. With it you can find a subroutine lost in one of the 50 modules making up the giant program that you're working on. You can find the misspelled name that your linker says is an undeclared function. Grep can number all the lines in a file or list all procedure declarations in a C program, as well as performing innumerable other things.

A good example of grep's utility is the history of this version, grep.c. At first, I wanted to expand the pattern-searching capabilities of Ed Ream's editor, RED ("RED: A Better C Screen Editor," *DDJ* #81). I wanted to add a pattern-searching capability similar to that of the Berkeley Unix editor, vi. So I set about converting into C the pattern-matching algorithms in *Software Tools in Pascal* by B.W. Kernighan and P.L. Plauger (Addison-Wesley, 1981, Chapter 5).

Along the way I ran into difficulties. My version of RED was written in BDS C, which has a nonstandard I/O library. I wanted to translate the editor to standard C so I could port it between different compilers and different machines. To do the translation, I needed to find all calls to the nonstandard library routines. So I turned my pattern matcher into a real program, linked the BDS version of RED without linking the library modules (to get a list of the library routines that RED used), then used grep to search all the modules of RED for procedure calls to the library functions.

The program presented here is most of the Unix grep. The only omissions are those command line switches that are Unix dependent, the -x switch (that performs an exact line match), and the +, ?, and ( ) regular expression operators (that are not essential).

The power of grep lies in its use of regular expressions as pattern templates rather than explicit strings. For example, the grep command line

```
grep^[a - z][a - z]*[\s\t]*.*([^;]*)[^;]*$ mod1.c mod2.c mod3.c
```

creates a cross-reference of a large C program. The three files mod1.c, mod2.c, and mod3.c are searched. Grep's output shows all subroutine declarations along with the name of the file in which the subroutine is declared. The regular expression is interpreted as follows: beginning of line (^), followed by one or more occurrences of any character in the range a to z ([a - z][a - z]*), followed by either a space or a tab repeated zero or more times ([\s\t]*), followed by any character repeated zero or more times (.*), followed by an open parenthesis (( ), followed by any character except a semicolon repeated zero or more times ([^;]*), followed by a close parenthesis ( )), followed by any character except a semicolon repeated zero or more times ([^;]*), followed by end of line ($).

You could also use grep to get a count of the number of procedures found and either have the matching lines printed out with line numbers or have all the lines not matching the pattern printed by including various command line switches in the program invocation.

Regular Expressions

Regular expressions are a way of representing text patterns in a symbolic shorthand. The * and ? that CP/M uses are examples of a crude regular expression syntax. The symbols grep uses to define regular expressions fall into five categories:

- Symbols that match a specific character

- Symbols that match any character

- Symbols that match a character's position on the line

- Symbols (called *character classes*) that match any of a set of characters or anything except a set of characters

- Symbols that let you match the previous symbol any number of times (called *closure*)

The rules for constructing regular expressions are given on the excerpted manual page (see Table 14-1, page 667). Some examples follow.

a.d	matches any word containing an *a*, followed by any character, followed by a *d*. This expression will match the substrings "and" in *and* and "ard" in a*ard*vark; this means that grep will print any *line* containing either word, along with any other match.
^a.d	matches the same strings but only if they occur at the beginning of the line. No characters, including spaces and tabs, are allowed in front of the *a*.
a.d$	matches the same strings if they occur at the end of the line. No character, including spaces and tabs, can follow the *d*.
^$	matches a beginning of line, followed by an end of line; this means it matches all lines containing nothing but a newline character.
an*d	matches any word containing an *a*, followed by an *n* repeated zero or more times. This expression will match *add* as well as *and*.
*	matches any character repeated any number of times. This expression will always succeed. For example, an invocation of grep with the line grep -n.* filename outputs every line in the file preceded by its line number.
aa*	matches one (rather than zero) or more occurrences of the letter *a*.
[abc]	defines a *character class*. A character class matches any one of the characters surrounded by the square brackets. This particular character class matches an *a*, *b*, or *c* in the corresponding position on the line.
who[ms]e	matches *who*, followed immediately by either an *m* or an *s*, followed by an *e*. That is, the words *whomever* and *whose* will be matched, but the word *whole* will not. Character class definitions may be abbreviated by using a dash. For example, [a - k] will be treated as if you had said [abcdefghijk]. Similarly, [0−9A−Fa−f] will be expanded to [0123456789ABCDEFabcdef]. This last character class will match any single hexadecimal digit. That is, any digit or any letter between *a* and *f* will be matched. Note that you have to say "A - Fa - f" to match both uppercase and lowercase.
0x[0 - 9a - fA - F][0 - 9 a - fA - F]*	matches all lines in a C program that contain hexadecimal numbers. This regular expression matches the characters 0x, followed by any of the characters 0123456789abcdefABCDEF repeated one or more times.

[^]	defines a *negative character class* (one that matches any character except those listed). For example, f[^o] finds all occurrences of an *f* not followed by an *o*. Be careful here with patterns at the end of line. Although [^o] matches any character that is not an *o*, a lone *f* at the end of line will not match the pattern because the end of line is not a character—it is a position. To find an *f* at the end of line position, use f[^o]*$ or f$¦f[^o].
[a - zA - Z]f\s¦[A - Z][A - Z]*\s	matches all lines containing words ending in *f* or all lines containing words composed only of uppercase characters. That is, if either of the regular expressions separated by the ¦ are satisfied, a match is returned.

If you need to match a character that is used as a symbol in the regular expression, precede it with a backslash (\). For example, * matches an asterisk, and \\ matches the backslash itself. Certain escape sequences (as these backslash sequences are called) are predefined; in particular, \s matches a space, and \t matches a tab (control-I). These are needed because of the irregularities of certain compilers and operating systems. A space in the command line makes many command-line interpreters break up the expression into two arguments. A tab in the command line confuses CP/M utterly; it won't execute your program at all. Other escape sequences are defined on the manual page (Table 14-1).

Technical Description

The routines in tools.c differ from those in *Software Tools* in three important ways. First, the routines were translated into C. Second, all references to array indexes were replaced with pointers in the interest of increased execution speed. Finally, the data structure used for the pattern template was changed significantly.

The reasons for this last change are somewhat complex. Grep breaks up the input expression into a pattern template, where each element of the template represents a single logical portion of the expression. For example, the expression [a - z]x.* requires four elements in the pattern template. One element is required for the character class ([a - z]), one element for the literal character match (x), one element to match any character (.), and one element for the closure (*). Processing the expression is much easier once it has been functionally divided in this way.

Kernighan and Plauger use a single ASCII string as their pattern template, and this data structure causes several problems. Varying numbers of characters are required to represent different types of elements in the template. To advance through the template, you need a subroutine that analyzes the current element and then advances the appropriate number of characters; this subroutine adds unnecessary overhead to the pattern-recognizing parts of grep. By replacing the ASCII string with a linked list of structures (which is how the templates are represented in my version of grep), you can advance to the next pattern with a single assignment operation.

Grep can be broken up into three distinct parts:

- Get the regular expression(s), the file list, and any switches from the command line.
- Translate the expression(s) into a pattern template.
- Go through the input files one line at a time, calling the routine matchs(), and produce the appropriate output on finding a match.

Getting the Expressions

Grep is divided into two main modules: grep.c and tools.c Grep.c does all of the I/O, and tools.c contains the pattern-matching routines. Grep translates the pattern strings into a special template representing the pattern (more about this later), and the routine matchs() does the actual pattern matching; it processes all symbols except the OR (|) operator, that separates the regular expressions.

Grep creates a template for every regular expression input and organizes these templates using an array of pointers to templates (similar to argv) called exprv[]; a count of the number of separate expressions in the array, exprc, is also available. Grep then calls matchs(), once for each template in exprv[], before getting the next input line.

The Pattern Template

The templates are a linked list of structures called TOKENs (Figure 14-1). Matchs() is passed a pointer to this linked list. A string holding a regular expression is converted to a template by the procedure makepat(). Since alloc() is used to allocate the (main) memory needed to contain the template, the expression can be any length, within reason. Using the routine unmakepat(), you can return the memory used by a template to the free list. Unmakepat() is not used by grep, but it may be useful for other applications (such as editors).

Some of the fields in a TOKEN are not always used; although using a union would have saved a small amount of (main) memory space, this would have added additional complexity to the program as a whole. The *tok* field identifies the type of symbol represented by this node (closure, character class, and so on). If the node is a literal character, *1char* holds the character itself, and if the node is a character class, *string* points at a string holding all the characters in the class. Classes defined with the dash notation (a - z) are expanded.

Note that a CLOSURE token is put into the chain in front of the node on which it operates (even though the closure symbol is put after the character in

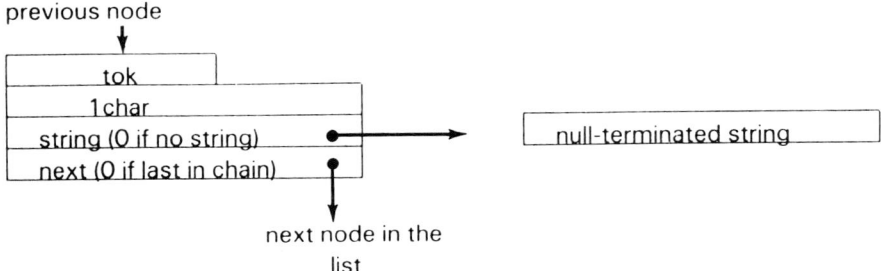

Figure 14-1. The TOKEN data structure.

the expression itself). This transposition eliminates the need for any sort of look-ahead in the searching routines. When you encounter the CLOSURE token, you know the next token should be repeated zero or more times. If the CLOSURE token did not come first, you would process the character on which the CLOSURE operates as if it were a literal match; that is, you would match a single occurrence of the character. Since closure represents zero or more matches, this first match would be incorrect. So, if the CLOSURE token did not come first, you could not process a token without having looked for a token following it.

Matchs()

The core of grep is the routine matchs() and the procedures that matchs() calls. This routine looks for a regular expression match in a string. It takes the string and a pointer to a pattern template as input and returns a pointer into the string upon success (or zero if no match is found). This pointer can point at either the beginning or the end of the matched string, depending on the value of the ret_endp parameter to matchs(). If ret_endp is zero, a pointer to the beginning of the matched string is returned; if ret_endp is nonzero, then a pointer to the end of the matched string is returned. For example, given the string abcdefghijklm and the pattern a.*j, matchs() can return a pointer to either the *a* or the *j*. This is a useful feature in an editor.

You must be careful with the $ symbol if you want to use the pointers returned by matchs(). Usually $ means *at* the end of line, not the end-of-line character itself; for example, if you are searching for f$, a pointer is returned to the *f*. However, if you are searching for $ itself, a pointer to the actual end-of-line character is returned. This takes care of the ^$ case. Matchs() must return a pointer to something, and the only character on the line is the newline character. A search for \n always returns a pointer to the newline. This last feature is nonstandard but, again, is useful in an editor application.

Matchs() advances through the input string, one character at a time, until it reaches the end of the string and failure is returned. It calls amatch() to do the comparisons, and when amatch() returns success, so does matchs().

Amatch() goes through the pattern template, one element at a time, comparing it with the text string. It advances to the next element of the template with each successful comparison, also advancing the text string as appropriate. If amatch() reaches the end of the template, the match is successful. Omatch() is called to do the simple comparisons: single characters against single elements in the pattern template.

Amatch() returns immediately on failure, so the performance of matchs() is not too slow in the general case (execution time is directly proportional to the length of the input stream). The worst-case performance, however, is an exponential function of the matched string's length. Given an input string of the form:

aaaaaaaaaaaaaaaaaaaaaaaaaaaaaaaaaaaaaaaaaaaab

along with a match string a*c, amatch() will be called n times, where n is the length of the input string. Each call to amatch() will look at the entire input string on the order of n^2 times; this means the total worst-case execution time is $O(n^3)$.

Most of this is the fault of closure processing, which is done by brute force. Amatch() first eliminates all the characters defined by the closure by scanning along the text string and calling omatch(), until a mismatch is found. It then tries to match the rest of the template against the rest of the text string. If amatch() fails to match the tail, it goes backwards through the characters it just processed, while trying to match the trailing string against the rest of the pattern template. This is necessary because the character following the closure could have been included in the closure itself.

For example, in the pattern [a-z]*t (which matches any lowercase word ending in a t), the final t will be absorbed by the first scan (t is included in the character class [a-z]). Since amatch() has scanned too far, an attempt to match the t will now fail. So it backs up a notch in the input string and then tries to match the rest of the pattern template again, repeating this process recursively until it gets back to the beginning of the closure. The recursion only goes one level deep.

Examples:

Makepat() takes two arguments. The first argument is an ASCII string holding the regular expression; the second argument is a character to use as a terminator in the expression string. That is, processing of the expression string will be terminated when the character specified by the second argument is encountered.

The template returned by makepat() when called with

```
makepat("^The qui",'\0')
```

is shown in Figure 14-2. If you had called makepat() with

```
makepat("^The quick",' ')
```

a template like that in Figure 14-2 would again be returned; however, this time the template would stop with the *e* LITCHAR because makepat() was passed a space as the input string terminator. A call to

```
makepat("a[0 - 9].*[^v]$",'\0')
```

returns a pointer to the template shown in Figure 14-3.

Matchs() looks for an expression on only one input line. Consequently, it has to be called several times, once for each line in the input file. Three arguments are required: the first is a pointer to the line being searched, the second is a pointer to a pattern template (returned by a previous call to makepat()), and the third determines whether matchs() will return a pointer to the beginning or to the end of the matched pattern (0 for a pointer to the beginning, 1 for the end).

Consider the program fragment:

```
#include "tools.h"
TOKEN *template; char *ptr;
template = makepat("456",'\0');
ptr = matchs("1234567890", template, 0);
ptr = matchs("1234567890", template, 1);
ptr = matchs("abcdefghij", template, 1);
```

The call to makepat() returns a pointer to a pattern template representing the string 456. This template will be three elements long, one element for each character in the string, and all three elements will be of type LITCHAR. The first call to matchs() will return a pointer to the 4 (because its third parameter is 0). The second call to matchs() will return a pointer to the 6 (because the third parameter is 1). The third call to matchs() returns 0 because the string 456 does not exist in the string abcdefghij.

A simplistic version of grep—using only gets(), makepat(), and matchs()—is shown in Figure 14-4. This version prints all input lines that match a pattern found on the command line. No attempt at any sort of error checking is made in this example, so it's not a very practical program. It does, however, illustrate how makepat() and matchs() may be used in a real program.

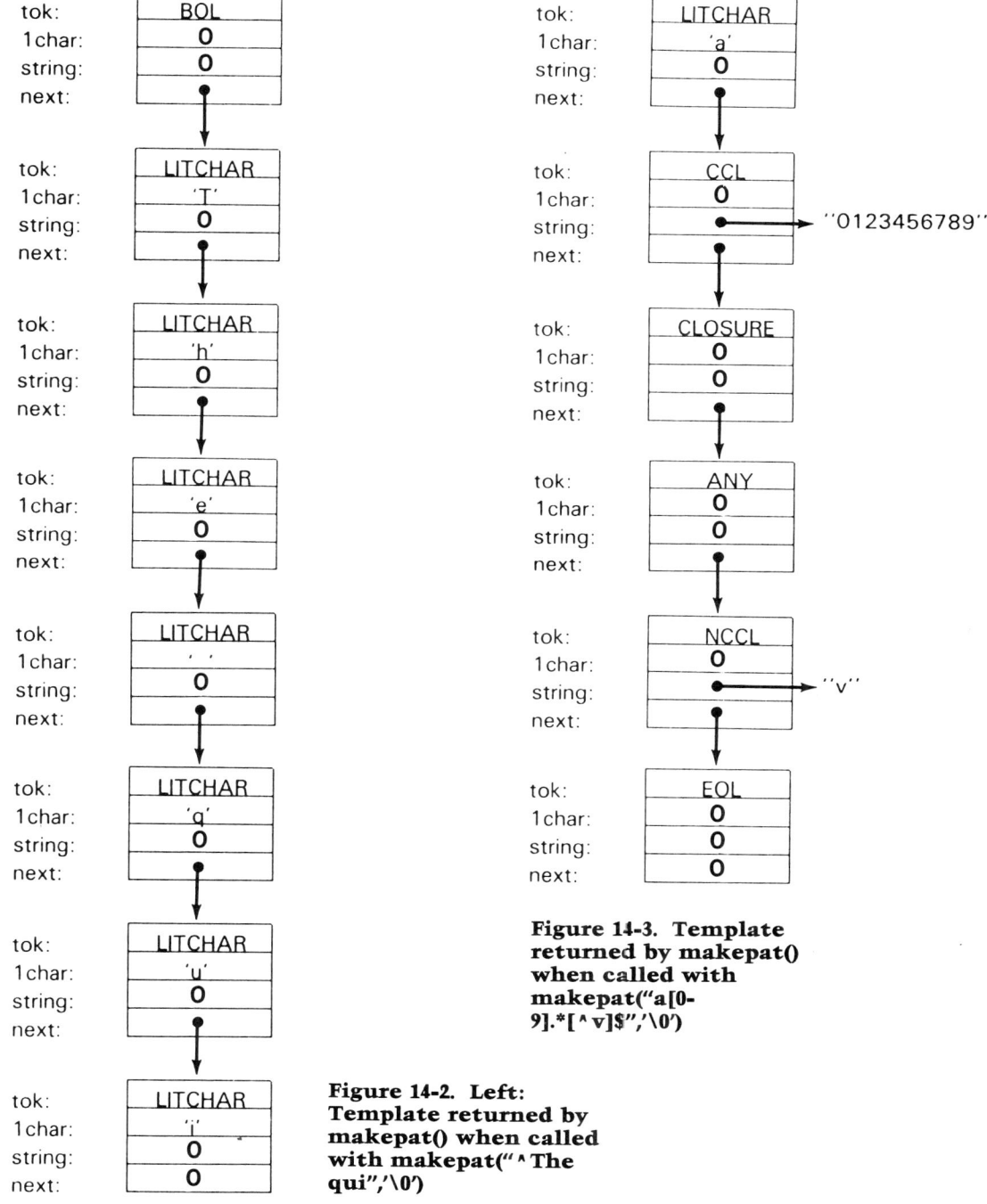

Figure 14-2. Left: Template returned by makepat() when called with makepat("^The qui",'\0')

Figure 14-3. Template returned by makepat() when called with makepat("a[0-9].*[^v]$",'\0')

Debugging Aids

Four routines are included here for debugging: pr_tok(), pr_line(), insert(), and delete(); all are in tools.c.

Pr_tok, when passed by a pointer to a linked list of TOKENs, prints out the list to stdout. You can use pr_tok to monitor the progress of amatch() as it works and to see if the expression is translated correctly to begin with.

Pr_line() prints out one line of text to stdout; however, any nonprintable characters are represented as numbers in the form:

    \0x<two hex digits>

Insert() puts a character into a string at a place pointed to by its str parameter. Delete() takes the character out again.

Some Implementation Notes

While bringing up grep on my system, I ran into a few problems worth mentioning. First, depending on which compiler you use, getting the expression from the command line may be unexpectedly difficult. The command-line parser for Aztec C II (the compiler I used on this version) doesn't allow quoted strings; that is, an argument of the form

    grep "this is a single argument" foo.bar

will be broken up into seven (rather than three) arguments by the compiler. So I modified the command-line parser in the module croot.c to accept quoted strings (See "C-Chest," *DDJ*, March '85, #101).

Figure 14-4. A simplistic version of grep that uses only gets(), makepat(), and matchs()

```
# include"stdio.h"
# include"tools.h"
main(argc,argv)
int     argc;
char    *argv[];
{
    TOKEN   *template;
    char    str[132];
    template = makepat(argv[1],'\0');
    while(gets(str)!=NULL)
        if(matches(str,template,0))
            printf("%s\n",str);
}
```

The BDS C compiler does give you quoted strings, but there are pitfalls here, too. As it parses the command line, BDS strips off the quotes. Because BDS wildcard expansion is done with a call to wildexp() inside the program proper (instead of inside the command-line parser where it belongs); wildexp() cannot differentiate between the quoted argument and the normal arguments: it does not have any quotes to work with. Consequently, it tries to expand the regular expression if the expression has a * or ? in it.

I got around this problem in a BDS version of grep by getting the regular expression from the command line *before* calling wildexp(). I then replaced the argv entry, that pointed at the expression, with a pointer to a null string and called wildexp(). You could also try to call wildexp() from inside the command-line parser itself. Since the parser is written in assembly language and wildexp() is in C, I didn't try this (though it would be a permanent solution to the problem).

A similar problem can be found in microshell which supports quoted strings, but still treats a backslash inside a quoted string as a special character. You need to double the backslash to pass it through to grep (that is, use \\ instead of \; and \\\\ instead of \\). One saving grace is that microshell lets you pass tabs through unmolested.

One final difficulty: you can use grep as a filter if you like. That is, if you are running microshell or some other environment that supports pipes, you may use grep as a general purpose filter, stripping out unwanted material from the input stream, and then passing the modified stream to another program. The problem is what happens to end-of-line terminators on their way through the pipe.

CP/M requires a carriage-return, line-feed (CR-LF) combination at the end of line. C, however, wants a single newline character (\n). Consequently, when getc() sees a CR, it echoes it as a CR-LF (so the screen looks nice) and then turns it into a \n. On output, putc() turns the \n back into a CR-LF.

This is fine until you use the output of one program as the input of another. The next program will see the CR-LF, echo it as CR-LF-LF, and map it to a \n\n (one \n for the CR, another for the LF). The output from the second program will have a CR-LF-CR-LF at the end of every line—instant double spacing. If you go through another layer of pipe you will get CR-LF-CR-LF-CR-LF-CR-LF at the end of each line, and so on.

A solution would be to have getchar() work as described above, and have getc() ignore the LF character entirely (not pass it through to the program). The BDS C compiler doesn't lend itself to this change because its I/O library has the two input routines functionally reversed (that is, getc() calls getchar(), which is the reverse of Unix). You could also use the BDS version 1.5 raw I/O routines, but then your code would be even more nonstandard. Alternately, you could enter all the characters from the console with direct bdos() calls.

Table 14-1.
Grep Manual Page

NAME
   grep — search a file for a pattern

SYNOPSIS
   grep [-options] ... [expression] [file list] ...

DESCRIPTION
   The algorithm used here is essentially that presented in *Software Tools in Pascal* by Kernighan and Plauger (Addison-Wesley, 1981, pp. 145f).

   This program is a healthy subset of the Unix program of the same name. The differences are as follows:

   - The -s, -x, and -b options are not supported.
   - The metacharacters ( ) + ? are not supported.
   - The -y option causes all lowercase characters in the file being searched to be mapped to uppercase before the match (as compared to "lowercase letters in the pattern will also match uppercase letters in the input").

   The program will find a string specified by a regular expression in a file or group of files. The following options are recognized:

-v	All lines except those matching are printed.
-c	Only a count of the matching lines is printed.
-l	The names of the files with matching lines are listed (once) separated by newlines.
-n	Each line is preceded by its line number in the file.
-h	Do not print filename headers with output lines.
-y	All characters in the file are mapped to uppercase before matching. This is the default if the regular expression is given on the command line (because CP/M maps everything on the command line to uppercase). Use the -f option if you need both lowercase and uppercase.
-e\<expression\>	Same as a simple expression argument, but useful when the expression begins with "-".
-f\<file\>	The regular expression is taken from the file. If several regular expressions are listed (separated by newlines or |s), then a match will be flagged if any of the regular expressions are satisfied. -e and -f are mutually exclusive. If -f is given, any regular expression on the command line is taken to be a filename.

   Regular expressions are composed of the following:

^	matches the beginning of a line
$	matches the end of a line

Table 14-1 (continued).

.   matches any character
\   followed by a single character matches that character. However, the following sequences are special:
\b   backspace (^H)
\n   linefeed (^J; this is not the same as $)
\r   carriage return (^M)
\s   space
\t   tab (^I)
\\   backslash

A single character not otherwise endowed with special meaning matches that character.

A string enclosed in brackets [] specifies a *character class*. Any single character in the string will be matched. For example, [abc] will match an a, b, or c. Ranges of ASCII character codes may be abbreviated, as in [a-z 0-9]. If the first symbol following the [is a ^ then a *negative character class* is specified. In this case, the string matches all characters except those enclosed in the brackets (that is, [^a-z] matches everything except lowercase letters). Note that a negative character class must match something, even though that something cannot be any of the characters listed. For example, ^$ is not the same as ^[^z]$. The first example matches an empty line (beginning of line followed by end of line); the second example matches a beginning of line followed by any character except a z followed by end of line. In the second example, a character must be present on the line, but that character cannot be a z. Note that the characters * . ^ $ are not special characters when inside a character class.

A regular expression followed by * matches zero or more matches of the regular expression.

Two regular expressions concatenated match a match of the first, followed by a match of the second.

Two regular expressions separated by | or a newline match either a match for the first, or a match for the second.

The order of precedence is [ ] then * then concatenation then | then newline.

Example:

The command line
    grep -n ^[a - z][a - z]*[\s\t]*.*([^;]*)[^;]*$<file list>
creates a cross-reference of a large C program. The <file list> should be replaced with a list of the modules to be searched. Grep's output will show all subroutine declarations in all the listed files. In addition, every output line will be preceded by both the name of the file in which the line was found (this is automatic if more than one file is searched) and by the appropriate line number (the -n causes line numbers to be shown).

The regular expression is interpreted as follows: beginning of line (^), followed by one or more occurrences of any character in the range a to z ([a - z][a - z]*), followed by either a space or a tab repeated zero or more times ([\s\t]*), followed by any character repeated zero or more times (.*), followed by an open parenthesis ((), followed by any character except a semicolon repeated zero or more times ([;]*),

Table 14-1 (continued).

followed by a close parenthesis ()), followed by any character except a semicolon repeated zero or more times ([;]*), followed by end of line ($).

BUGS

Arguments, if present, must be grouped together in the second position on the command line. The first character of the group must be a -. Unless the -f option is given, the next argument is always taken to be the expression. If -f is present, then the third argument is the name of the file containing the expression.

Beware of spaces or tabs in the expression, even if your compiler supports quoted arguments. CP/M will object to ^I anywhere on the command line. To be safe, use \s for spaces and \t for tabs.

Some of the command-line switches do mutually exclusive things (-ef and -lh). If you try to trick grep into doing something it is not supposed to do, the output will be undefined.

Grep's execution speed varies as a function of the type of expression being parsed. The speed will vary as follows (listed fastest to slowest):

- Simple expressions anchored to beginning of line (^<expression>).
- Expressions matching literal strings.
- Expressions including character classes ([]).
- Expressions including closure (*).

PC-DOS Update:

In the CP/M version of grep the command line is automatically mapped to uppercase by the operating system. Consequently, the -y switch is automatically turned on in the CP/M version of grep. This switch causes case to be ignored. Since PC-DOS does not map the command line to uppercase, this automatic invocation of the -y flag is not performed in the PC-DOS version of grep.

Conclusion

Despite the few implementation problems I encountered, grep remains an extremely useful program. It has saved me hours of rooting around in modular C programs looking for misspelled subroutine names. Its cross-referencing ability has also proved invaluable. When I get a new C compiler, the first thing I do is use grep to make a cross-reference of the runtime library sources. Using this cross-reference, it's easy to find the source code for the particular library subroutine that doesn't seem to be working correctly. The addition of matchs() to the RED editor has made it a much nicer editor, giving RED not only an extended search ability but also a powerful global substitution ability. Once you've used regular expressions in an editor, you won't settle for anything else. I hope you find this program as useful as I have.

LISTING 14-1

```c
/*--------------------------------------------------------------*
 *      TOOLS.H: Various #defines and typedefs for GREP         *
 *                                                              *
 *      Copyright   (c)   1984   by Allen Holub. All   rights   *
 *      reserved.                                               *
 *--------------------------------------------------------------*
 */

/*
 *      #defines for non-printing ASCII characters
 */

#define NUL         0x00        /* ^@ */
#define CR          0x0d        /* ^M */
#define SUB         0x1a        /* ^Z */
#define CPMEOF      SUB

#define islower(c)      ( 'a' <= (c) && (c) <= 'z' )
#define toupper(c)      ( islower(c) ? (c) - ('a' - 'A') : (c) )

/*      Definitions of meta-characters used in pattern matching routines.
 *      LITCHAR & NCCL are only used as token identifiers; all the others
 *      are also both token identifiers and the actual symbol used in
 *      the regular expression
 */

#define BOL         '^'
#define EOL         '$'
#define ANY         '.'
#define LITCHAR     'L'
#define ESCAPE      '\\'
#define CCL         '['         /* Character class:   [...]             */
#define CCLEND      ']'
#define NEGATE      '^'
#define NCCL        '!'         /* Negative character class [^...]      */
#define CLOSURE     '*'
#define OR_SYM      '|'

/*
 *      Tokens are used to hold pattern templates. (see makepat() in
 *      tools.h
 */

typedef struct token
{
        char            tok;
        char            lchar;
```

```
            char        *bitmap;
            struct token *next;
    }TOKEN;

    #define TOKSIZE sizeof(TOKEN)

    /*
     *      An absolute maximum for strings.
     */

    #define MAXSTR      132         /* Maximum number of characters in
                                     *      a line.
                                     */

    extern  char    *matchs     ();
    extern  char    *amatch     ();
    extern  char    *index      ();
    extern  TOKEN   *getpat     ();
    extern  int     esc         ();
    extern  char    *dodash     ();
    extern  TOKEN   *makepat    ();
    extern  int     unmakepat   ();
    extern  int     insert      ();
    extern  int     delete      ();
    extern  int     isalphanum  ();
    extern  char    *stoupper   ();
    extern  int     pr_tok      ();
    extern  int     pr_line     ();
```

LISTING 14-2

```
    /*----------------------------------------------------------------
     *
     *      TOOLS.C: The expression parser used by GREP
     *
     *
     *              Copyright (c) 1984 Allen Holub
     *                  All rights reserved.
     *
     *      Permission to copy this program or any part of this program
     *      is granted in the case of personal, non-commercial use only.
     *      Any use for profit or other commercial gain without written
     *      permission of the author is prohibited.
     *
     *      If you've been give this program by a friend, and you find
     *      it worthwhile, I'd appreciate your sending $35 to me for the
     *      program.
     *
```

```
 *      Software Engineering Consultants, P.O. Box 5679, Berkeley CA, 94705
 *
 *-------------------------------------------------------------------
 */

/*
 *      This module contains the various routines needed by grep
 *      to match regular expressions. Routines are ordered
 *      alphabeticaly.
 */

#include <stdio.h>
#include "tools.h"

char    *amatch( lin, pat, boln )
char    *lin, *boln;
TOKEN   *pat;
{
        /*      Scans through the pattern template looking for a match
         * with lin. Each element of lin is compared with the template
         * until either a mis-match is found or the end of the template
         * is reached. In the former case a 0 is returned; in the latter,
         * a pointer into lin (pointing to the last character in the
         * matched pattern) is returned.
         *
         *      "lin"   is a pointer to the line being searched.
         *      "pat"   is a pointer to a template made by makepat().
         *      "boln"  is a pointer into "lin" which points at the
         *              character at the beginning of line.
         */

        register char   *bocl, *rval, *strstart;

        if (pat == 0)
                return( (char *)0 );

        strstart = lin;

        while ( pat )
        {
                if (pat->tok == CLOSURE &&    pat->next)
                {
                        /*
                         * Process a closure:
                         * First skip over the closure token to the
                         * object to be repeated. This object can be
                         * a character class.
                         */
```

```
            pat = pat->next;

    /*      Now match as many occurrences of the
     *      closure pattern as possible.
     */

            bocl = lin;

            while ( *lin  &&  omatch(&lin, pat, boln) )
                    ;

    /*      'Lin' now points to the character that made
     *      made us fail. Now go on to process the
     *      rest of the string. A problem here is
     *      a character following the closure which
     *      could have been in the closure.
     *      For example, in the pattern "[a-z]*t" (which
     *      matches any lower-case word ending in a t),
     *      the final 't' will be sucked up in the while
     *      loop. So, if the match fails, we back up a
     *      notch and try to match the rest of the
     *      string again, repeating this process
     *      recursively until we get back to the
     *      beginning of the closure. The recursion
     *      goes, at most, two levels deep.
     */

            if (pat = pat->next)
            {
                    while ( bocl <= lin )
                    {
                            if (rval = amatch(lin, pat, boln) )
                            {
                                    /* success */
                                    return(rval);
                            }
                            else
                                    --lin;
                    }
                    return (0);     /* match failed */
            }
    }
    else if ( omatch(&lin, pat, boln) )
    {
            pat = pat->next;
    }
    else
    {
            return (0);
```

```
        }
    }

    /*
     *  Note that omatch() advances lin to point at the next
     *  character to be matched. Consequently, when we reach
     *  the end of the template, lin will be pointing at the
     *  character following the last character matched.
     *  The exceptions are templates containing only a
     *  BOLN or EOLN token. In these cases omatch doesn't
     *  advance.
     *
     *  So, decrement lin to make it point at the end of the
     *  matched string. Then, check to make sure that we haven't
     *  decremented past the beginning of the string.
     *
     *  A philosophical point should be mentioned here. Is $
     *  a position or a character? (i.e., does $ mean the EOL
     *  character itself or does it mean the character at the end of
     *  the line.) I decided here to make it mean the former, in
     *  order to make the behavior of amatch() consistent. If you
     *  give amatch the pattern ^$ (match all lines consisting only
     *  of an end of line) then, since something has to be returned,
     *  a pointer to the end of line character itself is returned.
     *
     *  The --lin is done outside the return statement because max()
     *  is often a macro (which has side-effects).
     */

    --lin;
    return ( max(strstart, lin) );
}

/* ------------------------------------------------------------------ */

#ifdef DEBUG

delete( ch, str )
int            ch;
register char  *str;
{
        /*      Delete the first occurrence of character from string
         *      moving everything else over a notch to fill the hole.
         */

        ch &= 0xff;

        while ( *str && *str != ch )
                str++;
```

```
        while ( *str )
        {
                *str = *(str+1);
                str++;
        }
}

#endif

/* ---------------------------------------------------------------------- */

setbit( c, field )
int     c;
char    field[];
{
        /*      Set a bit in the bit ASCII bit map corresponding to the
         *      character c. Field must be at least 16 bytes long.
         */

        field[ (c & 0x7f) >> 3 ] |= 1 << (c & 0x07) ;
}

/* ---------------------------------------------------------------------- */

testbit( c, field )
int     c;
char    *field;
{
        /*      See if the bit corresponding to c in field is set.
         */

        return (    field[ (c & 0x7f)>>3 ]  &  (1 << (c & 0x07))   );
}

/* ---------------------------------------------------------------------- */

char    *dodash( delim, src, map )
int     delim;
char    *src, *map;
{
        /*      Expand the set pointed to by "*src" into the bitmap "map."
         *      Stop at delim or end of string. Update *src to point
         *      at terminator. A set can have one element {x} or several
         *      elements ( {abcdefghijklmnopqrstuvwxyz} and {a-z}
         *      are equivalent ). Note that the dash notation is expanded
         *      as sequential numbers. This means (since we are using the
         *      ASCII character set) that a-Z will contain the entire alphabet
         *      plus the symbols: [\]^_`
         *
```

```
 *      The character classes are stored in a 16 byte wide bit field
 *      where each bit corresponds to an ASCII character.
 */

    register int   first, last;
    char           *start;

    start = src;

    while( *src  &&  *src != delim )
    {
        if( *src != '-')
                setbit( esc( &src ), map );

        else if( src == start || *(src+1) == delim )
                setbit( '-', map );

        else
        {
                src++;

                if( *src < *(src - 2) )
                {
                        first = *src;
                        last  = *(src-2);
                }
                else
                {
                        first = *(src - 2);
                        last  = *src;
                }

                while( ++first <= last )
                        setbit( first, map );

                src++;
        }
    }

    return( src );
}

/* ---------------------------------------------------------------- */

int     esc(s)
char    **s;
{
        /* Map escape sequences into their equivalent symbols. Returns the
         * Correct ASCII character. c is the character following the \.
```

```
                */

                register int    rval;

                if( **s != ESCAPE )
                        rval = *( (*s)++ );
                else
                {
                        (*s)++;

                        switch( toupper(**s) )
                        {
                        case '\0':      rval = ESCAPE;          break;
                        case 'B':       rval = '\b' ;           break;
                        case 'F':       rval = '\f' ;           break;
                        case 'N':       rval = '\n' ;           break;
                        case 'R':       rval = '\r' ;           break;
                        case 'S':       rval = ' '  ;           break;
                        case 'T':       rval = '\t' ;           break;
                        default:        rval = **s  ;           break;
                        }

                        (*s)++;
                }

                return (rval);
}

/* ----------------------------------------------------------------- */

TOKEN   *getpat( arg )
char    *arg;
{
        /*      Translate arg into a TOKEN string
         */

        return ( makepat(arg, '\000' ) );
}

/* ----------------------------------------------------------------- */

#ifdef DEBUG

insert( ch, str )
int        ch;
register char   *str;
{
        /*      Insert ch into str at the place pointed to by str. Move
         *      everything else over a notch
```

```
                */

        register char    *bp;

        bp = str;

        while (*str)                    /* Find the end of string      */
                str++;
        do                              /* Move the tail over one notch */
        {
                *(str+1) = *str;
                str--;

        } while (str >= bp);

        *bp = ch;                       /* Put the char in the hole.   */
}

#endif

/* ------------------------------------------------------------------ */

int isalphanum(c)
int     c;
{
        /*      Return true if c is an alphabetic character or digit,
         *      false otherwise.
         */

        return( ('a' <= c  &&  c <= 'z') ||
                ('A' <= c  &&  c <= 'Z') ||
                ('0' <= c  &&  c <= '9')
              );
}

/*------------------------------------------------------------------*/

TOKEN   *makepat(arg, delim)
char    *arg;
int     delim;
{
        /*      Make a pattern template from the string pointed to by arg.
         *      Stop when delim or '\000' or '\n' is found in arg.
         *      Return a pointer to the pattern template.
         *
         *      The pattern templates used here are somewhat different
         *      than those used in the book; each token is a structure
         *      of the form TOKEN (see tools.h). A token consists of
         *      an identifier, a pointer to a string, a literal
```

```
 *      character and a pointer to another token. This last is 0 if
 *      there is no subsequent token.
 *
 *      The one strangeness here is caused (again) by CLOSURE which
 *      has to be put in front of the previous token. To make this
 *      insertion a little easier, the 'next' field of the last
 *      token in the chain (the one pointed to by 'tail') is made
 *      to point at the previous node. When we are finished,
 *      tail->next is set to 0.
 */

TOKEN   *head, *tail;
TOKEN   *ntok;
int     error, i ;

/*      Check for characters that aren't legal at the beginning
 *      of a template.
 */

if (*arg=='\0' || *arg==delim || *arg=='\r' || *arg==CLOSURE)
        return(0);

error = 0;
head  = 0;
tail  = 0;

for(; *arg && *arg != delim && *arg != '\n' && !error; arg++)
{
        ntok = (TOKEN *) malloc(TOKSIZE) ;

        if( error = !ntok )
        {
                fprintf(stderr,
                        "Not enough memory for pattern template\n");
                break;
        }

        switch(*arg)
        {
        case ANY:
                ntok->tok = ANY;
                break;

        case BOL:

                if (head==0)    /* then this is the first symbol */

                        ntok->tok = BOL;
                else
```

```
                        error = 1;
                break;

        case EOL:
                if ( *(arg+1) == delim || *(arg+1) == '\0'
                                       || *(arg+1) == '\n'  )
                        ntok->tok = EOL;
                else
                        error = 1;
                break;

        case CCL:
                if (*(arg+1) == NEGATE)
                {
                        ntok->tok = NCCL;
                        arg += 2;
                }
                else
                {
                        ntok->tok = CCL;
                        arg++;
                }

                if( ntok->bitmap = (char *) calloc( 16, 1 ) )
                {
                        arg = dodash(CCLEND, arg, ntok->bitmap );
                }
                else
                {
                        fprintf(stderr,"Not enough memory for pat\n");
                        error = 1;
                }

                break;

        case CLOSURE:
                switch ( tail->tok )
                {
                case BOL:
                case EOL:
                case CLOSURE:
                        return(0);
                default:
                        ntok->tok = CLOSURE;
                }
```

```c
                    break;

        default:
                ntok->tok = LITCHAR;
                ntok->lchar = esc( &arg );
                --arg;  /* esc advances us past the character */
        }

        if( error )
        {
                unmakepat(head);
                return (0);
        }
        else  if (head == 0)
        {
                /*  This is the first node in the chain.
                 */

                ntok->next = 0;
                head = tail = ntok;
        }
        else if( ntok->tok != CLOSURE)
        {
                /* Insert at end of list (after tail) */

                tail->next = ntok;
                ntok->next = tail;
                tail = ntok;
        }
        else if( head != tail )
        {
                /* More than one node in the chain. Insert the
                 * CLOSURE node immediately in front of tail.
                 */

                (tail->next)->next = ntok;
                ntok->next = tail;
        }
        else
        {
                /* Only one node in the chain, Insert the CLOSURE
                 * node at the head of the linked list.
                 */

                ntok->next = head;
                tail->next = ntok;
                head = ntok;
        }
}
```

```
                tail->next = 0;
                return (head);
        }


        /* ------------------------------------------------------------------ */

        char    *matchs(line, pat, ret_endp)
        char    *line;
        TOKEN   *pat;
        int     ret_endp;
        {
                /*
                 *      Compares line and pattern. Line is a character string while
                 *      pat is a pattern template made by getpat().
                 *      Returns:
                 *              1. A zero if no match was found.
                 *              2. A pointer the last character
                 *                 satisfying the match if ret_endp is non-zero.
                 *              3. A pointer to the beginning of the matched string
                 *                 if ret_endp is 0;
                 *
                 *      For example:
                 *
                 *              matchs ("1234567890", getpat("4[0-9]*7"), 0);
                 *
                 *      will return a pointer to the '4', while
                 *
                 *              matchs ("1234567890", getpat("4[0-9]*7"), 1);
                 *
                 *      will return a pointer to the '7'.
                 */

                char    *rval, *bptr;

                bptr = line;

                while (*line)
                {
                        if ( (rval = amatch(line, pat, bptr)) == 0 )
                        {
                                line++;
                        }
                        else
                        {
                                rval = ret_endp ? rval : line ;
                                break;
                        }
                }
```

```
                return (rval);
        }

/* ---------------------------------------------------------------- */

        char    *stoupper(str)
        char    *str;
        {
                /*
                 *      Map the entire string pointed to by str to upper case
                 *      Return str.
                 */

                char    *rval;

                rval = str;

                while (*str)
                {
                        if ( 'a' <= *str  &&  *str <= 'z' )
                                *str -= ('a' - 'A');

                        str++;
                }

                return(rval);
        }

/* ---------------------------------------------------------------- */

        int     omatch (linp, pat, boln)
        char    **linp, *boln;
        TOKEN   *pat;
        {
                /*      Match one pattern element, pointed at by pat, with the
                 *      character at **linp. Return non-zero on match.
                 *      Otherwise, return 0. *Linp is advanced to skip over the
                 *      matched character; it is not advanced on failure. The
                 *      amount of the advance is 0 for patterns that match null
                 *      strings, 1 otherwise. "boln" should point at the position
                 *      that will match a BOL token.
                 */

                register int    advance;

                advance = -1;

                if ( **linp )
                {
```

```
                switch ( pat->tok )
                {
                case LITCHAR:
                        if ( **linp == pat->lchar )
                                advance = 1;
                        break;

                case BOL:
                        if ( *linp == boln )
                                advance = 0;
                        break;

                case ANY:
                        if ( **linp != '\n' )
                                advance = 1;
                        break;

                case EOL:
                        if ( **linp == '\n' )
                                advance = 0;
                        break;

                case CCL:
                        if( testbit( **linp, pat->bitmap ) )
                                advance = 1;
                        break;

                case NCCL:
                        if( !testbit( **linp, pat->bitmap) )
                                advance = 1;
                        break;

                default:
                        printf("omatch: can't happen\n");
                }
        }

        if (advance >= 0)
                *linp += advance;

        return( ++advance );
}
/* ---------------------------------------------------------------- */

#ifdef DEBUG

pr_line(ln)
register char    *ln;
```

```
{
        /*      Print out ln, if a non-printing character is found, print
         *      out its numerical value in the form "\0x<hex number>".
         *      Again, this is a debugging aid. It lets you see what's
         *      really on the line.
         */

        for ( ; *ln ; ln++ )
        {
                if ( (' ' <= *ln) && (*ln <= '~') )
                        putchar(*ln);
                else
                {
                        printf("\\0x%02x", *ln);

                        if (*ln == '\n')
                                putchar('\n');
                }
        }
}

/* ---------------------------------------------------------------------- */

pr_tok( head )
TOKEN   *head;
{
        /*      Print out the pattern template (linked list of TOKENs)
         *      pointed to by head. This is a useful debugging aid. Note
         *      that pr_tok() just scans along the linked list, terminating
         *      on a null pointer; so, you can't use pr_tok from inside
         *      makepat() because tail->next points to the previous
         *      node instead of being null. Note that NEGATE and OR_SYM
         *      are not listed because they won't occur in a template.
         */

        register char   *str;
        register int    i;

        for (; head ; head = head->next )
        {
                switch (head->tok)
                {
                case BOL:
                        str = "BOL";
                        break;

                case EOL:
                        str = "EOL";
                        break;
```

```c
        case ANY:
                str = "ANY";
                break;

        case LITCHAR:
                str = "LITCHAR";
                break;

        case ESCAPE:
                str = "ESCAPE";
                break;

        case CCL:
                str = "CCL";
                break;

        case CCLEND:
                str = "CCLEND";
                break;

        case NCCL:
                str = "NCCL";
                break;

        case CLOSURE:
                str = "CLOSURE";
                break;

        default:
                str = "**** unknown ****";
        }

        printf("%-8s at: 0x%x, ", str, head);

        if (head->tok == CCL || head->tok == NCCL)
        {
                printf("string (at 0x%x) =<", head->bitmap );

                for( i = 0; i < 0x7f ; i++)
                        if( testbit(i, head->bitmap) )
                                putchar(i);

                printf(">, ");
        }

        else if (head->tok == LITCHAR)
                printf("lchar = %c, ", head->lchar);

        printf("next = 0x%x\n", head->next);
```

```
                }

                putchar('\n');
        }

#endif

/* ---------------------------------------------------------------- */

unmakepat(head)
TOKEN   *head;
{
        /*      Free up the memory used for the token string    */

        register TOKEN  *old_head;

        while (head)
        {
                switch (head->tok)
                {
                case CCL:
                case NCCL:
                        free(head->bitmap);
                        /* no break, fall through to default */

                default:
                        old_head = head;
                        head = head->next;
                        free(old_head);
                        break;
                }
        }
}

/*----------------------------------------------------------------*/

char    *index( c, str )
char    *str;
{
        /*      Return true if c is in str.
         */

        while( *str )
                if( *str++ == c )
                        return str;
        return 0;
}
```

LISTING 14-3

```c
/*-----------------------------------------------------------------
 *
 *      GREP.C: A generalized regular expression parser
 *
 *
 *                  Copyright (c) 1984 Allen Holub
 *                        All rights reserved.
 *
 *      Permission to copy this program or any part of this program
 *      is granted in the case of personal, non-commercial use only.
 *      Any use for profit or other commercial gain without written
 *      permission of the author is prohibited.
 *
 *      If you've been give this program by a friend, and you find
 *      it worthwhile, I'd appreciate your sending $35 to me for the
 *      program.
 *
 * Software Engineering Consultants, P.O. Box 5679, Berkeley, CA 94705
 *
 *-----------------------------------------------------------------
 */

#include <stdio.h>
#include "tools.h"

/*
 *      GREP
 *
 *      Search a file for a pattern.
 *
 *      The algorithm used here is essentially the algorithm in
 *      Software Tools in Pascal (pp 145f.). Though the routines have
 *      been changed somewhat to put them into good 'C'. See tools1.c
 *      for details.
 *
 *      This program is a healthy subset of the UNIX program of the same
 *      name. The differences are as follows:
 *
 *              - the -s, -x and -b options are not supported.
 *              - the meta-characters ()+? are not supported.
 *              - the -y option cause case to be ignored.
 *
 *      usage is:
 *              grep [-vclnhyef] [expression] files ...
 *
 *      For more details see grep.doc
 */
```

GREP.C: A GENERALIZED, REGULAR EXPRESSION PARSER IN C

```c
#define MAXLINE   128           /*      Maximum size cf an input line
                                 */

#define MAX_EXPR  64            /*      The maximum number of regular
                                 *      expressions separated by
                                 *      newlines or ! allowed.
                                 */

/*      The following global flags are true if a switch was set
 *      in the command line, false otherwise.
 */

int     vflag, yflag, cflag, lflag, nflag, hflag, fflag;

/*----------------------------------------------------------------*/

main(argc, argv)
int     argc;
char    **argv;
{
        int     i, j, linenum, count;

        int     line[MAXLINE];
        int     numfiles;
        FILE    *stream;
        int     exprc;
        TOKEN   *exprv[MAX_EXPR];

        fprintf(stderr, "GREP - Copyright (C) 1984, Allen I. Holub,");
        fprintf(stderr, " all rights reserved\n");

        i = 1;

        if (argc < 2)
                abort( pr_usage(1) );

        if ( *argv[i] == '-')
        {
                /*
                 *      Expand the switches on the command line
                 */

                expand_sw( argv[i++] );

                if ( i == argc )
                        abort( pr_usage(1) );
        }

        /*      Get the pattern string.
```

```
                */

                if ( (exprc = get_expr( exprv, MAX_EXPR, &argv[i++])) == 0 )
                        abort( pr_usage(2) );

                numfiles = argc - i;            /* Get number of files left to
                                                 * process on the command line
                                                 */
                do
                {
                        if ( numfiles)
                        {
                                stream = fopen( argv[i], "r");
                                if (stream == NULL)
                                {
                                        fprintf(stderr, "Can't open %s\n", argv[i]);
                                        continue;
                                }
                        }
                        else
                        {
                                stream = stdin;
                        }

                        count = 0;
                        linenum = 1;

                        while ( fgets(line, MAXLINE, stream) )
                        {
#ifdef CPM
                                if (!fflag || yflag )
                                        stoupper(line);
#else
                                if ( yflag )
                                        stoupper(line);
#endif

                                for( j = exprc ; --j >= 0 ; )
                                {
                                        if ( matchs(line , exprv[j]) )
                                        {
                                                count++;
                                                pr_match(linenum, line, argv[i], 1,
                                                                        numfiles);
                                        }
                                        else
                                        {
                                                pr_match(linenum, line, argv[i], 0,
                                                                        numfiles);
```

```
                                }
                                linenum++;
                                cntrl_c();
                        }
                        if( lflag && count )
                                break;
                }
                pr_count( numfiles, argv[i], count );
                fclose (stream);

        } while (++i < argc);

        abort();
}

/*----------------------------------------------------------------*/

pr_count( fcount, fname, count)
int     fcount, count;
char    *fname;
{
        /*      Process the -c flag by printing out a count and,
         *      if more than one file was listed on the command line,
         *      the file name too.
         */

        if (!cflag)
                return;

        if (fcount > 1)
                printf("%-12s: ", fname );

        printf( "%d\n", count );
}

/*----------------------------------------------------------------*/

pr_match(linenum, line, fname, match, numfiles)
int     linenum, match;
char    *line, *fname;
{
        /*      If a match is found print the correct thing
         *      as specified by the command line switches.
         */

        char    buf[80];

        if (cflag)
```

```
                        return;

                if ( (vflag && !match) || (!vflag && match) )
                {
                        if (!hflag && ( (numfiles > 1) || lflag) )
                                printf("%s%s", fname, lflag ? "\n" : ":" );

                        if (nflag)
                                printf("%03d:", linenum );

                        if (!lflag)
                                printf("%s", line );
                }
}
/*------------------------------------------------------------------*/
pr_usage(num)
int     num;
{

#ifdef DEBUG
        fprintf(stderr,"%d ", num);
#endif
        fprintf(stderr,"usage: grep [-cefhlnvy] [expression] <files ...>\n");
}

/*------------------------------------------------------------------*/

abort()
{
        exit();
}

/*------------------------------------------------------------------*/

expand_sw( str )
char    *str;
{
        /*      Set global flags corresponding to specific switches
         *      if those switches are set
         */

        vflag = 0;
        cflag = 0;
        lflag = 0;
        nflag = 0;
        hflag = 0;
        fflag = 0;
```

```c
        yflag = 0;

        while (*str)
        {
                switch ( toupper(*str))
                {
                case '-':
                case 'E':
                        break;

                case 'C':
                        cflag = 1;
                        break;

                case 'F':
                        fflag = 1;
                        break;

                case 'H':
                        hflag = 1;
                        break;

                case 'L':
                        lflag = 1;
                        break;

                case 'N':
                        nflag = 1;
                        break;

                case 'V':
                        vflag = 1;
                        break;

                case 'Y':
                        yflag = 1;
                        break;

                default:
                        pr_usage(3);
                        abort();
                        break;
                }

                str++;
        }
}

/*----------------------------------------------------------------*/
```

```c
int do_or( lp, expr, maxexpr )
char    *lp;
TOKEN   **expr;
int     maxexpr;
{
        int     found;
        TOKEN   *pat;
        char    *op;

        found = 0;

        /*
         *      Extract regular expressions separated by OR_SYMs from
         *      lp and put them into expr. Extract only up to
         *      maxexpr expressions. If yflag is true map string to upper
         *      case first.
         */

        if( yflag )
                stoupper( lp );

        while ( op = index(OR_SYM, lp) )
        {
                if(found <= maxexpr && (pat = makepat(lp, OR_SYM)) )
                {
                        *expr++ = pat;
                        found++;
                }
                lp = ++op;

                if ( pat == 0 )
                        goto fatal_err;
        }

        if (found <= maxexpr   &&  (pat = makepat( lp, OR_SYM))  )
        {
                found++;
                *expr = pat;
        }

        if ( pat == 0 )
        {
fatal_err:
                printf("Illegal expression: %s\n", lp);
                exit();
        }

        return (found);
}
```

```
/*----------------------------------------------------------------*/

get_expr( expr, maxexpr, defexpr )
TOKEN   *expr[];
int     maxexpr;
char    **defexpr;
{
        FILE    *stream;
        int     count;
        char    line[MAXLINE];

#ifdef DEBUG
        int     i;
#endif

        /*      Get regular expressions separated by | or newlines
         *      either out of a file or off the command line depending
         *      on whether the -f flag is set. The expressions are
         *      converted into pattern templates (see tools.c) and
         *      pointers to the templates are put into the array expr[]
         *      (which works similar to argv).
         *
         *      Return the number of expressions found (which can be used
         *      in a similar fashion to argc).
         */

        count = 0;

        if ( fflag )
        {
                /*
                 *      Then *defexpr is the file name and expressions should
                 *      be taken from that file.
                 */

                if ( (stream = fopen(*defexpr, "r")) == NULL )
                {
                        fprintf(stderr, "Can't open %s\n", *defexpr);
                        abort();
                }

                while ( (maxexpr - count)  &&  fgets(line, MAXLINE, stream) )
                {
                        count += do_or(line, &expr[count], maxexpr - count );
                }

                fclose (stream);
        }
        else
```

```
        {
                /*
                 *      *defexpr is the expression itself.
                 */

                if ( count += do_or( *defexpr, &expr[count], maxexpr - count))
                        *defexpr = " ";
        }

#ifdef DEBUG

        /*      Print out all the regular expressions after they have been
         *      converted into pattern templates (see tools.c).
         */

        for (i = count; --i >= 0 ; )
        {
                pr_tok( expr[i] );
                printf("-------------------------------------------------\n");
        }

#endif
        return(count);
}


/*--------------------------------------------------------------------*/

cntrl_c()
{

#ifdef CPM

        /*      If any character was hit, and that character is a
         *      ^C, then abort.
         */

        if ( bdos(11) && ((bdos(1,0) & 0x7f) == 0x03) )
                abort();
#endif

}
```

LISTING 14-4

```
lc -ms  -i\lc\ -i\lc\s\ grep tools >err
linkgrep
```

Revisions to Listings

Revisions and changes made to grep.c and tools.c since publication in the October 1984 *Dr. Dobb's Journal.*

10/20/84 amatch in tools.c

```
change: while( *sptr && (*sptr != delim) && (dstart-dest < maxccl ))
to:     while( *sptr && (*sptr != delim) && (dest-dstart < maxccl ))
```

10/29/84 dodash in tools.c

```
change: while( *lin && omatch( &lin, pat ))
to:     while( *lin && omatch( &lin, pat, boln ))
```

11/3/84 stoupper in tools.c

explicitly declared stoupper() as returning a character pointer

11/21/84 dodash and makepat in tools.c

- added tests for error returns from the two calls to malloc().
- changed dodash to use a bit map rather than a string of characters.

15
OPTIMIZING STRINGS IN C

by Edward McDermott

This chapter originally appeared in DDJ #90 (April 1984).

The C programming language offers many advantages: flexibility, speed, and portability. Routines that would take months in assembler can be written and tested much more easily in C. It supports true recursion and allows users to optimize portions of code, since it produces assembly-language source.

Optimization is the process of improving the efficiency of a program—getting more bang for your buck, whether the buck is time or memory. In general, you can try to make the program smaller or faster, or both. Sometimes you have to trade size for speed, or vice versa. Optimization can apply to a particular program or to a group of programs. The problem with optimization is that it takes time and effort.

What methods exist to optimize a program or programs? The following approaches have advantages and disadvantages:

- Improving the compiler output by improving the compiler, or getting a better one
- Improving compiler output by tinkering
- Improving the individual program's algorithm
- Rewriting entire routines in assembler

To improve the compiler output, you must have the source for the compiler and know enough to improve the code-generation logic. If you have those skills, please try it and publish the results. As for the rest of us mere mortals, this is a foolhardy exercise that can bring disaster. Besides, it takes a lot of time. Buying a better compiler has one small problem: How do you know it's really better?

For C programmers, another alternative is to recognize a commonly used pattern of code that can be improved, and write a program that tinkers with the compiler's output to improve it. This approach is similar to the optimization portion of the Small-C compiler.

Improving a program by rewriting all or part of it is a perfectly valid approach. The problem is that the payback doesn't go any further. The rest of your programs are still the same.

The final approach is to write some commonly used routines in assembler to speed things up. You can generalize this approach to all your programs by recompiling them. It improves both execution speed and size (to some extent). The problem is that these routines are no longer portable from machine to machine.

If you choose this last approach, its success depends on which functions you select for optimization. The ideal candidates would contain tight loops, be used by almost every program, and be small enough to rework easily.

C is an ideal language for editors, compilers, operating systems, and so on. Indeed, that was what C was designed for. Although every one of those applications involves a good deal of string handling, C has no string manipulation verbs. All string handling is done on a character-by-character basis, often by very small functions, which contain some very tight loops.

Another consideration is any special commands of the CPU you are using. Can any functions built into the chip be taken advantage of by any other means? The Z80 chip has a few commands that are unavailable on the 8080, specifically LDIR, LDDR, LDI, LDD, CPIR, CPDR, CPI, and CPD. Each of these instructions is the equivalent of several 8080 instructions and, properly used, can be substituted for several instructions in C.

For example, the LDIR command takes the contents of the memory position pointed at by the HL register pair, transfers those contents to the memory position specified by the DE register pair, increments HL and DE, and decrements BC until the BC register pair is zero. That is a mouthful. Perhaps this makes it a little clearer:

```
WHILE (BC--) *DE++ = *HL++ ;
```

Does that seem familiar? It is, in fact, almost identical to the the STRCPY function in *The C Programming Language* by Kernighan and Ritchie. The principal difference lies in the delimitation of the loop.

If your computer runs on a Z80 chip, string manipulation is a natural choice. But the question that haunts all optimization efforts still remains: is the payback worth the effort? To try to answer that question, I chose the following four functions to optimize:

STRCPY	copy a string from one place to another
STRINIT	initialize a string to a specified value
STRLEN	find the length of a string
CMATCH	find a character within a string

Since the Small-C compiler produces assembler code, my first approach was to review its output. In small loops the compiler produces code that does not optimally use the registers, so I completely rewrote the functions; most of the speed gained can be attributed to this rewrite. This optimization should apply to 8080-based machines as well.

Listing 15-1 gives the new routines in Z80 code. I chose Z80 intentionally to take advantage of its special OP codes and to emphasize the major disadvantage of this type of optimization—the loss of portability. Readers can adapt these routines to the 8080 environment fairly easily, for use with C or other languages.

Usually you judge an optimization by the following criteria:

Is it faster? If so, how much?

Is it smaller? If so, how much?

Does it suggest other methods of improvement?

Was it worth the time and effort to do?

Faster

The timings involved executing each command 10,000 times on a string of 30 characters. The first set of timings is for the driver program, without any string manipulation at all, to see the impact of the code used in handling the test. The second set is using C routines, compiled under the Small-C compiler, version 2. The third set is for the same program, but using the assembler routines.

Test element	**Time/10,000**
Null test	3 seconds
Small-C (v2)	195 seconds
Assembler	16 seconds

I also compared the CMATCH routine to the rest, since this routine was significantly longer and more involved in both languages.

Test element	**Time/10,000**
Null test	1 second
Small-C (v2)	90 seconds
Assembler	6 seconds

If you remove the constant load of the code to drive the test program, you find the new routines are 14.8 times faster. Skeptics can ignore the impact of the loops, and still end up with new routines that are 12.2 times faster.

Smaller

The memory savings were as follows:

Language	Size in bytes
Small-C (v2)	254
Assembler	116

The assembler code for the four routines was less than half the size of the comparable C code. However, saving 138 bytes is not going to make anyone jump for joy. With fine tuning, this figure could be improved, but once again it is a matter of cost versus gain.

Other Improvements

My first thought was to optimize other small routines for handling strings. Part of the savings came from using all three register pairs and keeping the values in the registers throughout the loop. Where the number of parameters exceeds three (one for each of BC, DE, and HL register pairs), the potential savings drop and the effort begins to increase.

Another improvement would be to use these optimized routines as heavily as possible. That has some major implications to the style of C code a programmer uses. You must build up your functions out of smaller optimized functions instead of writing complex character-by-character processing.

Some other potential candidates for optimization are: convert to uppercase and convert to lowercase; find string; compare string; extract part of a string.

All string manipulation functions should not necessarily be optimized. The gain in speed achieved by improving screen and printer routines is hidden by the limited transmission speed to these devices for most small systems; you won't see any improvement. Most likely, your disk I/O routines are already in assembler to interface the language to your particular operating system.

By the way, the string copy and string init functions were designed to return the address of the resulting string. This may seem an unnecessary complication, but it does allow programmers to nest functions within each other when writing the C code.

Time and Effort

Whether the optimization was worth the effort depends on how you value your time and on your requirements for speed and/or memory. I expected a speed improvement on the order of five times faster. The improvement, however, was between 12 and 15 times faster. Since creating these routines, testing them, correcting them, and correcting them again resulted in more speed than I expected, the optimization proved successful. You have to decide if it's worth your time to type these routines in, and use them in your code.

The improvement you can achieve by converting small routines into assembler is significant, if not startling. Leaving the original C routine as a comment in the assembler code lets you combine the best of both worlds: the most efficient routine and the original portable routine. Any small, tight looping function that is concerned with three or fewer variables and that is commonly used is an ideal candidate. However, to get the most out of such an optimization, you must build more complex functions out of these smaller ones.

Some Further Thoughts

Rarely can an author or a programmer go back to reconsider what he or she has unleashed on the world after a year has passed. I was a little surprised to see that I had made almost no alterations in *Optimizing Strings in C.*

There was only one revision to the original four routines. Originally, CMATCH requested a zero relative offset into the string it searched, and returned a one relative position of the match it found. (A zero meant no match.) In other words, to start the search at the first byte of the string you specified 0, and if the first byte matched the desired character, it returned a 1. That inconsistency confused even me. The new version of the routine expects a 1 relative offset, so the offset and the returned value are now on the same basis. (See Listing 15-2.)

Assembler routines are like potato chips—you can't stop at one or two. One set of candidates for conversion I had overlooked before were routines used within tight loops. Tests to classify a character type were ideal candidates because each was short, used almost everywhere, and often within tight loops. Furthermore, since these tests made multiple comparisons to the same value, they could benefit from optimization. ISDIGIT, ISALPHA, ISASCII, and so forth could all benefit. Finally, since these routines were similar, once one was converted properly the rest could be built in the same manner.

When I did find a library of functions for C in the public domain, I found some of the functions to be distinctly similar to the ones I had already developed. That created a problem. I didn't want two functions that did the same thing on my system. I didn't want to change all my programs, and I certainly didn't want to change what I didn't really understand. The solution was simple: I just added one line of code to my assembler routine. By adding PAD:: before my routine, I had two names for the same function. Later I realized the DEFINE statement would achieve the same results.

Some functions in the public-domain library were almost identical to my assembler functions. They differed either in their scope or the construction of their pass parameters. Since my assembler routines were significantly faster (10 to 15 times faster) I wanted to get the most mileage out of them. So I revised the new functions to call my assembler routines, where possible.

Upon reviewing some of the code I have written, I realized that these optimized routines have had a significant impact on my programming style. Instead of writing one complex character-by-character analysis of a string, I use these optimized functions and subdivide the task. For instance, I wrote a function to verify that a filename would be a valid CP/M filename FN_F_NAME. The rules were as follows: it must be nonblank; it must not contain either a * or a ?; it must contain at most one ":"; any ":" must be the second character of the string; it must contain at most one "."; the name portion must have a length greater than 1 and less than 9; and the type portion of the name must have a length greater than 1 and less than 4 (I impose this restriction on myself even though CP/M doesn't insist on it). Writing such a routine is a breeze using the CMATCH function. I admit my code isn't the most efficient or elegant. However, it is a simple, straightforward function that works with a minimum of effort. Furthermore, I won't improve it because such a routine is executed only once or twice in a program.

My final suggestion is to leave the original C code in place as comments. This acts as documentation and allows you the option of moving to a new machine with a different assembler. Also, when you are debugging you might want to put displays into your program. Adding a display to an assembler routine can be time-consuming; I simply reinstall the original C code temporarily, with whatever displays I want.

LISTING 15-1

```
/*
 *  Optimizing Strings in C
 *
 *  Copyright 1983 by Edward McDermott
 *  12 Manor Haven Road
 *  Toronto, Ontario M6A 2H9, Canada
 *
 */

#asm
;/*
;strcpy(s,t) char *s, *t;
;{ int ret; ret = *s; while (*s++ = *t++); return(ret) ; }
STRCPY::
        POP     BC        ; POP return ADDRESS
        POP     HL        ; POP ADDRESS OF T
        POP     DE        ; POP ADDRESS OF S
        PUSH    DE        ; RESTORE STACK
        PUSH    HL
        PUSH    BC
        PUSH    DE        ; SAVE ADDRESS OF START OF S

STRLP:  LD      A,(HL)    ; TRANSFER LOOP
        OR      A         ; TEST FOR ZERO IN T
        JR      Z,STREXT  ; if SO EXIT
        LDI               ; MOVE INCREMENTING
                          ; S++ = T++
        JR      STRLP     ; continue LOOP

STREXT: LD      A,00      ; ZERO FINAL BITE IN S
        LD      (DE),A
        POP     HL        ; return  S
        RET
;
;PAD(DEST, CH, N) char *DEST, *N; int CH;
;{while(N--) *DEST++ = CH;}
;
;STRINIT(S,C,I ) char *S; char C ; int I ;
;{ int RET; RET = *S;
;   while (I-- ) *S++=C;
;   return(RET) ; }

PAD::
STRINIT::
        POP     IX        ; POP return ADDRESS
        POP     BC        ; POP I (LEN for INIT)
        POP     DE        ; POP C ( INIT charACTER
```

```
        POP     HL      ; POP ADDRESS OF STRING
        PUSH    HL      ; RESTORE STACK
        PUSH    DE
        PUSH    BC
        PUSH    IX
        PUSH    HL      ; SAVE ADDRESS OF START OF S
        LD      A,B     ; if BC = 0 return(s);
        OR      C       ;
        JR      Z,STRIN2

        LD      A,E     ; LOAD A WITH C charACTER
        LD      (HL),A  ; STORE charACTER IN BEGIN OF S
        POP     DE      ; SET DE TO BEGIN OF S
        PUSH    DE
        INC     DE      ; POint DE TO NEXT BYE
        DEC     BC      ; REDUCE for char TAKEN
        LD      A,B
        OR      C       ; MAKE SURE BC > 00
        JR      Z,STRIN2
        LDIR            ; while (BC--) DE++ = HL++
STRIN2: POP     HL      ; GET ADDRESS OF S TO return
        RET

;/* strlen -- return length of string s (page 98) */
;STRLEN(S) char *S;
;       { int P ;  P =S;
;         while (*S) ++S ;
;         return(S-P);}

STRLEN::
        POP     BC      ; POP return ADDRESS
        POP     HL      ; POP ADDRESS OF S
        PUSH    HL      ; RESTORE STACK
        PUSH    BC
        PUSH    HL       ; SAVE ADDRESS OF START OF S
        LD      BC,0FFFFH ; BC IS BYTE COUNT (DECREMENTED)
        XOR     A       ; SEARCHING FOR A  00
        CPIR            ; EQUIVALENT OF while (HL++)
        POP     DE      ; DE = S
        SBC     HL,DE   ; HL = HL - DE
        DEC     HL      ; CORRECTION FOR COUNT LAST char
        RET             ; return(HL);
;
;/* revised version */
;cmatch(S,P,FROM )
; char S[] ; int P, FROM ;
; { int ADV,I  ;
;   ADV = FROM; I= 0;
;   while (--ADV > 0) {if (S[I++] == 0) return(0);}
```

```
;       while (S[I] != 0 )  {if (P == S[I++])  return(I);}
;       return 0; }
;
;
CMATCH::
        POP     IX          ; POP RETURN ADDRESS
        POP     BC          ; POP I  (INDENT FOR INIT)
        POP     DE          ; POP P  (SEARCH CHARACTER
        POP     HL          ; POP ADDRESS OF STRING S
        PUSH    HL          ; RESTORE STACK
        PUSH    DE
        PUSH    BC
        PUSH    IX
        DEC     BC          ; FROM 1 RELATIVE TO ZERO RELATIVE BASE
        PUSH    BC          ; SAVE BC FOR COUNT OF BYTES
        LD      A,B         ;
        OR      C           ; IF BC == 0  THEN GO TO CMA1
        JR      Z,CMA1
        LD      A,0
CMA0:   CPIR                ; CHECK 00  BEFORE END OF BC
        LD      A,B         ; IF (BC != 0 ) RETURN 0
        OR      C
        JR      NZ,CMAX1    ; ELSE CONTINUE
CMA1:   POP     BC          ; RESTOR BC = I FOR OFFEST COUNT
                            ; I IS WITHIN   THE STRING ?
CMA2:   INC     BC          ; COUNT BYTES
        LD      A,(HL)
        OR      A           ; END OF STRING?
        JR      Z,CMAX
        CP      E           ; CHECK SEARCH CHARACTER
        JR      Z,CMAE      ; IF (HL = P) CONTIN
        INC     HL          ; HL ++
        JR      CMA2

CMAE:   LD      H,B         ; RETURN (HL = BC)
        LD      L,C
        RET

        ; I IS BEYOND THE STRING END
CMAX1:  POP     BC          ; RESTORE STACK
CMAX:   LD      HL,00H      ;RETURN (NULL);
        RET
#endasm
/* end of listing */
```

LISTING 15-2

```
    /*
     *
```

```
 *  Contributed by
 *  Edward McDermott, 12 Manor Haven Road,
 *  Toronto, Ontario M6A 2H9, Canada
 *
 */

/*************************************************/
/*  Various additional assembler routines for C  */
/*************************************************/

/*----- common C routines utilizing an assembler routine ----*/

/* return pointer to 1st occurrence of c in str, else 0  */
/* note this function is a special case of the CMATCH */
STRCHR(STR, C) char *STR, C;
  {return(CMATCH(STR,C,1));}

/* convert the string to uppercase */
STRUPPER(S) char *S;
{int T; T = S;
 while (*T) {*T=TOUPPER(*T); T++;}
 return(S);}

/* convert the string to lowercase */
STRLOWER(S) char *S;
{int T; T = S;
 while (*T) {*T=TOLOWER(*T); T++;}
 return(S);}

/* Test File name conforms to valid cp/m structure */
/* returns YES on error and NO for a valid name */
/* also sends an error message to stderr */
FN_F_NAME(ST) char  *ST;
{ int K,J,I ;
   if (CMATCH(ST,'?',1) || CMATCH(ST,'*',1))
                              {ERR_MSG("Ambig. Ref."); return(YES);}
   I = CMATCH(ST,':',1);
   if (I ==1 || I > 2)         {ERR_MSG("Bad Drive")   ; return(YES);}
   if (CMATCH(ST,':',I+1) > 0) {ERR_MSG("Double ':'")  ; return(YES);}
   J = CMATCH(ST,'.',1) - I;
   if (J < 2 || J > 9)         {ERR_MSG("Bad Name")    ; return(YES);}
   if (CMATCH(ST,'.',I+J+1)> 0){ERR_MSG("Double '.'")  ; return(YES);}
   K = STRLEN(ST) - J - I;
   if (K < 1 || K > 3)         {ERR_MSG("Bad Type")    ; return(YES);}
   return(NO);}

/* write error message to stderr with a carriage return */
ERR_MSG(ST) char *ST:
{ fputs(st,stderr); fputc(st,'\n'); return;}
```

Optimizing Strings in C

```
/*-------------- common assembler routine -----------*/
#asm
;/* return c, converted to uppercase is appropriate */
;TOUPPER(C) int C;
;{if(C<='z' && C>='a') return(C-32);
;  return(C);}

TOUPPER::
        POP     BC      ; POP return ADDRESS
        POP     HL      ; POP C
        PUSH    HL      ; RESTORE STACK
        PUSH    BC      ;
        LD      A,L     ; LOAD C INTO A-REG
        CP      123     ; if c >='z'+1 then go to second range
        JP      NC,NOUPPER      ;
        CP      96      ; if c <='a'-1 then go to second range
        JP      C,NOUPPER
        SUB     32      ; SUB 32 FROM Accumulator
        LD      L,A     ; load up date accumultor to L of HL
NOUPPER:RET

; revised version that uses a one offset
;CMATCH(S,P,FROM ) char S[] ; int P, FROM ;
; { int ADV,I ;
;   ADV = FROM; I= 0;
;   while (--ADV != 0) {if (S[I++] == 0) return(0);}
;   while (S[I] != 0 ) {if (P == S[I++])  return(I);}
;   return 0; }
;
CMATCH::
        POP     IX      ; POP RETURN ADDRESS
        POP     BC      ; POP I (INDENT FOR INIT)
        POP     DE      ; POP P (SEARCH CHARACTER
        POP     HL      ; POP ADDRESS OF STRING S
        PUSH    HL      ; RESTORE STACK
        PUSH    DE
        PUSH    BC
        PUSH    IX
        DEC     BC      ; FROM 1 RELATIVE TO ZERO RELATIVE BASE
        PUSH    BC      ; SAVE BC FOR COUNT OF BYTES
        LD      A,B     ;
        OR      C       ; IF BC == 0  THEN GO TO CMA1
        JR      Z,CMA1
        LD      A,0
CMA0:   CPIR            ; CHECK 00  BEFORE END OF BC
        LD      A,B     ; IF (BC != 0 ) RETURN 0
        OR      C
        JR      NZ,CMAX1 ; ELSE CONTINUE
CMA1:   POP     BC      ; RESTOR BC = I FOR OFFEST COUNT
```

```
                        ; I IS WITHIN  THE STRING ?
CMA2:   INC     BC      ; COUNT BYTES
        LD      A,(HL)
        CP      00      ; END OF STRING?
        JR      Z,CMAX
        CP      E       ; CHECK SEARCH CHARACTER
        JR      Z,CMAE  ; IF (HL = P) CONTIN
        INC     HL      ; HL ++
        JR      CMA2

CMAE:   LD      H,B     ; RETURN (HL = BC )
        LD      L,C
        RET

        ; I IS BEYOND THE STRING END
CMAX1:  POP     BC      ; RESTORE STACK
CMAX:   LD      HL,00H  ;RETURN (NULL);
        RET

;/* return 'true' if c is a decimal digit */
;ISDIGIT(C) int C;
;{return (C<='9' && C>='0');}
;
ISDIGIT::
        POP     BC      ; POP return ADDRESS
        POP     HL      ; POP  C
        PUSH    HL      ; RESTORE STACK
        PUSH    BC      ;
        LD      A,L     ; LOAD C INTO A-REG
        JP      IS3     ; use part of ISALNUM test
;/* return 'true' if c is alphabetic   */
;ISALPHA(C) INT C;
;{return((C<='z' && C>='a') || (C<='Z' && C>='A'));}
;
ISALPHA::
        POP     BC      ; POP return ADDRESS
        POP     HL      ; POP  C
        PUSH    HL      ; RESTORE STACK
        PUSH    BC      ;
        LD      A,L     ; LOAD C INTO A-REG
        CP      123     ; if c >='z'+1 then go to second range
        JR      NC,ISA2 ;
        CP      96      ; if c <='a'-1 then go to second range
        JR      C,ISA2  ;
        JP      ISTRUE  ; GO to IS TRUE
ISA2:
        CP      91      ; if c >='Z'+1 then go to second range
        JP      NC,ISNOT;
        CP      64      ; if c <='A'-1 then go to second range
```

```
                JP      C,ISNOT  ;
                JP      ISTRUE   ; GO to IS TRUE
;
;/* return 'true' if c is alphanumeric */
;ISALNUM(C) int C;
;{return (
;  (C<='z' && C>='a') || (C<='Z' && C>='A') || (C<='9' && C>='0'));}
;
ISALNUM::
                POP     BC       ; POP return ADDRESS
                POP     HL       ; POP  C
                PUSH    HL       ; RESTORE STACK
                PUSH    BC       ;
                LD      A,L      ; LOAD C INTO A-REG
                CP      123      ; if c >='z'+1 then go to second range
                JR      NC,IS2   ;
                CP      96       ; if c <='a'-1 then go to second range
                JR      C,IS2    ;
                JR      ISTRUE   ; GO to IS TRUE
IS2:
                CP      91       ; if c >='Z'+1 then go to second range
                JR      NC,IS3   ;
                CP      64       ; if c <='A'-1 then go to second range
                JR      C,IS3    ;
                JR      ISTRUE   ; GO to IS TRUE

IS3:            CP      58       ; if c >='9'+1 then go to second range
                JR      NC,ISNOT     ;
                CP      47       ; if c <='a'-1 then go to second range
                JR      C,ISNOT  ;
                JR      ISTRUE   ; go to IS TRUE

; Note, these two routine are used to exit all the IS tests.
; A JR command is used with within 128 by of the test else a JP
; command is used. That's why they're near the middle of the routine
ISNOT:  LD      HL,0000  ; ZERO FINAL BITE IN S
        RET
ISTRUE: LD      HL,1     ; SET HL TO TRUE (non zero)
        RET

; /*  return 'true' if c is an ASCII character (0-127)   */
;ISASCII(C) char *C;
;{ return (C <= 127);}
;
ISASCII::
                POP     BC       ; POP return ADDRESS
                POP     HL       ; POP  C
                PUSH    HL       ; RESTORE STACK
                PUSH    BC       ;
```

```
        LD      A,L     ; LOAD C INTO A-REG
        CP      128     ; if c >=127+1 then go to IS NO
        JR      NC,ISNOT
        JR      ISTRUE

;/* return 'true' if c is a control character (0-31 or 127) */
;ISCNTRL(C) char *C;
;{ return ((C <= 31) || (C == 127));}
;
ISCNTRL::
        POP     BC      ; POP return ADDRESS
        POP     HL      ; POP  C
        PUSH    HL      ; RESTORE STACK
        PUSH    BC      ;
        LD      A,L     ; LOAD C INTO A-REG
        CP      127     ; if c =127 then go to IS TRUE
        JR      Z,ISTRUE
        CP      31
        JR      NC,ISTRUE ; IF C <= 31 THEN GO TO IS TRUE
        JR      ISNOT

;/* return 'true' if c is lower-case alphabetic   */
;ISLOWER(C) int C;
;{return (C<='z' && C>='a');}
ISLOWER::
        POP     BC      ; POP return ADDRESS
        POP     HL      ; POP  C
        PUSH    HL      ; RESTORE STACK
        PUSH    BC      ;
        LD      A,L     ; LOAD C INTO A-REG
        CP      123     ; if c >='z'+1 then go to second range
        JP      NC,ISNOT        ;
        CP      96      ; if c <='a'-1 then go to second range
        JP      C,ISNOT ;
        JP      ISTRUE  ; GO to IS TRUE
#endasm

/* end of listing */
```

**PC WEEK'S PRODUCT OF THE YEAR
PC MAGAZINE'S AWARD FOR TECHNICAL EXCELLENCE**

Borland Introduces the Laws of *TURBO DYNAMICS*™

Laws That Work Like Magic. Whether considering technological excellence, or innovation in areas such as pricing, not copy-protection, licensing agreements, site licenses, 60 day money-back guarantee —Borland is clearly recognized as the software industry leader. The following three laws of *"Turbo Dynamics"*™ exemplify our pledge for excellence.

1ST LAW:
SPEED, POWER AND PRICE.
Borland products are known to be fast, powerful and to deliver an incredible price performance ratio. We only believe in absolutely superb software at rock bottom prices.

2ND LAW:
NOT COPY-PROTECTED SOFTWARE AND REASONABLE LICENSING AGREEMENTS.
We will always offer not copy-protected versions of our software. Also, our licensing agreement is now so simple that even a child can understand it.

3RD LAW:
60 DAY MONEY-BACK GUARANTEE.
This third law is actually a first in the industry! We are so sure that you will love our software that all of our products now come backed with a 60 day money-back guarantee. No questions asked.

Turbo Dynamics Applies to Turbo Pascal. Borland's Pascal family of products is growing by leaps and bounds. You can now join hundreds of thousands of users and enter the world of Turbo Pascal programming. And remember, all three laws of *Turbo Dynamics* apply to all Borland products.

TURBO PASCAL™ $69.95
The industry standard. With more than 350,000 users worldwide Turbo Pascal is the industry's de facto standard. Turbo Pascal is praised by more engineers, hobbyists, students and professional programmers than any other development environment in the history of microcomputing. And yet, Turbo Pascal is simple and fun to use. **Free spreadsheet** included on every Turbo disk with ready-to-compile source code. **Options:** We offer the exciting Binary Coded Decimal (BCD) option for your business applications as well as an 8087 option for your number-crunching applications at a very low charge. Please refer to the coupon. **Portability.** Turbo Pascal is available today for most computers running PC-DOS, MS-DOS, CP/M-80 or CP/M-86. **Jeff Duntemann, PC Magazine:** "In its simplicity it achieves an elegance that no other language compiler has ever displayed."

TURBO GRAPHIX TOOLBOX™ $54.95

High resolution monochrome graphics and window management for the IBM PC. The Turbo Graphix Toolbox will give even a beginning programmer the expert's edge. It's a complete library of Pascal procedures and functions. Tools that will allow you to draw and hatch pie charts, bar charts, circles, rectangles and a full range of geometric shapes. Procedures that will save and restore graphic images to and from disk. And much, much, more. You may incorporate part or all of these tools in your programs and yet we won't charge you any royalties. Best of all, these functions and procedures come complete with commented source code on disk ready to compile.

TURBO TUTOR™ $34.95
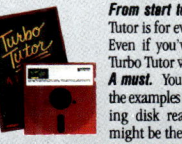
From start to finish in 300 pages. Turbo Tutor is for everyone from novice to expert. Even if you've never programmed before Turbo Tutor will get you started right away. **A must.** You'll find the source code for all the examples in the book on the accompanying disk ready to compile. Turbo Tutor might be the only reference on Pascal and programming you'll ever need.

TURBO DATABASE TOOLBOX™ $54.95

The Turbo Database Toolbox is the perfect complement to Turbo Pascal. It contains a complete library of Pascal procedures that allows you to sort and search your data and build powerful applications. It's another Borland set of tools that will give the beginning programmer the expert's edge. **Get started right away: free database!** Included on every Toolbox disk is the source code to a working data base which demonstrates how powerful and easy to use our search system, Turbo-Access, really is. Modify it to suit your individual needs or just compile it and run. **Remember, no royalties!**

BORLAND INTERNATIONAL
4585 Scotts Valley Drive, Scotts Valley CA 95066
Phone (408) 438-8400   Telex 172373

Copyright 1985 Borland International BI-1011
Turbo Pascal, Turbo Database Toolbox, Turbo Graphix Toolbox, Turbo Tutor and Turbo Dynamics are trademarks of Borland International, Inc.

TURBO PASCAL FAMILY — NOT COPY-PROTECTED

Available at better dealers nationwide. Call (800) 556-2283 for the dealer nearest you. To order by Credit Card call (800) 255-8008, CA (800) 742-1133

Pascal 3.0	$ 69.95
Pascal w/8087	$109.90
Pascal w/BCD	$109.90
Pascal w/8087 & BCD	$124.95
Turbo Database Toolbox	$ 54.95
Turbo Graphix	$ 54.95
Turbo Tutor	$ 34.95

*These prices include shipping to all U.S. cities. All foreign orders add $10 per product ordered.

60 DAY MONEY-BACK GUARANTEE

Carefully Describe your Computer System:
Mine is: ___ 8 bit   ___ 16 bit
I Use: ___ PC-DOS ___ MS-DOS
       ___ CP/M 80 ___ CP/M 86
My computer's name/model is: _____

The disk size I use is:
☐ 3½" ☐ 5¼" ☐ 8"

Name: _____
Shipping Address: _____
City: _____
State: ___ Zip: ___
Telephone: _____

Amount: _____ (CA 6% tax)
Payment: VISA MC BankDraft Check
Credit Card Expir. Date: ___/___
Card #: _____

COD's and Purchase Orders WILL NOT be accepted by Borland. California residents: add 6% sales tax. Outside USA: add $10 and make payment by bank draft, payable in US dollars drawn on a US bank.

Slash Programming Time in Half!
With FirsTime™

- Fast program entry through single keystroke statement generators.
- Fast editing through syntax oriented cursor movements.
- Dramatically reduced debugging time through immediate syntax checking.
- Fast development through unique programmer oriented features.
- Automatic program formatter.

FirsTime is a true syntax directed editor.

FirsTime ensures the integrity of your programs by performing all editing tasks like moves, inserts and deletes along the syntactic elements of a program. For example, when you move an IF statement, FirsTime will move the corresponding THEN and ELSE clauses with it.

Even FirsTime's cursor movements are by syntax elements instead of characters. The cursor automatically skips over blank spaces and required keywords and goes directly to the next editable position.

FirsTime is a Syntax Checker

FirsTime checks the syntax of your program statements, and also:

- Semantics like undefined variables and mismatched statement types.
- The contents of include files and macro expansions.
- Statements for errors as they are entered and warns you immediately.

FirsTime is a Program Formatter

FirsTime automatically indents statements as they are entered, saving you from having to track indentation levels and count spaces.

FirsTime has Unique Features

No other editor offer these features:

The *Zoom command* gives you a top down view of your program logic.

The *View command* displays the contents of include files and macro expansions. This is valuable to sophisticated programmers writing complex code or to those updating unfamiliar programs.

FirsTime's *Transform command* lets you change a statement to another similar one with just two keystrokes. For example, you can instantly transform a FOR statement into a WHILE statement.

The *Move at Same Level command* moves the cursor up or down to the next statement at the same indentation level. This is very useful. For example, you can use it to locate the ELSE clause that corresponds to a given THEN clause or to traverse a program one procedure at a time.

FirsTime is Unparalleled

FirsTime is the most advanced syntax directed editor available. It makes programming faster, easier and more fun.

TO ORDER CALL (201) 741-8188
or write:

Spruce Technology Corporation

189 E. Bergen Place
Red Bank, NJ 07701

Circle **no. 65** on reader service card.

In Germany, Austria and Switzerland contact:
Markt & Technik Software Verlag
Munchen, W. Germany
(089) 4613-0

FirsTime is a trademark of Spruce Technology Corporation • MS-DOS is a trademark of Microsoft Corporation
IBM is a trademark of International Business Machines, Inc. • Turbo Pascal is a trademark of Borland International

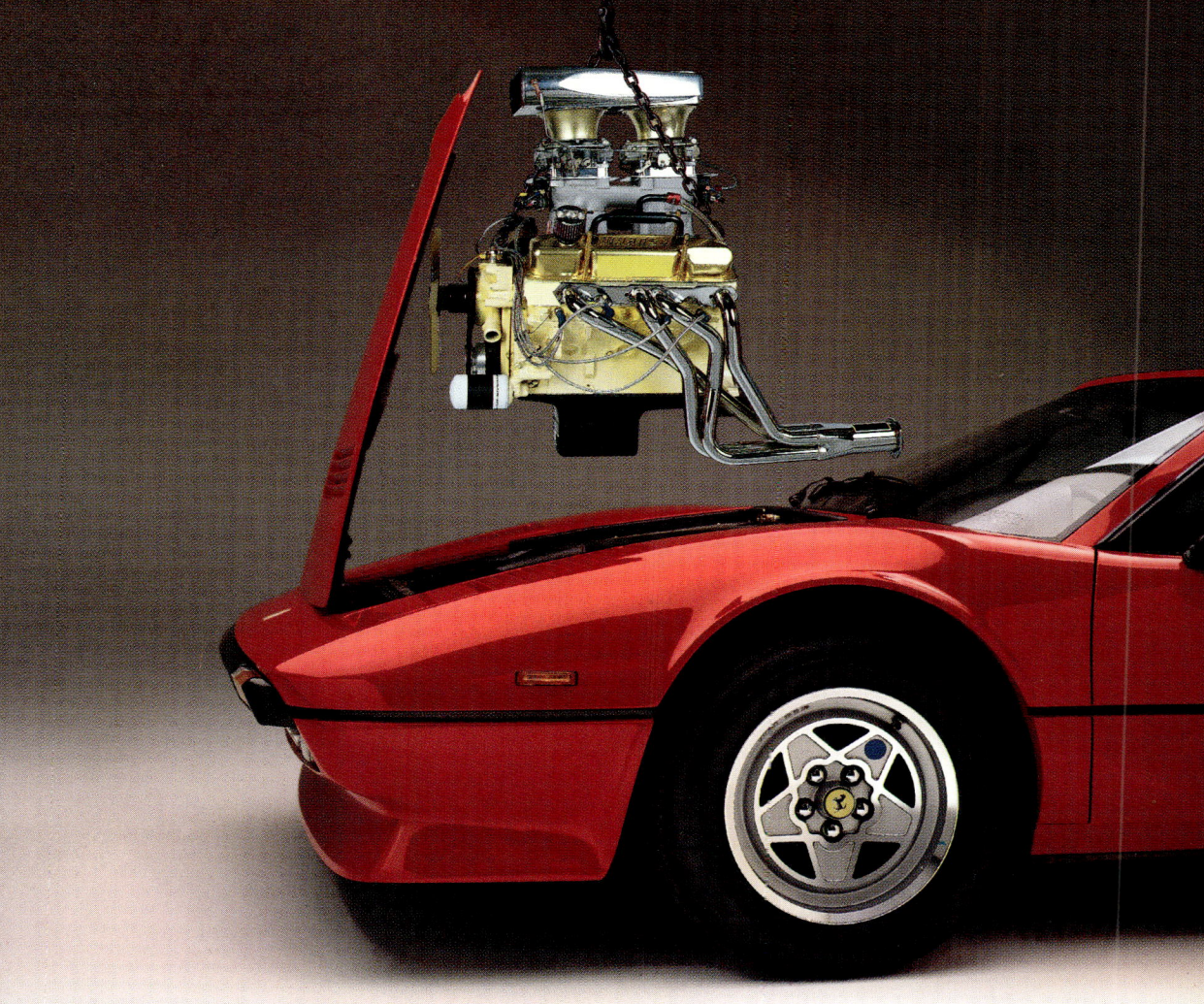

AT™ Pfantasies for your PC or XT.™

Want better speed and memory on your PC or XT without buying an AT?

You've got it!

Phoenix's new Pfaster™286 co-processor board turns your PC or XT into a high-speed engine 60 percent faster than an AT. Three times faster than an XT. It even supports PCs with third-party hard disks. But that's only the beginning.

You can handle spreadsheets and programs you never thought possible. Set up RAM disks in both 8088 and 80286 memory for linkage editor overlays or super-high-speed disk caching. All with Pfaster286's 1mb of standard RAM, expandable to 2mb, and dual-mode design.

You can develop 8086/186/286 software on your XT faster. Execute 95 percent of the application packages that run on the AT, excluding those that require fancy I/O capabilities your PC or XT hardware just isn't designed to handle. Queue multi-copy, multi-format print jobs for spooling. Or, switch to native 8088 mode to handle hardware-dependent programs and back again without rebooting. All with Pfaster286's compatible ROM software. And, Pfaster286 does the job unintrusively! No motherboard to exchange. No wires to solder. No chips to pull. Just plug it into a standard card slot, and type the magic word, "PFAST."

If you really didn't want an AT in the first place, just what it could do for you, call or write: Phoenix Computer Products Corp., 320 Norwood Park South, Norwood, MA 02062; (800) 344-7200. In Massachusetts, 617-762-5030.

Programmers' Pfantasies™ by

Phoenix

XT and AT are trademarks of International Business Machines Corporation. Pfaster286 and Programmers' Pfantasies are trademarks of Phoenix Computer Products Corporation.
For the Ferrari aficionado: yes, we know this is a rear engine car. We are showing the addition of a second engine to symbolize how Pfaster can be added to your PC or XT to increase performance.

Where did AT&T and SONY find the Tools to C them thru?

The Application Programmer's Toolkit!!!

A *WizardWare*™ product from Shaw☆American Technologies APT™ provides you with everything you need to increase your C programming productivity, including:

- COMPLETE SOURCE CODE (over 5000 lines!) no royalties required
- File handling with direct & keyed access
- Screen and Report Generators, with full screen handling for your programs
- Generic Terminal Driver for portable C
- String math functions, and string manipulation routines
- Reference Manual on Disk (over 50 pages)
- Tutorial Manual (over 25 pages) with Source for Mailing List Manager
- A host of useful Utilities, Database and File Editors
- Available for Microsoft (3.0), Lattice, Mark Williams, DeSmet, BDS, Eco, CI-C86
- C-STARTER Toolkit!: Binary APT, DeSmet C, "Programming in C on the IBM-PC"

NOW MORE AFFORDABLE!!
```
APT/MS-DOS versions .................................. $395
APT/DeSmet C & BDS C versions ........................ $295
C-Starter (binary APT, DeSmet Compiler and Book) ..... $295
Demo Disk with manual ................................ $  5
```

** NEW PRODUCTS! Available Now or Coming Soon: **
```
ADAPT: English-language, applications generator ...... $295
BIZ-WIZ: Comprehensive Accounting Package ............ $495
FLORA: Graphics Toolkit, with MAC-like capabilities .. $ 95
APT-WINDOWS!: APT-Compatible/stand-alone window mgt!.. $ 95
db2e: dBaseIII/II TO C Source Code Translator and Libraries! CALL
Dr. Shaw's DOS-Shell: a UNIX-like shell for DOS ...... $ 95
```

Call (502) 583-5527
Shaw☆American Technologies
WizardWare™
830 South Second St. - Box 488
Louisville, KY 40201, USA
(C.O.D. and Foreign Orders - Add $5 Shipping/Handling)
References: Bank of Louisville, Citizens Fidelity Bank, Louisville Chamber of Commerce

---

Advanced Trace86™

Symbolic Debugger & Assembler Combo

- Full-screen trace with single stepping; Even backstepping!
- Write & Edit COM & EXE programs
- Conditional breakpoints (programmable)
- Switch between trace and output screen; Or set up two monitors
- 8087, 80186, 80286, 80287 support
- Write labels & comments on code
- Polish hex/decimal calculator
- and more... Priced at $175.00

To order or request more information contact:

 Morgan Computing Co., Inc.

2520 Tarpley Rd. Suite 500
(214) 245-4763   Carrollton, TX 75006

EC Text Editor

...the Latest in Programming Environment Technology...
The DOS Interface — All Available Memory — Windows !!!

EC's DOS Interface is a major advance. It is far more sophisticated and useful than the "EXIT" to DOS provided by other editors.

Here's how you can use the DOS Interface:
1) Execute any DOS command you like.
2) Keep a history of all DOS output (you can even have EC automatically save it to a file if you want to keep a DOS Log.) EC displays the output in the DOS Interface. You can page through it, scroll it, etc.
3) You can re-execute or edit previous commands, even those very far back in the DOS history.
4) You can set a prompt, just like you would for DOS.

Here's how this can help you: You can run a database manager or a compiler inside the editor. Enter the command to execute your program just like you would in DOS. If you get error messages, exit the application, open a window on the error messages, and view the error messages as you edit your text.
Jump instantly to the lines with errors. Correct all of the syntax errors after one compile; it's faster and more convenient than getting thrown back in your text time and time again as the compiler finds each error.

The DOS Interface captures ALL DOS output — even from your application. When your program terminates, and you want to edit your source code, you can still view your program's previous output! Especially useful as a debugging trace.

Read in large files — limited by your PC's memory. Move text between windows and buffers.

There's more: List command — like a random access Find, wildcards for Find/Replace/List, tab size dependent on file extension, auto-indent for C, on-screen file-comparison, Path support, support for read-only files, extensive screen and printer support, International and other extended ASCII characters, support for International keyboards, garbage pile of deleted text, columnar editing. Keystroke macros are created merely by hitting the keys — no codes to remember.

On-line tables: ASCII, extended ASCII, extended keyboard codes, operator precedence for C, DOS and BIOS functions, PC Memory Map. **On-line Help** and a **Tutorial**. EC was written with the DeSmet C compiler on a PC.

Please note: EC's low price belies its quality. EC stands with the best! The price is low because we want everyone to try EC and find out why it is superior to editors costing $200 and more!

EC is not copy-protected. **30 day money back guarantee.** Full-featured demo: $5.00.

```
EC Editor........................ $ 49.50
DeSmet C Compiler................   99.50
DeSmet Debugger..................   50.00
BASIC__C Library.................  175.00
Lattice C Compiler...............  350.00
PC-Lint..........................   89.50
```

EC and BASIC__C run on PC compatibles.
We use and support all products we sell.

C Source
12801 Frost Road
Kansas City, MO 64138
(816) 353-8808

Shipping: $5.00 for orders under $50.00. MC, VISA, COD. Site licenses available. OEM's, dealers welcome.

Other Products

The DeSmet C Compiler — the fastest professional C compiler for the PC! DeSmet's program speed & efficiency are excellent. We chose DeSmet to develop EC and Basic__C, though, because of one factor: compile and link time. DESMET IS FOUR TIMES FASTER THAN LATTICE. 'Nuff said.

The Basic__C Library — the Convenience and Rich Function Set of BASIC for C.
The best way to move BASIC code over to C. The manual is regarded as the best tutorial for programmers moving from BASIC to C. You get a version for Lattice, DeSmet, and CI. No royalties. Includes source.

PC-Lint — A top quality lint checker at a quarter the price of the competition. Save hours of debugging by catching subtle bugs like function return mismatches.

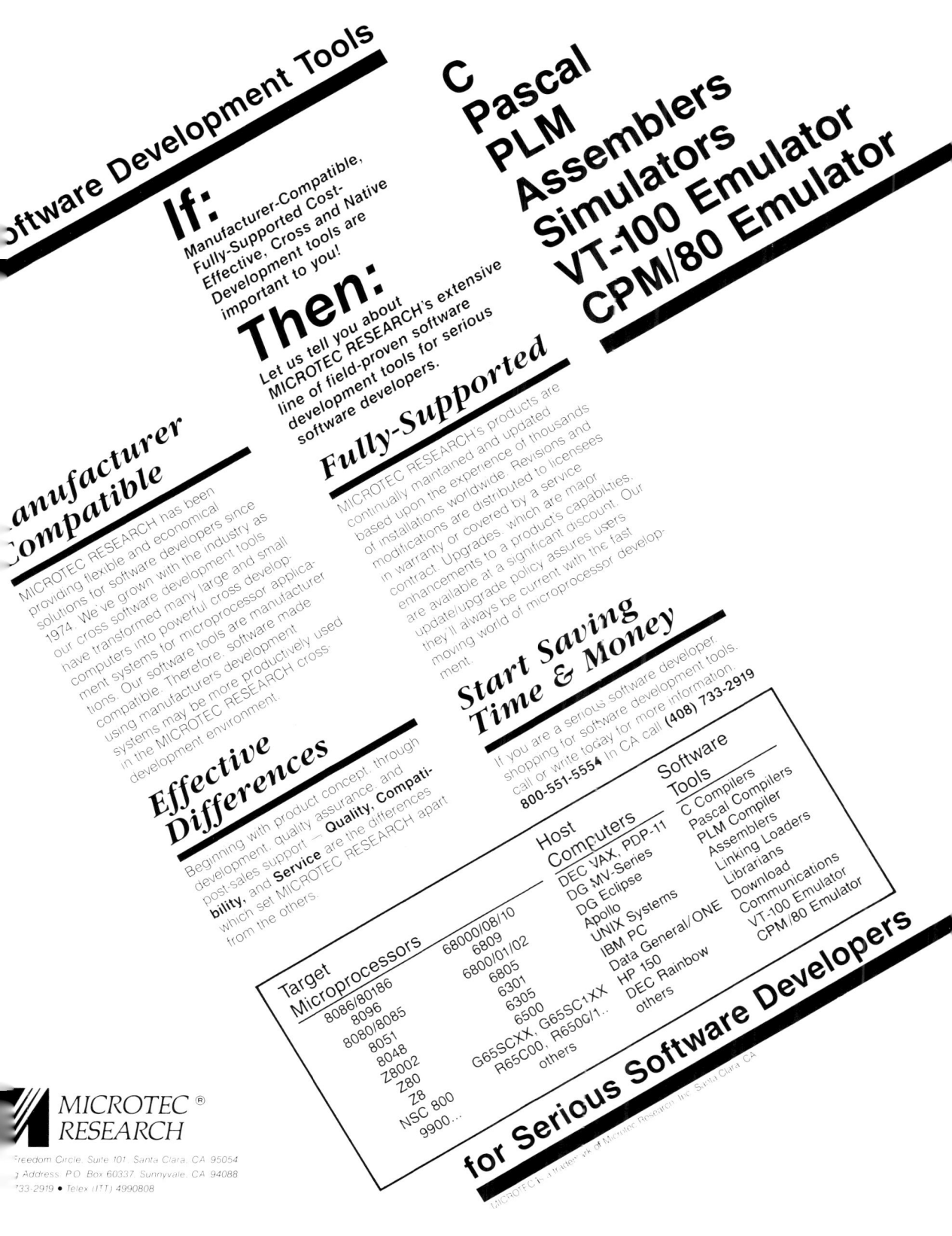

YOU NEED A GOOD LIBRARY

POWER PACKS™

COMPLETE SOURCES NO ROYALTIES

COMPREHENSIVE C Power Packs include over 1000 functions which provide an integrated environment for developing your applications efficiently. "This is a beautifully documented, incredibly comprehensive set of C Function Libraries."
— Dr. Dobb's Journal, July 1984

USEFUL "...can be used as an excellent learning tool for beginning C Programmers..."
— PC User's Group of Colorado, Jan. 1985

FLEXIBLE Most Compilers and all Memory Models supported.

RECOMMENDED "I have no hesitation in recommending it to any programmer interested in producing more applications code, using more of the PC capabilities, in much less time." — Microsystems, Oct. 1984

- **PACK 1: Building Blocks I** $149
  DOS, Keyboard, File, Printer, Video, Async

- **PACK 2: Database** $399
  B-Tree, Virtual Memory, Lists, Variable Records

- **PACK 3: Communications** $149
  Smartmodem™, Xon/Xoff, X-Modem, Modem-7

- **PACK 4: Building Blocks II** $149
  Dates, Textwindows, Menus, Data Compression, Graphics

- **PACK 5: Mathematics I** $99
  Log, Trig, Random, Std Deviation

- **PACK 6: Utilities I** $99
  (EXE files)
  Arc, Diff, Replace, Scan, Wipe

Master Card/Visa, $7 Shipping, Mass. Sales Tax 5%
ASK FOR FREE DEMO DISKETTE

NOVUM ORGANUM INC.   SOFTWARE HORIZONS INC.

165 Bedford St., Burlington, MA 01803
(617) 273-4711

Thinking of the C Language?

THINK COMPUTER INNOVATIONS

 **C86 VERSION 2.3 with Source Level Debugging Support**

The C language has rapidly become the development language of choice for applications ranging from Operating Systems to Accounting Packages. WHY? Its structured approach and extreme portability make it perfectly suited to today's fast-paced environment.

Of all of the C Compilers available for PC/MSDOS, more programmers choose COMPUTER INNOVATIONS' C86. WHY? Because it's part of a COMPREHENSIVE family of C products with an unparalleled reputation for performance, reliability, and stability.

C86 2.3 C COMPILER
C for PC/MSDOS began with C86 and today it remains perhaps the most solid, stable C Compiler available. Even competitor's ads show C86 as a consistent top level performer in benchmark testing.
Version 2.3 offers a host of new features including source level debugging support and a 40% boost in compilation speed. Call for complete specifications.
**COST: $395   UPDATE TO 2.3: $35 w/old diskettes NOT COPY PROTECTED
CALL ABOUT VOLUME DISCOUNTS**

LEARN C INTERACTIVELY WITH INTRODUCING C
Intimidated by rumors about the difficulty of learning C? Need to train your staff quickly? INTRODUCING C can help. INTRODUCING C combines a thorough, self-paced manual with a unique C interpreter to provide a fast, efficient method of learning C. Designed for both professional and casual programmers, it provides a comprehensive understanding of important C concepts such as standard K&R syntax and operators, full structures and unions, arrays, pointers, and data types. Requires IBM PC, XT, or AT with one disk drive and 192K bytes of memory.
COST: $125 - NOT COPY PROTECTED

CI PROBE SOURCE DEBUGGER
Take advantage of C86 2.3 source level debugging support with CI PROBE. Cut down program development time and save money! CI PROBE is highly economical yet has the features of debuggers costing far more.
COST: $225 - NOT COPY PROTECTED

C-TERP C86 COMPATIBLE INTERPRETER
The C-TERP INTERPRETER is a full K&R implementation that allows you to write code and execute it immediately without the compile and link steps. Once you have your program running with C-TERP you can compile the code (without alterations) with C86 for fast, efficient executable files. C-TERP requires 256K, 512K is recommended.
**COST: C86 version - List Price: $300, Special Computer Innovations Price $250.
Combined C86 & Lattice version - List Price: $400, Special Computer Innovations Price $350.**

Start With Us, Stay With Us
Computer Innovations offers a complete range of products that let you enter the C environment and create applications with the most advanced set of development tools available. Unparalleled tech support assures that you're always at the height of productivity.

To order call: 800-921-0169

980 Shrewsbury Ave., Tinton Falls, NJ 07724 • (201) 542-5920

C-TERP is a trademark of Gimple Software. Prices and specifications subject to change without notice.

whitesmith \ˈhwit-ˌsmith\ n:
a craftsman who finishes or polishes the work

The Whitesmith of today is every bit a perfectionist as his predecessor of a century ago. He is a high-tech software craftsman who takes the time to do the job well. The Whitesmiths, Ltd. product line of C and Pascal cross compilers reflects the time and polish that is associated with this age-old profession. It gives you the tools you need to be the software craftsman you've always wanted to be.

Whitesmiths offers compilers that are portable across more than 30 operating systems and six machine environments. Our cross compilers are just what you need to generate code for stand-alone environments. Or you can build programs to run on various flavors of CP/M, MS/PC-DOS, and VERSAdos. With the purchase of a Whitesmiths cross compiler you receive detailed documentation and technical phone support. Our most popular crosses include:

Host:	Crossing to:
IBM 370 (all models)	
All OS Operating Systems and CMS	8080, 8086, 68000
DEC PDP-11 (all models)	
RSX-11M, M+	8080, 8086, 68000, PDP-11 (POS)
RT-11	8080, 8086, 68000
PDP-11 UNIX	8080, 8086, 68000
VAX	
VMS	8080, 8086, 68000, PDP-11 (POS, RSX-11)
UNIX	8080, 8086, 68000
INTEL	
PC/MS-DOS	8080, 8086, 68000

For other hosts and targets contact Whitesmiths at 1-800-225-1030.

Contact Whitesmiths, Ltd., 97 Lowell Road, Concord, MA 01742, (617) 369-8499, TLX 750246 SOFTWARE CNCM.

Whitesmiths, Ltd.

INTERNATIONAL DISTRIBUTORS: **Australia**, Neology, Ltd., No. 1 Rosebery Ave., Rosebery 2018, N.S.W., (790) 74943; **France**, COSMIC s.a.r.l., 76 Quai Des Carrieres, 94227 Charenton Le Pont, (842) 232507; **Germany**, GEI, Albert-Einstein-Strasse 61, 5100 Aachen Walheim, (841) 8329745; **Japan**, Advanced Data Controls Corp., Nihon Seimei Otsuka Bldg., No. 13-4, Kita Otsuka 1-Chome, Toshima-Ku, Tokyo 170, (781) 32902; **Sweden**, Unisoft AB, Fiskhamnsgatan 10, S-41455 Goteborg, (854) 20120; **United Kingdom**, Real Time Systems Ltd., P.O. Box 70, Douglas, Isle of Man, (851) 628356. TECHNICAL AUTHORIZED REPRESENTATIVE: Praxtek Corporation, 880 Wellington St., Ottowa, Ontario, CANADA K1P5W7.

"C/80... the best software buy in America!" —MICROSYSTEMS

Now available in MS-DOS

Other technically respected publications like *Byte* and *Dr. Dobb's* have similar praise for **The Software Toolworks'** $49.95 full featured 'C' compiler for CP/M® and HDOS with:

- I/O redirection
- command line expansion
- execution trace and profile
- initializers
- Macro-80 compatability
- ROMable code
- and much more!

"We bought and evaluated over $1500 worth of 'C' compilers... C/80 is the one we use."
— Dr. Bruce E. Wampler
Aspen Software
author of "Grammatik"

The optional **C/80 MATHPAK** adds 32-bit floats and longs to the C/80 3.0 compiler. Includes I/O and transcendental function library all for only **$29.95!**

C/80 is only one of 41 great programs each **under sixty bucks.** Includes: LISP, Ratfor, assemblers and over 30 other CP/M® and MSDOS programs.

For your **free** catalog contact:

The Software Toolworks
15233 Ventura Blvd., Suite 1118,
Sherman Oaks, CA 91403 or call 818/986-4885 today!

CP/M is a registered trademark of Digital Research.

C-INDEX™   Release 2.0

Variable Length Record Management For C

C-INDEX is a state-of-the-art data management function library for C programmers. Ideal for all data and text based applications. No other package can give you the performance, capability, and portability of C-INDEX. To make sure you are a satisfied customer, we offer a 30 day money-back guarantee. Ask us about it.

- variable length data storage with B+Tree indexing
- high performance, easy to use
- large and small models, fully transportable source
- IBM PC format: Lattice, Microsoft, C86, others
- Macintosh format: Consulair, Manx, others

C-INDEX/FILE ($99)   Object code package.

C-INDEX/PRO ($195)   Partial source code, no royalties.

C-INDEX/PLUS ($395)   Complete transportable source code, no royalties.

Trio Systems

2210 Wilshire Blvd., Suite 289
Santa Monica, CA 90403
213/394-0796

Mac C™/Mac C Toolkit

A C Compiler and Support Library for the Macintosh™

From the creators of Apple's Macintosh 68000 Development System (MDS)

Mac C Features:

- **EFFICIENT** — Built-in interfaces with complete support of all ROM system calls
- **TESTED** — Used to create the MDS
- **FAST** — Up to 2500 lines per minute; Sieve time: 3.68 seconds
- **INCLUDES** — Standard C library, Floating point, Extensive Macintosh support libraries and all library sources
- No royalties, No copy protection
- Full technical support at no additional charge

Works With:

- Any Macintosh (128K, 512K, XL)
- Apple's MDS
- External disk drive, Hard disks, Ram disks, Extended memory

$425   Available directly from Consulair or your local computer store

" Powerful, flexible, fast! It's the best development system I've seen for the Macintosh. "
—*David S. Maynard, Electronic Arts*

" Consulair's version of C is the best C compiler I've seen so far for the Macintosh. "
—*Thom Hogan, A+ Magazine, May, 1985*

" ...It follows to buy a C from the guy who wrote the MDS... Even though we had a free review copy, we went out and bought another copy so it could be used in our own development efforts and so we could continue to get Bill Duvall's excellent phone support. It works, we like it, it's friendly — so what else can be said? "
—*Club Mac News, January, 1985*

Consulair

140 Campo Drive, Portola Valley, CA 94025 (415) 851-3272

Mac C is a trademark of Consulair Corp.
Macintosh is a trademark licensed to Apple Computer, Inc.

LATTICE
C Compiler

YOU GET MORE THAN LATTICE C FROM Lattice, Inc.

When you purchase a C Compiler from Lattice, you get the " compiler chosen by more than 26,000 professional software dev world-wide for its:

- Fast compile time
- Compatibility with proposed ANSI C standard
- Extremely efficient code generation
- Seven iAPX 86 memory models
- Comprehensive XENIX and UNIX-compatible library
- High-quality documentation
- Free periodic updates during the warranty period
- Support by more than 50 compatible software libraries and
- Unconditional money-back guarantee
- Competent telephone support

Join the thousands of Lattice C users. Call Lattice today for co information on the Lattice C Compiler, Lattice C Cross Compilers Libraries, and C Utilities!

Ask about our "Trade Up To Lattice C" Policy!

Lattice, Inc.
P.O. Box 3072, Glen Ellyn, IL 60138
Phone: (312) 858-7950 TWX: 910-291-2190

International Sales Offices:
BENELUX: DeVooght. Phone (32)-2-720.91.28 ENGLAND: Roundhill, Phone (0672) 54675
JAPAN: Lifeboat, Inc. Phone (03) 293-4711

Who Says You Can't Tell A Book By Its Cover?

Dr. Dobb's Sourcebook: A Reference Guide for the C Programming Language

For years, serious programmers have relied on Dr. Dobb's Journal for the technical tools of their trade. Now, Dr. Dobb's presents the definitive programmers guide to the who, what, where, when and why of C, the leading language among software developers. This comprehensive guide to new information, products and services specific to C will be your most often-used reference!

In this valuable guide you'll find:

- An extensive directory of hardware and software services—including classes and seminars, C programming opportunities, and on-line services

- A bibliography with over 300 listings of available articles and books on C

- A comprehensive C product listing—including C compilers, graphics modules, utilities, editors and development systems, and more!

- And much more practical C programming information

At only $7.95, no C programmer can afford to be without this unique reference.

TO ORDER: Mail this coupon, along with payment, to: **Dr. Dobb's Journal, 2464 Embarcadero Way, Palo Alto, CA 94303**

PAYMENT MUST ACCOMPANY YOUR ORDER

____ I enclose check/money order
____ Please charge my ___ VISA ___ M/C ___ American Express
Card #_____ Exp. Date _____
Signature _____
Name _____
Address _____
City _____ State _____ Zip _____

Please send me _____ copies of **Dr. Dobb's Sourcebook**

at $7.95 each = _____

+ Shipping & Handling = _____
(Must be included with order. Please add $1.50 per book in U.S. $3.25 each surface mail outside U.S. Foreign airmail rates available on request.)

TOTAL = _____

Please allow 6 to 12 weeks for delivery

4003

living C - personal ™

GIVES LIFE TO C PROGRAMMING

Living C™ is the fully integrated interactive programming environment for C. By replacing the headaches of programming in C with total control and understanding – whether new to C or an expert – Living C is the exciting solution to maximize your creativity and productivity.

$99

The Living C editor is a true full function commercial editor, fully menu-driven with help facilities on call. The editor is fully integrated and can be used at all times throughout the design, development, maintenance and debugging of your C application.

FULL SCREEN EDITOR

Living C allows you to execute all your C source code on the screen. You control the code you wish to examine and the speed of animation. The cursor demonstrates exactly how your source is executing, enabling you to understand instantly how the application or prototype works – or why it doesn't!

ANIMATING C INTERPRETER™

Living C conforms to the full Kernighan and Ritchie standard. Living C not only highlights all errors discovered, but also offers comprehensive error diagnostics and useful hints to solve the problem. Corrections can be made immediately, using the fully integrated Living C editor.

FULL C SOURCE DEBUG

The Living C windows allow you to constantly monitor the variables and I/O of your applications even when you are "zooming" to your next breakpoint!

WINDOWS

I understand that I can write my applications in Living C, but what if I want to debug or modify an existing application – bearing in mind that 75% of my programming time is taken up with maintenance?

You simply compile in your C source and leave the rest to Living C! Living C not only enables you to understand how your application works but also ensures you can interpret a colleague's application and understand why it works or doesn't!! Once in Living C, the full suite of programming tools are automatically available. Combined with your rapid increase in productivity and understanding, you will now find that maintenance time is dramatically reduced.

So now I have written and tested my application, how can I use it?

You have 3 choices:
 (i) Simply switch off the animation and use Living C as an interpreter
 (ii) Recompile your application into your favourite C compiler (eg Microsoft, Lattice, Computer Innovations, Aztec)
 (iii) Use the optional Living C code generator ($99)

What machines does Living C - Personal run on?

Living C - Personal is available for the IBM PC and all compatibles. You will need PCDOS, either twin floppy disk drives or a floppy and a hard disk with 192K RAM.

How do I order Living C - Personal?

Just fill out the coupon and send it to us along with $99 or call us on the toll free number

1 800 826-2612

Circle no. 122 on reader service card.

Living Software, 250 North Orange Avenue, Suite 820, Orlando, Florida 32801

Living C, Living C - Personal and Animating C Interpreter are trade marks of Living Software

---

Mail to: Living Software, 250 North Orange Avenue, Suite 820, Orlando, Florida 32801

To order your copy of Living C-Personal, please complete this form:

Please Send   Quantity
Living C – Personal @ $99 x _____ = $ _____
Code Generator @ $99 x _____ = $ _____
Handling & Shipping Orders $ _____
Florida residents please include   10.00
Florida Sales Tax $ _____
TOTAL   = $ _____
Payment   Visa☐ MC☐ Check☐ Money Order☐
Credit Card expiry date _____
Name on Card _____
Card# _____

Name _____
Shipping Address _____
City _____
State _____ Zip _____
Telephone _____

Living C - Personal is available for PC-DOS with min 192KB RAM. COD's and Purchase Orders will not be accepted by Living Software.

ANNOUNCING! DR. DOBB'S COMPLETE TOOLBOX OF C

Dr. Dobb's Journal, the most respected source of technical software information available, brings you this collection of powerful programming tools.

Available in October from M&T Publishing and Brady Communications—

Dr. Dobb's Toolbook for C

A comprehensive library of valuable C code

Many of Dr. Dobb's most popular articles on C from sold-out issues are updated and reprinted in this unique reference, along with new C programming tools. **THE TOOLBOOK** contains a complete C compiler, an assembler, text processing programs, and more! Dr. Dobb's Journal offers **THE TOOLBOOK** in a special hardbound edition for only $29.95. You'll find:

- James Hendrix's famous Small C Compiler v. 2 and A New Library for Small C (also available on disk)
- Ron Cain's original A Small-C Compiler for the 8080's
- Never before published: Hendrix's new *Small-Mac: An Assembler for Small C* and *Small Tools: Programs for Text Processing* (both available on disk)
- Plus many useful programming tools in C

Also from M&T Publishing and Brady Communications—

The Small-C Handbook

The Small-C Handbook by James Hendrix is a valuable source of information about the Small-C compiler. In addition to descriptions of the language and the compiler, **The Handbook** also contains the entire source listings of the compiler and its library arithmetic and logical routines.

A perfect companion to the Hendrix Small-C compiler offered by Dr. Dobb's on disk, **The Handbook** even tells how to use the compiler to generate new versions of itself. $17.95

Dr. Dobb's C Tools On Disk

To complement **The Toolbook** Dr. Dobb's also offers the following programs on disk for only $19.95 each. Full source code is included and, except where indicated, both CP/M and MS or PC DOS versions are available.

Small-C Compiler

Jim Hendrix's **Small-C Compiler** is the most popular piece of software published in Dr. Dobb's 10-year history. Like a home study course in compiler design, the **Small-C Compiler** and **The Small-C Handbook** provide all you need to learn how compilers are constructed, as well as teaching the C language at its most fundamental level. **The Small-C Handbook** provides documentation for both versions; however, an addendum is recommended in addition to **The Handbook** for MS or PC DOS-specific documentation. The addendum is available for $4.95.

Small Tools: Programs for Text Processing

This package consists of programs designed to perform specific functions on text files, including: editing; formatting; sorting; merging; listing; printing; searching; changing; transliterating; copying and concatenating; encrypting and decrypting; replacing spaces with tabs and tabs with spaces; counting characters, words, or lines; and selecting printer fonts. Documentation available for $9.95.

Small-Mac: An Assembler for Small-C

Small-Mac is a macro assembler designed to stress simplicity, portability, adaptability, and educational value. The package features simplified macro facility, C-language expression operators, descriptive error messages, object file visibility, and an externally defined machine instruction table. Included programs are: macro assembler, CPU editor, load-and-go loader, library manager, configuration utility, and dump relocatable files. This program is available for CP/M systems only. Documentation available for $9.95.

To order, send this order form with your payment to: **Dr. Dobb's Journal, 2464 Embarcadero Way, Palo Alto, CA 94303**

		QTY.	TOTAL
BOOKS			
Dr. Dobb's Toolbook	$29.95	X	=
Small-C Handbook	$17.95	X	=

Check Format
	CP/M	MS or PC DOS			
DISKS					
Small-C Compiler			$19.95	X	=
Small Tools Text Processor			$19.95	X	=
Small Mac Assembler (for CP/M only)		■	$19.95	X	=

MANUALS			
Small-C Compiler MSPC-DOS specific addendum to The Small-C Handbook (NOTE: The Small-C Handbook provides full documentation for the CP/M version)	$4.95	X	=
Small Tools	$9.95	X	=
Small Mac	$9.95	X	=

Sub Total $ _____

California residents add applicable sales tax   Tax _____

Add $1.75 per item for shipping in U.S., Shipping _____
$4.25 per item outside U.S.   TOTAL $ _____

For CP/M system disks only, please specify one of the following formats:

☐ Kaypro
☐ Apple
☐ Zenith Z-00 DS/DD
☐ Osborne
☐ 8" SS/SD
☐ Inquire about other formats

PAYMENT MUST ACCOMPANY YOUR ORDER

☐ Check enclosed
☐ Please charge my   ☐ VISA   ☐ M/C   ☐ Amer. Exp.

Card # _____

Exp. Date _____

Signature _____

Name _____

Address _____
(please use street address)
City _____

State _____ Zip _____

Allow 6–12 Weeks for delivery   4001

CONTINUING THE TRADITION

DR. DOBB'S JOURNAL ANNOUNCES THE RELEASE OF BOUND VOLUME 8

Every 1983 Issue together in one source

BOUND VOLUME 8
DDJ turns pro. Some of the most powerful, professional programmer's tools ever published in a magazine are in this volume. Jim Hendrix's Small C compiler. Ed Ream's RED screen editor. A microcomputer subset of the Defense Department's official programming language, Ada. C and Forth and 68000 software. Because the magazine increased in size in 1983, this volume is bigger and better than ever.

Vol. 1 1976
The material brought together in this volume chronicles the development in 1976 of Tiny BASIC as an alternative to the "finger blistering," front-panel, machine-language programming which was then the only way to do things. This is always pertinent for the bit crunching and byte saving, language design theory, home-brew computer construction and the technical history of personal computing.
Topics include: Tiny BASIC, the (very) first word on CP/M, Speech Synthesis, Floating Point Routines, Timer Routines, Building an IMSAI, and more.

Vol. 2 1977
1977 found DDJ still on the forefront. These issues offer refinements of Tiny BASIC, plus then state-of-the-art utilities, the advent of PILOT for microcomputers and a great deal of material centering around the Intel 6080, including a complete operating system. Products just becoming available for reviews were the H-8, KIM-1, MITS BASIC, Poly Basic, and NIBL.
Articles are about Lawrence Livermoore Lab's BASIC, Alpha Micro, String Handling, Cyphers, High Speed Interaction, I/O, Tiny Pilot & Turtle Graphics, many utilities, and even more.

Vol. 3 1978
The microcomputer industry entered into its adolescence in 1978. This volume brings together the issues which began dealing with the 6502, with mass-market machines and languages to match. The authors began speaking more in terms of technique, rather than of specific implementations; because of this, they were able to continue laying the groundwork industry would follow. These articles relate very closely to what is generally available today.
Languages covered in depth were SAM76, Pilot, Pascal, and Lisp, in addition to RAM Testers, S-100 Bus Standard Proposal, Disassemblers, Editors, and much, much more.

Vol. 4 1979
This volume heralds a wider interest in telecommunications, in algorithms, and in faster, more powerful utilities and languages, innovation is still present in every page, and more attention is paid to the best ways to use the processors which have proven longevity—primarily the 8080IZ80, 6502, and 6800. The subject matter is invaluable both as a learning tool and as a frequent source of reference.
Main subjects include: Programming Problems/Solutions, Pascal, Information Network Proposal, Floating Point Arithmetic, 8-bit to 16-bit Conversion, Pseudo-random Sequences, and Interfacing a Micro to a Mainframe—more than ever!

Vol. 5 1980
All the ground-breaking issues from 1980 in one volume! Systems software reached a new level with the advent of CP/M, chronicled herein by Gary Kildall and others (DDJ's all-CP/M issue sold out within weeks of publication). Software portability became a subject of greater import, and DDJ published Ron Cain's immediately famous Small-C compiler—reprinted here in full.
Contents include: The Evolution of CP/M, a CP/M-Flavored C Interpreter, Ron Cain's C Compiler for the 8080. Further with Tiny BASIC, a Syntax-Oriented Compiler Writing Language, CP/M to UCSD Pascal File Conversion, Run-time Library for the Small-C Compiler and, as always, even more!

Vol. 6 1981
1981 saw our first all-FORTH issue (now sold out), along with continuing coverage of CP/M, small-C, telecommunications, and new languages. Dave Cortesi opened "Dr. Dobb's Clinic" in 1981, beginning one of the magazine's most popular features.
Highlights: Information on PCNET, the Conference Tree, and The Electric Phone Book, writing your own compiler, a systems programming language, and Tiny BASIC for the 6809.

Vol. 7 1982
In 1982 we introduced several significant pieces of software, including the RED text editor and the Runic extensible compiler, and we continue to publish utility programs and useful algorithms. Two new columns, The CP/M Exchange and The 16-Bit Software Toolbox, were launched, and we devoted special issues to FORTH and telecommunications. Resident Intern Dave Cortesi supplied a year of "Clinic" columns while delivering his famous review of JRT Pascal and writing the first serious technical comparison of CP/M-86 and MSDOS. This was also the year we began looking forward to today's generation of microprocessors and operating systems, publishing software for the Motorola 68000 and the Zilog Z8000 as well as Unix code. And in December, we looked beyond, in the provocative essay, "Fifth-generation Computers."

Complete your reference library. Buy the entire set of Dr. Dobb's Journals from 1976 through 1983, Bound Volumes 1–8, for $195.00. That's $34.00 off the combined individual prices—a savings of almost 15%!

YES! ☐ Please send me the following Volumes of **Dr. Dobb's Journal.**
Payment must accompany your order.
Please charge my: ☐ Visa ☐ MasterCard ☐ American Express
I enclose ☐ Check/money order
Card # _____ Expiration Date _____
Signature _____
Name _____ Address _____
(please, no P.O. Boxes)
City _____ State _____ Zip _____

Mail to Dr. Dobb's Journal, 2464 Embarcadero Way, Palo Alto, CA 94303

4002   Allow 6 to 12 weeks for delivery.

Vol. 1 _____	x $27.75 =	_____
Vol. 2 _____	x $27.75 =	_____
Vol. 3 _____	x $27.75 =	_____
Vol. 4 _____	x $27.75 =	_____
Vol. 5 _____	x $27.75 =	_____
Vol. 6 _____	x $27.75 =	_____
Vol. 7 _____	x $30.75 =	_____
Vol. 8 _____	x $31.75 =	_____
All 8 _____	x $195.00 =	_____

Sub-total $ _____
California residents add applicable sales tax_____% _____

Postage & Handling Must be Included with order.
Please add $1.75 per book in U.S. ($4.25 each surface mail outside U.S. Foreign Airmail rates available on request.)

TOTAL $ _____

PROGRAMMERS—
YOUR DREAMS HAVE JUST COME TRUE!

Have you dreamed of having ONE BOOK that contains ESCAPE and CONTROL CODES for 100's of different printers???
Now the **Programmers' Handbook of Computer Printer Commands** is not a dream but a reality!!!

The handbook gives you:
- Codes for 100's of models of Personal Computer Printers made by over 40 Printer Manufacturers.
- Easy to use spiral bound book of over 250 pages of Programming Codes written in table form.
- Codes arranged by Written Code, Hex and Decimal equivalent, and with a brief description of what each code does.
- Manufacturers listed alphabetically. PLUS complete Manufacturers Address and Phone Number Section.
- Codes for either Daisy-Wheel or Dot Matrix Printers (Models through 1984).

ONLY $37.95 + $2.00 shpg. and hdlg. ppd.
with a two week approval guarantee. If not satisfied return in original carton for refund of book price only.
DEALER and USER GROUP INQUIRIES INVITED. FOR MORE INFORMATION OR TO ORDER CALL OR WRITE:

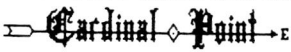
INCORPORATED
(812) 876-7811 (9-5 EST)
P.O. BOX 596, ELLETTSVILLE, IN 47429
We accept MasterCard, Visa, MO—
same day shipping. COD—$39.95 + $2 extra.
CKs—Allow extra 14 days before shipping.

VANCE info systems is pleased to announce
THE MOST COMPLETE C FUNCTION LIBRARY AVAILABLE TO DATE!

C FUNCTION LIBRARY

"C lib" is the most functional library available for software written in C, providing over 200 routines, extending the capabilities of C on the IBM PC. The library is available under the DeSmet (C Ware) C88 compiler, will soon be available in MicroSoft C, Lattice C and other C compilers; and runs using MS Dos 1.1 and later versions.

Featuring:
- Unix/Xenix Compatibility
- Windowing Library
- Math Functions
- String Functions
- Asychronous Buffered, Interrupt-driven Communications
- 8087/MicroSoft Floating Point conversions
- And much more

Documentation is offered in an easy to use printed manual or on disk for personal printing needs, complete with programming examples and follow-up demo programs.

The "C lib" C FUNCTION LIBRARY is offered at only **$195** less than most available today.

For further information on "C lib" please call or write us.

VANCE info systems
2818 clay street • san francisco, california 94115 • (415) 922-6539

IBM is a trademark of International Business Machines Corp. C88 is a trademark of Computer Innovations, Inc. Lattice is a trademark of Lattice Inc. Xenix, MicroSoft C and MS DOS are trademarks of MicroSoft. Unix is a trademark of Bell Labs, Inc. "C lib" is a trademark of VANCE info systems.

WIZARD C

LANGUAGE FEATURES
- Full K & R standard syntax
- enum, void, unsigned char, unsigned long supported
- Structure assignment
- Non-unique structure members
- Full Lint checking included

CODE OPTIONS
- 6 Memory models up to 1M Byte of Code & Data
- 8087/80186/80286 support
- In-line assembler using C symbols
- ROMable code

Fast execution speed: Sieve of Eratosthenes 6 seconds with 2 register variables on a PC

VAX/VMS, UNIX Cross-compilers Available

LIBRARY FEATURES:
- K & R Standard I/O supported
- DOS 2.0 & 3.0 interfaces
- Transcendental math library
- IBM ROM BIOS interface supported
- Library source code included

Only $450.
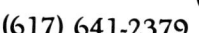

(617) 641-2379

systems software, inc.
11 willow court, arlington, ma 02174

ARITY/PROLOG AND C: THE POWERFUL COMBINATION

When you need the best of symbolic computation and conventional procedural processing, use Arity/Prolog with C. Arity/Prolog extends your C code with its symbolic processing, declarative style, and powerful data structures for faster execution.

Combine code you have already written in C with Arity/Prolog to build faster, more flexible, and serious applications, including databases, expert systems, natural language, and logical problem solving.

The *Arity/Prolog Compiler and Interpreter* includes these powerful features:

- Source level debugger
- Virtual databases, each with a workspace of 16 megabytes
- Floating-point arithmetic
- String support for efficient text handling

- Interface to assembly language and 'C'
- Text screen manipulation
- Integrated programming shell to MSDOS
- Comprehensive set of evaluable predicates
- Definite clause grammar support

The *Arity/Prolog Compiler and Interpreter* is available now at a price that makes sense. And you may distribute your compiled applications royalty-free.

Arity/Prolog Compiler and Interpreter $1950.00

Also available: *Arity/Prolog Interpreter* without compiler $495.00. *Arity/Prolog Demo Disk* $19.95. ■ Arity/Prolog products run on the IBM PC, XT, AT, and all IBM compatibles. ■ To order, call (617) 371-2422.

arity corporation 358 Baker Avenue, Concord, MA 01742

M-AD-09

Not long ago, *PC* Magazine called MDBS III "The most complete and flexible data base management system available for microcomputers." That's a powerful statement. But then, MDBS III is an amazingly powerful software package. So powerful, in fact, that it lets you build mainframe-quality application systems on your micro or mini. MDBS III is not for beginners. It's for application developers with large data bases or complex data interrelationships who want to define data base structures in the most natural way—without resorting to redundancy or artificial constructs. It's for professionals who can appreciate its extensive data security and integrity features, transaction logging, ad hoc query and report writing capability and its ability to serve multiple simultaneous users. And if you want the power and the glory that only the world's most advanced data management system can provide, MDBS III is for you. For information on MDBS III and our professional consulting services, write or call Micro Data Base Systems, Inc., MDBS/Application Development Products, 85 West Algonquin Road, Suite 400, Arlington Heights, IL 60005. (800) 323-3629, or (312) 981-9200. **MDBS III. ABSOLUTE POWER.**

WE'LL GIVE YOU THE POWER.

YOU TAKE THE GLORY.

C

HOW EASY DEVELOPING PROGRAMS CAN BE WITH THE C UTILITY LIBRARY!

COMPLETE. Over 300 tested and well documented functions. All features of the PC &AT are at your finger tips.

ADVANCED. Features like windows, data entry fields, switching displays, and batch file execution are supported.

GRAPHICS. A complete set of fast business graphics functions. Our low level graphics routines are the fastest in the business.

SOURCE. All source code is included. 95% of the library is written in C. Only functions demanding fast execution speed are in Assembler.

COMPATIBLE. With Lattice, Microsoft(3.0), CI-C86, Aztec, DeSmet, Wizard, and Mark Williams. All memory models are supported.

MUCH MORE. Dozens of string functions, the best time & date math and formatting, DOS directory and file mgmt., keyboard control, polled async communications, and more. **NO ROYALTIES.** We **SUPPORT** what we sell.

C UTILITY LIBRARY - $185
COMPILERS: Lattice $349, CI-C86 $329, Mark Williams $449. **Save $40-$50** with compiler & library package.

Specify compiler and version number when ordering. Add $4 for UPS or $7 for UPS 2-day shipping. NJ residents add 6% sales tax. VISA, MC, Chks & qualified PO's.

Essential Software, Inc.
P.O. Box 1003
Maplewood, New Jersey 07040
914/762-6605

The Best Source Debugger for C

Interactive testing: enter any C expression, statement, or function call, and it is immediately executed and the result displayed. **Direct execution** allows fast and thorough testing, makes learning C a snap.

Run-time checking: execution stops upon exception, and source code displayed. Exceptions include array reference bounds, stack overflow arithmetic or floating point error, etc. Pointers are checked for null or out of range values.

Breakpoints: *any* number of breakpoints can be set *anywhere* in your program; breakpoints are set with screen editor, not by line numbers. Breakpoints may be conditional. Single-step by statement. Interrupt execution from keyboard. Breakpoint, exception, or interruption is always shown with source code. Examine and modify data, look at stack history. Even change your program and then resume execution!

Lint-like **Compile-time checking:** argument number and sizes are checked for consistency. Never mismatch source and object code.

The best feature of all: the *fastest* C interpreter is right there when you're debugging. Make changes in seconds with the integrated screen editor. Test the changes immediately, running your program at compiled speed. Save source code for your favorite compiler, or make stand-alone executable programs. Nothing else is needed. **Instant-C is the fastest way to get working, fully debugged C programs available today.**

"We sincerely feel that *Instant-C* can have a major positive impact on programmer productivity." *Computer Language*, Feb. 85, pp. 82-83.

Instant-C is only $495. Money back for any reason in first 31 days.

Rational
Systems, Inc.

(617) 653-6194
P.O. Box 480
Natick, MA 07160

Circle **no.** 7 on reader service card.

DeSmet C

8086/8088 Development Package $109

FULL DEVELOPMENT PACKAGE
- Full K&R C Compiler
- Assembler, Linker & Librarian
- SEE™ A Full Screen Editor
- Execution Profiler
- Complete STDIO Library (>120 Func)

Automatic DOS 1.X/2.X SUPPORT
BOTH 8087 AND S/W FLOATING POINT OVERLAYS
OUTSTANDING PERFORMANCE
- First and Second in AUG '83 BYTE benchmarks

SYMBOLIC DEBUGGER $50
- Examine & change variables by name using C expressions
- Flip between debug and display screen
- Display C source during execution
- Set multiple breakpoints by function or line number

DOS LINK SUPPORT $35
- Uses DOS .OBJ Format
- LINKs with DOS ASM
- Uses Lattice® naming conventions

Check: ☐ Dev. Pkg (109)
☐ Debugger (50)
☐ DOS Link Supt. (35)

SHIP TO:
_____
_____
_____ ZIP_____

CWARE CORPORATION

P.O. BOX C
Sunnyvale, CA 94087
(408) 720-9696

All orders shipped UPS surface on IBM format disks. Shipping included in price. California residents add sales tax. Canada shipping add $5, elsewhere add $15. Checks must be on US Bank and in US Dollars. Call 9 a.m. – 1 p.m. to CHARGE by VISA/MC/AMEX
Street Address: 505 W. Olive, #767, (94086)

Breakthrough for C Programmers

H.E.L.P. Eliminates Every Bug known to Compilers ... As well as a few other species

H.E.L.P. is a completely interactive C programming environment with three innovative full-sized features that will revolutionize the way you write code.

A Clean Compile — Guaranteed!

Say Good-bye to all compiler-type errors. **H.E.L.P.**'s built-in program checker (which would embarrass LINT) not only hunts down bugs ... explains the proper syntax ... gives examples of usage ... but will even offer suggested corrections. If you want, **H.E.L.P.** will even make the corrections for you ... at the touch of a key.

H.E.L.P. also finds semantic errors as well as poor style and inefficiencies. You can even check the portability of your code!

Multi-Window Editing

Open as many windows as you want .... there's no limitation ... not even your own memory. Because **H.E.L.P.** uses a virtual memory system you can create programs larger than your machine capacity.

H.E.L.P.'s very powerful editor allows you the flexibility to work in several windows ... with several files at the same time.

Save Keystrokes

Hundreds of commands are bound to the keyboard to give you fast execution.

Always be in Control

Not only can you develop code in many windows at the same time, but you can show (and refer to) important definitions in one window while creating in another. Or open a window and keep notes about your program ... or type a memo ... or a letter.

Increase your Productivity by 300% or More .....

If you are a novice programmer, you'll begin writing code like an advanced programmer much faster with **H.E.L.P.**

Just imagine what **H.E.L.P.** will do for the ADVANCED PROGRAMMER.

You'll have more time to become creative with your algorithm (since **H.E.L.P.** will make sure your code compiles the "first time at bat").

H.E.L.P. tracks every step you make. If you are not sure about a command, just press a key, and you'll get the kind of help you need.

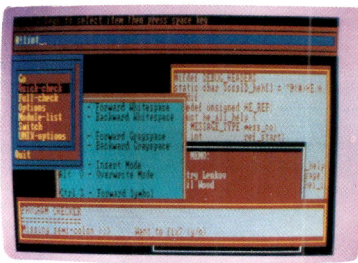

Check These Features

- Multi-window environment
- Interactive program checking
- Check syntax, semantic, type usage, intermodule inconsistencies and portability
- Multi-file editing
- Intelligent help sub-system
- User-definable keyboard bindings
- Supports color and monochrome
- H.E.L.P. supports the full C Language

NOW IN MS-DOS

Order now $395

Everest Solutions, Inc.
3350 Scott Boulevard
Building 58
Santa Clara, CA 95051
(408) 986-8977

If lightning still scares you, you're using the wrong file manager.

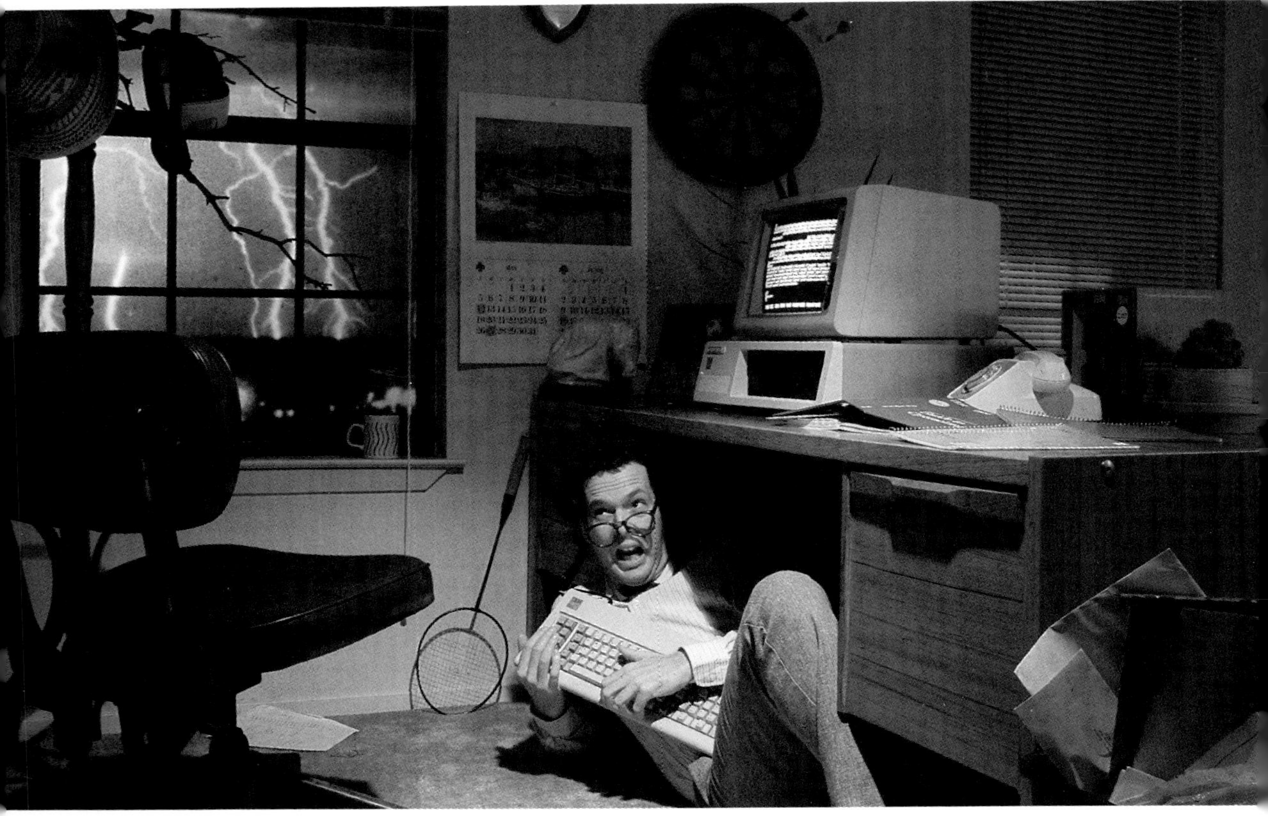

Be sure. Btrieve.™

Lightning may strike. But it doesn't have to destroy your database.

Btrieve™ file management offers automatic file recovery after a system crash. So accidents and power failures don't turn into database disasters. Your Btrieve-based applications will come up when the lights come back on.

Fast. Btrieve is lightning fast, too. Its b-tree file structure automatically balances—you never waste time reorganizing the index. And Btrieve is written in Assembly language especially for the IBM PC™. The result: electrifying speed on file maintenance routines. Applications that run fast. Users who don't waste time waiting.

The standard for networking. When your application requires multi-user file sharing, Btrieve/N (network version) sets the standard for the industry's most popular LANs: IBM's PC Network, Netware™, Davong MultiLink™, Omninet™, PC Net™, EtherSeries™, Nestar™, and NetOne™. Btrieve/N offers **safe** network file management that coordinates simultaneous updates and protects against lost data.

Fully-relational data management. Using SoftCraft's entire family of products gives you a complete, fully-relational database management system. Rtrieve™ adds report writing capabilities for generating the reports you need. Xtrieve™ speeds users through database queries with interactive, on-screen menus—no command language or special syntax.

For professional programmers. Btrieve is the fast, reliable answer for all your application development. In any development language—BASIC, Pascal, Cobol, C, Fortran, and APL. With multikey access to records. Unlimited records per file. Duplicate, modifiable, and segmented keys. Variable cache buffer.

With Btrieve, you can develop better applications faster. And know they'll be safe if lightning strikes.

Suggested retail prices: Btrieve, $245; Btrieve/N, $595; Xtrieve, $195; Xtrieve/N, $395; Rtrieve, $85; Rtrieve/N, $175. Requires PC-DOS or MS™-DOS 1.X, 2.X, or 3.X.

Btrieve, Xtrieve, and Rtrieve; IBM; ware; Davong MultiLink; Omninet; Net; EtherSeries; Nestar; NetOne; a MS are trademarks of SoftCraft Inc.; ternational Business Machines; Nove Data Systems; Davong Systems Inc. Corvus Systems; Orchid Technology; 3Com Corp.; Nestar Systems Inc.; Ungermann-Bass; and Microsoft Inc

SoftCraft Inc.
P.O. Box 9802 #917
Austin, Texas 78766
(512) 346-8380   Telex 358

Dr. Dobb's Journal
- Ian Ashdown, November 1984
"WINDOWS FOR C... has obviously been well thought out and very cleanly executed.
"WINDOWS FOR C is a professionally-oriented set of programming tools... that we can recommend."

Now for the IBM PC, XENIX, UNIX, VMS...

WINDOWS FOR C™

Advanced Screen Management Made Easy
A video tool kit for all screen tasks

- Pop-up menus and help files
- Unlimited files and windows
- Rapid screen changes
- Logical video attributes
- Complete color control
- Horizontal and vertical scrolling
- Word wrap
- Highlighting
- Plus a library of over 65 building block subroutines

So easy to learn and easy to use, you'll wonder how you ever managed without it.

Provides application portability between the IBM PC and XENIX, UNIX, VMS or any terminal-based system.

Full support for IBM PC/XT/AT and compatibles; Lattice C, C1-C86, Mark Wm. C, Aztec C, Microsoft C, DeSmet C (PC/MSDOS), PC/XENIX. Source version available for Unix and other OS.

NEW Ver. 4.0
Logical attributes
Easier menus
New pop-up functions
WINDOWS FOR C PCDOS
(specify compiler) **$195**
PC/XENIX $395
UNIX and other OS Call
Full Source Available

Vermont Creative Software

21 Elm Ave.
Richford, VT 05476
802-848-7738, ext. 71,

Master Card & Visa Accepted
Shipping $2.50
VT residents add 4% tax

Trademarks - UNIX, AT&T; XENIX, Microsoft; VMS, DEC.

¿C? ¡Sí!

If you're a C programmer (or want to be one), we speak your language. Subscribe to **The C Journal** today, and start increasing your productivity right away. We give you information you can **use** on **any** machine — IBM PC™, UNIX™-based, Macintosh™, or CP/M™ — micro, mini, or mainframe.

- in-depth reviews and feature articles — C compilers, editors, interpreters, function libraries, and books.

- hints and tips — help you work **better** and **faster**.

- interviews — with software entrepreneurs that **made it** — by using C.

- news and rumors — from the ANSI standards committee and the industry.

LIMITED TIME OFFER

Join our thousands of subscribers at the **Discount Rate** of only $18 for a full year (regularly $28)! Call us now at (201) 989-0570 for faster service — don't miss a single issue of **The C Journal!**

Please add $9 for overseas airmail.

Trademarks — CP/M: Digital Research Inc.   IBM PC: IBM Corp.   Macintosh: Apple Computer Corp.
The C Journal: InfoPro Systems.   UNIX: AT&T Bell Labs.

InfoPro Systems
3108 Route 10
Denville, NJ 07834
(201) 989-0570

HIPPO-C
The C compilers for the Macintosh™

Level 1:

The ideal C compiler: powerful, expandable, affordable.
- A friendly, integrated environment complete with a screen editor, full K&R C compiler, linker, source-level debugger, tutorial, standard C library, and structure definition files.
- Convenient access to over 400 Toolbox routines, serial ports and sound channels.
- Over 200 pages of documentation and many sample programs.
- Upgradable to Hippo-C Level 2 for $250.00 suggested retail price.
- New version 1.2.
- **$149.95** suggested retail price.

Level 2:

At last: a complete professional C compiler!
- Allows for the creation of large, stand-alone commercial applications.
- Comes with a screen editor, optimizing K&R C compiler, 68000 assembler, linker, C library, stdio package, full floating-point support, and structure definition files.
- "Glue" routines which allow easy access to Macintosh features.
- UNIX™-like shell which includes many powerful commands and utilities.
- Convenient access to over 500 Toolbox routines.
- Documentation, many sample programs, and sources.
- No royalties or license fees.
- You may obtain a non-copy protected disk by signing and returning a form along with $25.00 to Hippopotamus.
- **$399.95** suggested retail price.

HIPPOPOTAMUS
SOFTWARE, INC

985 University Avenue, Suite 12, Los Gatos, California 95030 • 408-395-3190 • Telex: 172211 HQSUVL

Available from your local dealer or directly from Hippopotamus Software

Dealer inquiries welcome. We accept credit cards, checks, and money orders. California residents add local sales tax. Please include $10 for shipping and handling. Macintosh is a trademark of Apple Computer, Inc. UNIX is a trademark of AT&T Bell Labs. Hippo-C is a trademark of Hippopotamus Software, Inc. Please allow 3-4 weeks for delivery. Price, availability, and specifications subject to change without notice.

Over 50 volumes of public domain software including:
- compilers
- editors
- text formatters
- communications packages
- many UNIX-like tools

Write or call for more details

The C Users' Group
Box 97
McPherson, KS 67460
(316) 241-1065

THE GREENLEAF FUNCTIONS™

The GREENLEAF FUNCTIONS GENERAL LIBRARY has over 200 functions in C and assembler. Strength in DOS, video, string, printer, async, and systems interface. All DOS 1 and 2 functions are in assembler for speed. All video capabilities of PC supported. All printer functions. 65 string functions. Extensive time and date. Directory searches. Polled mode async. (If you want interrupt driven, ask us about the **Greenleaf Comm Library**.) Function key support. Diagnostics. Rainbow Color Text series. Much, much more. **The Greenleaf Functions.** Simply the finest C library (and the most extensive). All ready for you!

THE GREENLEAF FUNCTIONS™
The Library of C Functions that probably has just what you need . . . **TODAY!**

- Over 200 functions for the IBM PC, XT, AT, and compatibles
- complete, tested, on the shelf – with demos and source code
- compatible with most compilers, supports all memory models, DOS 1.1, 2.0, 2.1, 3.0
- optimized for speed and density – parts in assembler
- in use by thousands of customers worldwide – available from stock – or your dealer
- it's called **The Greenleaf Functions**

The Library of C Functions is Waiting for You

Specify compiler when ordering. Add $7.00 for UPS second-day air (or $5.00 for ground). Texas residents add sales tax. MasterCard, VISA, check or P.O. In stock, shipped same day.

General Libraries	$185	CI C86 Compiler	$349	Mark Williams	$475
Comm Library	$185	Lattice C	$395	Microsoft 3.0	$400

Prices are subject to change without notice. For Information: 214-446-8641

2101 HICKORY DR.
CARROLLTON, TX 75006

Programmers' Pfantasi

Phoenix makes programmers' dreams come true. With the best-engineered, highest performance programming tools you can find. A full line of MS-DOS©/PC DOS programs and utilities no other company offers. All designed to help you write, test and deliver the best programs possible. Top-of-the-line quality at a price you can afford. And all these products are available for the IBM© PC, XT,™ AT™ and compatibles.

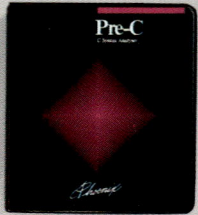

Finally, A Lint For MS-DOS.

Now you can get the full range of features C programmers working in UNIX™ have come to expect from their Lint program analyzer.

With Pre-C™ you can detect structural errors in C programs five times faster than you can with a debugger. Find usage errors almost impossible to detect with a compiler. Cross-check multiple source files and parameters passed to functions. Uncover interface bugs that are difficult to isolate. All in a single pass. Capabilities no C compiler, with or without program analyzing utilities, can offer. In fact, Pre-C outlints Lint, since you can handle analyses incrementally.

Pre-C's flexible library approach lets you maintain continuity across all the programs in your shop, whether you use Pre-C's pre-built libraries, pre-existing functions you already have, or some you might want to buy yourself.

Plus, you're not limited to one particular library, and Pre-C keeps track of all the libraries you're using to make sure that code calls them correctly. **$395.**

Outside the US, contact: Lifeboat Japan, Tokyo, Japan, Telex #2423296 LBJTYO, Telephone: 03-456-4101 • Repro Haganum (Stevis BV), Dinther, Netherlands, Telex #39581 REHAGNL, Telephone: 01-720-74543, 01-720-75543 • Memory Data, Sundbyberg, Sweden, Telephone: 46-8764-6700 • Roundhill Computer Systems, Marlborough, Wiltshire, UK, Telex #444453 AWARE G, Telephone: 44-467254675.

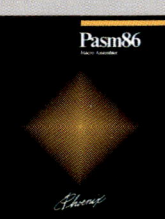

Assemble Programs Twice As Fast.

Pasm™86 will assemble MASM files two to three times faster than MASM 3.0. Pasm86 supports 8086/88, 8087, 80186 and 80286 processors.

With Pasm86's built-in defaults, you can write code quickly since you won't spend hours learning all the control statements needed at the beginning of your program. You can define symbols on the command line. Decide whether you want error messages or not. And, put local symbols within procedures. **$295.**

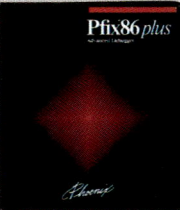

Still Fixing Bugs The Hard Way?

Pfix™86 Plus, the most advanced symbolic debugger on the market, eliminates the endless error searches through piles of listings. Locate instructions and data by symbolic name, using symbolic addresses. Handle larger, overlayed programs with ease.

An adjustable multiple-window display shows source, object code and data, breakpoint settings, current machine register and stack contents simultaneously. An in-line assembler allows program corrections directly in Assembly language. Powerful breakpoint features run a program full speed until a loop has been performed n times.

With a single keystroke you can trace an instruction and the action will be immediately reflected in source, object, data, stack, and register windows. Another key begins a special trace mode that executes call and loop instructions at full speed. Designed to work with both Plink™86 and MS© LINK linkage editors. **$395.**

Programmer's Pfantasies, Pre-C and Pfinish are trademarks of Phoenix Computer Products Corporation.
MS-DOS and MS are registered trademarks of Microsoft Corporation.
IBM is a registered trademark of International Business Machines Corporation.

by Phoenix

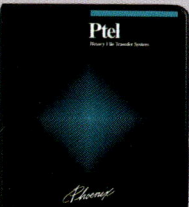

Get The Lead Out Of Binary File Transfer.

Ptel™ is the universal binary file transfer program for MS-DOS 2.0 or higher. You can move binary files fast and accurately. Upload or download groups of files from Bulletin Boards or remote computers. Move files between dissimilar machines and operating systems. Ptel's advanced binary protocol, Telink,™ offers better-than- Modem7 accuracy and performance. Faster transfer speeds. An on-screen update of error correction, blocks transferred, and transmission time.

Includes popular Modem7 and XModem protocols. With checksum or CRC. Plus Kermit and ASCII. **$195.**

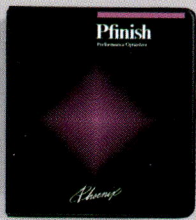

Maximize Your Program's Efficiency.

Pfinish™ delivers the fastest running programs possible. This performance analyzer lets you "zoom in" on the inefficient parts of your program. Whether written in Assembly language, C, PASCAL, FORTRAN, BASIC. Unlike profilers available today, Pfinish understands the structure of your program and reports the amount of activity and time spent in its subroutines or functional groups. Pfinish analyzes both overlaid and memory resident programs. Down to the instruction level. Reports are displayed. Stored on disk. Or printed out. In tabular form or histograms.

Do a dynamic program scan. Identify the most frequently executed subroutines. Find inefficient code that costs your program valuable time. Rank subroutines by execution frequency. **$395.**

Why Work With A Primitive Editor?

More than a powerful editor, Pmate™ is a text processing language. An emulator of other editors. A language-specific editor for C, PASCAL, and FORTRAN. Pmate can even run in the background!

You get full-screen, single-key editing. Ten editing buffers. Horizontal and vertical scrolling. A "garbage stack" buffer. A built-in macro language with variables, control statements, radix conversion, tracing and 120 commands that you can group and execute with a single keystroke. **$225.**

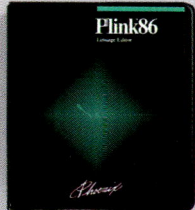

Why Squeeze Your Program More Than You Have To?

The Plink86 overlay linkage editor brings modular programming to 8086/88-based micros. Write large and complex programs without worrying about memory constraints. Work on modules individually, link them into executable files. Use the same module in different programs. Change the overlay structure of an existing program without recompiling. Use one overlay to access code and data in other overlays.

Plink86 links Intel©-format modules. **$395.**

Call (800) 344-7200. In Massachusetts (617) 762-5030. Or, write.

Phoenix

Phoenix Computer Products Corp.
320 Norwood Park South
Norwood, MA 02062

XT and AT are trademarks of International Business Machines Corporation.
UNIX is a trademark of AT&T Bell Laboratories.
Pasm86, Pfix86 Plus, Ptel, Telink, Pmate and Plink86 are trademarks of Phoenix Software Associates Ltd.
Intel is a registered trademark of Intel Corporation.

Program Editing with BRIEF™

is More Productive and Less Frustrating

because it will work YOUR way: BRIEF elegantly integrates:

- A high-level, readable **Macro Programming Language** - allows customization for programming languages . . . Complete, unlimited variables, etc.
- Edit **multiple** files of **unlimited size** (2 Meg is OK)
- Multiple **Windows** on screen with different or same file, fragments, etc.
- A bona-fide **UNDO** stack (up to 300) of **all operations**: deletions, reading files, search, translate, more

- Full **"regular expression search"** - wild cards, complex patterns
- A completely **reconfigurable keyboard**
- **Keystroke macros** - for common typing sequences
- Suspend BRIEF to execute, **exit to DOS** - run another program (like a compiler, dir, XREF, DIFF, or DEBUG) then resume BRIEF session
- **Compiler-specific** support like auto indent, syntax check, compile with-in BRIEF For PC, AT, and compatibles.

FREE WITH ORDER: "Best of BRIEF Macros" — includes Fortran, C, Calculator. Call before 11/30/85.

Only $195

Full Refund if not satisfied in 30 days.
CALL **800-821-2492**.

Solution Systems™
335-DD Washington St., Norwell, MA 02061
617-659-1571

Scrap your LINKER with FASTER C

Reliably:

CUT Compile times (by 15% to 55%)
CUT Testing times (by 12% to 37%)

HOW: FASTER C keeps the Lattice C or C86 library and any other functions you choose in memory. It manages a jump table to replace the LINKER and immediately execute your functions. You can also CALL active functions interactively to speed your program debugging. It includes many options for configuration and control.

"Automatic" support for new libraries by reading the .OBJ files makes support for new libraries quick and simple.

AVAILABLE FOR PC-DOS, IBM-AT, AND ANY 256K MSDOS SYSTEM.

ONLY $95.
Full Refund if not satisfied during first 30 days.
Call **800-821-2492**

Solution Systems™
335-DD Washington St., Norwell, Mass. 02061
617-659-1571

DeSmet C

MACINTOSH™ DEVELOPMENT PACKAGE $150 Includes Shipping

Runs on 128K and 512K Macintosh
- Produces FINDER/SHELL applications
- Dynamic OVERLAY support

Full K&R C Compiler
- Native Code Compiler
- In-line **asm** directive
- IEEE S/W Floating Point

Assembler, Linker, and Librarian

Machine Code Debugger

Source Code Editor

"SHELL" Interface
- Environmental Variables
- Wild-Card Expansion
- Many Built-in Functions
- Command History
- Runs Any Application

>120 Function STDIO Library

>450 Function Macintosh ROM Library

360 Page Manual

RAM Disk

Macintosh is a trademark licensed to Apple Computer, Inc.

Please Send Information.
Send Macintosh Development Package

Check # _____ Enclosed

SHIP TO

_____

_____

_____ ZIP

WARE
CORPORATION

P.O. BOX C
Sunnyvale, CA 94087
(408) 720-9696

All orders shipped UPS surface. California residents add sales tax. Canada shipping add $5, elsewhere add $15. Checks must be on U.S. Bank and in U.S. Dollars. Call 9 a.m - 1 p.m. to CHARGE by VISA MC AMEX.

Street Address: 505 W Olive #767 Sunnyvale CA 94086

Manx Aztec C86 is the best C for MS-DOS and you can prove it yourself!

"A compiler that has many strengths ... quite valuable for serious work"
Computer Language review, February 1985

Manx Aztec C86 - The C For MS-DOS

Manx Aztec C86 is clearly the best C software development system for MS-DOS. Aztec C86 is the only C compiler for MS-DOS that provides the level of performance, features, documentation, and support required for serious, professional software development. You can prove it yourself. All you have to do is order Aztec C86 from Manx, evaluate it, and, if you like it, keep it. If you don't like it, send it back within 30 days and we'll cancel your order.

If you keep your Manx Aztec C86, as 99% do, you'll be in with the best company.

Manx Aztec C86 Features:

Optimized C compiler: Unsurpassed for code quality and speed. Optionally generates 80186 and 80286 code. Full K & R.

Symbolic Debugger: Execution trace, break points, display data in floating point, integer, character, or hex format. Evaluate expressions. Detect illegal memory stores, modify memory/registers, disassemble code.

Manx AS86 Macro Assembler: Supports macroes, 8086, 80186, and 80286 instructions in Intel format. Fast execution.

LN86 Overlay Linker: Links small, large, and mixed memory model routines, supports overlays, and options for producing ROM based code.

Librarian: Build and modify personal or system run time libraries.

8087/80287 Sensing Library: One library simulates floating point, another assumes the presence of an 8086 or 80287 math chip, the third senses the existence of a math chip, and if it finds one it uses it.

Profiler: Provides a run time analysis of your code to pinpoint code segments to optimize.

UNIX Library: Compatible with UNIX C. Fast I/O. Terminal I/O can be buffered or unbuffered.

DOS Library: Time and date functions, program forking (exec), program chaining, directory commands, I/O port support, sysint support, BIOS functions, and BDOS functions.

Screen & Graphics Library: Screen and cursor functions. Fast routines for drawing lines, circles, elipses, points, and setting colors.

CP/M-86 Library (-c): Produce programs for CP/M-86.

Large Memory Model: Manx Aztec C86 supports programs and data of any size. Global data has a max size of 64k.

Intel Object Option: Interface to software that requires intel object format, such as PLINK86.

Z (vi) Source Editor (-c): Fast, powerful editor, Macro capabilities, undo, ctags, buffers for commands and data, and all the bells and whistles that make vi fanatics fanatical.

ROM Support Package (-c): Startup routine, linker options for separate placement of code and data, special utilities like the Intel HEX Utility, documentation, and library source.

Library Source Code (-c): UNIX, screen, graphics, and math function libraries.

Mixed Memory Models (-c): Mix large code and small data, small code and large data, or mix within type.

UniTools (-c): The UNIX utilities make, diff, and grep.

One year of updates (-c): As new versions are released, updates are automatically sent.

Technical Support: Manx has a full time staff to provide support via telephone & bulletin board.

Items marked -c are special features of the Aztec C86-c system.

Manx Aztec C86 is available in four configurations: Manx Aztec C86-c, Manx Aztec C86-d, Manx Aztec C86-p, and Manx Aztec C86-a. The -p and -a systems are not intended for commercial work and do not incorporate the same compilers as the -c and -d systems. All systems are upgradable.

Aztec C86-c Commercial System	$499
Aztec C86-d Developer's System	$299
Aztec C86-p Personal System	$199
Aztec C86-a Apprentice System	$ 49

Manx Cross Development Systems

Manx Aztec C compilers are available as native or as cross development systems for PC-DOS, MS-DOS, Macintosh, CP/M-86, CP/M-80, TRSDOS, Apple II, and Commodore 64/128.

Cross development involves two computer systems: the development system (HOST) and the execution system (TARGET). This method is useful when the TARGET machine is slower or more limited than the HOST.

HOSTS: VAX UNIX ($3000), PDP-11 UNIX ($2000), MS-DOS ($750), CP/M ($750), Macintosh ($750), CP/M-68k ($750), XENIX ($750).

TARGETS: MS-DOS, CP/M-86, Macintosh, CP/M-68k, CP/M-80, TRS-80 3 & 4, Apple II, Commodore C64, 8086/80x85 ROM, 68xxx ROM, 8080/8085/Z80 ROM, 65xx ROM.

Additional TARGETS are $300 to $500 (non VAX) or $1000 (VAX). Call for information, on cross development to the 68000, 65816, Amiga, C128, CP/M-68K, VRTX, and others.

How To Become a Manx Aztec C User

Call 1-800-221-0440 or 1-800-832-9273 (800-TEC WARE). In NJ or outside the USA call 201-530-7997. Orders can also be telexed to 4995812.

Payment can be by check, COD, American Express, VISA, Master Card, or Net 30 to qualified customers.

Orders can also be mailed to Manx Software Systems, Box 55, Shrewsbury, NJ 07701.

For More Information: call 1-800-221-0440, or 201-530-7997, or write to Manx Software Systems.

Manx maintains a large professional staff to service and support Manx users. You will get fast delivery and great service dealing directly with Manx.

Support Software for Manx Aztec C86

C-tree $395: B-tree database system. Easy to use. Available for Aztec C for MS-DOS, Macintosh, CP/M-86, CP/M-80, and others. Includes source.

PHACT $250: Powerful database system. Available for Manx Aztec C compilers for MS-DOS, CP/M-86, CP/M-80, and Macintosh.

PANEL $295: Create screens via simple, powerful editing commands. Select colors, edit fields. Directly input data to a multi-keyed file utility included with the system.

SunScreen $99: Create and modify formatted screens easily. Validate fields, select colors, create screens for both the color and monochrome cards. With library source SunScreen is $199.

WindScreen $149: Combines SunScreen with a powerful window utility.

Windows for C $195: Versatile window utility that supports IBM PC compatible and some non-compatible environments.

AMBER Windows $99: Powerful, low priced window package.

HALO $250: The ultimate C graphics package. It supports viewports, shapes, and multiple graphics cards. A less expensive version is available for just the PC mono and color cards.

FirsTime $295: Syntax checking while you edit greatly shortens compile time.

Pre-C $395: Powerful Lint-like utility locates structural and usage errors. Easily checks multiple files for bad parameter declarations and other interface errors. Lint users will find the user interface a dream come true.

PC-LINT $98: Lint-like utility that supports large memory models, has clear error messages, and executes quickly, has lots of options and features that you wouldn't expect at this low price.

Greenleaf Functions $185: Source for over 200 C and assembler functions. They are great, they work, they are used extensively, and are economically priced. Clear documentation and easy to use interface round out an impressive package.

C Utility Library $185: C and assembler source for screens, windows, color graphics, asynch communications, and more. The color graphics and speed of this package are impressive.

Plink-86 $395: MS-DOS linkage editor for producing and maintaining overlayed programs. It works with Aztec C86 in Intel object format mode.

30 Day Guaranty:

Any Manx Aztec development system can be returned within 30 days for a refund if it fails to meet your needs. Restrictions are that the original purchase must be directly from Manx, shipped within the USA, and the package must be in new condition. Returned items must be received by Manx within 30 days. A restocking fee may be required.

Discounts:

There are special discounts available to professors, students, and consultants. A discount is also available on a "trade in" basis for users of competing C systems.

Manx Aztec C Distribution:

In the USA, Manx Software Systems is the exclusive distributor of Aztec C. Telephone or mail order sales other than through Manx are unauthorized.

To order or for information call:
800-221-0440

Lifeboat.™

C is the language.
Lifeboat™ is the source.

Productivity Tools from the Leading Publisher of C Programs™

The Lattice® C Compiler

The cornerstone of a program is its compiler; it can make the difference between a good program and a great one. The Lattice C compiler features:
- Full compatibility with Kernighan and Ritchie's standards
- Four memory model options for control and versatility
- Automatic sensing and use of the 8087 math chip
- Choose from the widest selection of add-on options
- Renowned for speed and code quality
- Superior quality documentation

"Lattice C produces remarkable code...the documentation sets such a high standard that others don't even come close...in the top category for its quick compilation and execution time and consistent reliability."
Byte Magazine

Lattice Library source code also available.

Language Utilities

Pfix 86/Pfix 86 Plus — dynamic and symbolic debuggers respectively, these provide multiple-window debugging with breakpointing capability.
Plink 86 — a two-pass overlay linkage editor that helps solve memory problems.
Text Management Utilities — includes GREP (searches files for patterns), DIFF (differential text file comparator), and more.
LMK (UNIX "make") — automates the construction of large multi-module products.
Curses — lets you write programs with full screen output transportable among all UNIX, XENIX and PC-DOS systems without changing your source code.
BASTOC — translates MBASIC or CBASIC source code directly to Lattice C source code.
C Cross Reference Generator — examines your C source modules and produces a listing of each symbol and where it is referenced.

Editors

Pmate — a customizable full screen text editor featuring its own powerful macro command language.
ES/P for C — C program entry with automatic syntax checking and formatting.
VEDIT — an easy-to-use word processor for use with V-PRINT.
V-PRINT — a print formatting companion for VEDIT.
CVUE — a full-screen editor that offers an easy way to use command structure.
EMACS — a full screen multi window text editor.
Fast/C — speeds up the cycle of edit-compile-debug-edit-recompile.

Graphics and Screen Design

HALO — one of the industry's standard graphics development packages. Over 150 graphics commands including line, arc, box, circle and ellipse primitives. The **10 Fontpack** is also available.
Panel — a screen formatter and data entry aid.
Lattice Window — a library of subroutines allowing design of windows.

Functions

C-Food Smorgasbord — a tasty selection of utility functions for Lattice C programmers; includes a binary coded decimal arithmetic package, level 0 I/O functions, a Terminal Independence Package, and more.
Float-87 — supports the 8087 math chip to boost the speed of floating-point calculations.
The Greenleaf Functions — a comprehensive library of over 200 routines.
The Greenleaf Comm Library — an easy-to-use asynchronous communications library.
C Power Packs — sets of functions useful for a wide variety of applications.
BASIC C — This library is a simple bridge from IBM BASIC to C.

Database Record Managers

Phact — a database record manager library of C language functions, used in the creation and manipulation of large and small databases.
Btrieve — a sophisticated file management system designed for developing applications under PC-DOS. Data can be instantly retrieved by key value.
FABS — a Fast Access Btree Structure function library designed for rapid, keyed access to data files using multipath structures.
Autosort — a fast sort/merge utility.
Lattice dB-C ISAM — a library of C functions that enables you to create and access dBase format database files.

Cross-Compilers

For programmers active in both micro and mini environments we provide advanced cross-compilers which product Intel 8086 object modules. All were developed to be as functional — and reliable — as the native compilers. They are available for the following systems:

VAX/VMS, VAX/UNIX, 68K/UNIX-S, 68K/UNIX-L

Also, we have available:
Z80 Cross-Compiler for MS- and PC-DOS — produces Z80 object modules in the Microsoft relocatable format.

New Products

Run/C — finally, a C interpreter for all levels of C Programmers.
C Sprite — a symbolic debugger with break point capability.

Call LIFEBOAT: 1-800-847-7078. In NY, 1-212-860-0300.

YES! Please rush me the latest FREE Lifeboat™ catalog of C products.

Name_____ Title_____
Company Name_____ Business Phone_____
Address_____

Please check one of the following categories:
☐ Dealer/Distributor   ☐ End User   ☐ Other _____

Return Coupon to: Lifeboat™ Associates
1651 Third Avenue, New York, NY 10128
© 1985 Lifeboat Associates

DD

Vitamin C

A Healthy Supplement For C Programmers

SCREEN I/O FEATURES INCLUDE:
- dBase-like atsay(), atget(), readgets()
- Input formatting via picture clause
- Unlimited input validation
- Individual field color/attribute control
- Field specific help messages
- Status line for added field specific prompts
- Right-to-left numeric input with floating dollar signs, asteriks, and commas
- Insert/delete, next/previous field, etc
- Current field highlighting
- Fast, easy, and bulletproof

More than just another function library! A well planned, fully integrated programming system complete with pull down menus & user help system!

PERFECT WINDOWS
- Automatic interface with all screen I/O functions
- Full overlay and restore
- Multiple virtual screens
- Full collision protection
- Automatically keeps I/O within window boundries
- Grow, shrink and move
- Word wrap & margins
- Print to or scroll any window without colision even if it is overlayed by another!
- Much, much more!

Vitamin C • $149.95
Includes more features than there is room to mention, all source code, manual, tutorial and sample programs. No royalties on your applications. For most MS-DOS C compilers! Soon for UNIX / XENIX ! Include $3 shipping, $6 for second day. Phone orders with MC/Visa welcome! Prices & features subject to change without notice. Call for other products.

CREATIVE PROGRAMMING
(214)243-6197
Box 112097
Carrollton, Texas 75011-2097

A FULL C COMPILER FOR $49.95

The Eco-C88 C compiler is setting a new standard for price and performance. Compare Eco-C88's performance to compilers costing up to 10 times as much:

	Seive	Fib	Defref	Matrix
Execute	12.1 sec.	43.1 sec.	13.7 sec.	21.3 sec.
Code Size	7782	7754	7772	9120
Compile-link	76 Sec.	77 Sec.	77 Sec.	92 Sec.

Eco-C88 Rel. 2.20, on IBM PC with 2 floppy disks, 256K. Benchmarks from Feb., 1985 **Computer Language**.

Eco-C88 includes:
* All operators and data types (except bit fields)
* Error messages in English with page numbers that reference the **C Programming Guide** – a real plus if you're just getting started in C.
* Over 170 library functions, including color and transcendentals
* New library functions for treating memory as a file
* User-selectable ASM or OBJ output (no assembler required)
* 8087 support with 8087 sensed at *runtime*
* cc and "mini-make" for easy compiles (with source)
* Fast, efficient code for all IBM-PC, XT, AT and compatibles using MSDOS 2.1 or later.
* Complete user's manual

If ordered with the compiler, the C library source code (excluding transcendentals) is $10.00 and the ISAM file handler (as published in the **C Programmer's Library**, Que Corp) in OBJ format is an additional $15.00. Please add $4.00 for shipping and handling. To order, call or write:

Ecosoft Inc.
6413 N. College Avenue
Indianapolis, IN 46220
(317) 255-6476 • 8:30–4:30

Eco-C (Ecosoft), MSDOS (Microsoft), UNIX (Bell Labs), CP/M (Digital Research), Z80 (Zilog), 8086, 8087, 8088 (Intel).

C PROGRAMMERS' DBMS

db_VISTA

PREFERRED over **ISAM** and file utilities, **POWER** like a mainframe **DBMS**, **PRICE** like a microcomputer utility, **PORTABILITY** like only C provides.

MS-DOS/UNIX

db_VISTA FEATURES

- Written in C for C.
- Fast B*-tree indexing method.
- Maximum data efficiency using the network database model.
- Multiple key records—any or all data fields may be keys.
- Multi-user capability.
- Transaction processing.
- Interactive database access utility.
- Ability to import and export dBASE II/III and ASCII files.

**NO ROYALTIES
SOURCE CODE INCLUDED
MONEY BACK GUARANTEE**

db_VISTA PRICE

Single user without source	$195
Single user with source	$495
Multi-user without source	$495
Multi-user with source	$990

MC/VISA/COD

Available for the Lattice, Microsoft, Computer Innovations, DeSmet and Aztec C compilers under MS-DOS, and most UNIX systems.

RAIMA
CORPORATION

11717 Rainier Avenue South
Seattle, WA 98178, USA
(206) 772-1515 Telex 9103330300

**CALL TOLL-FREE
1-800-843-3313**
At the tone, touch 700-992.

C Programmers:
Consider 104 Ways To Be More Productive

If you find and choose the right development software, you can: cut development effort, make impractical projects feasible, and eliminate unproductive, frustrating aspects of programming.

Confused? We'll help you sort thru the huge number of alternatives. Call for comparisons or information.

We carry 27 C Compilers, 4 C Intepreters, 49 Support Libraries, 5 C source debuggers, and 19 other C Add-ons for programming with MSDOS, Macintosh, or CP/M — more than 104 products, really. Here are some of the best products available:

Learn C Programming Only $95
"Introducing C" Interpreter

Computer Innovations has done it again! This interactive implementation is combined with a full screen editor and a thorough, self-paced manual.

You can develop programs faster by getting immediate feedback. Programs will start instantly upon your command. There is no need to wait "for compile and link."

Introducing C includes demo programs, powerful C language interpreter, complete C function library, full screen editor, color graphics, and C language compatibility.   PCDOS $95

Inventive Programming Becomes Possible
with 300 + ESSENTIAL, tested, fast, rountines to Rely On.
C Utilities Library by Essential Software
Recent Enhancements to Graphics, Windows, AT Support

Every application you write is likely to require functions were you feel like you are "reinventing". Don't. Even if you use only 5% of this library, you will come out ahead on schedule and cost.

Full business Graphics, Window support, polled Communications, and Data Entry support have recently been added/upgraded along with more functions for DOS Interface and AT support. String handling, screen control, "word processor" functions, memory management, directory and path access, date handling, program chaining, keyboard and printer control are traditional strengths.

Full source code is included. No royalties are charged to include functions in your programs. 95% are C for portability and to make it practical for you to understand or modify them.

Lattice, Microsoft, C86, Mark Williams, Aztec, Desmet and Wizard C are supported. Specify which you need.

Substantial time, effort, testing and attention has been invested by Essential Software developing, documenting and supporting this comprehensive library. Make new projects practical and interesting. Use this tested and reliable library.

Some functions are PC-specific. Most support any MSDOS. $159.

SORT/MERGE Files for Clean, Fast Maintenance
with OPT-TECH SORT

Performance should not suffer with DOS or other "free" sorts. ISAMs alone are slow when 10% or even less is changed/added.
OPT-TECH includes:
 – CALLable and Standalone use
 – C, ASM, BAS, PAS, FTN, COBOL
 – Variable and fixed length
 – 1 to 9 fields to sort/merge
 – Autoselect of RAM or disk
 – Options: dBASE, BTrieve files
 – 1 to 10 files Input
 – No software max for # Records
 – All common field types
 – By pass headers, limit sort
 – Inplace sort option
 – Output = Record or keys
Try what you're using on an XT. 1,000 128 byte records, 10 byte key in 33 seconds.   MSDOS $90.

Which Compiler Features Do You Need?
Optimizing C86 Compiler

Over the years the Optimizing C86 has evolved to be the most complete set of C compiler tools. It includes utilities, a rich library, and thorough tech support. In line 8087/287 routines run up to 100 times faster than the 8086 math package. The source code to all routines is included, so you have complete control over how they work. Thorough ROM support, Intel UDI & VMS cross versions are available.

More of the features you want include:
- special IBM-PC library • 2 math and 2 I/O libraries
- full memory utilization of the 8086/88/186/286
- compatibility with most commercial libraries
- Version 2.3 has support for source level debuggers   MSDOS $339

Fast File Access with Source
C-Index +

C-Index + contains a high performance ISAM, balanced B + Tree indexing system with *source* and *variable length* fields. The result is a complete data storage system to eliminate tedious programming and add efficient performance to your programs.

Features include random and sequential data access, virtual memory buffering, and multiple key indexes.

With *no royalties* for programs you distribute, full source code, and variable length fields C-Index + fits what you are likely to need.

Save time and enhance your programs with C-Index +.   MSDOS $375

File Management: MultiUser/MultiLanguage
BTRIEVE

Billions and billions of bytes! That's what you can control with Btrieve's file manager. Btrieve gives you the ISAM capability you need without the maintenance headaches.

Using b-trees for optimum performance, Btrieve automatically maintains your files in sorted order on up to 24 different fields. And Btrieve offers you the fastest search algorithm available, to give you instantaneous access to any individual record. You can locate any record in 4 disk reads or less (thanks to Btrieve's RAM cache, usually less). With Btrieve you can stop wasting your time being a file clerk and concentrate on more productive tasks.

Btrieve's other features include:
- 4 gigabyte file size
- 4090 byte record length
- 255 byte key length
- duplicate, modifiable, and null keys
- up to 24 key indexes per file
- automatic file recovery after power failure

Btrieve's Local Area Network version lets you migrate your software to multiuser environments without changing your code. And offers you multiuser update capability beyond simple file locking schemes. Available *for all programming languages* as well as C. MSDOS.Single user $245 Multiuser $595.

Btrieve. Don't settle for less

Call for details, comparisons, or for our "C Extras Packet" with over 50 pages of information about C support products.

THE PROGRAMMER'S SHOP
The programmer's complete source for software, services and answers
128-DD Rockland Street, Hanover, MA 02339   (617) 826-7531   (800) 421-8006

Ask about COD and PO's. All formats available. Prices subject to change. Names of products and companies are generally their trademarks.

THE HAMMER
Software Tools in C

More than just BIOS/DOS access, THE HAMMER Library also provides routines for multi-level **123-like menus**, easy **data entry & verification** of strings, numbers, & dates, screen attribute control, date & time processing, AND MORE.

Super data entry routines give programmer a natural, strong interface with the user. They work in both "single-field" and "multi-field" (**full screen editing**) modes. This is NOT just another library of general purpose routines.

For: IBM/PC family with DOS 2.00+
C Compilers: CI-C86, Lattice, DeSmet, and new Microsoft V3.00

$195 with source code and manual. To order or inquire, **CALL OR WRITE:**

O.E.S. SYSTEMS
1906 Brushcliff Road
Pittsburgh, PA 15221
412/243-7365

Looking for the right tool for the job?
GET THE HAMMER

Finally. BSW-Make.

The Boston Software Works now brings a <u>complete</u> implementation of the Unix "make" facility to MS-DOS. No more recompiling every file in sight after a small edit; no more wondering if you've really rebuilt every module affected by an edit. Just type "make" and BSW-Make automatically builds your product quickly, efficiently and correctly.

BSW-Make supports:
- most compilers and assemblers
- MS-DOS or PC-DOS v2.00 or later
- macros for parameterized builds
- default rules
- MS-DOS pathnames
- any MS-DOS machine (192K minimum)

Only $69.95 postpaid (Mass. residents add 5% sales tax)

The Boston Software Works
120 Fulton Street, Boston, MA 02109
(617) 367-6846

Csharp Realtime Toolkit

Realtime on MSDOS? **Csharp** can do it! Get the tools without operating system overhead. Cut development time with C source code for realtime data acquisition and control. **Csharp** includes: graphics, event handling, procedure scheduling, state system control, and interrupt handling. Processor, device, and operating system independent. **Csharp** runs standalone or with: MSDOS, PCDOS, or RT11. **Csharp** runs on: PDP-11 and IBM PC. **Csharp** includes drivers for Hercules and IBM graphics boards, Data Translation and Metrabyte IO boards, real time clock, and more. Inquire for Victor 9000, Unix, and other systems. Price: $600

 Systems Guild, Inc., P.O. Box 1085, Cambridge, MA 02142
(617) 451-8479

C POWER
C LIBRARIES
C WINDOWS

Best You Can Get!
325 Fully Tested Functions

Best Documentation
(over 400 pages)

SIX C LIBRARIES
For IBM PC, XT, AT

All Source Code. No royalties.
- 51 screen handling / graphics
- 50 cursor/keyboard/data entry
- 85 superior string handling
- 25 system status & control
- 72 utility/DOS/BIOS/time/date
- 42 printer control

**RICHLY COMMENTED
EASY TO LEARN
EASY TO MODIFY**

NO MATTER WHAT ELSE
YOU HAVE
GET THESE!!

ALL 6 LIBRARIES $99.95
(ON FOUR DISKETTES)

POWER WINDOWS
PROFESSIONAL WINDOW MANAGEMENT

OVERLAYS, BORDERS, POPUP
MENUS, COLOR HIGHLIGHTING,
HELP WINDOWS, STATUS-LINE,
MONOCHROME OR COLOR,
FILE, CURSOR, KEYBOARD
CONTROL AND MORE!!

C WINDOWS: COMPLETE SOURCE CODE $99.95

**ALL LIBRARIES
PLUS
WINDOW $159.95**

Entelekon
SOFTWARE SYSTEMS

ENTELEKON 12118 KIMBERLEY
HOUSTON, TX 77024   (713) 468-4412

VISA • MASTERCARD • CHECK

HISOFT
COMPILERS $69

'One hell of a piece of software'

That's what one reviewer said. Get the facts before you buy. One phone call, or a brief letter is all it takes to get full specs of our range of languages.

Pascal C Assembler

form the current range, but we're always introducing new products and improving our existing ones. That's how we built our reputation throughout Europe for the quality of our products and the strength of our support. All our compilers are supplied with an editor and all of them are high-specification products at very fair prices. Our compilers are available for Z80 CP/M and many other Z80 machines — ask about yours.

180 High Street North, Dunstable, Beds LU6 1AT, England
(582) 696421

How much time can you buy for $49.95?

You know what your time is worth, but **MATIS**™ users know that they save long hours everyday in developing an attractive and efficient user interface for their programs.

If you think you spend too much time:

☐ Creating Windows   ☐ Defining large Virtual Screens
☐ Formatting Input Fields   ☐ Scrolling in four directions
☐ Setting independent Video Attributes   ☐ Controlling Keyboard input at run-time   ☐ Drawing lines and boxes
☐ Printing and maintaining your screens.

Buy yourself a well deserved rest!
With a copy of MATIS for only $49.95

ORDER BY MAIL — WRITE OR CALL FOR COMPLETE DESCRIPTION
No License Fee

Softway, Inc.

500 Sutter Street • Suite 222-T1 • San Francisco, CA 94102   (415) 397-4666
Credit Card Orders Only, 24 hours a day   (800) 227-2400 Ext. 989
* ADD $5.00 FOR SHPG CA RES. ADD SALES TAX